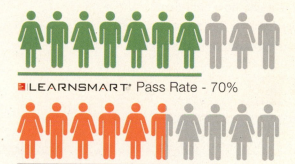
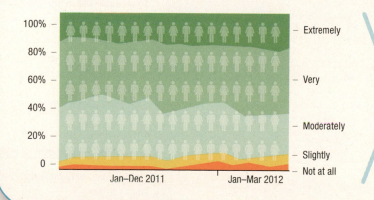

How do you rank against your peers?

What you know (green) and what you still need to review (yellow), based on your answers.

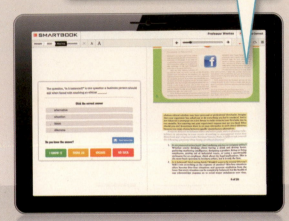

Let's see how confident you are on the questions.

COMPARE AND CHOOSE WHAT'S RIGHT FOR YOU

	BOOK	LEARNSMART	ASSIGNMENTS	
connect plus+	✓	✓	✓	LearnSmart, assignments, and SmartBook—all in one digital product for maximum savings!
connect plus+ Looseleaf	✓	✓	✓	Pop the pages into your own binder or carry just the pages you need.
connect plus+ Bound Book	✓	✓	✓	The #1 Student Choice!
SMARTBOOK Access Code	✓	✓		The first and only book that adapts to you!
LEARNSMART ADVANTAGE Access Code		✓		The smartest way to get from a B to an A.
CourseSmart eBook	✓			Save some green and some trees!
create	✓	✓	✓	Check with your instructor about a custom option for your course.

> Buy directly from the source at http://shop.mheducation.com.

Management

4th Edition

Thomas S. Bateman

McIntire School of Commerce,
University of Virginia

Scott A. Snell

Darden Graduate School of Business,
University of Virginia

Rob Konopaske

McCoy College of Business,
Texas State University

McGraw Hill Education

management

SENIOR VICE PRESIDENT, PRODUCTS & MARKETS: **KURT L. STRAND**

VICE PRESIDENT, GENERAL MANAGER, PRODUCTS & MARKETS: **MICHAEL RYAN**

VICE PRESIDENT, CONTENT DESIGN & DELIVERY: **KIMBERLY MERIWETHER DAVID**

MANAGING DIRECTOR: **SUSAN GOUIJNSTOOK**

DIRECTOR, MGMT & OB: **MIKE ABLASSMEIR**

DIRECTOR, PRODUCT DEVELOPMENT: **MEGHAN CAMPBELL**

PRODUCT DEVELOPER: **LAURA GRIFFIN**

MARKETING MANAGER: **ELIZABETH TREPKOWSKI**

DIRECTOR, CONTENT DESIGN & DELIVERY: **TERRI SCHIESL**

PROGRAM MANAGER: **MARY CONZACHI**

CONTENT PROJECT MANAGERS: **MARY CONZACHI, DANIELLE CLEMENT, JUDI DAVID**

BUYER: **MICHAEL R. MCCORMICK**

DESIGN: **MATT DIAMOND**

CONTENT LICENSING SPECIALIST: **KERI JOHNSON**

COVER IMAGE: **GETTY IMAGES, PHOTOGRAPHER TOM MERTON**

COMPOSITOR: **LASERWORDS PRIVATE LIMITED**

PRINTER: **R. R. DONNELLEY**

MANAGEMENT, FOURTH EDITION

Published by McGraw-Hill Education, 2 Penn Plaza, New York, NY 10121. Copyright © 2016 by McGraw-Hill Education. All rights reserved. Printed in the United States of America. Previous editions © 2013, 2011, and 2009. No part of this publication may be reproduced or distributed in any form or by any means, or stored in a database or retrieval system, without the prior written consent of McGraw-Hill Education, including, but not limited to, in any network or other electronic storage or transmission, or broadcast for distance learning.

Some ancillaries, including electronic and print components, may not be available to customers outside the United States.

This book is printed on acid-free paper.

4 5 6 7 8 9 DOW 21 20 19 18 17 16

ISBN 978-0-07-786259-6 (student edition)
MHID 0-07-786259-7 (student edition)
ISBN 978-1-25-930851-2 (instructor's edition)
MHID 1-25-930851-0 (instructor's edition)

All credits appearing on page or at the end of the book are considered to be an extension of the copyright page.

Library of Congress Control Number: 2014952745

The Internet addresses listed in the text were accurate at the time of publication. The inclusion of a website does not indicate an endorsement by the authors or McGraw-Hill Education, and McGraw-Hill Education does not guarantee the accuracy of the information presented at these sites.

www.mhhe.com

Brief Contents

Contents

part two   Planning 66

Chapter Changes

Chapter 1

- Expanded coverage on topics to emphasize global/international issues.
- Updated content via the addition of several new notes from 2012, 2013, and 2014.
- New organizations and topics, including Baidu's innovative approach to video; the growth of Pinterest, Google+, Tumblr, and Facebook as social networking sites; PepsiCo's plan to aid veterans; Starbucks mobile app card success; Mary Barra's leadership at GM; and Tesla sales.
- Updated research covering changing employee demographics through 2020.

Chapter 2

- Updated content via the addition of several new notes from 2012, 2013, and 2014.
- Added more global and international company examples.
- Updated concepts, including the inclusion of the concept "big data" to the quantitative management section.
- New applied examples and cases.
- Addition of new green case titled: "Are Companies Really Shifting to Green Power?"

Chapter 3

- Trimmed chapter length and revised content to include updated information.
- New coverage of the intense competition in the downloadable app industry and a new discussion of shoe industry competition between Nike and Reebok.
- Updated section on labor force projections from 2012 through 2022.
- New and updated features, cases, and notes.
- New current events include Oreo's tweet during the power outage of the 2013 Super Bowl, Google's new products including the smart watch, Alcoa's guilty plea to violating the Foreign Corrupt Practice Act, and the struggle between Russia and Ukraine over the control of Crimea.

Chapter 4

- Updated chapter coverage of ethical issues, including issues surrounding employees' use of social media in the workplace.
- New exhibit: "Partial List of Steps Organizations Can Take to Meet SOX Guidelines."
- New "Did You Know?" example about amount/type of unethical behavior in *Fortune* 500 companies.
- Updated content via the addition of several new notes from 2012, 2013, and 2014.
- Updated coverage of ethical issues, including Penn State's Sandusky situation, the garment factory building that collapsed in Bangladesh that killed more than 400 workers, and cyclist Lance Armstrong admitting to using performance-enhancing drugs and being stripped of his seven Tour de France titles.

Chapter 5

- Trimmed chapter length and revised content to include updated information.
- New and updated chapter cases, examples, and graphics.
- Updated content via the addition of several new notes from 2012, 2013, and 2014.
- New exhibits: "Three Common Plans Used by Organizations" and "Elements Included in an Environmental Analysis."
- Updated current events, including Wells Fargo's cross-selling strategy, GE Honda's jet engines, Unilever's and Google's mission statements, and Facebook's purchase of WhatsApp.

Chapter 6

- Trimmed chapter length and revised content to include updated information.
- Updated materials featuring the State New Economy Index, U.S. franchises, and a new green case on IKEA.
- New quotes from Zappos' Tony Hsieh and Virgin Group's Richard Branson.
- Updated organizations and topics, including Elon Musk and Tesla, Zazzle's customizable products, Oprah Winfrey's OWN turning a profit in 2013, and National Business Incubation Industry statistics.
- New section on long-lasting business partnerships, featuring Twitter's Evan Williams, Biz Stone, and Jack Dorsey; Microsoft's Bill Gates and Steve Ballmer; Imagine Entertainment's Brian Grazer and Ron Howard; the New York Yankees baseball franchise's Joe Torre and Don Zimmer; and Google's Sergei Brin and Larry Page.

Chapter 7

- Updated information and facts in several passages throughout chapter.
- New green case about New Belgium Brewing titled: "Can a Brewery Be a Force for Good?"
- Updated content via the addition of several new notes from 2012, 2013, and 2014.
- Updated featured organizations, including Facebook, King (Candy Crush Saga), John Deere, and Yahoo!.

Chapter 8

- Updated content via the addition of several new notes from 2012, 2013, and 2014.
- New exhibit: "Practical Guidelines for Conducting a Termination Interview" as well as three new updated or redesigned exhibits.
- Updated section on pensions.
- Addition of featured organizations, including Intuit, NetApp, USA Financial Services, FedEx, National Instruments, Best Buy, Old Navy, CollegeRecruiter, SimplyHired, Mashable Jobs, Dollar General, BMW, and Boeing.

Chapter 9

- Updated content via the addition of several new notes from 2012, 2013, and 2014.
- Updated sections on pensions and Equal Employment Opportunity.
- New exhibits: "Differences between Affirmative Action and Diversity Management Programs" and "Basic Components of a Company's Policy to Prevent Harassment."
- New featured current events, including a SHRM study reported that companies promote diversity by offering work/life balance policies internationally, updated NAFE's list of Top 10 companies for executive women, and an updated Global Diversity Readiness Index Top 5.

Chapter 10

- Trimmed chapter length and revised content to include updated information.
- Updated content via the addition of several new notes from 2012, 2013, and 2014.
- New exhibits: "Sources of Power in Organizations" and "The Path–Goal Framework."
- Featuring new current events, including the "1,000 Start-up Weekends across 100 Countries" event, Mars Exploration Program and Rover Curiosity's progress on the Red Planet, and why Elon Musk of Tesla Motors and SpaceX was named *Fortune*'s 2013 Businessperson of the Year.
- Green case features the green power initiatives of Cisco, Georgetown University, Microsoft, and Ohio State University.

Chapter 11

- Trimmed chapter length and revised content to include updated information.
- Updated content via the addition of several new notes from 2012, 2013, and 2014.
- New applied examples, including "Employee Engagement Percentages" and "Happiest Jobs in the United States."
- New people and organizations, including Zappos, TOMS, Madcap Coffee, SpaceX, Healthy Choice, and Anderson Cancer Center.

Chapter 12

- New research featuring the top five attributes of high-performance teams.

- New exhibits: "Superior Team Leaders Excel at These Behaviors" and "A Four-Stage Strategy to Resolve Disputes."
- Updated green case, notes, and research, including a new study on the team cohesion and high performance of the Blue Angels and how David Ogilvy played devil's advocate to the ads produced by his agency's staff.
- New people and organizations, including Ford, Creative Labs, Google Chromebooks, Google Glass, and Google Handouts.

Chapter 13

- Trimmed chapter length and revised content to include updated information.
- Updated content via the addition of several new notes from 2012, 2013, and 2014.
- New and redesigned exhibits, including "An Illustration of a Two-Way Communication Model," "Advantages of Using Electronic Media at Work," and "Example of Reflection in Action."
- New current events, including how Amazon is using informal communication and leaks to create buzz around the expected launch of its new smartphone, how a labor agreement in France prohibits employees from responding to work-related emails after leaving work each day and on weekends, and how Edward Snowden leaks classified National Security Agency documents and data.

Chapter 14

- Trimmed chapter length and revised content to include updated information.
- Included new exhibit, "Common Measures of Performance Standards."
- Updated content via the addition of several new notes from 2012, 2013, and 2014.
- New current events, including GM's 10-year delay in fixing/recalling automobiles with faulty ignition switches; how the scandal at the Phoenix Veterans Administration (VA) Medical Center suggests a lack of control from the VA bureaucracy and leadership; and how TerraCycle launched operations in Norway, Spain, Germany, Ireland, Switzerland, Denmark, Israel, Belgium, Argentina, and the Netherlands.

Chapter 15

- New green case entitled: "How 'Big Data' Contributes to Sustainable Farming."
- Updated content via the addition of several new notes from 2012, 2013, and 2014.
- Featuring new exhibits, including "Four Basic Types of OD Interventions" and "Motivating People to Change."
- New research featuring a text mini case about Uber, the fast-growing driver service company that wants to change the future of logistics, delivery, and travel.
- New current events, featuring the following companies: SSM Health Care, Amazon, Microsoft's Bing Translator, Intel, IQBG, Boeing, Volvo Group, Dongfeng Motor Group, Grey Advertising, American Express, and Whole Foods.

Management

1 chapter

Managing Effectively in a Global World

Learning Objectives

After studying Chapter 1, you should be able to

LO1 Describe the four functions of management.

LO2 Understand what managers at different organizational levels do.

LO3 Define the skills needed to be an effective manager.

LO4 Summarize the major challenges facing managers today.

LO5 Recognize how successful managers achieve competitive advantage.

Almost everyone has worked for a good supervisor, played for a good coach, or taken a class with a good professor. What made these managers so effective? Was it because they always had a plan and set goals to guide their people toward accomplishing what needed to get done? Maybe it had something to do with being organized and always prepared. Or maybe these managers were effective because of the way they motivated, inspired, and led their employees, players, or students. Of course, they were probably good at keeping things under control and making changes when needed.

Effective managers in companies from China, India, Germany, and Mexico do all of these things—plan, organize, lead, and control—to help employees reach their potential so organizations can succeed and thrive in the highly competitive and changing global marketplace.

Starbucks is an example of a successful global company. In 1971 it began as a single store that sold coffee, tea, and spices in Seattle's Pike Place Market. Since that time, the company has experienced dramatic growth in every sense of the word. In 2013 Starbucks reported $14.9 billion in revenue from its 1,700 stores 63 countries.[1] However, the company's 43-year journey has not always been smooth and predictable. No one knows this better than Howard Schultz, the current CEO of Starbucks. Having joined the company in 1982, Schultz worked his way up the ranks to become chief executive officer. In 2000 he stepped down from the post to oversee the company's international expansion. In 2008 Schultz decided to return to his previous role as chief executive officer because he felt that several changes and improvements were needed to get the company to the next level.[2] For example, Schultz's mobile and digital strategy to encourage more customers to pay for their mochas with a Starbucks' mobile app card is paying off. In 2013, customers used the app approximately 5 million times per week, making it the most popular digital payment app in the United States.[3] Some estimates suggest that the company generated $1 billion in revenue in 2013 from smartphone transactions at its stores.[4]

As the top manager of Starbucks, Schultz does a lot of *planning* regarding how fast the company should grow in the future: "I've learned that growth and success can cover up a lot of mistakes. So now, we seek disciplined, profitable growth for the right reasons." In terms of *organizing* the human resources and talent needed to support that growth, Schultz comments, "Our biggest growth constraint is attracting world-class people who have values that are aligned with our culture." *Leading* comes naturally to Schultz, as reflected by his approach to motivating employees: "It's vital to give people hope, to provide aspirations and a vision for the future." And like any good manager, he is also concerned about *controlling* key parts of the business: "Having gained full operating control, we now have the flexibility and the freedom to control our own destiny . . ." (Schultz is explaining why Starbucks settled with Kraft for $2.7 billion so it could push its own single-serve offerings).[5]

In business, there is no replacement for effective management. A company may fly high for a while, but it cannot maintain that success for long without good management. The goal of this book is to help you learn what it takes to become an effective and successful manager. It is organized into five major sections: introduction, planning, organizing, leading, and controlling. Also, several themes that can help managers differentiate themselves in today's workplace will be emphasized throughout the book: globalization; green and sustainability initiatives; entrepreneurship; e-management, social media, and mobile computing; changing demographics and diversity management; and study tips and career suggestions for your personal development.

● Starbucks CEO Howard Schultz and staff pose to photographers during the Starbucks Mexico 10th anniversary and opening of the new Starbucks store Bosque De Chapultepec at Av. Paseo De La Reforma in Mexico City, Mexico.

1 | THE FOUR FUNCTIONS OF MANAGEMENT

Management is the process of working with people and resources to accomplish organizational goals. Good managers do those things both effectively and efficiently:

- To be *effective* is to achieve organizational goals.

- To be *efficient* is to achieve goals with minimal waste of resources—that is, to make the best possible use of money, time, materials, and people.

Unfortunately far too many managers fail on both criteria, or focus on one at the expense of another. The best managers maintain a clear focus on both effectiveness *and* efficiency.

Although business is changing rapidly, there are still plenty of timeless principles that make managers great and companies thrive. While fresh thinking and new approaches are required now more than ever, much of what we already know about successful management practices (Chapter 2 discusses historical but still-pertinent contributions) remains relevant, useful, and adaptable to the current highly competitive global marketplace.

Great managers and executives like Howard Schultz of Starbucks not only adapt to changing conditions but also apply—passionately, rigorously, consistently, and with discipline—the fundamental management principles of planning, organizing, leading, and controlling. These four core functions remain as relevant as ever, and they still provide the fundamentals that are needed to manage effectively in all types of organizations, including private, public, nonprofit, and entrepreneurial (from microbusinesses to global firms).

Caption: Mary Barra, CEO of GM, speaks at the opening ceremony of the GM China Advanced Technical Center-Phase 1 in Shanghai, China.

As any exceptional manager, coach, or professor would say, excellence always starts with the fundamentals.

1.1 | Planning Helps You Deliver Value

Planning is specifying the goals to be achieved and deciding in advance the appropriate actions needed to achieve those goals. As Exhibit 1.1 illustrates, planning activities include analyzing current situations, anticipating the future, determining objectives, deciding on what types of activities the company will engage, choosing corporate and business strategies, and determining the resources needed to achieve the organization's goals. Plans set the stage for action.

For example, Mary Barra, the first woman to become CEO at General Motors, has several plans to make her firm the "the most valuable automotive company" in the world.[6] An engineer with 33 years of experience at GM, Barra's goals include strengthening the Cadillac and Chevrolet global brands, expanding the company's position in China, and empowering teams to be innovative. Her definition of innovative is "providing value to the customer."[7] A good example of delivering value to customers who want a more environmentally friendly luxury vehicle would be the launch of the 2014 Cadillac ELR, an electric battery–gaspowered hybrid

Exhibit 1.1 Examples of planning activities

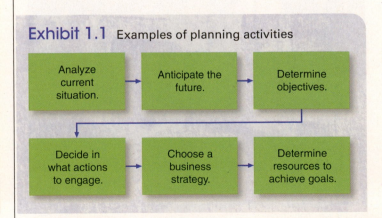

| Analyze current situation. | → | Anticipate the future. | → | Determine objectives. |

| Decide in what actions to engage. | → | Choose a business strategy. | → | Determine resources to achieve goals. |

that can be driven up to 345 miles between charges.[8] A final part of Barra's plan at GM is to reduce complexity at all levels of the organization. Her reputation for simplicity is well-established; while in a former role as HR director, Barra simplified GM's 10-page dress code to two words: "Dress appropriately."[9]

In today's highly competitive business environment, the planning function can also be described as *delivering strategic value.* Value is a complex concept.[10] Fundamentally, it describes the monetary amount associated with how well a job, task, good, or service meets users' needs. Those users might be business owners, customers, employees, governments, and even nations. When Steve Jobs, founder and CEO of Apple, died on October 5, 2011, many people around the world experienced a sense of loss both for him as a person and for the value that his transformational Apple products provided. The better you meet users' needs (in terms of quality, speed, efficiency, and so on), the more value you deliver. That value is "strategic" when it contributes to meeting the organization's goals. On a personal level, you should

1.2 | Organizing Resources Achieves Goals

Organizing is assembling and coordinating the human, financial, physical, informational, and other resources needed to achieve goals. Organizing activities include attracting people to the organization, specifying job responsibilities, grouping jobs into work units, marshaling and allocating resources, and creating conditions so that people and things work together to achieve maximum success.

management the process of working with people and resources to accomplish organizational goals

planning the management function of systematically making decisions about the goals and activities that an individual, a group, a work unit, or the overall organization will pursue

organizing the management function of assembling and coordinating human, financial, physical, informational, and other resources needed to achieve goals

> "Innovation distinguishes between a leader and a follower."
>
> —Steve Jobs

periodically ask yourself and your boss, "How can I add value?" Answering that question will enhance your contributions, job performance, and career.

Traditionally, planning was a top-down approach in which top executives established business plans and told others to implement them. For the best companies, delivering strategic value is a continual process in which people throughout the organization use their knowledge and that of their external customers, suppliers, and other stakeholders to identify opportunities to create, seize, strengthen, and sustain competitive advantage. (Chapter 3 discusses the external competitive environment of business and how managers can influence it.) This dynamic process swirls around the objective of creating more and more value for the customer. For example, Amazon is trying to create more value for its customers by offering a cutting-edge tablet computer that is designed to be faster and less expensive than those offered by the competition.

Effectively creating value requires fully considering a new and changing set of factors, including the government, the natural environment, global forces, and the dynamic economy in which ideas are king and entrepreneurs are both formidable competitors and potential collaborators. You will learn about these and related topics in Chapter 4 (ethics and corporate responsibility), Chapter 5 (strategic planning and decision making), and Chapter 6 (entrepreneurship).

LISTEN & LEARN ⊙ ONLINE

YOUNG MANAGERS
Speak Out!

"It's all about balance in this business. You really have to pay attention to what is going on . . . what you do well. What you can do better. At the same time, you do have to pay attention to what is going on outside and how you can keep up."

—Michael Kettner, Bar Manager

Traditional Thinking

Planning is a top-down approach where top executives establish business plans and tell others to implement them.

The Best Managers Today

Deliver strategic value that draws on the collective knowledge and ideas of a wide variety of people both inside and outside the organization.

The organizing function's goal is to *build a dynamic organization.* Traditionally, organizing involved creating an organization chart by identifying business functions, establishing reporting relationships, and having a personnel department that administered plans, programs, and paperwork. Now and in the future, effective managers will be using new forms of organizing and viewing their people as their most valuable resources. They will build organizations that are flexible and adaptive, particularly in response to competitive threats and customer needs.

Tony Hsieh, CEO of Zappos, has built a dynamic and successful online shoe and retail business by changing the rules of how to organize and treat its diverse employees and customers. After he founded the business in 2000, Hsieh's entrepreneurial approach was rewarded when Amazon purchased Zappos in 2009 for $1.2 billion.[11]

A major goal of Zappos is to treat its employees and customers with integrity, honesty, and commitment.[12] Hsieh encourages employees to develop themselves by checking out books stored at the company, post questions to the "Ask Anything" newsletter, make suggestions to improve how things get done, and contribute to making Zappos a positive and fun place to work. Employees have been known to volunteer to shave their heads (in a mullet style or in the shape of a "No. 1"), act in zany ways during job interviews, wear fun wigs, and blow horns and ring cowbells to entertain tour groups who visit the company.[13]

Employees aren't the only stakeholders who benefit from Hsieh's flexible and adaptive approach to organizing. Customers who call the online retailer often feel spoiled by the treatment they receive. Surprisingly, customer service employees at Zappos aren't told how long they can spend on the phone with customers. In a time when many call-in customer service operations are tightly controlled or outsourced, Hsieh encourages his employees to give customers a "wow" experience such as staying on the phone with a customer for as long as it takes to connect with them and make them happy (the longest recorded phone call lasted six hours), giving customers free shipping both ways, sending flowers and surprise coupons, writing thank-you notes, or even helping a customer find a pizza place that delivers all night.[14]

Progressive employee and customer-oriented practices such as those at Zappos help organizations organize and effectively deploy the highly dedicated, diverse, and talented human resources needed to achieve success. You will learn more about these topics in Chapter 7 (organizing for action), Chapter 8 (human resources management), and Chapter 9 (managing diversity and inclusion).

1.3 | Leading Mobilizes Your People

Leading is stimulating people to be high performers. It includes motivating and communicating with employees, individually and in groups. Leaders maintain close day-to-day contact with people, guiding and inspiring them toward achieving team and organizational goals. Leading takes place in teams, departments, and divisions, as well as at the tops of large organizations.

In earlier textbooks, the leading function described how managers motivate workers to come to work and execute top management's plans by doing their jobs. Today and in the future, managers must be good at *mobilizing and inspiring people* to engage fully in their work and contribute their ideas—to use their knowledge and experience in ways never needed or dreamed of in the past.

Ursula M. Burns, chair and CEO of Xerox since 2009, inspired her employees to change their thinking about the future direction of the $21.4 billion company and mobilized them to

● Online retail giant Zappos' zanny culture and work environment make it a great place to work.

apply their talents and energies in new ways.[15] The company's acquisition of Affiliated Computer Systems for $6.4 billion means that Burns is asking employees to help transform the copier manufacturer into a "formidable" services company that offers business and IT outsourcing.[16] Additional acquisitions and an investment of $185 billion has helped Xerox gain a larger share of the expanding business process outsourcing market than First Data, Accenture, IBM, and Paychex.[17] If Burns can continue to motivate Xerox employees to embrace the new direction of the firm, this new service side of the business may grow to as much as two-thirds of Xerox's revenues by 2015.[18]

Like Ursula Burns, today's managers must rely on a very different kind of leadership (Chapter 10) that empowers and motivates people (Chapter 11). Far more than in the past, great work must be done via great teamwork (Chapter 12), both within work groups and across group boundaries. Underlying these processes will be effective interpersonal and organizational communication (Chapter 13).

1.4 | Controlling Means Learning and Changing

Planning, organizing, and leading do not guarantee success. The fourth function, **controlling**, is about monitoring performance and making necessary changes in a timely

● Ursula Burns, Chairman and CEO of Xerox, smiles as she attends an interview at The Times Center in New York.

manner. By controlling, managers make sure the organization's resources are being used as planned and the organization is meeting its goals for quality and safety.

Control must include monitoring. If you have any doubts that this function is important, consider some control breakdowns that caused catastrophic problems for workers, the environment, and local economies. Consider the explosion of Transocean Ltd.'s Deepwater Horizon oil rig in the Gulf of Mexico on April 20, 2010, which killed 11 workers. Some argue that this worst offshore oil spill in U.S. history could have been prevented if tighter controls were in place. One recent report suggested that the rig's crew failed to react to multiple warning signs: ". . . the crew deviated from standard well-control and well-abandonment protocols by testing for pressure during the removal of the drilling mud, instead of prior to it, an operation that resulted in the drilling pipe being present in the blowout preventer at the time of the blowout, keeping it from closing properly to contain the outburst."[19] This was not the only oil well to go out of control in the Gulf of Mexico. According to an interview with William Reilly, former head of the U.S. Environmental Protection Agency, there have been "79 losses of well control" during the 2000–2009 period.[20] He suggests

that greater controls need to be put in place by both the U.S. government and the oil companies.[21]

When managers implement their plans, they often find that things are not working out as planned. The controlling function makes sure that goals are met. It asks and answers the question, "Are our actual outcomes consistent with our goals?" It then makes adjustments as needed. Elon Musk, chief executive officer of the premium electric car firm Tesla Motors, has applied this function to make needed changes at that firm. Like many start-ups, Tesla has hit a few potholes along the way. Conflicts with the firm's founder and technical problems during development pushed back the launch of the company's first car by more than a year, causing cash flow problems. Musk was forced to close one office and lay off nearly 25 percent of the company's workforce. But Musk also raised $55 million of capital from investors, and since production started in 2008, there are more than 25,000 Model S cars on the road in the United States and Europe.[22]

Successful organizations, large and small, pay close attention to the controlling function. But today and for the future, the key managerial challenges are far more dynamic than in the past; they involve *continually learning and changing*. Controls must still be in place, as described in Chapter 14. But new technologies and other innovations (Chapter 15) make it possible to achieve controls in more effective ways, to help all people throughout a company and across company boundaries change in ways that forge a successful future.

Exhibit 1.2 provides brief definitions of the four functions of management and the respective chapters in which these functions are covered in greater detail.

1.5 | Managing Requires All Four Functions

As a manager in the ever-changing global economy, your typical day will not be neatly divided into the four functions. You will be doing many things more or less simultaneously.[23] Your days will be busy and fragmented, with interruptions, meetings, and firefighting. If you work with heavy digital users who constantly

● A Tesla Model S electric car sits on display in the Tesla Motors, Inc., auto plant, formerly operated by New United Motor Manufacturing, Inc. (NUMMI), in Fremont, CA.

send texts and e-mails, then your workdays will require even more stop-and-go moments.[24] There will be plenty of activities that you wish you could be doing but can't seem to get to. These activities will include all four management functions.

Some managers are particularly interested in, devoted to, or skilled in one or two of the four functions. Try to devote enough time and energy to developing your abilities with *all four* functions. You can be a skilled planner and controller, but if you organize your people improperly or fail to inspire them to perform at high levels, you will not be realizing your potential as a manager. Likewise, it does no good to be the kind of manager who loves to organize and lead but doesn't really understand where to go or how to determine whether you are on the right track. Good managers don't neglect any of the four management functions. You should periodically ask yourself whether you are devoting adequate attention to *all* of them.

Exhibit 1.2	The four functions of management	
Function	**Brief Definition**	**See Chapters**
Planning	Systematically making decisions about which goals and activities to pursue.	4, 5, and 6
Organizing	Assembling and coordinating resources needed to achieve goals.	7, 8, and 9
Leading	Stimulating high performance by employees.	10, 11, 12, and 13
Controlling	Monitoring performance and making needed changes.	14 and 15

The four management functions apply to your career and other areas of your life, as well. You must find ways to create value; organize for your own personal effectiveness; mobilize your own talents and skills as well as those of others; monitor your performance; and constantly learn, develop, and change for the future. As you proceed through this book and this course, we encourage you to engage in the material and apply the ideas to your other courses (e.g., improve your teamwork skills), your part-time and full-time jobs (e.g., learn how to motivate coworkers and "wow" your customers), and use the ideas for your own personal development by becoming an effective manager.

> **LO2** Understand what managers at different organizational levels do

2 | FOUR DIFFERENT LEVELS OF MANAGERS

Organizations—particularly large organizations—have many levels. In this section, you will learn about the types of managers found at four different organizational levels:

- Top-level manager.
- Middle-level manager.
- Frontline manager.
- Team leader.

2.1 | Top Managers Strategize and Lead

Top-level managers are the organization's senior executives and are responsible for its overall management. Top-level managers, often referred to as *strategic managers,* focus on the survival, growth, and overall effectiveness of the organization.

Top managers are concerned not only with the organization as a whole but also with the interaction between the organization and its external environment. This interaction often requires managers to work extensively with outside individuals and organizations.

The chief executive officer (CEO) is one type of top-level manager found in large corporations. This individual is the primary strategic manager of the firm and has authority over everyone else. Others include the chief operating officer (COO), company presidents, vice presidents, and members of the top management team. As companies have increasingly leveraged technology and knowledge management to help them achieve and maintain a competitive advantage, they created the position of chief information officer (CIO). A relatively new top

"In a nationwide survey, employees had mixed reviews of their manager's leadership skills. As a result, a manager who excels in leadership is especially valuable."[25]

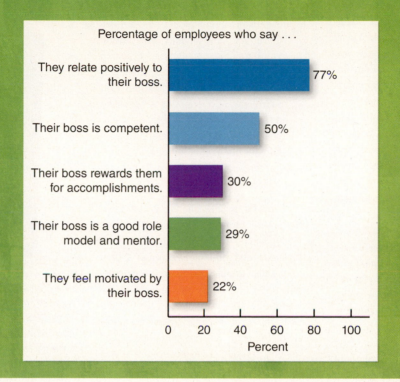

Percentage of employees who say . . .

- They relate positively to their boss. — 77%
- Their boss is competent. — 50%
- Their boss rewards them for accomplishments. — 30%
- Their boss is a good role model and mentor. — 29%
- They feel motivated by their boss. — 22%

Percent

manager position, chief ethics officer, has emerged in recent years. Kathleen Edmond holds that position for Best Buy. Her role is to "develop, market and support programs and strategies designed to support the enterprise's business initiatives and promote honest and ethical business conduct in its daily operations."[26]

Traditionally, the role of top-level managers has been to set overall direction by formulating strategy and controlling resources. But now more top managers are called on to be not only strategic architects but also true organizational leaders. Like Indra Nooyi of PepsiCo, leaders must create and articulate a broader corporate purpose with which people can identify—and one to which people will enthusiastically commit.

2.2 | Middle Managers Bring Strategies to Life

As the name implies, **middle-level managers** are located in the organization's hierarchy below top-level management and above the frontline managers and team leaders. Sometimes called *tactical managers,* they are responsible for translating the general goals and plans developed by strategic managers into more specific objectives and activities.

Traditionally the role of the middle manager is to be an administrative controller who bridges the gap between higher and lower levels. Today middle-level managers break corporate objectives down into business unit targets; put together separate business unit plans from the units below them for higher-level corporate review; and serve as nerve centers of internal communication, interpreting and broadcasting top management's priorities downward and channeling and translating information from the front lines upward.

As a stereotype, the term *middle manager* connotes mediocre, unimaginative people defending the status quo. Companies have been known to cut them by the thousands, and television often portrays them as incompetent (such as Michael Scott of NBC's *The Office*).[27] But middle managers

top-level managers senior executives responsible for the overall management and effectiveness of the organization

middle-level managers managers located in the middle layers of the organizational hierarchy, reporting to top-level executives

Indra Nooyi of PepsiCo Pushes for Sustainable, "Healthier" Growth

At a typical college, you wouldn't have to look far before seeing someone with a bag of Doritos and a can of Pepsi. These two products, along with Classic Lay's, Cheetos, Fritos, and Mountain Dew, are some of the best sellers from PepsiCo. While these products are still very important to the financial success of the company, Indra Nooyi, the Indian-born CEO, is encouraging the company to follow a dual-growth strategy: one focusing on maintaining the success of its salty snacks and sweet drinks, and the other focusing on a multifaceted sustainability initiative called "Performance with Purpose." Nooyi believes a major driver for the next level of PepsiCo's success will come from "delivering sustainable growth by investing in a healthier future for people and our planet."

At first this may seem like a major change in direction for a company that has made billions of dollars from selling sweet drinks and snack foods, but Nooyi doesn't see it that way. Perhaps concerned about the growing societal concerns about unhealthful foods and drinks that are seen as contributing to the childhood and adult obesity problem in the United States and elsewhere, she believes strongly that "ethics and growth are not just linked, but inseparable."

Two major components of PepsiCo's sustainability strategy include

1. *Human sustainability:* The company is encouraging people to live balanced and healthy lives through nonprofit initiatives and by expanding its product and drink lines to include more healthful choices. For example, Baked Lays have zero trans fats, and Propel Zero is water enhanced with vitamins and antioxidants.

2. *Environmental sustainability:* PepsiCo sells millions of products worldwide in packages, containers, or bottles. To reduce the impact on natural resources, the company is reducing water usage, increasing recycling levels, and minimizing its carbon footprint. In 2010 PepsiCo launched a recycling partnership with Waste Management, Greenopolis, and Keep America Beautiful with the goal of increasing beverage container recycling to 50 percent by 2018.

Even for a CEO, change is not easy. Some Wall Street analysts and critics feel Nooyi should focus less on health and wellness, and more on PepsiCo's "sugary and salty product portfolio." However, with total soft drink consumption in the United States dropping by 16 percent over the past decade, there's certainly room for both "fun for you" and "good for you" products and beverages at this forward-looking company.

PepsiCo, in partnership with Waste Management, has placed 4,000 Dream Machine recycling kiosks in schools, offices, stores, and malls around the United States. Since 2010, Dream Machines have collected 94 million plastic beverage bottles and aluminum cans. Proceeds provide career training, education, and job creation for returning U.S. veterans with disabilities.

Discussion Questions

- Indra Nooyi, as CEO of PepsiCo, faces some unique challenges as she advocates a dual-focus strategy for her company. Describe your reaction to her dual-focus strategy and whether you think it will help PepsiCo succeed in the future.

- To what degree do you think a "Performance with Purpose" strategy would be applicable to other organizations (using examples)? How could leaders of other organizations modify the strategy so it would fit their particular organizational cultures and industries?

SOURCES: See PepsiCo's 2010 Annual Report at www .pepsico.com; "Pepsico Reports Dream Machine Recycling Progress," *Plastic News,* April 20, 2012, www.plasticnews.com; "Bottoms Up!" *Newsweek,* October 10 and 17, 2011 (double issue), p. 29; A. Rappeport, "Pepsi Chief Faces Challenge of Putting Fizz Back into Brand," *Financial Times,* March 21, 2011, p. 19; A. Bary, "Sweet or Salty, PepsiCo Tastes Success," *Barron's* 91, no. 32 (August 8, 2011), pp. 15–17; and V. Bauerlein, "CEO Indra Nooyi Stands by Strategy to Promote 'Good for You' Foods," *The Wall Street Journal,* June 28, 2011, p. B1.

---

are closer than top managers to day-to-day operations, customers, frontline managers, team leaders, and employees, so they know the problems. They also have many creative ideas—often better than their bosses'. Good middle managers provide the operating skills and practical problem solving that keep the company working.[28]

2.3 | Frontline Managers Are the Vital Link to Employees

Frontline managers, or *operational managers,* are lower-level managers who execute the operations of the organization. These managers often have titles such as *supervisor* or *sales*

frontline managers lower-level managers who supervise the operational activities of the organization

team leaders employees who are responsible for facilitating successful team performance

manager. They are directly involved with nonmanagement employees, implementing the specific plans developed with middle managers. This role is critical because operational managers are the link between management and nonmanagement personnel. Your first management position probably will fit into this category.

Traditionally, frontline managers were directed and controlled from above to make sure that they successfully implemented operations to support the company strategy. But in leading companies, their role has expanded. Operational execution remains vital, but in leading companies, frontline managers are increasingly called on to be innovative and entrepreneurial, managing for growth and new business development.

● Actor Steve Carell played Michael Scott, the likeable, but often incompetent manager on NBC's The Office.

Managers on the front line—usually newer, younger managers—are crucial to creating and sustaining quality, innovation, and other drivers of financial performance.[29] In outstanding organizations, talented frontline managers are not only *allowed* to initiate new activities but are *expected* to do so by their top and middle-level managers. And they receive the freedom, incentives, and support to do so.[30]

2.4 | Team Leaders Facilitate Team Effectiveness

A relatively new type of manager, known as a **team leader**, engages in a variety of behaviors to achieve team effectiveness.[31] The use of teams (discussed in Chapter 12) has increased as organizations shift from hierarchical to flatter structures that require lower-level employees to make more decisions.[32] While both team leaders and frontline managers tend to be younger managers with entrepreneurial skills, frontline managers have direct managerial control over their non-managerial employees. This means that frontline managers

may be responsible for hiring, training, scheduling, compensating, appraising, and if necessary, firing employees in order to achieve their goals and create new growth objectives for the business.

In comparison, team leaders are more like project facilitators or coaches. Their responsibilities include organizing the team and establishing its purpose, finding resources to help the team get its job done, removing organizational impediments that block the team's progress, and developing team members' skills and abilities.[33] In addition, a good team leader creates and supports a positive social climate for the team, challenges the team, provides feedback to team members, and encourages the team to be self-sufficient.[34] Beyond their internally focused responsibilities, team leaders also need to represent the team's interests with other teams, departments, and groups within and outside of the organization. In this sense, the team leader serves as the spokesperson and champion for the team when dealing with external stakeholders.

Team leaders are expected to help their teams achieve important projects and assignments. In some ways, a team leader's job can be more challenging than frontline and other types of managers' jobs because team leaders often lack direct control (e.g., hiring and firing) over team members. Without this direct control, team leaders need to be creative in how they inspire, motivate, and guide their teams to achieve success.

Exhibit 1.3 elaborates on the changing roles and activities of managers at different levels within the organization. You will learn about each of these aspects of management throughout the course.

Exhibit 1.3 Transformation of management roles and activities

	Team Leaders	Frontline Managers	Middle-Level Managers	Top-Level Managers	
Changing Roles	From operational implementer to facilitator of team effectiveness.	From operational implementers to aggressive entrepreneurs.	From administrative controllers to supportive controllers.	From resource allocators to institutional leaders.	
Key Activities	Structuring teams and defining their purpose.	Attracting and developing resources.	Linking dispersed knowledge and skills across units.	Establishing high performance standards.	
	Finding resources and removing obstacles so teams can accomplish their goals.	Creating and pursuing new growth opportunities for the business.	Managing the tension between short-term purpose and long-term ambition.	Institutionalizing a set of norms to support cooperation and trust.	
	Developing team members' skills so teams can be self-managing.	Managing continuous improvement within the unit.	Developing individuals and supporting their activities.	Creating an overarching corporate purpose and ambition.	

Sources: Adapted from F. P. Morgeson, D. S. DeRue, and E. P. Karam, "Leadership in Teams: A Functional Approach to Understanding Leadership Structures and Processes," *Journal of Management* 36, no. 1 (January 2010), pp. 5–39; J. R. Hackman and R. Wageman, "A Theory of Team Coaching," *Academy of Management Review* 30, no. 2 (April 2005), pp. 269–87; and C. Bartlett and S. Goshal, "The Myth of the Generic Manager: New Personal Competencies for New Management Roles," *California Management Review* 40, no. 1 (Fall 1997), pp. 92–116.

2.5 | Three Roles That All Managers Perform

The trend today is toward less hierarchy and more teamwork. In small firms—and in large companies that have adapted to these highly competitive times—managers have strategic, tactical, operational responsibilities and team responsibilities. They are *complete* businesspeople; they have knowledge of all business functions, are accountable for results, and focus on serving customers both inside and outside their firms. All of this requires the ability to think strategically, translate strategies into specific objectives, coordinate resources, and do real work with lower-level people.

Today's best managers can do it all; they are adaptive and agile, and are "working leaders."[35] They focus on relationships with other people and on achieving results. They don't just make decisions, give orders, wait for others to produce, and then evaluate results. They get their hands dirty, do hard work themselves, solve problems, and create value.

What does all of this mean in practice? How do managers spend their time—what do they actually do? A classic study of top executives found that they spend their time engaging in 10 key activities, falling into three broad categories or roles:[36]

1. **Interpersonal roles:**

   - *Leader*—Staffing, training, and motivating people to achieve organizational goals.
   Example: The manager of a real estate company leads and manages 10 realtors.

   - *Liaison*—Maintaining a network of outside contacts and alliances that provide information and favors.
   Example: A human resources manager attends monthly HR association meetings.

   - *Figurehead*—Performing symbolic duties on behalf of the organization, like greeting important visitors and attending social events.
   Example: The president of a university presides over a graduation ceremony.

2. **Informational roles:**

   - *Monitor*—Seeking information to develop a thorough understanding of the organization and its environment.
   Example: A marketing researcher for a fast-food company tracks changing consumer tastes.

   - *Disseminator*—Sharing information between different people like employees and managers; sometimes interpreting and integrating diverse perspectives.
   Example: A team leader in an accounting firm shares her team's concerns with the managing partner.

   - *Spokesperson*—Communicating on behalf of the organization about plans, policies, actions, and results.
   Example: A public relations officer of a global company issues a news release detailing plans to expand operations in China and India.

3. **Decisional roles:**

   - *Entrepreneur*—Searching for new business opportunities and initiating new projects to create change.
   Example: A software engineer at a social networking website company identifies a new and more intuitive way to connect its users.

- *Disturbance handler*—Taking corrective action during crises or other conflicts.
  Example: An accounting manager at a firm disciplines a junior accountant for engaging in unethical behavior.

- *Resource allocator*—Providing funding and other resources to units or people; includes making major organizational decisions.
  Example: The chief financial officer at a company determines the size of each division's budget for the upcoming fiscal year.

- *Negotiator*—Engaging in negotiations with parties inside and outside the organization.
  Example: An account executive from an advertising company negotiates the purchase price and terms of an advertising campaign with a team from a large client.

This classic study of managerial roles remains highly descriptive of what all types of managers do today. As you review the list, you might ask yourself, "Which of these activities do I enjoy most (and least)? Where do I excel (and not excel)? Which would I like to improve?" Whatever your answers, you will be learning more about these activities throughout this course.

> **LO3** Define the skills needed to be an effective manager

3 | MANAGERS NEED THREE BROAD SKILLS

Performing management functions and roles, pursuing effectiveness and efficiency, and competitive advantage (discussed later in this chapter) are the cornerstones of a manager's job. However, understanding this fact does not ensure success. Managers need a variety of skills to *do* these things *well*. Skills are specific abilities that result from knowledge, information, aptitude, and practice. Although managers need many individual skills, which you will learn about throughout this text, three general categories are crucial:[37]

- Technical skills.

- Conceptual and decision skills.

- Interpersonal and communication skills.

First-time managers tend to underestimate the challenges of the many technical, human, and conceptual skills required.[38] However, with training, experience, and practice, managers can learn to apply each of these skills to increase their effectiveness and performance.

3.1 | Technical Skills

A **technical skill** is the ability to perform a specialized task that involves a certain method or process. Most people develop a set of technical skills to complete the activities that are part of their daily work lives. The technical skills you learn in school will give you the opportunity to get an entry-level position or change careers; they will also help you as a manager. For example, your accounting and finance courses will develop the technical skills you need to understand and manage an organization's financial resources.

Lower-level managers who possess technical skills earn more credibility from their subordinates than comparable managers without technical know-how.[39] Thus, newer employees may want to become proficient in their technical area (e.g., human resources management or marketing) before accepting a position as team leader or frontline manager.

3.2 | Conceptual Decision Skills

Conceptual and decision skills involve the ability to identify and resolve problems for the benefit of the organization and everyone concerned. Managers use these skills when they consider the overall objectives and strategy of the firm, the interactions among different parts of the organization, and the role of the business in its external environment. Managers (like Indra Nooyi of PepsiCo) are increasingly required to think out of their comfort zones to make "new connections between social and environmental challenges on the one hand and firm growth and innovation on the other, and to plan far beyond the quarter and into the future."[40]

As you acquire greater responsibility, you will be asked often to exercise your conceptual and decision skills. You will confront issues that involve all aspects of the organization and must consider a larger and more interrelated set of decision factors. Much of this text is devoted to enhancing your conceptual and decision skills, but experience also plays an important part in their development.

3.3 | Interpersonal and Communication Skills

Interpersonal and communication skills influence the manager's ability to work well with people. These skills are often called *people skills* or *soft skills*. Managers spend the great majority of their time interacting with people,[41] and they must develop their abilities to build trust, relate to, and communicate effectively with those around them. Your people skills often make a difference in the level of success you achieve. Management professor Michael Morris explains, "At a certain level in business, you're living and dying on your social

technical skills the ability to perform a specialized task involving a particular method or process

conceptual and decision skills skills pertaining to the ability to identify and resolve problems for the benefit of the organization and its members

interpersonal and communication skills people skills; the ability to lead, motivate, and communicate effectively with others

abilities. . . . gets you in the door, but social intelligence gets you to the top."[42] Supporting this view, a survey of senior executives and managers found that more than 6 out of 10 said they base hiring and promotion decisions on a candidate's "likeability." Roughly equal numbers (62 versus 63 percent) said they base these decisions on skills, presumably referring to technical skills.[43]

Professor Morris emphasizes that it is vital for future managers to realize the importance of these skills in getting a job, keeping it, and performing well, especially in this era when so many managers supervise independent-minded knowledge workers. He explains, "You have to get high performance out of people in your organization who you don't have any authority over. You need to read other people, know their motivators, know how you affect them."[44]

As Exhibit 1.4 illustrates, the importance of these skills vary by managerial level. Technical skills are most important early in your career when you are a team leader and frontline manager. Conceptual and decision skills become more important than technical skills as you rise higher in the company and occupy positions in the middle and top manager ranks. But interpersonal and communication skills are important throughout your career, at every level of management. One way to increase the effectiveness of your interpersonal and communication skills is by being emotionally intelligent at work.

Good, successful managers often demonstrate a set of interpersonal skills known collectively as **emotional intelligence**[45] (or EQ). EQ combines three skill sets:

- *Understanding yourself*—including your strengths and limitations as a manager.

- *Managing yourself*—dealing with emotions, making good decisions, seeking feedback, and exercising self-control.

- *Working effectively with others*—listening, showing empathy, motivating, and leading.

The basic idea is that before you can be an effective manager of other people, you need to be able to manage your own emotions and reactions to others. Maybe you already have a high EQ, but if you feel that you could use some improvement

in this area, observe how others connect with the people around them, handle stressful situations, and exercise self-control. This can help you build your own EQ so that you can be a more effective manager.

LO4 Summarize the major challenges facing managers today

4 | MAJOR CHALLENGES FACING MANAGERS

When the economy is soaring, business seems easy. Starting up an Internet company looked easy in the 1990s, and ventures related to the real estate boom looked like a sure thing during the early 2000s. Eventually investors grew wary of dot-com start-ups, and the demand for new homes cooled as the United States experienced a major economic recession. At such times, it becomes evident that management is a challenge that requires constantly adapting to new circumstances.

What defines the competitive landscape of today's businesses? You will be reading about many relevant issues in the coming chapters, but we begin here by highlighting five key elements that make the current business landscape different from those of the past:

1. Globalization.

2. Technological change.

3. The importance of knowledge and ideas.

4. Collaboration across organizational boundaries.

5. Increasingly diverse labor force.

4.1 | Business Operates on a Global Scale

Far more than in the past, today's enterprises are global, with offices and production facilities all over the world. Corporations such as Lenovo and Unilever transcend national borders. A key reason for this change is the strong demand coming from consumers and businesses overseas. Companies that want to grow often need to tap international markets where incomes are rising and demand is increasing. GE, which became a massive and profitable corporation by selling appliances, lightbulbs, and machinery to U.S. customers, recently announced that it expected its foreign sales to equal its sales within the United States. GE's biggest foreign customers are in Europe, but sales volume in China and India is rising fast.[46]

Globalization also means that a company's talent can come from anywhere. As with its sales, half of GE's employees work outside the United States.[47] Cisco, a San Jose, California–based leader in equipment for computer networking, considers staffing its ever-expanding operations in India to be an essential

Exhibit 1.4	Importance of skills at different managerial levels		
	Technical Skills	Conceptual/ Decision Skills	Interpersonal/ Communication Skills
Top manager	Low	High	High
Middle manager	Medium	High	High
Frontline manager	High	Medium	High
Team leader	High	Medium	High

Source: Adapted from R. Katz, "Skills of an Effective Administrator," *Harvard Business Review* 52, no. 5 (September–October 1974), pp. 90–102.

Take Charge of Your Career

Pursuing your passion!

Many people go through life tolerating (or worse, hating) their jobs and careers. Given the amount of time people spend working each day, this can feel like a life sentence. Whether you are just starting out or are thinking about switching careers, take the time to discover what you are passionate about. It takes a lot of research, but with persistence and focus, you can find your passion in life and get paid to follow it. A good starting point is to purchase a copy of *What Color Is Your Parachute?* by Richard Bolles. It's filled with exercises and suggestions designed to help readers understand their career and job preferences. The book will not tell you exactly what job or career is a perfect fit, but it will help you understand your preferences regarding the types of skills you want to use in the ideal job, with what types of people you want to work, and so on.

Furthermore, visit your school's career services office. Ask a career counselor if you could complete some *career* and *occupational interest inventories*. Most schools have several available (for free) online for students, including the Campbell Interest and Skill Survey, the Strong Interest Inventory, and Holland's Occupational Themes (this last one is also available for a fee through the U.S. Department of Labor O*Net Interest Profiler—www.onetcenter.org/IP.html).

How do these online inventories work? You answer several questions about yourself, such as whether you like talking to people at a party or working with numbers. After you submit your answers, you receive immediately an interpretive report that describes your preferences in terms of themes, skills, interests, personal style, and occupational preferences. For example, the report from the Strong Interest Inventory gives your highest-rated themes (investigative, social, artistic), your top interest areas (writing and mass communication, law, performing arts), your top occupations (attorney, editor, chef), and your personal style preferences (you are probably comfortable both leading by example and taking charge).

After reading the test results, make an appointment with the career counselor to ask for advice about any internships and full-time jobs that would fit well with your results and interests.

Parents, mentors, motivational speakers, and others often tell students to find their passions. But finding your passion is not easy. Do not get discouraged if your first couple of jobs or internships teach you what you *do not* want to do for the rest of your life. That is good information, too. It takes a lot of persistence to find the "right" internship or job that begins to feel like it is something you could do (and enjoy) for the rest of your career. If you keep asking yourself, "*What am I really passionate about?*" and pursue jobs and careers that fit better and better with that ideal, you will eventually find your passion.

---

tactic for staying competitive. Wim Elfrink, the company's industry solutions and chief globalization officer, recently returned from a four and a half year assignment in Bangalore, India. His job was to create and staff a second global headquarters in Bangalore so Cisco could "establish key resources closer to the world's fastest growing markets."[48] He accomplished his goal. As of May 2012, the Indian-based Globalisation Centre East has approximately 10,000 employees, and more than 20 percent of Cisco's global leadership is based there.[49] Many of these senior executives are from the United States and are helping Cisco take advantage of the fast-growing Indian Internet market.[50] Elfrink also reports that Cisco has transformed its focus for the Bangalore operation from cost savings and outsourcing to quality and innovation. Its talent has earned 420 patents and leads worldwide initiatives for creating new markets for the company's products and services.[51]

Another factor that is making globalization both more possible and more prevalent is the Internet. In 2012 it was estimated that an astounding 8.7 billion devices worldwide were connected to the Internet.[52] Many of these new users are from the emerging BRIC economies: Brazil, Russia, India, and China.[53] Global companies like Dell Computer and Johnson & Johnson are taking advantage of this trend in that a growing percentage of their international sales are to customers in the BRIC countries.[54] As people in developing nations turn to the power of the web, they develop content in their own languages and create

● Chief Globalization Officer Wim Elfrink, left, and Cisco Systems Inc. chairman and Chief Executive Officer John Chambers, right, help former Indian President A. P. J. Abdul Kalam, center, to cut the ribbon for the inauguration of the Cisco Globalization Centre East in Bangalore, India.

their own means of access, like Baidu, the search engine market leader in China.[55]

The Internet is a powerful force for connecting people without regard to time and space. The Internet enables people to connect and work from anywhere in the world on a 24/7 basis. Laura Asiala, a manager for Dow Corning, based in Midland, Michigan, supervises employees in Tokyo, Seoul, Hong Kong, Shanghai, and Brussels. To keep in touch with them, she starts working at 5:00 a.m. some days and ends as late as midnight. She takes a break from 3:30 to 9:30 each day, and technology lets her communicate from home.[56]

:::::::::::::::::

The global reach of the Internet pushed Mitch Free to expand his business, MFG.com, into China. MFG.com runs a website where manufacturers that need parts post their specifications online, and suppliers bid to provide those parts. The suppliers pay an annual fee for the right to submit bids. Free, who grew up in a small town in Georgia and had barely traveled outside the United States, had never planned to be an international manager, but Chinese suppliers soon began submitting requests to participate. At the same time, manufacturers were pressing MFG.com to include Asian suppliers, which often could offer the best prices.

So Free traveled to Shanghai, China, to meet some of the interested suppliers. He learned about the business culture, such as the importance of cultivating business relationships and networks. After a difficult search, he made a key hiring decision: general manager James Jin, who speaks fluent English, studied global management, and has experience in manufacturing both in the United States and in China. The effort was well rewarded. Jin has helped Free navigate the fast-growing business landscape of his native China. Sales in China accounted for more than 10 percent of MFG.com's total annual sales and are growing faster than the company's overall sales.[57]

:::::::::::::::::

Smaller firms are also engaged in globalization. Many small companies export their goods. Many domestic firms assemble their products in other countries, using facilities such as Mexico's maquiladora plants. And companies are under pressure to improve their products in the face of intense competition from foreign manufacturers. Firms today must ask themselves, "How can we be the best in the world?"

For students, it's not too early to think about the personal ramifications. In the words of chief executive officer Jim Goodnight of SAS, the largest privately held software company in the world, "The best thing business schools can do to prepare their students is to encourage them to look beyond their own backyards. Globalization has opened the world for many opportunities, and schools should encourage their students to take advantage of them."[58]

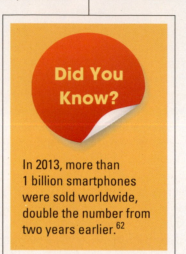

Did You Know?

In 2013, more than 1 billion smartphones were sold worldwide, double the number from two years earlier.[62]

4.2 | Technology Is Continuously Advancing

The Internet's impact on globalization is only one of the ways that technology is vitally important in the ever-changing business world. Technology both complicates things and creates new opportunities. The challenges come from the rapid rate at which communication, transportation, information, and other technologies change.[59] Until recently, for example, desktop computers were a reliable source of income, not only for computer makers but also for the companies that make keyboards and a whole host of accessories like wrist rests and computer desks. But after just a couple of decades of widespread PC use, customers switched to laptops, tablets, and even smartphones for their computing needs, requiring different accessories and using them in different ways.[60] Any company that still makes desktops has to rethink its customers' wants and needs, not to mention the possibility that these customers may be doing their work at the airport or a local coffee shop rather than in an office.

Later chapters will discuss technology further, but here we highlight the rise of the Internet and its effects. Why is the Internet so important to business?[61]

- It enables managers to be mobile and connected 24/7.

- It fulfills many business functions. It is a virtual marketplace, a means to sell goods and services, a distribution channel, an information service, and more.

- It speeds up globalization. Managers can see what competitors, suppliers, and customers are doing on the other side of the world.

- It provides access to information, allows better-informed decisions, and improves efficiency of decision making.

- It facilitates design of new products and services, from smartphones to online banking services.

While these advantages create business opportunities, they also create threats as competitors capitalize on new developments.

At the beginning, Internet companies dazzled people with financial returns that seemed limitless. Today investors and entrepreneurs have learned that not every business idea will fly, but many profitable online businesses have become a part of our day-to-day lives. Just a few years ago, it was novel to go online to order plane tickets, read the news, or share photos. Some online success stories, such as eBay, Amazon, Monster, and Google, are purely Internet businesses. Other companies, including Target, Barnes & Noble, and Office Depot, have incorporated online channels into an existing business strategy.

The Internet's impact is felt not only at the level of businesses as a whole but also by individual employees and their managers. Just as globalization has stretched out the workdays of some people, high-tech gadgets have made it possible to stay connected to work anytime and anywhere. Wi-Fi hotspots make connections available in shared working spaces, coffee shops, restaurants, hotels, airports, and libraries. Software lets users download and read files and e-mail over their phones and PDAs.

Social media and networking are also challenging the way businesses operate and managers connect. Facebook, the largest online social network, has reported 945 million active users as of December 2013, an increase of 39 percent over the previous year.[63] Facebook is not just an American phenomenon; about 70 percent of its users are located outside the United States. Other popular social networking sites, like Twitter, LinkedIn, Pinterest, Google+, and Tumblr, also connect people with one another.

Finding the time to build and maintain meaningful connections to a large and diverse network of contacts, clients, and other key stakeholders is a major challenge for managers today. While it can be time-consuming, connecting with people has never been easier because of online social networking sites that allow you to develop your **social capital**. The goodwill stemming from your social relationships is more important than ever and aids your career success, compensation, employment, team effectiveness, successful entrepreneurship, and relationships with suppliers and other outsiders.[64] Students should take time to build a large and diverse network while in school. This network may prove valuable in the future.

The stress comes when employees or their supervisors don't set limits on being connected. Real estate broker Ted Helgans calls his BlackBerry a "traveling office" and a valuable tool for getting and sharing information. Helgans emphasizes that users can and should decide when to turn off the devices.[65] Jean Chatzky, an editor for *Money* magazine, realized that the device had become more of a distraction than a help, and began reminding herself that the messages were not emergencies.[66] Thus using technology effectively is more than a matter of learning new skills; it also involves making judgments about when and where to apply the technology for maximum benefit.[67]

4.3 | Knowledge Is a Critical Resource

Companies and managers need new, innovative ideas. Because companies in advanced economies have become so efficient at producing physical goods, most workers have been freed up to provide services like training, entertainment, research, and advertising. Efficient factories with fewer workers produce the cereals and cell phones the market demands; meanwhile, more and more workers create software

and invent new products. These workers, whose primary contributions are ideas and problem-solving expertise, are often referred to as *knowledge workers.*

Managing these workers poses some particular challenges, which we will examine throughout this book. For example, determining whether they are doing a good job can be difficult because the manager cannot simply count or measure a knowledge worker's output. Also, these workers often are most motivated to do their best when the work is interesting, not because of a carrot or stick dangled by the manager.[68]

Because the success of modern businesses so often depends on the knowledge used for innovation and the delivery of services, organizations need to manage that knowledge. **Knowledge management** is the set of practices aimed at discovering and harnessing an organization's intellectual resources—fully utilizing the intellects of the organization's people. Knowledge management is about finding, unlocking, sharing, and capitalizing on the most precious resources of an organization: people's expertise, skills, wisdom, and relationships.

Typically knowledge management relies on software that lets employees contribute what they know and share that knowledge readily with one another. As a result, knowledge management may be the responsibility of an organization's information technology (IT) department, perhaps under the leadership of a chief information officer or chief knowledge officer.

In hospitals, important knowledge includes patients' histories, doctors' orders, billing information, dietary requirements, prescriptions administered, and much more. With lives at stake, many hospitals have embraced knowledge management. At Virginia Commonwealth University (VCU) Health System, a single information system lets doctors write prescriptions, look up patient information and lab results, and consult with one another. Billing also is automated as part of VCU's knowledge management system, making the process more efficient and connecting with patient data so that it can remind the physician of all the conditions being treated—and billed for.[69] Hospitals may also give patients access to the knowledge management system so they can schedule appointments, request prescription refills, and send questions to their doctors.

4.4 | Collaboration Boosts Performance

One of the most important processes of knowledge management is to ensure that people in different parts of the organization collaborate effectively. This requires communication among departments, divisions, or other subunits of the organization. As illustrated in Exhibit 1.5, BP tries to create "T-shaped" managers who break out of the traditional corporate hierarchy to share knowledge freely across the organization (the horizontal part of the "T") while remaining fiercely committed to the performance of their individual business units (the vertical part of the "T"). This emphasis on dual responsibilities for performance and knowledge sharing also occurs at Procter & Gamble, pharmaceutical giant Glaxo-SmithKline, the large German industrial company Siemens, and the London-based steelmaker Ispat International.[70]

Toyota keeps its product development process efficient by bringing together design engineers and manufacturing employees from the beginning. Often manufacturing employees can see ways to simplify a design so that it is easier to make without defects or unnecessary costs. Toyota expects its employees to listen to input from all areas of the organization, making this type of collaboration a natural part of the organization's culture. The collaboration is supported with product development software including an online database that provides a central, easily accessible source of information about designs and processes. Along with this information, employees use the software to share their knowledge—best practices they have developed for design and manufacturing.[71] At Toyota, knowledge management supports collaboration and vice versa.

Collaboration also occurs beyond the boundaries of the organization itself. Companies today must motivate and capitalize on the ideas of people outside the organization. AT&T, in an effort to connect with more small business owners (a key source of potential customers) over the Internet, is collaborating with an outside firm to develop over 100 how-to articles.[72] Topics include everything from writing a business plan to setting up a wireless network. AT&T is putting content like this on the web to attract these new customers when they use search engines and social media.[73]

Customers, too, can be collaborators. Creating outstanding products and services can start with involving customers in company decisions. Procter & Gamble has been getting customers to think creatively and talk with one another online to come up with new product and service ideas.[74] Tapping into the popularity of social networking websites like Facebook and Twitter, P&G set up two websites aimed at bringing its customers together. One site, the People's Choice Community, provides content about the winners of the People's Choice Awards, along with opportunities to join a "community" of people who want to share messages about those celebrities. The other site, called Capessa, is a discussion group for women where they can

Exhibit 1.5 The T-shaped manager at BP

T-shaped managers increase organizational effectiveness by *sharing knowledge with others across the organization . . .*

. . . .while simultaneously focusing on achieving strong performance in their own business units.

trade thoughts about health and other concerns. Although both sites offer advertising opportunities, P&G intends to use them primarily as a way to learn more about consumers' attitudes.[75]

4.5 | Diversity Needs to Be Leveraged

The labor force is becoming more and more diverse. This means that it is likely that your coworkers, customers, suppliers, and other stakeholders will differ from you in race, ethnicity, age, gender, physical characteristics, or sexual orientation. To be an effective manager, you'll need to understand, relate to, and work productively with these individuals. How diverse are we becoming at work? The following trends in the U.S. labor force are expected from 2010 through 2020:[76]

- The labor force will continue to grow more diverse.

- Fast growth of "older workers" will occur to the point that approximately 1 out of 4 workers will be 55 and older.

- Hispanics will grow to about 19 percent and Asians to about 6 percent of the labor force.

- A higher percentage of women than men will join the labor force.

- White (non-Hispanic) workers' participation in the labor force will drop from 68 to 62 percent.

The increase in gender, racial, age, and ethnic diversity in the workplace will accentuate the many differences in employees' values, attitudes toward work, and norms of behavior. In addition to leveraging the strengths of diverse employees, effective managers need to find ways to connect with diverse customers, suppliers, and government officials, both in the United States and internationally. As will be discussed in greater detail in later chapters, managers need to be acutely aware of these differences and be prepared to prevent (or deal with) miscommunication, insensitivity, and hostility on the part of an employee, customer, or other stakeholder who doesn't embrace the benefits of diversity management.

Fortunately, effective managers and organizations are taking steps to address these concerns and leverage the diversity of their resources and talent in new ways. IBM's board of directors and its Worldwide Executive Council (WEC) are 57 percent and 40 percent (respectively) female and multicultural (not U.S.-born). The WEC is responsible for overseeing the company's worldwide diversity initiatives, including recruiting, retaining, and promoting talent, and linking diversity initiatives to the global marketplace.[77] Accounting, taxation and consulting firm Deloitte LLP has undertaken several steps to break the "glass ceiling" and retain more of its talented female employees. The firm decreased the amount of travel for employees to allow them to have better work/life balance, provided enhanced career opportunities for women, and made diversity management a key priority for the entire organization. By making a concerted effort to retain and value female employees, Deloitte is managing its talent in a more effective and efficient manner. The company now has more than 1,000 female partners, principals, and directors.[78] By retaining valuable human resources, Deloitte avoids having to spend time and money on recruiting, selecting, orienting, and training new employees who may or may not fit the organizational culture or be able to do the job as well as a current employee.

Globalization, technological change, the monumental importance of new ideas, collaboration across disappearing boundaries, diversity—what are the effects of this tidal wave of new forces? The remainder of this chapter and the following chapters will answer this question with business and management principles, real-world examples, and insights from successful managers and leaders.

5 | SOURCES OF COMPETITIVE ADVANTAGE

Why do some companies lose their dominant positions while others manage to stay on top?[79] Blockbuster was a successful video rental chain until Netflix, cable companies, and online enterprises changed the delivery and pricing of videos and entertainment content. Then there's Eastman Kodak. For over 100 years, this company dominated the camera and film markets until being upended by the invention of digital photography, file sharing, and the like. On the other hand, how does a company like Apple continually excite customers with its "iGadget" offerings?[80] How does the Chinese electric car manufacturer BYD compete effectively in this emerging segment of the automobile industry? How does the Indian technology company Infosys compete effectively against its American rivals, Accenture and McKinsey?[81]

These successful companies have strong managers who know they are in a competitive struggle to survive and win. To do this, you have to gain advantage over your competitors and earn a profit. You gain competitive advantage by being better than your competitors at doing valuable things for your customers. But what does this mean, specifically? To succeed, managers must deliver the fundamental success drivers: innovation, quality, service, speed, and cost competitiveness.

5.1 | Innovation Keeps You Ahead of Competitors

Founded in 2000, Baidu is the number one Chinese-language Internet search engine. With 21,000 employees and $3.5 billion in sales in 2013, Baidu is hoping that its recent acquisition of an Internet video provider will help it maintain an innovative edge in China.[82]

Innovation is the introduction of new goods and services. Your firm must adapt to changes in consumer demand and to new competitors. Products don't sell forever; in fact, they

● The iPad page on the Apple.com UK website viewed on a 4th generation Apple iPad tablet computer.

don't sell for nearly as long as they used to because so many competitors are introducing so many new products all the time. Likewise, you have to be ready with new ways to communicate with customers and deliver products to them, as when the Internet forced traditional merchants to learn new ways of reaching customers directly. Globalization and technological advances have accelerated the pace of change and thus the need for innovation.

Sometimes the most important innovation isn't the product itself but the way it is delivered. Borrowing an idea that has proved popular in Europe, Opaque–Dining in the Dark has collaborated with the Braille Institute of America to present dining events at the Hyatt West Hollywood in total darkness. Diners select gourmet meals from a menu in a lighted lounge and then are led into a dark banquet room by blind or visually impaired waiters. The attraction is that diners experience the meal in a completely new way because they are forced to concentrate on their senses of taste, smell, and touch.[83]

Innovation is today's holy grail.[84] And like the other sources of competitive advantage, innovation comes from people, it must be a strategic goal, and it must be managed properly. Later chapters will show you how great companies innovate.

5.2 | Quality Must Continuously Improve

When Spectrum Health, a hospital chain based in Grand Rapids, Michigan, asked patients how well they were served, the hospital learned that it had a problem. Patients rated staff low on helpfulness and said they didn't get good information about the procedures they received in the hospital, or the way they were supposed to take care of themselves after being released to return home. Spectrum responded to the survey results by setting up an advisory council of patients and family members, making visiting hours more flexible, getting patient input on who was allowed to hear medical information and make decisions about treatment, and calling discharged patients at home to make sure they understood the directions they had received. Within two years of conducting the survey and beginning to make these changes, satisfaction scores of Spectrum patients improved dramatically.[85]

Spectrum Health's efforts reflect a commitment to quality. In general, **quality** is the excellence of your product or service. The importance of quality and the standards for acceptable quality have increased dramatically. Customers now demand high-quality goods and services, and often they will accept nothing less.

Historically, quality pertained primarily to the physical goods that customers bought, and it referred to attractiveness, lack of defects, reliability, and long-term dependability. The traditional approach to quality was to check work after it was completed and then eliminate defects. But then W. Edwards Deming, J. M. Juran, and other quality gurus convinced managers to take a more complete approach to achieving *total* quality. This includes several objectives:

- *Preventing* defects before they occur.
- *Achieving zero defects* in manufacturing.
- *Designing* products for quality.

The goal is to plan carefully, prevent from the beginning all quality-related problems, and live a philosophy of *continuous improvement* in the way the company operates. Deming and his ideas were actually rebuffed by U.S. managers; only when he found an audience in Japan, and Japan started grabbing big chunks of market share from the United States in vehicles, computer chips, and TVs, did U.S. managers start internalizing and practicing his quality philosophy.[86]

Although these principles were originally applied to manufacturing tangible goods, the experiences of Spectrum Health remind us that service quality is vital as well. Quality is also enhanced when companies customize goods and services to individual consumers' wishes. Choices at Starbucks give consumers literally thousands of variations on the drinks they can order, whether it's half-caff or full caffeine, skim milk or soy milk, or shots of espresso and any of a variety of flavored syrups. And for a premium price, candy lovers can select M&M's candies bearing the message of their own creation.[87]

Providing world-class quality requires a thorough understanding of what quality really is.[88] Quality can be measured in terms of product performance, customer service, reliability (avoidance of failure or breakdowns), conformance to standards, durability, and aesthetics. At the beginning of this section, we mentioned how hospitals are using patient surveys to measure quality. However, a study conducted by the University of Pennsylvania School of Medicine determined that a patient's risk of dying was not significantly less at hospitals that scored well on Medicare's quality measures.[89] Certainly, if you enter a hospital, you hope to come out alive! Only when you move beyond broad, generic concepts like "quality" and identify specific quality requirements can you identify problems, target needs, set performance standards more precisely, and deliver world-class value.

5.3 | Services Must Meet Customers' Changing Needs

As we noted in the discussion of quality, important quality measures often pertain to the level of service customers receive. This dimension of quality is particularly important because the service sector now dominates the U.S. economy. Services include intangible products like insurance, hotel accommodations, medical care, and haircuts. Between now and 2018, the Bureau of Labor Statistics forecasts that Americans will spend a higher percentage of their personal income on services than tangible goods.[90] The total number of jobs in service companies—not including retailing, wholesaling, and government workers—is nearly five times the number in manufacturing companies. And that pattern is expected to intensify. Between now and 2018, the fastest-growing job categories will be almost entirely services and retailing jobs, and the jobs expected to see the greatest declines are almost all in manufacturing.[91]

In a competitive context, **service** means giving customers what they want or need, when and where they want it. So service is focused on continually meeting the changing needs of customers to establish mutually beneficial long-term relationships. Service is also an important offering for many companies that sell tangible goods. Software companies, in addition to providing the actual programs, may help their customers identify requirements, set up computer systems, and perform maintenance.

Stores offer a shopping environment and customer service along with the goods on their shelves. To improve service for a wider customer base, Best Buy adjusted its store environment so it would be more inviting to female shoppers.

The chain's loud music and emphasis on high-tech features had been aimed at young men, but the store found that women

service the speed and dependability with which an organization delivers what customers want

speed fast and timely execution, response, and delivery of results

company a few million dollars, Google cofounder Larry Page responded to her explanation and apology by saying he was actually glad she had made the mistake. It showed that Sandberg appreciated the company's values. Page told her, "I want to run a company where we are moving too quickly and doing too much, not being too cautious and doing too little. If we don't have any of these mistakes, we're just not taking enough risks."[93]

While it's unlikely that Google actually favors mistakes over money-making ideas, Page's statement expressed an appreciation that in the modern business environment, **speed**—rapid execution, response, and delivery of results—often separates

> "Be everywhere, do everything, and never fail to astonish the customer."
>
> —Macy's Motto

influence 9 out of 10 consumer electronics purchases. Best Buy lowered the volume, dimmed the lighting, and trained staff to discuss what customers want the technology to do for them, rather than merely pointing out bells and whistles. The chain is also trying to hire more female salespeople.[92]

An important dimension of service quality is making it easy and enjoyable for customers to experience a service or to buy and use products. For example, Apple made it easy and enjoyable for online customers to sample their favorite music and then download it from the iTunes store. Amazon allows customers to look at a free sample of a book to help them decide whether they want to read and purchase the entire book. These innovations in service are changing the way companies do business.

5.4 | Do It Better *and* Faster

Google's culture, based on rapid innovation, is constantly trying to make improvements in its product. When Sheryl Sandberg (now chief operating officer of Facebook) was a vice president at Google, she once made a mistake by moving too fast to plan carefully. Although the mistake cost the

the winners from the losers. How fast can you develop and get a new product to market? How quickly can you respond to customer requests? You are far better off if you are faster than the competition—and if you can respond quickly to your competitors' actions.

Speed is no longer just a goal of some companies; it is a strategic imperative. Speed combined with quality is a measure that a company is operating efficiently. In the auto industry, getting faster is essential just for keeping up with the competition. A recent study found that the top assembly plant in the United States was Ford's Atlanta facility, where employees needed just 15.4 hours to assemble a vehicle. Compare that with the 1980s, when GM employees needed 40 hours to assemble a vehicle.[94] Another important measure of speed in the auto industry is the time a company takes to go from product concept to availability of a vehicle in the showroom. During the 1980s, that time was about 30 or 40 months. Today Toyota has cut the process to an average of 24 months; it needed just 22 months to launch its Tundra pickup.[95]

Speed isn't everything—you can't get sloppy in your quest to be first. But other things being equal, faster companies are more likely to be the winners, slow ones the losers.

5.5 | Low Costs Help Increase Your Sales

Walmart keeps driving hard to find new ways to cut billions of dollars from its already very low distribution costs. It leads the industry in efficient distribution, but competitors are copying Walmart's methods, so the efficiency no longer gives it as much of an advantage. To stay on top of the game, Walmart has urged its suppliers to use radio frequency ID (RFID) tags on products for instantaneous identification and better inventory tracking.[96] Walmart also has sought to keep costs down by scheduling store employees more efficiently. It introduced a computerized system that schedules employees based on each store's sales, transactions, units sold, and customer traffic. It compares seven weeks' worth of data in those areas with the prior year's performance and uses the results to determine how many employees will be needed during which hours. The system is intended to schedule just enough workers, with full staffing only at the busiest times and days of the week, so it requires more flexibility from Walmart's employees.[97]

Walmart's efforts are aimed at **cost competitiveness**, which means keeping costs low enough so the company can realize profits and price its products (goods or services) at levels that are attractive to consumers. Toyota's efforts to trim product development processes are also partly aimed at cost competitiveness. Making the processes more efficient through collaboration between design and manufacturing employees eliminates wasteful steps and procedures. Needless to say, if you can offer a desirable product at a lower price, it is more likely to sell.

Managing your costs and keeping them down require being efficient: accomplishing your goals by using your resources wisely and minimizing waste. Little improvements can save big money, but cost cuts involve trade-offs. That explains some of the growth in the market for private jets. Flying on a private jet is more expensive than buying a ticket on a commercial airline. But for a highly paid, frequently traveling business executive, the time spent hanging around an airport can become more costly than the cost of a jet. If the company can arrange to participate in a service such as NetJets, where the company buys only shares in a jet with the rights to use it, this can trim the price and make the arrangement even more beneficial.[98]

One reason every company must worry about cost is that consumers can easily compare prices on the Internet from thousands of competitors. DealTime, Shopzilla, and PriceGrabber are only a few of the search tools that can generate lists of prices at which a product is available from various suppliers. Consumers looking to buy popular items, such as cameras, printers, and plane fares, can go online to research the best models and the best deals. If you can't cut costs and offer attractive prices, you can't compete.

● Walmart controls costs by continuously improving the efficiency and speed of its inventory management system. One of its distribution centers is pictured above.

5.6 | The Best Managers Deliver All Five Advantages

Don't assume that you can settle for delivering just one of the five competitive advantages: low cost alone or quality alone, for example. The best managers and companies deliver them all.

Virginia Mason Medical Center, like many hospitals, felt challenged in delivering low costs along with high quality and superior services. Virginia Mason has a reputation for high-quality care, but it was losing money treating certain patients. Complicated, high-tech procedures generate higher fees, but they aren't necessarily what a patient needs the most. Some patients may benefit more from a simple doctor visit, but that's not as profitable. So Virginia Mason collaborated with Aetna, an insurer that pays for 10 percent of the medical center's business, and with local employers that provide coverage for their employees through Aetna. Together the companies renegotiated the standard procedures physicians would follow and the rates Aetna would pay so that some of the most expensive conditions could be treated in ways that were ultimately more economical to insure but paid for at higher rates that would be profitable for Virginia Mason. The facility presented the plan to its department heads, helping them pay attention to how their decisions affect the cost of care. Virginia Mason has also improved quality through measures that enhance speed—in this case, cutting waiting times for patients, such as a reduction in the four-hour wait for chemotherapy to 90 minutes.[99]

Trade-offs may occur among the five sources of competitive advantage, but this doesn't need to be a zero-sum game where one has to suffer at the expense of another. Columbia Hotel Management is in the business of managing hotel properties around the country. Some of these hotels include Best Western (Georgia), Holiday Inn (Illinois), Ramada Plaza (Texas), and the Quality Inn (Mississippi).[100] The director of human resources for the company focused on cost savings when he decided to outsource some of the more routine human resources tasks such as payroll and benefits management.[101] Turning over those responsibilities to a vendor that specializes in performing them efficiently freed the HR director to engage in higher-level HR strategies and projects that can help his organization provide outstanding services for the hotel properties it manages.

Making decisions about outsourcing and cost savings are just some important ways to help your organization achieve competitive advantage. As you read this chapter, you learned about several of the challenges facing managers today and what functions and activities managers engage in at different levels of the organization. The next chapter (Chapter 2) looks back to help provide a lens for understanding how we got to where we are today. It provides a brief look at the evolution of management thought and practice.

Study Checklist

- Did you tear out the perforated student review card at the back of the text to revisit learning objectives and key terms and definitions?

Connect® Management is available for M Management. Additional resources include:

- Interactive applications:
  - Case Analysis: Likely to Succeed as an Executive?
  - Drag & Drop: A Manager's Many Roles
  - Drag & Drop: The Four Functions of Management at Trader Joe's

- Video Case: Managing for the Future of State Farm Bank

- LearnSmart—Multiple choice questions help you determine what you already know, are not sure about, or need to practice based on your score. And with SmartBook, you can read the relevant section in the eBook as well as practice and recharge what you've learned.

- Chapter Videos: Redbox, Zappos.com

- Young Manager Speaks Out: Michael Kettner, Bar Manager

Want help studying?

SMARTBOOK—Make each minute count.

Go to: LearnSmartAdvantage.com

2 chapter

The Evolution of Management

Learning Objectives

After studying Chapter 2, you should be able to

LO1 Describe the origins of management practice and its early concepts and influences.

LO2 Summarize the five classical approaches to management.

LO3 Discuss the four contemporary approaches to management.

LO4 Identify modern contributors who have shaped management thought and practices.

What is a chapter about history doing in a management textbook? It provides context for understanding how managerial approaches have evolved over time. Today's taken-for-granted management practices—efficiency, division of labor, pay for performance, cooperative work environments, equitable treatment of employees, decentralized decision making, empowerment, autonomy, and teamwork—originated from earlier contributions to management thought.

Many of the historical contributors discussed in this chapter were colorful, interesting people. Frederick Taylor did not like seeing that processes at his company were disorganized and workers were slacking off. His ideas inspired the likes of Henry Ford, who perfected the assembly line and changed history. Lillian Gilbreth maintained quite a balancing act between her successful career, husband, and 12 children while still finding time to design kitchens and appliances as a consultant for General Electric. Henri Fayol saved a large mining and steel company that was on the brink of bankruptcy and turned it into a profitable, well-managed organization. He saved over 10,000 employees' jobs.

The management profession as we know it today is relatively new. This chapter explores the roots and influences of modern management theory. Understanding the origins of management thought will help you grasp the underlying contexts of the ideas and concepts presented in the chapters ahead.

Although this chapter is titled "The Evolution of Management" it might be more appropriately called "The Revolutions of Management" because it documents the wide swings in management approaches over the last 100 years. Parts of each of these approaches have survived and found their way into modern perspectives on management. Thus the legacy of past efforts, breakthroughs, and failures has become our guide to current and future management practice.

The remainder of this chapter discusses the classical and contemporary approaches to management, as well as modern contributions from current and well-known management thought leaders.

1 | ORIGINS OF MANAGEMENT

For several thousand years, managers have wrestled with some of the same issues and problems that confront executives today. As far back as 5000 BC, the Sumerians practiced the management function of controlling (discussed in Chapter 1) by keeping records of tax receipts, real estate holdings, and lists of farm animals.[1] Here are some other examples of the early application and use of management functions:[2]

- Around 4000 BC, the Egyptians used planning, organizing, leading, and controlling to build their great pyramids; one pyramid took over 100,000 laborers 20 years to complete.

● A limestone relief from the tomb of Ipi, Ipi, a relatively humble manager of estate, is being carried by attendants with sunshades. Egypt. Ancient Egyptian. 6th dynasty c 2345-2181 BC. Saqqara.

- As early as 1100 BC, the Chinese applied the managerial concepts of delegation, cooperation, efficiency, organization, and control.

- In 500 BC, Sun Tzu discussed the importance of planning and leading in his book *The Art of War.*

- Around 400–350 BC, the Greeks recognized management as a separate art and advocated a scientific approach to work.

- Around 1436, the Venetians standardized production through the use of an assembly line, building warehouses and using an inventory system to monitor the contents.

- In 1776 Adam Smith discussed control and the principle of specialization with regard to manufacturing workers.

However, throughout history most managers operated by a trial-and-error basis. The industrial revolution in the 18th and 19th centuries changed that. Fueled by major advances in manufacturing and transportation technologies like the steam engine, cotton gin, and railway networks, and the availability of large numbers of low-skilled laborers,[3] businesses and factories grew in size and became more complex to operate. Managers who could make minor improvements in management tactics produced impressive increases in production quantity and quality.[4]

The emergence of **economies of scale**—reductions in the average cost of a unit of production as the total volume produced increases—drove managers to strive for further growth. The opportunities for mass production created by the industrial revolution spawned intense and systematic thought about management problems and issues—particularly efficiency, production processes, and cost savings.[5] In the 1890s the newly formed General Electric Company was able to mass-produce several new products (many invented or refined by Thomas A. Edison), including incandescent lightbulbs, electric fans, and phonographs.[6]

Toward the end of the industrial revolution, management emerged as a formal discipline. The first university programs to offer management and business education, the Wharton School at the University of Pennsylvania and the Amos Tuck School at Dartmouth, were founded in the late 19th century. By 1914, 25 business schools existed.[7]

1.1 | The Evolution of Management

Exhibit 2.1 provides a timeline depicting the evolution of management thought through the decades. This historical perspective is divided into two major sections: classical approaches and contemporary approaches. Many of these approaches overlapped as they developed, and they often had a significant impact on one another. Some approaches were a direct reaction to the perceived deficiencies of previous approaches. Others developed as the needs and issues confronting managers changed over the years. All the approaches attempted to explain the real issues facing managers and provide them with tools to solve future problems.

Exhibit 2.1 will reinforce your understanding of the key relationships among the approaches and place each perspective in its historical context.

2 | CLASSICAL APPROACHES

The classical period extended from the mid-19th century through the early 1950s. The major approaches that emerged during this period were systematic management, scientific management, bureaucracy, administrative management, and human relations.

2.1 | Systematic Management

During the 19th century, growth in U.S. business centered on manufacturing.[8] Early writers such as Adam Smith believed the management of these firms was chaotic, and their ideas helped to systematize it. Most organizational tasks were subdivided and performed by specialized labor. However, poor coordination caused frequent problems and breakdowns of the manufacturing process.

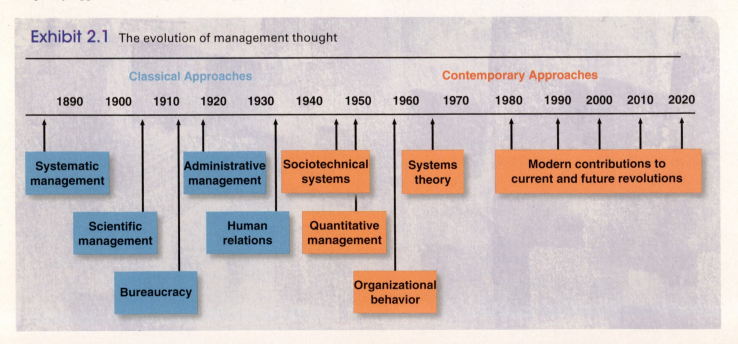

Exhibit 2.1 The evolution of management thought

Classical Approaches | Contemporary Approaches

1890 1900 1910 1920 1930 1940 1950 1960 1970 1980 1990 2000 2010 2020

Systematic management
Scientific management
Bureaucracy
Administrative management
Human relations
Sociotechnical systems
Quantitative management
Organizational behavior
Systems theory
Modern contributions to current and future revolutions

An Early Labor Contract

The following rules, taken from the records of Cocheco Company, were typical of labor contract provisions in the 1850s.

1. The hours of work shall be from sunrise to sunset, from the 21st of March to the 20th of September inclusively; and from sunrise until eight o'clock, P.M., during the remainder of the year. One hour shall be allowed for dinner, and half an hour for breakfast during the first mentioned six months; and one hour for dinner during the other half of the year; on Saturdays, the mill shall be stopped one hour before sunset, for the purpose of cleaning the machinery.

2. Every hand coming to work a quarter of an hour after the mill has been started shall be docked a quarter of a day; and every hand absenting him or herself, without absolute necessity, shall be docked in a sum double the amount of the wages such hand shall have earned during the time of such absence. No more than one hand is allowed to leave any one of the rooms at the same time—a quarter of a day shall be deducted for every breach of this rule.

3. No smoking or spiritous liquors shall be allowed in the factory under any pretense whatsoever. It is also forbidden to carry into the factory, nuts, fruits, etc., books, or papers during the hours of work.

Source: W. Sullivan, "The Industrial Revolution and the Factory Operative in Pennsylvania," *The Pennsylvania Magazine of History and Biography* 78 (1954), pp. 478–79.

The **systematic management** approach attempted to build specific procedures and processes into operations to ensure coordination of effort. Systematic management emphasized economical operations, adequate staffing, maintenance of inventories to meet consumer demand, and organizational control. These goals were achieved through

- Careful definition of duties and responsibilities.

- Standardized techniques for performing these duties.

- Specific means of gathering, handling, transmitting, and analyzing information.

- Cost accounting, wage, and production control systems to facilitate internal coordination and communications.

Systematic management emphasized internal operations because managers were concerned primarily with meeting the explosive growth in demand brought about by the industrial revolution. In addition, managers were free to focus on internal issues of efficiency, in part because the government did not constrain business practices significantly. Finally, labor was poorly organized. As a result, many managers were oriented more toward things than toward people.

Systematic management did not address all the issues 19th-century managers faced, but it tried to raise managers' awareness about the most pressing concerns of their job.

2.2 | Scientific Management

Systematic management failed to lead to widespread production efficiency. This shortcoming became apparent to a young engineer named Frederick Taylor, who was hired by Midvale

Steel Company in 1878. Taylor discovered that production and pay were poor, inefficiency and waste were prevalent, and most companies had tremendous unused potential. He concluded that management decisions were unsystematic and that no research to determine the best means of production existed.

In response, Taylor introduced a second approach to management, known as **scientific management**.[9] This approach advocated the application of scientific methods to analyze work and to determine how to complete production tasks efficiently. For example, U.S. Steel's contract with the United Steel Workers of America specified that sand shovelers should move 12.5 shovelfuls per minute; shovelfuls should average 15 pounds of river sand composed of 5.5 percent moisture.[10]

Taylor identified four principles of scientific management:

1. Management should develop a precise, scientific approach for each element of one's work to replace general guidelines.

2. Management should scientifically select, train, teach, and develop each worker so that the right person has the right job.

3. Management should cooperate with workers to ensure that jobs match plans and principles.

economies of scale
reductions in the average cost of a unit of production as the total volume produced increases

systematic management
a classical management approach that attempted to build into operations the specific procedures and processes that would ensure coordination of effort to achieve established goals and plans

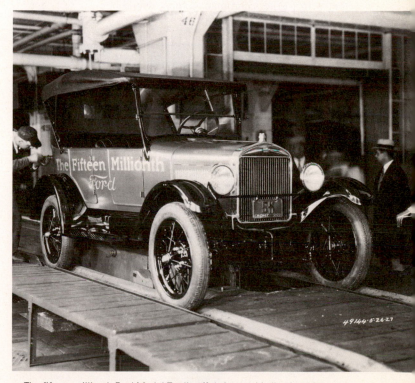

● The fifteen millionth Ford Model T rolls off the assembly line in 1927. Henry Ford revolutionized automobile manufacturing by applying the principles of scientific management.

4. Management should ensure an appropriate division of work and responsibility between managers and workers.

To implement this approach, Taylor used techniques such as time-and-motion studies. With this technique, a task was divided into its basic movements, and different motions were timed to determine the most efficient way to complete the task.

After the "one best way" to perform the job was identified, Taylor stressed the importance of hiring and training the proper worker to do that job. Taylor advocated the standardization of tools, the use of instruction cards to help workers, and breaks to eliminate fatigue.

Another key element of Taylor's approach was the use of the differential piecerate system. Taylor assumed workers were motivated by receiving money. Therefore, he implemented a pay system in which workers were paid additional wages when they exceeded a standard level of output for each job. Taylor concluded that both workers and management would benefit from such an approach.

Did You Know?

Frederick Taylor started as a common laborer at Midvale Steel company in Philadelphia. Within six years, he rose through the ranks (clerk, machinist, supervisor, and master mechanic) to become the chief engineer of the plant. His experiences at Midvale Steel informed many of his ideas about scientific management.

Source: D.A. Wren, *The History of Management Thought* (Upper Saddle River, NJ: Wiley, 2005), pp. 122–124.

● Frederick Taylor was an early expert in management efficiency.

Henry L. Gantt worked with and became a protégé of Frederick Taylor's.[11] Like Taylor, he believed in scientific management and the need for management and labor to cooperate. He expanded on the piecerate system by suggesting that frontline supervisors should receive a bonus for each of their workers who completed their assigned daily tasks.[12] Gantt believed that this would motivate supervisors to provide extra attention and training to those workers who were struggling with meeting their output goals. He is also known for creating the Gantt chart, which helps employees and managers plan projects by task and time to complete those tasks. An interesting aspect of the chart is that it illustrates how some tasks need to be done during the same time period. Today Gantt charts (available through Microsoft Project and other project software) are used in several fields for a wide variety of projects.[13] Exhibit 2.2 illustrates how students can use a Gantt chart to complete a semester-long team research project.

Frank B. and Lillian M. Gilbreth formed a productive husband and wife team. Frank was a strong believer in Taylor's philosophies. While working as a supervisor of bricklayers, Frank Gilbreth developed a system to lower costs and increase worker productivity by showing how employees could work smarter, not harder.[14] His analysis showed how the number of motions for the average bricklayer could be reduced from 18 to 4, allowing worker productivity to increase from 1,000 to 2,700 bricks laid each day.[15] This success inspired Gilbreth to use a motion picture camera (with a clock in the foreground) to capture the precise movements of workers as they accomplished tasks. These "motion studies" were used to identify and remove wasteful movements so workers could be more efficient and productive.

Lillian Gilbreth was also an influential contributor to management thought and practice. Known as the "mother of modern management," she earned a PhD in psychology and later taught at Purdue University as a professor of management and

LISTEN & LEARN ○ ONLINE

YOUNG MANAGERS
Speak Out!

"Look at big business people. I'll use Steve Jobs as an example . . . Looking at what other people are doing in business and saying 'wow!' That's something that someday I'd wish I could make that sort of splash."

—Tim Cote, Technology Services Manager

Exhibit 2.2 — Using a Gantt chart for a team research project at school

Step	Task	Assigned to	Accomplish Task				
			Aug	**Sept**	**Oct**	**Nov**	**Dec**
1	Review assignment.	All team members	-----8/28				
2	Meet as group to discuss and identify areas for clarification.	All team members	-----9/5				
3	Identify team leader.	All team members	-------9/8				
4	Meet with professor to clarify objectives of assignment.	Team leader	----9/12				
5	Meet as group to divide responsibilities.	Team leader and members	-------9/18				
6	Write sections 1–3.	Member B			---------------10/31		
7	Write sections 4–6.	Member C			---------------10/31		
8	Write introduction and conclusion and type bibliography.	Member D			---------------10/31		
9	Edit entire paper.	Team leader				-------11/15	
10	Prepare PPT slides for presentation.	Member E				-------11/20	
11	Practice/rehearse presentation.	Team leader and members				--------11/22	
12	Submit completed paper and deliver presentation.	Team leader and members					--12/1

the first female professor in the engineering school.[16] While supportive of her husband's work, Lillian Gilbreth eventually focused less on the technical and more on the human side of management. She was interested in how job satisfaction motivated employees, how motion studies could be used to help disabled individuals perform jobs, and how fatigue and stress affected workers' well-being and productivity.[17] Amazingly,

Scientific Management and the Model-T

At the turn of the century, automobiles were a luxury that only the wealthy could afford. They were assembled by craftspeople who put an entire car together at one spot on the factory floor. These workers were not specialized, and Henry Ford believed they wasted time and energy bringing the needed parts to the car. Ford took a revolutionary approach to automobile manufacturing by using scientific management principles.

After much study, machines and workers in Ford's new factory were placed in sequence so that an automobile could be assembled without interruption along a moving production line. Mechanical energy and a conveyor belt were used to take the work to the workers.

The manufacture of parts likewise was revolutionized. For example, formerly it had taken one worker 20 minutes to assemble a flywheel magneto. By splitting the job into 29 different operations, putting the product on a mechanical conveyor, and changing the height of the conveyor, Ford cut production time to 5 minutes.

By 1914 chassis assembly time had been trimmed from almost 13 hours to 1½ hours. The new methods of production required complete standardization, new machines, and an adaptable labor force. Costs dropped significantly, the Model-T became the first car accessible to the majority of Americans, and Ford dominated the industry for many years.

Source: H. Kroos and C. Gilbert, *The Principles of Scientific Management* (New York: Harper & Row, 1911).

Lillian Gilbreth achieved many of these accomplishments while raising 12 children and running a consulting business. Perhaps it would be more appropriate to refer to her as the "first superwoman" who balanced a successful career and family life.[18]

Scientific management principles were widely embraced. One of the most famous examples of the application of scientific management is the factory Henry Ford built to produce the Model-T.[19]

The legacy of Taylor's scientific management approach is broad and pervasive. Most important, productivity and efficiency in manufacturing improved dramatically. The concepts of scientific methods

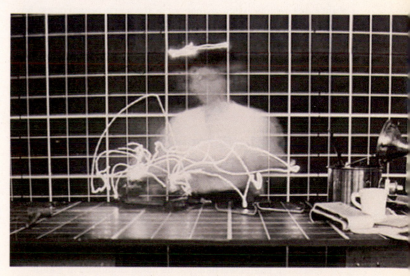

● Using time-lapse photography to capture this worker's physical movements while she worked, Frank B. and Lillian M. Gilbreth became famous for their "effort-versus-efficiency" research and analyses.

bureaucracy a classical management approach emphasizing a structured, formal network of relationships among specialized positions in the organization

administrative management a classical management approach that attempted to identify major principles and functions that managers could use to achieve superior organizational performance

and research were introduced to manufacturing. The piecerate system gained wide acceptance because it more closely aligned effort and reward. Taylor also emphasized the need for cooperation between management and workers. And the concept of a management specialist gained prominence.

Despite these gains, not everyone was convinced that scientific management was the best solution to all business problems. First, critics claimed that Taylor ignored many job-related social and psychological factors by emphasizing only money as a worker incentive. Second, production tasks were reduced to a set of routine, machinelike procedures that led to boredom, apathy, and quality control problems. Third, unions strongly opposed scientific management techniques because they believed management might abuse their power to set the standards and the piecerates, thus exploiting workers and diminishing their importance. Finally, although scientific management resulted in intense scrutiny of the internal efficiency of organizations, it did not help managers deal with broader external issues such as competitors and government regulations, especially at the senior management level.

2.3 | Bureaucracy

Max Weber, a German sociologist, lawyer, and social historian, showed how management itself could be more efficient and consistent in his book *The Theory of Social and Economic Organizations.*[20] The ideal model for management, according to Weber, is the **bureaucracy** approach.

Weber believed bureaucratic structures can eliminate the variability that results when managers in the same organization have different skills, experiences, and goals. As illustrated in Exhibit 2.3, Weber advocated that the jobs themselves be standardized so that

personnel changes would not disrupt the organization. He emphasized a structured, formal network of relationships among specialized positions in an organization. Rules and regulations standardize behavior, and authority resides in positions rather than in individuals. As a result, the organization need not rely on a particular individual, but will realize efficiency and success by following the rules in a routine and unbiased manner.

According to Weber, bureaucracies are especially important because they allow large organizations to perform the many routine activities necessary for their survival. Also, bureaucratic positions foster specialized skills, eliminating many subjective judgments by managers. In addition, if the rules and controls are established properly, bureaucracies should be unbiased in their treatment of people, both customers and employees. Many organizations today are bureaucratic. Bureaucracy can be efficient and productive. However, bureaucracy is not the appropriate model for every organization. Organizations or departments that need rapid decision making and flexibility may suffer under a bureaucratic approach. Some people may not perform their best with excessive bureaucratic rules and procedures.

Other shortcomings stem from a faulty execution of bureaucratic principles rather than from the approach itself. Too much authority may be vested in too few people; the procedures may become the ends rather than the means; or managers may ignore

● German Sociologist Max Weber believed that a bureaucracy approach would make management more efficient and consistent.

Exhibit 2.3 Characteristics of an effective bureaucracy

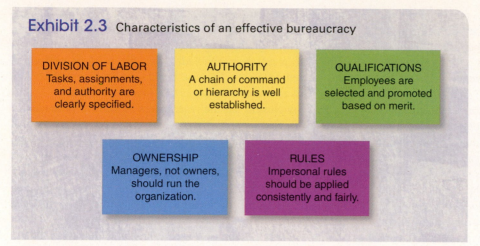

DIVISION OF LABOR
Tasks, assignments, and authority are clearly specified.

AUTHORITY
A chain of command or hierarchy is well established.

QUALIFICATIONS
Employees are selected and promoted based on merit.

OWNERSHIP
Managers, not owners, should run the organization.

RULES
Impersonal rules should be applied consistently and fairly.

Source: Adapted from M. Weber, *The Theory of Social and Economic Organization,* trans. T. Parsons and A. Henderson (New York: Free Press, 1947), pp. 324–341.

appropriate rules and regulations. Finally, one advantage of a bureaucracy—its permanence—can also be a problem. Once a bureaucracy is established, dismantling it is very difficult.

2.4 | Administrative Management

The **administrative management** approach emphasized the perspective of senior managers within the organization, and

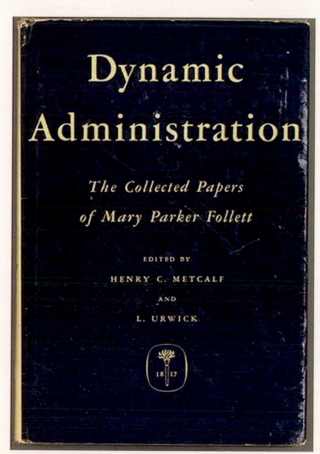

● Author of *Dynamic Administration* and other works, Mary Parker Follett was an influential writer, speaker, and management consultant.

argued that management was a profession and could be taught.

An explicit and broad framework for administrative management emerged in 1916, when Henri Fayol, a French mining engineer and executive, published a book summarizing his management experiences. Fayol identified five functions and 14 principles of management. The five functions, which are very similar to the four functions discussed in Chapter 1, are planning, organizing, commanding, coordinating, and controlling. Exhibit 2.4 lists and defines the 14 principles. Although some critics claim Fayol treated the principles as universal truths for management, he actually wanted them applied flexibly.[21]

A host of other executives contributed to the administrative management literature. These writers discussed a broad spectrum of management topics, including the social responsibilities of management, the philosophy of management, clarification of business terms and concepts, and organizational principles. Chester Barnard's and Mary Parker Follett's contributions have become classic works in this area.[22]

Exhibit 2.4   Fayol's 14 principles of management

1. *Division of work*—divide work into specialized tasks and assign responsibilities to specific individuals.
2. *Authority*—delegate authority along with responsibility.
3. *Discipline*—make expectations clear and punish violations.
4. *Unity of command*—each employee should be assigned to only one supervisor.
5. *Unity of direction*—employees' efforts should be focused on achieving organizational objectives.
6. *Subordination of individual interest to the general interest*—the general interest must predominate.
7. *Remuneration*—systematically reward efforts that support the organization's direction.
8. *Centralization*—determine the relative importance of superior and subordinate roles.
9. *Scalar chain*—keep communications within the chain of command.
10. *Order*—order jobs and material so they support the organization's direction.
11. *Equity*—fair discipline and order enhance employee commitment.
12. *Stability and tenure of personnel*—promote employee loyalty and longevity.
13. *Initiative*—encourage employees to act on their own in support of the organization's direction.
14. *Esprit de corps*—promote a unity of interests between employees and management.

Barnard, former president of New Jersey Bell Telephone Company, published his landmark book *The Functions of the Executive* in 1938. He outlined the role of the senior executive: formulating the purpose of the organization, hiring key individuals, and maintaining organizational communications.[23] Mary Parker Follett's 1942 book *Dynamic Administration* extended Barnard's work by emphasizing the continually changing situations that managers face.[24] Two of her key contributions—the notion that managers desire flexibility and the differences between motivating groups and individuals—laid the groundwork for the modern contingency approach discussed later in the chapter.

All the writings in the administrative management area emphasize management as a profession along with fields such as law and medicine. In addition, these authors offered many recommendations based on their personal experiences, which often included managing large corporations. Although these perspectives and recommendations were considered sound, critics noted that they might not work in all settings. Different types of personnel, industry conditions, and technologies may affect the appropriateness of these principles.

2.5 | Human Relations

A fourth approach to management, **human relations**, developed during the 1930s. This approach aimed at understanding how psychological and social processes interact with the work situation to influence performance. Human relations was the first major approach to emphasize informal work relationships and worker satisfaction.

This approach owes much to other major schools of thought. For example, many of the ideas of the Gilbreths (scientific management) and Barnard and Follett (administrative management) influenced the development of human relations from 1930 to 1955. In fact, human relations emerged from a research project that began as a scientific management study.

Western Electric Company, a manufacturer of communications equipment, hired a team of Harvard researchers led by Elton Mayo and Fritz Roethlisberger. They were to investigate the influence of physical working conditions on workers' productivity and efficiency in one of the company's factories outside Chicago. This research project, known as the *Hawthorne Studies,* provided some of the most interesting and controversial results in the history of management.[25]

The Hawthorne Studies were a series of experiments conducted from 1924 to 1932. During the first stage of the project (the Illumination Experiments), various working conditions, particularly the lighting in the factory, were altered to determine the effects of those changes on productivity. The researchers found no systematic relationship between the factory lighting and production levels. In some cases, productivity continued to increase even when the illumination was reduced to the level of moonlight. The researchers concluded that the workers performed and reacted differently because the researchers were observing them. This reaction is known as the **Hawthorne Effect**.

This conclusion led the researchers to believe productivity may be affected more by psychological and social factors than by physical or objective influences. With this thought in mind, they initiated the other four stages of the project. During these stages, the researchers performed various work group experiments and had extensive interviews with employees. Mayo and his team eventually concluded that productivity and employee behavior were influenced by the informal work group.

Human relations proponents argued that managers should stress primarily employee welfare, motivation, and communication. They believed social needs had precedence over economic needs. Therefore, management must gain the cooperation of the group and promote job satisfaction and group norms consistent with the goals of the organization.

Another noted contributor to the field of human relations was Abraham Maslow.[26] In 1943 Maslow suggested that humans have five levels of needs. The most basic needs are the physical

A Human Relations Pioneer

In 1837 William Procter, a ruined English retailer, and James Gamble, son of a Methodist minister, formed a partnership in Cincinnati to make soap and candles. Both were known for their integrity, and soon their business was thriving.

By 1883 the business had grown substantially. When William Cooper Procter, grandson of the founder, left Princeton University to work for the firm, he wanted to learn the business from the ground up. He started working on the factory floor. "He did every menial job from shoveling rosin and soap to pouring fatty mixtures into crutchers. He brought his lunch in a paper bag . . . and sat on the floor [with the other workers] and ate with them, learning their feelings about work."

By 1884 Cooper Procter believed, from his own experience, that increasing workers' psychological commitment to the company would lead to higher productivity. His passion to increase employee commitment to the firm led him to propose a scandalous plan: share profits with workers to increase their sense of responsibility and job satisfaction. The surprise was audible on the first "Dividend Day," when workers held checks equivalent to seven weeks' pay.

Still, the plan was not complete. Workers saw the profit sharing as extra pay rather than as an incentive to improve. In addition, Cooper Procter recognized that a fundamental issue for the workers, some of whom continued to be his good friends, was the insecurity of old age. Public incorporation in 1890 gave Procter a new idea. After trying several versions, by 1903 he had discovered a way to meet all his goals for labor: a stock purchase plan. For every dollar a worker invested in P&G stock, the company would contribute four dollars' worth of stock.

Finally, Cooper Procter had resolved some key issues for labor that paid off in worker loyalty, improved productivity, and an increasing corporate reputation for caring and integrity. He went on to become CEO of the firm, and P&G today remains one of the most admired corporations in the United States.

Sources: O. Schisgall, *Eyes on Tomorrow* (Chicago: J. G. Ferguson, 1981): T. Welsh, "Best and Worst Corporate Reputations," *Fortune,* February 7, 1994, pp. 58–66.

Take Charge of Your Career

Using history to your advantage!

Many senior executives and entrepreneurs have not only read many of the famous books and writings (discussed later in this chapter) by modern writers like Peter Drucker, Michael Porter, and Stephen Covey, but also know the classic works of Frederick Taylor, Elton Mayo, and Abraham Maslow. By familiarizing yourself with these influential works, you will be able to discuss them with senior managers, who will probably be impressed to discover that you have taken the time to learn "where we have come from."

You might take this approach a step further by learning everything you can about the *history of the industry* in which your organization competes. This may give you insights into your firm's growth and position relative to its competitors. Next you could dig into the *history of the company* and learn about the key people and founders who shaped its culture and direction. This will help you learn about the firm's values and how things really work inside its walls. Last, try to learn about the *history of your supervisor and coworkers* since they joined the organization. This information will give you insight and could prove helpful in many ways during your tenure at the organization. For example, maybe you find out that your supervisor was instrumental is stopping some unethical practices in the department a few years ago. This should tell you that she or he takes these issues very seriously, and thus you and your coworkers should do the same.

History is a source of information, and information is powerful when it is turned into actionable knowledge that can help you develop an excellent reputation and successful career within an organization.

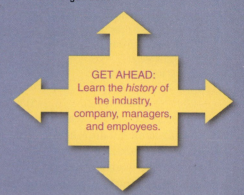

GET AHEAD:
Learn the *history* of the industry, company, managers, and employees.

● Employees working at a Western Electric plant circa 1930.

needs for food, water, and shelter; the most advanced need is for self-actualization, or personal fulfillment. Maslow argued that people try to satisfy their lower-level needs and then progress upward to the higher-level needs. Managers can facilitate this process and achieve organizational goals by removing obstacles and encouraging behaviors that satisfy people's needs and organizational goals simultaneously.

Although the human relations approach generated research into leadership, job attitudes, and group dynamics, it drew heavy criticism.[27] Critics believed that one result of human relations—a belief that a happy worker was a productive worker—was too simplistic. While scientific management overemphasized the economic and formal aspects of the workplace, human relations ignored the more rational side of the worker and the important characteristics of the formal organization. However, human relations was a significant step in the development of management thought because it prompted managers and researchers to consider the psychological and social factors that influence performance.

LO3 Discuss the four contemporary approaches to management

3 | CONTEMPORARY APPROACHES

The contemporary approaches to management include **sociotechnical systems theory**, quantitative management, organizational behavior, and systems theory. The contemporary approaches have developed at various times since World War II, and they continue to represent the cornerstones of modern management thought.

3.1 | Sociotechnical Systems Theory

Drawing on several classical approaches, sociotechnical systems theory suggests that organizations are effective when their employees (the social system) have the right tools, training, and knowledge (the technical system) to make products and services that are valued by customers.[28] Developed in the early 1950s by researchers from the London-based Tavistock Institute of Human Relations, sociotechnical systems theory explained how important it was to understand how coal miners' social behaviors interacted with the technical production system of their organizations. The researchers found that when there was a good fit between these two important internal dimensions and the demands of customers external to the organization, the organizations could reach higher levels of effectiveness.[29]

While research on sociotechnical systems theory was a precursor to the total quality management (TQM) movement (discussed in other chapters), it also promoted the use of teamwork and semiautonomous work groups as important factors for creating efficient production systems. The researchers believed that workers should be given the freedom to correct problems at early stages of the production process rather than after products were made, when errors would create waste.[30]

Sociotechnical systems theory was put into action back in the late 1980s and 1990s when each of the large U.S. automakers—General Motors, Ford, and Chrysler—created cooperative ventures with the major Japanese automakers. General Motors and Toyota set up in Fremont, California, Ford and Mazda in Flat Rock, Michigan, and Chrysler and Mitsubishi in Bloomington, Illinois.[31] Both sides wanted to learn from the other, with American managers being especially interested in understanding how the Japanese integrated the different management and technical subsystems to achieve high performance. At that time, managers at these Japanese companies were applying sociotechnical systems to achieve competitive advantage.[32]

3.2 | Quantitative Management

Although Taylor introduced the use of science as a management tool early in the 20th century, most organizations did not adopt the use of quantitative techniques for management problems until the 1940s and 1950s.[33] During World War II, military planners began to apply mathematical techniques to defense and logistic problems. After the war, private corporations began assembling teams of quantitative experts to tackle many of the complex issues confronting large organizations. This approach, referred to as **quantitative management**, emphasizes the application of quantitative analysis to management decisions and problems.

Quantitative management helps a manager make a decision by developing formal mathematical models of the problem. Computers facilitated the development of specific quantitative methods. These include such techniques as statistical decision theory, linear programming, queuing theory, simulation, forecasting, inventory modeling, network modeling, and breakeven analysis. Organizations apply these techniques in many areas, including production, quality control, marketing, human resources, finance, distribution, planning, and research and development. One particular area of quantitative management known as "big data" (discussed in Chapter 15) is increasingly being used by managers to analyze patterns in structured and unstructured data.[34] The idea is that more accurate analyses and decision making can result in "greater operational efficiencies, cost reductions, and reduced risk."[35]

Despite the promise quantitative management holds, managers do not rely on these methods as the primary approach to decision making. Typically they use these techniques as a supplement or tool in the decision process. Many managers will use results that are consistent with their experience, intuition, and judgment, but they often reject results that contradict their beliefs. Also, managers may use the process to compare alternatives and eliminate weaker options.

organizational behavior
a contemporary management approach that studies and identifies management activities that promote employee effectiveness by examining the complex and dynamic nature of individual, group, and organizational processes

systems theory a theory stating that an organization is a managed system that changes inputs into outputs

inputs goods and services organizations take in and use to create products or services

outputs the products and services organizations create

Several explanations account for the limited use of quantitative management. Many managers have not been trained in using these techniques. Also, many aspects of a management decision cannot be expressed through mathematical symbols and formulas. Finally, many of the decisions managers face are nonroutine and unpredictable.

3.3 | Organizational Behavior

During the 1950s, a transition took place in the human relations approach. Scholars began to recognize that worker productivity and organizational success are based on more than the satisfaction of economic or social needs. The revised perspective, known as **organizational behavior**, studies and identifies management activities that promote employee effectiveness through an understanding of the complex nature of individual, group, and organizational processes. Organizational behavior draws from a variety of disciplines, including psychology and sociology, to explain the behavior of people on the job.

During the 1960s, organizational behaviorists heavily influenced the field of management. Douglas McGregor's Theory X and Theory Y marked the transition from human relations.[36] According to McGregor, Theory X managers assume workers are lazy and irresponsible and require constant supervision and external motivation to achieve organizational goals. Theory Y managers assume employees *want* to work and can direct and control themselves. An important implication for managers who subscribe to Theory X is known as a *self-fulfilling prophecy*. This occurs when a manager treats employees as lazy, unmotivated, and in need of tight supervision; then the employees eventually fulfill the manager's expectations by acting that way. This cycle can have several negative implications for managers, employees, and organizations. McGregor advocated a Theory Y perspective, suggesting that managers who encourage participation and allow opportunities for individual challenge and initiative would achieve superior performance.

Other major organizational behaviorists include Chris Argyris, who recommended greater autonomy and better jobs for workers,[37] and Rensis Likert, who stressed the value of participative management.[38] Through the years, organizational behavior has consistently emphasized development of the organization's human resources to achieve individual and organizational goals. Like other approaches, it has been criticized for its limited perspective, although more recent contributions have a broader and more situational viewpoint. In the past few years, many of the primary issues addressed by organizational behavior have experienced a rebirth with a greater interest in leadership, employee involvement, and self-management.

3.4 | Systems Theory

The classical approaches as a whole were criticized because they (1) ignored the relationship between the organization and its external environment and (2) usually stressed one aspect of the organization or its employees at the expense of other considerations. In response to these criticisms, management scholars during the 1950s stepped back from the details of the organization to attempt to understand it as a whole system. These efforts were based on a general scientific approach called **systems theory**.[39] Organizations are open systems, dependent on **inputs** from the outside world, such as raw materials, human resources, and capital. They transform these inputs into **outputs** that (ideally) meet the market's needs for goods and services. The environment reacts to the outputs through a feedback loop; this feedback provides input for the next cycle of the system. The process repeats itself for the life of the system, and is illustrated in Exhibit 2.5.

Systems theory also emphasizes that an organization is one system in a series of subsystems. For instance, Southwest

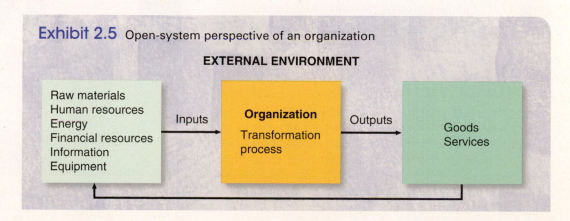

Exhibit 2.5 Open-system perspective of an organization

EXTERNAL ENVIRONMENT

Raw materials
Human resources
Energy
Financial resources
Information
Equipment

Inputs →

Organization
Transformation process

Outputs →

Goods
Services

contingency perspective an approach to the study of management proposing that the managerial strategies, structures, and processes that result in high performance depend on the characteristics, or important contingencies, or the situation in which they are applied

contingencies factors that determine the appropriateness of managerial actions

Airlines is a subsystem of the airline industry, and the flight crews are a subsystem of Southwest. Systems theory points out that each subsystem is a component of the whole and is interdependent with other subsystems.

Building on systems theory ideas, the **contingency perspective** refutes universal principles of management by stating that a variety of factors, both internal and external to the firm, may affect the organization's performance.[40] Therefore, there is no "one best way" to manage and organize because circumstances vary.

Situational characteristics are called **contingencies**. Understanding contingencies helps a manager know which sets of circumstances dictate which management actions. You will learn recommendations for the major contingencies throughout this text. The contingencies include

1. Circumstances in the organization's external environment.

2. The internal strengths and weaknesses of the organization.

3. The values, goals, skills, and attitudes of managers and workers in the organization.

4. The types of tasks, resources, and technologies the organization uses.

With an eye to these contingencies, a manager may categorize the situation and then choose the proper competitive strategy, organization structure, or management process for the circumstances.

Researchers continue to identify key contingency variables and their effects on management issues. As you read the topics covered in each chapter, you will notice similarities and differences among management situations and the appropriate responses. This perspective should represent a cornerstone of your own approach to management. Many of the things you will learn about throughout this course apply a contingency perspective.

LO4 Identify modern contributors who have shaped management thought and practices

---

4 | MODERN CONTRIBUTORS

In addition to the historical figures that we discussed earlier in this chapter, several individuals from more recent times have influenced (through their leadership, interviews, presentations, or writing) the way management is practiced in today's organizations.

In 2001 Jim Collins authored an influential book titled *Good to Great* in which he and his research team analyzed 1,435 companies to understand why some companies reach high levels of sustained performance while other companies fail to reach greatness.[41] He discovered that great companies are managed by "level 5 leaders" who often display humility while simultaneously inspiring those in the organization to apply self-discipline and self-responsibility while pursuing high standards. These leaders often leave enduring legacies without drawing a lot of attention to themselves.[42]

Several CEOs have left an impact on modern management thought. Ex-CEO Jack Welch transformed General Electric from a $13 billion company into a $500 billion company over a 20-year period.[43] Though sometimes criticized for his controversial practices (e.g., selling off underperforming divisions and forced rankings of employees by performance),[44] he is widely viewed as having mastered "all of the critical aspects of leadership: people, process, strategy and structure."[45] Welch has written several books about this management philosophies and successes. Other exceptional leaders who have left their mark

● Jack Welch, former CEO of General Electric, signs his book *Winning* at Borders in New York, NY.

Traditional Thinking

Leaders adapt to change by relying on one or two favorite managerial approaches.

The Best Managers Today

Embrace change by drawing on classic, contemporary, and modern managerial approaches to guide their decisions and actions.

● Peter Drucker was an influential contributor of modern management ideas and practices.

on management practice include Herb Kelleher, cofounder of Southwest Airlines, Sam Walton, founder of Walmart, and Lou Gerstner, former CEO of IBM.

Michael Porter, professor at Harvard University, is a well-known and influential expert on competitive strategy. He has published more than 125 research articles and 18 books on the subject and related areas, including *Competitive Strategy: Creating and Sustaining Superior Performance.* Two of his influential research articles are titled "What Is Strategy?" and "The Five Competitive Forces That Shape Strategy" (discussed in Chapter 3).[46]

Gary Hamel, professor, consultant, and management educator, was recently ranked as the "world's most influential business thinker" by *The Wall Street Journal.* As a member of the London Business School faculty since 1983, Hamel has published numerous influential articles, including "The Core Competence of the Corporation" (with C.K. Prahalad) and "The Why, What, and How of Management Innovation." His

most recent book, *The Future of Management,* was selected by Amazon.com as the best business book of 2007.[47]

Peter Drucker was a respected management guru who, through his writings and consulting, made several lasting contributions to the practice of management. One of his major contributions was the need for organizations to set clear objectives and establish the means of evaluating progress toward those objectives.[48] He was the first person to discuss "management by objective" (MBO), by which a manager should be self-driven to accomplish key goals that link to organizational success (as opposed to being controlled by a supervisor).[49] Drucker also championed several ideas that continue to be influential to this day, including decentralization, employees as assets (not liabilities), corporation as a human community, and the importance of knowledge workers in the new information economy."[50]

In addition to these modern contributors, several more individuals have made a lasting impact on current thought and practices. Peter Senge of MIT Sloan School of Management has made several significant contributions to the areas of organizational learning and change. In addition to founding the "Society of Organizational Learning," Senge wrote *The Fifth Dimension: The Art and Practice of The Learning Organization,* which has sold more than 1 million copies worldwide (2006) (MIT Sloan bio);[51] Christopher A. Bartlett of Harvard University has focused on the "strategic and organizational challenges confronting managers in multinational corporations."[52] With coauthor Sumatra Ghoshal, he wrote the influential *Managing Across Borders: The Transnational Solution* (1998), named by the *Financial Times* as one of the 50 most influential business books of the 20th century.[53] In his 1990 best-selling book, the *Seven Habits of Highly Effective People: Powerful Lessons in Personal Change,* Stephen Covey discussed how a leader's success hinges on balancing between personal and professional effectiveness.[54] In 1982 Thomas J. Peters and Robert H. Waterman wrote the best-selling book *In Search of Excellence,* which urged U.S. firms to fight their

> "Management means, in the last analysis, the substitution of thought for brawn and muscle, of knowledge for folklore and tradition, and of cooperation for force."
>
> —Peter Drucker

Are Companies Really Shifting to Green Power?

It seems the answer is "yes." While some critics in the United States see "green power" as an alternative source of energy that is only used by a handful of environmentally conscious companies, many organizations are increasingly tapping this alternative source of power. In contrast to conventional power that includes the combustion of fossil fuels (coal, natural gas, and oil) and nuclear fission of uranium, *green power* refers to renewable energy resources and technologies that produce electricity from solar, wind, geothermal, biogas, and so forth. A major advantage of companies using more green (and less conventional) power sources is that they restore themselves over brief periods of time and do not diminish. Ultimately, companies that use green power are helping the environment by reducing the emissions of greenhouse gases like carbon dioxide.

In an effort to encourage organizations to purchase and develop more green power, the U.S. Environmental Protection Agency created the voluntary Green Power Partnership (GPP) in 2001. The GPP currently has more than 1,500 partner organizations (*Fortune* 500 companies, local-state-federal governments, and colleges and universities) that use billions of kilowatt-hours of green power annually.

According to a GPP report released on January 27, 2014, the top 10 users of green power include Intel, Microsoft, Kohl's Department Stores, Whole Foods, Walmart Stores, Google, U.S. Department of Energy, Staples, City of Houston, and

Starbucks. These 10 organizations purchased approximately 11 billion kilowatt-hours of green power over the previous 12 months.

Annise Parker, the mayor of Houston summed up the benefits of using green power: "Purchasing green power reduces the environmental impacts of electricity use, decreases the cost of renewable power over item, and supports the development of new renewable generation."

Companies like Apple are taking the idea of green power to the next level. The company supplies all of its data

centers with 100 percent renewable energy through a combination of green power purchases and its own onsite generation. Apple's onsite projects not only power its data centers, but also provide energy to local grids. The company's long-term goal is to use 100 percent clean, renewable energy for all of its operations.

Discussion Questions

1. Knowing that the majority of companies and organizations in the United States rely on conventional energy sources like coal, natural gas, and oil to power their operations, to what extent is the growing use of green power a passing fad or a fundamental shift in energy consumption? Defend your position.

2. Compare and contrast the use of conventional (coal, natural gas, and oil) and green energy sources and technologies (wind, solar, geothermal, and biogas). In other words, why should a company consider shifting part/all of its energy consumption from conventional to green power?

SOURCES: The Green Power Partnership at www.epa.gov/greenpower/; "EPA Partnerships Cut Greenhouse Gas Emissions and Save Businesses Money," Environmental Protection Agency Documents and Publications, Press Release on January 31, 2014, www.epa.gov; "EPA Announces U.S. Organizations Using the Most Green Power," Environmental Protection Agency Documents and Publications, Press Release on April 17, 2013, www.epa.gov; and "Intel No. 1 on EPA's Green Power List," *Sacramento Business Journal* (August 13, 2013), www.bizjournals.com.

---

competition by refocusing their business strategies on several drivers of success: people, customers, values, culture, action, and an entrepreneurial spirit.[55]

4.1 | An Eye on the Future

All of these historical perspectives have left legacies that affect contemporary management thought and practice. Their undercurrents continue to flow, even as the context and the specifics change.

Times do pass, and things do change. This may sound obvious, but it isn't to those managers who sit by idly while their

firms fail to adapt to changing times. Business becomes global. New technologies and flexible work arrangements like virtual teamwork, mobile communications, and social networking change how we work, produce goods, and deliver services. Change continually creates both new opportunities and new demands for lowering costs and for achieving greater innovation, quality, and speed. Employee skills are also changing. Increasing global competition requires employees to develop key 21st-century skills such as problem solving, critical thinking, communication, collaboration, and self-management; along with a global perspective, foreign language proficiency, and cross-cultural knowledge.[56] Management knowledge and practices evolve accordingly.

The essential facts about change are these: First, change is happening more rapidly and dramatically than at any other time in history. Second, if you don't anticipate change and adapt to it, you and your firm will not thrive in a competitive business world. The theme of change—what is happening now, what lies ahead, how it affects management, and how you can deal with it—permeates this entire book.

What are the implications of these changes for you and your career? How can you best be ready to meet the challenges? You must ask questions about the future, anticipate changes, know your responsibilities, and be prepared to meet them head-on. We hope you study the remaining chapters with these goals in mind.

Study Checklist

- Did you tear out the perforated student review card at the back of the text to revisit learning objectives and key terms and definitions?

Connect® Management is available for M Management. Additional resources include:

- Interactive applications:
  - Drag & Drop: Fayol's Principles in the Cupcake Kingdom
  - Drag & Drop: Contemporary Theories Used Today
  - Drag & Drop: Creating Products as Open Systems

- Sequencing/Timeline: The Historic Approaches to Management
- LearnSmart—Multiple choice questions help you determine what you already know, are not sure about, or need to practice based on your score. And with SmartBook, you can read the relevant section in the eBook as well as practice and recharge what you've learned.
- Chapter Video: Teachers and Performance Incentives
- Young Manager Speaks Out: Tim Cote, Technology Services Manager

3 chapter

The Organizational Environment **and Culture**

Learning Objectives

After studying Chapter 3, you should be able to

LO1 Describe the five elements of an organization's macroenvironment.

LO2 Explain the five components of an organization's competitive environment.

LO3 Understand how managers stay on top of changes in the external environment.

LO4 Summarize how managers respond to changes in the external environment.

LO5 Discuss how organizational cultures can be leveraged to overcome challenges in the external environment.

Bob Stiller, founder and former chairman of Green Mountain Coffee Roasters (now called Keurig Green Mountain), brought his company a long way since its beginnings in a small Vermont café more than 30 years ago. He expanded his business by surveying the competition and choosing avenues that looked most promising. With the retail coffee market crowded by Starbucks, Seattle's Best Coffee, Dunkin' Donuts Coffee, Caribou Coffee, and others, Stiller chose to focus on the quality of his coffee—offering more than 100 gourmet varieties—and to sell through retail stores, wholesale outlets, direct-mail catalogs, and on the web. Recognizing consumers' growing interest in organic foods, KGM also began offering organically grown coffees that were produced through fair trade practices—ensuring that farmers receive a fair price for their crops.[1] The company also makes the best-selling single-cup coffee machine in the United States. Tripling in size since 2011, the single-cup coffee market accounted for half of the $11.7 billion in sales in the United States in 2013.[2] Leveraging the popularity of its Keurig single-cup brewers, KGM has entered into partnerships with several competitors. In 2014, the company extended its agreement with Starbucks to sell SB's coffee in Keuring K-cup packs in grocery stores. Other recent partnerships include offering Unilever's Lipton hot and iced tea in K-cup packs and to distribute Peet's Coffee & Tea in the popular single-cup offerings.[3]

Executives such as Stiller must keep a sharp watch on their external environment, or developments outside their organizations. As we suggested in the first two chapters, organizations are **open systems**—that is, they are affected by and in turn affect their external environments. They use *inputs* like goods and services from their environment to create goods and services that are *outputs* to their environment. When we use the term **external environment** here, we mean more than an organization's customers, competitive partnerships, or supplier relationships: the external environment includes all relevant forces outside the organization's boundaries.

Many external factors are uncontrollable. Managers and their organizations are often battered by recession, government interference, and competitors' actions. But their lack of control does not mean that managers can ignore such forces, use them as excuses for poor performance, and try to just get by. Managers must stay abreast of external developments and react effectively. In addition, as we will discuss later in this chapter, sometimes managers can influence components of the external environment.

This chapter discusses the major components of an organization's macroenvironment and competitive environment. It covers several methods that managers use to gather information to better understand uncertainties in their firm's external environment. Next the chapter discusses how leaders respond to and attempt to manage this uncertainty in their environment. It also examines the internal environment, or culture, of the organization and how a culture can help the organization respond to its environment. Later chapters elaborate on many of the basic environmental forces introduced here. For example, technology will be discussed again in Chapters 5 and 15. Other chapters focus on ethics, social responsibility, and the natural environment. And Chapter 15 reiterates the theme that recurs throughout this text: organizations must change continually because environments change continually.

1 | THE MACRO-ENVIRONMENT

All organizations operate in a **macroenvironment**, which includes the general elements in the external environment that potentially can influence strategic decisions. As Exhibit 3.1 illustrates, the five components of an organization's macroenvironment include laws and regulations, the economy, technology, demographics, and social values.

1.1 | Laws and Regulations Protect and Restrain Organizations

U.S. government policies impose strategic constraints on organizations but may also provide opportunities. For example, while the *Patient Protection and Affordable Care Act of 2010* (PPACA) imposes several changes in the way that certain employers administer and pay for health insurance for their workers, companies involved with supporting the

enrollment portal, Healthcare.gov, have benefited. For example, Terremark, a subsidiary of Verizon, hosts several parts of the website as well as an information exchange among state-run insurance exchanges, federal agencies, and insurance companies. The United States government has paid $55.4 million to Verizon for its support services.[4]

The government can affect business opportunities through tax laws, economic policies, labor laws, and international trade rulings. In some countries, for example, bribes and kickbacks are common and expected ways of doing business. However, the *Foreign Corrupt Practices Act* (FCPA) prohibits Americans from bribing foreign officials.[5] In 2014, after a subsidiary of lightweight metals manufacturer Alcoa pleaded guilty to paying bribes to government officials in Bahrain, it agreed to pay $384 million in penalties.[6] Under the auspices of the FCPA, U.S. officials are looking into whether JPMorgan Chase hired the children of Chinese elite as a way to attract business from the Chinese govenment.[7] Hewlett-Packard recently agreed to pay $108 million to U.S. government authorities to settle allegations that HP's Russian, Polish, and Mexican subsidiaries bribed government officials in those countries to win lucrative contracts.[8] But laws can also assist organizations. Because U.S. federal and state governments protect property rights, including copyrights, trademarks, and patents, it is economically more attractive to start businesses in the United States than in countries where laws and law enforcement offer less protection.

Regulators are specific government organizations in a firm's more immediate task environment. Here are some example of regulatory agencies:

- Equal Employment Opportunity Commission (www.eeoc.gov).
- Occupational Safety and Health Administration (www.osha.gov).
- Federal Aviation Administration (www.faa.gov).
- Food and Drug Administration (www.fda.gov).
- National Labor Relations Board (www.nlrb.gov).
- Office of Federal Contract Compliance Programs (www.ofccp.gov).
- Environmental Protection Agency (www.epa.gov).

These agencies have the power to investigate company practices and take legal action to ensure compliance with laws. For example, the U.S. National Labor Relations Board (which regulates union activities) has proposed the Employee Free Choice Act that would make sweeping changes to labor law, effectively making it easier for employees to form unions.[9] As of the writing of this book, the proposed amendment has not been passed and is being opposed by several pro-business groups.

Often the corporate community sees government as an adversary. However, many organizations realize that government can be a source of competitive advantage for an individual company or an entire industry. Public policy may prevent or limit new foreign or domestic competitors from entering an industry. Government may subsidize failing companies or provide tax breaks to some. Federal patents protect innovative products or production technologies. Legislation may be

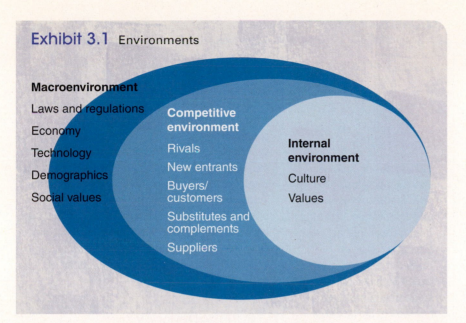
macroenvironment the general environment; includes governments, economic conditions, and other fundamental factors that generally affect all organizations

passed to support industry prices, thereby guaranteeing profits or survival. The government may even intervene to ensure the survival of certain key industries or companies, as it has done to help auto companies, airlines, and agricultural businesses.

1.2 | The Economy Affects Managers and Organizations

Although most Americans think in terms of the U.S. economy, the economic environment for organizations is much larger—created by complex interconnections among the economies of different countries. Several events in the world have had far-reaching influence: the post-tsunami nuclear meltdown in Japan, the European financial crisis and social unrest,

● Police officers, who retreated into the prosecutor's office, fire gas and stun grenades at pro-Russian activists who take cover behind shields taken from the police on May 1, 2014, in Donetsk, Ukraine. Activists marched to the prosecutor's office and overran the police guarding the building. After taking control of the building and confiscating the police riot gear, police officers were set free.

antigovernment protests throughout several nations, Syria's civil war, and the intense struggle between Russia and the Ukraine over the sovereignty of Crimea.

∙∙∙∙∙∙∙∙∙∙∙∙∙∙∙∙

The economic environment dramatically affects managers' ability to function effectively and influences their strategic choices. Interest and inflation rates affect the availability and cost of capital, growth opportunities, prices, costs, and consumer demand for products. Unemployment rates affect labor availability and the wages the firm must pay, as well as product demand. Steeply rising energy and health care costs have limited companies' ability to hire and have raised the cost of doing business. Changes in the value of the dollar on world exchanges may make American products cheaper or more expensive than their foreign competitors.

∙∙∙∙∙∙∙∙∙∙∙∙∙∙∙∙

An important economic influence is the stock market. When investors bid up stock prices, they are paying more to own shares in companies, so the companies have more capital to support their strategies. Observers of the stock market watch trends in major indexes such as the Dow Jones Industrial Average, Standard & Poor's 500, and NASDAQ Composite, which combine many companies' performance into a single measurement. In recent years, the indexes had risen to great heights, but then they dropped rapidly. The falling prices reflected an economy in which demand for homes and cars had shriveled, credit was difficult to obtain, exports tumbled, and unemployment rates soared.[10] Governments launched a variety of stimulus efforts to help companies get financing and to encourage consumers to start spending again. Since then, the stock markets have rebounded as a result of investors having confidence in renewed business growth.

The stock market may also affect the behavior of individual managers. In publicly held companies, managers throughout the organization may feel required to meet Wall Street's earnings expectations. It is likely that you, too, at some point in your career will be asked to improve budget or sales numbers because your company does not want to disappoint "the Street." Such external pressures usually have a positive effect—they help make many firms more efficient and profitable. But failure to meet those expectations can cause a company's stock price to drop, making it more difficult for the firm to raise additional capital for investment. The compensation of managers may also be affected, particularly if they have been issued stock options. These pressures sometimes lead managers to focus

demographics statistical characteristics of a group or population such as age, gender, and education level

on short-term results at the expense of the long-term success of their organizations, or even worse, to engage in unethical or unlawful behavior that misleads investors.[11]

1.3 | Technology Is Changing Every Business Function

Today a company cannot succeed without incorporating into its strategy the astonishing technologies that exist and are under development. As technology evolves, new industries, markets, and competitive niches develop. Advances in technology also permit companies to enter markets that would otherwise be unavailable to them, such as when Apple's iPhone technology spurred exponential growth among application developers. New technologies also provide new production techniques. In automobile and other types of capital-intensive manufacturing, sophisticated robots perform jobs without suffering fatigue, requiring vacations or weekends off, or demanding wage increases. New methods, such as drilling horizontal wells to reach new oil and natural gas deposits in Texas, Oklahoma, and North Dakota have led to a boom in production and the need for U.S.-based refining companies

Did You Know?

Texting during lecture may be hazardous to your grades. A research study published in *Research in Higher Education Journal* divided a group of undergraduate business students into two groups: one-half of participants were allowed to text during lecture and the other half were not. Exam scores of the "texting" students were significantly lower than those students who focused only on lecture.[14]

to expand production capabilities.[12] In this case, technological and economic forces overlap: the rising price of oil has made it worthwhile for companies to develop and try new technology.[13]

In addition, new technologies provide more efficient ways to manage and communicate. Advanced information technology and telecommunication systems make information available when and where it's needed around the clock. Productivity software monitors employee performance and detects deficiencies. Telecommunications allow conferences to take place without requiring people to travel to the same location. As we will discuss in Chapter 5, strategies developed around cutting-edge technological advances can create a competitive advantage.

1.4 | Demographics Describe Your Employees and Customers

Demographics are statistical characteristics of a group or population. An organization's customers, a university's faculty and staff, or a nation's current labor force can all be described statistically in terms of their members' ages, genders, education levels, incomes, occupations, and so forth.

Managers must consider workforce demographics in formulating their human resources strategies. The labor force participation rate measures the percentage of the population working or looking for work. From early 2007 (before the recession hit) to March 2014, this rate decreased from 66.4 to 63.2 percent. Fewer workers contributed to a 13.3 percent reduction in productivity growth during that same period.[15] Population growth influences the size and composition of the labor force. In the decade from 2012 to 2022, the U.S. civilian labor force is expected to grow at a rate of 10.8 percent, reaching nearly 163 million in 2022.[16] This growth is slower than during the previous decade, partly because young workers—those between the ages of 16 and 24—are declining in numbers. The fastest-growing age group will be workers who are 55 and older, who are expected to represent one out of four workers in the labor force in 2022. What does this mean for employers? They will need to find ways to retain and fully use the talents of their experienced workers while competing for relatively scarce entry-level workers. Perhaps their older employees will be willing to work past the traditional retirement age of 65, at least on a part-time basis; research suggests that a lack of pensions and adequate savings will make retirement unaffordable for many of today's baby boomers.[17] Eventually, however, declining participation in work by older people will force managers to find replacements for these highly experienced workers.

LISTEN & LEARN ● ONLINE

YOUNG MANAGERS
Speak Out!

"Within . . . my specific store, we have a relatively flat organization. My associates report directly to me, and I report up to a more senior level of management. I also have indirect relationships with department heads in other areas of my organization."

Kevin Wielgus, General Manager, Carpet Company

Toms Shoes Makes Impact with Its "One-for-One" Model

By now many people have heard of Blake Mycoskie, the 34-year-old "social entrepreneur" and founder of Toms Shoes (short for Tomorrow's Shoes). Before becoming famous, Mycoskie started several entrepreneurial ventures. As a business school student at Southern Methodist University in Dallas, he started a door-to-door laundry service for students. Later he created an outdoor media company that was purchased by Clear Channel. In 2002 he teamed up with his sister to compete in the CBS reality show The Amazing Race, which brought him to Argentina where he witnessed large-scale poverty.

While traveling back to Argentina in 2006, Mycoskie met an American woman who was coordinating a shoe drive to deliver donated shoes to poor Argentinean children. Barefoot children are exposed to dangerous hookworm, tetanus, and other soil-based ailments. Mycoskie noticed that children who received donated shoes often got the wrong size. He had a "lightbulb" moment and came up with the idea of creating a sustainable, for-profit business that could fund donations of new shoes for poor children. Known as the "one-for-one" sustainability model, for every pair of shoes that the company sells, it donates a pair of shoes to a poor child somewhere in the world.

Modeled after a popular Argentinean shoe known as an *alpargata,* Toms Shoes are available in many colors and styles for men, women, and children online and through retail outlets like Whole Foods and Nordstrom. The company is in the process of expanding its product offerings and now also donates eyeglasses.

Wanting to help children have adequate shoes to protect their feet, founder Blake Mycoskie created TOMS Shoes. The company matches every pair of shoes purchased with a pair of new shoes for a child in need, creating the model of One for One.®

Toms Shoes was not the first company to use the "one-for-one" sustainability model, but its success is inspiring many other entrepreneurs to create their own socially conscious ventures that make profit while helping others. In 2011 Mycoskie wrote a book titled *Start Something That Matters,* in which he offers six suggestions that others can follow to develop a sustainable venture that is meaningful. His six suggestions are to find your story, face your fears, be resourceful without resources, keep it simple, build trust, and realize that giving is good business.

The Toms Shoes socially conscious and sustainable business model is having impact. As of June 2013, Toms Shoes had given more than 10 million pairs of new shoes to children in 60 countries. Blake Mycoskie is proving that a company can do well by doing good.

Discussion Questions

- Some critics believe that sustainable and socially oriented business models like the one at Toms Shoes are a passing fad. To what degree do you agree or disagree with this claim? Can you think of some other examples of organizations that are doing well by doing good?
- What are some areas in which you have thought about making a difference? Do you envision yourself ever starting a venture that matters to you and others?

SOURCES: See Toms Shoes 2013 Giving Report at www.toms.com/media/TOMS_Giving_Report_2013.pdf; B. Mycoskie, *Start Something That Matters* (New York: Spiegel & Grau, 2011); P. D. Broughton, "Doing Good by Shoeing Well," *The Wall Street Journal* (online), September 10, 2011, www.wsj.com; J. Schectman, "Good Business," *Newsweek* 156, no. 15 (October 11, 2010), p. 8; "In Toms' Shoes: Start-Ups Copy 'One-for-One' Model," *The Wall Street Journal* (online), September 29, 2010, www.wsj.com; and J. Shambora, "Blake Mycoskie, Founder of TOMS Shoes," *Fortune* 161, no. 4 (March 22, 2010), p. 72.

The education and skill levels of the workforce are another demographic factor managers must consider. The share of the U.S. labor force with at least some college education has been increasing steadily over the past several decades, from less than one-fourth of the workforce in 1970 to close to 70 percent today.[18] Even so, many companies invest heavily in training their entry-level workers and send them through their own corporate universities, common at hundreds of large organizations like Apple, Boeing, Motorola, Amazon, and General Electric. Also, as college has become a more popular option, employers are having difficulty recruiting employees for jobs that require knowledge of a skilled trade, such as machinists and toolmakers, especially in areas where the cost of living is so high that most residents are professionals.[19]

Traditional Thinking

Twenty-somethings interested in a business career will join companies and work their way up the ranks. In exchange for performing well, companies will reward employees with pay raises, benefits, and job security.

Source: Adapted from M. J. Cetron and O. Davies, "Trends Shaping Tomorrow's World: Forces in the Natural and Institutional Environments," *The Futurist* 44, no. 4 (July/August 2010), pp. 38–53.

The Best Managers Today

Are increasingly starting their own entrepreneurial ventures, often before turning 30 years old. Millennials' command of technology and social networking will create many opportunities for new businesses.

However, as education levels improve around the globe, more organizations may send technical tasks to lower-priced but highly trained workers overseas. For example, some U.S. hospitals, to avoid paying higher wages to U.S.-based radiologists, outsource radiology services (called "teleradiology") to Indian specialists who analyze patients' images and provide written reports of the results—all via telecommunications technology.[20]

Another factor that significantly influences the U.S. population and labor force is immigration. For each year between now and 2020, it is estimated that 1.5 million immigrants will become residents of the United States. In recent years, immigrants have accounted for approximately 40 percent of recent U.S. population growth.[21] Immigrants are frequently of working age, but some have different educational and occupational backgrounds from the rest of the labor force. The demographic importance of immigration intersects with legal issues governing who is permitted to work in the United States. For example, the federal government recently cracked down not only on undocumented workers but also on the managers who hired them. It established a new program by which businesses are required to check prospective hires' legal status by submitting their names to a database called "E-Verify."[22] Some companies have asked the U.S. government to admit more foreign workers with technical expertise that may be hard to find in the United States.

Immigration is one reason why the labor force in the future will be more ethnically diverse than it is today. The biggest percentage of employment increases will be by Asian Americans and Hispanic populations, followed by African Americans.

In the last quarter of the 20th century, women joined the U.S. labor force in record numbers. Throughout the 1970s and 1980s, they became much more likely to take paying jobs. In the 1970s only about one-third of women were in the labor force, but 60 percent had jobs in 1999. Since then, women's labor force participation rate has stayed near that level, declining slightly.[23]

A more diverse workforce has many advantages, but managers have to ensure they provide equality for women and minorities with respect to employment, advancement opportunities, and compensation. They must recruit, retain, train, motivate, and effectively utilize people of diverse demographic backgrounds who have the skills to achieve the company's mission.

1.5 | Social Values Shape Attitudes Toward Your Company and Its Products

Societal trends regarding how people think and behave have major implications for management of the labor force, corporate social actions, and strategic decisions about products and markets. For example, during the 1980s and 1990s women in the workforce often chose to delay having children as they focused on their careers, but today more women are having children and then returning to the workforce. As a result, at companies like Bank of America and PricewaterhouseCoopers, parents who work just 20 hours per week receive full benefits.[24] General Mills has introduced more supportive policies, including family leave, flexible working hours, less travel, and child care assistance.[25] Firms provide these benefits as a way of increasing a source of competitive advantage: an experienced workforce.

A prominent issue today pertains to natural resources: drilling for oil in formerly protected areas in the United States. Firms in the oil industry like ExxonMobil, Royal Dutch Shell, British Petroleum, ConocoPhillips, and Chevron face considerable public opinion both in favor of preserving the natural environment and against U.S. dependence on other countries for fuel. Protection of the natural environment will factor into social concerns and many types of management decisions.

How companies respond to these and other social issues may affect their reputation in the marketplace, which in turn may help or hinder their competitiveness. The public health issue of childhood obesity has given video games a bad name among those who advocate for children to get off the couch and move. But two games have generated favorable publicity: Konami's Dance Dance Revolution (DDR), where players compete with dance moves, and Nintendo's Wii Sports, where players swing a remote control containing motion sensors to move a virtual tennis racket, golf club, bowling ball, baseball bat, or boxing gloves. Exercise-oriented video games like DDR have been shown to help increase the mobility of older patients with major, debilitating diseases.[26] These games have also been praised as an alternative to games with violent themes. Dean Bender, the public relations agent for

DDR, said of his client, "With all the bad PR about violence, we became the white knights."[27] And Wii Sports players have reported breaking into a sweat and even straining muscles.[28]

LO2 Explain the five components of an organization's competitive environment

2 | THE COMPETITIVE ENVIRONMENT

All managers are affected by the components of the macroenvironment we just discussed. As Exhibit 3.2 illustrates, each organization also functions in a closer, more immediate **competitive environment**, consisting of rivalry among existing competitors and the threat of new entrants, the threat of substitute and complementary products, and the bargaining power of suppliers and buyers. This model was originally developed by Michael Porter, a Harvard professor and a noted authority on strategic management.[29] According to Porter, successful managers do more than simply react to the environment; they act in ways that actually shape or change the organization's environment. Porter's model is an excellent method for analyzing the competitive environment and adapting to or influencing the nature of the competition.

2.1 | Rivals Can Be Domestic or Global

Among the various components of the competitive environment, competitors within the industry must first deal with one another. When organizations compete for the same customers and try to win market share at the others' expense, all must react to and anticipate their competitors' actions.

Identify the Competition The first question to consider is this: Who is the competition? Sometimes the answer is obvious.

The major competitors in the market for video game consoles are Sony (whose brand is the PlayStation), Microsoft (Xbox 360), and Nintendo (maker of the Wii). But if organizations focus exclusively on traditional rivalries, they miss the emerging ones. Back in the 1990s, many of the large music companies were so busy competing against one another for sales and market share that they underestimated the long-term impact of new technologies like MP3 files and music swapping services like Napster. Then the launch of iTunes by Apple that allowed customers to purchase (for about $.99) single songs represented another competitive blow to the traditional music industry. In-store sales of CDs have never recovered. Apple's game changing strategy didn't stop there. In 2007, Apple released it's first iPhone which played MP3 files along with performing countless other functions. The music player industry didn't expect a computer manufacturer (Apple) to create a smartphone with multifunctionality that could compete with stand alone MP3 players.[30]

As a first step in understanding their competitive environment, organizations must identify their competitors. Competitors may include many types of companies:

- Small domestic firms, especially upon their entry into tiny, premium markets.
- Strong regional competitors.
- Big new domestic companies exploring new markets.

competitive environment the immediate environment surrounding a firm; includes suppliers, customers, rivals, and the like

Exhibit 3.2 Porter's five forces: The organization's competitive environment

Threat of new entrants

Bargaining power of suppliers

Rivalry among existing competitors

Bargaining power of buyers/customers

Threat of substitute products or services

Source: Adapted from M. E. Porter, "The Five Competitive Forces That Shape Strategy," *Harvard Business Review* (online), www.hbr.org (January 2008), pp. 78–93. Copyright © 2008 by the Harvard Business School Publishing Corporation; all rights reserved. Reprinted by permission of *Harvard Business Review*.

- Global firms, especially those that try to solidify their position in small niches (a traditional Japanese tactic) or can draw on an inexpensive labor force on a large scale (as in India and China).

- Newer ventures launched by all types of entrepreneurs.

The growth in competition from other countries has been especially significant with worldwide reduction in international trade barriers. For example, the North American Free Trade Agreement (NAFTA) sharply reduced tariffs on trade between the United States, Canada, and Mexico. Managers today confront a particular challenge from low-cost producers abroad.

● Nike spokesperson Michelle Wie teeing off at the Swingin Skirts event.

Analyze How They Compete Once competitors have been identified, the next step is to analyze how they compete. Competitors use tactics such as price reductions, new product introductions, and advertising campaigns to gain advantage over their rivals. Consider the market for athletic shoes. Nowadays, the Nike brand frequently comes to consumers' minds when it's time to purchase a new pair of shoes for the gym or sports. That wasn't always the case. For 30 years, Nike and Reebok competed fiercely with one another over the lucrative footwear market. Founded in 1964 by Phil Bowerman and Phil Knight, Nike quickly gained a foothold in the market by importing quality athletic footwear and "aggressively courting male customers."[31] Paul Fireman, who bought Reebok in 1984, instead focused on the growing market for female sneakers; a strategy that led to Reebok surpassing Nike in sales in 1987.

Nike took a different approach by signing the world-famous athlete, Michael Jordan, as a spokesperson for the company. The Air Jordan brand was a hit and earned the company annual sales of $1 billion. In later years, Nike signed other well-known athletes like Tiger Woods, Ronaldinho, Andre Agassi,

high-growth industries offer enormous opportunities for profits. When an industry matures and growth slows, profits drop. Then intense competition causes an industry shakeout: weaker companies are eliminated, and the strong companies survive.[33] We will discuss competitors and strategy further in Chapter 5.

2.2 | New Entrants Increase When Barriers to Entry Are Low

New entrants into an industry compete with established companies. A relatively new global industry, downloadable apps have become big business. In 2013, 102 billion app store downloads were made worldwide, resulting in $26 billion in sales.[34] In June of that year, the top 5 paid for apps were: Minecraft (Mojang), Dentist Office Kids (Beansprites), Plants vs. Zombies (PopCap Games), Scribblenauts Remix (Warner Bros.), and Temple Run: Brave (Disney).[35]

If many factors prevent new companies from entering an industry, the threat to established firms is less serious. If there are few such **barriers to entry**, the threat of new entrants is greater. Several major barriers to entry are common:

- *Government policy*—When a firm's patent for a drug expires, other companies can enter the market. The patents recently expired on several drugs made by Pfizer, including antidepressant Zoloft and allergy medicine Zyrtec. At the same time, several research projects to introduce new, patented medicines failed, so Pfizer had to lay off employees and close some facilities to cut costs.[36]

- *Capital requirements*—Getting started in some industries, such as building aircraft or operating a railroad, may cost so much that companies won't even try to raise such large amounts of money. This helps explain why Boeing and Airbus have no direct competitors in manufacturing large, long-haul aircraft.[37]

> **"Your most unhappy customers are your greatest source of learning."**
>
> — Bill Gates

Mia Hamm, Rory McIlroy, and so forth. Eventually, with the help of celebrity endorsements and strong branding, Nike beat out Reebok to become the $25.3 billion powerhouse that it is today.[32]

Competition is most intense when there are many direct competitors (including global contenders), industry growth is slow, and the product or service cannot be differentiated. New,

- *Brand identification*—When customers are loyal to a familiar brand, new entrants have to spend heavily. Imagine, for example, the costs involved in trying to launch a new chain of fast-food restaurants to compete against McDonald's or Subway. Similarly, Google's recent entry into the market for business software, with a package called Google Apps for Business, surprised many people because Microsoft has dominated that segment for many years.[38]

final consumer a customer who purchases products in their finished form

intermediate consumer a customer who purchases raw materials or wholesale products before selling them to final customers

- *Cost disadvantages*—Established companies may be able to keep their costs lower because they are larger, have more favorable locations, and have existing assets and so forth.

- *Distribution channels*—Existing competitors may have such tight distribution channels that new entrants struggle to get their goods or services to customers. For example, established food products have supermarket shelf space. New entrants must displace existing products with promotions, price breaks, intensive selling, and other tactics.

2.3 | Buyers/Customers Determine Your Success

Buyers (customers) purchase the goods or services an organization offers. Without them, a company won't survive. You are a **final consumer** when you buy a buy a book from Amazon or new home speakers from Bose. **Intermediate consumers** buy raw materials or wholesale products and then sell to final consumers, as when Sony buys components from IBM and ATI Technologies and uses them to make PS3 consoles. Types of intermediate customers include retailers, who buy from wholesalers and manufacturers' representatives and then sell to consumers, and industrial buyers, who buy raw materials (such as chemicals) to be converted into final products. Intermediate customers make more purchases than individual final consumers do.

Customers do much more than simply purchasing goods and services. They can demand lower prices, higher quality, unique product specifications, or better service. They also can play competitors against one another, as occurs when a car buyer (or a purchasing agent) collects different offers and negotiates for the best price. Often today's customers want to be actively involved with their products, as when Nike launched its "NikeiD" program that lets customers customize their shoes by choosing the color of the swoosh, stitching, tread, and upper material.[39]

Social networking and media sites have further empowered customers. They provide an easy source of information—both about product features and pricing. In addition, today's social media users informally create and share messages about a product, which provide flattering free "advertising" at best or embarrassing and even erroneous bad publicity at worst. For example, when the power went out for about 30 minutes during Super Bowl XLVII in the Superdome (New Orleans) on February 3, 2013, the Oreo's social media team swooped into action by tweeting: "You can still dunk in the dark."[40] The "brilliant and bold" idea made quite a splash; within minutes the clever post had 16,000 retweets and 20,000 likes on Facebook.[41] Another example of engaging customers online is what Hasbro has done with its game, Cranium. Fans can either play the board game in their living rooms or on social networks, and the "craniacs" can enjoy reading online posts of factoids about everything from Einstein's theory of relativity to how Buenos Aires received its name.[42] However, viral posts and videos can also work against companies. Out of frustration over a customer service dispute with United Airlines, musician Dave Carroll wrote a song titled "United Breaks Guitars" and posted it on YouTube.[43] As of July 2014 that video had received approximately 14 million hits. Today's companies may find it difficult to identify, much less respond to, these unofficial messages.

As we discussed in Chapter 1, customer service means giving customers what they want or need in the way they want it. This usually depends on the speed and dependability with which an organization can deliver its products. Actions and attitudes that provide excellent customer service include the following:

- Speed of filling and delivering normal orders.

- Willingness to meet emergency needs.

- Merchandise delivered in good condition.

- Readiness to take back defective goods and resupply quickly.

- Availability of installation and repair services and parts.

- Service charges (i.e., whether services are free or priced separately).[44]

An organization is at a disadvantage if it depends too heavily on powerful customers—those who make large purchases or can easily find alternative places to buy. If you are a firm's largest customer and can buy from others, you have power over that firm and probably can negotiate with it successfully. Your firm's biggest customers, especially if they can buy from other sources, will have the greatest negotiating power over you.

2.4 | Products Can Be Substitutes or Complements of Yours

Besides products that directly compete, other products can affect a company's performance by being substitutes for or complements of the company's offerings. A *substitute* is a potential threat; customers use it as an alternative, buying less of one kind of product but more of another. For example, substitutes for coffee could be tea, energy drinks, cola, or water. A *complement* is a potential opportunity because customers buy more of a given product if they also demand more of the complementary product. Examples include ink cartridges as a complement for printers; when people buy more printers, they buy more ink cartridges.

Substitutes Technological advances and economic efficiencies are among the ways that firms can develop substitutes for existing products. Internet offerings such as YouTube and World of Warcraft have attracted video game players away from their TV sets to interact with one another online. This example shows that substitute products or services can limit another industry's revenue potential. Founded in Austin, Texas, in 1980, Whole Foods positions itself as a substitute to more traditional grocery chains like Kroger, Wegman, and Albertsons. Providing natural and organic foods that cater to health-conscious consumers and vegetarians, Whole Foods has grown dramatically in recent years to 360 stores in the United States and United Kingdom.[45] Rumors of soon-to-be available substitutes can garner attention. Amazon is rumored to be close to entering the smartphone market with a product that has six cameras and other sensors to produce a 3D depth effect without needed 3D glasses.[46]

In addition to current substitutes, companies need to think about potential substitutes that may be viable in the future. For example, possible alternatives to fossil fuels include nuclear fusion, solar power, and wind energy. The advantages promised by each of these technologies are many: inexhaustible fuel supplies, inexpensive electricity, zero emissions, universal public acceptance, and so on. Yet each of these faces economic and technical hurdles.

Complements Besides identifying and planning for substitutes, companies must consider complements for their products. When the Wii became popular, some programmers saw an opportunity to offer a niche service: tweaking the software to offer customized avatars. Wii players can use Nintendo's software to select from a range of facial characteristics, height, and other features, but some users want a more customized look or perhaps a character modeled after a famous figure. An entrepreneur in Tokyo created Mii Station, which uses a customer-supplied photo to create a Mii lookalike for a $5 fee.

● The picture of a virtual applicant appears on the screen of recruiters at the cyber café, Le Milk, in Paris during its first virtual job fair on the 3-D "Second Life" online game.

A web developer in Boston started Mii Plaza, a website where users can tap a database of more than 8,000 characters to collect and share Miis. Nintendo could have viewed these efforts as copyright infringement, but the company's initial response has been to treat Mii-related businesses as harmless.[47]

2.5 | Suppliers Provide Your Resources

Recall from our earlier mention of open systems that organizations must acquire resources (inputs) from their environment and convert those resources into products or services (outputs) to sell. Suppliers provide the resources needed for production, and those resources may come in several forms:

- *People*—supplied by trade schools and universities.

- *Raw materials*—from producers, wholesalers, and distributors.

- *Information*—supplied by researchers and consulting firms.

- *Financial capital*—from banks and other sources.

But suppliers are important to an organization for reasons beyond the resources they provide. Suppliers can raise their prices or provide poor-quality goods and services. Labor unions can go on strike or demand higher wages. Workers may produce defective work. Powerful suppliers, then, can reduce an organization's profits, particularly if the organization cannot pass on price increases to its customers.

Organizations are at a disadvantage if they become overly dependent on any powerful supplier. A supplier is powerful if the buyer has few other sources of supply or if the supplier has many other buyers. Intel has a dominant hold on a key part of the microprocessor chip market. The company supplies the x86 chip designed for servers that run Web-based applications. In 2012, x86 servers accounted for 70 percent of worldwide server sales.[48]

Switching costs are fixed costs buyers face if they change suppliers. For example, once a buyer learns how to operate a supplier's equipment, such as computer software, the buyer faces both economic and psychological costs in changing to a new supplier.

In recent years many companies have improved their competitiveness and profitability through **supply chain management**, the management of the entire network of facilities and people that obtain raw materials from outside the organization, transform them into products, and distribute them to customers.[49] Increased global competition has required managers to pay close attention to their costs; they can no longer afford to hold large inventories, waiting for orders to come in. Also, once orders do come in, some products sitting in inventory might be out of date.

With the emergence of the Internet, customers look for products built to their specific needs and preferences—and they want them delivered quickly at the lowest available price. This requires the supply chain to be not only efficient but also flexible, so that the organization's output can quickly respond to changes in demand.

Today the goal of effective supply chain management is to have the right product in the right quantity available at the right place at the right cost. Boeing, the aircraft and defense systems company, forges partnerships with its suppliers to share knowledge that will help them learn how to operate more efficiently. Rick Behrens is senior manager of supplier development, charged with building close supplier relationships and helping them understand Boeing's commitment to "lean" operations, aimed at eliminating waste. He educates some suppliers in the basics of how to run lean operations; for others, he sends a team to the organization to help them streamline certain activities. Behrens helps suppliers develop their abilities so they can move from simply selling parts to providing complete subassemblies. In Behrens's words, "We need suppliers that can grow with us."[50]

In sum, choosing the right supplier is an important strategic decision. Suppliers can affect manufacturing time, product quality, costs, and inventory levels. The relationship between suppliers and the organization is changing in many companies. The close supplier relationship has become a new model for many organizations that are using a just-in-time manufacturing approach. And in some companies, innovative managers are forming strategic partnerships with their key suppliers in developing new products or new production techniques.

LO3 Understand how managers stay on top of changes in the external environment

3 | KEEP UP WITH CHANGES IN THE ENVIRONMENT

If managers do not understand how the environment affects their organization or cannot identify opportunities and threats that are likely to be important, their ability to make decisions and execute plans will be severely limited. For example, if little is known about customer likes and dislikes, organizations will have difficulty designing new products, scheduling production, or developing marketing plans. In short, timely and accurate environmental information is critical for running a business.

But information about the environment is not always readily available. For example, even economists have difficulty predicting whether an upturn or a downturn in the economy is likely. Moreover, managers find it difficult to forecast how well their own products will sell, let alone how a competitor might respond. In other words, managers often operate under conditions of uncertainty. **Environmental uncertainty** means that managers do not have enough information about the environment to understand or predict the future. Uncertainty arises from two related factors:

- *Complexity*—the number of issues to which a manager must attend, and the degree to which they are interconnected. Industries (e.g., the automotive industry) with many different firms that compete in vastly different ways tend to be more complex—and uncertain—than industries (e.g., airplane manufacturers) with only a few key competitors.

- *Dynamism*—the degree of discontinuous change that occurs within the industry. High-growth industries (e.g., smartphones) with products and technologies that change rapidly are more uncertain than stable industries (e.g., utilities) where change is less dramatic and more predictable.[51]

● The x86 (or 80x86) is the generic name of a microprocessor architecture first developed and manufactured by Intel. It has dominated the desktop computer, portable computer, and small server markets since the 1980s. Although some challengers have hit the market, none have so far supplanted the x86 for its core markets.

environmental scanning searching for and sorting through information about the environment

competitive intelligence information that helps managers determine how to compete better

scenario a narrative that describes a particular set of future conditions

As environmental uncertainty increases, managers need methods for collecting, sorting through, and interpreting information about the environment. We discuss some of these approaches in this section of the chapter. (In Chapter 5 we will also discuss how managers make decisions under conditions of uncertainty.) By analyzing forces in both the macroenvironment and the competitive environment, managers can identify opportunities and threats that might affect the organization.

3.1 | Environmental Scanning Keeps You Aware

The first step in coping with uncertainty in the environment is to pin down what might be important. Frequently organizations and individuals act out of ignorance, only to regret those actions in the future. IBM, for example, had the opportunity to purchase the technology behind xerography but turned it down. Xerox saw the potential and took the lead in photocopying. Later, Xerox researchers developed the technology for the original computer mouse but failed to see its potential and missed an important opportunity.

To understand and predict changes, opportunities, and threats, organizations such as Verizon, Marriott, and Kelly Services spend a good deal of time and money monitoring events in the environment. **Environmental scanning** includes searching for information that is unavailable to most people and sorting through that information to interpret what is important. Managers can ask questions such as these:

- Who are our current competitors?

- Are there few or many entry barriers to our industry?

- What substitutes exist for our product or service?

- Is the company too dependent on powerful suppliers?

- Is the company too dependent on powerful customers?[52]

Answers to these questions help managers develop **competitive intelligence**, the information necessary to decide how best to manage in the competitive environment they have identified. Porter's competitive analysis, discussed earlier, can guide environmental scanning and help managers evaluate the competitive potential of different environments. Exhibit 3.3 describes two extreme environments: an attractive environment, which gives a firm a competitive advantage, and an unattractive environment, which puts a firm at a competitive disadvantage.[53]

3.2 | Scenario Development Helps You Analyze the Environment

As managers try to determine the effect of environmental forces on their organizations, they often develop different

Exhibit 3.3 Attractive and unattractive environments

Environmental Factor	Attractive	Unattractive
Competitors	Few; high industry growth; unequal size differentiated.	Many; low industry growth; equal size; commodity.
Threat of entry	Low threat; many barriers.	High threat; few entry barriers.
Substitutes	Few.	Many.
Suppliers	Many; low bargaining power.	Few; high bargaining power.
Customers	Many; low bargaining power.	Few; high bargaining power.

Sources: Adapted from S. Ghoshal, "Building Effective Intelligence Systems for Competitive Advantage," *Sloan Management Review* 28, no. 1 (Fall 1986), pp. 49–58; and K. D. Cory, "Can Competitive Intelligence Lead to a Sustainable Competitive Advantage?" *Competitive Intelligence Review* 7, no. 3 (Fall 1996), pp. 45–55.

outcomes that are uncertain in the future—alternative combinations of different factors that form a total picture of the environment and the firm. For example, before Samsung launched the Galaxy S5 with fingerprint scanner, heart rate monitor, 50 GB of free dropbox storage, and a one-inch larger screen than the iPhone 5 in early 2014, company planners developed several "best guesses" about the level of sales the new product would attract. Though precise projections are not available, Samsung hopes the S5 will build on the company's previous sales of more than 200 million units of the Galaxy S line since 2010.[54] Frequently organizations develop a best-case scenario (the occurrence of events that are favorable to the firm), a worst-case scenario (the occurrence of unfavorable events), and some middle-ground alternatives. The value of **scenarios** is that they help managers develop contingency plans for what they might do given different outcomes.[55] For example, as a manager, you will quite likely be involved in budgeting for your area. You will almost certainly be asked to list initiatives you would eliminate in case of an economic downturn and new investments you would make if your firm does better than expected.

Effective managers regard the scenarios they develop as living documents, not merely prepared once and put aside. They constantly update the scenarios to take into account relevant new factors that emerge, such as significant changes in the economy or actions by competitors. Also, managers try to identify strategies that are the most robust across all of the different scenarios.

3.3 | Forecasting Predicts Your Future Environment

Whereas environmental scanning identifies important factors and scenario development develops alternative pictures of the future, **forecasting** predicts exactly how some variable or variables will change in the future. For example, in making capital investments, firms may forecast interest rates. In deciding to expand or downsize a business, firms may forecast the demand for goods and services or forecast the supply and demand of labor. Publications such as Businessweek's Business Outlook provide forecasts to businesses both large and small.

The accuracy of forecasts varies from application to application. Because they extrapolate from the past to project the future, forecasts tend to be most accurate when the future ends up looking a lot like the past. Of course we don't need sophisticated forecasts in those instances. Forecasts are most useful when the future will look radically different from the past. Unfortunately that is when forecasts tend to be less accurate. The more things change, the less confidence we have in our forecasts. Here is some practical advice for using forecasts:

- Use multiple forecasts, and consider averaging their predictions.
- Remember that accuracy decreases as you go further into the future.
- Collect data carefully. Forecasts are no better than the data used to construct them.
- Use simple forecasts (rather than complicated ones) where possible.
- Keep in mind that important events often are surprises that depart from predictions.[56]

3.4 | Benchmarking Helps You Become Best in Class

Besides trying to predict changes in the environment, firms can intensively study the best practices of various firms to understand their sources of competitive advantage. **Benchmarking** means identifying the best-in-class performance by a company in a given area—say, product development or customer service—and then comparing your processes with theirs. A benchmarking team collects information about its own company's operations and those of the other firm in order to determine gaps. These gaps serve as a point of entry to learn the underlying causes of performance differences. Ultimately, the team maps out a set of best practices that lead to world-class performance. We will discuss benchmarking further in Chapter 5.

> **LO4** Summarize how managers respond to changes in the external environment

4 | RESPONDING TO THE ENVIRONMENT

For managers and organizations, responding effectively to their environments is almost always essential. Clothing retailers who pay no attention to changes in the public's style preferences,

and manufacturers who fail to ensure they have steady sources of supply, are soon out of business. To respond to their environment, managers and companies have a number of options, which can be grouped into three categories:

1. Adapting to the environment.
2. Influencing the environment.
3. Selecting a new environment.

4.1 | Adapt to the External Environment

To cope with environmental uncertainty, organizations frequently adjust their structures and work processes. Exhibit 3.4 shows four different approaches that organizations can take in adapting to environmental uncertainty, depending on whether it arises from complexity, dynamism, or both.

When uncertainty arises from environmental complexity, organizations tend to adapt by decentralizing decision making. For example, if a company faces a growing number of competitors in various markets, if different customers want different things, if product features keep increasing, and if production facilities are being built in different regions of the world, executives probably cannot keep abreast of all activities and understand all the operational details of a business. In these cases, the top management team is likely to give lower-level managers authority to make decisions that benefit the firm. The term **empowerment** is used frequently today to talk about this type of decentralized authority.

∷∷∷∷∷∷∷∷

To compete in volatile environments, organizations rely on knowledgeable and skilled workers. One way to develop such workers is to sponsor training programs. Alliances among employers, community colleges, universities, and nonprofit training programs are producing workers with much-needed skills in many industries.

forecasting method for predicting how variables will change the future

benchmarking the process of comparing an organization's practices and technologies with those of other companies

empowerment the process of sharing power with employees to enhance their confidence in their ability to perform their jobs and contribute to the organization

Exhibit 3.4 Four structural approaches for managing uncertainty

		Stable	Dynamic
Complex		Decentralized Bureaucratic (standardized skills)	Decentralized Organic (mutual adjustment)
Simple		Centralized Bureaucratic (standardized work processes)	Centralized Organic (direct supervision)

One program in New York, Per Scholas, trains computer repair technicians in one of the country's poorest areas—the Bronx. Funded by grants from private foundations and the New York City Council, the program gained momentum through its collaboration with Time Warner Cable and other companies looking for skilled employees. To date, Per Scholas has trained more than 3,800 low-income adults to obtain jobs in the technology field.

Per Scholas boasts a job placement rate of 80 percent of its graduates, who earn about $12 per hour in the first year and $15 per hour in two years—often double what they would have earned without the training. One graduate, Cristina Rodriguez, works at Time Warner Cable as a broadband specialist. Her new skills have empowered her to become a high-performing employee. "What feels great is when I resolve someone's issue," she says. Rodriguez, fluent in both English and Spanish, is able to solve customers' problems in both languages.

Training programs such as Per Scholas have grown more sophisticated in the last few years because of their close association with the companies that hire their graduates. These relationships give the programs insight into how the employers operate and what they need. Connie Ciliberti, vice president of human resources for Time Warner Cable, confirms the importance of this collaboration. "Per Scholas has spent time learning our business, understanding our measures of success," she says.[57]

● Per Scholas hosted hands-on workshops to help 1,500 senior citizens in New York City learn how technology can improve the quality of their lives.

In response to uncertainty arising from a dynamic environment, organizations tend to establish more flexible structures. Today the term bureaucracy generally has a bad connotation. While bureaucratic organizations may be efficient and controlled if the environment is stable, they tend to react slowly to changes in products, technologies, customers, or competitors. Because bureaucratic organizations tend to be formal and stable, they often cannot adjust to change or exceptional circumstances that "don't fit the rules." In these cases, more organic structures give organizations the flexibility to adapt. Organic structures are less formal than bureaucratic organizations; decisions are made through interaction and mutual adjustment among individuals rather than from a set of predefined rules.

Adapting at the Boundaries Because they are open systems, organizations are exposed to uncertainties from both their inputs and outputs. In response, they can create buffers on both the input and output boundaries with the environment. **Buffering** creates supplies of excess resources to meet unpredictable needs. On the input side, organizations establish relationships with employment agencies to hire part-time and temporary help during rush periods when labor demand is difficult to predict. In the U.S. labor force, these workers, known as contingent workers, include 2.5 million on-call workers, 1.2 million temporary-help agency workers, and more than 800,000 workers provided by contract firms, suggesting widespread use of this approach to buffering labor input uncertainties.[58] On the output side of the system, most organizations use some type of ending inventories, keeping merchandise on hand in case a rush of customers decides to buy their products. Auto dealers are a common example of this practice; other companies that use buffer inventories include fast-food restaurants, bookstores, and even real estate agencies.[59]

In addition to buffering, organizations may try **smoothing** or leveling normal fluctuations at the boundaries of the environment. For example, during winter months in the north, when automobile sales drop off, dealers commonly cut the price of their in-stock vehicles to increase demand. At the end of each clothing season, retailers discount their merchandise to clear it out and make room for incoming inventories. These are examples of smoothing environmental cycles to level off fluctuations in demand.

Adapting at the Core While buffering and smoothing manage uncertainties at the boundaries of the organization, firms also can establish **flexible processes** that allow for adaptation in their technical core. For example, firms increasingly try to customize their goods and services to meet customers' varied and changing demands. Health care companies like Blue Cross and Blue Shield and Aetna offer a variety of coverage options to customers. Even in manufacturing, where it is difficult to change basic core processes, firms are creating flexible factories. Instead of mass-producing large quantities of a "one-size-fits-all" product, organizations can use mass customization to produce customized products at an equally low cost. Whereas Henry Ford used to claim that "you could have a Model T in any color you wanted, as long as it was black," auto companies now offer a wide array of colors and trim lines, with different options and accessories. Customers who purchase a Ford Mustang can choose from a wide variety of exterior colors, and interior design features that suit their style.[60] The process of mass customization involves the use of a network of independent operating units in which each performs a specific process or task such as making a dashboard assembly on an automobile. When an order comes in, different modules join forces to deliver the product or service as specified by the customer.[61]

4.2 | Influence Your Environment

In addition to adapting or reacting to the environment, managers and organizations can develop proactive responses aimed at changing the environment. Two general types of proactive responses are independent action and cooperative action.

Independent Action A company uses **independent strategies** when it acts on its own to change some aspect of its current environment. As illustrated in Exhibit 3.5, several independent strategies are possible:[62]

- *Competitive aggression*—exploiting a distinctive competence or improving internal efficiency for competitive advantage (e.g., aggressive pricing and comparative advertising). Southwest Airlines cuts fares when it enters a new market, and Sony positioned itself as the gaming industry's technological leader with the launch of the PS3.

- *Competitive pacification*—independent action to improve relations with competitors (e.g., helping competitors find raw materials). Kellogg Company promotes the cereal

industry as a whole, as well as advertising its various brands.

- *Public relations*—establishing and maintaining favorable images in the minds of those making up the environment (e.g., sponsoring sporting events). The oil and natural gas industry advertises its role in national independence.

- *Voluntary action*—voluntary commitment to various interest groups, causes, and social problems (e.g., donating supplies to tsunami victims). Converse, Apple, Gap, Dell, Nike, Shazam, and other companies have signed on to Product Red, a program in which they market special Red-themed products and donate a percentage of the profits to the Global Fund, a project to help end AIDS in Africa.

independent strategies strategies that an organization acting on its own uses to change some aspect of its current environment

Exhibit 3.5 Ways that managers can influence their environment

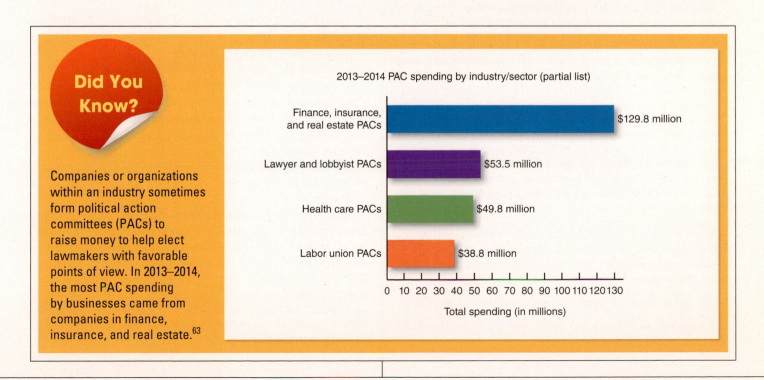

Did You Know?

Companies or organizations within an industry sometimes form political action committees (PACs) to raise money to help elect lawmakers with favorable points of view. In 2013–2014, the most PAC spending by businesses came from companies in finance, insurance, and real estate.[63]

2013–2014 PAC spending by industry/sector (partial list)

Industry/Sector	Total spending (in millions)
Finance, insurance, and real estate PACs	$129.8 million
Lawyer and lobbyist PACs	$53.5 million
Health care PACs	$49.8 million
Labor union PACs	$38.8 million

Total spending (in millions)

- *Legal action*—engaging the company in a private legal battle (e.g., lawsuits against illegal music copying). Viacom sued Google for allowing users to post copyrighted video clips on the Google-owned YouTube website.

- *Political action*—efforts to influence elected representatives to create a more favorable business environment or limit competition (e.g., issue advertising or lobbying at state and national levels). In 2013, special interest groups like companies, labor unions, and other organizations spent a total of $3.2 billion to lobby elected official and candidates in the United States.[64]

Each of these examples shows how organizations—on their own—can have an impact on the environment.

Cooperative Action In some situations, two or more organizations work together using **cooperative strategies** to influence the environment.[65] Several types of cooperative strategies are common:[66]

- *Contracts*—negotiating an agreement between the organization and another group to exchange goods, services, information, patents, and so on. Suppliers and customers, or managers and labor unions, may sign formal agreements about the terms and conditions of their future relationships. These contracts are explicit attempts to make their future relationship predictable.

- *Cooptation*—absorbing new elements into the organization's leadership structure to avert threats to its stability or existence. Many universities invite wealthy alumni to join their boards of directors.

- *Coalition*—groups that act jointly with respect to a set of political initiatives for some period. Local businesses may band together to curb the rise of employee health care costs, and organizations in some industries have formed industry associations and special interest groups. Life Is Good, a New England–based T-shirt company, used the latest economic downturn to strengthen cooperative action with the retailers that stock its products. Employees at Life Is Good began calling retailers to ask how they could help them through the slow times. Based on the feedback, the firm identified a need to establish online networks that retailers—the company's customers—could use for sharing ideas.[67]

At the organizational level, firms establish strategic alliances, partnerships, joint ventures, and mergers with competitors to deal with environmental uncertainties. Cooperative strategies such as these make most sense when two conditions exist:

1. Taking joint action will reduce the organizations' costs and risks.

2. Cooperation will increase their power (their ability to successfully accomplish the changes they desire).

4.3 | Change the Boundaries of the Environment

Besides changing themselves (environmental adaptation) or their environment, organizations can redefine or change which environment they are in. We refer to this last category as **strategic maneuvering**. By making a conscious effort to change the boundaries of its competitive environment, a firm can maneuver around potential threats and capitalize on opportunities.[68] Managers can use several strategic maneuvers, including domain selection, diversification, merger and acquisition, and divestiture.[69]

Domain selection is the entrance by a company into another suitable market or industry. For instance, the market may have limited competition or regulation, ample suppliers and customers, or high growth. An example is Nintendo's decision to create products such as the Wii that appeal to customer segments that have not been enthusiastic to purchase video games, such as people intimidated by complicated game controllers and parents concerned about the violent content and sedentary play involved in video games. By avoiding head-on competition to be the product with the best graphics or most advanced play, Nintendo was able to enjoy immediate profits from its new console. Thus Nintendo has used an existing expertise to broaden the goods and services it offers.

Diversification occurs when a firm invests in different types of businesses or products or when it expands geographically to reduce its dependence on a single market or technology. Google, which earns the bulk of its revenues from advertising on its ubiquitous search engine, has diversified into such new products as Google Glass, self-driven cars, high-speed fiber optic cable, the Nexus line of smartphones and tablets, the Chromebook laptop, and the Chromecast Internet connector for TVs. In March 2014, Google's Motorola unit and LG Electronics released a smartwatch to compete in the broader 45-million unit wearable device market.[70]

A **merger** or **acquisition** takes place when two or more firms combine, or one firm buys another, to form a single company. Mergers and acquisitions can offer greater efficiency from combined operations or can give companies relatively quick access to new markets or industries. Swedish automaker Volvo was recently acquired by Geely Holding Group in China.[71] Li Zhejiang, the CEO of Geely, has announced plans to build several manufacturing plants in China to serve its growing demand for cars.

Divestiture occurs when a company sells one or more businesses. At Ford Motor Company, recent operating losses and the costs of restructuring its workforce have brought about a cash shortage. To raise cash and focus on meeting changing consumer tastes in the U.S. automotive market, Ford recently dismantled its Premier Automotive Group by selling Aston Martin to a British-led group of investors, Land Rover and Jaguar to Tata of India, and Volvo to Geely of China.[72]

Organizations engage in strategic maneuvering when they move into different environments. Some companies, called **prospectors**, are more likely than others to engage in strategic maneuvering.[73] Aggressive companies like Amazon, Google, and Apple continuously change the boundaries of their competitive environments by seeking new products and markets, diversifying, and merging or acquiring new enterprises.

In these and other ways, corporations put their competitors on the defensive and force them to react. **Defenders**, in contrast, stay within a more limited, stable product domain.

4.4 | Three Criteria Help You Choose the Best Approach

Three general considerations help guide management's response to the environment:

1. *Managers need to change what can be changed.* Environmental responses are most useful when aimed at elements of the environment that cause the company problems, provide opportunities, and allow the company to change successfully. Thus Nintendo recognized that its game console would have difficulty competing on superior graphics, so it addressed underserved segments of the market, where customers and favorable publicity made the Wii successful.

2. *Managers should use the appropriate response.* If a company wants to better manage its competitive environment, competitive aggression and pacification are viable. Political action influences the legal

● LG engineers worked closely with Google from the initial stages of development to ensure that the LG G Watch worked perfectly with Android Wear. It will be compatible with a wide-range of Android™ smartphones and will present relevant information to users just when they need it or whenever they say "OK Google" to ask questions or get stuff done.

environment, and contracting helps manage customers and suppliers.

No business likes bad press, but if it occurs, managers must choose a response. They can ignore the negative publicity or address it in such a way that the incident is viewed as neutral, or even positive. When Washington, DC, restaurateur Mark Sakuta discovered criticisms of his restaurant on the website for the Washington Post, he was at first puzzled. About 10 negative reviews appeared simultaneously, accusing the restaurant of using cookbook recipes instead of its own original concoctions, claiming that the floor was unstable, and more. A month later, another harsh review criticized the gratuity policy for large groups.

Sakuta knew that the first group of accusations was simply untrue. He suspected they were written by disgruntled former employees. So he called customer service at the website and asked to have the postings removed. The site manager agreed. But Sakuta did not ask to have the comment about the tipping policy removed because it was accurate. Instead he decided to adjust the policy. He reasoned that if customers were uncomfortable with it, they might choose to dine elsewhere. Now Sakuta keeps closer tabs on food-related websites and blogs, looking for any comments about his business.[74]

3. *Managers should choose responses that offer the most benefit at the lowest cost.* Return-on-investment calculations should incorporate short-term financial considerations and long-term impact.

Proactive managers who consider these factors carefully will guide their organizations to competitive advantage more effectively.

In addition, effective managers also look to their internal environment for ways to respond to changes that are occurring outside their organization. This leads to a discussion of how an organization's culture can be used to address those changes in the external environment.

LO5 Discuss how organizational cultures can be leveraged to overcome challenges in the external environment

5 | CULTURE AND THE INTERNAL ENVIRONMENT OF ORGANIZATIONS

An organization's **internal environment** refers to all relevant forces inside a firm's boundaries, such as its managers, employees, resources, and organizational culture.

As we have discussed, an organization's managers serve a critical role in scanning and responding to threats and opportunities in the external environment. Financial, physical, and human resources also play a key role when it comes to achieving competitive advantage. One of the most important factors that influence an organization's response to its external environment is its culture.

5.1 | What Is an Organization Culture?

Organization culture is the set of assumptions about the organization and its goals and practices that members of the company share.[75] It is a system of shared values about what is important and beliefs about how the world works. It provides a framework that organizes and directs people's behavior on the job.[76] The culture of an organization may be difficult for an observer to define easily, yet like an individual's personality, an astute observer can decipher the clues of the culture over time. As illustrated in Exhibit 3.6, there are three layers of organization culture.[77] The first level is like the exposed part of an iceberg and consists of **visible artifacts**, which are the components of an organization that can be seen and heard such as office layout, dress, orientation, stories, and written material (e.g., annual reports and strategic plans). Though seemingly easy to interpret, these clues to understanding the culture often take time to figure out. The second level of

culture refers to its **values**, which are the underlying qualities and desirable behaviors that are important to the organization. Values are akin to that part of the iceberg that is just below the surface of the water. They can't be directly observed, but rather values need to be inferred from the behavior of managers. For example, acting on the value of wanting to become a "green" automobile company, the top management team may decide to build a line of fuel-efficient electric automobiles. The third and deepest level of an organization's culture refers to **unconscious assumptions**, which are strongly held and taken-for-granted beliefs that guide behavior in the firm. In the case of the automobile executives, they'll be willing to "go green" only to the extent that this new sustainability initiative is profitable.

Cultures can be strong or weak; *strong cultures* can greatly influence the way people think and behave. A strong culture is one in which everyone understands and believes in the firm's goals, priorities, and practices. A strong culture can be a real advantage to the organization if the behaviors it encourages and facilitates are appropriate. Zappo's culture encourages extraordinary devotion to customer service; the culture at Cirque du Soleil encourages innovation, and the culture at Walmart stresses low cost and frugality. Employees in these companies don't need rule books to dictate how they act because these behaviors are conveyed as "the way we do things around here," rooted in their companies' cultures.

Exhibit 3.6 The three levels of organizational culture

1: Visible Artifacts
Office layout, dress code, written documents.

2: Values
"We need to become a 'green' company."

3: Unconscious Assumptions
"But we have to be profitable."

Source: Adapted from E. H. Schein, "Coming to a New Awareness of Organizational Culture," *Sloan Management Review* 25, no. 2 (Winter 1984), pp. 3–16. Copyright © 1984 from MIT *Sloan Management Review*/Massachusetts Institute of Technology. All rights reserved. Distributed by Tribune Content Agency, LLC.

● Annie's CEO John Foraker pictured. Everyone at Annie's shares a common passion for food, people, and the planet we all share.

In contrast, a strong culture that encourages inappropriate behaviors can severely hinder an organization's ability to deal effectively with its external environment—particularly if the environment is undergoing change, as is almost always the case today. A culture that was suitable and even advantageous in a prior era may become counterproductive in a new environment. For instance, a small start-up may have an informal culture that becomes less suitable when the company grows, faces more competition, and requires decision making by a wide range of specialized employees spread out over many locations.

:::::::::::::::::

In its relatively short life as a company, Google quickly became a role model for its brainy culture of innovation. Software writers and engineers were attracted to Google not just for its famous perks, such as free meals and laundry facilities, but also for a climate in which they were encouraged to let their imaginations roam free, dreaming up ideas that could be crazy but just might be the next big thing on the Internet. During a long-running business boom, that culture served Google well. The best engineers were thrilled to work for a company that let them spend one-fifth of their time on new projects of their own choosing. But when the economy slowed and the stock market nosedived, Google's managers had to cope with a new reality in which money was tight. Google could no longer afford its free-spending culture. Managers had to figure out how to maintain the best of the culture while innovating at a more prudent pace.

Google's modified culture now values setting priorities. New ideas are still welcome if they are focused on core businesses of search, advertising, and web-based software applications. Managers are reassigning employees away from teams working on unrelated projects and using them to staff teams working on profitable ideas in the core areas. Employees who have an idea that can improve the computer user's experience are asked to consider also what impact that idea might have on Google's bottom line. Similarly, hiring has slowed because managers must not only justify the talent of a candidate but also target hiring to particular business needs. The challenge will be to keep employees as excited about targeted innovation as they have been about freewheeling innovation.[78]

:::::::::::::::::

In contrast, at a company with a *weak culture,* different people hold different values, there is confusion about corporate goals, and it is not clear from one day to the next what principles should guide decisions. Some managers may pay lip service to some aspects of the culture ("we would never cheat a customer") but behave very differently ("don't tell him about the flaw"). As you can guess, such a culture fosters confusion, conflict, and poor performance. Most managers would agree that they want to create a strong culture that encourages and supports goals and useful behaviors that will make the company more effective. In other words, they want to create a culture that is appropriately aligned with the organization's competitive environment.[79]

5.2 | Companies Give Many Clues About Their Culture

Let's say you want to understand a company's culture. Perhaps you are thinking about working there and you want a good "fit," or perhaps you are working there right now and want to deepen your understanding of the organization and determine whether its culture matches the challenges it faces. How would you go about making the diagnosis? As the "Take Charge of Your Career" feature discusses, a variety of things will give you useful clues about culture:

- *Corporate mission statements and official goals* are a starting point because they will tell you the firm's desired public image. Most companies have a mission statement—even the CIA (you can find it at http://www.cia.gov). Your school has one, and you can probably find it online. But are these statements a true expression of culture? A study of hospital employees and their managers found that managers rated their mission statement more positively than nonmanagers (even though employees had participated in developing it), and 3 out of 10 employees were not even aware that the hospital had a mission statement (even though the hospital had processes for communicating about it).[80] So even after reading statements of mission and goals, you still need to figure out whether the statements truly reflect how the firm conducts business.

- *Business practices can be observed.* How a company responds to problems, makes strategic decisions, and treats employees and customers tells a lot about what top management really values. When an unknown person(s) laced some Extra Strength Tylenol capsules with cyanide in the Chicago area back in the early 1980s, Jim Burke

Take Charge of Your Career

Figure out the organizational culture, and fast!

Starting a new job or career is never easy. If you moved as a child, it may bring up memories of being the new kid in town. Here's an idea. During the first few days, weeks, and months on the new job, try to "hit the ground listening." There's an old saying that suggests that because we've been given two ears and one mouth, we should probably try to listen twice as much as we talk. That makes a lot of sense, especially when trying to figure out the ins and outs of an organization you recently joined.

Think of yourself as a private investigator or cultural anthropologist whose job is to figure out answers to questions like these:

1. *The who's:* Who on staff is respected the most? Who seems to have the most influence? Whom do people go to with problems? Whom do I need to impress?

2. *The what's:* What skills, abilities, and knowledge does this organization value? What kind of attitudes do successful people display here?

3. *The why's:* Why is this organization successful? Why does it hire people like me? Why do people get fired from here? Why is there talk about changing the culture to better align with the external environment?

4. *The how's:* How good is the fit between the organizational culture and my values? How can I make a positive impact on this organization?

The questions are probably not the hardest part to figure out. Getting accurate answers to the questions is more challenging. How can you go about collecting information so that you can arrive at the answers?

First, find (or download) and read everything you can about the organization. Start with its website, but don't stop there. Use your school's library databases and Internet search engines to unearth articles, news releases, complaints, and other tidbits about your organization. Getting facts and opinions from diverse sources will give you a more complete picture of the organization than just relying on internal documents.

Second, start talking to people. When you start getting to know your supervisor, coworkers, customers, or suppliers, ask them for their opinions about some of the questions listed here. You might be surprised at what people are willing to tell you. Being new has advantages—most folks like imparting their wisdom to someone who's willing to listen to them.

Last, observe people's behaviors and listen to what they say (and how they say it). If you're a good observer of people, you'll be able to piece together the puzzle that makes up an organization's culture. If you find you often miss what people say or struggle with interpreting nonverbal cues, it may take you longer to arrive at the same point of understanding. That's okay. Everyone moves at his or her own pace. The important point is to make a direct and conscious effort to decipher your organization's culture so you can decide whether it's a good fit for you in the long term. If not, there are a virtually unlimited number of different organizations in the world. By finding one that fits well with your preferences, personality, values, and passion, you will feel at home while at work.

---

and the other leaders of Johnson & Johnson reacted to the crisis by recalling all related products throughout the United States. This decisive move, though not good for short-term profitability, was respected throughout the company and business community.

- *Symbols, rites, and ceremonies give further clues about culture.* For instance, status symbols can give you a feel for how rigid the hierarchy is and for the nature of relationships between lower and higher levels. Who is hired and fired—and why—and the activities that are rewarded indicate the firm's real values.

- *The stories people tell carry a lot of information about the company's culture.* Every company has its myths, legends, and true stories about important past decisions and actions that convey the company's main values. The stories often feature the company's heroes: people once or still active who possessed the qualities and characteristics that the culture especially values and who act as models for others about how to behave. Sam Walton, founder of Walmart, was a bigger-than-life presence for his employees. Well into his senior years, Walton would drive an old red pickup truck from store to store, where he'd meet and joke with employees and even lead them in a company cheer.

A strong culture combines these measures in a consistent way. The Ritz-Carlton hotel chain gives each employee a laminated card listing its 12 service values. Each day it carries out a type of ceremony: a 15-minute meeting during which employees from every department resolve problems and discuss areas of potential improvement. At these meetings, the focus is on the day's "wow story," which details an extraordinary way that a Ritz-Carlton employee lived up to one of the service values. For example, a family arrived at the Bali Ritz-Carlton with special eggs and milk because of their son's allergies, but the food had spoiled. The manager and dining staff couldn't find replacements in town, so the executive chef called his mother-in-law in Singapore and asked her to buy the necessary products and fly with them to Bali.[81]

5.3 | Four Different Types of Organizational Cultures

In general, cultures can be categorized according to whether they emphasize flexibility versus control and whether their focus is internal or external to the organization. Keep in mind that organizations can have characteristics of more than one culture. In order to understand their culture, managers should discuss this issue with other managers to compare notes on how the culture is evolving and its strengths and weaknesses relative to the demands of the external environment. By juxtaposing these two dimensions, we can describe four types of organizational cultures, depicted in Exhibit 3.7:

- *Group culture.* The New Belgium Brewery in Fort Collins, Colorada, is an example of a group culture that is internally oriented and flexible. It tends to be based on the values and norms associated with the firm. The employees (i.e., organizational members) comply with organizational directives that flow from trust, tradition, and long-term commitment. Their culture emphasizes member development and values participation in decision making. The strategic orientation associated with this cultural type is one of implementation through consensus building. Its leaders tend to act as mentors and facilitators.

- *Hierarchical culture.* The U.S. armed forces are based on a hierarchical culture that is internally oriented by more focus on control and stability. It has the values and norms associated with a bureaucracy. It values stability and assumes that individuals will comply with organizational mandates when roles are stated formally and enforced through rules and procedures.

- *Rational culture.* Oil and natural gas companies tend to have rational cultures that are externally oriented and focused on control. This type of culture's primary objectives are productivity, planning, and efficiency. Organizational members are motivated by the belief that performance that leads to the desired organizational objectives will be rewarded.

- *Adhocracy.* Apple is an example of an adhocracy that is externally oriented and flexible. This culture type emphasizes change in which growth, resource acquisition, and innovation are stressed. Organizational members are motivated by the importance or ideological appeal of the task. Leaders tend to be entrepreneurial and risk takers. Other members tend to have these characteristics as well.[82]

This type of diagnosis is important when two companies are considering combining operations, as in a merger, acquisition, or joint venture, because as we noted, cultural differences can sink these arrangements. In some cases, organizations investigating this type of change can benefit from setting up a "clean team" of third-party experts who investigate the details of each company's culture. For example, they might conduct employee focus groups, look for systems that empower employees to

Exhibit 3.7 Competing-values model of culture

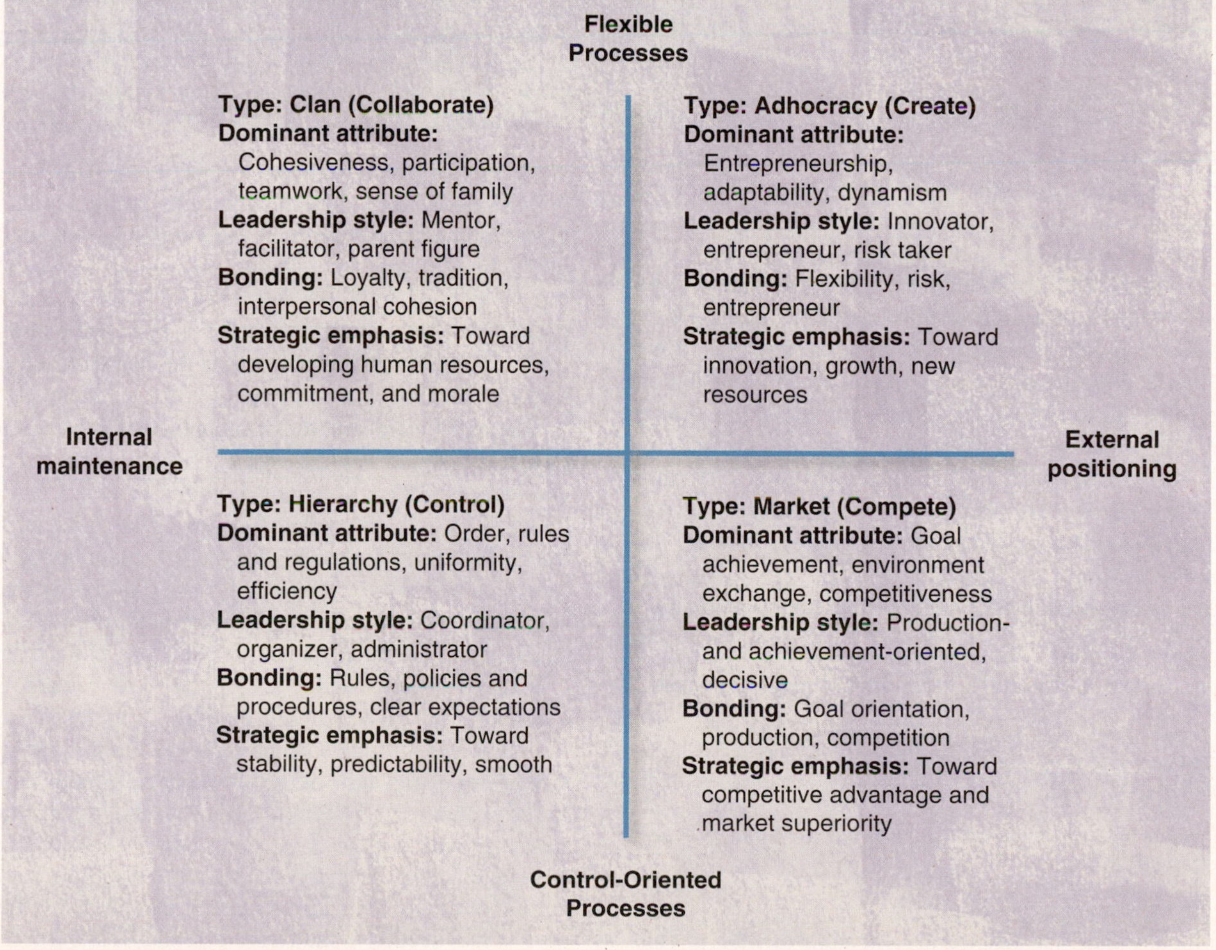

Flexible Processes

Internal maintenance

Type: Clan (Collaborate)
Dominant attribute: Cohesiveness, participation, teamwork, sense of family
Leadership style: Mentor, facilitator, parent figure
Bonding: Loyalty, tradition, interpersonal cohesion
Strategic emphasis: Toward developing human resources, commitment, and morale

Type: Adhocracy (Create)
Dominant attribute: Entrepreneurship, adaptability, dynamism
Leadership style: Innovator, entrepreneur, risk taker
Bonding: Flexibility, risk, entrepreneur
Strategic emphasis: Toward innovation, growth, new resources

External positioning

Type: Hierarchy (Control)
Dominant attribute: Order, rules and regulations, uniformity, efficiency
Leadership style: Coordinator, organizer, administrator
Bonding: Rules, policies and procedures, clear expectations
Strategic emphasis: Toward stability, predictability, smooth

Type: Market (Compete)
Dominant attribute: Goal achievement, environment exchange, competitiveness
Leadership style: Production- and achievement-oriented, decisive
Bonding: Goal orientation, production, competition
Strategic emphasis: Toward competitive advantage and market superiority

Control-Oriented Processes

Source: Adapted from K. S. Cameron and R. E. Quinn, *Diagnosing and Changing Organizational Culture* 3rd edition, 2011, Jossey-Bass. Reprinted with permission of the author.

> ### "Be the change you want to see in the world."
> — Mahatma Gandhi

make independent decisions, and note how management talks about the company's founder, customers, and employees. In this way, the clean team can identify for the organizations' leaders the types of issues they will have to resolve and the values they must choose among as they try to establish a combined culture.[83]

What type of company culture is important to you in your career?

Teamwork ⇐ or ⇒ Efficiency?
Creativity ⇐ or ⇒ Competitiveness?

5.4 | Cultures Can Be Leveraged to Meet Challenges in the External Environment

We mentioned earlier in this chapter that one important way organizations have of responding to the external environment is to adapt to it by changing the organization itself. One of the most important tools managers have for implementing internal changes lies in their management of their organization's culture. For example, a strong focus on customer service will be difficult to establish in a culture that has always focused on its own internal processes and goals. Simple directives alone are often ineffective; the underlying values of the organization also have to be shifted in the desired direction. Most companies today know that making moves necessary to remain competitive is so essential that they require deep-rooted cultural changes. When that kind of change occurs, organization members may begin to internalize the new values and display the appropriate behaviors.

Effective managers can take several approaches to managing culture:

- Craft an inspirational vision of "what can be" for the organizational culture.

- "Walk the talk" and show members of the culture that you are serious about and committed to long-term change.

- Celebrate and reward members who behave in ways that exemplify the desired culture.

First, effective managers should espouse ideals and visions for the company that will inspire organization members. That vision should be articulated over and over until it becomes a tangible presence throughout the organization. For example,

Coca-Cola's vision statement provides a clear idea of what the company stands for:

Our vision serves as the framework for our roadmap and guides every aspect of our business by describing what we need to accomplish in order to continue achieving sustainable, quality growth.

- ***People:*** *Be a great place to work where people are inspired to be the best they can be.*

- ***Portfolio:*** *Bring to the world a portfolio of quality beverage brands that anticipate and satisfy people's desires and needs.*

- ***Partners:*** *Nurture a winning network of customers and suppliers; together we create mutual, enduring value.*

- ***Planet:*** *Be a responsible citizen that makes a difference by helping build and support sustainable communities.*

- ***Profit:*** *Maximize long-term return to shareowners while being mindful of our overall responsibilities.*

- ***Productivity:*** *Be a highly effective, lean, and fast-moving organization.*[84]

Second, executives need to "walk the talk" of the new organizational direction by communicating regularly, being visible and active throughout the company, and setting examples. The CEO not only should talk about the vision but also should embody it day in and day out. This makes the CEO's pronouncements credible, creates a personal example others can emulate, and builds trust that the organization's progress toward the vision will continue over the long run.

Important here are the moments of truth requiring hard choices. Imagine top management trumpeting a culture that emphasizes quality and then discovering that a part used in a batch of assembled products is defective. Whether to replace the part at great expense in the interest of quality or to ship the defective part to save time and money is a decision that will reinforce or destroy a quality-oriented culture.

To reinforce the organization's culture, the CEO and other executives should routinely celebrate and reward those who exemplify the new values. Another key to managing culture involves hiring, socializing newcomers, and promoting employees on the basis of the new corporate values. In this way, the new culture will begin to permeate the organization. While this may seem a time-consuming approach to building a new culture, effective managers recognize that replacing a long-term culture of traditional values with one that embodies the competitive values needed in the future can take years. But the rewards of that effort will be an organization much more effective and responsive to its environmental challenges and opportunities.

Study Checklist

✔ Did you tear out the perforated student review card at the back of the text to revisit learning objectives and key terms and definitions?

Connect® Management is available for M Management. Additional resources include:

✔ Interactive Applications:
- Comprehension Case: Rubio's Competitive Environment
- Drag & Drop: Elements of Organizational Culture
- Drag & Drop: Model of Organizational Culture

- Video Case: Nordstrom's External and Internal Environment

✔ LearnSmart—Multiple choice questions help you determine what you already know, are not sure about, or need to practice based on your score. And with SmartBook, you can read the relevant section in the eBook as well as practice and recharge what you've learned.

✔ Chapter Video: CH2M Hill

✔ Young Manager Speaks Out: Kevin Wielgus, General Manager, Carpet Company

part two

4

Ethics and Corporate Responsibility

Learning Objectives

After studying Chapter 4, you should be able to

LO1 Describe how different ethical perspectives guide managerial decision making.

LO2 Identify the ethics-related issues and laws facing managers.

LO3 Explain how managers influence their ethics environment.

LO4 Outline the process for making ethical decisions.

LO5 Summarize the important issues surrounding corporate social responsibility.

LO6 Discuss the growing importance of managing the natural environment.

For an increasing number of people, tweeting, snap chatting, texting, downloading apps, checking Facebook walls, posting selfies on Pinterest, or endorsing skills on LinkedIn are a 24/7 activity. For the majority of Millennial (born between 1980 and 2000) employees, in particular, social media connectivity is both an obsessive habit and frequent necessity.

Consider the intersection of social media use at work and ethical behavior. Is it ethical for a manager, before making an offer to a job applicant, to search the applicant's online social media pages? What if she discovers (from her search) that the applicant appears to be affiliated with a non-mainstream religious entity? How about when employees spend company time texting friends or checking Twitter?

What about employees who post or blog (or have companies or their friends do it for them) fake positive online reviews about their company's services or products to create buzz? Is this practice ethical or misleading? Is it okay if everyone does it?

Organizations are increasingly addressing these sticky ethical issues surrounding the use of social media at work. A surprisingly high percentage of companies have disciplined employees for inappropriate behavior on social media sites.[1] One famous instance was when Virgin Atlantic Airlines fired 13 flight attendants for badmouthing customers and the airline's safety standards on a Facebook blog.[2]

Also, employers in some states are asking lawmakers for the right to ask for an employee's username and password if they're suspected of online misbehavior. This request is a controversial part of a growing debate over social media privacy laws. As of 2013, 35 states have introduced laws concerning social media privacy at the workplace. So far, five states have passed laws that prohibit companies from obtaining employees' passwords to social media websites.[3]

In contrast to the challenges presented here, many companies like Zappos and Amazon expertly leverage social media to promote their brands, increase customer engagement, and boost sales revenue. Other employers like IBM and Google harness social media to increase social learning and intercompany cohesion among employees and team members. And, let's not forget companies like Perfetti Van Melle (Mentos candies) and Speed Stick (deodorant) that have benefited through relatively low-cost marketing campaigns that went viral as a result of social media.[4]

Employers and employees alike have to come to terms with what's ethical (and legal) when it comes to using social media tools at work. According to Natalie C. Rougeux, JD, SPHR (www.rougeuxpllc.com): "Our employers are struggling more than ever with how to bridge the gap between: (i) the company's need to protect company data; and (ii) employees who consider the unfettered use of technology to be essential to their work/life balance. Quite simply, technology, employee/employer expectations, and the law are not in sync on this issue."

This chapter addresses the values and manner of doing business adopted by managers as they carry out their organizational and business strategies. In particular, we will explore ways of applying **ethics**, the moral principles and standards that guide the behavior of an individual or group. We do so based on the premise that employees, their organizations, and their communities thrive over the long term when managers apply ethical standards that direct them to act with integrity. In addition, we consider the idea that organizations have a responsibility to meet social obligations beyond earning profits within legal and ethical constraints. Professor Edward Freeman, an early champion of stakeholder theory[5] (discussed later in the chapter), and business and academic thought leaders from the Business Roundtable Institute for Corporate Ethics at the University of Virginia believe that managers benefit their organizations not

> *"In matters of style, swim with the current. In matters of principle, stand like a rock."*
>
> — Thomas Jefferson

only by growing profits, but also by behaving ethically when dealing with individuals and groups (known as stakeholders) that interact with their organizations.[6] As you study this chapter, consider what kind of manager you want to be. What reputation do you hope to have? How would you like others to describe your behavior as a manager?

It's a Big Issue

It seems ethics-related scandals are becoming a part of everyday life. While business leaders and managers commit many of these unethical acts, bad behavior can occur anywhere at anytime. Recent examples of business-related scandals include the conviction of Raj Rajaratnam, founder of the hedge fund Galleon Group, for securities fraud and conspiracy.[7] He is currently serving an 11-year jail term. In Bangladesh, a multistory garment factory collapsed recently, killing more than 400 workers. The owner of the factor is accused of violating building and safety codes.[8] In an unrelated scandal, Bernie Madoff was convicted of running a $50 billion Ponzi scheme in which he deceived his investors into thinking that they were earning legitimate returns on their investments; in reality, Madoff was taking investor's money to pay "returns" to other investors. After pleading guilty to 11 felony charges, Madoff is currently serving a 150-year prison term.[9]

What other news disturbs you about managers' behavior? Tainted products in the food supply . . . damage to the environment . . . price fixing . . . Internet scams . . . employees pressured to meet lofty sales or production targets by any means? The list goes on, and the public becomes cynical. In a survey by public relations firm Edelman, the percentage of Americans who trust business dropped from 59 percent in 2008 to 44 percent in 2014. They're even suspicious of their own company's management; only 43 percent said they trust their own CEO.[10] Try to imagine the challenge of leading employees who don't trust you.

Unethical behavior can happen anywhere, not just in business. It occurs when police officers "take care of parking tickets" so friends and family members do not have to pay fines.[11] While this may seem relatively minor at first glance, many citizens feel this is an unfair practice and an abuse of power.

Recently prosecutors have brought criminal charges related to "ticket fixing" against 13 members of the Patrolmen's Benevolent Association, a powerful police union in New York City.[12]

Sports have seen their share of unethical behavior. The aftershocks following the child sexual abuse trial of Jerry Sandusky, the former defensive coordinator of the Penn State University football team, have rocked the university and its community. For years, eyewitness information was known by some people at the university but not properly conveyed to the police. After the allegations were finally made public, Sandusky was found guilty of 45 felony counts of sexual abuse against 10 boys over a 15-year period.[13] He is serving a 30- to 60-year state prison sentence. Tim Curley, the athletic director, and Gary Schultz, the now-retired vice president of finance and business, were charged with perjury and for failing to report what they knew about the alleged crimes.[14] Acting to "restore trust in the university," the school's board of trustees dismissed the popular, longtime head coach Joe Paterno and the university's president, Graham Spanier.[15] The former head coach (who died in early 2012) and ex-university president were not charged in the case. The fallout from this tragic set of events, including the university's settlement of $59.7 million for Sandusky's victims,[16] will undoubtedly be felt for many years at Penn State University and throughout the university's community.

LISTEN & LEARN ● ONLINE

YOUNG MANAGERS
Speak Out!

"I think socially responsible organizations appear more mature and reliable than others. Our customers recognize that aspect, and they can tell the difference between genuine awareness and care for the human community. In being socially responsible, I think we gain a like-minded audience, and like-minded consumers generally show brand loyalty."

—Megan Gates, Market Development Manager

● Jerry Sandusky, center, is escorted from his sentencing at the Centre County Courthouse in Bellefonte in October 2012. Sandusky, maintaining his innocence, was sentenced to at least 30 years in prison (effectively a life sentence) in the child sexual abuse scandal that brought shame to Penn State and led to coach Joe Paterno's downfall.

The list of bad behavior goes on, whether it is allegations about the role that 38 principals and 178 teachers played in tampering with elementary and middle school students' scores on standardized tests in Atlanta[17] or cyclist Lance Armstrong who after admitting to using performance-enhancing drugs was stripped of his 7 Tour de France titles and banned from professional sports.[18]

Still, simply talking about recent examples of lax ethics does not get at the heart of the problem. Simply saying "I would never do anything like that" or "I would have reported it if it were me" is too easy. The fact is that temptations and levels of silence exist in all organizations. In a survey called the Spherion Workplace Snapshot, more than one-third of U.S. adults said they had observed unethical conduct at work. About one out of five reported seeing abuse or intimidation of employees; lying to employees, customers, vendors, or the public; or situations in which employees placed their own interests ahead of their company's interests.[19]

The motivations are not always as obvious as greed. Another survey, conducted by the American Management Association and the Human Resource Institute, found that the top justification given for unethical behavior was "pressure to meet unrealistic goals and deadlines."[20] Many of the decisions you will face as a manager will pose ethical dilemmas, and the right thing to do is not always clear.

It's a Personal Issue

"Answer true or false: 'I am an ethical manager.' If you answered 'true,' here's an uncomfortable fact: You're probably not."[21] These sentences are the first in a *Harvard Business Review* article called "How (Un)Ethical Are You?" The point is that most of us think we are good decision makers, ethical, and unbiased. But the fact is, most people have unconscious biases that favor themselves and their own group. For example, managers often hire people who are like them, think they are immune to conflicts of interest, take more credit than they deserve, and blame others when they deserve some blame themselves.

Knowing that you have biases may help you try to overcome them, but usually that's not enough. Consider the basic ethical issue of telling a lie. Many people lie—some more than others, and in part depending on the situation, usually presuming that they will benefit from the lie. At a basic level, we all can make ethical arguments against lying and in favor of honesty. Yet it is useful to think thoroughly about the real consequences of lying.[22] Exhibit 4.1 summarizes the possible outcomes of telling the truth or lying in different situations. People often lie or commit other ethical transgressions somewhat mindlessly, without realizing the full array of negative personal consequences.

Exhibit 4.1	Lying vs. telling the truth	
Reasons Why People Lie	**Results of Lying**	**Results of Telling the Truth**
Negotiating	• Short-term gain. • Economically positive. • Harms long-term relationship. • Must rationalize to oneself.	• Supports high-quality long-term relationship. • Develops reputation of integrity. • Models behavior to others.
Keeping a confidence (that may require at least a lie of omission)	• Protects whatever good reason there is for the confidence. • Maintains a long-term relationship with the party for whom confidence is kept. • May project deceitfulness to the deceived party.	• Violates a trust to the confiding party. • Makes one appear deceitful to all parties in the long run. • Creates the impression of honesty beyond utility.
Reporting your own performance within an organization	• Might advance oneself or one's cause. • Develops dishonest reputation over time. • Must continue the sequence of lies to appear consistent.	• Creates reputation of integrity. • May not always be positive.

Source: Adapted from S. L. Grover, "The Truth, the Whole Truth, and Nothing but the Truth: The Causes and Management of Workplace Lying," *Academy of Management Executive* 19 (May 2005), pp. 148–57, table 1, p. 155. Reprinted with permission of *Academy of Management Executive*. Permission conveyed through Copyright Clearance Center.

Ethics issues are not easy, and they are not faced only by top corporate executives and CEOs. You will face them; no doubt, you already have. You've got your own examples, but consider this one: more and more people at work use computers with Internet access. If the employer pays for the computer and the time you spend sitting in front of it, is it ethical for you to use the computer to do tasks unrelated to your work? Would you bend the rules for certain activities or certain amounts of time? Maybe you think it's OK to do a little online shopping during your lunch hour or to check scores during the World Series or March Madness. But what if you stream video of the games for your own and your coworkers' enjoyment or take a two-hour lunch to locate the best deal on a flat-panel TV?

Besides lost productivity, employers are most concerned about computer users introducing viruses, leaking confidential information, and creating a hostile work environment by downloading inappropriate web content. Sometimes employees write blogs or post comments online about their company and its products. Obviously companies do not want their employees to say bad things about them Also, some companies are concerned about employees who plug their companies and products on comments pages without disclosing their relationship with their company. Another practice considered deceptive is when companies create fictional blogs as a marketing tactic without disclosing their sponsorship. And in a practice known as Astroturfing—because the "grassroots" interest it builds is fake—businesses pay bloggers to write positive comments about them. A Florida company known as PayPerPost will match advertisers with bloggers but now requires bloggers to disclose the relationship. Companies such as Coca-Cola, UPS, and IBM have established guidelines directing employees to identify themselves accurately in online communications so that they can participate in online conversations about their companies without being accused of deception.[23]

Are these examples too small to worry about? What do you do that has potential ethical ramifications? This chapter will help you think through decisions with ethical ramifications.

LO1 Describe how different ethical perspectives guide managerial decision making

1 | FIVE PERSPECTIVES SHAPE YOUR ETHICS

The aim of ethics is to identify both the rules that should govern people's behavior and the "goods" that are worth seeking. Ethical decisions are guided by the underlying values of the individual. Values are principles of conduct such as caring, being honest, keeping promises, pursuing excellence, showing loyalty, being fair, acting with integrity, respecting others, and being a responsible citizen.[24]

Most people would agree that all of these values are admirable guidelines for behavior. However, ethics becomes a more complicated issue when a situation dictates that one value overrules others. An **ethical issue** is a situation, problem, or opportunity in which an individual must choose among several actions that must be evaluated as morally right or wrong.[25] Ethical issues arise in every facet of life; we concern ourselves here with business ethics in particular. **Business ethics** comprises the moral principles and standards that guide behavior in the world of business.[26]

Moral philosophy refers to the principles, rules, and values people use in deciding what is right or wrong. This seems to be a simple definition but often becomes terribly complex and difficult when facing real choices. How do you decide what is right and wrong? Do you know what criteria you apply and how you apply them?

Ethics scholars point to various major ethical systems as guides.[27] We will consider five of these:

1. Universalism.
2. Egoism.
3. Utilitarianism.
4. Relativism.
5. Virtue ethics.

These major ethical systems underlie personal moral choices and ethical decisions in business.

1.1 | Universalism

According to **universalism**, all people should uphold certain values, such as honesty and other values that society needs to function. Universal values are principles so fundamental to human existence that they are important in all societies—for example, rules against murder, deceit, torture, and oppression.

Some efforts have been made to establish global, universal ethical principles for business. The Caux Roundtable, a group of international executives based in Caux, Switzerland, worked with business leaders from Japan, Europe, and the United States to create the **Caux Principles for Business**.[28] Two basic ethical ideals underpin the Caux Principles: *kyosei* and human dignity. *Kyosei* means living and working together for the common good, allowing cooperation and mutual prosperity to coexist with healthy and fair competition. Human dignity concerns the value of each person as an end, not a means to the fulfillment of others' purposes. Research conducted by the Institute for Global Ethics identified five core ethical values that are found in all human cultures, including truthfulness, responsibility, fairness, respectfulness, and compassion.[29]

Universal principles can be powerful and useful, but what people say, hope, or think they would do is often different from what they *really* do, faced with conflicting demands in real situations. Before we describe other ethical systems, consider the following example, and think about how you or others would resolve it.

:::::::::::::::::

Suppose that Sam Colt, a sales representative, is preparing a sales presentation on behalf of his firm, Midwest Hardware, which manufactures nuts and bolts. Colt hopes to obtain a large sale from a construction firm that is building a bridge across the Missouri River near St. Louis. The bolts manufactured by Midwest Hardware have a 3 percent defect rate, which, although acceptable in the industry, makes them unsuitable for use in certain types of projects, such as those that might be subject to sudden, severe stress. The new bridge will be located near the New Madrid Fault line, the source of a major earthquake in 1811. The epicenter of that earthquake, which caused extensive damage and altered the flow of the Missouri, is about 190 miles from the new bridge site.

Bridge construction in the area is not regulated by earthquake codes. If Colt wins the sale, he will earn a commission of $25,000 on top of his regular salary. But if he tells the contractors about the defect rate, Midwest may lose the sale to a competitor whose bolts are slightly more reliable. Thus Colt's ethical issue is whether to point out to the bridge contractor that in the event of an earthquake, some Midwest bolts could fail.[31]

:::::::::::::::::

1.2 | Egoism

According to **egoism**, individual self-interest is the actual motive of all conscious action. "Doing the right thing," the focus of moral philosophy, is defined by egoism as "do the act that promotes the greatest good for oneself." If everyone follows this system, according to its proponents, the well-being of society as a whole should increase. This notion is similar to Adam Smith's concept of the invisible hand in business. Smith argued that if every organization follows its own economic self-interest, the total wealth of society will be maximized.

An example of egoism is how individual self-interest may have contributed to the subprime mortgage crisis. According to Adam Smith, individual financial and mortgage professionals should have acted in their own best interest, and ultimately the invisible hand of the mortgage and financial markets would be the best control mechanism to ensure the greater good. If that were the case, why did the housing market reach an unsustainable level that could not be maintained? Did opportunism and the deceptive use of information play a role? Stated differently, did unethical managerial behavior contribute to the subprime mortgage crisis?

Some financial and mortgage experts encouraged prospective home buyers to purchase homes that they could not afford by applying for adjustable-rate mortgages (ARMs). ARMs allow home buyers to pay a low introductory monthly payment for a few years; after this period expires, the monthly payment increases significantly.[32] The experts convinced many home buyers to assume this risk by pointing out that as long as the value of their homes continued to rise, their wealth would increase. Home owners were also told they could manage their risk by selling their homes anytime they wanted for a profit.

How did these financial and mortgage professionals benefit? They received commissions and other fees from the loans they sold. Higher compensation became a driving force for these managers to continue pushing high-risk loans. Others in the financial industry also profited, including banks, mortgage firms, and investment companies.[33]

---

universalism the ethical system stating that all people should uphold certain values that society needs to function

Caux Principles for Business ethical principles established by international executives based in Caux, Switzerland, in collaboration with business leaders from Japan, Europe, and the United States

egoism an ethical principle holding that individual self-interest is the actual motive of all conscious action

---

Did You Know?

A 2012 survey by the Ethics Resource Center found that approximately half of employees of *Fortune* 500 companies witnessed misconduct at work during the past 12 months. The most common forms of unethical behaviors included personal business on company time, abusive behavior, and lying to employees. The study also found that employees are more likely to engage in bribery and delivering goods not up to specifications when they feel pressure to keep their jobs, meet personal financial obligations, and reach quarterly earnings targets.[30]

In 2007–2008 the housing bubble burst as the economy went into a recession and home owners began to struggle to pay their "adjusted" mortgage payments. The large number of foreclosures and defaults contributed to a historic shake-up of the financial industry, including the collapse of Lehman Brothers, huge losses at Morgan Stanley, Citigroup, and Merrill Lynch, and unprecedented governmental intervention to help firms like JP Morgan to purchase Bear Stearns.[34] The fallout of the subprime mortgage and ensuing financial crises will be felt for many years to come. It is useful to ask yourself the following questions: To what degree did egoism motivate individuals in the mortgage and financial markets to make and sell loans that became toxic assets? Is there an alternative explanation for what caused the subprime mortgage crisis?

1.3 | Utilitarianism

Unlike egoism, **utilitarianism** directly seeks the greatest good for the greatest number of people. Refer back to the subprime mortgage crisis that was just discussed. It may be possible that certain utilitarian policies and practices that were implemented after 9/11/2001 and the dot-com meltdown inadvertently contributed to the subprime mortgage crisis. In an effort to do the greatest good for the greatest number of people, the Federal Reserve slashed the federal funds rate from 6.5 percent in May 2000 to 1.75 percent in December 2001. In 2004 the Fed lowered the rate to 1.0 percent.[35] The period from 2001 to 2004 became known as the "credit boom" when mortgages, bank loans, and credit cards were easily obtained at low interest rates.[36] The goal of these rate cuts was to spur the economy and job creation while also encouraging people to buy homes. An outcome of this low interest rate policy was that home ownership was made available to those whose income level or credit history placed them into a higher-risk category of borrower.

While some subprime loans were properly documented and executed, many of these "mortgage loans were created without

● The Securities and Exchange Commission has charged six former executives (including the former CEOs pictured above) of Fannie Mae and Freddie Mac for allegedly committing securities fraud.

any or little supervision."[37] This allowed opportunistic financial and mortgage experts to convince borrowers to assume subprime mortgages that had "teaser" introductory interest rates for a couple of years before automatically adjusting upward. Adding to the rapid growth of the subprime market were the Federal National Mortgage Association (Fannie Mae) and the Federal Home Loan Mortgage Corporation (Freddie Mac), two government-sponsored entities that bought many of these high-risk loans from banks and then packaged and sold them (as a way to diversity the risk of the loans) to U.S. and foreign investors. These two companies ran afoul of U.S. regulators. In 2003 Freddie Mac admitted that it "underreported earnings by over $5 billion," and in 2004 Fannie Mae was under investigation for allegedly committing several widespread accounting errors.[38] Several former executives from these firms are facing one or more civil charges ranging from manipulating earnings to fraud.[39]

In 2006 the housing market began to weaken as housing prices started to decline and inflation started to increase. Contributing to the decline was the Federal Reserve's decision to raise interest rates in order to decrease inflation. This move led banks to tighten credit and require borrowers to make larger down payments on homes, while many subprime mortgage owners saw their adjustable-rate mortgages increase to unexpectedly high levels. The net effect was that many home owners could not make their mortgage payments and began to default on their loans.[40]

Students may want to ask themselves whether decisions made at the Federal Reserve, Fannie Mae and Freddie Mac, and other institutions achieved utilitarian outcomes: Did these decisions result in the greatest good for the greatest number of home owners? Were the decisions completely rational, or did subjectivity lead to a suboptimal set of consequences? Was it egoism on the part of individuals or utilitarianism on the part of institutions that ultimately caused the subprime mortgage meltdown?

● Real estate signs at foreclosed properties.

● Former senior National Security Agency (NSA) senior executive Thomas Drake speaks to reporters during the Stop Watching Us Rally protesting surveillance by the United States NSA in October 2013 in front of the U.S. Capitol building in Washington, D.C. The demonstration was in support of American NSA whistleblower Edward Snowden who pleaded for new international norms on surveillance to avoid the kinds of abuses committed by the NSA, especially as high-tech surveillance practices become widespread worldwide.

1.4 | Relativism

It may seem that an individual makes ethical choices by applying personal perspectives. But this view is not necessarily true. **Relativism** defines ethical behavior based on the opinions and behaviors of relevant other people.

Relativism acknowledges the existence of different ethical viewpoints. For example, *norms,* or standards of expected and acceptable behavior, vary from one culture to another. A recent study found that the perceived effectiveness of *whistleblowing*—telling others, inside and outside the organization, about wrongdoing—differs across cultures.[41] While U.S. managers believe that whistleblower hotlines are effective at reducing unethical behaviors, managers in the Far East and Central Europe do not believe they are effective. For example, Chinese employees are less likely to report that their superiors have engaged in fraud or corruption. The Chinese government considers this a major problem. It is believed that *guanxi,* a Chinese term for personal relationships, prevents many Chinese employees from acting in an independent manner when it comes to blowing the whistle on unethical managers.[42] Relativism defines ethical behavior according to how others behave.

1.5 | Virtue Ethics

The moral philosophies just described apply different types of rules and reasoning. **Virtue ethics** is a perspective that goes beyond the conventional rules of society by suggesting that what is moral must also come from what a mature person with good "moral character" would deem right. Society's rules provide a moral minimum; moral individuals can transcend rules by applying their personal virtues such as faith, honesty, and integrity.

Yet individuals differ in their moral development. As illustrated in Exhibit 4.2, **Kohlberg's model of cognitive moral development** classifies people into categories based on their level of moral judgment.[43] People in the *preconventional* stage make decisions based on concrete rewards and punishments and immediate self-interest. People in the *conventional* stage conform to the expectations of ethical behavior held by groups or institutions such as society, family, or peers. People in the *principled* stage see beyond authority, laws, and norms and follow their self-chosen ethical principles.[44] Some people forever reside in the preconventional stage, some move into the conventional stage, and some develop even further into the principled stage. Over time, and through education and experience, people may change their values and ethical behavior.

∷∷∷∷∷∷∷∷∷

Returning to the bolts-in-the-bridge example, *egoism* would result in keeping quiet about the bolts' defect rate. *Utilitarianism* would dictate a more thorough cost–benefit analysis and possibly the conclusion that the probability of a bridge collapse is so low compared

Exhibit 4.2	Kohlberg's stages of moral development
Preconventional stage	• Make decisions based on immediate self-interest. • Example: You take a flash drive home from work because you need one and do not want to pay for it.
Conventional stage	• Make decisions that conform to expectations of groups and institutions like family, peers, and society. • Example: You think about taking the flash drive home, but decide against it because it would not look right.
Principled stage	• Make decisions based on self-chosen ethical principles. • Example: You do not consider taking the flash drive from work because you believe that would be wrong.

Source: Adapted from L. Kohlberg, "Moral Stages and Moralization: The Cognitive-Development Approach," in T. Lickona (ed.), *Moral Development and Behavior Theory, Research, and Social Issues* (New York: Holt, Rinehart & Winston, 1976), pp. 31–53.

to the utility of jobs, economic growth, and company growth that the defect rate is not worth mentioning. The *relativist* perspective might prompt the salesperson to look at company policy and general industry practice, and to seek opinions from colleagues and perhaps trade journals and ethics codes. Whatever is then perceived to be a consensus or normal practice would dictate action. Finally, *virtue ethics*, applied by people in the principled stage of moral development, would likely lead to full disclosure about the product and risks, and perhaps suggestions for alternatives that would reduce the risk.[45]

LO2 Identify the ethics-related issues and laws facing managers

2 | BUSINESS ETHICS MATTER

Insider trading, illegal campaign contributions, bribery and kickbacks, famous court cases, and other scandals have created a perception that business leaders use illegal means to gain competitive advantage, increase profits, or improve their personal positions. Neither young managers nor consumers believe top executives are doing a good job of establishing high ethical standards.[47] Some even joke that *business ethics* has become a contradiction in terms. Too often, these opinions are borne out by actual workplace experiences. In a recent survey of 700 employees holding a variety of jobs, 39 percent said their supervisor sometimes didn't keep promises, 24 percent said their supervisor had invaded their privacy, and 23 percent said their supervisor covered up his or her own mistakes by blaming someone else.[48]

2.1 | Ethical Dilemmas

Most business leaders believe they uphold ethical standards in business practices.[49] But many managers and their organizations must deal frequently with ethical dilemmas, and the issues are becoming increasingly complex. Here are just a few of the dilemmas challenging managers and employees today:[50]

- *Brands*—In-your-face marketing campaigns have sparked antibrand attitudes among people who see tactics as manipulative and deceptive.

Did You Know?

In a recent survey ranking 177 nations from most to least honest, the United States came in 19th (tied with Uruguay). The U.S. rating of 7.3 on a 10-point scale placed it among only 22 countries that scored at least a 7.0. The top ratings went to Denmark, New Zealand, and Finland. The bottom-ranked nations, including Afganihstan, North Korea, and Somalia, tend to be among the poorest. Sadly, the combination of corruption and poverty in these nations can literally amount to a death sentence for many of their citizens.[46]

- *CEO pay*—Nearly three-fourths of Americans say executives' pay packages are excessive.

- *Commercialism in schools*—Parent groups in hundreds of communities have battled advertising in the public schools.

- *Religion at work*—Many people seek spiritual renewal in the workplace, in part reflecting a broader religious awakening in America, while others argue that this trend violates religious freedom and the separation of church and boardroom.

- *Sweatshops*—At many colleges, students have formed antisweatshop groups, which picket clothing manufacturers, toymakers, and retailers.

- *Wages*—More than half of workers feel they are underpaid, especially because wages since 1992 have not grown as fast as productivity levels.

On Valentine's Day in 2007, a bad winter storm led to the cancellation or delay of several airline flights throughout the country. While most of the airlines did the best they could to get through this difficult situation, JetBlue made the headlines when 21 of its aircraft were delayed on the runway at Kennedy Airport in New York for up to 11 hours. Passengers were forced to stay in the stranded planes, and some bloggers went so far as to call it a "hostage situation." As snack supplies withered and rest room facilities turned unpleasant, many passengers felt trapped and angry with JetBlue. After passengers were eventually allowed to deplane, many found themselves stuck in the airport for long hours waiting for the weather to clear and flights to resume.[51]

In the wake of this fiasco, JetBlue compensated passengers and then introduced a Passengers' Bill of Rights to guard against this type of poor treatment of passengers from happening again.[52] Inspired by this initiative, the governments of the United States, European Union, Canada, and Australia are taking this issue seriously by considering or adopting laws to protect airline passenger rights.[53]

2.2 | Ethics and the Law

Responding to a series of corporate scandals—particularly the high-profile cases of Enron and WorldCom—Congress passed the **Sarbanes-Oxley Act** in 2002 to improve and maintain investor confidence. The law requires companies to do the following:

- Have more independent board directors, not just company insiders.

- Adhere strictly to accounting rules.

- Have senior managers personally sign off on financial results.

Violations could result in heavy fines and criminal prosecution. One of the biggest impacts of the law is the requirement for companies and their auditors to provide reports to financial statement users about the effectiveness of internal controls over the financial reporting process.

Companies that make the effort to meet or exceed these requirements can reduce their risks by lowering the likelihood of misdeeds and the consequences if an employee does break the law. Responding to a directive in the Sarbanes-Oxley Act, the U.S. Sentencing Commission modified the sentencing guidelines to say that organizations convicted of federal criminal laws may receive more lenient sentences if they are shown to have established an effective compliance and ethics program. See Exhibit 4.3 for ways that organizations can meet the requirements of these guidelines.

Some executives say Sarbanes-Oxley distracts from their real work and makes them more risk averse. Some complain about the time and money needed to comply with the internal control reporting—reportedly spending millions of dollars for technology upgrades. Others point out that unethical behavior has negative consequences, especially when it includes illegal actions that later come to light. For example, companies that set up a hot-line with which employees can report illegal or unethical conduct can find out when employees are engaged in fraud. Not only can fraud hurt customers, but it can also hurt the company itself when employees find ways to defraud or steal from the company. The Association of Certified Fraud Examiners found that U.S. companies lose about 5–6 percent of their annual sales to fraud, but the losses are less than half that at organizations with a mechanism for reporting misconduct.[54] Regardless of managers' attitudes toward Sarbanes-Oxley, it creates legal requirements intended to improve ethical behavior.

2.3 | The Ethical Climate Influences Employees

Ethics are not shaped only by laws and by individual development and virtue. They also may be influenced by the company's work environment. The **ethical climate** of an organization refers to the processes by which decisions are evaluated and made on the basis of right and wrong.[55] For example, General Electric's top executives have demonstrated a commitment to promoting high levels of integrity without sacrificing the company's well-known commitment to business results. The measures taken by GE to maintain a positive ethical climate include establishing global standards for behavior to prevent ethical problems such as conflicts of interest and money laundering. Managers at all levels are rewarded for their performance in meeting both integrity and business standards, and when violations occur, even managers who were otherwise successful are disciplined, sending a powerful message that ethical behavior is truly valued at GE.[56]

When people make decisions that are judged by ethical criteria, certain questions always seem to get asked: Why did she do it? Good motives or bad ones? So often, responsibility for unethical acts is placed squarely on the individual who commits them. But the work environment has a profound influence, as well. When employees feel pressured to meet unreasonable goals or deadlines, they may act unethically; but managers are in part responsible for setting the right standards, selecting employees with the ability to meet standards, and providing employees with the resources required for success. Managers also need to keep the lines of communication open so that employees will discuss problems in meeting goals, rather than resorting to unethical and possibly illegal behavior.

Unethical corporate behavior may be the responsibility of an unethical individual, but it often also reveals a company culture that is ethically lax.[57] Maintaining a positive ethical climate is always challenging, but it is especially complex for organizations with international activities. Different cultures and countries may have different standards of behavior, and managers have to decide when relativism is appropriate, rather than adherence to firm standards. Electronics giant Siemens Corporation of Germany recently agreed to pay $1.6 billion to the U.S. and German governments for bribing officials in several countries—Bangladesh, Argentina, Nigeria, Israel, and China—to win business contracts. Given that the bribery permeated several parts of the company, the permissive ethical climate of the firm undoubtedly influenced its managers to engage in this behavior.

> **ethical climate** in an organization, the processes by which decisions are evaluated and made on the basis of right and wrong

---

Exhibit 4.3   Partial list of steps organizations can take to meet SOX guidelines

Establish written standards of ethical conduct and controls for enforcing them.

Assign responsibility to top managers to ensure that the program is working as intended.

Exclude anyone who violates the standards from holding management positions.

Provide training in ethics to all employees and monitor compliance.

Give employees incentives for complying and consequences for violating the standards.

Respond with consequences and more preventive measures if criminal conduct occurs.

Sources: "2010 Report to the Nations on Occupational Fraud and Abuse," Association of Certified Fraud Examiners, www.acfe.com/; Thompson Hine LLP, "U.S. Sentencing Commission Announces Stiffened Organization Sentencing Guidelines in Response to the Sarbanes-Oxley Act," advisory bulletin, June 1, 2004, last modified August 31, 2006, www.thompsonhine.com; R. J. Zablow, "Creating and Sustaining an Ethical Workplace," *Risk Management* 53, no. 9 (September 2006).

Take Charge Of Your Career

Why settle? Find a great place to work!

The weak job market for college graduates is not going to last forever. Over the next 5 to 10 years, the retirement of millions of baby boomers will create a wide variety of job opportunities. It is a good time to start looking for a great place to work.

There are many lists available to help you find good companies, but one of the most famous lists is the "Fortune's 100 Best Companies to Work for." It is coauthored by Robert Levering and Milton Moskowitz of the Great Place to Work Institute.

Which companies made the list in 2011? In first place was SAS, an information technology

SAS employees staying fit at the firm's Recreation and Fitness Center in Cary, NC.

and software company, that spoils its employees with lavish benefits. Next was the Boston Consulting Group, which avoided layoffs during the recent recession while providing its

employees with extensive training and development opportunities. In third place was Wegman's Food Market, known for taking good care of its employees. Two high-tech firms, Google and NetApp, rounded off the top five best companies to work for thanks to their excellent pay, perquisites, and organizational cultures.

Want to learn more about great places to work? Try "Fortune's Best Small and Medium Companies to work for," "Fortune's Best Companies to work for: Minorities," and "Fortune's Best Companies to work for: Women."

SOURCE: www.greatplacetowork.com; www.moneycnn.com/magazines/fortune/2011; L. Petrecca, "Tech Companies Top List of 'Great Workplaces,'" *USA Today,* October 31, 2011, p. 7B.

Siemens has a long history of engaging in such practices. Prior to 1999, bribery was not illegal in Germany, and as a result, many firms used it as a competitive advantage to land contracts from foreign officials. After the law was changed, Siemens continued to engage in bribery but became more secretive in how it was used; Swiss bank accounts were used to make payments, and

consultants were hired to handle bribery payments. After investigators from several countries—Italy, Germany, Switzerland, and the United States—discovered the bribery, Siemens agreed to pay the huge fine, and several of its executives were sent to jail.[58]

2.4 | Danger Signs

In organizations, maintaining consistent ethical behavior by all employees is an ongoing challenge. What are some danger signs that an organization may be allowing or even encouraging unethical behavior? Many factors, including the following, create a climate conducive to unethical behavior:

- Excessive emphasis on short-term revenues over longer-term considerations.
- Failure to establish a written code of ethics.
- Desire for simple, "quick fix" solutions to ethical problems.
- Unwillingness to take an ethical stand that may impose financial costs.
- Consideration of ethics solely as a legal issue or a public relations tool.

> "It takes many good deeds to build a good reputation, and only one bad one to lose it."
>
> —Benjamin Franklin

ethical leader one who is both a moral person and a moral manager influencing others to behave ethically

- Lack of clear procedures for handling ethical problems.
- Responsiveness to the demands of shareholders at the expense of other constituencies.[59]

To understand your organization's ethics climate, think about issues from the employees' perspective. What do people think is required to succeed? Do they think that ethical people "finish last" and that the "bad guys win"? Or vice versa, that the company rewards ethical behavior and won't tolerate unethical behavior?[60] Lynn Brewer, who brought to light the financial misdeeds of Enron, also heard Enron's management advocate values such as respect and integrity, but she later determined that these messages were just "window-dressing" and that people would undermine one another as they looked out for their self-interests. She eventually concluded that "no one cared" about unethical and illegal behavior in support of the company's stock price.[61]

LO3 Explain how managers influence their ethics environment

3 | MANAGERS SHAPE BEHAVIOR

People often give in to what they perceive to be the pressures or preferences of powerful others. In the workplace, that means managers influence their employees for good or for ill. As we'll see in the discussions of leadership and motivation later in the text, managers formally and informally shape employees' behavior with money, approval, good job assignments, a positive work environment, and in many other ways. That means managers are a powerful force for creating an ethical culture.

To create a culture that encourages ethical behavior, managers must be more than ethical people. They also should lead others to behave ethically.[62] Sharon Allen, former chair of the board of the accounting and taxation firm Deloitte LLP, is convinced that being ethical can give organizations a competitive advantage. She believes that "the shared language of ethical values that enables people to conduct business with each other, where a deal can be sealed with a handshake and your word is your bond," is essential. Ethical leadership is also important when it comes to retaining employees. According to Deloitte LLP's *2010 Ethics & Workplace Survey,* about one-third of Americans plan to look for a new job when the economy improves. Respondents blamed the loss of trust in their employer and lack of transparent communication from their organization's leaders as the primary reasons for wanting to quit. Given that turnover can be costly and good replacements hard to find, Allen recommends that leaders work hard to rebuild an ethical climate characterized by trust and open communication.[63]

3.1 | Ethical Leadership

It's been said that your reputation is your most precious asset. Here's a suggestion: set a goal for yourself to be seen by others as both a "moral person" and also as a "moral manager," someone who influences others to behave ethically. When you are both personally moral and a moral manager, you will truly be an **ethical leader**.[64] You can have strong personal character, but if you pay more attention to other things, and ethics is "managed" by "benign neglect," you won't have a reputation as an ethical leader.

IBM uses a guideline for business conduct that asks employees to determine whether under the full glare of examination by associates, friends, and family, they would remain comfortable with their decisions. One suggestion is to imagine how you would feel if you saw your decision and its consequences on the front page of the newspaper.[65] This "light of day" or "sunshine" ethical framework can be powerful.

Such fear of exposure compels people more strongly in some cultures than in others. In Asia, anxiety about losing face often makes executives resign immediately if they are caught in ethical transgressions or if their companies are embarrassed by revelations in the press. By contrast, in the United States, exposed executives might respond with indignation, intransigence, pleading the Fifth Amendment, stonewalling, an everyone-else-does-it self-defense, or by not admitting wrongdoing and giving no sign that resignation ever crossed their minds. Partly because of legal tradition, the attitude often is never explain, never apologize, don't admit the mistake, and do not resign, even if the entire world knows exactly what happened.[66]

3.2 | Ethics Codes

The Sarbanes-Oxley Act, described earlier, requires that public companies periodically disclose whether they have adopted a code of ethics for senior financial officers—and if not, why not. Often the statements are just for show, but when implemented well they can change a company's ethical climate for the better and truly encourage ethical behavior. Executives say they pay most attention to their company's code of ethics when they feel that stakeholders (customers, investors, lenders, and suppliers) try to influence them to do so, and their reasons for paying attention to the code are that doing so will help create a strong ethical culture and promote a positive image.[67]

Ethics codes must be carefully written and tailored to individual companies' philosophies. For example, Coca-Cola's 44-page code of business conduct covers a variety of topics, from when written approval is necessary to how to prevent conflict of interest.[68] Aetna Life & Casualty believes that tending to the broader needs of society is essential to fulfilling its economic role.

Most ethics codes address subjects such as employee conduct, community and environment, share-holders, customers, suppliers and contractors, political activity, and technology. Often the codes are drawn up by the organizations' legal departments and begin with research into other companies' codes. The Ethics Resource Center in Arlington, Virginia, assists companies interested in establishing a corporate code of ethics.[69]

compliance-based ethics programs company mechanisms typically designed by corporate counsel to prevent, detect, and punish legal violations

integrity-based ethics programs company mechanisms designed to instill in people a personal responsibility for ethical behavior

To make an ethics code effective, apply the following principles:

- Involve those who have to live with the code in writing it.

- Focus on real-life situations that employees can relate to.

- Keep it short and simple, so it is easy to understand and remember.

- Write about values and shared beliefs that are important and that people can really believe in.

- Set the tone at the top, having executives talk about and live up to the statement.[70]

When reality differs from the statement—as when a motto says people are our most precious asset or a product is the finest in the world, but in fact people are treated poorly or product quality is weak—the statement becomes a joke to employees rather than a guiding light.

3.3 | Ethics Programs

Corporate ethics programs commonly include formal ethics codes articulating the company's expectations regarding ethics; ethics committees that develop policies, evaluate actions, and investigate violations; ethics communication systems giving employees a means of reporting problems or getting guidance; ethics officers or ombudspersons who investigate allegations and provide education; ethics training programs; and disciplinary processes for addressing unethical behavior.[72]

Ethics programs can range from compliance-based to integrity-based.[73] **Compliance-based ethics programs** are designed by corporate counsel to prevent, detect, and punish legal violations. Compliance-based programs increase

surveillance and controls on people and impose punishments on wrongdoers.

Yahoo! is struggling with an ethical dilemma as it makes decisions about how to operate in China. The Chinese government arrested Wang Xiaoning for "inciting subversion" in his prodemocracy e-journal and sentenced him to 10 years in prison. According to the case filed against Yahoo! in the United States, the Chinese subsidiary of Yahoo! claimed that Wang provided the information that enabled officials to track him down. How can an Internet company that values free expression justify support for a repressive government? Yahoo!'s Jim Cullinan points out that the company has to obey the laws of the countries where it operates but adds that the company has been trying to develop operating principles that will help its people make ethical decisions in countries where governments have different values.[74]

Integrity-based ethics programs go beyond the mere avoidance of illegality; they are concerned with the law but also with instilling in people a personal responsibility for ethical behavior. With such a program, companies and people govern themselves through a set of guiding principles that they embrace.

For example, the Americans with Disabilities Act (ADA) requires companies to change the physical work environment so it will allow people with disabilities to function on the job. Mere compliance would involve making the changes necessary to avoid legal problems. Integrity-based programs would go further by training people to understand and perhaps change attitudes toward people with disabilities and sending clear signals that people with disabilities also have valued abilities. This effort goes far beyond taking action to stay out of trouble with the law.

When top management has a personal commitment to responsible ethical behavior, programs tend to be better integrated into operations, thinking, and behavior. For example, at a meeting of about 25 middle managers at a major financial services firm, every one of them told the company's general

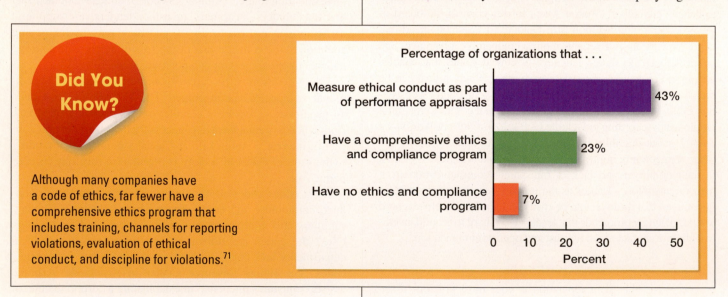

Did You Know?

Although many companies have a code of ethics, far fewer have a comprehensive ethics program that includes training, channels for reporting violations, evaluation of ethical conduct, and discipline for violations.[71]

Percentage of organizations that . . .

Measure ethical conduct as part of performance appraisals	43%
Have a comprehensive ethics and compliance program	23%
Have no ethics and compliance program	7%

Percent (0 10 20 30 40 50)

counsel that they had never seen or heard of the company's ethics policy document.[75] The policies existed but were not a part of the everyday thinking of managers. In contrast, a health care products company bases one-third of managers' annual pay raises on how well they carry out the company's ethical ideals. Their ethical behavior is assessed by superiors, peers, and subordinates—making ethics a thoroughly integrated aspect of the way the company and its people do business.

Acting with integrity is important not only to managers in organizations but also to MBA students. On June 3, 2009, over 400 graduating students of the Harvard Business School's MBA program took an oath stating that as future managers they would "act with the utmost integrity" and avoid "decisions and behavior that advance my own narrow ambitions, but harm the enterprise and the societies it serves." Created by then-MBA student Max Anderson with encouragement from a few faculty members, the oath is meant to signal that graduating MBA students are committed to applying ethics and integrity in all of their future managerial and leadership endeavors.[76]

MBA OATH

— Therefore, I Promise —

❖ I will act with utmost integrity and pursue my work in an ethical manner

❖ I will safeguard the interests of my shareholders, co-workers, customers and the society in which we operate.

❖ I will manage my enterprise in good faith, guarding against decisions and behavior that advance my own narrow ambitions but harm the enterprise and societies it serves.

❖ I will understand and uphold, both in letter and in spirit, the laws and contracts governing my own conduct and that of my enterprise.

❖ I will take responsibility for my actions, and will represent the performance and risks of my enterprise accurately and honestly.

❖ I will develop both myself and other mangers under my supervision so that the profession continues to grow and contribute to the well-being of society.

❖ I will strive to create sustainable economic, social, and environmental prosperity worldwide.

❖ I will be accountable to my peers and they will be accountable to me for living by this oath.

This oath I make freely, and upon my honor.

WWW.MBAOATH.ORG

LO4 Outline the process for making ethical decisions

4 | YOU CAN LEARN TO MAKE ETHICAL DECISIONS

We've said it's not easy to make ethical decisions. Such decisions are complex. For starters, you may face pressures that are difficult to resist. Also, it's not always clear that a problem has ethical dimensions; they don't hold up signs that say, "Hey, I'm an ethical issue, so think about me in moral terms!"[77] Making ethical decisions takes three things:

1. *Moral awareness*—realizing the issue has ethical implications.

2. *Moral judgment*—knowing what actions are morally defensible.

3. *Moral character*—the strength and persistence to act in accordance with your ethics despite the challenges.[78]

Moral awareness begins with considering whether a decision has ramifications that disadvantage employees, the environment, or other stakeholders. Then the challenge is to apply moral judgment.

The philosopher John Rawls created a thought experiment based on the "veil of ignorance."[79] Imagine you are making a decision about a policy that will benefit or disadvantage some groups more than others. For example, a policy might provide extra vacation time for all employees but eliminate flex time, which allows parents of young children to balance their work and family responsibilities. Or you're a university president considering raising tuition or cutting financial support for study abroad.

Now pretend that you belong to one of the affected groups, but you don't know which one—for instance, those who can afford to study abroad or those who can't, or a young parent or a young single person. You won't find out until after the decision is made. How would you decide? Would you be willing to risk being in the disadvantaged group? Would your decision be different if you were in a group other than your own? Rawls maintained that only a person ignorant of his or her own identity can make a truly ethical decision. A decision maker can tactically apply the veil of ignorance to help minimize personal bias.

4.1 | The Ethical Decision-Making Process

To resolve ethical problems, you can use the process illustrated in Exhibit 4.4. Understand the various moral standards (universalism, relativism, etc.), as described earlier in the chapter. Begin to follow a formal decision-making process. As we will discuss in more detail in Chapter 5, you identify and diagnose your problem, generate alternative solutions, and evaluate each alternative. Your evaluation should recognize the impacts of your alternatives: which people do they benefit and harm, which are able to exercise their rights, and whose rights are denied? You now know the full scope of the moral problem.

As you define the problem, it's easy to find excuses for unethical behavior. People can rationalize unethical behavior by denying responsibility ("What can I do? They're twisting my arm"), denying injury ("No one was badly hurt; it could have been worse"), denying the victim ("They deserved it"), social weighting ("Those people are worse than we are"), and

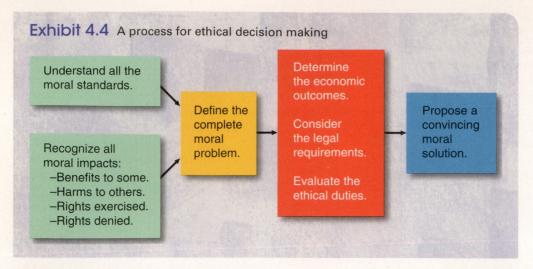

Exhibit 4.4 A process for ethical decision making

Understand all the moral standards.

Recognize all moral impacts:
–Benefits to some.
–Harms to others.
–Rights exercised.
–Rights denied.

Define the complete moral problem.

Determine the economic outcomes.

Consider the legal requirements.

Evaluate the ethical duties.

Propose a convincing moral solution.

Source: L. T. Hosmer, *The Ethics of Management*, 4th ed. (New York: McGraw-Hill/Irwin, 2003), p. 32. © 2003 Reprinted with permission of McGraw-Hill Education.

appealing to higher loyalties ("It was for a higher purpose," or "I'm too loyal to my boss to report it").[80] Only days after the U.S. government had posted $85 billion to keep insurance giant American International Group from collapsing, AIG sent executives on a luxurious retreat. When asked to justify this, executives initially replied with excuses: the $440,000 spent was far, far less than the amount of the government bailout, and the executives who participated in the retreat did not work in

the AIG division where the company's financial problems had originated. Eventually they had to concede that these responses did not really address the question of whether the retreat was an ethical use of company money at a time when the company— along with many of the taxpayers whose money was bailing out AIG—was undergoing an economic crisis.[81]

4.2 | Outcomes of Unethical Decisions

You must also consider legal requirements to ensure full compliance, and the economic outcomes of your options, including costs and potential profits. Exhibit 4.5 shows some of the costs associated with unethical behavior.[82] Some are obvious: fines and penalties. Others, like administrative costs and corrective actions, are less obvious. Ultimately the effects on customers, employees, and government reactions can be huge. Being fully aware of the potential costs can help prevent people from straying into unethical terrain.

Evaluating your ethical duties requires looking for actions that meet the following criteria:

- You would be proud to see the action widely reported in newspapers.

- It would build a sense of community among those involved.

- It would generate the greatest social good.

- You would be willing to see others take the same action when you might be the victim.

- It doesn't harm the "least among us."

- It doesn't interfere with the right of all others to develop their skills to the fullest.[83]

As you can see, making ethical decisions is complex, but considering all these factors will help you develop the most convincing moral solution.

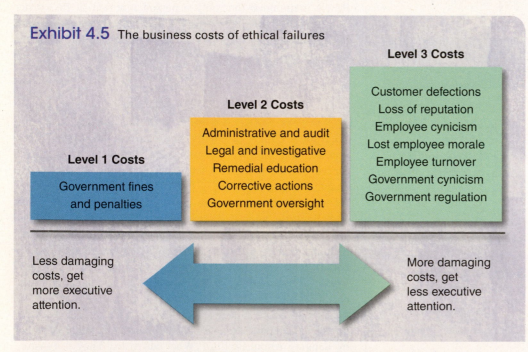

Exhibit 4.5 The business costs of ethical failures

Level 3 Costs
Customer defections
Loss of reputation
Employee cynicism
Lost employee morale
Employee turnover
Government cynicism
Government regulation

Level 2 Costs
Administrative and audit
Legal and investigative
Remedial education
Corrective actions
Government oversight

Level 1 Costs
Government fines and penalties

Less damaging costs, get more executive attention.

More damaging costs, get less executive attention.

Source: T. Thomas, J. Schermerhorn Jr., and J. Dienhart, "Strategic Leadership of Ethical Behavior in Business," *Academy of Management Executive* (May 2004), p. 58. Reprinted with permission of Academy of Management. Permission conveyed through Copyright Clearance Center.

4.3 | Ethics Requires Courage

Behaving ethically requires not just moral awareness and moral judgment but also moral character, including the courage to take actions consistent with your ethical decisions. Think about how hard it can be to do the right thing.[84] As you're growing up, you have plenty of peer pressure to conform to others' behavior, and it's not cool to be a snitch. On the job, how hard would it be to walk away from lots of money in order to "stick to your ethics"? To tell colleagues or your boss that you believe they've crossed an ethical line? To disobey a boss's order? To go over your boss's head to someone in senior management with your suspicions about accounting practices? To go outside the company to alert others if someone is being hurt and management refuses to correct the problem?

PepsiCo managers faced a difficult choice when an executive secretary from Coca-Cola Company's headquarters contacted them to offer confidential documents and product samples for a price. Rather than seek an unethical (and illegal) advantage, Pepsi's managers notified Coca-Cola. There, management fired the secretary and contacted the FBI. Eventually the secretary and two acquaintances were convicted of conspiring to steal trade secrets.[85] PepsiCo still doesn't have the secret recipe for Coke, but it did maintain its reputation as a competitor with integrity. Choosing integrity over short-term business gain took courage.

At Marvin Windows and Doors, which has thousands of employees working in a dozen facilities in the United States and Honduras, workers can go online to submit anonymous tips and suggestions in English or Spanish. The company's general counsel says the system not only provides an early warning in case of problems as diverse as theft and safety concerns, but also maintains an overall culture of valuing ethics.[87]

Besides online reporting systems, such as e-mail and web-based tools, companies can use drop boxes and telephone hotlines. Often these channels of communication are administered by third-party organizations, whose employees protect whistleblowers' identity and have procedures to follow if the complaint involves higher-level executives who might be part of the usual group charged with responding to reports.[88] Under the recently passed Dodd-Frank Act, reporting systems should be expanded to give access to customers, suppliers, shareholders, associates of employees, and others who could potentially report fraudulent acts and violations of the law.[89]

FINANCIAL REFORM SERIES

CONSUMER PROTECTION AND MORTGAGE REGULATION UNDER DODD-FRANK

2011 EDITION

MITCHEL H. KIDER, MICHAEL Y. KIEVAL AND LESLIE A. SOWERS

KIDER KIEVAL SOWERS

WEST.

● Signed into law on July 21, 2010, one of the aims of the Dodd-Frank Wall Street Reform and Consumer Protection Act is to increase the amount of regulation over financial institutions that operate in the United States.

LO5 Summarize the important issues surrounding corporate social responsibility

5 | CORPORATE SOCIAL RESPONSIBILITY

Should business be responsible for social concerns beyond its own economic well-being? Do social concerns affect a corporation's financial performance? The extent of business's responsibility for noneconomic concerns has been hotly debated for years. In the 1960s and 1970s, the political and social environment became more important to U.S. corporations as society focused on issues like equal opportunity, pollution control, energy and natural resource conservation, and consumer and worker protection.[90] Public debate addressed these issues and the ways business should respond. This controversy focused on the concept of **corporate social responsibility**—the obligation toward society assumed by business. A socially responsible business maximizes its positive effects on society and minimizes its negative effects.[91]

5.1 | Four Levels of Corporate Social Responsibility

Social responsibilities can be categorized more specifically,[92] as shown in Exhibit 4.6. The **economic responsibilities** of business are to produce goods and services that society wants at a price that perpetuates the business and satisfies its obligations to investors. For Smithfield Foods, the largest pork producer in the United States, this means selling bacon, ham, and other products to customers at prices that maximize Smithfield's profits and keep the company growing over the long term. Economic responsibility may also extend to offering certain products to needy consumers at a reduced price.

Legal responsibilities are to obey local, state, federal, and relevant international laws. Laws affecting Smithfield cover a wide range of requirements, from filing tax returns to meeting worker safety standards. **Ethical responsibilities** include meeting other societal expectations, not written as law. Smithfield took on this level of responsibility when it responded to requests by major customers, including McDonald's and Walmart, that it discontinue the practice of using gestation crates to house its sows. The customers were reacting to pressure from animal rights advocates who consider it cruel for sows to live in the two-foot by seven-foot crates during their entire gestation period, which means they cannot walk, turn around, or stretch their legs for months at a time. The practice had been to move the sows to a farrowing crate to give birth and then return them to the

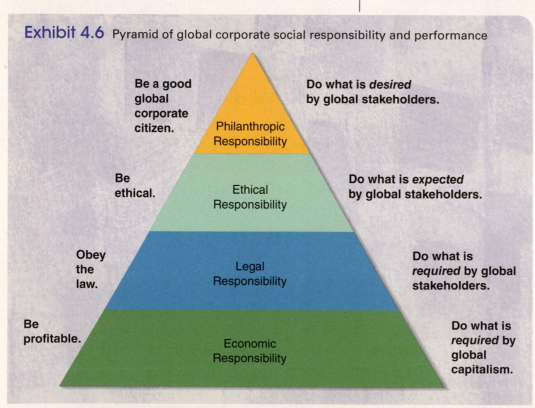

Exhibit 4.6 Pyramid of global corporate social responsibility and performance

Be a good global corporate citizen. — **Philanthropic Responsibility** — Do what is *desired* by global stakeholders.

Be ethical. — **Ethical Responsibility** — Do what is *expected* by global stakeholders.

Obey the law. — **Legal Responsibility** — Do what is *required* by global stakeholders.

Be profitable. — **Economic Responsibility** — Do what is *required* by global capitalism.

Source: A. Carroll, "Managing Ethically with Global Stakeholders: A Present and Future Challenge," *Academy of Management Executive* (May 2004), pp. 116, 114–20. Reprinted with permission of Academy of Management. Permission conveyed through Copyright Clearance Center.

gestation crate soon after, when they became pregnant again. Smithfield plans to exchange the crates for "group housing," which allows the animals to socialize, even though group housing costs more.[93] Smithfield is not legally required to make the change (except in two states), and the arrangement may not maximize profits, but the company's actions help it maintain good customer relationships and a positive public image.

Finally, **philanthropic responsibilities** are additional behaviors and activities that society finds desirable and that the values of the business support. Examples include supporting community projects and making charitable contributions. Philanthropic activities can be more than mere altruism; managed properly, "strategic philanthropy" can become not an oxymoron but a way to build goodwill in a variety of stakeholders and even add to shareholder wealth.[94]

Robert Giacalone, who teaches business ethics at Temple University, believes that a 21st-century education must help students think beyond self-interest and profitability. A real education, he says, teaches students to leave a legacy that extends beyond the bottom line—a transcendent education.[95] A **transcendent education** has five higher goals that balance self-interest with responsibility to others:

1. *Empathy*—feeling your decisions as potential victims might feel them, to gain wisdom.

2. *Generativity*—learning how to give as well as take, to others in the present as well as to future generations.

3. *Mutuality*—viewing success not merely as personal gain, but a common victory.

4. *Civil aspiration*—thinking not just in terms of "don'ts" (lie, cheat, steal, kill), but also in terms of positive contributions.

5. *Intolerance of ineffective humanity*—speaking out against unethical actions.

5.2 | Do Businesses Really Have a Social Responsibility?

Two basic and contrasting views describe principles that should guide managerial responsibility. The first, known as the **shareholder model**, holds that managers act as agents for shareholders and, as such, are obligated to maximize the present value of the firm. This tenet of capitalism is widely associated with the early writings of Adam Smith in *The Wealth of Nations,* and more recently with Milton Friedman, the Nobel Prize–winning economist of the University of Chicago. With his now-famous dictum "The social responsibility of business is to increase profits," Friedman contended that organizations may help improve the quality of life as long as such actions are directed at increasing profits.

Some considered Friedman to be "the enemy of business ethics," but his position was ethical: he believed it is unethical for unelected business leaders to decide what is best for society, and unethical for them to spend shareholders' money on projects unconnected to key business interests.[96] In addition, the context of Friedman's famous statement includes the qualifier that business should increase its profits while conforming to society's laws and ethical customs.

The alternative view of corporate social responsibility, called the **stakeholder model**, assumes that managers are obliged to look beyond profitability to help their organizations succeed by interacting with groups that have a stake in the organization.[97] A firm's stakeholders include shareholders, employees, customers, suppliers, competitors, society, and the government.[98] As members of society, organizations should actively and responsibly participate in the community and in the larger environment. From this perspective, many people criticized insurance companies after Hurricanes Katrina and Rita devastated homes and businesses along the Gulf Coast. From a social responsibility perspective, it was wrong for companies to watch out for their bottom line and avoid paying claims where they could make a case that the damage wasn't covered; the insurers should have been more concerned about their devastated customers. Or consider how companies have responded to public criticism that products manufactured in low-wage countries are produced in "sweatshops," where employees work in conditions widely viewed as unacceptable in developed nations such as the United States. Do U.S. companies have a social responsibility to insist on better working conditions? Walmart and other companies that buy products made in China have written codes of conduct and conducted onsite audits. Unfortunately some enterprising Chinese consultants have set up services that help factories hide violations instead of correcting them. Still, as demand for Chinese-made products and pressure from multinational corporations have both intensified, observers say pay and working conditions in China have generally improved.[99]

5.3 | You Can Do Good and Do Well

Profit maximization and corporate social responsibility used to be regarded as leading to opposing policies. But in today's business climate, which emphasizes both doing good and doing well, the two views can converge.[100] The Coca-Cola Company has set up about 70 charitable projects to provide clean water in 40 countries. These projects are helping some of the 1.2 billion people without access to safe drinking water. The company is building structures to "harvest" rainwater in India, expanding the

philanthropic responsibilities additional behaviors and activities that society finds desirable and that the values of the business support

transcendent education an education with five higher goals that balance self-interest with responsibility to others

shareholder model theory of corporate social responsibility that holds that managers are agents of shareholders whose primary objective is to maximize profits

stakeholder model theory of corporate social responsibility that suggests that managers are obliged to look beyond profitability to help their organizations succeed by interacting with groups that have a stake in the organization

● Barclays Cycle Hire scheme (or Borris Bikes) part of a green initiative by Transport for London.

municipal water supply in Mali, and delivering water purification systems and storage urns to Kenya. These projects are aimed at burnishing the company's image and targeting complaints that the company is using too much of the world's water supply to manufacture its beverages. From a practical perspective, Coca-Cola's strategic planners have identified water shortages as a strategic risk; from a values perspective, water conservation remains a key long-term priority.[101]

Earlier attention to corporate social responsibility focused on alleged wrongdoing and how to control it. More recently, attention has also been centered on the possible competitive advantage of socially responsible actions. DuPont has been incorporating care for the environment into its business in two ways it hopes will put it ahead of the competition. First, the company has been reducing its pollution, including a 72 percent cut in greenhouse gas emissions since 1990. It hopes these efforts will give it an advantage in a future where the government regulates emissions, requiring competitors to play catch-up. Second, DuPont has been developing products that are sustainable, meaning they don't use up the earth's resources. Examples include corn-based fabrics and new applications of its Tyvek material to make buildings more energy-efficient. DuPont expects these innovations to give the

company profitable access to the growing market for environmentally friendly products.[102]

The real relationship between corporate social performance and corporate financial performance is highly complex; socially responsible organizations do not necessarily become more or less successful in financial terms.[103] Some advantages are clear, however. For example, socially responsible actions can have long-term benefits. Companies can avoid unnecessary and costly regulation if they are socially responsible. Honesty and fairness may pay great dividends to the conscience, to the personal reputation, and to the public image of the company as well as in the market response.[104] In addition, society's problems can offer business opportunities, and profits can be made from systematic and vigorous efforts to solve these problems. Firms can perform a cost–benefit analysis to identify actions that will maximize profits while satisfying the demand for corporate social responsibility from multiple stakeholders.[105] In other words, managers can treat corporate social responsibility as they would treat all investment decisions. This has been the case as firms attempt to reconcile their business practices with their effect on the natural environment.

For a clearer link between social and business goals, companies can benefit from integrating social responsibility with corporate strategy—and society can benefit as well. Applying the principles of strategic planning (described in Chapter 5), organizations can identify the specific areas in which they can capitalize on their strengths to neutralize threats and benefit from opportunities that result from serving the society of which they are a part.[106] For example, suppose a company is interested in exercising social responsibility for the environment by reducing its carbon emissions. The extent to which this choice is strategic varies from one company to another. Reducing carbon emissions would be a good deed for Bank of America but not directly related to its strategy, except to the extent it might (or might not) lower its operating costs. For UPS, reducing carbon emissions would directly affect its day-to-day activities but still might not give the company a competitive advantage. For Toyota, reducing carbon emissions—say, by leading in the development and marketing of hybrid technology as well as by operating more efficiently—can be a significant part of its competitive advantage.

> "The essential test that should guide corporate social responsibility is not whether a cause is worthy but whether it presents an opportunity to create shared value—that is, a meaningful benefit for society that is also valuable to the business."
>
> —Michael E. Porter and Mark R. Kramer[107]

LO6 Discuss the growing importance of managing the natural environment

6 | THE NATURAL ENVIRONMENT

Most large corporations developed in an era of abundant raw materials, cheap energy, and unconstrained waste disposal.[108] But many of the technologies developed during that era are contributing to the destruction of ecosystems. Industrial-age systems follow a linear flow of extract, produce, sell, use, and discard—what some call a "take-make-waste" approach.[109] But perhaps no time in history has offered greater possibilities for a change in business thinking than the 21st century.

Business used to look at environmental issues as a no-win situation: either you help the environment and hurt your business, or else you help your business at a cost to the environment. But now a shift is taking place as companies deliberately incorporate environmental values into competitive strategies and into the design and manufacturing of products.[110] Why? In addition to philosophical reasons, companies "go green" to satisfy consumer demand, react to a competitor's actions, meet requests from customers or suppliers, comply with guidelines, and create a competitive advantage.

General Electric CEO Jeff Immelt used to view environmental rules as a burden and a cost. Now he sees environmentally friendly technologies as one of the global economy's most significant business opportunities. Under a business initiative called Ecomagination, GE is looking for business opportunities from solving environmental problems. Recently General Electric announced an "Ecomagination Challenge" in China in which it (along with seven other firms) will provide $100 million to support innovations in gas power, including natural gas and biogas.[111]

6.1 | Economic Activity Has Environmental Consequences

We live in a risk society. That is, the creation and distribution of wealth generate by-products that can cause injury, loss, or danger to people and the environment. The fundamental sources of risk in modern society are the excessive production of hazards and ecologically unsustainable consumption of natural resources.[112] Risk has proliferated through population explosion, industrial pollution, and environmental degradation.[113]

Industrial pollution risks include air pollution, global warming, ozone depletion, acid rain, toxic waste sites, nuclear hazards, obsolete weapons arsenals, industrial accidents, and hazardous products. More than 30,000 uncontrolled toxic waste sites have been documented in the United States alone, and the number is increasing by perhaps 2,500 per year. The situation is far worse in other parts of the world. The pattern, for toxic waste and many other risks, is one of accumulating risks and inadequate remedies.

ecocentric management its goal is the creation of sustainable economic development and improvement of quality of life worldwide for all organizational stakeholders

sustainable growth economic growth and development that meet present needs without harming the needs of future generations

6.2 | Development Can Be Sustainable

Ecocentric management has as its goal the creation of sustainable economic development and improvement of quality of life worldwide for all organizational stakeholders.[114] **Sustainable growth** is economic growth and development that meet the organization's present needs without harming the ability of future generations to meet their needs.[115] Sustainability is fully compatible with the natural ecosystems that generate and preserve life.

Some believe that the concept of sustainable growth can be applied in several ways:

- As a framework for organizations to use in communicating to all stakeholders.

- As a planning and strategy guide.

- As a tool for evaluating and improving the ability to compete.[116]

The principle can begin at the highest organizational levels and be made explicit in performance appraisals and reward systems.

High-Tech Greenhouses Are the Next Big Thing

Since early Roman days, people have used greenhouses to grow plants—particularly to enjoy fruits and vegetables out of season. But not until the 1990s did greenhouses begin to gain popularity in the United States. The timing couldn't be better. The amount of farmable land per capita in the world continues to shrink, and over the next 50 years world population is expected to increase by 3 billion. At the same time, economists estimate, the demand for farm products will double.

As more regions suffer from drought from climate change and as power shortfalls increase, the notion of using glass houses to grow fruits and vegetables has become increasingly attractive. A leader in greenhouse-grown produce, Houweling Nurseries (now Houweling's Tomatoes) was founded in 1974 by Cornelius Houweling, a Dutch immigrant to the United States and professional horticulturist. Today the business includes farms in British Columbia and Oxnard, California.

In 2009 the company expanded its Oxnard site with a $53 million, 40-acre greenhouse facility that uses sustainable practices to grow tomatoes year-round. Located in the center of California's $36 billion farming economy, the greenhouses stand as a triumph of 21st-century agricultural science. They are believed to be the world's first energy-neutral, commercial greenhouses. More than 90 percent of waste is recycled at the nurseries. Solar panels generate most of the electricity needed to power the greenhouse pumps and climate controls. Energy screens reduce heat loss. Should the temperature drop during the night, the greenhouses are heated with waste heat collected from refrigeration exhaust. The 2.1 megawatts of electricity generated by the greenhouses could power 1,500 homes.

Fully enclosed, the greenhouses are nearly dust-free. Crops grow herbicide-free and nearly pesticide-free, using only about half the fertilizer of conventional crops. Colonies of bumblebees reside on-site and pollinate the crops. Houweling greenhouses use about 20 percent as much water as a field farm and only about a third as much as an ordinary greenhouse. Rainwater and irrigation runoff are captured in a pond, filtered, and recirculated as needed. Watered individually through a complex computerized piping system, greenhouse-tended tomato plants live far longer than field crops. The plants grow to the ceiling; workers stand on ladders to harvest the fruit.

High-tech growing facilities like Houweling Nurseries yield as much as 24 times more tomatoes per acre than does a conventional farm. It would take more than 3,000 acres of open fields to match the tomato output of Houweling's 125 acres "under glass." In addition, at the Oxnard facility alone, Houweling has generated more than 450 full-time, year-round jobs in an industry that, like many in recessionary times, has been hard-hit by unemployment.

Discussion Questions

- How does Houweling's Tomatoes serve as a forward-looking example for other agricultural businesses?
- Emerging environmental issues have created significant challenges for farming. Although costly, what could the construction of more greenhouses like the Houwelings mean for today's farmers? For the agricultural industry as a whole?

SOURCES: Company website, www.houwelings.com; Oppenheimer company website, "Casey Houweling: Growing with Oppenheimer," www.oppyproduce.com; T. Burfield, "Opening of Houweling Nurseries Greenhouse Draws VIPs," *The Packer,* May 15, 2009, www.thepacker.com; S. Hoops, "Environmentally Friendly Greenhouses in Camarillo Impresses Experts," *Ventura County Star,* May 15, 2009, www.venturacountystar.com; J. Hirsch, "Greener Greenhouses Produce 21st Century Crops," *Los Angeles Times,* May 14, 2009, www.newsday.com; D. Babcock, "Grown under Glass: The Future of Greenhouse-Grown Products," *Produce Merchandising,* March 2009, http://producemerchandising.com.

With two-thirds of the world's population expected to experience water scarcity by 2025 and shortages forecast for 36 U.S. states by 2013, businesses are becoming concerned about this essential natural resource. If you haven't experienced a water shortage, water usage might not seem to be an obvious area of concern, but it should be. For example, Levi Strauss & Company determined that making a pair of jeans requires about 500 gallons of water for growing, dying, and processing cotton.

Brewer SABMiller is a leader in making water conservation part of its strategy. Using an online computer application, the company submitted the GPS coordinates of factory and farm locations and learned where its operations are located in areas of water scarcity. About 30 SABMiller sites were in vulnerable areas. Executives decided to target one of those areas and develop a process they could apply elsewhere. They selected South Africa, whose breweries produce about one-sixth of the company's beer. Not only is South Africa facing water shortages, but its government has yet to provide access to safe drinking water for 5 million of its people.

To get hard information about its water consumption, the company measured water usage at each stage of its processes, from growing crops to rinsing out used bottles before recycling. SABMiller hired a consulting firm for this task. The most water was used in growing barley, maize (corn), and hops. Together with the water used in factories, 20 gallons of water are needed to produce each pint of beer. Based on the data, SABMiller's initial efforts are focusing on identifying and using more efficient irrigation technology, preventing waste from runoff and evaporation.[117]

::::::::::::::::

Increasingly, firms are paying attention to the total environmental impact throughout the life cycle of their products.[118] **Life cycle analysis (LCA)** is a process of analyzing all inputs and outputs, through the entire "cradle-to-grave" life of a product, to determine the total environmental impact of its production and use. LCA quantifies the total use of resources and the releases into the air, water, and land.

LCA considers the extraction of raw materials, product packaging, transportation, and disposal. Consider packaging alone. Goods make the journey from manufacturer to wholesaler to retailer to customer; then they are recycled back to the manufacturer. They may be packaged and repackaged several times, from bulk transport, to large crates, to cardboard boxes, to individual consumer sizes. Repackaging not only creates waste but also costs time. The design of initial packaging in sizes and formats adaptable to the final customer can minimize the need for repackaging, cut waste, and realize financial benefits.

Profitability need not suffer and may be increased by ecocentric philosophies and practices. Some, but not all, research has shown a positive relationship between corporate environmental performance and profitability.[119] Of course, whether the relationship is positive, negative, or neutral depends on the strategies chosen and the effectiveness of implementation. And managers of profitable companies may feel more comfortable turning their attention to the environment than are managers of companies in financial difficulty.

6.3 | Some Organizations Set Environmental Agendas

In the past, most companies were oblivious to their negative environmental impact. More recently, many began striving for low impact. Now some strive for positive impact, eager to sell solutions to the world's problems. IBM has three decades of experience in lowering its environmental impact through efforts such as reducing waste in packaging and measuring carbon emissions. It has begun to use that experience as a strength—a basis for expertise it can sell to other organizations, along with its computing power and other consulting services. Thus one application might be to help clients measure and forecast the carbon emissions of their entire supply chain. By running calculations on its supercomputers, IBM consultants could help the clients find ways to lower their energy use.[120]

You don't have to be a manufacturer or a utility to jump on the green bandwagon. Web search giant Google is applying a three-pronged strategy aimed at reducing its "carbon footprint,"—that is, its output of carbon dioxide and other greenhouse gases. At Google, most greenhouse gas emissions are related to electricity consumption by its buildings and computers. So Google is first seeking ways to make buildings and computers more energy-efficient, such as by using high-efficiency lighting and installing power management software in its computers. Second, the company is developing ways to get more of its power from renewable sources, such as the solar power system at its facility in Mountain View, California. Finally, recognizing that its other efforts cannot yet eliminate Google's release of greenhouse gases, the company is purchasing "offsets"—funding projects that reduce greenhouse gas emissions elsewhere.[121]

Webs of companies with a common ecological vision can combine their efforts into high-leverage, impactful action.[122] In Kalundborg, Denmark, such a collaborative alliance exists among an electric power generating plant, an oil refiner, a biotech production plant, a plasterboard factory, cement producers, heating utilities, a sulfuric acid producer, and local agriculture and horticulture. Chemicals, energy (for heating and cooling), water, and organic materials flow among companies. Resources are conserved, "waste" materials generate revenues, and water, air, and ground pollution all are reduced.

Companies not only have the *ability* to solve environmental problems; they are coming to see and acquire the *motivation* as well. Some now believe that solving environmental problems is one of the biggest opportunities in the history of commerce.[123]

life cycle analysis (LCA)
a process of analyzing all inputs and outputs, through the entire "cradle-to-grave" life of a product, to determine total environmental impact

Study Checklist

- Did you tear out the perforated student review card at the back of the text to revisit learning objectives and key terms and definitions?

Connect® Management is available for M Management. Additional resources include:

- Interactive Applications:
  - Case Analysis: Danger Signs of Unethical Behavior
  - Drag & Drop: Ethics and Moral Philosophies
  - Self Assessment: Your Ethical Decision-Making Skills
  - Video Case: A Bakery with a Conscience

- LearnSmart—Multiple choice questions help you determine what you already know, are not sure about, or need to practice based on your score. And with SmartBook, you can read the relevant section in the eBook as well as practice and recharge what you've learned.
- Chapter Video: Cell Phones for Soliders
- Young Manager Speaks Out: Megan Gates, Market Development Manager

5 chapter

Planning and Decision Making

Learning Objectives

After studying Chapter 5, you will be able to

LO1 Summarize the basic steps in any planning process.

LO2 Discuss how strategic planning should be integrated with tactical and operational planning.

LO3 Describe the strategic management process and the importance of SWOT analysis in strategy formulation.

LO4 Analyze how companies can achieve competitive advantage through business strategy.

LO5 Identify the keys to effective strategy implementation.

LO6 Explain how to make effective decisions as a manager.

LO7 Give examples of some individual barriers that affect rational decision making.

LO8 Summarize principles for group decision making.

Senior executives at Royal Dutch Shell (the world's second largest oil company) have decided that China is their number one strategic business priority. In 2010 China passed the United States to become the top energy—consuming country in the world, and over the next 20 years China is expected to "account for almost half of the world's growth in oil consumption." To gain access to this massive market, Shell is part-nering with PetroChina, China's largest oil company, in a $1.3 billion joint venture at the Changbei gas field. The gas field, managed by Shell, produces over 3 billion cubic meters of gas annually. What does PetroChina gain? Knowledge. The Chinese want to learn Shell's techniques and methods for tapping "unconventional gas and oil resources, such as shale gas, that require new technolo-gies to extract." Similarly, Shell wants more than just access to the Chinese natural gas and oil markets: senior executives hope that the Changbei joint venture will help them "gain influence over the flow of all global resources destined for China, from the Middle East to Australia." However, every strategic plan has risks. Shell's foray into China may one day backfire if PetroChina, after learning many of Shell's extraction techniques and methods, decides that it does not need a "partner" as much as it once thought.[1]

It's almost impossible to imagine Royal Dutch Shell—or any organization—meeting significant challenges without develop-ing a plan beforehand. Planning is a formal expression of man-agerial intent. It describes what managers decide to do and how they will do it. It provides the framework, focus, and direction required for a meaningful effort. Without planning, any improve-ments in an organization's innovation, speed, quality, service, and cost will be accidental, if they occur at all.

● View of a Shell gas station in Chongqing, China. In an effort to expand its oil network in the country, Royal Dutch Shell is planning on building approximately 100 gas stations in Shaanxi province with its Chinese partners.

> ## "Manage your destiny, or someone else will."
> —Jack Welch, *former CEO, General Electric*

This chapter examines the most important concepts and processes involved in planning and strategic management. By learning these concepts and reviewing the steps outlined, you will be on your way to understanding the current approaches to strategically managing today's organizations. Also, whether or not managers are directly involved in strategic planning for their firms, they make key decisions that contribute to the suc-cessful implementation of that strategy. The chapter explores the types of decisions managers face, the ways they are made, and the ways they *should* be made.

1 | THE PLANNING PROCESS

Planning is the conscious, systematic process of making decisions about goals and activities that an individual, group, work unit, or organization will pursue in the future. Planning is not an informal or haphazard response to a crisis; it is a purposeful effort that is directed and controlled by managers and often draws on the knowledge and experience of employees at all levels. Exhibit 5.1 shows the steps in this process. Notice that planning moves in a *cycle*. The outcomes of plans are evaluated and, if necessary, revised.

Planning gives individuals and work units a clear map to follow in their future activities yet is flexible enough to allow for unique circumstances and changing conditions. We now describe the basic planning process in more detail. Later in this chapter, we will discuss how managerial decisions and plans fit into the larger purposes of the organization—its ultimate strategy, mission, vision, and goals.

Step 1: Analyze the Situation

Planning begins with a **situational analysis**. Within their time and resource constraints, planners should gather, interpret, and summarize all information relevant to the planning issue in question. They study past events, examine current conditions, and try to forecast future trends. The analysis focuses on the internal forces at work in the organization or work unit and, consistent with the open-systems approach (see Chapter 3), examines influences from the external environment. The outcome of this step is the identification and diagnosis of planning assumptions, issues, and problems.

A thorough situational analysis will provide information about the planning decisions you need to make. For example, if you are a manager in a magazine company considering the launch of a sports publication for the teen market, your analysis will include such factors as the number of teens who subscribe to magazines, the appeal of the teen market to advertisers, your firm's ability to serve this market effectively, current economic conditions, the level of teen interest in sports, and any sports magazines already serving this market and their current sales. Such an analysis will help you decide whether to proceed with the next step in your magazine launch.

Step 2: Generate Alternative Goals and Plans

Based on the findings from situational analysis, the planning process should generate alternative goals that may be pursued and alternative plans for achieving those goals. This step should stress creativity and encourage managers and employees to think broadly. Once a range of alternatives has been developed, their merits and feasibility will be evaluated. Continuing with our

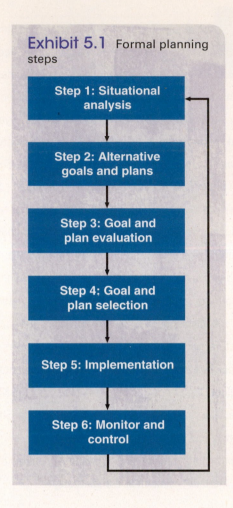

Exhibit 5.1 Formal planning steps

Step 1: Situational analysis

Step 2: Alternative goals and plans

Step 3: Goal and plan evaluation

Step 4: Goal and plan selection

Step 5: Implementation

Step 6: Monitor and control

magazine publishing example, the alternatives you might want to consider could include whether the magazine should be targeted at young men, young women, or both groups, and whether it should be sold mainly online, through subscriptions, or on newsstands.

Goals are the targets or ends the manager wants to reach. To be effective, goals should have certain qualities, which are easy to remember with the acronym SMART:

- *Specific*—When goals are precise, employees know what they need to do to accomplish them.

- *Measurable*—As much as possible, the goal should quantify the desired results, so that there is no doubt whether it has been achieved.

- *Attainable (but challenging)*—Employees need to recognize that they can attain their goals, so they won't become discouraged. However, they also should feel challenged to work hard and be creative.

- *Relevant*—Each goal should contribute to the organization's overall mission (discussed later in this chapter) and be consistent with its values, including ethical standards.

- *Time-bound*—Effective goals specify a target date for completion.

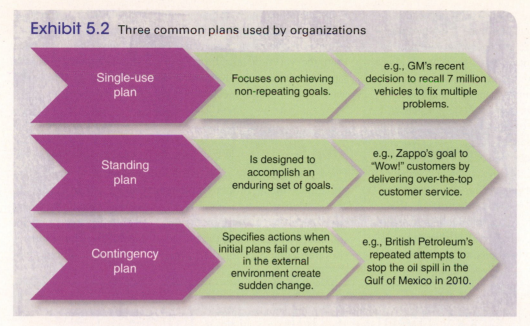

Exhibit 5.2 Three common plans used by organizations

Single-use plan	Focuses on achieving non-repeating goals.	e.g., GM's recent decision to recall 7 million vehicles to fix multiple problems.
Standing plan	Is designed to accomplish an enduring set of goals.	e.g., Zappo's goal to "Wow!" customers by delivering over-the-top customer service.
Contingency plan	Specifies actions when initial plans fail or events in the external environment create sudden change.	e.g., British Petroleum's repeated attempts to stop the oil spill in the Gulf of Mexico in 2010.

Sources: C. Isidore, "GM Recalls Reach Nearly 7 Million," *CNN Money* (online), April 1, 2014, http://money.cnn.com; B. Glassman, "What Zappos Taught Us About Creating The Ultimate Client Experience," *Forbes* (online), May 13, 2013, www.forbes.com; "BP Oil Spill Timeline," *The Guardian* (online), July 22, 2010, www.theguardian.com.

General Electric's goal of being first or second in all its markets is a well-known example of a goal that is specific, measurable, and challenging. SMART goals such as these not only point employees in the direction they should be going but also foster acceptance by those who are charged with achieving them. In other words, they both direct and motivate employees.

Plans are the actions or means the manager intends to use to achieve goals. In this chapter, we will talk about three plans commonly used by organizations (see Exhibit 5.2). At a minimum, planning should outline alternative actions that may lead to the attainment of each goal, the resources required to reach the goal, and the obstacles that may develop. IBM has goals to increase its profits, and the fastest-growing area of growth is in software. To meet profit goals, the software unit acquires existing software companies that have high-potential products but lack the means to promote them aggressively enough. IBM's software group plans how its gigantic sales force will sell the new products. Those plans include training the salespeople in what the new software does and how it can help IBM's clients. To improve the effectiveness of the sales force, the software group planned a selling system for categorizing and keeping track of each salesperson's leads.[2]

Step 3: Evaluate Goals and Plans

Next managers evaluate the advantages, disadvantages, and potential effects of each alternative goal and plan. They must prioritize the goals and even eliminate some of them. Also, managers consider how well alternative plans meet high-priority goals, considering the cost of each initiative and the likely investment return. In our magazine publishing example, your evaluation might determine that newsstand sales alone

wouldn't be profitable enough to justify the launch. Perhaps you could improve profits with an online edition supplemented by podcasts.

Step 4: Select Goals and Plans

Once managers have assessed the goals and plans, they select the most appropriate and feasible alternative. The evaluation process identifies the priorities and trade-offs among the goals

LISTEN & LEARN ONLINE

YOUNG MANAGERS

Speak Out!

"Be true to yourself. I've found when I waiver from my own thoughts and beliefs, that is when I find myself in situations that I'm not comfortable with and don't come naturally to me."

—Sheryl Freeman, Program Manager

and plans. For example, if your plan is to launch a number of new publications and you're trying to choose among them, you might weigh the different up-front investment each requires, the size of each market, and which one fits best with your existing product line or company image. Experienced judgment plays an important role in this process. As you will discover later in the chapter, however, relying on judgment alone may not be the best way to proceed.

Typically a formal planning process leads to a written set of goals and plans that are appropriate and feasible for a particular set of circumstances. In some organizations, the alternative generation, evaluation, and selection steps generate planning **scenarios**. A different contingency plan is attached to each scenario. The manager pursues the goals and implements the plans associated with the most likely scenario. However, the

Business's managers were doing—move beyond their fear of change to find new opportunities in challenging times. Hull counseled the owner of a real estate investment company to set aside his fears about the real estate downturn, reevaluate his data on the prospects for converting a warehouse into a restaurant, and go ahead with plans for what was in fact a well-researched, practical idea.[3]

Step 5: Implement the Goals and Plans

Once managers have selected the goals and plans, they must implement them. Proper implementation is key to achieving goals. Managers and employees must understand the plan, have the resources to implement it, and be motivated to do so. Including employees in the previous steps of the planning process paves the way for the implementation phase. Employees

> *"Plans are only good intentions unless they immediately degenerate into hard work."*
>
> —Peter Drucker

manager should also be prepared to switch to another set of plans if the situation changes and another scenario becomes relevant. This approach helps the firm anticipate and manage crises and allows greater flexibility and responsiveness.

Looking back to the chapter opening example, Shell managers undoubtedly developed several contingency plans for each scenario related to gaining access to Chinese oil and natural gas markets. A pioneer of scenario planning, Shell needed to have alternative plans ready in case PetroChina refused to work as its partner.

If a company hasn't already considered possible scenarios, managers must be prepared to restart the planning process when an unexpected change brings disappointing results. This flexible approach to planning can help a company survive and even thrive in a turbulent environment. For example, when the economy recently took a downturn, major clients stopped calling on Cor Business, a management coaching firm, for help in developing their managers. Jeffrey Hull and the other partners of Cor Business realized their firm's survival required a new plan for bringing in business.

The partners brainstormed ideas for a new business plan. Looking over the prior year's results, they noticed that most of Cor Business's growth that year had come from small businesses, even though the partners had been directing most of their energy toward large companies like MasterCard and AT&T. As a matter of fact, as the economy had slowed, more and more nervous small business owners had been looking for help from their firm.

Hull and the other partners drew up a new plan in which they would focus on serving small clients, helping them do what Cor

usually are better informed, more committed, and more highly motivated when a goal or plan is one that they helped develop.

Finally, linking the plan to other systems in the organization, particularly the budget and reward systems, helps ensure its successful implementation. If the manager does not have or cannot find the financial resources to execute the plan, the plan is probably doomed. Similarly, linking goal achievement to the organization's reward system, such as bonuses or promotions, encourages employees to achieve goals and to implement plans properly.

Wells Fargo's top management saw the importance of linking its employees' pay to a new strategy. Ex-Chairman of the Board Dick Kovacevich saw that one of the nation's largest banks could stay competitive by excelling at "cross-selling," that is, encouraging the bank's existing customers to use more of its financial services. Bank customers typically go to different institutions for different services, but Wells Fargo beat the odds by getting employees at all levels to focus on customer needs rather than product lines. Tellers and branch managers receive training aimed at this goal, and pay systems reward employees for cross-selling. As a result, Wells Fargo customers use an average of 5.7 of the bank's products, roughly double the average for the industry. Selling to existing customers is much more profitable than winning new ones, so this strategy might seem obvious. Perhaps it is, but Wells Fargo board member Robert Joss says, "It's simple in concept but very hard in execution," adding that this successful implementation reflected Kovacevich's "great capacity to motivate people."[4] This strategy has helped Wells Fargo to become one of the world's largest banks (by market capitalization).[5]

Step 6: Monitor and Control Performance

Although it is sometimes ignored, the sixth step in the formal planning process—monitoring and controlling—is essential. Without it, you would never know whether your plan is succeeding. As we mentioned earlier, planning works in a cycle. Managers must continually monitor the actual performance of their work units against the unit's goals and plans. They also need to develop control systems to measure that performance and allow them to take corrective action when plans are implemented improperly or the situation changes. In our magazine publishing example, newsstand and subscription sales reports let you know how well your new magazine launch is going. If subscription sales are below expectations, you may need to revise your marketing plan. We will discuss control systems in greater detail later.

strategic planning a set of procedures for making decisions about the organization's long-term goals and strategies

strategic goals major targets or end results relating to the organization's long-term survival, value, and growth

strategy a pattern of actions and resource allocations designed to achieve the organization's goals

● Wells Fargo rolled out a plan that links employee pay to the practice of cross-selling; encouraging the bank's existing customers to use more of its financial services. Selling to existing customers is more profitable than winning new ones.

efficiency (a high ratio of outputs to inputs). Typical strategic goals include growing, increasing market share, improving profitability, boosting return on investment, fostering quantity and quality of outputs, increasing productivity, improving customer service, and contributing to society.

A **strategy** is a pattern of actions and resource allocations designed to achieve the organization's goals. An effective strategy provides a basis for answering five broad questions about how the organization will meet its objectives:

1. Where will we be active?

2. How will we get there (e.g., by increasing sales or acquiring another company)?

3. How will we win in the marketplace (e.g., by keeping prices low or offering the best service)?

4. How fast will we move, and in what sequence will we make changes?

5. How will we obtain financial returns (low costs or premium prices)?[6]

Later in this chapter we discuss how managers try to craft a strategy by matching the organization's skills and resources to the opportunities found in the external environment.

LO2 Discuss how strategic planning should be integrated with tactical and operational planning

---

2 | LEVELS OF PLANNING

Planning is used by managers at all four levels described in Chapter 1: top-level (*strategic* managers), middle-level (*tactical* managers), frontline (*operational* managers), and team leaders. However, the scope and activities of the planning process tend to differ at each level.

2.1 | Strategic Planning Sets a Long-Term Direction

Strategic planning involves making decisions about the organization's long-term goals and strategies. Strategic plans have a strong external orientation and cover major portions of the organization. Senior executives are responsible for the development and execution of the strategic plan, although they usually do not formulate or implement the entire plan personally.

Strategic goals are major targets or end results that relate to the long-term survival, value, and growth of the organization. Strategic managers—top-level managers—usually establish goals aimed at effectiveness (providing appropriate outputs) and

2.2 | Tactical and Operational Planning Support the Strategy

The organization's strategic goals and plans serve as the foundation for planning by middle-level and frontline managers. Exhibit 5.3 shows that as goals and plans move from the strategic level to the tactical level and then to the operational level, they become more specific and involve shorter time periods. A strategic plan typically has a time horizon of three to seven years, but sometimes it spans decades, as with the successful plan to land a probe on Titan, Saturn's moon. Tactical plans may have a time horizon of a year or two, and operational plans may cover several months.

managers usually focus on routine tasks such as production runs, delivery schedules, and human resource requirements.

The formal planning model is hierarchical, with top-level strategies flowing down through the levels of the organization into more specific goals and plans and an ever-more-limited timetable. But in today's complex organizations, planning is often more dynamic and flexible. Managers throughout an organization may be involved in developing the strategic plan and contributing critical elements. Also, in practice, lower-level managers may make decisions that shape strategy, whether or not top executives realize it.

When Intel's former CEO and current senior adviser Andy Grove suggested that the company exit the computer memory business, Intel was directing about one-third of its research dollars to memory-related projects. Yet on a practical level, the company had already been exiting the business; only 4 percent of its total sales were for computer memory products. Why was this occurring, if it wasn't a defined strategy? Finance executives had directed manufacturing managers to set up factories in a way that would generate the biggest margins (revenues minus costs) per square inch of microchips produced. As com-

> "Think small and act small, and we'll get bigger. Think big and act big, and we'll get smaller."
>
> —Herb Kelleher, *Southwest Airlines*

Tactical planning translates broad strategic goals and plans into specific goals and plans relevant to a particular portion of the organization, often a functional area such as marketing or human resources. Tactical plans focus on the major actions a unit must take to fulfill its part of the strategic plan. Suppose a strategy calls for the rollout of a new product line. The tactical plan for the manufacturing unit might involve the design, testing, and installation of the equipment needed to produce the new line.

Operational planning identifies the specific procedures and processes required at lower levels of the organization. Frontline

puter memory became a money-losing commodity, manufacturing made fewer of those products. So when Intel announced it would get out of the memory business, its strategy was catching up with its operational planning, which had been driven by tactical plans.[7] The lesson for top managers is to make sure they are communicating strategy to all levels of the organization and paying attention to what is happening at all levels in the organization.

2.3 | All Levels of Planning Should Be Aligned

To be fully effective, the organization's strategic, tactical, and operational goals and plans must be *aligned*—that is, they must be consistent, mutually supportive, and focused on achieving the common purpose and direction. Whole Foods Market, for example, links its tactical and operational planning directly to its strategic planning. The strategic goal of Whole Foods is "to sell the highest-quality products that also offer high value for our customers." Its operational goals focus on ingredients, freshness, taste, nutritional value, safety, and appearance that meet or exceed its customers' expectations, including guaranteeing product satisfaction.

Exhibit 5.3 Three levels of planning in organizations

Level of planning	Who develops the plan?	How detailed is it?	How long is the plan?
Strategic	Top-level managers	Low	Long (3–7 years)
Tactical	Middle managers	Medium	Medium (1–2 years)
Operational	Frontline managers	High	Short (< 1 year)

Tactical goals include store environments that are "inviting, fun, unique, informal, comfortable, attractive, nurturing, and educational" and safe and inviting work environments for its employees.

:::::::::::::::::

At times, a temporary misalignment among the different levels of planning can ultimately result in a positive outcome for a company. After founding the Honda Motor Company in 1948, Soichero Honda wanted to gain a significant share of the motorcycle market in the United States. Honda leaders decided that a larger motorcycle was their best bet to compete against American firms like Harley-Davidson. However, Honda soon discovered that the larger bikes were not an immediate hit with American bikers. Quite by accident, the smaller 50 cc Super Cub caught the attention of a new, young group of American motorcycle customers, who wanted "inexpensive, convenient, individual transportation for short trips around town." This was in stark contrast to the existing customer base of hardcore enthusiasts who preferred large, long-haul motorcycles. This tactical move of first selling smaller motorcycles helped Honda gain a foothold in the American market that eventually led to gaining market share of larger bikes. Essentially, these adaptive tactics led to an adjustment in the company's strategy for the U.S. market. Honda went from practically no presence in 1959 to more than 60 percent of the current motorcycle market.

Flash forward to today. One of Honda Motor Company's strategies is to be on the "leading edge by creating new value and providing products of the highest quality at a reasonable price, for worldwide customer satisfaction." Two examples of recent innovations reinforce Honda's commitment to their company strategy. First, Honda and General Motors have agreed to work together to develop next-generation fuel cell system and hydrogen storage technology for automobiles. By 2020, the two companies hope to be able to mass-produce small, medium, and large fuel cell–powered vehicles that will offer a 400-mile driving range and be refueled within three minutes. A second example is Honda's new HA-420 HondaJet, the "world's most advanced light business jet." The HA-420's turbo fan engines and jet production facility are expected to be fully certified by the end of 2014. HondaJet, whose manufacturing facilities are located in Greensboro, North Carolina, plans to produce 80 to 90 jets per year. If he were alive today, Soichero Honda would undoubtedly be proud of how his strategic vision continues to make impact in the automobile, motorcycle, power products, and now aviation industries.[8]

:::::::::::::::::

Even the best strategies (like at Honda) have to rely on managers' ability to set tactical and operational priorities, allocate resources, analyze market conditions, and ensure proper implementation. The next section discusses six steps that managers can follow to convert strategic ideas into successful outcomes like higher profits, new products, and greater efficiencies.

● The Honda HA-420 HondaJet is the first general aviation aircraft developed by the Honda Aircraft Company. The maiden flight took place in late 2010. Having achieved FAA certification, the Honda Aircraft Company began production in fall 2012. With the price tag around $3.65 million, Honda plans to build 70 jets per year.

strategic management a process that involves managers from all parts of the organization in the formulation and implementation of strategic goals and strategies

LO3 Describe the strategic management process and the importance of SWOT analysis in strategy formulation

3 | STRATEGIC PLANNING PROCESS

Many organizations are changing the ways they develop and execute their strategic plans. Traditionally, strategic planning flowed from the top. Senior executives and specialized planning units developed goals and plans for the entire organization. Tactical and operational managers received those goals and plans, and then simply prepared procedures and budgets for their units. Today, however, senior executives increasingly are involving managers throughout the organization in strategy formulation.[9] In the current highly competitive and rapidly changing environment, executives need to look for ideas from all levels of the organization. Although top managers continue to furnish the organization's strategic direction, or "vision," tactical and operational managers provide valuable inputs to the organization's strategic plan. These managers also may formulate or change their own plans, making the organization more flexible and responsive.

Because of this trend, a new term for the strategic planning process has emerged: *strategic management.* **Strategic management** involves managers from all parts of the organization in the formulation and implementation of strategic goals and strategies. It integrates strategic planning and management into a single process. Strategic planning becomes an ongoing activity in which all managers are encouraged to think strategically and focus on long-term, externally oriented issues as well as short-term tactical and operational issues.

mission an organization's basic purpose and scope of operations

strategic vision the long-term direction and strategic intent of a company

As shown in Exhibit 5.4, the strategic management process has six steps: (1) establishment of mission, vision, and goals; (2) analysis of external opportunities and threats; (3) analysis of internal strengths and weaknesses; (4) SWOT analysis and strategy formulation; (5) strategy implementation; and (6) strategic control. This planning and decision process resembles the planning framework discussed earlier.

First, Establish a Mission, Vision, and Goals

The first step in strategic planning is establishing a mission, a vision, and goals for the organization. The **mission** is a clear and concise expression of the organization's basic purpose. It describes what the organization does, whom it does it for, its basic good or service, and its values. Here are some mission statements from firms you will recognize:[10]

IDEO: "We create impact through design."

Unilever: "To meet the everyday needs of people everywhere."

Google: "To organize the world's information and make it universally accessible and useful."

The mission describes the organization as it currently operates. The **strategic vision** points to the future; it provides a perspective on where the organization is headed and what it can become. Here are some actual vision statements:[11]

DuPont: "To be the world's most dynamic science company, creating sustainable solutions essential to a better, safer and healthier life for people everywhere."

City of Redmond, Washington: "Together we create a community of good neighbors."

Smithsonian: "Shaping the future by preserving our heritage, discovering new knowledge, and sharing our resources with the world."

The most effective vision statements inspire organization members. They offer a worthwhile target for the entire organization to work together to achieve. Often these statements are not strictly financial because financial targets alone may not motivate all organization members. Thus DuPont's vision refers to being a "dynamic science company" that works toward a "better, safer and healthier life" for people. This vision inspires innovation aimed at making the world better—the type of work that is likely to motivate the scientists and other knowledge workers who can give the company an edge, ultimately improving DuPont's competitive position.

Strategic goals evolve from the organization's mission and vision. For example, in support of its vision that "creating a community of good neighbors" is best done "together" with all sectors of the community, the City of Redmond has established goals such as these:

- Enhance citizen engagement in city issues.

- Sustain the natural systems and beauty of the community.

- Sustain a safe community with a coherent, comprehensive, cohesive approach to safety.

- Maintain economic vitality.

Different city departments would contribute to various aspects of this vision in the way they carry out their operational plans with an emphasis on collaborating with local businesses and residents.

Lofty words in a vision and mission statement cannot be meaningful without strong leadership support. At McDonald's,

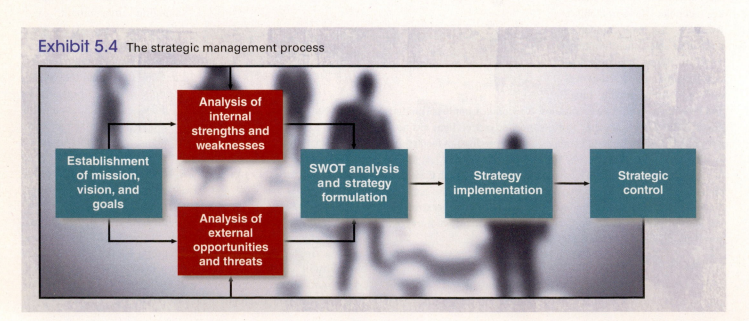

Exhibit 5.4 The strategic management process

Establishment of mission, vision, and goals → Analysis of internal strengths and weaknesses → SWOT analysis and strategy formulation → Strategy implementation → Strategic control

Establishment of mission, vision, and goals → Analysis of external opportunities and threats → SWOT analysis and strategy formulation

the commitment of past and present CEOs has played a large role in the success of the company's strategy implementation. Several years ago, the company was floundering as it lost sight of its commitment to quality, value, speed, and convenience. Under the leadership of James Cantalupo, the company created a customer-focused mission statement, "To be our customers' favorite place and way to eat." In support of this mission, McDonald's is pursuing strategic goals such

whether the firm's purposes and values are compatible with your own.

Second, Analyze External Opportunities and Threats

The mission and vision drive the second component of the strategic management process: analysis of the external environ-

> "Leadership is the capacity to translate vision into reality."
>
> —Warren G. Bennis

as revamping restaurants for a better drive-through experience and improving the quality of the menu. When Jim Skinner took the job of chief executive, he enthusiastically backed the mission statement and its supporting Plan to Win, not hesitating to share credit for the company's continued success.[12]

Large firms generally provide public formal statements of their missions, visions, goals, and even values. The concepts and information within these statements should be communicated to everyone who has contact with the organization. Strong leadership provides statements of vision and goals to clarify the organization's purpose to key constituencies outside the organization. Clear vision and goals also help employees focus their talent, energy, and commitment. When you seek employment with a firm, review the firm's statements of mission, vision, and goals; they can help you determine

ment. Successful strategic management depends on an accurate and thorough evaluation of the competitive environment and macroenvironment, described in Chapter 3.

As illustrated in Exhibit 5.5, an environmental analysis includes many elements.

Exhibit 5.5 — Elements included in an environmental analysis

Industry growth	Growth rates for the entire industry and key market segments, and projected changes in patterns and determinants of growth.
Industry forces	Threat of new industry entrants, threat of substitutes, economic power of buyers/customers, economic power of suppliers, and internal industry rivalry.
Competitor analysis	Goals, strategies, strengths, and weaknesses of each major competitor.
Legal trends	Legislation and regulatory activities and their effects on the industry.
Political activity	The level of political activity undertaken by organizations and associations within the industry.
Social issues	Current and potential social issues and their effects on the industry.
Social interest groups	Social interest groups: consumer, environmental, and other activist groups that try to influence the industry.
Labor issues	Key labor needs, shortages, opportunities, and problems confronting the industry.
Macro economic conditions	Economic factors that affect supply, demand, growth, competition, and profitability within the industry.
Technological factors	Scientific or technical methods that affect the industry, particularly recent and potential innovations.

The analysis begins with an examination of the industry. Next organizational stakeholders are examined. **Stakeholders** are groups and individuals who affect and are affected by achievement of the organization's mission, goals, and strategies. They include buyers, suppliers, competitors, government and regulatory agencies, unions and employee groups, the financial community, owners and shareholders, and trade associations. The environmental analysis provides a map of these stakeholders and the ways they influence the organization.[13]

:::::::::::::::

Collaborating with key stakeholders can help organizations successfully develop and implement their strategic plan. At software company Intuit (maker of Quickbooks and Quicken), President and CEO Brad Smith launched strategy development by learning what was on the minds of some key stakeholders. He visited with his board of directors and investors and set up meetings with groups of employees who work directly with Intuit's customers.

Smith asked each group of stakeholders some key questions related to strategic analysis: "What is Intuit's biggest untapped opportunity? What is the biggest risk facing Intuit that keeps you up at night?" From the answers, Smith gained insights that helped him establish priorities for Intuit's strategy.

Smith learned that a sizable number of Intuit's business customers have international activities, so he determined that Intuit would have to become a more global company. Its QuickBooks financial software now handles multiple currencies for international transactions. In response to the competitive threat of a new release of financial software from Microsoft, Smith assembled managers to craft a marketing strategy that would convince customers to wait two more months for the next version of QuickBooks. That campaign caused QuickBooks sales to jump despite of Microsoft's efforts.[14]

:::::::::::::::

The environmental analysis also should examine other forces in the environment, such as economic conditions and technological factors. One critical task in environmental analysis is forecasting future trends. As noted in Chapter 3, forecasting techniques range from simple judgment to complex mathematical models that examine systematic relationships among many variables. Because of biases and limits on human thinking, even simple quantitative techniques can outperform the intuitive assessments of experts.

Frequently the difference between an opportunity and a threat depends on how a company positions itself strategically. For example, some states have required that electric utilities get a certain share of their power from renewable sources, such as wind and solar energy, rather than from fossil fuels, including coal, oil, and natural gas. This requirement poses an obvious threat to utilities because the costs of fossil fuel energy are less,

and customers demand low prices. However, some companies see strategic opportunities in renewable power. German conglomerate Schott has developed a solar thermal technology in which sunlight heats oil in metal tubes enclosed in coated glass; the heated oil makes steam, which powers a turbine and generates electricity. Solar thermal energy, although it now costs more than fossil fuels, is more efficient than the solar panels installed on some buildings, and it can store extra power to be used on cloudy days.[15] Similarly, overflowing landfills are an expensive challenge for many municipalities, but a growing number are seeing an opportunity in the form of energy generation. As garbage decomposes, it produces methane gas, which is used as a fuel to power generators. In East Brunswick, New Jersey, for example, the Edgeboro landfill generates electricity that powers the county's wastewater treatment plant.[16]

Third, Analyze Internal Strengths and Weaknesses

As managers conduct an external analysis, they should also assess the strengths and weaknesses of major functional areas inside their organization. This internal resource analysis has several components:

- *Financial analysis*—Examines financial strengths and weaknesses through financial statements such as a balance sheet and an income statement and compares trends to historical and industry figures.

- *Human resources assessment*—Examines strengths and weaknesses of all levels of managers and employees and focuses on key human resources activities, including recruitment, selection, placement, training, labor (union) relationships, compensation, promotion, appraisal, quality of work life, and human resources planning.

- *Marketing audit*—Examines strengths and weaknesses of major marketing activities and identifies markets, key market segments, and the organization's competitive position (market share) within key markets.

- *Operations analysis*—Examines the strengths and weaknesses of the organization's manufacturing, production, or service delivery activities.

- *Other internal resource analyses*—Examine, as appropriate, the strengths and weaknesses of other organizational activities, such as research and development (product and process), management information systems, engineering, and purchasing.

Is your firm strong enough financially to invest in new projects, and can your existing staff carry out its part of the plan? Is your firm's image compatible with its strategy, or will it have to persuade key stakeholders that a change in direction makes sense? This type of internal analysis provides an inventory of the organization's existing functions, skills, and resources as well as its overall performance level. Many of your other business courses will prepare you to conduct an internal analysis.

Resources and Core Capabilities Without question, strategic planning has been strongly influenced in recent years by a focus on internal resources. **Resources** are inputs to production (recall systems theory) that can be accumulated over time to enhance the performance of a firm. Resources can take many forms, but they tend to fall into two broad categories:

1. *Tangible assets* such as real estate, production facilities, raw materials, and so on.

2. *Intangible assets* such as company reputation, culture, technical knowledge, and patents, as well as accumulated learning and experience.

The Walt Disney Company, for example, has developed its strategic plan based on combinations of tangible assets (including hotels and theme parks) and intangible assets (brand recognition, talented craftspeople, culture focused on customer service).[17]

Effective internal analysis provides a clearer understanding of how a company can compete through its resources. Resources are a source of competitive advantage only under all of the following circumstances:

- The resources are instrumental for creating customer *value*—that is, they increase the benefits customers derive from a good or service relative to the costs they incur.[18] For example, Amazon's powerful search technology, ability to track customer preferences and offer personalized recommendations, and quick product delivery are valuable resources.

- The resources are *rare* and not equally available to all competitors. At Roche, W.L. Gore, and BASF, patented formulas represent rare resources. Amazon similarly sought a patent for its one-click shopping technique. If competitors have equal access to a resource, it can be valuable but cannot provide a competitive advantage.

- The resources are *difficult to imitate.* Earlier in this chapter, we saw that Wells Fargo has competed with much larger banks by developing expertise in cross-selling. Unlike, say, free checking accounts, this intangible resource is difficult to imitate because the bank has to train and motivate employees at all levels to adopt customer-oriented thinking and collaborate across divisions.[19] As in this example, where success relies on leadership and collaboration practices, resources tend to be harder to imitate if they are complex, with many interdependent variables and no obvious links between behaviors and desired outcomes.[20]

- The resources are well *organized.* For example, IBM, known primarily for computer hardware until it became more of a commodity than a source of competitive advantage, has organized its staff and systems to efficiently produce a consolidated technology product for its corporate clients—hardware, software, and service in one package. This spares its clients the cost of managing technology on their own.

When resources are valuable, rare, inimitable, and organized, they can be viewed as a company's core capabilities. Simply stated, a **core capability** is something a company does especially well relative to its competitors. Honda, for example, has a core capability in small engine design and manufacturing, and Federal Express has a core capability in logistics and customer service. As in these examples, a core capability typically refers to a set of skills or expertise in some activity, rather than physical or financial assets.

● Imagine how skilled Coca-Cola's global network of bottlers are to be able to deliver their product worldwide and more efficiently than any of their competitors. Shown here is a truck delivering Coke in India.

For the past five years, IBM has been developing its "Smarter Planet" initiative, which focuses on the company's core capabilities in business analytics, e-commerce, and cloud computing. "Smarter Planet" is a business platform that is aimed at helping "make the world better through intelligent, connected systems." Whether it's working to improve the efficiency of the Stockholm traffic system or designing a smart electric grid for the island of Malta, IBM is staying ahead of the competition by using its resources in ways that create value while being unique and difficult to imitate. For example, IBM deploys large cross-functional, cross-company teams that have the right skills, knowledge, and experience to address complex client problems. These teams can be formed, disbanded, and reconfigured to meet the changing and diverse needs of clients. IBM's leaders are hoping that the "Smarter Planet" initiative will make the world more intelligent and interconnected.[21]

Benchmarking To assess and improve performance, some companies use benchmarking, the process of assessing how well one company's basic functions and skills compare with those of another company or set of companies. The goal of benchmarking is to thoroughly understand the "best practices" of other firms and to undertake actions to achieve better performance and lower costs. Benchmarking programs have helped Ford, Corning, Hewlett-Packard, Xerox, and other companies make great strides in eliminating inefficiencies and improving competitiveness.

SWOT analysis a comparison of strengths, weaknesses, opportunities, and threats that helps executives formulate strategy

Most college students have probably eaten a fast-food meal while driving between school and work, or while taking a break from studying. A recent benchmarking study compared the overall service quality of several popular fast-food restaurant chains in the United States, including McDonald's, Burger King, Wendy's, Subway, Arby's, and Hardee's.[22] As illustrated in Exhibit 5.6, these six restaurant chains were compared against one another and rank ordered on several criteria, with the following results (listed with first being best):

There are many uses for benchmarking data. For example, managers at McDonald's may be pleased to learn their restaurant was ranked first in service response time, proximity to customer's home, and price, but not as high as some of its competitors in the other important dimensions of overall service quality. Customers like Subway for its cleanliness, employee courtesy, and taste of food; however, the chain failed to make the top three in terms of service response time and price. As a result of such benchmarking, managers at Subway may look for ways to serve customers faster and provide additional discounts like the popular $5 "sub of the month" specials.

Benchmarking against competitors only helps a company perform as well as they do, but strategic management aims to surpass those companies. Besides benchmarking against leading organizations in other industries, companies may address this problem by engaging in internal benchmarking. That approach involves benchmarking internal operations and departments against one another to disseminate the company's best practices throughout the organization and thereby gain a competitive advantage.

Fourth, Conduct a SWOT Analysis and Formulate Strategy

Once managers have analyzed the external environment and the organization's internal resources, they have the information needed for a **SWOT analysis**: an assessment of the organization's strengths, weaknesses, opportunities, and threats. Strengths and weaknesses refer to internal resources. An organization's *strengths* might include skilled management, positive cash flow, and well-known and highly regarded brands. *Weaknesses* might

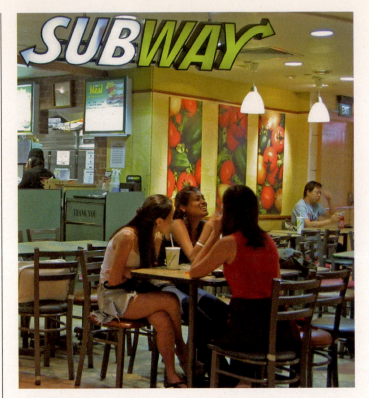

● Young adults eating at Subway.

be lack of spare production capacity and the absence of reliable suppliers. Opportunities and threats arise in the macroenvironment and competitive environment. Examples of *opportunities* are a new technology that could make the supply chain more efficient and a market niche that is currently underserved. *Threats* might include the possibility that competitors will enter the underserved niche once it has been shown to be profitable.

SWOT analysis helps managers summarize the relevant, important facts from their external and internal analyses. Based on this summary, they can identify the primary and secondary strategic issues their organization faces. The managers then formulate a strategy that will build on the SWOT analysis to take advantage of available opportunities by capitalizing on the organization's strengths, neutralizing its weaknesses, and countering potential threats.

As an example, consider how SWOT analysis might be conducted at Sony (see Exhibit 5.7). The company's size $72 billion in sales and 146,300 employees worldwide (in 2013), is an obvious strength. Also, the firm sells more than 2,000 diversified products from headphones and printers to movies and televisions. Sony has a history of "hit products" such as the Walkman, Trinitron television, Spider Man movie franchise, the PlayStation 4 video console, Xperia smartphones and tablets, and VAIO personal computers. As for weaknesses, the company's separate divisions prefer to act independently and resist change that might hurt their profitability. Several

Exhibit 5.6	Results of study comparing overall service quality of six fast-food restaurants		
Criteria	**Ranked 1st Place**	**Ranked 2nd Place**	**Ranked 3rd Place**
Cleanliness	Subway	McDonald's	Wendy's
Service response time	McDonald's	Wendy's	Burger King
Employee courtesy	Subway	Arby's	McDonald's
Healthful food	Subway	Wendy's	Arby's
Taste of food	Subway	Wendy's	Arby's
Competitive price	McDonald's	Wendy's	Burger King
Proximity to customer	McDonald's	Wendy's	Subway

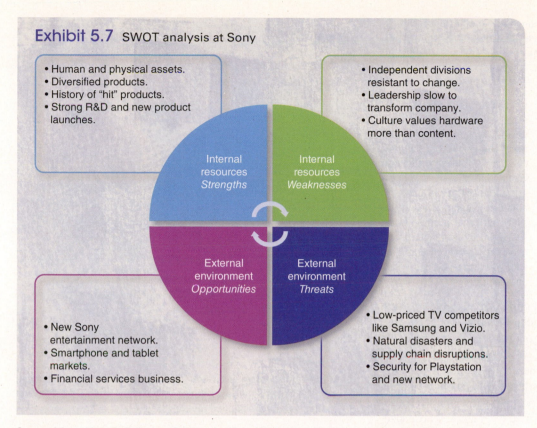

Exhibit 5.7 SWOT analysis at Sony

Internal resources *Strengths*
- Human and physical assets.
- Diversified products.
- History of "hit" products.
- Strong R&D and new product launches.

Internal resources *Weaknesses*
- Independent divisions resistant to change.
- Leadership slow to transform company.
- Culture values hardware more than content.

External environment *Opportunities*
- New Sony entertainment network.
- Smartphone and tablet markets.
- Financial services business.

External environment *Threats*
- Low-priced TV competitors like Samsung and Vizio.
- Natural disasters and supply chain disruptions.
- Security for Playstation and new network.

Source: Adapted from B. Gruley and C. Edwards, "Sony Needs a Hit," *Bloomberg BusinessWeek* (November 21–27, 2011), pp. 72–77.

corporate strategy the set of businesses, markets, or industries in which an organization competes and the distribution of resources among those entities

concentration a strategy employed for an organization that operates a single business and competes in a single industry

vertical integration the acquisition or development of new businesses that produce parts or components of the organization's product

related diversification a strategy used to add new businesses that produce related products or are involved in related markets and activities

recent leaders have tried unsuccessfully to transform the company into one that is more adaptive and aligned with consumer interests. Sony's organizational culture has traditionally placed more value on hardware than on content like songs and movies.

Beyond internal strengths and weaknesses, the firm's macroenvironment presents several opportunities. The Internet age has ushered in consumer demand for connectivity. To tap this demand, Sony plans to connect all of its devices with all of its content, including Sony's 90 million PlayStation users, via a new Sony entertainment network. This network will allow a PlayStation user to download music or movies onto a Sony Tablet or a soon-to-be launched smartphone. (Sony recently announced that it would be entering the smartphone market in the United States, where it is currently nonexistent.) Another opportunity for Sony is to continue to offer financial services like life and automobile insurance; surprisingly, this area has been Sony's most profitable business over the past nine years. Sony faces many threats from its macroenvironment including low-priced televisions from competitors Samsung and Vizio. This is making it very difficult for Sony to compete profitably in this product category that it once dominated.

Unpredictable natural disasters, like the tsunami and earthquake that rocked eastern Japan and floods in Thailand, recently led to temporary closings of several of both Sony's and its suppliers' plants. These supply chain disruptions contributed to a net loss of $3.1 billion. Other unforeseen factors have hurt the company's profitability, including the burning of a CD and DVD warehouse in London by a rioting mob and a hacker attack that shut down the PlayStation network.[23]

Corporate Strategy A **corporate strategy** identifies the set of businesses, markets, or industries in which the organization competes and the distribution of resources among those businesses. The four basic alternatives for a corporate strategy range from very specialized to highly diverse:

1. **Concentration**—focusing on a single business competing in a single industry. Frequently companies pursue concentration strategies to gain entry into an industry when industry growth is good or when the company has a narrow range of competencies. C. F. Martin & Company pursues a concentration strategy by focusing on making the best possible guitars and guitar strings, a strategy that has enabled the family-owned business to operate successfully for more than 150 years.

2. **Vertical integration**—expanding the organization's domain into supply channels or to distributors, generally to eliminate uncertainties and reduce costs associated with suppliers or distributors. At one time, Henry Ford had fully integrated his company from the ore mines needed to make steel all the way to the showrooms where his cars were sold.

3. **Related diversification**—moving into new businesses related to the company's original core business. Since its beginnings as a cartoon studio in the 1920s, Disney has expanded into a global firm known for its broadcast (ABC) and cable (ESPN) television networks, movies, books, TV shows, retail stores, theme parks, music, cruise lines, and more. Each of these businesses within the entertainment industry is related in terms of the products and services it provides, and the customers it attracts. Related diversification applies

strengths in one business to gain advantage in another. Success requires adequate management and other resources for operating more than one business.

4. **Unrelated diversification**—expansion into unrelated businesses, typically to minimize risks due to market fluctuations in one industry. General Electric has diversified from its original base in electrical and home appliance products to such wide-ranging industries as health, finance, insurance, truck and air transportation, and even energy, including oil, gas, wind, and electric.

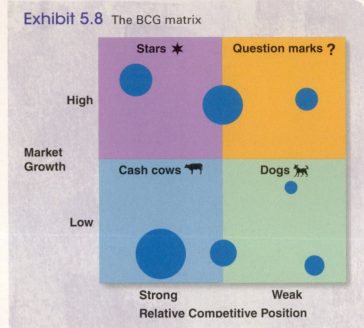

Exhibit 5.8 The BCG matrix

The diversified businesses of an organization are sometimes called its business *portfolio*. A popular technique for analyzing a corporation's strategy for managing its portfolio is the BCG matrix, developed by the Boston Consulting Group and shown in Exhibit 5.8. Each business in the corporation is plotted on the matrix on the basis of the growth rate of its market and the relative strength of its competitive position in that market (market share). The business is represented by a circle whose size depends on the business's contribution to corporate revenues.

There are four categories of businesses in the BCG matrix:

- *Question marks*—These high-growth, weak-competitive-position businesses require substantial investment to improve their position, or else they should be divested.

- *Stars*—Businesses with high growth and a strong competitive position require heavy investment, but their strong position lets them generate the needed revenues.

- *Cash cows*—These low-growth businesses with a strong competitive position generate revenues in excess of their investment needs, so they fund other businesses.

- *Dogs*—These low-growth, weak-competitive-position businesses should be divested after their remaining revenues are realized.

The BCG matrix is not a substitute for management judgment, creativity, insight, or leadership. But along with other techniques, it can help managers evaluate their strategy alternatives.[24] This type of thinking has recently helped Abbott Laboratories succeed. When Miles White took over as Abbott's CEO, he began restructuring the company's portfolio to emphasize growth. He sold off much of the company's diagnostics business, which was earning low returns, and purchased businesses with higher risks but potential to be stars. White says his goal is a portfolio of businesses that are innovative, growing, and delivering high returns.[25]

LO4 Analyze how companies can achieve competitive advantage through business strategy

● Kristen Bell and Idina Menzel, voice talent of Anna and Elsa in the Walt Disney Animation Studios film "Frozen," pose with Mattel's feature fashion dolls during the D23 Expo.

4 | BUSINESS STRATEGY

After the top management team and board make the corporate strategic decisions, executives must determine how to compete in each business area. **Business strategy** defines the major actions by which an organization builds and strengthens its competitive position in the marketplace. A competitive

Zero Motorcycles Leads the Pack

Motorcycles make noise, right? They did until California-based Zero Motorcycles rolled out its new electric models, including one designed to revolutionize urban commuting. The Zero S is different from the other motorcycles you see on the road in the morning. It is lightweight at 225 pounds and accelerates quickly, with the high performance associated with larger motorcycles. But it has just a barely audible hum that is lost in the background noise of commuter traffic. There's more to this innovative electric motorcycle. Able to reach speeds of 90 miles per hour, the 2014 models will include a power pack that is designed to last for over 300,000 miles and is capable of exceeding 130 miles on a single battery charge. For many consumers, these two attributes will make the motorcycle an attractive transportation option. The Zero's low maintenance costs and green appeal makes it an attractive option for the 20 police departments that have purchased it for their patrol officers.

Since the Zero S relies on electricity for power instead of fossil fuels, its emissions are—you guessed it—zero. "Although there is some pollution associated with the production of electricity, a Zero motorcycle produces less than an eighth of the CO_2 pollution per mile [produced by a gasoline-powered] motorcycle," says the company. In addition, the Zero S has a nontoxic lithium ion battery, and most of the motorcycle body is completely recyclable. The power pack is approved for disposal in landfills and recharges in less than four hours when plugged into a standard household outlet, which means that owners can easily recharge overnight or while at work, if necessary. All of these

features are vastly different from those of traditional gasoline-powered motorcycles.

How did Zero Motorcycles differentiate itself from its competitors? Through innovative management thinking. Founder Neal Saiki is also an inventor. He believes in his vision of an environmentally friendly, economical motorcycle. With a base price of $13,000—with no costs for fuel—the Zero S is about as inexpensive as transportation can get, except for a bicycle or walking shoes. In addition, the Zero S qualifies for a 10 percent federal plug-in tax credit, a sales tax deduction, and other incentives offered by different state governments. All of these features are attractive, but Saiki had to convince investors to back the Zero S venture. Saiki recalls: "My wife and I put all our savings into the company."

Yet Saiki didn't give up. Instead he pressed ahead with what he knew was a good product that was different from anything else on the market. "Our goal from the beginning was to engineer a high-performance electric urban street motorcycle that would change the face of the industry. The Zero S is a revolutionary motorcycle that is designed to tackle any city street, hill, or obstacle," Saiki says. "The innovation behind the Zero S is a high-performance motorcycle that also happens to be fully electric and green. The fact that it's electric means not having to get gas and reduced maintenance." That's something different.

A photo of Zero Motorcycles' electric motorcycle, the Zero S. The 2012 model can reach speeds of 88 miles per hour and travel approximately 100 miles on a single battery charge.

Discussion Questions

- The differentiation strategy of Zero S has its advantages. But what might be some of the disadvantages of being a "first mover" in this market?

- How does Neal Saiki's role as inventor and innovator affect the company's business strategy? How might the company's strategy be different if its founder's main area of expertise was finance or advertising instead?

SOURCES: Company website, www.zeromotorcycles.com; S. McKinney, "Why Does Zero Motorcycles' Sales Strategy Include Going After Police Departments?" *Forbes* (online), March 17, 2014, www.forbes.com; New 'Life of Motorcycle' Power Pack," *Marketing Weekly News* (November 26, 2011), p. 1612; J. Welsh, "Motorcycle Review: The Zero S," *The Wall Street Journal*, May 25, 2009, http://online.wsj.com; J. Madslien, "Electric Bikemaker Woos Commuters," *BBC News*, May 12, 2009, http://news.bbc.co.uk; "Zero Motorcycles Zero S First Look," *Motorcycle USA*, April 7, 2009, www.motorcycle-usa.com; A. Schwartz, "The Zero S All-Electric Street Motorcycle Goes to Market," *Fast Company*, April 7, 2009, www.fastcompany.com; C. Squatriglia, "Zero Takes Electric Motorcycles to the Street," *Wired*, April 7, 2009, www.wired.com.

advantage typically results from business strategies based on either keeping costs low or offering products that are unique and highly valued.[26]

Businesses using a **low-cost strategy** try to be efficient and offer a standard, no-frills product. Southwest Airlines' low-cost strategy is simply stated: "to be *the* low-fare airline." That strategy helps with operational planning; when someone suggested offering passengers chicken salad instead of peanuts on some flights, the chief executive asked whether chicken salad would help Southwest be "*the* low-fare airline."[27] Companies that succeed with a low-cost strategy often are large and take advantage of economies of scale—reductions in unit cost from large purchases or manufacturing runs—in production or distribution. Their scale may allow them to buy and sell goods and services

differentiation strategy a strategy an organization uses to build competitive advantage by being unique in its industry or market segment along one or more dimensions

functional strategies strategies implemented by each functional area of the organization to support the organization's business strategy

at a lower price, which leads to higher market share, volume, and ultimately profits. To succeed, an organization using this strategy generally must be the cost leader in its industry or market segment. However, even a cost leader must offer a product that is acceptable to customers.

With a **differentiation strategy**, a company tries to be unique in its industry or market segment along dimensions that customers value. This unique or differentiated position within the industry often is based on high product quality, excellent marketing and distribution, or superior service. The commitment of Zappos (owned by Amazon) to providing customers with a "wow" experience is an excellent example of a differentiation strategy. While other online retailers often skimp on this part of their businesses, Zappos CEO Tony Hsieh is passionate about using every opportunity to connect with and relate to customers. Customer service representatives are encouraged to stay on the line as long as it takes to make the customer happy. Representatives often delight customers with free shipping (both ways), discounts, flowers, and thank-you notes. To date, the longest customer service call lasted approximately six hours.[28] Outstanding customer service is a source of sustainable competitive advantage for Zappos.

Innovation is another ingredient of many differentiation strategies. In the market for toilet paper, Scott Paper Company once determined that it could not afford to compete for institutional sales based on price. Instead the company began offering institutions a free dispenser that would hold larger rolls of paper, reducing the labor cost of replacing empty rolls. Scott initially was the only company selling the larger rolls, so it gained market share while competitors scrambled to catch up.[29]

New technology can support either of these strategies. It can give the business a cost advantage through pioneering lower-cost product designs and low-cost ways to perform needed operations, or it can support differentiation with unique goods or services that increase buyer value and thus command premium prices.

Industry leaders such as Xerox, 3M, Google, PlayStation and Apple built and now maintain their competitive positions through early development and application of new technologies. However, technology leadership also imposes costs and risks:[30]

For example, being a "first mover"—first to market with a new technology—may allow a company to charge a premium price because it faces no competition. Higher prices and greater profits can defray the costs of developing new technologies. This one-time advantage of being the technology leader can be turned into a sustainable advantage if competitors cannot duplicate the technology and the organization can keep building on the lead quickly enough to outpace competitors.

Advantages of Leading	Disadvantages of Leading
First-mover advantage	Greater risks
Little or no competition	Cost of technology development
Greater efficiency	Costs of market development and customer education
Higher profit margins	
Sustainable advantage	Infrastructure costs
Reputation for innovation	Costs of learning and eliminating defects
Establishment of entry barriers	
Occupation of best market niches	Possible cannibalization of existing products
Opportunities to learn	

Patents and scientific expertise can keep an organization in the lead for years.

Being the first to develop or adopt a new technology does not always lead to immediate advantage and high profits, however. Technology leadership imposes high costs and risks that followers do not have to bear. Interestingly, technology followership also can be used to support both low-cost and differentiation strategies. If the follower learns from the leader's experience, it can avoid the costs and risks of technology leadership, thereby establishing a low-cost position. The makers of generic drugs use this type of strategy.

Followership can also support differentiation. By learning from the leader, the follower can adapt the products or delivery systems to fit buyers' needs more closely. Microsoft is famous for having built a successful company on this type of followership. The company's original operating system, MS-DOS, was purchased for $50,000 from Seattle Computer Works to compete with the industry's first desktop operating system, CP/M, sold by Digital Research. Marketing strength, combined with incremental product innovations, enabled Microsoft to take the lead in software categories (for example, Excel's spreadsheet program beat Lotus 1-2-3, which had taken share from the first mover, VisiCalc).[31] Microsoft products, including music players, video game consoles, and web browsers, have been launched after technology leaders paved the way.

Whatever strategy managers adopt, *the most effective strategy is one that competitors are unwilling or unable to imitate.* If the organization's strategic plan is one that could easily be adopted by industry competitors, it may not be sufficiently distinctive or, in the long run, contribute significantly to the organization's competitiveness. For example, in some industries, such as computers, technology advances so fast that the first company to provide a new product is quickly challenged by later entrants offering superior products.[32]

Functional Strategy The final step in strategy formulation is to establish the major functional strategies. **Functional strategies** are implemented by each functional area of the organization to support the business strategy. Major functional areas include production, human resources, marketing, research and development, finance, and distribution. At Wells Fargo, the strategy to grow through cross-selling requires functional strategies for advertising, training employees to cross-sell, and developing systems for sharing information across department boundaries.[33]

Functional strategies typically are developed by functional area executives with input of and approval from the executives responsible for business strategy. Senior strategic decision makers review the functional strategies to ensure that each major department is operating consistently with the organization's business strategies. For example, automated production techniques—even if they save money—would not be appropriate for a piano company like Steinway, whose products are strategically positioned (and priced) as high-quality and handcrafted.

At companies that compete based on product innovation, strategies for research and development are especially critical. But in the recession that occurred at the beginning of the 2000s, General Electric cut back on research in lighting technology just as other companies were making advances in LED lighting. When the economy recovered, customers were looking for innovative lighting, but GE had fallen behind. Based on that experience, GE committed itself to an R&D strategy of maintaining budgets even when sales slow down. In the latest economic downturn, the company continued to fund a project involving the development of new aircraft engines with Honda Motor Company.[34] That investment resulted in the creation of the HF 120 turbofan jet engine that is being used on the new HondaJet aircraft.[35]

● The GE Honda HF120 engine program was launched in 2006 and was selected to power Honda Aircraft Company's advanced light jet, the HondaJet.

corporations and strategy consultants have been paying more attention to implementation. They realize that clever techniques and a good plan do not guarantee success.

Organizations are adopting a more comprehensive view of implementation. The organization structure, technology, human resources, employee reward systems, information systems, organization culture, and leadership style must all support the strategy. Just as an organization's strategy must be matched to the external environment, so must it also fit the multiple factors through which it is implemented. The remainder of this section discusses these factors and the ways they can be used to implement strategy.

Many organizations also are involving more employees in implementing strategies. Managers at all levels are formulating strategy and identifying and executing ways to implement it. Senior executives still may oversee the implementation process but are placing much greater responsibility and authority in the hands of others.

In general, strategy implementation involves four related steps:

1. *Define strategic tasks.* Articulate in simple language what a particular business must do to create or sustain a competitive advantage. Define strategic tasks to help employees understand how they contribute to the organization.

2. *Assess organization capabilities.* Evaluate the organization's ability to implement the strategic tasks. Typically a task force interviews employees and managers to identify issues that help or hinder effective implementation, and then it summarizes the results for top management.

3. *Develop an implementation agenda.* Management decides how it will change its own activities and procedures, how critical interdependencies will be managed, what skills and individuals are needed in key roles, and what structures, measures, information, and rewards might ultimately support the needed behavior.

4. *Create an implementation plan.* The top management team, employee task force, and others develop the implementation plan. The top management team then monitors progress. The employee task force provides feedback about how others in the organization are responding to the changes.

This process, though straightforward, does not always go smoothly.[36] To prevent problems, top managers need to be actively involved, developing a statement of strategy and priorities that employees will accept. Communication is essential, including plenty of information shared by top management

5 | IMPLEMENT THE STRATEGY

As with any plan, simply formulating a good strategy is not enough. Strategic managers also must ensure that the new strategies are implemented effectively and efficiently. Recently

strategic control system a system designed to support managers in evaluating the organization's progress regarding its strategy and, when discrepancies exist, taking corrective action

certainty the state that exists when decision makers have accurate and comprehensive information

uncertainty the state that exists when decision makers have insufficient information

risk the state that exists when the probability of success is less than 100 percent and losses may occur

with all levels of the organization. Managers responsible for strategy implementation should ensure that the organization's various groups are coordinating their work rather than working at cross-purposes. Also, lower-level managers need coaching and training to help them lead their groups effectively. If strategy implementation lacks solid leadership, managers who cannot improve their skills will have to be replaced. Paying close attention to the processes by which strategies are implemented helps executives, managers, and employees ensure that strategic plans are actually carried out.[37]

Finally, Control Your Progress

The final component of the strategic management process is strategic control. A **strategic control system** is designed to support managers in evaluating the organization's progress with its strategy and, when discrepancies exist, taking corrective action. The system must encourage efficient operations that are consistent with the plan while allowing flexibility to adapt to changing conditions. As with all control systems, the organization must develop performance indicators, an information system, and specific mechanisms to monitor progress. More than 20 years in development, the HondaJet had to pass a series of performance milestones before it could be certified as ready for commercial use.[38]

Most strategic control systems include a budget to monitor and control major financial expenditures. In fact, as a first-time manager, you will most likely work with your work unit's budget—a key aspect of your organization's strategic plan. Your executive team may give you budget assumptions and targets for your area, reflecting your part in the overall plan, and you may be asked to revise your budget once all the budgets in your organization have been consolidated and reviewed.

The dual responsibilities of a control system—efficiency and flexibility—often seem contradictory with respect to budgets. The budget usually establishes spending limits, but changing conditions or the need for innovation may require different financial commitments during the period. To solve this dilemma, some companies have created two budgets: strategic and operational. For example, at Texas Instruments the strategic budget is used to create and maintain long-term effectiveness, and the operational budget is tightly monitored to achieve short-term efficiency. The topic of control in general—and budgets in particular—is discussed in more detail in Chapter 14.

6 | MANAGERIAL DECISION MAKING

Managers constantly face problems and opportunities, ranging from simple and routine decisions to problems requiring months of analysis. However, managers often ignore problems because they are unsure how much trouble will be involved in solving the problems, they are concerned about the consequences if they fail, and many management problems are so much more complex than routine tasks.[39] For these reasons, managers may lack the insight, courage, or will to act.

Why is decision making so challenging? Most managerial decisions lack structure and entail risk, uncertainty, and conflict.

Lack of structure is typical of managerial decisions.[40] Usually there is no automatic procedure to follow. Problems are novel and unstructured, leaving the decision maker uncertain about how to proceed. In other words, a manager's decisions most often have the characteristics of nonprogrammed decisions:[41]

With nonprogrammed decisions, *risk and uncertainty* are the rule. If you have all the information you need, and can predict precisely the consequences of your actions, you are operating under a condition of **certainty**.[42] But perfect certainty is rare. More often managers face **uncertainty**, meaning they have insufficient information to know the consequences of different actions. Decision makers may have strong opinions—they may feel sure of themselves—but they are still operating under uncertainty if they lack pertinent information and cannot estimate accurately the likelihood of different results.

When you can estimate the likelihood of various consequences but still do not know with certainty what will happen, you are facing **risk**. Risk exists when the probability of

Programmed Decisions	Nonprogrammed Decisions
Problem is frequent, repetitive, and routine, with much certainty regarding cause-and-effect relationships.	Problem is novel and unstructured, with much uncertainty regarding cause-and-effect relationships.
Decision procedure depends on policies, rules, and definite procedures.	Decision procedure needs creativity, intuition, tolerance for ambiguity, and creative problem solving.
Examples: periodic reorders of inventory; procedure for admitting patients.	Examples: diversification into new products and markets; purchase of experimental equipment; reorganization of departments.

● John Chambers, chief executive officer of Cisco Systems, Inc., the world's largest maker of networking equipment.

an action succeeding is less than 100 percent and losses may occur. If the decision is the wrong one, you may lose money, time, reputation, or other important assets. Risk as a quality of managerial decision making differs from *taking* a risk. Although it sometimes seems as though risk takers are admired and that entrepreneurs and investors thrive on taking risks, good decision makers prefer to *manage* risk. Knowing that their decisions entail risk, they anticipate the risk, minimize it, and control it.

For example, Facebook took a risk when it recently purchased WhatsApp for $19 billion. At the time of Facebook's largest purchase ever, WhatsApp reported having 450 million users of its popular chat app. Seventy percent of WhatsApp users send texts on a daily basis (which is a higher engagement rate than Facebook users). Adding to its attractiveness is the fact that WhatsApp is dominant in several countries outside of the United States. Facebook is hoping this acquisition of WhatsApp will help the company get closer to reaching its mission of "connecting everyone in the world."[43] Was Facebook's decision to acquire WhatsApp made under conditions of uncertainty or risk?

Formal Decision Making Has Six Stages

Faced with these challenges, how can you make good decisions? The ideal decision-making process moves through six stages:

1. Identify and diagnose the problem.
2. Generate alternative solutions.
3. Evaluate alternatives.
4. Make the choice.
5. Implement the decision.
6. Evaluate the decision.

These stages are general and applicable to any decision.

6.1 | Identifying and Diagnosing the Problem

The decision-making process begins with recognition that a problem (or opportunity) exists and must be solved (or should be pursued). Typically a manager realizes some discrepancy between the current state (the way things are) and a desired state (the way things ought to be). To detect such discrepancies, managers compare current performance against (1) *past* performance, (2) the *current* performance of other organizations or units, or (3) *future* expected performance as determined by plans and forecasts.[44] Larry Cohen, who founded Accurate Perforating with his father, knew his company was having difficulty making a profit because costs at the metal company were rising while the prices customers were willing to pay remained unchanged. However, when the company's bank demanded immediate payment of its $1.5 million loan, Cohen realized the problem had to be solved, or the company would have to sell off all its assets and close.[45] You will learn more about how Cohen solved this problem as we look at the subsequent stages of the decision process.

The "problem" may actually be an opportunity that needs to be exploited—a gap between what the organization is doing now and what it can do to create a more positive future. In that case, decisions involve choosing how to seize the opportunity. To recognize important opportunities as a manager, you will need to understand your company's macro and competitive environments (described in Chapter 3), including the opportunities offered by technological developments. According to Cisco Systems CEO John Chambers, managers who are ignorant about technology risk missing important transitions— dramatic shifts in the ways companies serve customers and work with their suppliers. Chambers advises managers to stay current by talking to people who challenge you and are willing to teach you.[46]

Recognizing that a problem or opportunity exists is only the beginning of this stage. The decision maker also must want to do something about it and must believe that the resources and abilities necessary for solving the problem exist.[47] Then the decision maker must dig in deeper and attempt to *diagnose* the true cause of the situation. Asking why, of yourself and others, is essential. Unfortunately, in the earlier example of Accurate Perforating, Larry Cohen did not ask why profits were declining; he simply assumed that the company's costs were too high.[48] A more thorough approach would include questions such as these:[49]

- Is there a difference between what is actually happening and what should be happening?

- How can you describe the deviation, as specifically as possible?

- What is/are the cause(s) of the deviation?

- What specific goals should be met?

- Which of these goals are absolutely critical to the success of the decision?

ready-made solutions
ideas that have been seen or tried before

custom-made solutions
new, creative solutions designed specifically for the problem

maximizing a decision realizing the best possible outcome

6.2 | Generating Alternative Solutions

The second stage of decision making links problem diagnosis to the development of alternative courses of action aimed at solving the problem. Managers generate at least some alternative solutions based on past experiences.[50]

Solutions range from ready-made to custom-made.[51] Decision makers who search for **ready-made solutions** use ideas they have tried before or follow the advice of others who have faced similar problems. **Custom-made solutions**, by contrast, must be designed for specific problems. This technique often combines ideas into new, creative solutions. Potentially, custom-made solutions can be devised for any challenge.

Often, many more alternatives are available than managers realize. For example, what would you do if one of your competitors reduced prices? An obvious choice would be to reduce your own prices, but the only sure outcome of a price cut is lower profits. Fortunately, cutting prices is not the only alternative. If one of your competitors cuts prices, you should generate multiple options and thoroughly forecast the consequences of these different options. Options include emphasizing consumer risks to low-priced products, building awareness of your products' features and overall quality, and communicating your cost advantage to your competitors so they realize that they can't win a price war. If you do decide to cut your price as a last resort, do it fast—if you do it slowly, your competitors will gain sales in the meantime, which may embolden them to employ the same tactic again in the future.[52]

The example of Accurate Perforating shows the importance of looking for every alternative. The company had become successful by purchasing metal from steel mills, punching many holes in it to make screenlike sheets, and selling this material in bulk to distributors, who sold it to metal workshops, which used it to make custom products. Cohen admits, "We wound up in a very competitive situation where the only thing we were selling was price." Management cut costs wherever possible, avoiding investment in new machinery or processes. The result was an out-of-date factory managed by people accustomed to resisting change. Only after the bank called in its loan did Cohen begin to see alternatives. The bank offered one painful idea: liquidate the company. It also suggested a management consultant, who advised renegotiating payment schedules with the company's suppliers. Cohen also received advice from managers of a company Accurate had purchased a year before. That company, Semrow Perforated & Expanded Metals, sold more sophisticated products directly to manufacturers, and Semrow's managers urged Cohen to invest more in finished metal products such as theirs.[53]

6.3 | Evaluating Alternatives

The third stage of decision making involves determining the value or adequacy of the alternatives that were generated. In other words, which solution will be the best?

Too often, alternatives are evaluated with insufficient thought or logic. At Accurate Perforating, Cohen made changes to cut costs but dismissed the idea to invest in marketing finished metal products, even though these product lines were more profitable. Accurate's general manager, Aaron Kamins (also Cohen's nephew), counseled that money spent on finished metal products would be a distraction from Accurate's core business. That reasoning persuaded Cohen, even though it meant focusing on unprofitable product lines.[54]

Obviously alternatives should be evaluated more carefully. Fundamental to this process is to predict the consequences that will occur if the various options are put into effect. Managers should consider several types of consequences. They include quantitative measures of success, such as lower costs, higher sales, lower employee turnover, and higher profits. Also, the decisions made at all levels of the organization should contribute to, and not interfere with, achieving the company's overall strategies. Business professors Joseph Bower and Clark Gilbert say that when it comes to decisions about investing in new projects, managers typically focus on whether alternatives generate the most sales or savings without asking the more basic question: In light of our strategy, is this investment an idea we should support at all?[55] When the recent downturn in the U.S. economy required cutbacks, many organizations as diverse as the University of California system, the State of North Carolina, American Airlines, and United Parcel Service evaluated the alternatives of layoffs (permanent job cuts) versus furloughs (requiring employees to take some unpaid time off until demand picks up again). In 2009, the total number of furloughed employees in the United States reached 6.5 million.[56] While layoffs save more money per employee because the company doesn't have to continue paying for benefits, furloughs attempt to maintain relationships with talented employees, who are more likely than laid-off workers to return when the company needs them again. Furloughs may seem kinder to employees, who can hope to return to work eventually, but workers may not be eligible for unemployment compensation during the furlough period.[57]

The success or failure of the decision will go into the track records of those involved in making it. That means, as Cohen eventually learned, the decision maker needs to know when to call on others to provide expertise. The mistake of not fully evaluating alternatives and identifying consequences is not limited to small family businesses. When John Sculley was Apple's chief executive, he convinced himself that he was a technology expert and made some poor decisions related to Apple's pioneering launch of a personal digital assistant (PDA), the now-forgotten Newton. Under Sculley's direction, Apple packed the Newton with features, such as handwriting recognition, that customers didn't care about and didn't want to pay the Newton's high price to obtain. In contrast, Steve Jobs

Take Charge of Your Career

Baby Boomers Launch Alternative Careers

In the United States there are approximately 78 million baby boomers, born between 1946 and 1964. Known for their work ethic, independent thinking, and growth orientation, many share the belief that with hard work, anything is possible. Without a doubt, boomers have accomplished a great deal in their careers over the past few decades. It is no wonder that, prior to this recent economic downturn, many of these individuals were planning to retire and enjoy life more by traveling, being with family, pursuing hobbies, and the like.

The recent recession has changed that for many boomers. The persistently high unemployment rate, layoffs, frozen pensions, declining equity in homes, age discrimination in hiring, and shrinking value of 401(k) portfolios have caused many boomers to postpone their retirement plans and continue working for many more years.

According to the Bureau of Labor Statistics, the fastest-growing segment of the U.S. workforce between now and 2018 will be employees aged 55 and older. For those who have been laid off, many older workers have difficulty finding full-time, permanent employment with an existing organization. This is motivating a growing number of boomers to follow the "road less traveled" and shift to part-time status, provide consulting services (sometimes for their ex-employers), go back to school, dive into a new "always wanted to do that" career, or start their own ventures. In essence, boomers are reinventing themselves as in a "Career 2.0" sort of way. Consider Lori Bitter, a 50-year-old marketing manager who ran a unit for J. Walter Thompson, the world's largest advertising agency. After being laid off, she and three other former JWT employees used their severance pay to start a new advertising firm, Continuum Crew. To date, the new venture has grown to 15 employees and plans to expand further as soon as it raises the capital. Bitter is enjoying her alternative career and relishes the flexible schedule that allows her to spend more time with her husband and grandchildren.

Younger generations at work can learn something from baby boomers' tenacity and can-do attitude. As the old adage says, "when one door closes, another one opens." Always take charge of your career.

SOURCES: Adapted from D. Rosato, "The Best Reason to Rethink Retirement," *Money* (June 2012), p. 98; E. Brandon, "7 Tips for Baby Boomers Turning 65 in 2011," *U.S. News and World Report* (January 10, 2011), http://money.usnews.com; D. L. Jacobs, "In a Brutal Economy, Boomers Rewrite the Next Chapter," Investment Guide Issue, *Forbes* (December 5, 2011), www.forbes.com; M. Toosi, "Labor Force Projections to 2018: Older Workers Staying More Active," *Monthly Labor Review* (November 2009), http://bls.gov/opub/mlr/2009/11/art3full.pdf; T. J. Erickson, *Retire Retirement: Career Strategies for the Boomer Generation* (Cambridge, MA: Harvard Business School Press, 2008).

---

charged a hardware engineer, Tony Fadell, with the development of the iPod, and Fadell decided to collaborate with a firm that had already developed much of the technology that would be used in that successful portable music player.[58]

To evaluate alternatives, refer to your original goals, defined in the first stage. Which goals does each alternative meet and fail to meet? Which alternatives are most acceptable to you and to other important stakeholders? If several alternatives may solve the problem, which can be implemented at the lowest cost or greatest profit? If no alternative achieves all your goals, perhaps you can combine two or more of the best ones. Several more questions help:[59]

- Is our information about alternatives complete and current? If not, can we get more and better information?

- Does the alternative meet our primary objectives?

- What problems could we have if we implement the alternative?

Of course results cannot be forecast with perfect accuracy. But sometimes decision makers can build in safeguards against an uncertain future by considering the potential consequences of several different scenarios. Then they generate contingency plans, described earlier in the discussion of strategic planning. Some scenarios will seem more likely than others, and some may seem highly improbable. Ultimately one of the scenarios will prove to be more accurate than the others. The process of considering multiple scenarios raises important "what if?" questions for decision makers and highlights the need for preparedness and contingency plans. As you read this, what economic scenario is unfolding? What are the important current events and trends? What scenarios could evolve six or eight years from now? How will *you* prepare?

6.4 | Making the Choice

Once you have considered the possible consequences of your options, it is time to make your decision. Some managers are more comfortable with the analysis stage. Especially with all the advanced technology that is available, quantitatively inclined people can easily tweak the assumptions behind every scenario in countless ways. But the temptation can lead to "paralysis by analysis"—that is, indecisiveness caused by too much analysis rather than the kind of active, assertive decision making that is essential for seizing new opportunities or thwarting challenges. The decision will differ according to the criteria and method used:[60]

- **Maximizing** is achieving the best possible outcome, the one that realizes the greatest positive consequences and the fewest negative consequences. In other words, maximizing results in the greatest benefit at the lowest cost, with the largest expected total return.

satisficing choosing an option that is acceptable, although not necessarily the best or perfect

optimizing achieving the best possible balance among several goals

Maximizing requires searching thoroughly for a complete range of alternatives, carefully assessing each alternative, comparing one to another, and then choosing or creating the very best. As a manager, you won't always have time to maximize; many decisions require quick responses, not exhaustive analysis. The necessary analysis requires money as well as time. But for decisions with large consequences, such as determining the company's strategy, maximizing is worthwhile—even essential.

- **Satisficing** is choosing the first option that is minimally acceptable or adequate; the choice appears to meet a targeted goal or criterion. When you satisfice, you compare your choice against your goal, not against other options, and you end your search for alternatives at the first one that is okay. When the consequences are not huge, satisficing can actually be the ideal approach. But when managers satisfice, they may fail to consider important options. For example, if you need a new sales manager and your goal is to get this person hired within two weeks, you are satisficing if you hire the first adequate candidate you interview. By not interviewing more candidates, you will miss out on other, potentially better-qualified individuals that could have led your sales team to achieve higher performance over the next few years.

- **Optimizing** means achieving the best possible balance among several goals. Perhaps, in purchasing equipment, you are interested in quality and durability as well as price. Instead of buying the cheapest piece of equipment that works, you buy the one with the best combination of attributes, even though some options may be better on the price criterion and others may offer better quality and durability. Likewise, for achieving business goals, one marketing strategy could maximize sales while a different strategy maximizes profit. An optimizing strategy achieves the best balance among multiple goals.

6.5 | Implementing the Decision

The decision-making process does not end once a choice is made. The chosen alternative must be implemented. Sometimes the people involved in making the choice must put it into effect. At other times, they delegate the responsibility for implementation, as when a top management team changes a policy or operating procedure and has operational managers carry out the change.

Unfortunately people sometimes make decisions but don't take action. Implementing may fail to occur when talking a lot is mistaken for doing a lot; if people just assume that a

Did You Know?

A scenario may use numbers that sound reasonable, but you should look at the data in different ways to check your assumptions. As Dean Kamen's company developed the Segway scooter, Kamen decided that each year Segway could capture 0.1 percent of the world's population. That percentage might sound conservative, but consider that 0.1 percent of 6 billion people is 6 million Segways a year! Kamen decided to build a factory that could produce 40,000 units a month; five years later, sales had reached fewer than 25,000.[61]

decision will "happen"; when people forget that merely making a decision changes nothing; when meetings, plans, and reports are seen as "actions," even if they don't affect what people actually do; and if managers don't check to ensure that what was decided was actually done.[62]

Those who implement the decision should *understand* the choice and why it was made. They also must be *committed* to its successful implementation. These needs can be met by involving those people in the early stages of the decision process. At Federal Warehouse Company, located in East Peoria, Illinois, executives decided to teach all the employees how to interpret the company's financial statements. Managers routinely review the company's performance in detail, and they invite all employees to participate in solving problems, including how to reduce costs by making the workplace safer. Employees—who had once assumed that if everyone was busy, the company must be profitable—have begun making many creative decisions that are helping profits climb.[63] By including all employees in the decision making, Federal fosters full understanding and total commitment.

Managers should plan implementation carefully by taking several steps:[64]

1. Determine how things will look when the decision is fully operational.

2. Chronologically order, perhaps with a flow diagram, the steps necessary to achieve a fully operational decision.

3. List the resources and activities required to implement each step.

4. Estimate the time needed for each step.

5. Assign responsibility for each step to specific individuals.

Decision makers should presume that implementation will *not* go smoothly. It is very useful to take a little extra time to *identify potential problems* and *identify potential opportunities* associated with implementation. Then you can take actions to prevent problems and also be ready to seize on unexpected opportunities.

Many of the chapters in this book address implementation issues: how to allocate resources, organize for results, lead and motivate people, manage change, and so on. View the chapters from that perspective, and learn as much as you can about how to implement properly.

6.6 | Evaluating the Decision

The final stage in the decision-making process is evaluating the decision. It involves collecting information on how well the decision is working. If you set quantifiable goals—a 20 percent increase in sales, a 95 percent reduction in accidents, 100 percent on-time deliveries—before implementation of the solution, you can gather objective data for accurately determining the decision's success or failure.

Decision evaluation is useful whether the conclusion is positive or negative. Feedback that suggests the decision is working implies that the decision should be continued and perhaps applied elsewhere in the organization. Negative feedback means one of two things:

1. Implementation will require more time, resources, effort, or thought.

2. The decision was a bad one.

If the decision appears inappropriate, it's back to the drawing board. Then the process cycles back to the first stage: (re)definition of the problem. The decision-making process begins anew, preferably with more information, new suggestions, and an approach that attempts to eliminate the mistakes made the first time around. This is the stage where Accurate Perforating finally began to see hope. When cost-cutting efforts could not keep the company ahead of the competition or in favor with the bank, Larry Cohen turned the problem over to his general manager, Aaron Kamins. He gave Kamins 90 days to show that he could keep the business from going under. Kamins hired a consultant to help him identify more alternatives and make more professional decisions about investment and marketing. This stage of the implementation showed Kamins that the company needed better-educated management, and he began taking courses in an executive education program. With what he learned in school and from his consultant, Kamins realized that the advice he had received from the managers at the Semrow subsidiary—to invest in producing finished metal products—was wiser than he had realized. He arranged new financing to purchase modern equipment, hired salespeople, developed a website, and finally began to see profits from his improved decision making.[65]

> **LO7** Give examples of some individual barriers that affect rational decision making

7 | HUMAN NATURE ERECTS BARRIERS TO GOOD DECISIONS

Vigilant and full execution of the six-stage decision-making process is the exception rather than the rule. But when managers use such rational processes, better decisions result.[66] Managers who make sure they engage in these processes are more effective.

Why don't people automatically invoke such rational processes? It is easy to neglect or improperly execute these processes, and decisions are influenced by subjective psychological biases, time pressures, and social realities.

7.1 | Psychological Biases

Decision makers are far from objective in the way they gather, evaluate, and apply information in making their choices. People have biases that interfere with objective rationality. Here are just a few of the many documented subjective biases:[67]

- **Illusion of control**—a belief that one can influence events even when one has no control over what will happen. Such overconfidence can lead to failure because decision makers ignore risks and fail to evaluate the odds of success objectively. In addition, they may believe they can do no wrong, or hold a general optimism about the future that can lead them to believe they are immune to risk and failure.[68] In addition, managers may overrate the value of their experience. They may believe that a previous project met its goals because of their decisions, so they can succeed by doing everything the same way on the next project. Rohit Girdhar admits that he held this type of bias until he tried a computer simulation that he assumed would confirm his skills as an experienced manager of software programmers. In the simulation, the workload increased, and he hired more workers, as he had in his prior jobs. But the added workers weren't as productive as his experience told him they would be, and his project fell behind. Girdhar learned to question his assumptions before making decisions.[69] Managers can correct for this problem by developing a realistic picture of their strengths and weaknesses and seeking out advisers who can point out consequences they may not have considered.

- **Framing effects**—phrasing or presenting problems or decision alternatives in a way that lets subjective influences override objective facts. In one example, managers indicated a desire to invest more money in a course of action that was reported to have a 70 percent chance of profit than in one said to have a 30 percent chance of loss.[70] The choices had equivalent chances of success; the way the options were expressed determined the managers' choices. Managers may also frame a problem as similar to problems they have already handled, so they don't search for new alternatives. When CEO Richard Fuld tackled financial problems at Lehman Brothers as the mortgage market tumbled, he assumed that the situation was much the same as a financial crisis in the late 1990s. Unfortunately for Lehman Brothers, the recent crisis was far worse. The firm declared bankruptcy—the largest in U.S. history—helping to send global financial markets into a tailspin. Similarly, when the head of the operations center of the Department of Homeland Security prepared for Hurricane Katrina as it headed for New Orleans, he assumed the storm would be like Florida hurricanes he had prepared for in the past. As information came in, he focused on the data that fit his expectations, but Katrina turned out to be far more devastating.[71]

illusion of control people's belief that they can influence events, even when they have no control over what will happen

framing effects a decision bias influenced by the way in which a problem or decision alternative is phrased or presented

● In 2005, the large-scale flooding and damage caused by Hurricane Katrina in New Orleans and surrounding areas caught many governmental decision makers by surprise. One reason for the miscalculation was that officials prepared for the storm and its potential effects by framing it like other, less damaging hurricanes that had recently hit Florida.

- **Discounting the future**—in evaluating alternatives, weighing short-term costs and benefits more heavily than longer-term costs and benefits. This bias applies to students who don't study, workers who take the afternoon off to play golf when they really need to work, and managers who hesitate to invest funds in research and development programs that may not pay off until far into the future. In all these cases, avoiding short-term costs or seeking short-term rewards yields problems in the long term. Discounting the future partly explains government budget deficits, environmental destruction, and decaying urban infrastructure.[72]

7.2 | Time Pressures

In today's rapidly changing business environment, the premium is on acting quickly and keeping pace. The most conscientiously made business decisions can become irrelevant and even disastrous if managers take too long to make them.

To make decisions quickly, many managers rely on simple rule-of-thumb techniques that have worked in the past and in so doing, reduce the amount of time they spend analyzing information relevant to the decision.[73] These strategies may speed up decision making, but they reduce decision *quality*. Carl Camden, CEO of Kelly Services, believed that rapid-fire decisions were the sign of a dynamic executive until he saw how this approach could hurt decision quality. After Camden joined Kelly, managers presented a proposal for expanding the temporary services firm into the business of placing substitute teachers. Camden quickly came up with a half dozen reasons to say no. However, the managers kept returning with similar

proposals until he gave in and launched the new division. It became one of the company's fastest-growing operations.[74]

Can managers under time pressure make decisions that are timely and high quality? A recent study of decision-making processes in microcomputer firms showed some important differences between fast-acting and slower firms.[75] The fast-acting firms realized significant competitive advantages without sacrificing the quality of their decisions. They used three important tactics:

1. Instead of relying on old data, long-range planning, and futuristic forecasts, they focus on *real-time information:* current information obtained with little or no time delay. For example, they constantly monitor daily operating measures like work in process rather than checking periodically the traditional accounting-based indicators such as profitability.

2. They *involve people more effectively and efficiently* in the decision-making process. They rely heavily on trusted experts, and this yields both good advice and the confidence to act quickly despite uncertainty.

3. They take a *realistic view of conflict:* they value differing opinions, but they know that if disagreements are not resolved, the top executive must make the final choice in the end. Slow-moving firms, in contrast, are stymied by conflict. Like the fast-moving firms, they seek consensus, but when disagreements persist, they fail to come to a decision.

7.3 | Social Realities

Many decisions are made by a group rather than by an individual manager. In slow-moving firms, interpersonal factors decrease decision-making effectiveness. Even the manager acting alone is accountable to the boss and to others and must consider the preferences and reactions of many people. Important managerial decisions are marked by conflict among interested parties. Therefore, many decisions are the result of intensive social interactions, bargaining, and politicking.

LO8 Summarize principles for group decision making

8 | GROUPS MAKE MANY DECISIONS

Sometimes a manager convenes a group of people to make an important decision. Some advise that in today's complex business environment, significant problems should *always* be tackled by groups.[76] As a result, managers must understand how groups operate and how to use them to improve decision making.

8.1 | Groups Can Help

The basic philosophy behind using a group to make decisions is captured by the adage "Two heads are better than one." But is this statement really valid? Yes, it is—potentially. If enough time is available, groups usually make higher-quality decisions than most individuals acting alone. However, groups often are inferior to the *best* individual.[77]

As summarized in Exhibit 5.9, how well the group performs depends on how effectively it capitalizes on the potential advantages and minimizes the potential problems of using a group. Using groups to make a decision offers at least five potential advantages:[78]

1. More *information* is available when several people are making the decision. If one member doesn't have all the facts or the pertinent expertise, another member might.

2. A greater number of *perspectives* on the issues, or different *approaches* to solving the problem, are available. The problem may be new to one group member but familiar to another. Or the group may need to consider several viewpoints—financial, legal, marketing, human resources, and so on—to achieve an optimal solution.

3. Group discussion provides an opportunity for *intellectual stimulation*. It can get people thinking and unleash their creativity to a far greater extent than would be possible with individual decision making.

4. People who participate in a group discussion are more likely to *understand* why the decision was made. They will have heard the relevant arguments both for the chosen alternative and against the rejected alternatives.

5. Group discussion typically leads to a higher level of *commitment* to the decision. Buying into the proposed solution translates into high motivation to ensure that it is executed well.

The first three potential advantages of using a group suggest that better-informed, higher-quality decisions will result when managers involve people with different backgrounds, perspectives, and access to information. The last two advantages imply that decisions will be implemented more successfully when managers involve the people responsible for implementing the decision as early in the deliberations as possible.

8.2 | Groups Can Hurt

Things *can* go wrong when groups make decisions. Most of the potential problems concern the process through which group members interact with one another:[79]

• Sometimes one group member *dominates* the discussion. When this occurs—as when a strong leader makes his or her preferences clear—the result is the same as it would have been if the dominant individual had made the decision alone. However, the dominant person does not necessarily have the most valid opinions, and even if that person leads the group to a good decision, the process will have wasted everyone else's time.

• *Satisficing* is more likely with groups. Most people don't like meetings and will do what they can to end them. This may include criticizing members who want to continue exploring new and better alternatives. The result is a satisficing, not an optimizing or maximizing, decision.

discounting the future a bias weighting short-term costs and benefits more heavily than longer-term costs and benefits

● Groups spur creative thinking, effective problem solving, and goal commitment. However, not all groups perform to their full potential, as they are susceptible to domination by a few members, satisficing, and groupthink. Strong leadership and engaged group members can increase the odds that the group performs effectively.

Exhibit 5.9   Advantages and disadvantages of using groups

Advantages	Disadvantages
1. More information improves decisions.	1. One person dominates the discussion and undermines the group process.
2. Different perspectives enhance problem solving.	2. Group produces a satisficing, not optimizing or maximizing, decision.
3. Group discussion spurs thinking.	3. Pressure to avoid disagreement leads to groupthink.
4. Involvement in group process leads to enhanced understanding of decisions.	4. Original goals are displaced by new, less important goals.
5. Participation in problem solving increases commitment to decisions.	

Source: Adapted from N. R. F. Maier, "Assets and Liabilities in Group Problem Solving: The Need for an Integrative Function," *Psychological Review* 74 (1967), pp. 239–49.

groupthink a phenomenon that occurs in decision making when group members avoid disagreement as they strive for consensus

goal displacement a condition that occurs when a decision-making group loses sight of its original goal and a new, less important goal emerges

devil's advocate a person who has the job of criticizing ideas to ensure that their downsides are fully explored

dialectic a structured debate comparing two conflicting courses of action

brainstorming a process in which group members generate as many ideas about a problem as they can; criticism is withheld until all ideas have been proposed

- *Pressure to avoid disagreement* can lead to a phenomenon called groupthink. **Groupthink** occurs when people choose not to disagree or raise objections because they don't want to break up a positive team spirit. Some groups want to think as one, tolerate no dissension, and strive to remain cordial. Such groups are overconfident, complacent, and perhaps too willing to take risks. Pressure to go along with the group's preferred solution stifles creativity and other behaviors characteristic of vigilant decision making.

- *Goal displacement* often occurs in groups. Group members' goal should be to come up with the best possible solution. With **goal displacement**, new goals emerge to replace the original ones. When group members have different opinions, attempts at rational persuasion might become a heated disagreement, and then winning the argument becomes the new goal.

8.3 | Groups Must Be Well Led

Effective managers pay close attention to the group process; they manage it carefully. Effectively managing group decision making has three requirements:

1. *Appropriate leadership style:* The group leader must try to keep process-related problems to a minimum by ensuring that everyone has a chance to participate, not allowing the group to pressure individuals to conform, and keeping everyone focused on the decision-making objective.

2. *Constructive use of disagreement and conflict:* Total and consistent agreement among group members can be destructive, leading to groupthink, uncreative solutions, and a waste of the knowledge and diverse viewpoints that individuals bring to the group. A certain amount of *constructive* conflict should exist.[80] Conflict should be task-related, involving differences in ideas and viewpoints, rather than personal.[81] Still, even task-related conflict can hurt performance;[82] disagreement is good only when managed properly. Managers can increase the likelihood of constructive conflict by assembling teams of different types of people, creating frequent interactions and active debates, and encouraging multiple alternatives from a variety of perspectives.[83] Methods for encouraging different views include assigning someone the role of **devil's advocate**—the job of criticizing ideas. Or the leader may use a process called **dialectic**, a structured debate between two conflicting courses of action.[84] Structured debates between plans and counterplans can be useful before making a strategic decision—one team might present the case for acquiring a firm while another team advocates not making the acquisition.

3. *Enhancement of creativity:* To "get" creativity out of other people, give creative efforts the credit they are due, and don't punish creative failures.[85] Avoid extreme time pressure if possible.[86] Support some innovative ideas without heeding projected returns. Stimulate and challenge people intellectually, and give people some creative freedom. Listen to employees' ideas, and allow enough time to explore different ideas. Put together groups of people with different styles of thinking and behaving. Get your people in touch with customers, and let them bounce ideas around. Protect your people from managers who demand immediate payoffs, don't understand the importance of creative contributions, or try to take credit for others' successes. People are likely to be more creative if they believe they are capable, know that their coworkers expect creativity, and believe that their employer values creativity.[87] A common technique for eliciting creative ideas is brainstorming. In **brainstorming**, group members generate as many ideas about a problem as they can. As the ideas are presented, they are posted so everyone can read them and use the ideas as building blocks. The group is encouraged to say anything that comes to mind, except to criticize other people or their ideas.

Study Checklist

- Did you tear out the perforated student review card at the back of the text to revisit learning objectives and key terms and definitions?

Connect® Management is available for M Management. Additional resources include:

- Interactive Applications:
  - Comprehension Case: SWOT Analysis
  - Drag & Drop: Psychological Bias in a Job Search
  - Sequencing/Timeline: Decision Making at Borders Books
  - Video Case: Strategy in Action at Panera Bread

- LearnSmart—Multiple choice questions help you determine what you already know, are not sure about, or need to practice based on your score. And with SmartBook, you can read the relevant section in the eBook as well as practice and recharge what you've learned.

- Chapter Videos: PODS, Ball Corporation

- Young Manager Speaks Out: Sheryl Freeman, Program Manager

SmartBook:

The First Personalized Reading and Learning Experience

Go to: LearnSmartAdvantage.com

6 chapter

Entrepreneurship

Learning Objectives

After studying Chapter 6, you will be able to

LO1 Describe why people become entrepreneurs and what it takes, personally.

LO2 Summarize how to assess opportunities to start new businesses.

LO3 Identify common causes of success and failure.

LO4 Discuss common management challenges.

LO5 Explain how to increase your chances of success, including good business planning.

LO6 Describe how managers of large companies can foster entrepreneurship.

Some extraordinary individuals have founded companies that have become famously successful:[1]

- Bill Gates and Paul Allen started Microsoft.
- Oprah Winfrey founded Harpo Productions.
- Steve Jobs and Steve Wozniak created Apple Computer.
- Mary Kay Ash established Mary Kay.
- N. R. Narayana Murthy founded Infosys.
- Martha Stewart started Martha Stewart Living Omnimedia.
- Larry Page and Sergey Brin founded Google.
- Estée Lauder created her namesake company.
- Elon Musk founded Tesla Motors and Space X.
- Mark Zuckerberg started Facebook.
- Vera Wang founded her namesake firm.

As they and countless others have demonstrated, great opportunity is available to talented people who are willing to work hard to achieve their dreams. **Entrepreneurship** occurs when an enterprising individual pursues a lucrative opportunity under conditions of uncertainty.[2] To be an entrepreneur is to initiate and build an organization, rather than being only a passive part of one.[3] It involves creating *new* systems, resources, or processes to produce *new* goods or services and/or serve *new* markets.[4]

Richard Branson is a perfect example. He seems to have business in his blood. He was only a teen when he started his first company, a magazine called *Student,* in the mid-1960s. In 1970 Branson launched his next enterprise, the iconic Virgin Records, which generated his first fortune. Since then, Branson has built 300 other businesses, all under the Virgin umbrella: a space travel venture, a global airline, a mobile phone enterprise, and companies in financial services, publishing, and retailing. Today the Virgin empire has nearly 50,000 employees in 50 countries, and Branson has a mind-boggling net worth of more than $5 billion. In 1999 he was knighted by Queen Elizabeth.[5]

Entrepreneurs differ from managers generally. An entrepreneur *is* a manager but engages in additional activities that not all managers do.[6] Traditionally, managers operate in a formal management hierarchy with well-defined authority and responsibility. In contrast, entrepreneurs use networks of contacts more than formal authority. And although managers usually prefer to own assets, entrepreneurs often rent or use assets on a temporary basis. Some say that managers often are slower to act and tend to avoid risk, whereas entrepreneurs are quicker to act and actively manage risk.

An entrepreneur's organization may be small, but it differs from a typical small business:[7]

- A **small business** has fewer than 100 employees, is independently owned and operated, is not dominant in its field, and is not characterized by many innovative practices. Small business owners tend not to manage particularly aggressively, and they expect normal, moderate sales, profits, and growth.

LISTEN & LEARN ● ONLINE

YOUNG MANAGERS
Speak Out!

"I encourage my employees to be entrepreneurial. To think. To be creative. I encourage them by asking the hard questions and making sure they have a solid plan going forward."

—Joe Gaspar, Bicycle Shop Owner/Manager

---

study tip 6

Engage your professors

Even though you are extremely busy, you should find time to visit with your professors when you have questions about the reading material or a challenging assignment. Similarly, you should go to office hours within a few days of taking an exam to see what questions you missed. This is a good time to ask the professor's advice regarding how to improve your studying strategy to make a higher grade on the next exam.

> ## "Chase the vision, not the money. The money will end up following you."
>
> —Tony Hsieh, CEO of Zappos

• An **entrepreneurial venture** has growth and high profitability as its primary objectives. Entrepreneurs manage aggressively and develop innovative strategies, practices, and products. They and their financial backers usually seek rapid growth, immediate and high profits, and sometimes a quick sellout with large capital gains.

Entrepreneurship Excitement Consider these words from Jeffry Timmons, a leading entrepreneurship scholar and author: "During the past 30 years, America has unleashed the most revolutionary generation the nation has experienced since its founding in 1776. This new generation of entrepreneurs has altered permanently the economic and social structure of this nation and the world . . . . It will determine more than any other single impetus how the nation and the world will live, work, learn, and lead in this century and beyond."[8]

Overhype? Sounds like it could be, but it's not. Entrepreneurship is transforming economies all over the world, and the global economy in general. In the United States since 1980, more than 95 percent of the wealth has been created by entrepreneurs.[9] It has been estimated that since World War II, small entrepreneurial firms have generated 95 percent of all radical innovation in the United States. The Small Business Administration has found that in states with more small business start-ups, statewide economies tend to grow faster and employment levels tend to be higher than in states with less entrepreneurship.[10] An estimated 20 million Americans are running a young business or actively trying to start one.[11]

The self-employed love the entrepreneurial process, and they report the highest levels of pride, satisfaction, and income. Importantly, entrepreneurship is not about the privileged descendants of the Rockefellers and the Vanderbilts; instead it provides opportunity and upward mobility for anyone who performs well.[12]

Myths about Entrepreneurship Simply put, entrepreneurs generate new ideas and turn them into business ventures.[13] But entrepreneurship is not simple, and it is frequently misunderstood. Exhibit 6.1 describes 12 myths and realities regarding entrepreneurship.[14]

Here is another myth: being an entrepreneur is great because you can "get rich quick" and enjoy a lot of leisure time while your employees run the company. But the reality is much more difficult. During the start-up period, you are likely to have a lot of bad days. It's exhausting. Even if you don't have employees, you should expect communications breakdowns and other "people problems" with agents, vendors, distributors, family,

subcontractors, lenders, whomever. Dan Bricklin, the founder of VisiCalc, advises that the most important thing to remember is this: "You are not your business. On those darkest days when things aren't going so well—and trust me, you will have them—try to remember that your company's failures don't make you an awful person. Likewise, your company's successes don't make you a genius or superhuman."[15]

As you read this chapter, you will learn about two primary sources of new venture creation:

1. Independent **entrepreneurs** are individuals who establish a new organization without the benefit of corporate support.

2. **Intrapreneurs** are new venture creators working inside big companies; they are corporate entrepreneurs, using their company's resources to build a profitable line of business based on a fresh new idea.[16]

● Ryan Clark (bottom) who won the Student Leadership Award from the Black Engineer of the Year Awards, poses with his twin brother, Ashton, at the Coordinated Science Laboratory in Urbana, IL. The Clark brothers (a.k.a., Dynamik Duo) graduated from the University of Illinois and in the past 12 years have formed more than a dozen successful web-based businesses, with products ranging from online music to sports apparel to parking place reservations.

1 | ENTREPRENEURSHIP

Two young entrepreneurs who recently founded a highly successful business are Tony Hsieh and Nick Swinmurn. In 1999 Swinmurn had the then-new idea to sell shoes online, but he needed money to get started. Hsieh, who at age 24 had already just sold his first start-up (LinkExchange, sold to Microsoft for $265 million), agreed to take a chance on the new venture. Swinmurn has moved on, but Hsieh remains at the helm of the online shoe retailer, Zappos. The successful online retail venture attracted Amazon, which purchased Zappos for $1.2 billion in 2009.[17]

Exceptional though their story may be, the real, more complete story of entrepreneurship is about people you've probably never heard of. They have built companies, thrived personally, created jobs, and contributed to their communities through their businesses. Or they're just starting out. Consider Shama Kabani, a 20-something who

entrepreneurial venture a new business having growth and high profitability as primary objectives

entrepreneur an individual who establishes a new organization without the benefit of corporate sponsorship

intrapreneurs new venture creators working inside big companies

Exhibit 6.1	Myths and realities about entrepreneurship

Myths	Realities
1. "Anyone can start a business."	Starting is easy. The hard part is building and sustaining a successful venture.
2. "Entrepreneurs are gamblers."	They take careful, calculated risks and are not afraid to act on those decisions.
3. "Entrepreneurs want the whole show to themselves."	Higher-potential entrepreneurs build a team, an organization, and a company.
4. "Entrepreneurs are their own bosses and independent."	They have to answer to many stakeholders, including partners, investors, customers, suppliers, creditors, employees, and families.
5. "Entrepreneurs work harder than managers in big firms."	There is no evidence to support this claim. Some work more, some less.
6. "Entrepreneurs experience a great deal of stress."	Entrepreneurs experience stress, but they also have high job satisfaction. They tend to be healthier and less likely to retire than those who work for others.
7. "Entrepreneurs are motivated solely by the quest for the dollar."	More are driven by building high-potential ventures and realizing long-term capital gains than instant gratification from high salaries. Feeling in control of their own destinies and realizing vision and dreams are powerful motivators.
8. "Entrepreneurs seek power and control over others."	Many are driven by responsibility, achievement, and results. Successful entrepreneurs may become powerful and influential, but these are by-products.
9. "If an entrepreneur is talented, than success will happen quickly."	Actually, many new businesses take three to four years to solidify. A saying from venture capitalists sums it up: "The lemons ripen in two and a half years, but the pearls take seven or eight."
10. "Any entrepreneur with a good idea can raise venture capital."	In practice, only 1 to 3 (out of 100) ventures are funded.
11. "If an entrepreneur has enough start-up capital, s/he can't miss."	Too much money at the beginning often leads to impulsive or undisciplined spending that usually result in serious problems or failure.
12. "Unless you attained a high score on your SATs or GMATs, you'll never be a successful entrepreneur."	Entrepreneurial IQ is actually a unique combination of creativity, motivation, integrity, leadership, team building, analytical ability, and ability to deal with ambiguity and adversity.

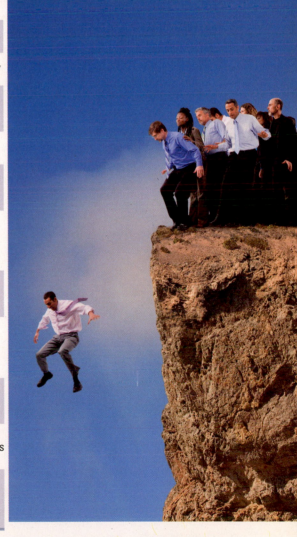

Source: Adapted from J. A. Timmons and S. Spinelli, *New Venture Creation,* 6th ed., pp. 67–68. Copyright © 2004. Reproduced with permission of McGraw-Hill Education.

went from graduate student to social media millionaire. An early proponent of using social media to market firms' products and services, Kabani wrote her masters' thesis on "why people use Twitter and other social networking sites." After applying and being rejected for jobs at large management consulting firms, she decided to trust her own entrepreneurial instincts and founded a web marketing company, The Marketing Zen Group. In just three years, Kabani has grown the company to 30 employees and $1.2 million in revenue.[18] In 2012, Kabani accepted an award at the White House for being one of Empact's top 100 companies started by an entrepreneur under the age of 35.[19] As president of The Marketing Zen Group, Kabani is a constant learner who provides strategy and implementation services for businesses that want to leverage the power of the Internet. Her company operates virtually with 30 employees in different countries and offers a range of services to clients, including social media marketing, search engine optimization, website design, content marketing, and consulting.[20]

1.1 | Why Become an Entrepreneur?

Bill Gross has started dozens of companies. When he was a boy, he devised homemade electronic games and sold candy for a profit to friends. In college he built and sold plans for a solar heating device, started a stereo equipment company, and sold a software product to Lotus. Then, he started Idealab, which hatched dozens of start-ups on the Internet. Recently launched Idealab companies include one that is making a three-dimensional printer, and another that sells robotics technology to supermarkets and toy companies. Through its Energy Innovations subsidiary, Idealab also has branched out into the now-hot markets for alternative energy, personal robotics, and advanced mobile advertising platform technologies.[21]

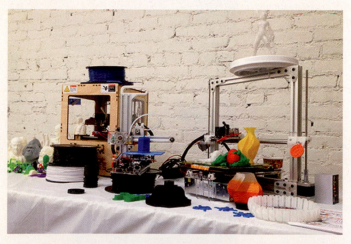

● Idealab startup, New Matter, thinks its Mod T printer can bring 3D printing to the mainstream by addressing what it sees as the biggest challenges: accessibility, relevance, and price. The Mod T is up for preorder for $249 via an Indiegogo campaign.

Why do Bill Gross and other entrepreneurs do what they do? Entrepreneurs start their own firms because of the challenge, profit potential, and enormous satisfaction they hope lies ahead. People starting their own businesses are seeking a better quality of life than they might have at big companies. They seek independence and a feeling that they are part of the action. They get tremendous satisfaction from building something from nothing, seeing it succeed, and watching the market embrace their ideas and products.

People also start their own companies when they see their progress or ideas blocked at big corporations. When people are laid off, believe they will not receive a promotion, or are frustrated by bureaucracy or other features of corporate life, they may become entrepreneurs. Years ago Philip Catron became disillusioned with his job as a manager at ChemLawn because he concluded that the lawn care company's reliance on pesticides contributed to illness in its employees, its customers' pets, and even the lawns themselves. Catron left to start NaturaLawn of America, based on the practice of integrated pest management (IPM), which uses natural and nontoxic products as much as possible, reducing pesticide use on lawns by 93 percent. Over nearly 25 years, Catron built NaturaLawn into 64 franchises in 23 states—and helped take IPM into the mainstream, as even his former employer has changed many of its practices.[22]

Immigrants may find conventional paths to economic success closed to them and turn to entrepreneurship.[23] The Cuban community in Miami has produced many successful entrepreneurs, as has the Vietnamese community throughout the United States. Sometimes the immigrant's experience gives him or her useful knowledge about foreign suppliers or markets that present an attractive business opportunity. Rakesh Kamdar immigrated to the United States from India to study computer science but noticed a way he could meet the huge U.S. demand for nursing talent. He set up DB Healthcare to recruit nurses from India to work in the United States. Unlike U.S. competitors that had failed, Kamdar set up meetings at DB's Indian offices, and he invited nurses to attend with their husbands, parents, and in-laws. His staff discussed family and individual questions related to the American jobs. Within a few years, DB Healthcare expanded its service offerings to staffing other medical personnel and IT professionals for the health care industry, ultimately earning the firm millions of dollars.[24]

::::::::::::::::

Born Josephine Esther Mentzer, the beauty company entrepreneur Estée Lauder was raised in Queens, New York, by her Hungarian mother and Czech father. Living on the floor above her father's hardware store, Lauder was always interested in beauty. In 1946 Lauder's chemist uncle created a handful of skin creams that she began selling to beauty salons and hotels. Two years after starting her business, she expanded her enterprise by convincing the managers at New York City department stores to give her counter space to sell her beauty products. Holding strong to the belief that

The Estee Lauder Companies Inc. launched the Jo Malone London brand in Bejing, China. The brand is now available in 34 countries worldwide and continues to inspire a loyal following.

"every woman can be beautiful," Lauder developed and perfected personal selling techniques that included advising customers and working with Beauty Advisors.

Lauder had a keen sense for marketing. At a time when her competitors were selling French perfumes to be applied in drops behind women's ears, Lauder's company launched *Youth Dew*, a combination bath oil and perfume that was consumed much faster as people poured it into their bath water. *Youth Dew* went from selling 50,000 in 1953 to over 150 million in 1984. Such business instincts, combined with strong selling and leadership skills, led to Estée Lauder being honored with many awards such as the United States' Presidential Medal of Freedom and France's Legion of Honor.

Estée Lauder left a legacy of success. The company's products are sold in over 150 countries under brand names such as Estée Lauder, Aramis, and Clinique. As of 2011, the company reported $8.8 billion in sales and continued to be a leader in skin care, makeup, fragrance, and hair care products.[25]

1.2 | What Does It Take to Succeed?

What can we learn from the people who start their own companies and succeed? Let's start with the example of Ken Hendricks, founder of ABC Supply.[26] As he acquired buildings and businesses, he saw opportunities where others saw problems. Several years after the town's largest employer, Beloit Corporation, closed its doors, Hendricks bought its property, where he discovered almost a half million patterns (wooden molds) used to make a variety of machine parts. Although a bankruptcy court ordered that he be paid to move the patterns to the dump, Hendricks called on a friend, artist Jack De Munnik, and offered him the patterns as free material to create art. De Munnik fashioned them into tables, clocks, sculptures, and other pieces. Hendricks calculated, "Even if we only got $50 apiece for them, 50 times 500,000 is $25 million," and he noted that that amount could have "taken the Beloit Corporation out of bankruptcy."[27] This example shows how Hendricks viewed business success: problems can be fixed. "It's how you look at something and how it's managed that make the difference."[28]

Ken Hendricks is a good example of what talents enable entrepreneurs to succeed. We express these characteristics in general terms with Exhibit 6.2. Successful entrepreneurs are innovators and also have good knowledge and skills in management, business, and networking.[29] In contrast, inventors may be highly creative but often lack the skills to turn their ideas into a successful business. Manager—administrators may be great at ensuring efficient operations but aren't necessarily innovators. Promoters have a different set of marketing and selling skills—useful for entrepreneurs, but those skills can be hired, whereas innovativeness and business management skills remain the essential combination for successful entrepreneurs.

LO2 Summarize how to assess opportunities to start new businesses

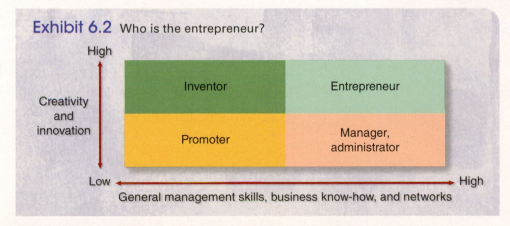

Exhibit 6.2 Who is the entrepreneur?

Source: J. Timmons and S. Spinelli, *New Venture Creation,* 6th ed., p. 65. © 2004 Reprinted with permission of McGraw-Hill Education.

2 | WHAT BUSINESS SHOULD YOU START?

You need a good idea, and you need to find or create the right opportunity. The following discussion offers some general considerations for choosing a type of business. For guidance in matching your unique strengths and interests to a business type, another helpful resource is *What Business Should I Start? Seven Steps to Discovering the Ideal Business for You* by Rhonda Abrams.

2.1 | The Idea

Many entrepreneurs and observers say that in contemplating your business, you must start with a great idea. A great product, a viable market, and good timing are essential ingredients in any recipe for success. For example, Tom Stemberg knew that the growing number of small businesses in the 1980s had no one dedicated to selling them office supplies. He saw his opportunity, so he opened his first Staples store, the first step toward a nationwide chain. Staples' sales now reach more than $18 billion annually.

:::::::::::::::::

Some of the best ideas start of as simple ideas. Thirty-five years ago, Debbie Fields, a 20-year-old housewife with no business experience, had a dream of opening a chocolate chip cookie bakery and store. After convincing a bank to finance her business idea, *Mrs. Fields* was founded. Fast-forward to today. *Mrs. Fields* makes about $450 million in revenue and has more than 600 company-owned and franchise stores in the United States and 10 foreign nations. Debbie Fields attributes her success to her motto that **"Good enough never is,"** which is reflected in her reputation for providing quality products and superior customer service.[30]

:::::::::::::::::

Many great organizations have been built on a different kind of idea: the founder's desire to build a great organization, rather than offering a particular product or product line.[31] Examples abound. Bill Hewlett and David Packard decided to start a company and then figured out what to make. J. Willard Marriott knew he wanted to be in business for himself but didn't have a product in mind until he opened an A&W root beer stand. Oprah Winfrey founded a successful production company, Harpo Productions, that produced her popular and

> **"Many now-great companies had early failures. But the founders persisted; they believed in themselves and in their dreams of building great organizations."**

● Over 35 years ago, Debbie Fields acted on her dream of opening a chocolate chip cookie bakery and store by founding Mrs. Fields.

influential talk show. Masaru Ibuka had no specific product idea when he founded Sony in 1945. Sony's first product attempt, a rice cooker, didn't work, and its first product (a tape recorder) didn't sell. The company stayed alive by making and selling crude heating pads.

Many now-great companies had early failures. But the founders persisted; they believed in themselves and in their dreams of building great organizations. Although the conventional logic is to see the company as a vehicle for your products, the alternative perspective sees the products as a vehicle for your company. Be prepared to kill or revise an idea, but never give up on your company—this has been a prescription for success for many great entrepreneurs and business leaders. At organizations including Disney, Procter & Gamble, Estée Lauder, Harpo Productions, and Walmart, the founders' greatest achievements—their greatest ideas—were their organizations.[32]

2.2 | The Opportunity

Entrepreneurs spot, create, and exploit opportunities in a variety of ways.[33] Entrepreneurial companies can explore domains that big companies avoid and introduce goods or services that capture the market because they are simpler, cheaper, more accessible, or more convenient. While Shayne McQuade was touring Spain, he noticed that he had a problem figuring out

Take Charge of Your Career

Why Wait? Start a Business While Still in College

Most of us are familiar with famous individuals who started businesses while still in college, like Michael Dell of Dell Computer and Mark Zuckerberg of Facebook. Less well known are the growing number of college student entrepreneurs who are busy launching businesses while taking normal courseloads. For example, while still in high school, Caroline Rooney designed a T-shirt for herself with a "Peace and Love" theme. After starting college at the University of Michigan, she wore the T-shirt around campus, and soon several friends were asking her where they could buy one. This lead to Rooney's decision to purchase and design 25 T-shirts for a total initial investment of $300. She sold all of the shirts. This initial success encouraged Rooney to sell cool T-shirts directly from her website and with the help of salespeople at six other college campuses. She founded The Bearon, a socially conscious clothing line.

Another college start-up took a different direction. After years of long swim practices followed by countless less-than-savory energy drinks, Indiana University student Zac Workman decided that he would try to use a three-generation-old family recipe for punch to create a more natural, better-tasting energy drink. With the support of his parents, Workman traveled to Los Angeles to convince a beverage development firm that worked on successful drinks like Gatorade and Sierra Mist to help him develop his new product concept.

The firm hooked up Workman with scientists who tweaked the ingredients of the punch drink so that it would be commercially viable. After a family investment of $200,000, the 21-year-old Workman launched ZW Enterprises to make and sell his energy drink, Punch. The firm is on track to make $1 million in sales revenue.

There are countless other examples of college students who turned into entrepreneurs while still in school. Talk to your family, friends, professors, current entrepreneurs, and other people who are willing to listen to your ideas and serve as sounding boards. Most important is to not be afraid to take that first step and try out your cool idea.

Sources: Adapted from "The Coolest College Start-ups," *Inc.*, 31, no. 2 (March 2009), pp. 78–89; company websites, The Bearon, www.bearon.com and ZW Enterprises, www.punchenergy.com.

---

how to recharge his cell phone. After his trip, McQuade developed a way to make backpacks and messenger bags containing solar panels that provide power to run personal electronics from anywhere. His company, Voltaic Systems, contracts to have the bags manufactured in China from material made out of recycled plastic. The products are sold in sporting goods stores, and McQuade is trying to get them stocked by Sam's Club.[34]

To spot opportunities, think carefully about events and trends as they unfold. Consider, for example, the following possibilities:

- *Technological discoveries.* Start-ups in biotechnology, microcomputers, and nanotechnology followed technological advances. Scotland-based Touch Bionics provides high tech prosthetics to patients with missing limbs. Their leading product, the *i-limb*, responds to muscular signals from the residual limb while featuring longer-lasting batteries and more power-efficient microprocessors. Also, Touch Bionics has developed functioning prototypes of artificial organs to replace one's spleen, pancreas, or lungs.[35]

- *Demographic changes.* As the population ages, many organizations have sprung up to serve the older demographic, from specially designed tablet and smartphone apps for seniors to assisted-living facilities. A business that targets both the aging population and the growth in single-parent and dual-career households is Errands Done Right. The service, launched by Donna Barber and Dawn Carter, targets those who are pressed for time or have difficulty getting around.[36]

- *Lifestyle and taste changes.* In recent years, more consumers want to help take care of the environment, and more businesses are concerned about showing consumers that they care, too. This trend has opened a niche for Affordable Internet Services Online. Featured in *Inc.* magazine's Top 50 Green Companies, the web-hosting company, based in Romoland, California, is powered by 120 solar panels. Clients' websites can boast, "Site hosted with 100% solar energy."[37]

- *Economic dislocations,* such as booms or failures. Rising oil prices have spurred a variety of developments related to alternative energy or energy efficiency. Howard Berke, the entrepreneur behind Konarka Technologies' solar cells, says, "I don't come at this as an environmentalist. I come at this from good business sense. The cost of renewables . . . is more competitive when compared with fossil fuel."[38]

- *Calamities* such as wars and natural disasters. The terrorist attacks of September 2001 spurred concern about security, and entrepreneurs today are still pursuing ideas to help government agencies prevent future attacks. Approximately one out of five United States service members returning from the wars in Iraq and Afghanistan have posttraumatic stress disorder, depression, or traumatic brain injuries. America's Heroes at Work, a new resource-based website sponsored by the U.S. Department of Labor, provides employers with information and tools to encourage the hiring of veterans with "invisible wounds of war."[39]

- *Government initiatives and rule changes.* Deregulation spawned new airlines and trucking companies. Whenever the government tightens energy efficiency requirements, opportunities become available for entrepreneurs developing ideas for cutting energy use.

* * *

A decade ago, Ryan Black was surfing in Brazil where he noticed many Brazilians gulping huge bowls of frozen purple slush. He followed his curiosity and learned that the slush was made from acai

Traditional Thinking

Facebook, Twitter and LinkedIn help entrepreneurs market their goods and services to "friends."

Source: Adapted from S. E. Needleman and A. Loten, "When 'Friending' Becomes a Source of Start-up Funds," *The Wall Street Journal,* November 1, 2011, p. B1.

The Best Managers Today

Are anticipating legislation that may permit "crowdfunding" or raising capital from social networking sites in exchange for an equity stake in the business.

● Entrepreneurs can help service members returning from war by providing them with employment opportunities, or services and products that meet their needs.

berries, which grow in abundance in the area and can be turned into smoothie-like drinks when they are crushed, blended with water, and frozen. As Brazilians already know, the berries contain antioxidants and healthy omega fats. Reflecting on U.S. consumers' demand for more healthful foods, Ryan believed that he and his brother could deliver a new taste sensation that was also nutritious.

The brothers founded Sambazon to develop and market frozen acai drinks but had to educate the public, including restaurants, store owners, and other potential customers, about the product. "They'd put on quite a show, going from store to store and putting on this Barnum and Bailey act," recalls Larry Sidoti, vice president of development for Juice It Up! Franchise Corp., which agreed to carry Sambazon. Sambazon, now worth over $100 million, manufacturers its products in Brazil and purchases its fruit directly from local farmers.[40]

2.3 | Franchises

One important type of opportunity is the franchise. You may know intuitively what franchising is, or at least you can name some prominent franchises: Supercuts, Pizza Hut, 7-Eleven, Hampton Hotels, and Quiznos. **Franchising** is an entrepreneurial alliance between two parties:[41]

1. The *franchisor*—an innovator who has created at least one successful store and seeks partners to operate the same concept in other local markets.

2. The *franchisee*—the operator of one or more stores according to the terms of the alliance.

franchising an entrepreneurial alliance between a franchisor (an innovator who has created at least one successful store and wants to grow) and a franchisee (a partner who manages a new store of the same type in a new location)

For the franchisee, the opportunity is wealth creation via a proven (but not failure-proof) business concept, with the added advantage of the franchisor's expertise. For the franchisor, the opportunity is wealth creation through growth. The partnership is manifest in a trademark or brand, and together the partners' mission is to maintain and build the brand. The Noodles & Company chain of fast-casual restaurants, which serve pasta dishes, soups, and sandwiches, first grew by opening 79 company-owned locations. Management concluded that it could grow faster through franchising. Establishing standard menus and prices took a year, but franchising helped the company grow to approximately 350 restaurants over a 10-year period.[43]

People often assume that buying a franchise is less risky than starting a business from scratch, but the evidence is mixed. A study that followed businesses for six years found the opposite of the popular assumption: 65 percent of the franchises studied were operating at the end of the period, while 72 percent of independent businesses were still operating. One reason may be that the franchises involved mostly a few, possibly riskier industries. A study that compared only restaurants over a three-year period found that 43 percent of the franchises and 39 percent of independent restaurants remained in business.[44]

If you are contemplating a franchise, consider its market presence (local, regional, or national), market share and profit margins, national programs for marketing and purchasing, the nature of the business, including required training and degree of field support, terms of the license agreement (e.g., 20 years with automatic renewal versus less than 10 years or no renewal), capital required, and franchise fees and royalties.[45] You can learn more from plenty of useful sources, including these:

- International Franchise Association (www.franchise.org).
- The Small Business Administration (www.sba.gov).
- Franchise Chat (www.franchise-chat.com).
- Franchise & Business Opportunity Directory (www.franchise.com).

In addition, the Federal Trade Commission investigates complaints of deceptive claims by franchisors and publishes information about those cases.

2.4 | The Next Frontiers

The next frontiers for entrepreneurship—where do they lie? When a business magazine asked prominent investors in new businesses to name the best ideas for a new start-up, their responses included next-generation batteries with enough juice to power cars after a seconds-long charge, longer-lasting tiny batteries to keep cell phones and cameras running for more hours, implantable wireless devices that can monitor heartbeats or blood sugar levels, and online social networking sites that allow artists and musicians to share and promote their work.[46] Another high-potential area for entrepreneurs includes nanotechnology, or the engineering of matter at a molecular scale. Though still in its infancy, this technology has potential applications for medicine, defense, consumer products, energy, construction, and electronics.[47]

One fascinating opportunity for entrepreneurs is outer space. Historically the space market was driven by the government and was dominated by big defense contractors like Boeing and Lockheed Martin. But now, with demand for satellite launches and potential profits skyrocketing, smaller entrepreneurs are entering the field. Some of the most dramatic headlines involve space tourism. Zero Gravity already operates flights in converted Boeing 727 jets that simulate the experience of weightlessness by flying up and down like a roller-coaster 10,000 feet above the earth. Famous passengers who signed up for the $3,500 flights included business owner Martha Stewart, Google co-founder Sergei Brin, and physicist Stephen Hawking.[48]

Virgin Galactic's mothership, the *White Knight Two,* is a specially designed jumbo jet that will carry the firm's passenger vehicle, the *Space Ship Two,* into sub-orbit. While regulatory delays continue to push back the first launch date, $70 million in deposits have been collected from 580 customers from the United States, China, Japan, Singapore, and Malaysia have plunked down $200,000 each for the ride.[49] Other recent ventures in space have included using satellites for automobile navigation, tracking trucking fleets, and monitoring flow rates and leaks in pipelines; testing designer drugs in the near-zero-gravity environment; and using remote sensing to monitor global warming, spot fish concentrations, and detect crop stress for precision farming.

2.5 | The Internet

The Internet is a business frontier that continues to expand. With Internet commerce, as with any start-up, entrepreneurs need sound business models and practices. You need to watch costs carefully, and you want to achieve profitability as soon as possible.[50]

Did You Know?

There are over 825,000 franchised businesses in the United States that supply over 7.9 million jobs. Franchises contribute approximately $2.1 trillion to the economy.[42]

At least five successful business models have proven successful for e-commerce:[51]

1. **Transaction fee model**—Companies charge a fee for goods or services. Amazon.com and online travel agents are prime examples.

2. **Advertising support model**—-Advertisers pay the site operator to gain access to the demographic group that visits the operator's site. More than one-third of online ads are for financial services, and another 22 percent are for web media. More than half of the ads appear on e-mail pages.[52]

3. **Intermediary model**—A website brings buyers and sellers together and charges a commission for each sale. The premier example is eBay.

4. **Affiliate model**—Sites pay commissions to other sites to drive business to their own sites. Zazzle.com, Spreadshirt.com, and CafePress.com are variations on this model. They sell custom-decorated gift items such as mugs and T-shirts. Designers are the affiliates; they choose basic, undecorated products (such as a plain shirt) and add their own designs. Visitors to a designer's website can link to, say, Zazzle and place an order, or they can go directly to Zazzle to shop. Either way, Zazzle sets the basic price, and the designer gets about 10 percent. Spreadshirt and CafePress let designers choose how much above the base price they want to charge consumers for the decorated product.[53]

5. **Subscription model**—The website charges a monthly or annual fee for site visits or access to site content. Newspapers and magazines are good examples.

> "My biggest motivation? just to keep challenging myself. i see life almost like one long university education that i never had—everyday i'm learning something new."
>
> —Richard Branson, *CEO, Virgin Group*[57]

● Mario, Nintendo's iconic video game character, floats with ZERO-G coaches in zero-gravity atmosphere to train for his upcoming game set in space, Super Mario Galaxy for Wii in Las Vegas, Nevada.

2.6 | Side Streets

Trial and error can also be useful in starting new businesses. Some entrepreneurs start their enterprises and then let the market decide whether it likes their ideas. This method is risky, of course, and should be done only if you can afford the risks. But even if the original idea doesn't work, you may be able to capitalize on the **side street effect**.[54] As you head down a road, you come to unknown places, and unexpected opportunities begin to appear. And while you are looking, *prepare* so you can act quickly and effectively on any opportunity that presents itself.

LO3 Identify common causes of success and failure

3 | WHAT DOES IT TAKE, PERSONALLY?

Many people assume that there is an "entrepreneurial personality." No single personality type predicts entrepreneurial success, but you are more likely to succeed as an entrepreneur if you have certain characteristics:[55]

1. *Commitment and determination:* Successful entrepreneurs are decisive, tenacious, disciplined, willing to sacrifice, and able to immerse themselves totally in their enterprises.

2. *Leadership:* They are self-starters, team builders, superior learners, and teachers. Communicating a vision for the future of the company—an essential component of leadership—has a direct impact on venture growth.[56]

3. *Opportunity obsession:* They have an intimate knowledge of customers' needs, are market driven, and are obsessed with value creation and enhancement.

4. *Tolerance of risk, ambiguity, and uncertainty:* They are calculated risk takers and risk managers, tolerant of stress, and able to resolve problems.

5. *Creativity, self-reliance, and ability to adapt:* They are open-minded, restless with the status quo, able to learn quickly, highly adaptable, creative, skilled at conceptualizing, and attentive to details.

6. *Motivation to excel:* They have a clear results orientation, set high but realistic goals, have a strong drive to achieve, know their own weaknesses and strengths, and focus on what can be done rather than on the reasons why things can't be done.

Bill Gross—whom you met in our earlier discussion of "Why become an entrepreneur?" exemplifies many of these characteristics. He persevered even after his brainchild, Idealab, apparently crashed and burned. The company was launched in the mid-1990s to nurture Internet start-ups as they were being formed left and right. Companies that Idealab invested in included eToys, Eve.com, and PetSmart.com. If you haven't heard of them, it's probably because they went out of business because sales couldn't keep up with the hype and the hopes. Today Gross explains that he hadn't intended for Idealab to help exclusively dot-com businesses, but that's what entrepreneurs were all starting in the 1990s. When the Internet boom crashed several years ago, Gross laid off employees and shuttered offices, but he maintained his vision of helping entrepreneurs. Instead of giving up, Gross established stricter criteria for funding companies in the future—and determined that he would choose companies whose activities make a difference. Of the company's near failure, Gross says, "We have a lot more wisdom now."[58]

characterized by low or high *risk*, including the probability of major financial loss, as well as psychological risk perceived by the entrepreneur, including risk to reputation and ego.[59] Combining these two variables, we can identify four kinds of new ventures:

1. In the upper left quadrant, innovation is high (ventures are truly novel ideas), and there is little risk. For example, a pioneering product idea from Procter & Gamble might fit here if there are no current competitors and because, for a company of that size, the financial risks of new product investments can seem relatively small.

2. In the upper right quadrant, novel product ideas (high innovation) are accompanied by high risk because the financial investments and competition are great. Virgin Galactic's space tourism venture would likely fall into this category.

3. Most small business ventures are in the lower right, where innovation is low and risk is high. They are fairly conventional entries in well-established fields. New restaurants, retail shops, and commercial outfits involve a sizable investment by the entrepreneur and face direct competition from similar businesses.

4. Finally, the low-innovation/low-risk category includes ventures that require minimal investment and/or face minimal competition for strong market demand. Examples are some service businesses having low start-up costs and those involving entry into small towns if there is no competitor and demand is adequate.

This matrix helps entrepreneurs think about their venture and decide whether it suits their particular objectives. It also helps identify effective and ineffective strategies. You might find one cell more appealing than others. The lower left cell is likely to have relatively low payoffs but to provide more security. The possible risks and returns are higher in other cells, especially the upper right. So you might place your new venture idea in the appropriate cell and pursue it only if it is in a cell where you would prefer to operate. If it is not, you can reject the idea or look for a way to move it toward a different cell.

The matrix also can help entrepreneurs remember a useful point: successful companies do not always require a cutting-edge technology or an exciting new product. Even companies offering the most mundane products—the type that might reside in

3.1 | Making Good Choices

Success is a function not only of personal characteristics but also of making good choices about the business you start. Exhibit 6.3 presents a model for conceptualizing entrepreneurial ventures and making the best choices. According to this model, a new venture may involve high or low levels of *innovation*, or the creation of something new and different. It can also be

Exhibit 6.3 Entrepreneurial innovation-risk strategies

	Low Risk	High Risk
High Innovation	Subway launches an online service to pre-order sandwiches.	Medical researchers try to use 3D printing technology to create organs.
Low Innovation	A college student launches a resume writing and interviewing tips venture.	An entrepreneur opens a pub in a downtown nightclub area.

Source: Adapted from Sonfield and Lussier, "Entrepreneurial Strategy Matrix: A Model of New and Ongoing Ventures," *Business Horizons*, May–June 1997.

the lower left cell—can gain competitive advantage by doing basic things better than competitors.

::::::::::::::::::

Oprah Winfrey is an award-winning entrepreneur with a long track record of success. From 1986 to 2011, her nationally syndicated talk show *The Oprah Winfrey Show* became the highest-rated talk show in television history by reaching over 40 million viewers each month. Not only did many of the show's topics spur nationwide debate on such topics as sexual abuse, discrimination, adoption, and homelessness, but it also served as a launch pad for several other shows like *Dr. Phil, Rachel Ray, The Dr. Oz Show,* and *The Nate Berkus Show.* Her monthly magazine *O, The Oprah Magazine* is also successful and has a monthly circulation of 2.35 million readers. Oprah also acts, produces movies, and leads

● Oprah Winfrey's exclusive no-holds-barred interview with controversial cyclist Lance Armstrong, "Oprah and Lance Armstrong: The Worldwide Exclusive," aired as a two-night event on OWN: Oprah Winfrey Network.

several philanthropic activities like the Angel Network and the Leadership Academy for Girls in South Africa.

In January 2011 Oprah launched the Oprah Winfrey Network (OWN) on cable. In partnership with Discovery Communications, OWN provides 24-hour-a-day programming and shows, including *Our America with Lisa Ling, The Haves and Have Nots,* and *Oprah Prime.* While many believed the Oprah brand would immediately translate into success with the new network, this has not been the case. Since its inception, OWN has received more than $500 million from its partner, Discovery. This working capital gave Winfrey some breathing room to learn the ins and outs of managing a network. Her skill and experience as an entrepreneur are beginning to pay off; OWN turned its first profit in 2013.[61]

::::::::::::::::::

3.2 | Failure Happens, But You Can Improve the Odds of Success

Success or failure lies ahead for entrepreneurs starting their own companies, as well as for those starting new businesses within bigger corporations. Entrepreneurs succeed or fail in private, public, and not-for-profit sectors, as well as in nations at all stages of development and of all political types.[62]

Estimated failure rates for start-ups vary. Most indicate that failure is more the rule than the exception. The failure rate is high for certain businesses like restaurants, and lower for successful franchises. Start-ups have at least two major liabilities: newness and smallness.[63] New companies are relatively unknown and must learn how to beat established competitors at doing something customers value. The odds of survival improve if the venture grows to at least 10 or 20 people, has revenues of $2 million or $3 million, and is pursuing opportunities with growth potential.[64]

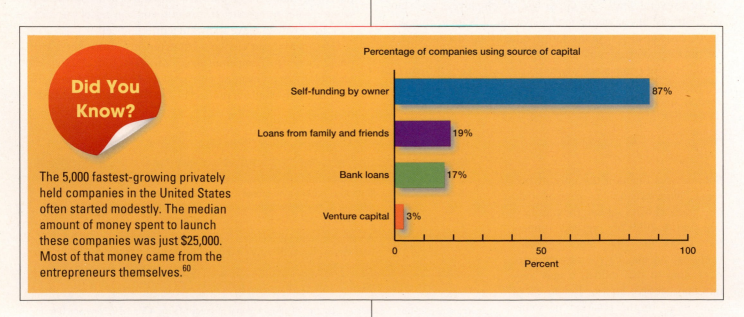

Did You Know?

The 5,000 fastest-growing privately held companies in the United States often started modestly. The median amount of money spent to launch these companies was just $25,000. Most of that money came from the entrepreneurs themselves.[60]

Percentage of companies using source of capital

Source	Percent
Self-funding by owner	87%
Loans from family and friends	19%
Bank loans	17%
Venture capital	3%

Acquiring venture capital is not essential to the success of most start-up businesses; in fact, it is rare. Recent numbers from the Census Bureau say that more than three-fourths of start-up companies with employees were financed by entrepreneurs' own assets or assets of their families. Approximately one-tenth of businesses were financed with the owners' credit cards.[65] Still, in 2013, venture capitalists invested $29.4 billion in approximately 4,000 deals;[66] that's a sizable amount of money, even if the fraction of total new companies is small. And venture capital firms often provide expert advice that helps entrepreneurs improve the odds for success.

Further factors that influence success and failure include risk, the economic environment, various management-related hazards, and initial public stock offerings (IPOs).

Risk It's a given: Starting a new business is risky. Entrepreneurs with plenty of business experience are especially aware of this. When Chris McGill was evaluating his idea for Mixx.com, a news website that could be personalized based on recommendations by users, he was *USA Today*'s vice president of strategy. To make Mixx succeed, McGill knew he would be leaving a well-paying job for an uncertain future in which he had to line up financing and hire talented people in a turbulent business environment. But McGill also concluded that his experience at *USA Today* and prior management experience with *Yahoo News* gave him knowledge and connections for a successful Internet business.[67]

3.3 | The Role of the Economic Environment

Entrepreneurial activity stems from the economic environment as well as the behavior of individuals. For example, money is a critical resource for all new businesses. Increases in the money supply and the supply of bank loans, real economic growth, and improved stock market performance lead to both improved prospects and increased sources of capital. In turn, the prospects and the capital increase the rate of business formation. Under favorable conditions, many aspiring entrepreneurs find early success. But economic cycles soon change favorable conditions into downturns. To succeed, entrepreneurs must have the foresight and talent to survive when the environment becomes more hostile.

Although good economic times may make it easier to start a company and to survive, bad times can offer a chance to expand. Ken Hendricks of ABC Supply found a business opportunity in a grim economic situation: a serious downturn in the manufacturing economy of the Midwest contributed to the shutdown of his town's largest employer, the Beloit Corporation. Hendricks purchased the company's buildings and lured a diverse group of new employers to town, despite the economic challenges. In fact, Hendricks has a track record of turning around the struggling suppliers that ABC acquires.[68]

Another silver lining in difficult economic times is that it's easier to recruit talent.

3.4 | Business Incubators

The need to provide a nurturing environment for fledgling enterprises has led to the creation of business incubators. **Business incubators**, often located in industrial parks or abandoned factories, are protected environments for new, small businesses. Incubators offer benefits such as low rents and shared costs. Shared staff costs, such as for receptionists and administrative assistants, avoid the expense of a full-time employee but still provide convenient access to services. The staff manager is usually an experienced businessperson or consultant who advises the new business owners. Incubators often are associated with universities, which provide technical and business services for the new companies.

The heyday of business incubators came in the 1990s, when around 700 of them were financing start-ups, mainly emphasizing technology. Eight out of 10 shut down following the collapse of the Internet bubble, but the idea of nurturing new businesses persists. Naval Ravikant is developing a company tentatively named Hit Forge, which resembles the dot-com incubators. Hit Forge hired four engineers with experience in launching successful Internet concepts. The engineers have wide latitude to try ideas, but they work under strict deadlines. They must go from concept to product within 90 days, and any enterprises that aren't growing after a year will be terminated. Unlike the older-style incubator, Hit Forge lets engineers work from the location of their choice, and the engineers retain half ownership in the ventures they develop. Also, whereas incubators in the 1990s might have spent $2 million developing an idea, today's launches might cost just $50,000.[70]

::::::::::::::::

One business incubator is thriving in Lebanon, New Hampshire. The Dartmouth Regional Technology Center (DRTC) offers young technology companies the business development support and services they need to grow. Funding for the incubator originally came from state and federal agencies, and nearby Dartmouth College sent some of the first businesses to the $8 million facility, which provides lab and office space, as well as shared conference areas.

When creative people gather, sparks fly, producing ideas for new solutions, goods and services, or processes. The DRTC is no exception. Some of the businesses that got their start there include PreventAGE Health Care, whose purpose is to improve diabetes care by providing patients and doctors with the necessary tools to predict and more effectively manage diabetic complications. Another company, segTEL, has built one of the largest telecommunications networks in northern New England.[71]

::::::::::::::::

> "The National Business Incubation Industry estimates that United States-based incubators assisted 49,000 start-up companies that provided full-time employment for nearly 200,000 workers and generated annual revenue of almost $15 billion."[69]

LO4 Discuss common management challenges

4 | COMMON MANAGEMENT CHALLENGES

As an entrepreneur, you are likely to face several common challenges that you should understand before you face them, and then manage effectively when the time comes. Exhibit 6.4 illustrates eight common management challenges.

4.1 | You Might Not Enjoy It

Big company managers and employees can specialize in what they love, whether it's selling or strategic planning. But entrepreneurs usually have to do it all, at least in the beginning. If you love product design, you also have to sell what you invent. If you love marketing, get ready to manage the money too. This last challenge was almost a stumbling block for Elizabeth Busch, Anne Frey-Mott, and Beckie Jankewicz when they launched The Event Studio to run business conferences for their clients. All three women had experience with some aspect of running conferences, but when they started their company, they didn't fully think out all the accounting decisions they would need for measuring their income and cash flow. With some practical advice, they learned the basic accounting lessons that helped them avoid tax troubles later on.[72]

4.2 | Survival Is Difficult

Zappos cofounder Tony Hsieh says, "We thought about going under every day—until we got a $6 million credit line from Wells Fargo."[73] Companies without much of a track record tend to have trouble lining up lenders, investors, and even customers. When economic conditions cool or competition heats up, a small start-up serving a niche market may have limited options for survival. Gary Gottenbusch worried when orders slowed at his Servatii Pastry Shop and Deli, located in Cincinnati. As a recession hit Ohio hard, customers were deciding that fancy breads and cakes were a luxury they could go without. Servatii might have closed, but Gottenbusch was willing to change his vision. He kept afloat and even added to sales by cultivating new distribution channels (sales in hospitals), new products (distinctive pretzel sticks), and cost-cutting measures (a purchasing association with other bakers in the area).[75]

Failure can be devastating. When Mary Garrison wanted to own a business, she chose the women's fitness industry and decided to buy a franchise from Lady of America Franchise Corporation. But when she held her grand opening, not a single person stopped by. Three months later, she closed. Garrison blames the franchisor for not providing the necessary promotional support, a complaint that Lady of America denies.[76]

4.3 | Growth Creates New Challenges

Just one in three *Inc.* 500 companies keeps growing fast enough to make this list of fastest-growing companies two years running. The reason: they are facing bigger challenges, competing with bigger firms, stretching the founders' capacities, and probably burning cash.[77] It's a difficult transition.

The transition is particularly complex for entrepreneurs who quickly face the possibility of expanding internationally. Whether a firm should expand internationally soon after it is created or wait until it is better established is an open question. Entering international markets should help a firm grow, but going global creates challenges that can make survival more difficult, especially when the company is young.

For instance, when Lou Hoffman decided to expand his public relations (PR) firm to China, he couldn't find anyone familiar with both Chinese business and the creative business culture that had served his agency well. So he hired a Chinese PR staffer who was willing to spend a year at his California headquarters, just absorbing the business culture. That method worked for the Chinese market but flopped when Hoffman tried it for opening

> "Inc. Magazine's list of best industries for starting a business in 2013 includes health and specialty food, digital forensics services like detecting phishing scams, mobile health apps, and green construction."[74]

a London office; the British employee didn't want to leave the California lifestyle and return home.[78] Of course, the risks tend to be lower when entrepreneurs (or their company's managers) have experience in serving foreign markets.[79]

In the beginning, the start-up mentality tends to be "we try harder."[80] Entrepreneurs work long hours at low pay, deliver great service, get good word-of-mouth, and their business grows. At first, it's "high performance, cheap labor." But with growth comes the need to pay higher wages to hire more people who are less dedicated than the founders. Then it's time to raise prices, establish efficient systems, or accept lower profits. The founder's talents may not spread to everyone else. You need a unique value proposition that will work as well with 100 employees, because hard work or instincts alone no longer will get the job done. Complicating matters is the continuing growth in customers' needs and expectations.[81]

4.4 | It's Hard to Delegate

As the business grows, entrepreneurs often hesitate to delegate work they are used to doing. Leadership deteriorates into micromanagement. For example, during the Internet craze, many company founders with great technical knowledge but little experience became "instant experts" in every phase of business, including branding and advertising.[82] Turns out, they didn't know as much as they thought, and their companies crashed. In contrast, Darren Herman kept his focus on what he knows. While still in his early 20s, Herman combined his passion for video games and his knowledge of marketing and came up with a business idea: IGA Worldwide, which works with advertisers and game developers to place advertising within video games. Shortly after he launched IGA, Herman

turned over the job of CEO to a more experienced person and named himself "senior business development director," which means he focuses on spotting new ideas and promoting the company to investors.[83]

4.5 | Misuse of Funds

Many unsuccessful entrepreneurs blame their failure on inadequate financial resources. Yet failure due to a lack of financial resources doesn't necessarily indicate a real lack of money; it could mean a failure to use the available money properly. A lot of start-up capital may be wasted—on expensive locations, great furniture, fancy stationery. Entrepreneurs who fail to use their resources wisely usually make one of two mistakes: they apply financial resources to

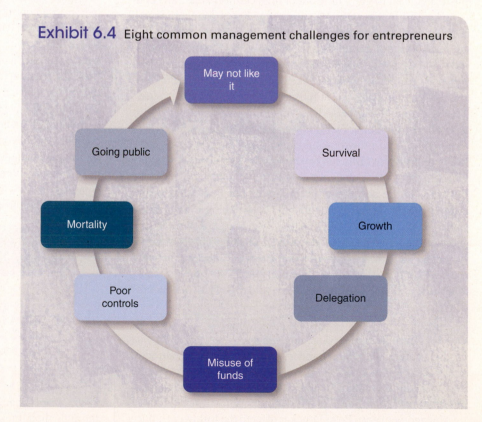

Exhibit 6.4 Eight common management challenges for entrepreneurs

May not like it — Survival — Growth — Delegation — Misuse of funds — Poor controls — Mortality — Going public

the wrong uses, or they maintain inadequate control over their resources.

This problem may be more likely when a lucky entrepreneur gets a big infusion of cash from a venture capital firm or an initial offering of stock. For most start-ups, where the money on the line comes from the entrepreneur's own assets, he or she has more incentive to be careful. Tripp Micou, founder of Practical Computer Applications, says, "If all the money you spend is based on what you're bringing in [through sales], you very quickly focus on the right things to spend it on."[84] Micou, an experienced entrepreneur who expects the company's revenues to double each year for the next few years, believes that this financial limitation is actually a management advantage.

4.6 | Poor Controls

Entrepreneurs, in part because they are very busy, often fail to use formal control systems. One common entrepreneurial malady is an aversion to record keeping. Expenses mount, but records do not keep pace. Pricing decisions are based on intuition without adequate reference to costs. As a result, the company earns inadequate margins to support growth.

Sometimes an economic slowdown provides a necessary alarm, warning business owners to pay attention to controls. When Servatii Pastry Shop and Deli's sales deteriorated while the prices of ingredients were rising, owner Gary Gottenbusch pushed himself to go "a little out of [his] comfort zone" and consulted with advisers at the Manufacturing Extension Partnership. Besides encouraging him to innovate, the advisers helped him set goals and monitor progress. One problem Gottenbusch tackled was the price of baking commodities, such as shortening and flour. He partnered with other local bakeries to form a purchasing association that buys in bulk and passes along the savings. Keeping costs down helped Servatii stay profitable when customers were trimming their budgets for baked goods.[85]

Even in high-growth companies, great numbers can mask brewing problems. Blinded by the light of growing sales, many entrepreneurs fail to maintain vigilance over other aspects of the business. In the absence of controls, the business veers out of control. So don't get overconfident; keep asking critical questions. Is our success based on just one big customer? Is our product just a fad that can fade away? Can other companies easily enter our domain and hurt our business? Are we losing a technology lead? Do we really understand the numbers, know where they come from, and have any hidden causes for concern?

4.7 | Mortality

One long-term measure of an entrepreneur's success is the fate of the venture after the founder's death. Founding entrepreneurs often fail to plan for succession. When death occurs, the lack of a skilled replacement for the founder can lead to business failure.

Management guru Peter Drucker offered the following advice to help family-managed businesses survive and prosper:[86]

- Family members working in the business must be at least as capable and hard-working as other employees.
- At least one key position should be filled by a nonfamily member.
- Someone outside the family and the business should help plan succession.

Family members who are mediocre performers are resented by others; outsiders can be more objective and contribute expertise the family might not have. Issues of management succession are often the most difficult of all, causing serious conflict and possible breakup of the firm.

4.8 | Going Public

Sometimes companies reach a point at which the owners want to "go public." **Initial public stock offerings (IPOs)** offer a way to raise capital through federally registered and underwritten sales of shares in the company.[87] You need lawyers and accountants who know current regulations. The reasons for going public include raising more capital, reducing debt or improving the balance sheet and enhancing net worth, pursuing otherwise unaffordable opportunities, and improving credibility with customers and other stakeholders—"you're in the big leagues now." Disadvantages include the expense, time, and effort involved; the tendency to become more interested in the stock price and capital gains than in running the company properly; and the creation of a long-term relationship with an investment banking firm that won't necessarily always be a good one.[88]

Many entrepreneurs prefer to avoid going public, feeling they'll lose control if they do. States Yvon Chouinard of sports and apparel firm Patagonia, "There's a certain formula in business where you grow the thing and go public. I don't think it has to be that way. Being a closely held company means being able to take risks and try new things—the creative part of business. If I were owned by a bunch of retired teachers, I wouldn't be able to do what I do; I'd have to be solely concerned with the bottom line."[89]

Executing IPOs and other approaches to acquiring capital is complex and beyond the scope of this chapter. Sources for more information include *The Ernst & Young Guide to Raising Capital,* the National Venture Capital Association (www.nvca.org), VentureOne (www.ventureone.com), and *VentureWire* (link to this publication from www.venturecapital.dowjones.com/).

LO5 Explain how to increase your chances of success, including good business planning

5 | PLANNING AND RESOURCES HELP YOU SUCCEED

Aside from financial resources, entrepreneurs need to think through their business idea carefully to help ensure its success.[90] This calls for good planning and nonfinancial resources.

5.1 | Planning

So you think you have identified a business opportunity and have the potential to make it succeed. Now what? Should you act on your idea? Where should you begin?

The Business Plan Your excitement and intuition may convince you that you are on to something. But they might not convince anyone else. You need more thorough planning and analysis. This effort will help convince others to get on board and help you avoid costly mistakes.

The first formal planning step is to do an **opportunity analysis.** This analysis includes a description of the good or service, an assessment of the opportunity, an assessment of the entrepreneur (you), a specification of activities and resources needed to translate your idea into a viable business, and your source(s) of capital.[91] Your opportunity analysis should include the following questions:[92]

- What market need does my idea fill?
- What personal observations have I experienced or recorded with regard to that market need?
- What social condition underlies this market need?
- What market research data can be marshaled to describe this market need?
- What patents might be available to fulfill this need?
- What competition exists in this market? How would I describe the behavior of this competition?
- What does the international market look like?
- What does the international competition look like?
- Where is the money to be made in this activity?

The opportunity analysis, or opportunity assessment plan, focuses on the opportunity, not the entire venture. It provides the basis for deciding whether to act. Then the **business plan** describes all the elements involved in starting the new venture.[93] The business plan describes the venture and its market, strategies, and future directions. It often has functional plans for marketing, finance, manufacturing, and human resources. Exhibit 6.5 outlines a typical business plan.

The business plan serves several purposes:

- It helps determine the viability of your enterprise.
- It guides you as you plan and organize.
- It helps you obtain financing.

It is read by potential investors, suppliers, customers, and others. Get help in writing a sound plan!

Key Planning Elements Most business plans devote so much attention to financial projections that they neglect other important information—information that matters greatly to astute investors. In fact, financial projections tend to be overly optimistic. Investors know this and discount the figures.[94] In addition to the numbers, the best plans convey—and make certain that the entrepreneurs have carefully thought through—five key factors:[95]

1. *The people:* The new organization's people should be energetic and have skills and expertise directly relevant to the venture. For many astute investors, the people are the most important element, more important even than the idea. Venture capital firms often receive 2,000 business plans per year; many believe that ideas are a dime a dozen and what counts is the ability to execute. Arthur Rock, a legendary venture capitalist who helped start Intel, Teledyne, and Apple, stated, "I invest in people, not ideas. If you can find good people, if they're wrong about the product, they'll make a switch."[96]

2. *The opportunity:* You need a competitive advantage that can be defended. The focus should be on customers. Who is the customer? How does the customer make decisions? What price will the customer pay? How will the venture reach all customer segments? How much does it cost to acquire and support a customer, and to produce and deliver the product? How easy or difficult is it to retain a customer?

3. *The competition:* The plan must identify current competitors and their strengths and weaknesses, predict how they will respond to the new venture, indicate how the new venture will respond to the competitors' responses, identify future potential competitors, and consider how to collaborate with or face off against actual or potential competitors. The original plan for Zappos was for its website to compete with other online shoe retailers by offering a wider selection than they did. However, most people buy shoes in stores, so Zappos cofounders Nick Swinmurn and Tony Hsieh soon realized that they needed a broader view of the competition. They began focusing more on service and planning a distribution method that would make online shopping as successful as visiting a store.[97]

4. *The context:* The environment should be favorable from regulatory and economic perspectives. Such factors as tax policies, rules about raising capital, interest rates, inflation, and exchange rates will affect the viability of the new venture. The context can make it easier or harder to get backing. Importantly, the plan should make clear that you know that the context inevitably will change, forecast how the changes will affect the business, and describe how you will deal with the changes.

5. *Risk and reward:* The risk must be understood and addressed as fully as possible. The future is uncertain, and the elements described in the plan will change. Although you cannot predict the future, you must contemplate head-on the possibilities of key people resigning, interest rates changing, a key customer leaving, or a powerful competitor responding ferociously. Then describe what you will do to prevent, avoid, or cope with such possibilities. You should also speak to the end of the process: how to get money out of the business eventually. Will you go public? Will you sell or liquidate? What are the various possibilities for investors to realize their ultimate gains?[98]

Exhibit 6.5 Outline of a business plan

I. **EXECUTIVE SUMMARY**
   A. Description of the Business Concept and the Business.
   B. The Opportunity and Strategy.
   C. The Target Market and Projections.
   D. The Competitive Advantages.
   E. The Economics, Profitability, and Harvest Potential.
   F. The Team.
   G. The Offering.

II. **THE INDUSTRY AND THE COMPANY AND ITS PRODUCT(S) OR SERVICE(S)**
   A. The Industry.
   B. The Company and the Concept.
   C. The Product(s) or Service(s).
   D. Entry and Growth Strategy.

III. **MARKET RESEARCH AND ANALYSIS**
   A. Customers.
   B. Market Size and Trends.
   C. Competition and Competitive Edges.
   D. Estimated Market Share and Sales.
   E. Ongoing Market Evaluation.

IV. **THE ECONOMICS OF THE BUSINESS**
   A. Gross and Operating Margins.
   B. Profit Potential and Durability.
   C. Fixed, Variable, and Semivariable Costs.
   D. Months to Breakeven.
   E. Months to Reach Positive Cash Flow.

V. **MARKETING PLAN**
   A. Overall Marketing Strategy.
   B. Pricing.
   C. Sales Tactics.
   D. Service and Warranty Policies.
   E. Advertising and Promotion.
   F. Distribution.

VI. **DESIGN AND DEVELOPMENT PLANS**
   A. Development Status and Tasks.
   B. Difficulties and Risks.
   C. Product Improvement and New Products.
   D. Costs.
   E. Proprietary Issues.

VII. **MANUFACTURING AND OPERATIONS PLAN**
   A. Operating Cycle.
   B. Geographical Location.
   C. Facilities and Improvements.
   D. Strategy and Plans.
   E. Regulatory and Legal Issues.

VIII. **MANAGEMENT TEAM**
   A. Organization.
   B. Key Management Personnel.
   C. Management Compensation and Ownership.
   D. Other Investors.
   E. Employment and Other Agreements and Stock Option and Bonus Plans.
   F. Board of Directors.
   G. Other Shareholders, Rights, and Restrictions.
   H. Supporting Professional Advisers and Services.

IX. **OVERALL SCHEDULE**

X. **CRITICAL RISKS, PROBLEMS, AND ASSUMPTIONS**

XI. **THE FINANCIAL PLAN**
   A. Actual Income Statements and Balance Sheets.
   B. Pro Forma Income Statements.
   C. Pro Forma Balance Sheets.
   D. Pro Forma Cash Flow Analysis.
   E. Breakeven Chart and Calculation.
   F. Cost Control.
   G. Highlights.

XII. **PROPOSED COMPANY OFFERING**
   A. Desired Financing.
   B. Offering.
   C. Capitalization.
   D. Use of Funds.
   E. Investor's Return.

XIII. **APPENDIXES**

Source: J. A. Timmons, *New Venture Creation,* 5th ed., p. 374. Copyright © 1999. Reprinted with permission of McGraw-Hill Education.

Selling the Plan Your goal is to get investors to support the plan. The elements of a great plan, as just described, are essential. Also important is whom you decide to try to convince to back your plan.

Many entrepreneurs want passive investors who will give them money and let them do what they want. Doctors and dentists generally fit this image. Professional venture capitalists do not, as they demand more control and more of the returns. But when a business goes wrong—and chances are, it will—nonprofessional investors are less helpful and less likely to advance more (needed) money. Sophisticated investors have seen sinking ships before and know how to help. They are more likely to solve problems, provide more money, and also navigate financial and legal waters such as going public.[100]

View the plan as a way for you to figure out how to reduce risk and maximize reward, and to convince others that you understand the entire new venture process. Don't put together a plan built on naïveté or overconfidence or one that cleverly hides major flaws. You might not fool others, and you certainly would be fooling yourself.

5.2 | Nonfinancial Resources

Also crucial to the success of a new business are nonfinancial resources, including legitimacy in the minds of the public and the ways other people can help.

Legitimacy An important resource for the new venture is **legitimacy**—people's judgment of a company's acceptance, appropriateness, and desirability.[101] When the market confers legitimacy, it helps overcome the "liability of newness" that creates a high percentage of new venture failure.[102] Legitimacy helps a firm acquire other resources such as top managers, good employees, financial resources, and government support. In a three-year study tracking business start-ups, the likelihood that a company would succeed at selling products, hiring employees, and attracting investors depended most on how skillfully entrepreneurs demonstrated that their business was legitimate.[103]

A business is legitimate if its goals and methods are consistent with societal values. You can generate legitimacy by visibly conforming to rules and expectations created by governments, credentialing associations, and professional organizations; by visibly endorsing widely held values; and by visibly practicing widely held beliefs.[104]

Networks The entrepreneur is aided greatly by having a strong network of people. **Social capital**—being part of a social network and having a good reputation—helps entrepreneurs gain access to useful information, win trust and cooperation from others, recruit employees, form successful business alliances, receive funding from venture capitalists, and become more successful.[105] Social capital provides a lasting source of competitive advantage.[106]

To see just some of the ways social capital can help entrepreneurs, consider a pair of examples. Brian Ko, an engineer who founded Integrant Technologies, got useful advice from his investors, including private investors, a bank, and venture capital firms. One adviser taught Ko that acquiring patents during the start-up phase would help the company stay competitive during the long term, so Integrant spent the money to file applications for 150 patents in six years, positioning the company to protect its ideas as it gains market share and competitors' attention.[107]

A second example of the benefits of a strong network can be seen in Victoria Colligan's "Ladies Who Launch," a media firm that provides resources and connections to female entrepreneurs. Members receive advice about promoting and growing their new businesses, network with several other women entrepreneurs, and are teamed up with expert business coaches.[108]

Top Management Teams The top management team is another crucial resource. Consider one of Sudhin Shahani's two start-ups, MyMPO, whose digital media services include Musicane, which lets musicians sell audio and video files and ringtones online at storefronts they create for themselves. The company's head of marketing was a singer.[109] Having a musician in that top spot may help Musicane build client relationships with other artists. Also, in companies that have incorporated, a board of directors improves the company's image, develops longer-term plans for expansion, supports day-to-day activities, and develops a network of information sources.

Advisory Boards Whether or not the company has a formal board of directors, entrepreneurs can assemble a group of people willing to serve as an advisory board. Board members with business experience can help an entrepreneur learn basics like how to do cash flow analysis, identify needed strategic changes, and build relationships with bankers, accountants,

Did You Know?

According to the State New Economy Index, the most hospitable states for starting an innovative, new economy business are Massachusetts, Delaware, Washington, California, and Maryland.[99]

and attorneys. Karen Usher, founder of human resources out-sourcing firm TPO, recently reported $5 million in revenue and sales growth at 10 percent per year for the past decade. Usher attributes TPO's success to her advisory board of three veteran executives, who give management and investment advice and make introductions to potential clients.[110]

Partners Often two people go into business together as partners. Partners can help one another access capital, spread the workload, share the risk, and share expertise.

While some partnerships fall apart over time, others endure and become very successful. Some examples of high-performance business partnerships include Twitter's Evan Williams, Biz Stone, and Jack Dorsey; Microsoft's Bill Gates and Paul Allen; Imagine Entertainment's Brian Grazer and Ron Howard; the New York Yankees baseball franchise's Joe Torre and the late Don Zimmer; and Google's Sergei Brin and Larry Page.

What factors contribute to successful, long-lasting business relationships? Some experts suggest that the answer includes trust, mutual respect, shared vision and values, and honest and open communication.[111] For example, Berkshire Hathaway's CEO, Warren Buffett, values the fact that his vice chairman, Charlie Munger, plays devil's advocate by looking at "every possible business deal skeptically, always looking for a reason to say no." In contrast, Buffett uses every argument possible to convince Munger to support a given deal.[112] By the end of these discussions, the partners decide whether to invest or not in a given company. This strategy has helped Berkshire Hathaway grow from a start-up in 1965 to an influential investment company that reported a net worth of $34.2 billion in 2013.[113]

6 | CORPORATE ENTREPRENEURSHIP

Large corporations are more than passive bystanders in the entrepreneurial explosion. Consider Microsoft. Every spring, the company hosts Techfest, essentially a three-day science fair that spotlights innovations the company may pursue. About half of Microsoft's researchers come from around the world to be inspired and energized by the glimpse at their colleagues' creative projects.[114]

Even established companies try to find and pursue profitable new ideas—and they need in-house entrepreneurs (often called intrapreneurs) to do so. If you work in a company and are considering launching a new business venture, Exhibit 6.6 can help you decide whether the new idea is worth pursuing.

6.1 | Build Support for Your Ideas

A manager with an idea to capitalize on a market opportunity will need to get others in the organization to buy in or sign on. In other words, you need to build a network of allies who support and will help implement the idea.

If you need to build support for a project idea, the first step involves *clearing the investment* with your immediate boss or bosses.[115] At this stage, you explain the idea and seek approval to look for wider support.

Higher executives often want evidence that the project is backed by your peers before committing to it. This involves *making cheerleaders*—people who will support the manager before formal approval from higher levels. Managers at General Electric refer to this strategy as "loading the gun"—lining up ammunition in support of your idea.

Next, *horse trading* begins. You can offer promises of payoffs from the project in return for support, time, money, and other resources that peers and others contribute.

Finally, you should *get the blessing* of relevant higher-level officials. This usually involves a formal presentation. You will need to guarantee the project's technical and political feasibility. Higher management's endorsement of the project and promises of resources help convert potential supporters into an enthusiastic team. At this point, you can go back to your boss and make specific plans for going ahead with the project.

Along the way, expect resistance and frustration—and use passion and persistence, as well as business logic, to persuade others to get on board.

● Berkshire Hathaway Inc. Chairman Warren Buffett (right) talks to Microsoft Corp. Chairman Bill Gates at the Berkshire Hathaway annual meeting. Buffett usually laments that his company has more cash than investment opportunities, but announced that he envisioned an acquisition so big that he'd have to sell some stocks to free up funds.

6.2 | Build Intrapreneurship in Your Organization

Since taking over as CEO of Google in April of 2011, Larry Page has been busy reviving the organization's entrepreneurial culture. He's speeding up the pace of change; and in over the six months he's been at the helm, he has made social media integration (Google+) a priority, acquired Motorola Mobility, launched Google Wallet, and shut down underperforming projects like Google Labs, Aardvark, Slide, and Fast Flip.[116]

Two common approaches used to stimulate intrapreneurial activity are skunkworks and bootlegging. **Skunkworks** are project teams designated to produce a new product. A team is formed with a specific goal within a specified time frame. A respected person is chosen to be manager of the skunkworks. In this approach to corporate innovation, risk takers are not punished for taking risks and failing—their former jobs are held for them. The risk takers also have the opportunity to earn large rewards. Adam Gryglak, chief engineer at Ford Motor Company, led a skunkworks team to develop an all-new Ford diesel engine in a record-setting 36 months.[117]

Bootlegging refers to informal efforts—as opposed to official job assignments—in which employees work to create new products and processes of their own choosing and initiative. Informal can mean secretive, such as when a bootlegger believes the company or the boss will frown on those activities. But companies should tolerate some bootlegging, and some even encourage it. To a limited extent, they allow people freedom to pursue pet projects without asking what they are or monitoring progress, figuring bootlegging will lead to some lost time but also to learning and to some profitable innovations.

Merck, desiring entrepreneurial thinking and behavior in research and development, explicitly rejects budgets for planning and control. New product teams don't *get* a budget. They must persuade people to join the team and commit *their* resources. This creates a survival-of-the-fittest process, mirroring the competition in the real world.[118] At Merck, as at Wells Fargo TPA, intrapreneurship derives from deliberate strategic thinking and execution.

6.3 | Managing Intrapreneurship is Risky

Organizations that encourage intrapreneurship face an obvious risk: the effort can fail.[119] However, this risk can be managed. In fact, failing to foster intrapreneurship may represent a subtler but greater risk than encouraging it. The organization that resists entrepreneurial initiative may lose its ability to adapt when conditions dictate change.

The most dangerous risk in intrapreneurship is the risk of overrelying on a single project. Many companies fail while awaiting the completion of one large, innovative project.[120] The successful intrapreneurial organization avoids overcommitment to a single project and relies on its entrepreneurial spirit to produce at least one winner from among several projects.

Organizations also court failure when they spread their entrepreneurial efforts over too many projects.[121] If there are many projects, each effort may be too small in scale. Managers

---

| Exhibit 6.6 | Checklist for choosing ideas |

Fit with Your Skills and Expertise

Do you believe in the product or service?

Does the need it fits mean something to you personally?

Do you like and understand the potential customers?

Do you have experience in this type of business?

Do the basic success factors of this business fit your skills?

Are the tasks of the enterprise ones you could enjoy doing yourself?

Are the people the enterprise will employ ones you will enjoy working with and supervising?

Has the idea begun to take over your imagination and spare time?

Fit with the Market

Is there a real customer need?

Can you get a price that gives you good margins?

Would customers believe in the product coming from your company?

Does the product or service you propose produce a clearly perceivable customer benefit that is significantly better than that offered by competing ways to satisfy the same basic need?

Is there a cost-effective way to get the message and the product to the customers?

Fit with the Company

Is there a reason to believe your company could be very good at the business?

Does it fit the company culture?

Does it look profitable?

Will it lead to larger markets and growth?

What to Do When Your Idea Is Rejected

As an intrapreneur, you will frequently find that your idea has been rejected. There are a few things you can do.

1. Give up and select a new idea.

2. Listen carefully, understand what is wrong, improve your idea and your presentation, and try again.

3. Find someone else to whom you can present your idea by considering:

   a. Who will benefit most if it works? Can they be a sponsor?

   b. Who are potential customers? Will they demand the product?

   c. How can you get to the people who really care about intrapreneurial ideas?

Source: G. Pinchot III, *Intrapreneuring*, Copyright © 1985 by John Wiley & Sons, Inc. Reprinted by permission of the author, www.pinchot.com.

Intrapreneurship at IKEA

Many college students have probably shopped at IKEA to buy affordable furnishings for their apartments, dormitory rooms, or homes. The popular Swedish retailer has more than 151,000 employees working in 345 stores in 42 countries. IKEA's approach to business is captured in its vision:

> At IKEA, our vision is to create a better everyday life for the many people. Our business idea supports this vision by offering a wide range of well designed, functional home furnishing products at prices so low that as many people as possible will be able to afford them.

In order to keep costs low for customers, intrapreneurs at IKEA look for innovative and creative ways to be more efficient. Sometimes these ideas are exciting, but more times than not they are simple improvements that can have real impact in the long run. Consider the ubiquitous wooden pallet. For over 50 years, IKEA has shipped its merchandise on 55-pound wooden pallets. Using about 10 million each year, the pallets are rented from suppliers and used many times before they have to be replaced.

In January 2012 the company began switching to a "paper variant that's lighter, thinner, and—the company says—cheaper to use." The new corrugated cardboard pallet is 90 percent lighter and one-third the height of the wooden version, but can carry up to 1,650 pounds (the same as a wooden pallet). Lighter pallets can reduce the size of the environmental footprint related to transporting products from IKEA's factories to stores. Another difference is that the cardboard version is good for only one shipment and then needs to be recycled.

IKEA is making this change because it expects the lighter and shorter pallets to decrease transportation costs by about $193 million or 10 percent per year.

Intrepreneurship at IKEA is helping the firm become more efficient with its transportation, which, if successful, will have a positive impact on the bottom line.

IKEA is switching from wood to paper pallets to transport its products around the globe. The lighter paper pallets are expected to decrease transportation costs by about $193 million or 10 percent per year.

Discussion Questions

1. IKEA has been using wooden pallets for several decades. Why do you think it took until 2011 for the company to pursue the idea of switching from wooden to paper pallets?

2. The expected savings related to transportation costs were discussed in this feature. What are some potential negative consequences of the company's decision?

SOURCES: R. Leblanc, "Paper Pallets for Export," *Packaging Revolution* (online), July 22, 2013, http://packagingrevolution.net; "IKEA's Challenge to the Wooden Pallet," *Bloomberg Businessweek*, November 28–December 4, 2011, p. 67; company website, IKEA, http://www.ikea.com.

---

will consider the projects unattractive because of their small size. Or those recruited to manage the projects may have difficulty building power and status within the organization.

6.4 | An Entrepreneurial Orientation Encourages New Ideas

Not only can we distinguish characteristics of individual entrepreneurs, but we can do the same for companies. Companies that are highly entrepreneurial differ from those that are not. CEOs play a crucial role in promoting entrepreneurship within large corporations.[122]

Entrepreneurial orientation is the tendency of an organization to engage in activities designed to identify and capitalize successfully on opportunities to launch new ventures by entering new or established markets with new or existing goods or services.[123] Entrepreneurial orientation is determined by five tendencies:

1. *Independent action*—The organization grants individuals and teams the freedom to exercise their creativity, champion promising ideas, and carry them through to completion.

2. *Innovativeness*—The firm supports new ideas, experimentation, and creative processes that can lead to new products or processes; it is willing to depart from existing practices and venture beyond the status quo.

3. *Risk taking*—The organization is willing to commit significant resources and perhaps borrow heavily, to venture into the unknown. The tendency to take risks can be assessed by considering whether people are bold or cautious, whether they require high levels of certainty before taking or allowing action, and whether they tend to follow tried-and-true paths.

4. *Proactiveness*—The organization acts in anticipation of future problems and opportunities. A proactive firm changes the competitive landscape; other firms merely react. Proactive firms, like proactive individuals, are forward-thinking and fast to act, and are

leaders rather than followers.[125] Proactive firms encourage and allow individuals and teams to *be* proactive.

5. *Competitive aggressiveness*—The firm tends to challenge competitors directly and intensely to achieve entry or improve its position. In other words, it has a competitive tendency to outperform its rivals in the marketplace. This might involve striking fast to beat competitors to the punch, tackle them head-to-head, and analyze and target competitors' weaknesses.

Entrepreneurial orientation should enhance the likelihood of success and may be particularly important for conducting business internationally.[126]

Thus an "entrepreneurial" firm engages in an effective combination of independent action, innovativeness, risk taking, proactiveness, and competitive aggressiveness.[127] The relationship between these factors and the performance of the

lack of competitive fire—will undermine entrepreneurial activities. And without entrepreneurship, how would firms survive and thrive in a constantly changing competitive environment?

Thus management can create environments that foster more entrepreneurship. If your bosses are not doing this, consider trying some entrepreneurial experiments on your own.[128] Seek out others with an entrepreneurial bent. What can you learn from them, and what can you teach others? Sometimes it takes individuals and teams of experimenters to show the possibilities to those

entrepreneurial orientation the tendency of an organization to identify and capitalize successfully on opportunities to launch new ventures by entering new or established markets with new or existing goods or services

> ## "I had to make my own living and my own opportunity! but I made it! don't sit down and wait for the opportunities to come. Get up and make them."
>
> —Madam C.J. Walker, *Founder of Walker Cosmetics Line*[124]

firm is complicated and depends on many things. Still, you can imagine how the opposite profile—too many constraints on action, business as usual, extreme caution, passivity, and a

at the top. Ask yourself, and ask others: Between the bureaucrats and the entrepreneurs, who is having a more positive impact? And who is having more fun?

Study Checklist

- ☑ Did you tear out the perforated student review card at the back of the text to revisit learning objectives and key terms and definitions?

Connect® Management is available for M Management. Additional resources include:

- ☑ Interactive Applications:
  - Case Analysis: To Be, or Not to Be, an Entrepreneur
  - Drag & Drop: Opportunity Analysis for Shoes With Soul
  - Self-Assessment: Assessing Your Flexibility
  - Video Case: Entrepreneurship at 1154 Lill Studio

- ☑ LearnSmart—Multiple choice questions help you determine what you already know, are not sure about, or need to practice based on your score. And with SmartBook, you can read the relevant section in the eBook as well as practice and recharge what you've learned.

- ☑ Chapter Video: Pillow Pets

- ☑ Young Manager Speaks Out: Joe Gaspar, Bicycle Shop/Owner

part three

7
chapter

Organizing **for Success**

Learning Objectives

After studying Chapter 7, you will be able to

LO1 Define the fundamental characteristics of organization structure.

LO2 Distinguish among the four dimensions of an organization's vertical structure.

LO3 Give examples of four basic forms of horizontal structures of organizations.

LO4 Describe important mechanisms used to coordinate work.

LO5 Discuss how organizations can improve their agility through strategy, commitment to customers, and use of technology.

The worldwide mobile gaming market for smartphones and tablets is expected to reach 22 billion in 2015, an increase of nearly 30 percent over the previous year.[1] How many people play these mobile games? According to AppData, a research firm that tracks this information, as of May 2013,[2]

- 43.5 million people play Candy Crush Saga (King).
- 38.4 million people play Farmville 2 (Zynga).
- 30.2 million people play Texas HoldEm Poker (Zynga).
- 24.7 million people play Pet Rescue Saga (King).
- 23.3 million people play Dragon City (Social Point).

The competition for market-leader Zynga is heating up as companies like King develop and launch popular games like Candy

As with Zynga and Electronic Arts, an organization's success often depends on the way work and responsibilities are organized. Ideally managers make decisions that align their company's structure with its strategy, so employees have the authority, skills, resources, and motivation to focus on the activities where they can contribute most to the company's success.

This chapter focuses on the vertical and horizontal dimensions of organization structure. We begin by covering basic principles of *differentiation* and *integration*. Next we discuss the vertical structure, which includes issues of authority, hierarchy, delegation, and decentralization. Then we describe various forms of horizontal structure, including functional, divisional, and matrix forms. We illustrate the ways in which organizations can integrate their structures: achieving coordination by standardization, by plan, and by mutual adjustment. Finally, we focus on the importance of organizational flexibility and responsiveness—that is, the organization's ability to change

> "Good order is the foundation of all things."
>
> —Edmund Burke

Crush Saga, currently the top-rated app on Facebook. Virtually unknown in 2012, King recently filed an initial public offering rumored to be valued at $5 billion.[3] Intense competition, nonexistent brand loyalty, and low barriers to entry make competing in the mobile gaming market challenging. Companies like Electronic Arts (FIFA and Madden) and ATVI (World of Warcraft) are reorganizing their design, social media, and marketing efforts to capture more players from Facebook.[4] EA's gamble is paying off: since its launch in 2012, The Simpsons: Tapped Out has generated $50 million in revenue and has more than 5 million daily active users.[5]

There are no guarantees that these organizational structuring efforts will produce the next blockbuster game. For example, Zynga's Mafia Wars 2, which had a group of up to 80 specialized employees working on its development for more than a year, lost 900,000 daily players since its peak of 2.5 million daily players in October 2011.[6] However, given Zynga's track record of social virtual game hits, specialists and design experts within the firm are undoubtedly working on the next big thing to be played on mobile devices like smartphones and tablets.

its form and adapt to new strategies, technology innovations, changes in the environment, and other challenges.

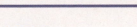

YOUNG MANAGERS
Speak Out!

"We (our team) know how to basically delegate the different tasks because we know what each other's strengths are. Having that knowledge and being able to leverage the talent on our team really helps us to have more successful outcomes..."

—Stephanie Weber, Sales Analytics Manager

organization chart the reporting structure and division of labor in an organization

mechanistic organization a form of organization that seeks to maximize internal efficiency

organic structure an or ganizational form that emphasizes flexibility

differentiation an aspect of the organization's internal environment created by job specialization and the division of labor

integration the degree to which differentiated work units work together and coordinate their efforts

● King Inc., makers of Candy Crush Saga, is the largest skill-gaming company in the world. 150 billion games of Candy Crush have been played to date and 500 million people have installed the game.

LO1 Define the fundamental characteristics of organization structure

1 | FUNDAMENTALS OF ORGANIZING

We often begin to describe a firm's structure by looking at its organization chart. The **organization chart** depicts the positions in the firm and the way they are arranged. The chart provides a picture of the reporting structure (who reports to whom) and the various activities that are carried out by different individuals. Most companies have official organization charts drawn up to give people this information.

Exhibit 7.1 shows a traditional organization chart. Note the various types of information that are conveyed in a simple way:

- The boxes represent different work.

- The titles in the boxes show the work performed by each unit.

- Reporting and authority relationships are indicated by solid lines showing superior–subordinate connections.

- Levels of management are indicated by the number of horizontal layers in the chart. All persons or units that are at the same rank and report to the same person are on one level.

The organization chart in Exhibit 7.1 resembles the structure of organizations that German sociologist Max Weber addressed when he wrote about the concept of bureaucracy at the beginning of the 20th century. Many years later, two British management scholars (Burns and Stalker) described this type of structure as a **mechanistic organization**, a formal structure intended to promote internal efficiency.[7] But they went on to suggest the modern corporation has another option: the **organic structure**, which is much less rigid and, in fact, emphasizes flexibility. Differences between these two types of structures are listed in Exhibit 7.2.

An organic organization depends heavily on an informal structure of employee networks. Astute managers are keenly aware of these interactions, and they encourage employees to work more as teammates than as subordinates who take orders from the boss.[8] As we will discuss later in this chapter, the more organic a firm is, the more responsive it is to changing competitive demands and market realities.

study tip 7

Get organized—form a study group

Many students feel they can earn a good grade on their own and don't need others to help them study. While that may be true, teaming up with other students and meeting for an hour or two on a regular basis can help you learn the material better. How does it work? Meeting with peers helps you get organized and focus on the material instead of putting it off until later. Also, you will hear others' ideas and interpretations about "what's going to be on the exam," "what a topic in the book means," and "what the professor thinks is important." Discussing course topics with others should help you learn it more thoroughly, ultimately preparing you for the next exam.

Exhibit 7.1 A conventional organization chart

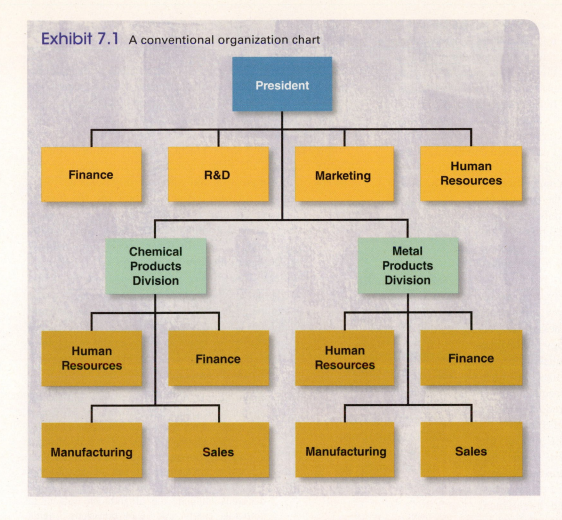

1.1 | Differentiation Creates Specialized Jobs

Within an organization's structure, differentiation is created through division of labor and job specialization. **Division of labor** means the work of the organization is subdivided into smaller tasks to be performed by individuals and units throughout the organization. **Specialization** means different people or groups perform specific parts of the larger task. The two concepts are, of course, closely related. Administrative assistants and accountants specialize in, and perform, different jobs; similarly, marketing, finance, and human resources tasks are divided among their respective departments. Specialization and division of labor are necessary because of the many tasks that must be carried out in an organization. The overall work of the organization would be too complex for any individual.[10]

Differentiation is high when an organization has many subunits and many specialists who think differently. Harvard professors Lawrence and Lorsch found that organizations in a complex, dynamic environment developed a high degree of differentiation to cope with the challenges. Companies in a simple, stable environment had low levels of differentiation. Companies in an intermediate environment had intermediate differentiation.[11]

Besides differing in their reliance on informal networks and formal organization charts, company structures can vary in terms of their differentiation and integration:

- **Differentiation** means the organization is composed of many different units that work on different kinds of tasks, using different skills and work methods.

- **Integration** means these differentiated units are put back together so that work is coordinated into an overall product.[9]

1.2 | Integration Coordinates Employees' Efforts

As organizations differentiate their structures, managers must simultaneously consider issues of integration. The specialized tasks in an organization cannot be performed completely independently; they require some degree of communication and

Exhibit 7.2 Comparison of mechanistic and organic organizations

Characteristic	Mechanistic	Organic
Degree of formality	Formal	Informal
Primary emphasis	Efficiency	Flexibility
Job responsibilities	Narrowly defined	Broad and evolving
Communication	Orders and instructions	Advice and information
Decision making	Centralized	Decentralized
Expression of commitment	Obedience to authority	Commitment to organization
Source of guidance	Rules	Personal judgment
Employee interdependence	Limited, when necessary	Employees feel interconnected

Source: Adapted from T. Burns and G. Stalker, *The Management of Innovation* (London: Tavistock, 1961).

coordination the procedures that link the various parts of an organization to achieve the organization's overall mission

authority the legitimate right to make decisions and to tell other people what to do

cooperation. Integration and its related concept, **coordination**, refer to the procedures that link the various parts of the organization to achieve the organization's overall mission.

Integration is accomplished through structural mechanisms that enhance collaboration and coordination. Any job activity that links work units performs an integrative function. The more highly differentiated the firm, the greater the need for integration among its units. Lawrence and Lorsch found that highly differentiated firms were successful if they also had high levels of integration and were more likely to fail if they existed in complex environments but failed to integrate their activities adequately.[12] However, focusing on integration may slow innovation, at least for a while. In a study tracking the outcomes at information technology companies that acquired other firms, companies with more structural integration were less likely to introduce new products soon after the acquisition, but integration had less impact on product launches involving more experienced target companies.[13]

These concepts permeate the rest of the chapter. First we discuss *vertical differentiation* within organization structure—authority within an organization, the board of directors, the chief executive officer, and hierarchical levels, as well as issues pertaining to delegation and decentralization. Next we turn to *horizontal differentiation* in an organization's structure, exploring issues of departmentalization that create functional, divisional, and matrix organizations. Then we cover issues relating to structural integration, including coordination, organizational roles, interdependence, and boundary spanning. Finally we look at how these issues apply to organizations seeking greater agility.

Did You Know?

A recent survey of 100 large public companies in the United States found that more than half of boards had between 10 and 12 directors, the average cash retainer for serving a one-year term was $79,000, and 16 percent of directors were female and 15 percent of directors were ethnic minorities.[15]

LO2 Distinguish among the four dimensions of an organization's vertical structure

2 | THE VERTICAL STRUCTURE

The four dimensions of a firm's vertical structure—authority, span of control, delegation, and centralization—shape the company's reporting relationships, responsibility, and accountability.

2.1 | Authority Is Granted Formally and Informally

At the most fundamental level, the functioning of every organization depends on the use of **authority**, the legitimate right to make decisions and to tell other people what to do. For example, a boss has the authority to give an order to a subordinate. Traditionally authority resides in *positions* rather than in people. The job of vice president of a particular division has authority over that division, regardless of how many people come and go in that position and who currently holds it.

In private business enterprises, the owners have ultimate authority. In most small, simply structured companies, the owner also acts as manager. Sometimes the owner hires another person to manage the business and its employees. The owner gives this manager some authority to oversee the operations, but the manager is accountable to—that is, reports and defers to—the owner, who retains the ultimate authority. In larger companies the principle is the same, but the structure of top management has several components:

- *Board of directors*—In corporations, the owners are the stockholders. But because there are numerous stockholders and these individuals generally lack timely information, few are directly involved in managing the organization. Stockholders elect a board of directors to oversee the organization. The board, led by the chairperson, makes major decisions affecting the organization, subject to corporate charter and bylaw provisions. Boards select, assess, reward, and perhaps replace the CEO; determine the firm's strategic direction and review financial performance; and assure ethical, socially responsible, and legal conduct.[14] The board's membership usually includes some top executives—called *inside directors*. Outside members of the board typically are executives at other companies. Successful boards tend to be those who are active, critical participants in determining company strategies.

- *Chief executive officer*—The authority officially vested in the board of directors is assigned to a chief executive officer (CEO), who occupies the top of the organizational pyramid. The CEO is personally accountable to the board and to the owners for the organization's performance. In some corporations, one person holds the three positions of CEO, chair of the board of directors, and president.[16] More commonly, however, the CEO holds two of those positions, serving as either the chair of the board or the president of the organization. When the CEO is president, the chair may be honorary and do little more than conduct meetings. If the chair is the CEO, the president is second in command.

- *Top management team*—CEOs may share their authority with other key members of the top management team. Top management teams typically consist of the CEO, president, chief operating officer, chief financial officer, and other key executives. Rather than make critical decisions on their own, CEOs at companies such as Shutterfly, Infosys, Walt Disney, and ConocoPhillips regularly meet with their top management teams to make decisions as a unit.[17]

Formal position authority is generally the primary means of running an organization. An order that a boss gives to a lower-level employee is usually carried out. As this occurs throughout the organization day after day, the organization can move forward and achieve its goals.[18] However, authority in an organization is not always position-dependent. People with particular expertise, experience, or personal qualities may have considerable *informal* authority—scientists in research companies, for example, or employees who are computer-savvy.

Authority is directly related to the three broad levels of the organizational pyramid, commonly called the *hierarchy*. The CEO occupies the top position as the senior member of top management. The top managerial level also includes presidents and vice presidents—the strategic managers in charge of the entire organization. The second broad level of the organization

the authority to make decisions and tell lower-level people what to do. For example, middle managers can give orders to first-line supervisors; first-line super-visors, in turn, direct operative-level workers.

A powerful trend for U.S. businesses over the past few decades has been to reduce the number of hierarchical layers. General Electric used to have 29 levels; today it has only a handful of layers, and its hierarchical structure is basically flat. Most executives today believe that fewer layers create a more efficient, fast-acting, and cost-effective organization. This also holds true for the subunits of major corporations. A study of 234 branches of a financial services company found that branches with fewer layers tended to have higher operating efficiency than did branches with more layers.[19]

This trend and research might seem to suggest that hierarchy is a bad thing, but entrepreneur Joel Spolsky learned that a completely flat structure is not necessarily ideal. When Spolsky and Michael Pryor started Fog Creek Software, they decided

> ## "The key to successful leadership today is influence, not authority."
>
> —Kenneth Blanchard

is middle management. At this level, managers are in charge of facilities or departments. The lowest level, made up of lower management and workers, includes office managers, sales managers, supervisors, and other first-line managers, as well as the employees who report directly to them. This level is also called the *operational level* of the organization.

An authority structure is the glue that holds these levels together. Generally, but not always, people at higher levels have

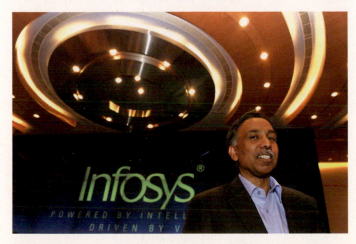

● S.D. Shibulal, co-founder, managing director, and CEO of Infosys, makes major decisions in concert with key members of his top management team. Founded in India in 1981 by seven people and an initial investment of $250, the global technology and outsourcing firm reports 2014 revenues of $8.25 billion.

they would empower employees by having everyone report to the two owners. The system worked fine for a few years until Fog Creek grew to 17 full-time employees. At that size, the company was no longer one small, happy family; employees had concerns and were finding it difficult to approach the partners and set up three-way meetings with them. So Spolsky and Pryor tapped two of the employees to serve as leaders of programming teams. Employees found it easier to talk to their team leader, and Spolsky concluded that this layer of "middle management" helps his company run more smoothly.[20]

2.2 | Span of Control Determines a Manager's Authority

The number of people under a manager is an important feature of an organization's structure. The number of subordinates who report directly to an executive or supervisor is called the **span of control**. Differences in the span of control affect the shape of an organization. Holding size constant, narrow spans build a *tall* organization with many reporting levels. Wide spans create a *flat* organization with fewer reporting levels. The span of control can be too narrow or too wide. The optimal span of control maximizes effectiveness by balancing two considerations:

1. It must be narrow enough to permit managers to maintain control over subordinates.

2. It must not be so narrow that it leads to overcontrol and an excessive number of managers overseeing a few subordinates.

delegation the assignment of new or additional responsibilities to a subordinate

responsibility the assignment of a task that an employee is supposed to carry out

accountability the expectation that employees will perform a job, take corrective action when necessary, and report upward on the status and quality of their performance

The optimal span of control depends on a number of factors. The span should be wide under the following conditions:

- The work is clearly defined and unambiguous.

- Subordinates are highly trained and have access to information.

- The manager is highly capable and supportive.

- Jobs are similar, and performance measures are comparable.

- Subordinates prefer autonomy to close supervisory control.

If the opposite conditions exist, a narrow span of control may be more appropriate.[21]

2.3 | Delegation Is How Managers Use others' Talents

As we recognize that authority in organizations is spread out over various levels and spans of control, we see the importance of **delegation**, the assignment of authority and responsibility to a subordinate at a lower level. Delegation often requires a subordinate to report back to his or her boss about how effectively the assignment was carried out. Delegation is perhaps the most fundamental feature of management at all levels because it entails getting work done through others. The process can occur between any two individuals in any type of structure with regard to any task. Some managers are comfortable fully delegating an assignment to subordinates; others are not.

Responsibility, Authority, and Accountability When delegating work, it is helpful to distinguish among the concepts of authority, responsibility, and accountability. **Responsibility** means that a person is assigned a task that he or she is supposed to carry out. When delegating work responsibilities, the manager also should delegate to the subordinate enough authority to get the job done. *Authority* means that the person has the power and the right to make decisions, give orders, draw on resources, and do whatever else is necessary to fulfill the responsibility. Ironically, people often have more responsibility than authority; they must perform as well as they can through informal influence tactics instead of relying purely on authority.

As the manager delegates responsibilities, subordinates are held accountable for achieving results. **Accountability** means the subordinate's manager has the right to expect the subordinate to perform the job, and the right to take corrective action if the subordinate fails to do so. The subordinate must report upward on the status and quality of his or her performance.

However, the ultimate responsibility—accountability to higher-ups—lies with the manager doing the delegating. Managers remain responsible and accountable not only for their own actions but also for the actions of their subordinates. Managers should not use delegation to escape their own responsibilities; however, sometimes managers refuse to accept responsibility for subordinates' actions. They "pass the buck" or take other evasive action to ensure they are not held accountable for mistakes.[22] Ideally, empowering employees to make decisions or take action results in an increase in employee responsibility.

Advantages of Delegation As illustrated in Exhibit 7.3, delegating work offers important advantages, particularly when it is done effectively. Effective delegation leverages the manager's energy and talent and those of his or her subordinates. It lets managers accomplish much more than they could do on their own. Conversely, lack of or ineffective delegation sharply reduces what a manager can achieve. Delegation also conserves one of the manager's most valuable assets—his or her time. It frees the manager to devote energy to important, higher-level activities such as planning, setting objectives, and monitoring performance.

Another significant advantage of delegation is that it develops effective subordinates. Delegation essentially gives the subordinate a more important job. The subordinate gains an opportunity to develop new skills and demonstrate potential for additional responsibilities and perhaps promotion—in effect, a vital form of on-the-job training that may pay off in the future. In addition, at least for some employees, delegation promotes a sense of being an important, contributing member of the organization, so these employees tend to feel a stronger commitment, perform their tasks better, and engage in more innovation.[23]

:::::::::::::::::::

Richard Semler has taken delegation and empowerment to a whole new level at his Brazilian company, Semco. Since taking over the struggling manufacturing company from his father 30 years ago, Semler's goal has been to create a work environment in which employees feel "exhilaration and fulfillment." His actions have been much more than the typical lip service some companies pay to empowerment initiatives. Semco does not have any of the following: HR department, organizational chart, job descriptions, fixed working hours, multiyear plans, or a permanent CEO.[24] Employees are encouraged to pursue their own ideas without having to ask for their managers' approval. Employees are given a few parameters of what's expected from them in terms of performance and then are given the autonomy and freedom to accomplish their jobs.[25]

Exhibit 7.3	Advantages of delegation

LEVERAGES managers' energy and talent

CONSERVES managers' most valuable asset: time

DEVELOPS subordinates' managerial skills and knowledge

PROMOTES subordinates' sense of importance and commitment

Source: Adapted from Z. X. Chen and S. Aryee, "Delegation and Employee Work Outcomes: An Examination of the Cultural Context of Mediating Processes in China," *Academy of Management Journal* 50, no. 1 (2007), pp. 226–38.

How has Semco done as a company? Very well. Though precise sales figures are not available to the public (Semco is a private firm), average annual revenue growth has been reported at 40 percent. Another report states that the company has grown from $35 million and several hundred employees when Semler took over as CEO to more than $200 million and 3,000 employees in recent years.[26] Semco's unusual approach to delegation and empowerment has led to more than 80 universities publishing case studies about the company and Semler writing *Maverick,* a best-selling management book about "the world's most unusual workplace."[27]

••••••••••••••••

Through delegation, the organization also receives payoffs. When managers can devote more time to important managerial functions while lower-level employees carry out assignments, jobs are done more efficiently and cost-effectively. In addition, as subordinates develop and grow in their own jobs, their ability to contribute to the organization increases.

How Should Managers Delegate? To achieve the advantages we have just discussed, managers must delegate properly. As Exhibit 7.4 shows, effective delegation follows several steps.[28]

The first step in the delegation process, defining the goal, requires a manager to clearly understand the outcome he or she wants. Then the manager should select a person who is capable of performing the task. Delegation is especially beneficial when you can identify an employee who would benefit from developing skills through the experience of taking on the additional responsibility.

The person who gets the assignment should be given the authority, time, and resources to carry out the task successfully. The required resources usually involve people, money, and equipment, but they may also involve critical information that will put the assignment in context. Throughout the delegation process, the manager and the subordinate must work together and communicate about the project. The manager should seek the subordinate's ideas at the beginning and inquire about progress or problems at periodic meetings and review sessions. Even though the subordinate performs the assignment, the manager needs to be available and aware of its current status. These checkups also provide an important opportunity to offer encouragement and praise.

Some tasks, such as disciplining subordinates and conducting performance reviews, should not be delegated. But when managers err, it usually is because they delegated too little rather than too much. The manager who wants to learn how

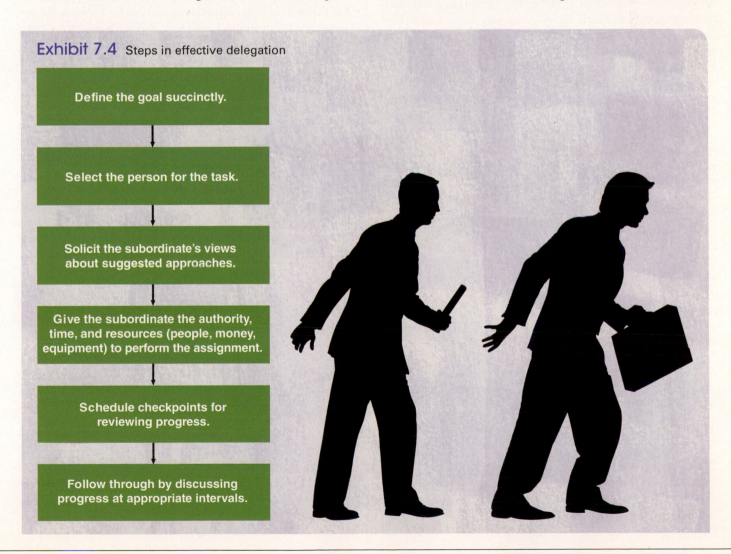

Exhibit 7.4 Steps in effective delegation

Define the goal succinctly.

Select the person for the task.

Solicit the subordinate's views about suggested approaches.

Give the subordinate the authority, time, and resources (people, money, equipment) to perform the assignment.

Schedule checkpoints for reviewing progress.

Follow through by discussing progress at appropriate intervals.

centralized organization an organization in which high-level executives make most decisions and pass them to lower levels for implementation

decentralized organization an organization in which lower-level managers make important decisions

line departments units that deal directly with the organization's primary goods and services

staff departments units that support line departments

departmentalization subdividing an organization into smaller subunits

to delegate more effectively should remember this distinction: If you are not delegating, you are merely *doing* things; but the more you delegate, the more you are truly *building* and *managing* an organization.[29]

2.4 | Decentralization Spreads Decision-Making Power

The delegation of responsibility and authority *decentralizes* decision making. In a **centralized organization**, important decisions usually are made at the top. In **decentralized organizations**, more decisions are made at lower levels. Ideally decision making occurs at the level of the people who are most directly affected and have the most intimate knowledge about the problem. This is particularly important when the business environment is fast-changing and decisions must be made quickly and well. Balanced against these criteria, centralization may be valuable when departments have different priorities or conflicting goals, which need to be mediated by top management. For example, when researchers modeled the search for new ideas in organizations, they found that the worst performance occurred in decentralized organizations where the search for new ideas was carried out at lower levels, because ideas were presented for approval only if they benefited the particular department doing the search.[30]

Sometimes organizations change their degree of centralization, depending on the particular challenges they face. Tougher times often cause senior management to take charge, whereas in times of rapid growth, decisions are pushed farther down the chain of command. When Jeff Harvey took over Burgerville, a 39-unit restaurant chain in Vancouver, Washington, he needed to figure out a way to keep sales from declining. His solution was to give more freedom and autonomy to the employees and managers of the individual restaurants. As part of this decentralization effort, he removed the regional manager position from the organizational structure. In the past, some of the regional managers were known to "micromanage"

● Burgerville was founded in 1961 by George Propstra in Vancouver, WA. Burgerville is known for its progressive business practices and commitment to local resources.

the general managers of each restaurant. Employees have responded well to the decentralized environment by suggesting several initiatives that the company has implemented over the past five years, including 100 percent wind power for all of the chain's locations; health insurance for both full- and part-time employees; drive-through lanes for cars and bicyclists; and new limited-time-only products like Ale-Battered Albacore and Summer Slaw, Fresh Strawberry Lemonade, and Rosemary Shoestring Potatoes.[31] Harvey's leadership approach is paying off. Annual sales revenue at Burgerville increased from $55 million in 2005 to $68 million in 2009. Harvey's efforts were recognized in 2010 when he was chosen as *Restaurant Business*'s Entrepreneur of the Year.[32]

Most executives today understand the advantages of pushing decision-making authority down to the point of the action. The level that deals directly with problems and opportunities has the most relevant information and can best foresee the consequences of decisions. Executives also see how the decentralized approach allows people to take timelier action.[33]

According to Raj Gupta, president of Environmental Systems Design (ESD), the engineering design firm decentralized as a necessary response to growth. A traditional "command-and-control" approach to management worked fine when the company was starting out, but now with 220 engineering and design professionals designing for diverse clients working on commercial, transportation, residential, manufacturing, energy, and other projects, it would be impossible for a few people at the top to dictate solutions. In fact, it wouldn't even be desirable, given the diverse expertise of its employees. So instead of grouping staff into functional departments such as sustainable design or electrical work, ESD has a structure in which studios of professionals serve particular clients, making decisions to meet their specialized needs.[34]

LO3 Give examples of four basic forms of horizontal structures of organizations

3 | THE HORIZONTAL STRUCTURE

As the tasks of organizations become increasingly complex, the organization inevitably must be subdivided—that is, *departmentalized*. **Line departments** are those that have responsibility for the principal activities of the firm. Line units deal directly with the organization's primary goods or services; they make things, sell things, or provide customer service. At General Motors, line departments include product design, fabrication,

Traditional Thinking

It is inevitable that line managers bump heads with staff professionals because the latter are too focused on monitoring, controlling, and avoiding risk.

Source: Adapted from E. E. Lawler III, "New Roles for the Staff Function: Strategic Support and Services," in *Organizing for the Future*, J. Galbraith, E. E. Lawler III, & Associates (San Francisco: Jossey-Bass, 1993).

The Best Managers Today

Expect staff professionals to contribute to the success of the business through their expertise and strategic thinking.

---

assembly, distribution, and the like. Line managers typically have much authority and power in the organization, and they have the ultimate responsibility for making major operating decisions. They also are accountable for the "bottom-line" results of their decisions.

Staff departments are those that provide specialized or professional skills that support line departments. They include research, legal, accounting, public relations, and human resources departments. In large companies, each of these specialized units may have its own vice president, some of whom are vested with a great deal of authority, as when accounting or finance groups approve and monitor budgetary activities.

In traditionally structured organizations, conflicts often arose between line and staff departments. One reason was that career paths and success in many staff functions have depended on being an expert in that particular functional area, whereas success in line functions is based more on knowing the organization's industry. So while line managers might be eager to pursue new products and customers, staff managers might seem to stifle these ideas with a focus on requirements and procedures. Line managers might seem more willing to take risks for the sake of growth, while staff managers seem more focused on protecting the company from risks. But in today's organizations, staff units tend to be less focused on monitoring and controlling performance and more interested in providing strategic support and expert advice.[35] For example, human resource managers have broadened their focus from merely creating procedures that meet legal requirements to helping organizations plan for, recruit, develop, and keep the kinds of employees who will give the organization a long-term competitive advantage. This type of strategic thinking not only makes staff managers more valuable to their organizations but also can reduce the conflict between line and staff departments.[36]

As organizations divide work into different units, we can detect patterns in the way departments are clustered and arranged. The three basic approaches to **departmentalization** are functional, divisional, and matrix.

> **functional organization**
> departmentalization around specialized activities such as production, marketing, and human resources

3.1 | Functional Organizations Foster Efficient Experts

In a **functional organization**, jobs (and departments) are specialized and grouped according to *business functions* and the skills they require: production, marketing, human resources, research and development, finance, accounting, and so forth. Exhibit 7.5 is a basic functional organization chart.

The traditional functional approach to departmentalization has a number of potential advantages:[37]

1. *Economies of scale can be realized.* When people with similar skills are grouped, the company can buy more efficient equipment and obtain discounts for large purchases.

2. *Monitoring of the environment* is more effective. Each functional group is more closely attuned to developments in its own field, so it can adapt more readily.

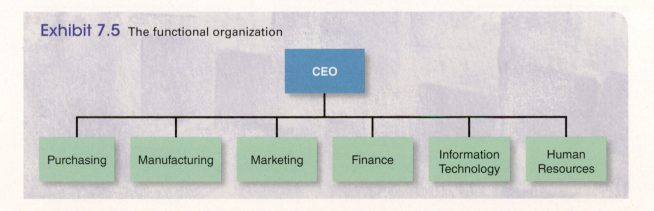

Exhibit 7.5 The functional organization

CEO — Purchasing | Manufacturing | Marketing | Finance | Information Technology | Human Resources

3. *Performance standards* are better maintained. People with similar training and interests may develop a shared concern for performance in their jobs.

4. People have greater opportunity for *specialized training* and *in-depth skill development.*

5. Technical specialists are relatively *free of administrative work.*

6. *Decision making* and *lines of communication* are simple and clearly understood.

The functional form does have disadvantages, however. People may care more about their own function than about the company as a whole, and their attention to functional tasks may reduce their focus on overall product quality and customer satisfaction. Managers develop functional expertise but lack knowledge of the other areas of the business; they become specialists, not generalists. Between functions, conflicts arise, and communication and coordination fall off. In short, this structure may promote functional differentiation but not *functional integration.*

As a consequence, the functional structure may be most appropriate in rather simple, stable environments. If the organization becomes fragmented (or *dis*integrated), it may have difficulty developing and bringing new products to market and responding quickly to customer demands and other changes. Particularly when companies are growing and business environments are changing, organizations need to integrate work areas more effectively for flexibility and responsiveness. Other forms of departmentalization can be more flexible and responsive than the functional structure.

Demands for total quality, customer service, innovation, and speed have highlighted the shortcomings of the functional form.

Functional organizations, being highly differentiated, create barriers to coordination across functions. The functional organization will not disappear, in part because functional specialists will always be needed; but functional managers will make fewer decisions. The more important units will be cross-functional teams with integrative responsibilities for products, processes, or customers.[38]

3.2 | Divisional Organizations Develop a Customer Focus

As organizations grow and become increasingly diversified, their functional departments have difficulty managing a wide variety of products, customers, and geographic regions. In this case, organizations may restructure by creating a **divisional organization**, which groups all functions into a single division and duplicates functions across all the divisions. In the divisional organization chart in Exhibit 7.6, each division has its own operations, marketing, and finance departments. Separate divisions may act almost as separate businesses or profit centers and work autonomously to accomplish the goals of the entire enterprise. Here are some examples of how the same tasks would be organized under functional and divisional structures:[39]

Organizations can create a divisional structure in several ways:

- *Product divisions*—All functions that contribute to a given product are organized under one product manager. Johnson & Johnson is an example of this form. It has more than 250 independent company divisions, many of which are responsible for particular product lines. One of its companies, McNeil Consumer Health Care, sells Tylenol products, while Vistakon develops and markets ACUVUE contact lenses.

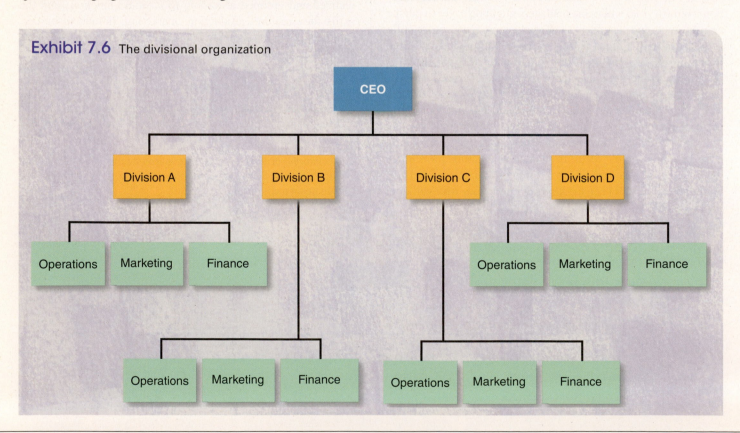

Exhibit 7.6 The divisional organization

The product approach to departmentalization offers a number of potential advantages.[40]

1. *Information needs are managed more easily* because people work closely on only one product.

2. *People are committed* full-time to a particular product line, so they are aware of how their jobs fit into the broader scheme.

3. *Task responsibilities are clear,* and managers are more independent and accountable.

4. *Managers receive broader training.* Because the product structure is more flexible than the functional structure, it is best suited for unstable environments, when an ability to adapt rapidly to change is important.

The product form does have some disadvantages, however. Coordination across product lines and divisions is difficult. And although managers learn to become generalists, they may not acquire the depth of expertise that develops in the functional structure. Functions are not centralized at headquarters, and the duplication of effort is expensive. And because decision making is decentralized, top management can lose control over decisions made in the divisions. Proper management of all the issues surrounding decentralization and delegation, as discussed earlier, is essential for this structure to be effective.[41]

- *Customer divisions*—Divisions are built around groups of customers. Pfizer recently replaced divisions based on location with three based on customer groups: primary care, specialty care, and emerging markets. The pharmaceutical company hopes that this structure will make the company more responsive to the needs of doctors and their patients in each group.[42] Similarly, a hospital may organize its services around child, adult, psychiatric, and emergency cases. Bank loan departments commonly have separate groups handling consumer and business needs.

- *Geographic divisions*—Divisions are structured around geographic regions. Geographic distinctions include district, territory, region, and country. Headquartered in Moline, Illinois, John Deere is a well-known manufacturer and supplier of farming equipment. To better serve its customers in Latin America and Europe, the company also maintains regional headquarters in Brazil and Germany. Given that the company predicts that 75 percent of its future growth will occur in seven parts of the world— the United States, Canada, Europe, Brazil, Russia, India, and China—it is possible that Deere will be opening additional regional headquarters over the next decade.[43]

The primary advantage of the product, customer, and regional approaches to departmentalization is the ability to focus on customer needs and provide faster, better service. But again, duplication of activities across many customer groups and geographic areas is expensive.

divisional organization departmentalization that groups units around products, customers, or geographic regions

matrix organization an organization composed of dual reporting relationships in which some managers report to two superiors—a functional manager and a divisional manager

3.3 | Matrix Organizations Try to Be the Best of Both Worlds

A **matrix organization** is a hybrid form of organization in which functional and divisional forms overlap. Managers and staff personnel report to two bosses—a functional manager and a divisional manager—creating a dual line of command. In Exhibit 7.7, for example, each project manager draws employees from each functional area to form a group for the project. The employees working on those projects report to the individual project manager as well as to the manager of their functional area.

A good example of the matrix structure can be found at Time Inc., the top magazine publisher in the United States and United Kingdom. At major Time Inc. titles like *Time, Sports Illustrated,* and *Fortune,* production managers who are responsible for getting the magazines printed report both to the individual publishers and editors of each title *and* to a senior corporate executive in charge of production. At the corporate level, Time Inc. achieves enormous economies of scale by buying paper and printing in bulk and by coordinating production activities for the company as a whole. At the same time, production managers working at each title ensure that the different needs and schedules of their individual magazines are met. Similar matrix arrangements are in place for other key managers, like circulation and finance. In this way, the company attempts to benefit from both the divisional and functional organization structures.

Like other organization structures, the matrix approach has a number of strengths:[44]

1. *Cross-functional problem solving* leads to better-informed and more creative decisions.

2. *Decision making is decentralized* to a level where information is processed properly and relevant knowledge is applied.

3. *Extensive communications networks* help process large amounts of information.

4. With decisions delegated to appropriate levels, *higher management levels are not overloaded* with operational decisions.

5. *Resource utilization is efficient* because key resources are shared across several important programs or products at the same time.

Functional Organization	Divisional Organization
A central purchasing department	A purchasing unit for each division
Separate companywide marketing, production, design, and engineering departments	Each product group's own experts in marketing, design, production, and engineering
A central city health department	Separate health units for the school district and the prison
Plantwide inspection, maintenance, and supply departments	Inspection, maintenance, and supply conducted by each production team

Take Charge of Your Career

Be a specialist first, then a generalist

If you think your career will be as a specialist, think again. Chances are, you will not want to stay forever in strictly technical jobs with no managerial responsibilities. Accountants are promoted to accounting department heads and team leaders, sales representatives become sales managers, writers become editors, and nurses become nursing directors. As your responsibilities increase, you must deal with more people, understand more about other aspects of the organization, and make bigger and more complex decisions. Beginning to learn now about these managerial challenges may yield benefits sooner than you think.

It will help if you can become both a specialist and a generalist. However, first seek to become a specialist: you should be an expert in something. This expertise will give you specific skills that help you provide concrete, identifiable value to your firm and to customers. And over time, you should learn to be a generalist, knowing enough about a variety of business disciplines so you can think strategically and work with different perspectives.

Patricia Calkins broadened her focus gradually and ambitiously from specialties in the sciences, expanding first to engineering and then to management. She started her career with AT&T's Western Electric subsidiary as a chemist. When she was considering a master's degree in chemistry, she heeded advice to develop her career opportunities by studying engineering. Once Calkins had her master's degree in civil and environmental engineering, the company saw her management talent and wanted to promote her. So she returned to school for another master's degree, this time in business administration. She developed her generalist skills by consulting and from that work moved to her current—and favorite—position as global vice president of environment, health, and safety at Xerox.

Sources: Company website, www.xerox.com; E. Garone, "Leading the Environmental Charge at Xerox," *The Wall Street Journal,* March 25, 2009, http://onlinewsj.com; and W. Kiechel III, "A Manager's Career in the New Economy," *Fortune,* April 4, 1994, pp. 68–27.

6. *Employees learn the collaborative skills* needed to function in an environment characterized by frequent meetings and more informal interactions.

7. *Dual career ladders* are elaborated as more career options become available on both sides of the organization.

As with the other structures, the matrix form also has disadvantages. Confusion can arise because people do not have a single superior to whom they feel primary responsibility. The design encourages managers who share subordinates to jockey for power, so conflict can occur. The mistaken belief can arise

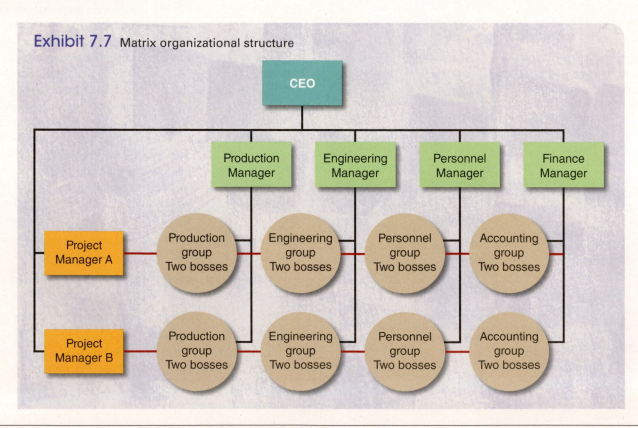

Exhibit 7.7 Matrix organizational structure

Can a Brewery Be a Force for Good?

In 2013, the U.S. beer market was approximately $100 billion. Though there are many different types of breweries, craft brewing is growing in popularity. With nearly 3,000 craft brewers reporting total sales of $14 billion in 2013, these operations tend to be local, innovative, independent, and creative in how they connect with their customers.

A large craft brewer, Colorado-based New Belgium Brewing, produces more than 23 million gallons of beer per year that is distributed in 28 states and Washington, DC. Beer enthusiasts know the company for its popular beers like Fat Tire Amber Ale and Ranger India Pale Ale, but it is also receiving kudos for its cutting-edge sustainability and green practices. Founded by Jeff Lebesch and Kim Jordan in 1991, New Belgium Brewing immediately differentiated itself from other brewers (and companies) by its socially and environmentally responsible approach as evidenced by its purpose statement: "To manifest our love and talent by crafting our customers' favorite brands and proving business can be a force for good." Part of doing good for the environment is captured in one of the company's core values: "Environmental stewardship: Honoring nature at every turn of the business."

How does New Belgium Brewing honor and protect the environment? The company fosters a high-involvement culture in which employees are treated like owners. Actually, as of 2012, New Belgium Brewing is 100 percent employee owned. The employee owners are involved in all major decisions and take responsibility for being effective environmental stewards. For example, on a quarterly basis, all managers and employees meet to identify ways to reduce the company's consumption of natural resources like water, electricity, natural gas, and greenhouse gas emissions.

By 2015, New Belgium Brewing hopes to accomplish the following green goals:

- Reduce CO_2 emissions by 25 percent.
- Work toward becoming a zero waste facility by conducting waste stream audits, replacing dumpsters with recycling containers, and tracking key data. and,
- Decrease water use (it's the primary ingredient in beer) by 18 percent.

New Belgium Brewing Company emphasizes eco-friendly practices and employee ownership in its marketing materials.

A recent decision provides further evidence of how New Belgium Brewing tries to minimize damage to the environment. The brewery needed to replace some of the trucks that it uses to make deliveries of beer to local restaurants and pubs. After analyzing several options, the employees suggested that the company lease Kenworth T370s, diesel-electric hybrids. Not only are the trucks powerful enough to haul beer, but they also get better gas mileage and produce fewer CO_2 emissions than non-hybrid trucks. In addition, New Belgium Brewing owns two other hybrid vehicle types: two Nissan Leaf electric vehicles and five Toyota Prius hybrids.

Is environmental stewardship working for New Belgium Brewing? It would seem the answer is yes. The company reported $180 million in revenue in 2012, a 41 percent increase over sales in 2009. Its reputation as a green pioneer continues to flourish. And, by all accounts, the nearly 500 employee-owners are engaged in their work and environment and take pride in crafting innovative, tasty beers.

Discussion Questions

- How would you characterize the organizational structure of New Belgium Brewing: mechanistic or organic? Explain your answer.
- What factors contribute to New Belgium Brewing's employees feeling empowered to pursue the company's core value: "Environmental stewardship: Honoring nature at every turn of the business"?
- To what degree would you like to work for a company like the one featured in this mini-case? Why or why not?

SOURCES: Company website, www.newbelgium.com; "New Belgium Brewing," company profile, (online), April 25, 2014, www.inc.com; "Craft Brewing Facts," Brewers Association (online), *Inc.* March 17, 2014, www.brewersassociation.org; T. Kelley, "New Belgium Crafts a Green Fleet," *Beverage Industry* 105, no 1 (January 2014), pp. 74-75; and "New Belgium Brewing, Maker of Fat Tire Beer, Is Now Completely Employee-Owned," *Huffington Post* (online), January 15, 2013, www.huffingtonpost.com.

unity-of-command principle a structure in which each worker reports to one boss, who in turn reports to one boss

network organization a collection of independent, mostly single-function firms that collaborate on a good or service

modular network temporary arrangements among partners that can be assembled and reassembled to adapt to the environment; also called virtual network

that matrix management is the same thing as group decision making—in other words, everyone must be consulted for every decision; this can lead to slower decision making. And too much democracy can lead to not enough action.[45]

Many of the disadvantages stem from the matrix's inherent violation of the **unity-of-command principle**, which states that a person should have only one boss. Reporting to two superiors can create confusion and a difficult interpersonal situation unless steps are taken to prevent these problems.

Matrix Survival Skills To a large degree, problems can be avoided if the key managers in the matrix learn the behavioral skills demanded in the matrix structure.[46] These skills vary depending on the manager's job. The *top executive* must learn to balance power and emphasis between the product and functional orientations. The middle managers, who are *product* or *division managers* and *functional managers,* must learn to collaborate and manage their conflicts constructively. Finally, the *two-boss managers,* who report to a product or division manager and to a functional manager, must learn how to be responsible to two superiors. This means having a high level of maturity, prioritizing multiple demands, and sometimes even reconciling conflicting orders. Some people function poorly under this ambiguous circumstance, which signals the end of their careers with the company. Others learn to be proactive, communicate effectively with both superiors, rise above the difficulties, and manage these work relationships constructively.

The Matrix Form Today Recently the matrix form has been regaining some of its popularity. Reasons for this resurgence include pressures to consolidate costs and be faster to market, creating a need for better coordination across functions in the business units, and a need for coordination across countries for firms with global business strategies. Many of the challenges created by the matrix form are particularly acute in an international context, mainly because of the distances involved and the differences in local markets.[47] For example, pharmaceutical firm Bristol-Myers Squibb uses a matrix structure to ensure proper coordination among its many subsidiaries around the globe. Jane Luciano, vice president of global learning and organization development, explains, "Based on our size and [the fact that we are] in a highly regulated industry, the matrix helps us to gain control of issues as they travel around the globe."[48]

The key to managing today's matrix is not the formal structure itself but the realization that the matrix is a *process.* Among managers who have adopted the matrix structure because of

the complexity of the challenges they confront, many who had trouble implementing it failed to change the employee and managerial relationships within their organizations. Flexible organizations cannot be created merely by changing their structure. To allow information to flow freely throughout an organization, managers must also attend to the norms, values, and attitudes that shape people's behavior.[49]

3.4 | Network Organizations Are Built on Collaboration

So far we have been discussing variations of the traditional, hierarchical organization, within which all the business functions of the firm are performed. In contrast, a **network organization** is a collection of independent, mostly single-function firms that collaborate to produce a good or service. As depicted in Exhibit 7.8, the network organization describes not one organization but a web of relationships among many firms. Network organizations are flexible arrangements among designers, suppliers, producers, distributors, and customers in which each firm is able to pursue its own distinctive core capability yet work effectively with other members of the network. Often members of the network share information electronically to respond quickly to customer demands. The normal boundary of the organization becomes blurred or porous as managers within the organization interact closely with network members outside it. The network as a whole, then, can display the technical specialization of the functional structure, the market responsiveness of the product structure, and the balance and flexibility of the matrix.[50]

A very flexible version of the network organization is the **modular network**—also called the *virtual* corporation. It is composed of temporary arrangements among members that can

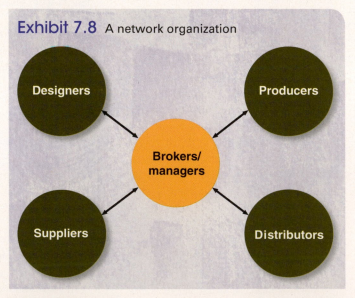

Exhibit 7.8 A network organization

Designers · Producers · Brokers/managers · Suppliers · Distributors

Source: From R. Miles and C. Snow, "Organizations: New Concepts for New Forms," *California Management Review,* Spring 1986, p. 65. vol. 28, no. 3. Copyright © 1986 by The Regents of the University of California. Republished by permission of the University of California Press.

be assembled and reassembled to meet a changing competitive environment. The members of the network are held together by contracts that stipulate results expected (market mechanisms), rather than by hierarchy and authority. Poorly performing firms can be removed and replaced.

Such arrangements are common in the aerospace, electronics, toy, and apparel industries, each of which creates and sells trendy products at a fast pace. Modular networks also are suited to organizations in which much of the work can be done independently by experts. For example, Canada-based Bombardier Aerospace makes and sells business jets. Instead of manufacturing everything by itself in Canada, Bombardier uses a virtual network of contractors to make the jets. The firm designed the aircraft into "12 large chunks," with some of these modules (cockpit and forward fuselage) being made in-house and other components (wings, engines, and landing gear) manufactured by contractors from countries like Australia, Taiwan, and Japan. After the different components arrive at one of the firm's production sites in Wichita, Kansas, it takes employees about four days to assemble the final aircraft. This modular approach to making jets has allowed Bombardier to beat the price of its nearest competitor by about $3 million.[51]

Successful networks potentially offer flexibility, innovation, quick responses to threats and opportunities, and reduced costs and risk. But for these arrangements to be successful, several things must occur:

- The firm must choose the right specialty. It must be something (good or service) that the market needs and that the firm is better at providing than other firms—its core capability.

- The firm must choose collaborators that also are excellent at what they do and that provide complementary strengths.

- The firm must make certain that all parties fully understand the strategic goals of the partnership.

- Each party must be able to trust all the others with strategic information and also trust that each collaborator will deliver quality products even if the business grows quickly and makes heavy demands.

The role of managers shifts in a network from that of command and control to more like that of a broker. Broker/managers serve several important boundary roles that aid network integration and coordination:[52]

- *Designer role:* The broker serves as a network architect who envisions a set of groups or firms whose collective expertise could be focused on a particular good or service.

- *Process engineering role:* The broker serves as a *network cooperator* who takes the initiative to lay out the flow of resources and relationships and makes certain that everyone shares the same goals, standards, payments, and the like.

- *Nurturing role:* The broker serves as a network developer who nurtures and enhances the network (like team building) to make certain the relationships are healthy and mutually beneficial.

LO4 Describe important mechanisms used to coordinate work

4 | ORGANIZATIONAL INTEGRATION

Besides structuring their organization around *differentiation*—the way the organization is composed of different jobs and tasks, and the way they fit on an organization chart—managers also need to consider *integration* and *coordination*—the way all parts of the organization work together. Often the more differentiated the organization, the more difficult integration may be. Because of specialization and the division of labor, different groups of managers and employees develop different orientations. Employees think and act differently depending on whether they are in a functional department or a divisional group, are line or staff, and so on. When they focus on their particular units, it is difficult for managers to integrate all their activities.

Managers can use a variety of approaches to foster coordination among interdependent units and individuals. In some situations, managers might see that employees need to work closely together to achieve joint objectives, so they build mutual trust, train employees in a common set of skills, and reward teamwork. In other situations, organizations might rely more on individuals with unique talents and ideas, so they set up flexible work arrangements and reward individual achievements, while encouraging employees to share knowledge and develop respect for one another's contributions.[53] In general, however, coordination methods include standardization, plans, and mutual adjustment.[54]

● Canadian jet manufacturer, Bombardier Aerospace, relies on a modular network of contractors to supply some of the 12 large components needed to assemble the firm's jets.

standardization establishing common routines and procedures that apply uniformly to everyone

formalization the presence of rules and regulations governing how people in the organization interact

coordination by plan interdependent units are required to meet deadlines and objectives that contribute to a common goal

coordination by mutual adjustment units interact with one another to make accommodations in order to achieve flexible coordination

4.1 | Standardization Coordinates Work Through Rules and Routines

When organizations coordinate activities by establishing routines and standard operating procedures that remain in place over time, we say that work has been standardized. **Standardization** constrains actions and integrates various units by regulating what people do. People often know how to act—and how to interact—because standard operating procedures spell out what they should do. For example, managers may establish standards for which types of computer equipment the organization will use. This simplifies the purchasing and training processes (everyone is on a common platform) and helps the different parts of the organization communicate.

To improve coordination, organizations may also rely on **formalization**—the presence of rules and regulations governing how people in the organization interact. Simple, often written, policies regarding attendance, dress, and decorum, for example, may help eliminate a good deal of uncertainty at work.

An important assumption underlying both standardization and formalization is that the rules and procedures should apply to most (if not all) situations. These approaches, therefore, are most appropriate in situations that are relatively stable and unchanging. In some cases, when the work environment requires flexibility, coordination by standardization may not be very effective. Who hasn't experienced a time when rules and procedures—frequently associated with a slow bureaucracy—prevented timely action to address a problem? In these instances, we often refer to rules and regulations as "red tape."[55]

4.2 | Plans Set a Common Direction

If laying out the exact rules and procedures by which work should be integrated is difficult, organizations may provide more latitude by establishing goals and schedules for interdependent units. **Coordination by plan** does not require the same high degree of stability and routinization required for coordination by standardization. Interdependent units are free to modify and adapt their actions as long as they meet the deadlines and targets required for working with others.

In writing this textbook, for example, we (the authors) sat down with a publication team that included the editors, the marketing staff, the production group, and support staff. Together we ironed out a schedule for developing this book that covered approximately a two-year period. That development plan included dates and "deliverables" that specified what was to be accomplished and forwarded to the others in the organization. The plan gave each subunit enough flexibility, and the overall approach allowed us to work together effectively.

4.3 | Mutual Adjustment Allows Flexible Coordination

Ironically, the simplest and most flexible approach to coordination may just be to have interdependent parties talk to one another. **Coordination by mutual adjustment** involves feedback and discussions to jointly figure out how to approach problems and devise solutions that are agreeable to everyone. The popularity of teams today is in part due to the fact that they allow for flexible coordination; teams can operate under the principle of mutual adjustment.

::::::::::::::::

The Chinese motorcycle industry has figured out how to coordinate hundreds of suppliers in the design and manufacturing of motorcycles. Together these small firms collaborate by working from rough blueprints to design, construct, and assemble related components, and then deliver them to another plant for final

● Organizations of all types have established routines and standard operating procedures so employees, customers, and other stakeholders know how to act and interact with one another.

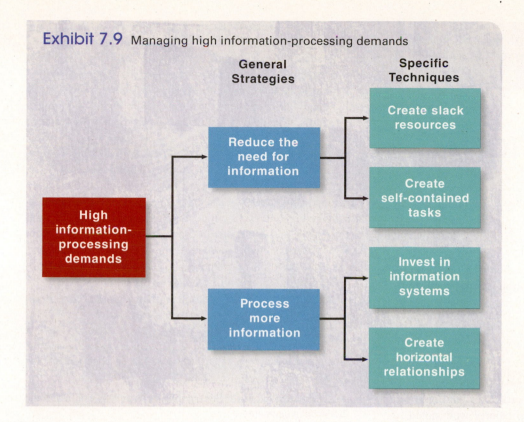

Exhibit 7.9 Managing high information-processing demands

General Strategies — Specific Techniques

High information-processing demands → Reduce the need for information → Create slack resources / Create self-contained tasks

High information-processing demands → Process more information → Invest in information systems / Create horizontal relationships

external environment to the organization and back. To cope, organizations must acquire, process, and respond to that information. To function effectively, organizations need to develop structures for processing information.

To cope with high uncertainty and heavy information demands, managers can use the two general strategies shown in Exhibit 7.9:[57]

1. *Reduce the need for information.* Managers can do this by creating slack resources. *Slack resources* are extra resources that organizations can rely on in a pinch. For example, a company that carries inventory does not need as much information about sales demand or lead time. Part-time and temporary employees are another type of slack resource because using them helps employers get around perfectly forecasting sales peaks.

2. *Increase information-processing capability.* An organization may do this by *investing in information systems* or engaging in *knowledge management*—capitalizing on the intellect and experience of the organization's human assets to increase collaboration and effectiveness. Managers may foster knowledge management by creating horizontal relationships. These may be as simple as assigning someone to serve as a *liaison* between groups, or they may be more complex, such as an interdepartmental task force or team.[58]

assembly. Because design and assembly are decentralized, suppliers can move quickly to make adjustments, try out new components, and make more changes if necessary before delivering a product for final assembly.

Using this approach, the Chinese motorcycle industry is now designing and building new motorcycles faster and less expensively than any other country in the world. In fact, production has quadrupled from 5 million motorcycles a year to 23 million which gives China about 50 percent of the worldwide motorcycle market.[56]

••••••••••••••••

But the flexibility of mutual adjustment as a coordination device carries some cost. Hashing out every issue takes time and may not be the most expedient approach for organizing work. Imagine how long it would take to accomplish even the most basic tasks if subunits had to talk through every situation. Still, mutual adjustment can be very effective when problems are novel and cannot be programmed in advance with rules, procedures, or plans. Particularly during crises, in which rules and procedures don't apply, mutual adjustment is likely to be the most effective approach to coordination.

4.4 | Coordination Requires Communication

Today's environments tend to be complex, dynamic, and therefore uncertain. Huge amounts of information flow from the

● Information sharing is vital at the National Counterterrorism Center. Technology is used to enable the efficient and safe execution of information sharing.

5 | ORGANIZATIONAL AGILITY

Managers today place a premium on *agility*—being able to act fast to meet customer needs and respond to other outside pressures. They want to correct past mistakes quickly and also to prepare for an uncertain future. They need to respond to threats and capitalize on opportunities when they come along. The particular structure the organization adopts to accomplish agility will depend on its *strategy,* its *customers,* and its *technology.*

5.1 | Strategies Promote Organizational Agility

Certain strategies, and the structures, processes, and relationships that accompany them, seem particularly well suited to improving an organization's ability to respond quickly and effectively to the challenges it faces. They reflect managers' determination to fully leverage people and assets to make the firm more agile and competitive. These strategies and structures are based on the firm's core capabilities, strategic alliances, and abilities to learn to engage all its people in achieving its objectives and to adapt its structure to its size.

⋯⋯⋯⋯⋯⋯⋯⋯

Advertising agency mcgarrybowen is not letting its size or age (it's been in business about nine years) get in the way of its success. Founded by three industry veterans who spent the earlier part of their careers in much larger firms, this 2009 winner of *Advertising Age's* U.S. Agency of the Year has built a reputation for being creative, relationship-oriented, and responsive. Shortly before the first anniversary of the September 11, 2001, attacks, CEO John McGarry was asked by Verizon Communications to create a last-minute television ad (within two weeks!) that would capture the spirit and sacrifice of both the tragedy of 9/11 and the round-the-clock commitment that Verizon's employees made to restore phone reception and communications to businesses and residences in the affected area of New York City. In record time, McGarry and his team developed a two-minute 9/11 tribute that featured children gathering around the Statue of Liberty accompanied by a moving song that ended with the words "in gratitude for those who served." Verizon's leaders and employees were so proud and moved that the company decided to give all of their corporate brand and image advertising to mcgarrybowen, which currently accounts for about one-fifth of the ad agency's $176 million in revenue.[59]

⋯⋯⋯⋯⋯⋯⋯⋯

Organizing Around Core Capabilities A recent and important perspective on strategy and organization hinges on the concept of *core capability.*[60] As you learned in Chapter 5, a core capability is the ability—knowledge, expertise, skill—that underlies a company's ability to be a leader in providing a range of goods or services. It allows the company to compete on the basis of its core strengths and expertise, not just on what it produces.

Successfully developing a world-class core capability opens the door to a variety of opportunities; failure means being foreclosed from many markets. Thus a well-understood, well-developed core capability can enhance a company's responsiveness and competitiveness. Strategically, companies must commit to excellence and leadership in capabilities and strengthen them before they can win market share for specific products. Organizationally, the corporation should be viewed as a portfolio of capabilities, not just of specific businesses.

Managers who want to strengthen their firms' competitiveness need to focus on several related issues:

- Identify existing core capabilities.

- Acquire or build core capabilities that will be important for the future.

- Keep investing in capabilities, so the firm remains world-class and better than competitors.

- Extend capabilities to find new applications and opportunities for the markets of tomorrow.[61]

Keep in mind that it's not enough for an organization to *have* valuable resources that provide capabilities; those resources have to be *managed* in a way that gives the organization an advantage.[62] That means managers have to do three things:

1. *Accumulate the right resources (such as talented people).* Managers must determine what resources they need, acquire and develop those resources, and eliminate resources that don't provide value.

● Apple and Starbucks have a new partnership that allows customers to use the T-Mobile HotSpot Wi-Fi Network to wirelessly download music onto their wireless devices. The iTunes Wi-Fi Music Store offers the service with no Wi-Fi connection fees or HotSpot login required.

2. *Combine the resources in ways that give the organization capabilities,* such as researching new products or resolving problems for customers. These combinations may involve knowledge sharing and alliances between departments or with other organizations.

3. *Leverage or exploit their resources.* Managers must identify the opportunities where their capabilities deliver value to customers (say, by creating new products or delivering existing products better than competitors) and then coordinate and deploy the employees and other resources needed to respond to those opportunities.

Strategic Alliances The modern organization has a variety of links with other organizations that are more complex than traditional stakeholder relationships. Today even fierce competitors are working together at unprecedented levels to achieve their strategic goals. In early 2014, Yahoo! CEO Marissa Mayer announced that as a strategy to compete more effectively against Google and Bing search engines, the company had formed an alliance with online review site Yelp. Yahoo! will integrate listings and reviews of local businesses—from restaurants to stores—into results on its search engine.[63]

A **strategic alliance** is a formal relationship created with the purpose of joint pursuit of mutual goals. In a strategic alliance, individual organizations share administrative authority, form social links, and accept joint ownership. Such alliances are blurring firms' boundaries. They occur between companies and their competitors, governments, and universities. Such partnering often crosses national and cultural boundaries. Companies form strategic alliances to develop new technologies, enter new markets, and reduce manufacturing costs through outsourcing. Not only can alliances enable companies to move ahead faster and more efficiently, but they also are sometimes the only practical way to bring together the variety of specialists needed for operating in today's complex and fast-changing environment. Rather than hiring the experts who understand the technology and market segments for each new product, companies can form alliances with partners that already have those experts on board.[64]

Managers must devote plenty of time to developing the human relationships in the partnership. The best alliances are true partnerships that meet the criteria shown in Exhibit 7.10.

Most of these ideas apply not only to strategic alliances but to any type of relationship.[65]

Learning Organizations Being responsive requires continually changing and learning new ways to act. Some experts say the only sustainable advantage is learning faster than the competition. This has led to interest in an idea called the learning organization.[66] A **learning organization** is an organization skilled at creating, acquiring, and transferring knowledge, and at modifying its behavior to reflect new knowledge and insights.[67] L.L. Bean, Apple, Google, and GM are good examples of learning organizations. Such organizations are skilled at solving problems, experimenting with new approaches, learning from their own experiences, learning from other organizations, and spreading knowledge quickly and efficiently.

How do firms become true learning organizations? There are a few important ingredients:[68]

- Their people engage in disciplined thinking and attention to details, making decisions based on data and evidence rather than guesswork and assumptions.

- They search constantly for new knowledge and ways to apply it, looking for expanding horizons and opportunities, not just quick fixes to current problems. The organization values and rewards individuals who expand their knowledge and skill in areas that benefit the organization.

- They carefully review successes and failures, looking for lessons and deeper understanding.

- They benchmark—that is, identify and implement the best practices of other organizations, stealing ideas shamelessly.

- They share ideas throughout the organization via reports, information systems, informal discussions, site visits, education, and training. Employees work with and are mentored by more experienced employees.

High-Involvement Organizations Another increasingly popular way to create a competitive advantage is participative management. Particularly in high-technology companies facing stiff international competition, the aim is to generate high levels of commitment and involvement as employees and managers work together to achieve organizational goals.

Exhibit 7.10 Criteria for forming alliances

Individual excellence	Partners add value, and their motives are to pursue opportunity.
Importance	Partners want alliance to help them reach long-term objectives.
Interdependence	Partners need each other and help each other reach its goals.
Investment	Partners dedicate financial and other resources to relationship.
Information	Partners communicate openly about goals, data, and changing situations.
Integration	Partners develop shared ways of operating and learn from each other.
Institutionalization	Relationship is formal with clear responsibilities.
Integrity	Partners are trustworthy and honorable.

Source: Adapted and reprinted by permission of *Harvard Business Review.* From R. M. Kanter, "Collaborative Advantage: The Art of Alliances," *Harvard Business Review,* July–August 1994, pp. 96–108. Copyright © 1994 by the Harvard Business School Publishing Corporation; all rights reserved.

In a **high-involvement organization**, top management ensures that there is a consensus about the direction in which the business is heading. The leader seeks input from his or her top management team and from lower levels of the company. Task forces, study groups, and other techniques foster participation in decisions that affect the entire organization. Participants receive continual feedback regarding how they are doing compared with the competition and how effectively they are meeting the strategic agenda.

Structurally, this usually means that even lower-level employees have a direct relationship with a customer or supplier and thus receive feedback and are held accountable for delivering a good or service. The organization has a flat, decentralized structure built around a customer, good, or service. Employee involvement is particularly powerful when the environment changes rapidly, work is creative, complex activities require coordination, and firms need major breakthroughs in innovation and speed—in other words, when companies need to be more responsive.[69]

Impact of Organizational Size Large organizations are typically less organic and more bureaucratic. Jobs become more specialized, and distinct groups of specialists are created because large organizations can add a new specialty at lower proportional expense. The resulting complexity makes the organization harder to control, so management adds more levels to keep spans of control from becoming too large. Rules, procedures, and paperwork are also introduced.

But a huge, complex organization can find it hard to manage relationships with customers and among its own units. Larger companies also are more difficult to coordinate and control. While size may enhance efficiency, it also may create administrative difficulties that inhibit efficiency.

Nimble, small firms frequently outmaneuver big bureaucracies, but size offers market power in buying and selling. The

● In an effort to exceed customers' expectations, L.L. Bean now offers free shipping to addresses in the United States and Canada. There is no minimum purchase and no expiration date.

challenge, then, is to be both big and small to capitalize on the advantages of each. Solutions include decentralized decision making and the use of teams empowered to respond quickly to a changing environment.

As large companies try to regain the responsiveness of small companies, they often consider *downsizing,* the planned elimination of positions, for example, by eliminating functions, hierarchical levels, or even whole units.[70] Recognizing that people will be unemployed and frightened, managers usually opt for downsizing only in response to pressure. Traditionally, companies have downsized when demand falls and seems unlikely to rebound soon. These layoffs save money so that the company can remain profitable—or at least viable—until the next upturn. More recently, however, global competition has forced companies to cut costs even when sales are strong and when, through technological advances, the same output can be produced by fewer employees. As a result, many companies have used downsizing to become more efficient. Whereas downsizing in response to a slowdown in demand has tended to have the most impact on operating-level jobs in manufacturing firms, downsizing to improve efficiency has focused on eliminating layers of management, so those layoffs target "white-collar" middle managers.

⋯⋯⋯⋯⋯⋯

The recent recession has forced widespread downsizing across a variety of industries, not just manufacturing. For example, in response to a severe downturn in demand, Microsoft announced that, for the first time in its history, it would have to downsize, laying off about 5,000 employees (about 5 percent of its workforce). In a memo to employees, CEO Steve Ballmer acknowledged the risks of such an approach: "Our success at Microsoft has always been the direct result of the talent, hard work, and commitment of our people."[71] In effect, downsizing risks eliminating the very source of a company's success.

⋯⋯⋯⋯⋯⋯

Done appropriately, downsizing can in fact make firms more agile. But even under the best circumstances, downsizing can be traumatic for an organization and its employees. Interestingly, the people who lose their jobs because of downsizing are not the only ones deeply affected. Those who keep their jobs tend to exhibit what has become known as *survivor's syndrome.*[72] They struggle with heavier workloads, wonder who will be next to go, try to figure out how to survive, lose commitment to the company and faith in their bosses, and become narrow-minded, self-absorbed, and risk-averse.

Managers can engage in a number of positive practices to ease the pain and increase the effectiveness of downsizing:[73]

- Use downsizing only as a last resort, when other methods of improving performance by innovating or changing procedures have been exhausted.

- In choosing positions to eliminate, engage in careful analysis and strategic thinking.

- Train people to cope with the new situation.

- Identify and protect talented people.

- Give special attention and help to those who have lost their jobs.

- Communicate constantly with people about the process, and invite ideas for alternative ways to operate more efficiently.

- Identify how the organization will operate more effectively in the future, and emphasize this positive future and the remaining employees' new roles in attaining it.

5.2 | Agile Organizations Focus on Customers

In the end, the point of structuring a responsive, agile organization lies in enabling it to meet and exceed the expectations of its customers. Customers are vital to organizations because they purchase goods and services, and their continued relationships with the firm constitute the fundamental driver of sustained, long-term competitiveness and success. To meet customer needs, organizations focus on quality improvement.

Organizing for Quality Improvement Managers may embed quality programs within any organizational structure. **Total quality management (TQM)** is a way of managing in which everyone is committed to continuous improvement of his or her part of the operation. TQM is a comprehensive approach to improving product quality and thereby customer satisfaction. It is characterized by a strong orientation toward customers (external and internal) and has become a theme for organizing work. TQM reorients managers toward involving people across departments in improving all aspects of the business. Continuous improvement requires mechanisms that facilitate group problem solving, information sharing, and cooperation across business functions. The walls that separate stages and functions of work tend to come down, and the organization operates in a team-oriented manner.[74]

One of the founders of the quality management movement was W. Edwards Deming. As illustrated in Exhibit 7.11,

Deming's "14 points" of quality emphasize a holistic approach to management:

One of the most important contributors to total quality management has been the introduction of statistical tools to analyze the causes of product defects, in an approach called *six sigma quality.* Sigma is the Greek letter used to designate the estimated standard deviation or variation in a process. (The higher the "sigma level," the lower the amount of variation.) The product defects analyzed may include anything that results in customer dissatisfaction—for example, late delivery, wrong shipment, or poor customer service, as well as problems with the product itself. When the defect has been identified, managers then engage the organization in a comprehensive effort to eliminate its causes and reduce it to the lowest practicable level. At six sigma, a product or process is defect-free 99.99966 percent of the time. Reaching that goal almost always requires managers to restructure their internal processes and relationships with suppliers and customers in fundamental ways. For example, managers may have to create teams from all parts of the organization to implement the process improvements that will prevent defects from arising.

Related to this is the *lean six sigma* approach, which combines six sigma quality improvement techniques with initiatives that eliminate waste in time, complex processes, and materials. As a way to be more efficient and keep budgets under control, city planners in Irving, Texas, have used lean six sigma analysis to reduce the time it takes to complete a cycle of street repairs from an average of 14 weeks to 6 weeks. Instead of maintaining three separate 40-year-old, inefficient community pools (used by about 9,700 residents each year), city planners built a new energy-efficient pool that is now used by 110,000 visitors annually.[75]

The influence of TQM on the organizing process has become even more acute with the emergence of ISO standards. **ISO 9001** is a series of voluntary quality standards developed by a committee working under the International Organization for Standardization (known as ISO), a network of national standards institutions in more than 150 countries. In contrast to most ISO standards, which describe a particular material, product,

total quality management (TQM) an integrative approach to management that supports the attainment of customer satisfaction through a wide variety of tools and techniques that result in high-quality goods and services

ISO 9001 a series of quality standards developed by a committee working under the international organization for standardization to improve total quality in all businesses for the benefit of producers and consumers

Exhibit 7.11	Deming's 14 points of quality

1. *Create constancy of purpose*—strive for long-term improvement (vs. short-term profit).
2. *Adopt the new philosophy*—don't tolerate delays and mistakes.
3. *Cease dependence on mass inspection*—build quality into the process on the front end.
4. *End the practice of awarding business on price tag alone*— build long-term relationships.
5. *Improve constantly and forever the system of production and service*—at each stage.
6. *Institute training and retraining*—continually update methods and thinking.
7. *Institute leadership*—provide the resources needed for effectiveness.
8. *Drive out fear*—people must believe it is safe to report problems or ask for help.
9. *Break down barriers among departments*—promote teamwork.
10. *Eliminate slogans and arbitrary targets*—supply methods, not buzzwords.
11. *Eliminate numerical quotas*—they are contrary to the idea of continuous improvement.
12. *Remove barriers to pride in work*—allow autonomy and spontaneity.
13. *Institute a vigorous program of education and retraining*—people are assets, not commodities.
14. *Take action to accomplish the transformation*—provide a structure that enables quality.

● Guided by the results of a lean six sigma analysis, city planners in Irving, TX, decided to build an 11,000 square-foot energy efficient aquatic center to serve all age groups. The analysis suggested that thousands more people would visit the new aquatic center than the three separate inefficient pools that served the community for the past 40 years.

or process, the ISO 9001 standards apply to management systems at any organization and address eight principles:[76]

1. Customer focus—learning and addressing customer needs and expectations.

2. Leadership—establishing a vision and goals, establishing trust, and providing employees with the resources and inspiration to meet goals.

3. Involvement of people—establishing an environment in which employees understand their contribution, engage in problem solving, and acquire and share knowledge.

4. Process approach—defining the tasks needed to successfully carry out each process and assigning responsibility for them.

5. Systems approach to management—putting processes together into efficient systems that work together effectively.

6. Continual improvement—teaching people how to identify areas for improvement and rewarding them for making improvements.

7. Factual approach to decision making—gathering accurate performance data, sharing the data with employees, and using the data to make decisions.

8. Mutually beneficial supplier relationships—working in a cooperative way with suppliers.

U.S. companies first became interested in ISO 9001 because overseas customers, particularly those in the European Union, embraced it. Now some U.S. customers are making the same demand. As a result, hundreds of thousands of companies in manufacturing and service industries around the world are ISO certified. For example, UniFirst Corporation, a Massachusetts-based provider of workplace uniforms and protective work clothing, obtained ISO certification for its two Mexican plants through a process that included documenting all the facilities' processes and training employees in quality control.[77]

5.3 | Technology Can Support Agility

Another critical factor affecting an organization's structure and responsiveness is its *technology*. Broadly speaking, **technology** can be viewed as the methods, processes, systems, and skills used to transform resources (inputs) into products (outputs). Although we will discuss technology—and innovation—more fully later, in this chapter we want to highlight some of the important influences technology has on organizational design.

technology the systematic application of scientific knowledge to a new product, process, or service

small batch technologies that produce goods and services in low volume

large batch technologies that produce goods and services in high volume

continuous process a process that is highly automated and has a continuous production flow

mass customization the production of varied, individually customized products at the low cost of standardized, mass-produced products

Technology Configurations Research by Joan Woodward laid the foundation for understanding technology and structure. According to Woodward, three basic technologies characterize how work is done in service as well as manufacturing companies:[78]

- *Small batch technologies*—When goods or services are provided in very low volume or **small batches**, a company that does such work is called a *job shop*. For example, PMF Industries, a small custom metalworking company in Williamsport, Pennsylvania, produces stainless steel assemblies for medical and other uses. In the service industry, local restaurants and doctors' offices provide a variety of low-volume, customized services. In a small batch organization, structure tends to be organic, with few rules and formal procedures, and decision making tends to be decentralized. The emphasis is on mutual adjustment among people.

- *Large batch technologies*—Companies with higher volumes and lower varieties than a job shop tend to be characterized as **large batch**, or mass production technologies. Examples include the computer assembly operations at Lenovo and Apple, and in the service sector, McDonald's and Burger King. Their production runs tend to be standardized, and customers receive similar (if not identical) products. Machines may replace people in the physical execution of work. Structure tends to be more mechanistic. There are more rules and formal procedures, and decision making is more centralized with higher spans of control. Communication tends to be more formal, and hierarchical authority more prominent.

- *Continuous process technologies*—At the high-volume end of the scale are companies that use **continuous process** technologies, technologies that do not stop and start. International Paper and Air Products and Chemicals, for example, use continuous process technologies to produce a very limited number of products. People are completely removed from the work itself, which is done by machines and computers. People may run the computers that run the machines. Structure can return to a more organic form because less supervision is needed. Communication tends to be more informal, and fewer rules and regulations are established.

Organizing for Flexible Manufacturing Although issues of volume and variety are often seen as trade-offs in a technological sense, today organizations are trying to produce both high-volume and high-variety products at the same time. This is referred to as **mass customization**.[79] Automobiles, clothes, computers, and other products are increasingly being manufactured to match each customer's taste, specifications, and budget. You can now buy clothes cut to your proportions, supplements with the exact blend of the vitamins and minerals you like, CDs with the music tracks you choose, and textbooks whose chapters are picked by your professor.

How do companies manage this type of customization at such low cost? They organize around a dynamic network of relatively independent operating units.[80] Each unit performs a specific process or task—called a *module*—such as making

> "Information technology and business are becoming inextricably interwoven. I don't think anyone can talk meaningfully about one without talking about the other."
>
> —Bill Gates

a component, performing a credit check, or performing a particular welding method. Some modules may be performed by outside suppliers or vendors.

Different modules join forces to make the good or provide a service. How and when the various modules interact with one another are dictated by the unique requests of each customer. The manager's responsibility is to make it easier and less costly for modules to come together, complete their tasks, and then recombine to meet the next customer demand. The ultimate goal of mass customization is a never-ending campaign to expand the number of ways a company can satisfy customers.

One technological advance that has helped make mass customization possible is *computer-integrated manufacturing (CIM)*, which encompasses a host of computerized production efforts, including computer-aided design and computer-aided manufacturing. These systems can produce high-variety and high-volume products at the same time.[81] They may also offer greater control and predictability of production processes, reduced waste, faster throughput times, and higher quality. But managers cannot "buy" their way out of competitive trouble simply by investing in superior technology alone. They must also ensure that their organization has the necessary strategic and people strengths and a well-designed plan for integrating the new technology within the organization.

lean manufacturing an operation that strives to achieve the highest possible productivity and total quality, cost-effectively, by eliminating unnecessary steps in the production process and continually striving for improvement

just-in-time (JIT) a system that calls for subassemblies and components to be manufactured in very small lots and delivered to the next stage of the production process just as they are needed

As the name implies, *flexible factories* provide more production options and a greater variety of products. They differ from traditional factories in three primary ways:[82]

1. The traditional factory has long production runs, generating high volumes of a standardized product. Flexible factories have much shorter production runs, with many different products.

2. Traditional factories move parts down the line from one location in the production sequence to the next. Flexible factories are organized around products, in work cells or teams, so that people work closely together and parts move shorter distances with shorter or no delays.

3. Traditional factories use centralized scheduling, which is time-consuming, inaccurate, and slow to adapt to changes. Flexible factories use local or decentralized scheduling, in which decisions are made on the shop floor by the people doing the work.

Another organizing approach is **lean manufacturing**, based on a commitment to making an operation both efficient and effective; it strives to achieve the highest possible productivity and total quality, cost-effectively, by eliminating unnecessary steps in the production process and continually striving for improvement. Rejects are unacceptable, and staff, overhead, and inventory are considered wasteful. In a lean operation, the emphasis is on quality, speed, and flexibility more than on cost, efficiency, and hierarchy. If an employee spots a problem, the employee is authorized to halt the operation and signal for help to correct the problem at its source, so processes can be improved and future problems avoided. With a well-managed lean production process, a company can develop, produce, and distribute products with half or less of the human effort, space, tools, time, and overall cost.[83]

St. Agnes Hospital in Baltimore has used lean principles to reduce costs and patient waiting times while improving safety, and the ThedaCare health system in Wisconsin saved more than $3 million in one year of using lean methods.[84]

For the lean approach to result in more effective operations, the following conditions must be met:[85]

- People are broadly trained rather than specialized.
- Communication is informal and horizontal among line workers.
- Equipment is general-purpose.
- Work is organized in teams, or cells, that produce a group of similar products.
- Supplier relationships are long-term and cooperative.
- Product development is concurrent, not sequential, and is done by cross-functional teams.

Organizing for Speed: Time-Based Competition Companies worldwide have devoted so much energy to improving product quality that high quality is now the standard attained by all top competitors. Competition has driven quality to such heights that quality products no longer are enough to distinguish one company from another. Time has emerged as the key competitive advantage that can separate market leaders from also-rans.[86]

One way to compete based on time is to set up **just-in-time (JIT)** operations. JIT calls for subassemblies and components to be manufactured in very small lots and delivered to the next stage in the process precisely at the time needed, or "just in time." A customer order triggers a factory order and the production process. The supplying work centers do not produce the next lot of product until the consuming work center requires it. Even external suppliers deliver to the company just in time.

Just-in-time is a companywide philosophy oriented toward eliminating waste and improving materials through-out all operations. In this way, excess inventory is eliminated and costs are reduced. The ultimate goal of JIT is to serve the customer better by providing higher levels of quality and service. For example, by making products perfectly, companies eliminate the need for costly and time-consuming inspections. Likewise, production processes are shortened when they are streamlined so that parts are actually being worked on every minute they are in production, rather than sitting on a table, waiting for an operator.

Many believe that only a fraction of JIT's potential has been realized and that its impact will grow as it is applied to other processes, such as service, distribution, and new product development.[87] However, it's important to keep in mind that JIT offers efficiency only when the costs of storing items are greater than the costs of frequent delivery.[88]

While JIT concentrates on reducing time in manufacturing, companies are speeding up research and product development through the use of *simultaneous engineering*. Traditionally, when R&D completed its part of the project, the work was "passed over the wall" to engineering, which completed its task and passed it over the wall to manufacturing, and so on. In contrast, simultaneous engineering incorporates the issues and perspectives of all the functions—and customers and suppliers—from the beginning of the process.

This team-based approach results in a higher-quality product that is designed for efficient manufacturing *and* customer needs.[89] In the automobile industry, tools such as computer-aided design and computer-aided manufacturing (CAD/CAM) support simultaneous engineering by letting various engineers submit elements and showing how these submissions affect the overall design and the manufacturing process. With a modern CAD system, automobile engineers can enter performance requirements into a spreadsheet, and the system will identify a design that meets cost and manufacturing requirements. This technology has helped automakers slash product development time.[90] In the realm of computing, some organizations have taken this idea much further, making the programming code for their products available to the public so that anyone at any time can develop new ideas to use with their product, and the organization can decide to license any ideas that seem to have market potential.

Study Checklist

- Did you tear out the perforated student review card at the back of the text to revisit learning objectives and key terms and definitions?

Connect® Management is available for M Management. Additional resources include:

- Interactive Applications:
  - Drag & Drop: Organizational Structures
  - Drag & Drop: The Organizational Chart
  - Sequencing/Timeline: Delegating
  - Video Case: Organizing at The Container Store

- LearnSmart—Multiple choice questions help you determine what you already know, are not sure about, or need to practice based on your score. And with SmartBook, you can read the relevant section in the eBook as well as practice and recharge what you've learned.

- Chapter Videos: New Belgium Brewery

- Young Manager Speaks Out: Stephanie Weber, Sales Analytics Manager

8 chapter

Managing Human Resources

Learning Objectives

After studying Chapter 8, you should be able to:

LO1 Discuss how companies use human resources management to gain competitive advantage.

LO2 Give reasons why companies recruit both internally and externally for new hires.

LO3 Understand various methods for selecting new employees and HR-related laws.

LO4 Evaluate the importance of spending on training and development.

LO5 Explain alternatives for who appraises an employee's performance.

LO6 Describe the fundamental aspects of a reward system.

LO7 Summarize how unions and labor laws influence human resources management.

In 1981 Pam Nicholson was a senior in college, and graduation was looming. So when recruiters from Enterprise Rent-A-Car appeared on campus, she jumped at the chance to interview. For Nicholson, who hoped to manage a small business someday, getting an offer to work behind the counter at an Enterprise rental location seemed ideal. Today, as chief executive officer of the $15.4 billion private company, Nicholson is responsible for 75,000 employees in 40 countries and a fleet of 1.3 million rental vehicles. She has been named to *Fortune's* "Most Powerful Women in Business" in each of the past six years. Industry observers might say that Nicholson's career success has something to do with the firm's formula for running a business: hire recent college grads looking for management experience, provide training and mentoring, promote from within, and put customers and employees first.[1]

Enterprise's approach to business is based on the expectation that success will follow from effective human resources management. **Human resources management (HRM)** focuses on activities that attract, develop, and motivate people at work—which are fundamental aspects of organizational and managerial life. Your first formal interaction with an organization you wish to join will likely involve some aspect of its human resources function, and throughout your career as a manager you will be a part of, as well as be affected by, your organization's human resources management.

We begin this chapter by describing HRM as it relates to strategic management. Then we discuss the "nuts and bolts" of HRM: staffing, training, performance appraisal, rewards, and labor relations. Throughout the chapter, we discuss legal issues that affect each aspect of HRM.

LO1 Discuss how companies use human resources management to gain competitive advantage

1 | STRATEGIC HUMAN RESOURCES MANAGEMENT

Human resources management plays a vital strategic role as organizations attempt to compete through people. You already know that firms can create a competitive advantage when they possess or develop resources that are valuable, rare, inimitable, and organized. The same criteria apply to the strategic impact of human resources:

human resources management (HRM) system of organizational activities to attract, develop, and motivate an effective and qualified workforce. Also known as talent, human capital, or personnel management

1. *People create value.* People can increase value by helping lower costs, providing something unique to customers, or both. Through empowerment, total quality initiatives, and continuous improvement, people at Intuit, NetApp, USAA Financial Services, and other companies add to the bottom line.

2. *Talent is rare.* People are a source of competitive advantage when their skills, knowledge, and abilities are not equally available to all competitors. Top companies invest in hiring and training the best and the brightest employees to gain a competitive advantage.

3. *A group of well-chosen, motivated people is difficult to imitate.* Competitors have difficulty matching the unique cultures of SAS, W. L. Gore, and The Container Store, which get the most from their employees.

4. *People can be organized for success.* People can deliver a competitive advantage when their talents are combined and deployed rapidly to work on new assignments at a moment's notice, as in the effective use of teamwork and collaboration.

These four criteria highlight the importance of people and show the close link between HRM and strategic management. Evidence is mounting that this focus brings positive business results. For example, a study by Deloitte & Touche associated the use of effective human resources practices with higher valuation of a company in the stock market.[2] Because employee skills, knowledge, and abilities are among an organization's most distinctive and renewable resources, strategic management of people is more important than ever.

As more executives realize that their employees can be their organization's most valuable resources, human resources managers have played a greater role in strategic planning. HR specialists are challenged to know their organization's business, and line managers are challenged to excel at selecting and motivating the best people. As contributors to the organization's strategy, HR managers also face greater ethical challenges. Strategy decisions require them to be able to link decisions about staffing, benefits, and other HR matters to the organization's business success. For example, as members of the top management team, HR managers may need to implement drastic downsizing while still retaining top executives through generous salaries or bonuses, or they may hesitate to risk aggressively investigating and challenging corrupt management practices. In the long run, however, organizations are best served when HR leaders strongly advocate at least four sets of values: strategic, ethical, legal, and financial.[3]

Traditional Thinking

Managers see the HR department as being primarily concerned with filling out paperwork, administering benefits, and complying with laws.

Source: Adapted from S. E. Needleman and A. Loten, "When 'Friending' Becomes a Source of Start-up Funds," *The Wall Street Journal,* November 1, 2011, p. B1.

The Best Managers Today

Think of HR as a business partner within the firm who helps align HR activities—hiring, training, and compensation— with organizational strategy.

Tough economic times deliver exciting HR opportunities as well as tough HR challenges. For example, companies that can hire during a recession gain access to a huge pool of talented people. Well-managed firms seize the opportunities and meet the challenges.

Family Dollar Stores is one of the companies that found opportunities during the recent recession. As shoppers switched to dollar stores from higher-priced retailers, Family Dollar opened more stores, receiving applications from workers with better-than-usual credentials. To meet a need for specialists for its information technology department, the company found experienced IT workers who had left Circuit City when that chain went out of business. Companies that, like Family Dollar, build up their staff when talented people are hungry for work can boost sales, improve efficiency, and gain an advantage over competitors—if they can keep and motivate these employees.[4]

Managing human capital to sustain a competitive advantage may be the most important part of an organization's HR function. But on a day-to-day basis, HR managers have many other concerns regarding their workers and the entire personnel puzzle: attracting talent; maintaining a well-trained, highly motivated, and loyal workforce; managing diversity; devising effective compensation systems; managing layoffs; and containing health care and pension costs. The best approaches depend on the circumstances of the organization, such as whether it is growing, declining, or standing still.

1.1 | HR Planning Involves Three Stages

"Get me the right kind and the right number of people at the right time." It sounds simple enough, but meeting an organization's staffing needs requires strategic human resources planning—an activity with a strategic purpose derived from the organization's plans. The HR planning process occurs in three stages, shown in Exhibit 8.1:

1. *Planning*—To ensure that the right number and types of people are available, HR managers must know the organization's business plans— where the company is headed, in what businesses it plans to be, what future growth is expected, and so forth.

2. *Programming*—The organization implements specific human resources activities, such as recruitment, training, and pay systems.

3. *Evaluating*—Human resources activities are evaluated to determine whether they are producing the results needed to contribute to the organization's business plans.

In this chapter, we focus on human resources planning and programming. Many of the other factors listed in Exhibit 8.1 are discussed in later chapters.

● *Southwest Airlines is known for creating a unique culture that gets the most from employees. Southwest rewards its employees for excellent performance and maintains loyalty by offering free airfare, profit sharing, and other incentives. What benefits would you need to stay motivated?*

> "When talent, capabilities, and leadership align with external expectations, organizations sustain their competitive advantage."[5]
>
> —Dave Ulrich, Professor (University of Michigan)

Demand Forecasts Perhaps the most difficult part of HR planning is conducting *demand* forecasts—that is, determining how many and what type of people are needed. Demand forecasts are derived from organizational plans. To develop the iPhone, Apple had to determine how many engineers and designers it needed to ensure that such a complex product was ready to launch. Managers also needed to estimate how many iPhones the company would sell. Based on their forecast, they had to determine how many production employees would be required, along with the staff to market the phone, handle publicity for the product launch, and answer inquiries from customers learning how to use the new product. Similarly, companies selling an existing product consider current sales and projected future sales growth as they estimate the plant capacity for future demand, the sales force required, the support staff needed, and so forth. They calculate the number of labor-hours required and then use those estimates to determine the demand for specific types of workers.

Labor Supply Forecasts Along with forecasting demand, managers must forecast the *supply of labor*—how many and what types of employees the organization actually will have. In performing a supply analysis, the organization estimates the number and quality of its current employees and the available external supply of workers. To estimate internal supply, the company typically relies on its experiences with turnover, terminations, retirements, promotions, and transfers. A computerized human resources information system can help considerably.

Externally, organizations look at workforce trends to make projections. Worldwide, the highly skilled, higher-paid jobs have been generated mostly in the cities of the industrialized world, where companies have scrambled to find enough qualified workers. At the same time, companies in industrialized nations have used offshoring to move much of their routine and less skilled work to nations with a large population willing to work for lower pay. However, the resulting demand for overseas talent has made it difficult to fill a variety of jobs throughout the world, from factory workers in China to engineering positions in India.[6]

In the United States, demographic trends have contributed to a shortage of skilled and highly educated workers. Traditional labor-intensive jobs in agriculture, mining, and assembly-line manufacturing have made way for jobs in technical, financial, and customized goods and service industries. These jobs often require much more training and schooling than the jobs they replace. Other trends may worsen this situation. For example, the upcoming retirement of the baby boomer generation will remove many educated and trained employees from the workforce. And in math, science, and engineering graduate schools, fewer than half the students receiving graduate degrees are American-born. To fill U.S. jobs, companies must hire U.S. citizens or immigrants with permission to work in the United States.

Some managers have responded to this skills shortage by significantly increasing their remedial and training budgets.[7] Many companies have increased their labor supply by recruiting workers from other countries. However, this strategy is limited by the number of visas issued by the U.S. government. Retraining downsized workers is yet another approach to increasing the workforce labor pool.

LISTEN & LEARN ● ONLINE

YOUNG MANAGERS
Speak Out!

"... It is easy to form relationships with your colleagues because you work so closely with them, but keeping in mind that a business is a business."

—Blair Root, Nonprofit Director

Exhibit 8.1 HR planning process

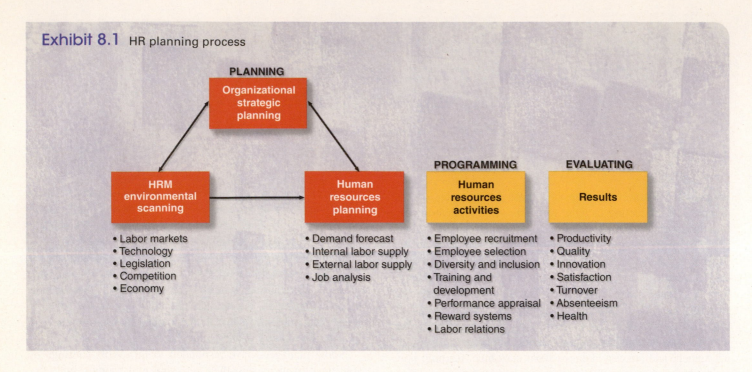

PLANNING

Organizational strategic planning

HRM environmental scanning

- Labor markets
- Technology
- Legislation
- Competition
- Economy

Human resources planning

- Demand forecast
- Internal labor supply
- External labor supply
- Job analysis

PROGRAMMING

Human resources activities

- Employee recruitment
- Employee selection
- Diversity and inclusion
- Training and development
- Performance appraisal
- Reward systems
- Labor relations

EVALUATING

Results

- Productivity
- Quality
- Innovation
- Satisfaction
- Turnover
- Absenteeism
- Health

Not limited to the United States, there is also a skills shortage in several other countries like Brazil, Japan, India, and China. A survey of 35,000 employers in 36 countries found that 31 percent of responding companies are having difficulty filling positions due to lack of qualified employees. The top 10 jobs that employers are having difficulty filling include these:

1. Skilled trades.

2. Sales representatives.

Hiring College Hunks to Haul Junk

It takes brains to manage brawn. And that's exactly what the cofounders of College Hunks Hauling Junk do daily. College Hunks Hauling Junk was established by high school friends Omar Soliman and Nick Friedman over summer vacation from college—they needed work, so they created a company. The young men borrowed a delivery truck from Soliman's mother's furniture store and offered to haul away people's unwanted junk. When they graduated, Soliman and Friedman decided to turn their project into something bigger, and College Hunks Hauling Junk hit the road.

For a fee, crew members will pick up unwanted furniture and other household, construction, or office debris from individuals or businesses. The College Hunks then recycle or donate whatever items they can, transporting to the dump only what cannot possibly be recycled or reused. Although some skeptics point out that many towns will collect large items left curbside as part of regular trash pickup (for an added cost), so demand for College Hunks will fall off, that doesn't seem to be happening. Home owners and small business owners seem to appreciate the convenience of the service as well as the knowledge that many of their items will be recycled or reused. Friedman identifies an additional reason: "We recognized that people placed a premium on having young, friendly, personable, and courteous teams coming in to do the work."

Omar Soliman is cofounder and CEO of College Hunks Hauling Junk.

From the beginning, Soliman and Friedman envisioned a business that would expand through franchising. This requires forecasts of labor demand and supply in more than one location. It also requires the ability to select the right franchise owners

3. Technicians (especially production operations or maintenance).

4. Engineers.

5. Accounting and finance staff.

6. Production operators.

7. Administrative assistants, physician assistants, and office support staff.

8. Management and executives.

9. Drivers.

10. Laborers.

The problem is not due to an insufficient number of applicants, but rather a mismatch between employer needs and applicant qualifications. Employers increasingly want applicants to have combinations of skills as opposed to just technical skills. For example, an employer may hire only salespeople who can also be team leaders and trainers of other salespeople. Or a firm may reject several candidates for an HR position because even though the applicants have the required technical training in staffing, legal compliance, and compensation, they may lack other important skills like critical thinking and knowing how to align HR initiatives with the company's business strategy.

There are no easy solutions to this problem of not having the right people in the right place at the right time. It's a long-term and complex problem that is affecting developed and emerging

● *LinkedIn, the popular online professional networking site, has approximately 300 million members in over 200 countries.*

economies as "increasingly sophisticated production systems require a better-trained and more capable workforce."[8]

In contrast, earlier forecasts of an increasingly diverse workforce have become fact, adding greatly to the pool of available talent. Minorities, women, immigrants, older and disabled workers, and other groups have made the management of diversity a fundamental activity of today's manager. Because managing the "new workforce" is so essential, the next chapter is devoted to this topic.

Reconciling Supply and Demand Once managers can estimate the supply of and demand for various types of employees, they develop approaches for reconciling the two. If organizations need more people than they currently have (a labor deficit), they can hire new employees, promote current employees to new positions, or outsource work to contractors. When organizations have more people than they need (a labor surplus), they can use attrition—the normal turnover of employees—to reduce the surplus if they have planned far enough in advance. The organization also may lay off employees or transfer them to other areas.

When managers need to hire, they can use their organization's compensation policy to attract talent. Large companies spend a lot of time gathering information about pay scales for the jobs they have available and making sure their

to manage these franchises, including the junk-hauling hunks themselves. New franchise owners are put through a five-day training program at "Junk University." They learn every facet of the business, ranging from recruiting and hiring a workforce to management, sales, and marketing. Franchisees tend to recruit their junk haulers from nearby colleges. And while employees don't need to look like male runway models, they are required to be well groomed, with no visible piercings or tattoos. Female "hunkettes" are beginning to make their way from the corporate offices onto the trucks as well.

To date, the company has sold nearly 47 franchises that operate bright green and orange trucks in towns across the United States. The business made $12.3 million in

2012, which was about 360 percent more than in 2009. What's next? "We grew super, super fast," notes CEO Omar Soliman.

"Now we're playing catch-up, getting all the systems in place so everything works smoother."

Discussion Questions

- What factors might affect the demand for the services provided by College Hunks Hauling Junk? How might individual franchise owners deal with fluctuations in labor demand?

- The labor supply for College Hunks Hauling Junk is mainly college students. What are some risks and benefits of relying on college students as a workforce? How should this source of labor affect the ways that franchise owners recruit, select, and train workers?

SOURCES: Company website, www.1800junkusa.com; 2013 Inc. 5000 List, *Inc.* (online), www.inc.com, accessed May 15, 2014; S. E. Needleman, "How I Built It: 'Hunks' Take Summer Gig, Turn It into Real Business," *The Wall Street Journal,* September 15, 2011, p. B8; L. Gerdes, "Creative Career of the Week: College Hunks Hauling Junk," *BusinessWeek,* May 11, 2009, www.businessweek.com; L. Rosellini, "Dreamers: Hunks of Junk," *Reader's Digest,* April 2009, www.rd.com; D. Gill, "Hauling Junk (with a Touch of Class)," *The New York Times,* October 1, 2008, www.nytimes.com; and J. Leiser, " College Hunks Hauling Junk Relocates to Tampa Bay," *Tampa Bay Business Journal,* March 21, 2008, http://tampabay.bizjournals.com.

compensation systems are fair and competitive. We discuss pay issues later in this chapter.

Job Analysis Although issues of supply and demand are conducted at an organizational level, HR planning also focuses on individual jobs, using *job analysis*. **Job analysis** does two things:[9]

1. A *job description* tells about the job itself—the essential tasks, duties, and responsibilities involved in performing the job. The job description for an accounting manager might specify that the position will be responsible for monthly, quarterly, and annual financial reports, getting bills issued and paid, preparing budgets, ensuring the company's compliance with laws and regulations, working closely with line managers on financial issues, and supervising an accounting department of 12 people.

2. A *job specification* describes the knowledge, skills, abilities, and other characteristics (KSAOs) needed to perform the job. For an assistant manager at a retail store like Best Buy or Old Navy, the job requirements might include a degree in management, motivational skills, knowledge of customer service, retail managerial experience, and excellent communication skills.

Job analysis provides the information required by virtually every human resources activity. It assists with the essential HR programs: recruitment, training, selection, appraisal, and reward systems. It may also help organizations defend themselves in lawsuits involving employment practices—for example, by clearly specifying what a job requires if someone claims unfair dismissal.[10] Ultimately, job analysis helps increase the value added by employees to the organization because it clarifies what is required to perform effectively.

LO2 Give reasons why companies recruit both internally and externally for new hires

2 | STAFFING THE ORGANIZATION

Once HR planning is completed, managers can focus on staffing the organization. The staffing function consists of three related activities: recruitment, selection, and outplacement.

2.1 | Recruitment Helps Find Job Candidates

Recruitment activities increase the pool of candidates that might be selected for a job. Recruitment may be internal to the organization (considering current employees for promotions and transfers) or external. Each approach has advantages and disadvantages.[11]

Internal Recruiting The advantages of internal recruiting are that employers know their employees, and employees know their organization. External candidates who are unfamiliar with the

organization may find they don't like working there. Also, the opportunity to move up within the organization may encourage employees to remain with the company, work hard, and succeed. Recruiting from outside the company can be demoralizing to employees. Many companies, such as FedEx and National Instruments, prefer internal to external recruiting for these reasons.

Internal staffing has some drawbacks. If employees lack skills or talent, it yields a limited applicant pool, leading to poor selection decisions. Also, an internal recruitment policy can inhibit a company that wants to change the nature or goals of the business by bringing in outside candidates. In changing from a rapidly growing, entrepreneurial organization to a mature business with more stable growth, Dell went outside the organization to hire managers who better fit those needs.

Many companies that rely heavily on internal recruiting use a *job-posting system* to advertise open positions. Shell Oil and AT&T use job posting. Employees complete a request form indicating interest in a posted job. The posted job description includes a list of duties and the minimum skills and experience required.

External Recruiting External recruiting brings in "new blood" and can inspire innovation. Among the most frequently used sources of outside applicants are Internet job boards, company websites, employee referrals, newspaper advertisements, and college campus recruiting.

Recent surveys suggest that employers place the greatest emphasis on referrals by current employees and online job boards.[12] Some companies actively encourage employees to refer their friends by offering cash rewards. In fact, surveys show that word-of-mouth recommendations are the way most job positions get filled. Not only is this method relatively inexpensive, but employees also tend to know who will be a good fit with the company.

Web job boards such as CareerBuilder, Monster, CollegeRecruiter, SimplyHired, and Mashable Jobs have exploded in popularity as a job recruitment tool because they easily reach a large pool of job seekers. They have largely supplanted newspaper want ads, although print recruiting has grown somewhat, partly as a result of forming alliances with the job boards. Most companies also let people apply for jobs at their corporate website, and many even list open positions. Some companies also are buying search engine ads to display next to the results for relevant terms such as *nurse*. Another online tool is to obtain leads through networking sites such as LinkedIn, Twitter, Facebook, and Craigslist.

Employment agencies are another common recruitment tool, and for important management positions, companies often use specialized executive search firms. Campus recruiting can be helpful for companies looking for applicants who have up-to-date training and innovative ideas. However, companies that rely heavily on campus recruiting and employee referrals must take extra care to ensure that these methods do not discriminate by generating pools of applicants who are, say, mostly women or primarily white.[13]

• A U.S. Army soldier attends the Hiring our Heroes job fair in New York. It was started by the U.S. Chamber of Commerce to help service members, veterans, and military spouses obtain information on veteran benefits, employment, or upgrade their current job situations. There have been 610 fairs across the 50 states since program started in 2011.

of thousands of U.S. troops have recently returned home from Iraq and Afghanistan. Many of these men and women will be leaving the military and rejoining the civilian workforce. To help these veterans, JPMorgan Chase, with the involvement of 11 other companies, committed to hire or help find jobs for 100,000 military members. Having surpassed that goal, the mission has been expanded to place 200,000 veterans by 2020. Known as the "100,000 Jobs Mission," a website (http://100000jobsmission.com) was launched to help transitioning military members match their military expertise to job openings. Also, the participating companies have hired many of these veterans themselves; they have agreed to share best practices and hiring/retention statistics.[14]

Some organizations go beyond the call of duty to help certain groups of people find gainful employment. Finding jobs for veterans is an important goal given that the unemployment rate among veterans who have served since 2001 is higher than that of the general population. In the next year or two, the number of veterans seeking civilian positions is likely to increase given that tens

Most companies use some combination of the methods we have been discussing, depending on the particular job or situation. For example, they might use internal recruiting for existing jobs that need replacements, and external recruiting when the firm is expanding or needs to acquire some new skill.

Did You Know?

According to a recent survey,[15] U.S. employees would leave their current organizations for the following five reasons (in descending order of importance):

1. Work-related stress is too high.
2. Base pay is too low.
3. Promotion opportunity is available in another organization.
4. Trust/confidence in management is lacking.
5. Incentive pay opportunity is offered in another organization.

LO3 Understand various methods for selecting new employees and HR-related laws

3 | SELECTION CHOOSES APPLICANTS TO HIRE

Selection builds on recruiting and involves decisions about whom to hire. As important as these decisions are, they are at times made carelessly or quickly.

3.1 | Selection Methods

To help you in your own career, we describe a number of selection instruments you may encounter.

Applications and Résumés Application blanks and résumés provide basic information that help prospective employers make a first cut through candidates. Applications and résumés typically include the applicant's name, educational background, citizenship, work experiences, certifications, and the like. Their appearance and accuracy also say something about the applicant—spelling mistakes, for example, almost always disqualify you immediately. While providing important information, applications and résumés tend not to be useful as a basis for final selection decisions.

Interviews The most popular selection tool is interviewing, and every company uses some type of interview. Employment interviewers must be careful about what they ask and how they ask it. As we will explain later, federal law requires employers to avoid discriminating on criteria such as sex and race; questions that distinguish candidates according to protected categories may be seen as evidence of discrimination.

In an *unstructured* (or nondirective) interview, the interviewer asks different interviewees different questions. The interviewer may also use probes—that is, ask follow-up questions to learn more about the candidate.[16]

In a **structured interview**, the interviewer conducts the same interview with each applicant. There are two basic types of structured interview:

1. The *situational interview* focuses on hypothetical situations. Zale Corporation, a major jewelry chain, uses this type of interview to select sales clerks. Here is sample question: "A customer comes into the store to pick up a watch he had left for repair. The watch is not back yet from the repair shop, and the customer becomes angry. How would you handle the situation?" Answering "I would refer the customer to my supervisor" might suggest that the applicant felt incapable of handling the situation independently.

2. The *behavioral description interview* explores what candidates have actually done in the past. In selecting accountants, Bill Bufe of Plante & Moran asks candidates how they handled a difficult person they have worked with, and Art King asks how candidates have handled a stressful situation because he believes this shows how candidates "think on their feet."[17] Because behavioral questions are based on real events, they often provide useful information about how the candidate will actually perform on the job.

Each of these interview techniques offers different advantages and disadvantages, and many interviewers use more than one technique during the same interview. Unstructured interviews can help establish rapport and provide a sense of the applicant's personality, but they may not generate specific information about the candidate's ability. Structured interviews tend to be more reliable predictors of job performance because they are based on the job analysis that has been done for the position. They are also more likely to be free of bias and stereotypes. And because the same questions are being asked of all candidates for the job, an interview that is at least partly structured allows the manager to compare responses across different candidates.[18]

Reference Checks Résumés, applications, and interviews rely on the applicant's honesty. To make an accurate selection decision, employers have to be able to trust the words of each candidate. Unfortunately some candidates may exaggerate their qualifications or hide criminal backgrounds that could pose a risk to the employer. In a highly publicized incident, the dean of admissions at the Massachusetts Institute of Technology resigned after nearly three decades on the job because the school learned she had provided false information about her educational background.[19] She had demonstrated an ability to perform the job functions but could no longer claim the level of integrity required by that position. Once lost, a reputation is hard to regain.

Because these and more ambiguous ethical gray areas arise, employers supplement candidate-provided information with other screening devices, including *reference checks*. Virtually all organizations contact references or former employers and educational institutions listed by candidates

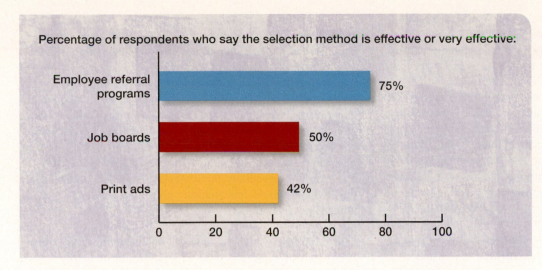

Percentage of respondents who say the selection method is effective or very effective:

Employee referral programs	75%
Job boards	50%
Print ads	42%

to at least confirm dates of employment (or attendance), positions held, and job duties performed. Although checking references makes sense, reference information is becoming increasingly difficult to obtain as a result of several highly publicized lawsuits. In one case, an applicant sued a former boss on the grounds that the boss told prospective employers the applicant was a "thief and a crook." The jury awarded the applicant $80,000.[20] Still, talking to an applicant's previous supervisor is a common practice and often does provide useful information, particularly if specific job-related questions are asked ("Can you give me an example of a project candidate X handled particularly well?").

Background Checks For a higher level of scrutiny, background investigations also have become standard procedure at many companies. Some state courts have ruled that companies can be held liable for negligent hiring if they fail to do adequate background checks. Types of checks include Social Security verification, past employment and education verification, and a criminal records check. A number of other checks can be conducted if they pertain to the specific job, including a motor vehicle record check (for jobs involving driving) and a credit check (for money-handling jobs).

Internet tools have made basic background checks fast and easy. A recent survey of executive recruiters learned that more than three-quarters use search engines such as Google to find out about

● When based on a job analysis, structured interviews tend to be more reliable predictors of job performance than are unstructured interviews.

candidates.[21] Such searches can turn up a variety of information, including what people have written on blogs or posted under their name on Twitter, LinkedIn, or Facebook. Internet users are advised to remember that anything carrying their name online may become information for potential employers, even years down the road. ChoicePoint, a 4,200-employee company specializes in conducting background checks, sells a preemployment self-check to job seekers who want to see what prospective employers will learn about them. The cost of this service is between $25 and $75.[22]

Personality Tests Employers have been hesitant to use personality tests for employee selection, largely because they are hard to defend in court.[23] Some personality types have been associated with greater job satisfaction and performance, especially where the organization can build groups of people with similar positive traits.[24] As a result, personality tests are regaining popularity, and at some point in your career you will probably complete some personality tests. A number of well-known paper-and-pencil inventories measure personality traits such as sociability, adjustment, and energy. Typical questions are "Do you like to socialize with people?" and "Do you enjoy working hard?" Some personality tests try to determine the type of working conditions that the candidate prefers, to see if he or she would be motivated and productive in the particular job. For example, if the candidate prefers making decisions on his or her own but the job requires gaining the cooperation of others, another candidate might be a better fit.

Drug Testing Drug testing is now a frequently used screening instrument. Since the passage of the Drug-Free Workplace Act of 1988, applicants and employees of federal contractors and Department of Defense contractors and those under Department of Transportation regulations have been subject to testing for illegal drugs. Well over half of all U.S. companies conduct preemployment drug tests.

Cognitive Ability Tests

Among the oldest employment selection devices are cognitive ability tests. These tests measure a range of intellectual abilities, including verbal comprehension (vocabulary, reading) and numerical aptitude (mathematical calculations). About 20 percent of U.S. companies use cognitive ability tests for selection purposes.[25] Exhibit 8.2 shows some examples of cognitive ability test questions.

Performance Tests

In a performance test, the test taker performs a sample of the job. Most companies use some type of performance test, typically for administrative assistant and clerical positions. The most widely used performance test is the typing test. However, performance tests have been developed for almost every occupation, including manage rial positions.

Assessment centers are the most notable offshoot of the managerial performance test.[26] A typical **assessment center** consists of 10 to 12 candidates who participate in a variety of exercises or situations; some of the exercises involve group interactions, and others are performed individually. Each exercise taps a number of critical managerial dimensions, such as leadership, decision-making skills, and communication ability. Assessors, generally line managers from the organization, observe and record information about the candidates' performance in each exercise.

Integrity Tests

To assess job candidates' honesty, employers may administer integrity tests. Polygraphs, or lie detector tests,

---

Exhibit 8.2 Sample measures of cognitive ability

Verbal

1. What is the meaning of the word surreptitious?
   - a. covert
   - b. winding
   - c. lively
   - d. sweet

2. How is the noun clause used in the following sentence: "I hope that I can learn this game."
   - a. subject
   - b. predicate nominative
   - c. direct object
   - d. object of the preposition

Quantitative

3. Divide 50 by .5 and add 5. What is the result?
   - a. 25
   - b. 30
   - c. 95
   - d. 105

4. What is the value of 144^2?
   - a. 12
   - b. 72
   - c. 288
   - d. 20736

Reasoning

5. _____ is to boat as snow is to _____
   - a. sail, ski
   - b. water, winter
   - c. water, ski
   - d. engine, water

6. Two women played 5 games of chess. Each woman won the same number of games, yet there were no ties. How can this be so?
   - a. There was a forfeit.
   - b. One player cheated.
   - c. They played different people.
   - d. One game was still in progress.

Mechanical

7. If gear A and gear C are both turning counterclockwise, what is happening to gear B?
   - a. It is turning counterclockwise.
   - b. It is turning clockwise.
   - c. It remains stationary.
   - d. The whole system will jam.

A   B   C

Answers: 1a, 2c, 3d, 4d, 5c, 6c, 7b.

Source: G. Bohlander, S. Snell, and A. Sherman, *Managing Human Resources,* 12th ed. © 2001. Reprinted with permission of South-Western, a part of Cengage Learning, Inc. Reproduced by permission. www.cengage.com/permissions.

have been banned for most employment purposes.[27] Paper-and-pencil honesty tests are more recent instruments for measuring individuals' propensity to engage in dishonesty or other counterproductive behaviors at work. The tests include questions such as whether a person has ever thought about stealing and whether he or she believes other people steal. Although companies including Payless ShoeSource reported that losses due to theft declined following the introduction of integrity tests, the accuracy of these tests is still debatable.[28]

3.2 | Both Reliability and Validity Are Important

A good selection technique, like a structured interview or assessment center, needs to be consistent and accurate. The basic objective of achieving competitive advantage through human capital can be compromised if the reliability and validity of the firm's selection techniques are in doubt. The first step is to understand the difference between these two concepts:

1. **Reliability** refers to the consistency of test scores over time and across alternative measurements. For example, if three different interviewers talked to the same job candidate but drew very different conclusions about the candidate's abilities, there could be problems with the reliability of one or more of the selection tests or interview procedures.

2. **Validity** moves beyond reliability to assess the accuracy of the selection test.

Criterion-related validity refers to the degree to which a test actually predicts or correlates with job performance. Such validity is usually established through studies comparing test performance and job performance for a large enough sample of employees to enable a fair conclusion to be reached. For example, if a high score on a cognitive ability test strongly predicts good job performance, then candidates who score well will tend to be preferred over those who do not. Still, no test by itself perfectly predicts performance. Managers usually consider other criteria before making a final selection.

Content validity concerns the degree to which selection tests measure a representative sample of the knowledge, skills, and abilities required for the job. The best-known example of a content-valid test is a keyboarding test for administrative assistants because keyboarding is a task a person in that position almost always performs. However, to be completely content-valid, the selection process also should measure other skills the assistant would likely perform, such as answering the telephone, duplicating and faxing documents, and dealing with the public. Content validity is more subjective (less statistical) than evaluations of criterion-related validity but is no less important, particularly when an organization is defending employment decisions in court.

3.3 | Sometimes Employees Must Be Let Go

Unfortunately staffing decisions do not simply focus on hiring employees. As organizations evolve and markets change, the demand for certain employees rises and falls. Also, some employees simply do not perform at the level required. For these reasons, managers sometimes must make difficult decisions to terminate their employment.

Layoffs As a result of the massive restructuring of American industry, many organizations have been *downsizing*—laying off large numbers of managerial and other employees. Dismissing any employee is tough, but when a company lays off a substantial portion of its workforce, the results can rock the foundations of the organization.[29] The victims of restructuring face all the difficulties of being let go—loss of self-esteem, demoralizing job searches, and the stigma of being out of work. Employers can help by offering **outplacement,** the process of helping people who have been dismissed from the company to regain employment elsewhere. Even then, the impact of layoffs goes further than the employees who leave. Many who remain will experience disenchantment, distrust, and lethargy. The way management deals with dismissals affects the productivity and satisfaction of those who remain. A well-thought-out dismissal process eases tensions and helps remaining employees adjust to the new work situation.

Organizations with strong performance evaluation systems benefit because the survivors are less likely to believe the decision was arbitrary. In addition, if laid-off workers are offered severance pay and help in finding a new job, remaining workers will be comforted. Companies also should avoid stringing out layoffs by dismissing a few workers at a time.

study tip 8

"Productivity requires sufficient sleep"

Do you ever feel like you have too much on your plate? Between school, work, volunteer/community activities, and social/family life, you may not be getting enough sleep. Another factor that may negatively affect your sleep is consuming caffeinated drinks in the late afternoon or evening. What's the bottom line? Getting sufficient sleep on a regular basis can help you study more efficiently and possibly earn higher grades in your courses.

Termination People sometimes "get fired" for poor performance or other reasons. Should an employer have the right to fire a worker? In 1884 a Tennessee court ruled "All may dismiss their employee(s) at will for good cause, for no cause, or even for cause morally wrong." The concept that an employee may be fired for any reason is known as **employment-at-will** or *termination-at-will* and was upheld in a 1908 Supreme Court ruling.[30] The logic is that if the employee may quit at any time, the employer is free to dismiss at any time.

Since the mid-1970s, courts in most states have made exceptions to this doctrine based on public policy—a policy or ruling designed to protect the public from harm. Under the public policy exception, employees cannot be fired for such actions as refusing to break the law, taking time off for jury duty, or "whistle-blowing" to report illegal company behavior. So if a worker reports an environmental violation to the regulatory agency and the company fires him or her, the courts may argue that the firing was unfair because the employee acted for the good of the community. Another major exception is union contracts that limit an employer's ability to fire without cause.

Employers can avoid the pitfalls associated with dismissal by developing progressive and positive disciplinary procedures.[31] Progressive means the manager takes graduated steps in trying to correct a workplace behavior. For example, an employee who has been absent receives a verbal reprimand for the first offense, and a written reprimand for the second offense. A third offense results in counseling and probation, and a fourth results in a paid-leave day to think over the consequences of future infractions. The employer is signaling to the employee that this is the "last straw." Arbitrators are more likely to side with an employer that fires someone when they believe the company has made sincere efforts to help the person correct his or her behavior.

The **termination interview,** in which the manager discusses the company's termination decision with the employee, is stressful for both parties. Most experts believe that the immediate superior should be the one to deliver the bad news to employees. However, it is wise to have a third party, such as an HR manager, present for guidance and note-taking. Because announcing a termination is likely to upset the employee and occasionally leads to a lawsuit, the manager should prepare carefully. Preparation should include learning the facts of the situation and reviewing any documents to make sure they are consistent with the reason for the termination. During the termination interview, ethics and common sense dictate that the manager should be truthful but respectful, stating the facts and avoiding arguments. Exhibit 8.3 provides some additional practical guidelines for conducting a termination interview:[32]

3.4 | Legal Issues and Equal Employment Opportunity

Many laws have been passed governing employment decisions and practices. They will directly affect a good part of your day-to-day work as a manager, as well as the human resource function of your organization. It is important for managers to be familiar with Equal Employment Opportunity laws in order to follow best practices and avoid the negative consequences of noncompliance. In 2012, there were nearly 100,000 charges of illegal discrimination filed with the U.S. government, costing employers $365.4 million in settlement costs. In 2013, the government filed charges against Dollar General and BMW for "allegedly implementing and utilizing a criminal background

---

Exhibit 8.3	Practical guidelines for conducting a termination interview

Do give as much warning as possible for mass layoffs.

Do sit down one-on-one with the individual, in a private office.

Do complete a termination session within 15 minutes.

Do provide written explanations of severance benefits.

Do provide outplacement services away from company headquarters.

Do be sure the employee hears about the termination from a manager, not a colleague.

Do express appreciation for what the employee has contributed, if appropriate.

Don't leave room for confusion when firing. Tell the individual in the first sentence that he or she is terminated.

Don't allow time for debate during a termination session.

Don't make personal comments when firing someone; keep the conversation professional.

Don't rush a fired employee off site unless security is an issue.

Don't fire people on significant dates, like the 25th anniversary of their employment or the day their mother died.

Don't fire employees when they are on vacation or have just returned.

Exhibit 8.4 U.S. equal employment laws

Act	Major Provisions	Enforcement and Remedies
Fair Labor Standards Act (1938)	Creates exempt (salaried) and nonexempt (hourly) employee categories, governing overtime and other rules; sets minimum wage, child labor laws.	Enforced by Department of Labor, private action to recover lost wages; civil and criminal penalties also possible.
Equal Pay Act (1963)	Prohibits gender-based pay discrimination between two jobs substantially similar in skill, effort, responsibility, and working conditions.	Fines up to $10,000, imprisonment up to 6 months, or both; enforced by Equal Employment Opportunity Commission (EEOC); private actions for double damages up to 3 years' wages, liquidated damages, reinstatement, or promotion.
Title VII of Civil Rights Act (1964)	Prohibits discrimination based on race, sex, color, religion, or national origin in employment decisions: hiring, pay, working conditions, promotion, discipline, or discharge.	Enforced by EEOC; private actions, back pay, front pay, reinstatement, restoration of seniority and pension benefits, attorneys' fees and costs.
Executive Orders 11246 and 11375 (1965)	Requires equal opportunity clauses in federal contracts; prohibits employment discrimination by federal contractors based on race, color, religion, sex, or national origin.	Established Office of Federal Contract Compliance Programs (OFCCP) to investigate violations; empowered to terminate violator's federal contracts.
Age Discrimination in Employment Act (1967)	Prohibits employment discrimination based on age for persons over 40 years; restricts mandatory retirement.	EEOC enforcement; private actions for reinstatement, back pay, front pay, restoration of seniority and pension benefits; double unpaid wages for willful violations; attorneys' fees and costs.
Vocational Rehabilitation Act (1973)	Requires affirmative action by all federal contractors for persons with disabilities; defines disabilities as physical or mental impairments that substantially limit life activities.	Federal contractors must consider hiring disabled persons capable of performance after reasonable accommodations.
Americans with Disabilities Act (1990)	Extends affirmative action provisions of Vocational Rehabilitation Act to private employers; requires workplace modifications to facilitate disabled employees; prohibits discrimination against disabled.	EEOC enforcement; private actions for Title VII remedies.
Civil Rights Act (1991)	Clarifies Title VII requirements: disparate treatment impact suits, business necessity, job relatedness; shifts burden of proof to employer; permits punitive damages and jury trials.	Punitive damages limited to sliding scale only in intentional discrimination based on sex, religion, and disabilities.
Family and Medical Leave Act (1991)	Requires 12 weeks' unpaid leave for medical or family needs: paternity, maternity, family member illness.	Private actions for lost wages and other expenses, reinstatement.

policy that results in employees being fired and others being screened out for employment."[33] Exhibit 8.4 summarizes many of these major employment laws.

The 1938 *Fair Labor Standards Act* (FLSA), among other provisions, creates two employee categories: exempt and nonexempt. Employees are normally exempt from overtime pay if they have considerable discretion in how they carry out their jobs and if their jobs require them to exercise independent judgment. Managers usually fall in this category. Nonexempt employees are usually paid by the hour and must be paid overtime if they work more than 40 hours in a week. As a manager you will almost certainly need to specify the exempt or nonexempt status of anyone you hire.

Laws aimed at protecting employees from discrimination include the 1964 *Civil Rights Act*, which prohibits discrimination in employment based on race, sex, color, national origin, and religion. Title VII of the act specifically forbids discrimination in such employment practices as recruitment,

hiring, discharge, promotion, compensation, and access to training.[34] Title VII also prohibits a specific form of discrimination, *sexual harassment*, which refers to "unwelcome sexual advances, requests for favors, and other verbal or physical conduct of a sexual nature" that impacts an individual's employment, interferes with work performance, or creates a hostile work environment.[35] The *Americans with Disabilities Act* prohibits employment discrimination against people with disabilities. Recovering alcoholics and drug abusers, cancer patients in remission, and AIDS patients are covered by this legislation. The 1991 *Civil Rights Act* strengthened all these protections and permitted punitive damages to be imposed on companies that violate them. The *Age Discrimination in Employment Act* of 1967 and its amendments in 1978 and 1986 prohibit discrimination against people age 40 and over. One reason for this legislation was the practice of dismissing older workers to replace them with younger workers earning lower pay.

● Walmart employee Betty Dukes was the first "named plaintiff" in the Dukes v. Walmart case. Approximately 1.5 million current and former female employees of the giant retailer filed the largest gender bias class action lawsuit in U.S. history.

One common reason why employers are sued for discrimination is **adverse impact**—when a seemingly neutral employment practice has a disproportionately negative effect on a group protected by the Civil Rights Act.[36] For example, if equal numbers of qualified men and women apply for jobs but a particular employment test results in far fewer women being hired, the test may be considered to cause an adverse impact, making it subject to challenge on that basis. For example, 1.5 million current and former female employees from Walmart pressed a class action lawsuit against the retailer, claiming that it has a discriminatory pay and promotion policy against women. In 2011 the U.S. Supreme Court (in a split decision) rejected this class action lawsuit.[37]

Because of the importance of these issues, many companies have established procedures to ensure compliance with labor and equal opportunity laws. For example, they may monitor and compare salaries by race, gender, length of service, and other categories to make sure employees across all groups are being fairly paid. Written policies can also help ensure fair and legal practices in the workplace, although the company may also have to demonstrate a record of actually following those procedures and making sure they are implemented. In this sense, effective management practices not only help managers motivate employees to do their best work but often help provide legal protection as well. For example, managers who give their employees regular, specific evaluations can prevent misunderstandings that lead to lawsuits. A written record of those evaluations is often useful in demonstrating fair and objective treatment.

Another law that affects staffing practices is the *Worker Adjustment and Retraining Notification Act* of 1989, commonly known as the *WARN Act* or *Plant Closing Bill*. It requires covered employers to give affected employees 60 days' written notice of plant closings or mass layoffs.

LO4 Evaluate the importance of spending on training and development

4 | TRAINING AND DEVELOPMENT

Today's competitive environment requires managers to upgrade the skills and performance of employees—and themselves. Continual improvement increases both personal and organizational effectiveness. It makes organization members more useful in their current job and prepares them for new responsibilities. And it helps the entire organization handle new challenges and take advantage of new methods and technologies. These training and development activities are supported by appraising employees' performance and giving them effective feedback, as we will discuss in the next section.

U.S. businesses spend more than $60 billion to provide their employees with formal training annually. As shown in Exhibit 8.5, the greatest increase in training expenditures has been in management/supervisory, onboarding, and sales training.[38] But competitive pressures require that companies consider the most efficient training methods. That means traditional classroom settings are often giving way to computerized methods.

4.1 | Training Programs Include Four Phases

Although we use the general term *training* here, training sometimes is distinguished from development. **Training** usually

Exhibit 8.5 Percentage of companies increasing spending on training areas in 2014

29%	• Management/supervisory
22%	• Onboarding
21%	• Sales training
20%	• Interpersonal skills (e.g., communication and teamwork)
20%	• Customer service
19%	• IT/Systems (e.g., enterprise software)
18%	• Mandatory or compliance
16%	• Executive development

Source: Adapted from "2013 Training Industry Report," *Training* (online), November/December 2013, www.trainingmag.com.

development teaching managers and professional employees broad skills needed for their present and future jobs

needs assessment an analysis identifying the jobs, people, and departments for which training is necessary

orientation training training designed to introduce new employees to the company and familiarize them with policies, procedures, culture, and the like

team training training that provides employees with the skills and perspectives they need to collaborate with others

diversity training programs that focus on identifying and reducing hidden biases against people with differences and developing the skills needed to manage a diversified workforce

refers to teaching lower-level employees how to perform their present jobs, whereas **development** involves teaching managers and professional employees broader skills needed for their present and future jobs.

Phase one of training usually starts with a **needs assessment.** Managers conduct an analysis to identify the jobs, people, and departments for which training is necessary. Job analysis and performance measurements are useful for this purpose.

Phase two involves the design of training programs. Training objectives and content are established from the needs assessment. For example, Recreational Equipment Inc. (REI) wants its sales associates to learn how to tell whether they are being approached by a "transactional customer," who simply wants to find and pay for a specific product, or a "consultative customer," who wants to spend some time discussing alternative features and benefits.[39]

Phase three involves decisions about the training methods and location—whether the training will be provided on or off the job. Common training methods include lectures, role-playing, business simulation, behavior modeling (watching a video and imitating what is observed), conferences, vestibule training (practicing in a simulated job environment), and apprenticeships. Another popular method is job rotation, or assigning employees to different jobs in the organization to broaden their experience and improve their skills. Smart managers often request assignment to jobs where they can be challenged and their skills broadened. The training method should be suited to the objectives defined in phase two. At REI, where the company wants sales associates to identify and respond to various interpersonal situations, much of the training involves role-playing, supplemented with video presentations. And Home Depot emphasizes mentoring for sales associates who work the aisles but has a more efficient computer-based training program for the cashiers, whose jobs are more routine.[40]

Finally, *phase four* of training should evaluate the program's effectiveness. Measures of effectiveness include employee reactions (surveys), learning (tests), improved behavior on the job, and bottom-line results (e.g., an increase in sales or reduction in defect rates following the training program).

4.2 | Training Options Achieve Many Objectives

Companies invest in training to enhance individual performance and organizational productivity. Programs to improve an employee's computer, technical, or communication skills are common, and some types of training have become standard across many organizations. **Orientation training** familiarizes new employees with their jobs, work units, and the organization in general. Done well, orientation training can increase morale and productivity and can lower employee turnover and the costs of recruiting and training.

Team training teaches employees the skills they need to work together and helps them interact. After General Mills acquired Pillsbury, it used a team training program called Brand Champions to combine the marketing expertise of the two companies and share knowledge among employees handling various functions such as sales and research and development. Most of the time, trainees engaged in team exercises to analyze brands, target customers, and develop marketing messages.[41]

Diversity training focuses on building awareness of diversity issues and providing the skills employees need to work with others who are different from them. Managing diversity is discussed in the next chapter.

As today's decentralized and leaner organizations have put more demands on managers, *management training programs* have become widespread. Such programs often seek to improve managers' *people skills*—their ability to delegate effectively, motivate their subordinates, and communicate and inspire others to achieve organization goals. *Coaching*—being trained by a superior—is usually the most effective and direct management development tool. Managers may also participate in training programs that are used for all employees, such as job rotation, or attend seminars and courses specifically designed to help them improve supervisory skills or prepare for future promotion.

:::::::::::::::::

NetApp, a data management company based in Sunnyvale, California, has an engaging approach to management training. The company hired BTS Group to develop a simulation game, modeled on NetApp's real-life business. NetApp first used the simulation at a strategy meeting of its top managers. The executives were so enthusiastic and creative about solving the simulation problem that the company invited middle managers to play the game as training for top posts, where strategic thinking is essential.

In the simulation, the managers were divided into five teams, bringing together managers from various functions. Each team was told to run an imaginary high-growth company named Pet-a-Toaster for three years, competing against the other teams. A year's worth of events were packed into each day of the training program. Each team received a booklet with details about Pet-a-Toaster, based on the market conditions actually facing

NetApp. Teams allocated their resources, selected from among possible strategies, and reacted to events posed by the game (for example, a request from a big customer). BTS's simulation software analyzed the actions and provided feedback.

At the end of the simulation, BTS reported each team's results, including total sales and operating profits. Now NetApp's middle managers appreciate what it takes to run a company—and have greater respect for their leaders.[42]

::::::::::::::::

LO5 Explain alternatives for who appraises an employee's performance

5 | PERFORMANCE APPRAISAL

One of the most important responsibilities you will have as a manager is **performance appraisal (PA),** the assessment of an employee's job performance. Done well, it can help employees improve their performance, pay, and chances for promotion; foster communication between managers and employees; and increase the employees' and the organization's effectiveness. Done poorly, it can cause resentment, reduce motivation, diminish performance, and even expose the organization to legal action.

Performance appraisal has two basic, equally important purposes:

1. *Administrative*—It provides managers with the information they need to make salary, promotion, and dismissal decisions; helps employees understand and accept the basis of those decisions; and provides documentation that can justify those decisions in court.

2. *Developmental*—The information gathered can be used to identify and plan the additional training, experience, or other improvement that employees require. Also, the manager's feedback and coaching based on the appraisal help employees improve their day-to-day performance and can help prepare them for greater responsibilities.

5.1 | What Do You Appraise?

Performance appraisals can assess three basic categories of employee performance: traits, behaviors, and results. *Trait appraisals* involve judgments about employee performance. The rater indicates the degree to which the employee possesses a trait such as initiative, leadership, and attitude. Usually the manager uses a numerical *ratings scale*. For example, if the measured trait is "attitude," the employee might be rated anywhere from 1 (very negative attitude) to 5 (very positive

attitude). Trait scales are common because they are simple to use and provide a standard measure for all employees. But they are often not valid as performance measures. Because they tend to be ambiguous as well as highly subjective—does the employee really have a bad attitude, or is he or she just shy?—they often lead to personal bias and may not be suitable for providing useful feedback.

Behavioral appraisals, while still subjective, focus on observable aspects of performance. They use scales describing specific, prescribed behaviors, which can help ensure that all parties understand what the ratings are really measuring. Because they are less ambiguous, they also can provide useful feedback. Exhibit 8.6 shows an example of a behaviorally anchored rating scale (BARS) for evaluating quality. Another common approach is the *critical incident* technique, in which the manager keeps a regular log by recording each significant employee behavior that reflects the quality of his or her performance ("Juanita impressed the client with her effective presentation today"; "Joe was late with his report"). This approach can be subjective and time-consuming, and it may give some employees a sense that everything they do is being recorded. However, it reminds managers preparing a performance review what the employee actually did.

Results appraisals tend to be more objective and can focus on production data such as sales volume (for a salesperson), units produced (for a line worker), or profits (for a manager). One approach, **management by objectives (MBO),** involves a subordinate and a supervisor agreeing in advance on specific performance goals (objectives). They develop a plan describing the time frame and criteria for determining whether the objectives have been reached. The aim is to agree on a set of objectives that are clear, specific, and reachable. An objective of a marketing manager might be "Develop a new advertising campaign using social media and YouTube videos."

MBO has several important advantages. First, it avoids the biases and measurement difficulties of trait and behavioral appraisals. At the end of the review period, the employee either has or has not achieved the specified objective. The employee is judged on actual job performance. Second, because the employee and manager have agreed on the objective at the outset, the employee is likely to be committed to the outcome, and misunderstanding is unlikely. Third, because the employee is directly responsible for achieving the objective, MBO supports empowerment of employees to adapt their behavior so they achieve the desired results. But the approach has disadvantages as well. Objectives may be unrealistic, frustrating the employee and the manager, or too rigid, leaving the employee without enough flexibility if circumstances change. Finally, MBO often focuses too much on short-term achievement at the expense of long-term goals.

None of these performance appraisal systems is easy to conduct properly, and all have drawbacks. In choosing an appraisal method, the following guidelines may prove helpful:

- Base performance standards on job analysis.
- Communicate performance standards to employees.

Exhibit 8.6 Example of BARS used for evaluating quality

Performance Dimension: Total Quality Management. This area of performance concerns the extent to which a person is aware of, endorses, and develops proactive procedures to enhance product quality, ensure early disclosure of discrepancies, and integrate quality assessments with cost and schedule performance measurement reports to maximize clients' satisfaction with overall performance.

OUTSTANDING	7	**Uses measures of quality and well-defined processes to achieve project goals.** **Defines quality from the client's perspective.**
	6	**Looks for/identifies ways to continually improve the process.**
	5	**Clearly communicates quality management to others.** **Develops a plan that defines how the team will participate in quality.**
		Appreciates TQM as an investment.
AVERAGE	4	**Has measures of quality that define tolerance levels.**
	3	**Views quality as costly.** **Legislates quality.**
	2	**Focuses his/her concerns only on outputs and deliverables, ignoring the underlying processes.**
POOR	1	**Blames others for absence of quality.** **Gives only lip service to quality concerns.**

Source: Reprinted with permission of Rick Jacobs.

- Evaluate employees on specific performance-related behaviors rather than on a single global or overall measure.

- Document the performance appraisal process carefully.

- If possible, use more than one rater.

- Develop a formal appeal process.

- Always take legal considerations into account.[43]

- *Managers* and *supervisors* are the traditional source of appraisal information because they are often best positioned to observe an employee's performance.

- *Peers* and *team members* see different dimensions of performance and may be best at identifying leadership potential and interpersonal skills. Companies are therefore turning to peers and team members to provide input to the performance appraisal.

> "Outstanding leaders go out of their way to boost the self-esteem of their personnel. If people believe in themselves, it's amazing what they can accomplish."
>
> —Sam Walton

5.2 | Who Should Do the Appraisal?

Just as multiple methods can be used to gather performance appraisal information, several different sources can provide that information:

- *Subordinates* are becoming a more popular source of appraisal information, used by companies such as Xerox and IBM to give superiors feedback on how their employees view them. Often this information is given in confidence to the manager and not shared with superiors. Even so, this approach can make managers uncomfortable

Take Charge of Your Career

Tips for Providing Constructive Feedback

For many managers, supervisors, and team leaders, giving performance feedback to their employees can be uncomfortable. Maybe it's not as stressful as going to the dentist, but there are some tips available for making the process less painful.

According to Eileen Chadnick of Big Cheese Coaching, providing constructive feedback to employees may not only help them develop and improve their performance, but it may also build trust between you and your employees. First, she recommends reframing your thinking to envisioning the meeting as a way to help your employees, not to demoralize them. Spend time and practice phrasing questions so you do not put the employee on the defensive. For example, "Can you help me understand why your sales numbers were down by 10 percent this year?" sounds better than "Tell me why you're not pulling your weight in sales this year?" Chadnick also suggests that you be prepared for a two-way conversation, not just a one-way lecture about how the employee needs to improve. Giving employees room to comment and clarify performance issues will generally make the process seem more fair and transparent. Also, focus on employees' behaviors, not their character or personalities. For example, "When you arrived late to the call center, your coworkers had to take extra calls to cover for you" focuses on the behavior that needs to be changed. In contrast, avoid saying things like "Only slackers arrive late. Be on time so you don't stress out your coworkers." A final tip for giving constructive feedback is to show empathy with your employees. It needs to be sincere. You may consider saying things like "I know some customers can be unreasonable" or "I bet that can be challenging." Showing empathy signals to your employees that you hear them and understand what they are going through.

Source: E. Chadnick, "Giving Feedback That Fuels Success," *Canadian HR Reporter* 23, no. 15 (September 6, 2010), pp. 19–21.

---

initially, but the feedback is often practical and can help them significantly improve their management style. Because this process gives employees power over their bosses, it is generally used for development purposes only, not for salary or promotion decisions.

- *Internal and external customers* are relevant sources of performance appraisal information in companies, such as Ford and Honda, that are focused on total quality management. External customers have been used for some time to appraise restaurant employees. Internal customers can include anyone inside the organization who depends on an employee's work output.

- *Self-appraisals,* in which employees evaluate their own performance, usually are a good idea. Although they may be biased upward, the process of self-evaluation helps increase the employee's involvement in the review process and is a starting point for setting future goals.

Because each source of information has some limitations, and since different people may see different aspects of performance, Westinghouse, Dell, and many other companies have involved more than one source for appraisal information. In a process known as **360-degree appraisal,** feedback is obtained from subordinates, peers, and superiors—every level involved with the employee. Often the person being rated can select the appraisers, subject to a manager's approval, with the understanding that the individual appraisals are kept confidential; returned forms might not include the name of the appraiser, for example, and the results may be consolidated for each level.

The 360-degree appraisal delivers a fuller picture of the employee's strengths and weaknesses, and it often captures qualities other appraisal methods miss. For example, an employee may have a difficult relationship with his or her supervisor yet be highly regarded by peers and subordinates. The approach can lead to significant improvement, with employees often motivated to improve their ratings. On the downside, employees may be unwilling to rate colleagues harshly, so a certain uniformity of ratings may result. Also, the 360-degree appraisal is less useful than more objective criteria, like financial targets. It is usually aimed at employee development, rather than being a tool for administrative decisions like raises. For those, results appraisals like MBO are more appropriate.[44]

5.3 | How Do You Give Employees Feedback?

Giving performance feedback can be stressful for managers and subordinates because its purposes conflict to some degree. Providing growth and development requires understanding and support, but the manager must be impersonal and able to make tough decisions. Employees want to know how they are doing, but typically they are uncomfortable about getting feedback. Finally, the organization's need to make HR decisions conflicts with the individual employee's need to maintain a positive image.[45] These conflicts often make performance interviews difficult, so managers should conduct them thoughtfully.

In general, appraisal feedback works best when it is *specific* and *constructive*—related to clear goals or behaviors and clearly intended to help the employee rather than simply criticize. Managers have an interest not just in rating performance but in raising it, and effective appraisals take that into account. In addition, the appraisal is likely to be more meaningful and satisfying when the manager gives the employee a chance to discuss his or her performance and respond to the appraisal.

360-degree appraisal process of using multiple sources of appraisal to gain a comprehensive perspective on one's performance

• *Performance appraisal feedback tends to be more effective when it's specific and constructive.*

Interviews are most difficult with an employee who is performing poorly. Here is a useful interview format for when an employee is performing below acceptable standards:

1. Summarize the employee's specific performance. Describe the performance in behavioral or outcome terms, such as sales or absenteeism. Don't say the employee has a poor attitude; rather, explain which employee behaviors indicate a poor attitude.

2. Describe the expectations and standards, and be specific.

3. Determine the causes for the low performance; get the employee's input.

4. Discuss solutions to the problem, and have the employee play a major role in the process.

5. Agree to a solution. As a supervisor, you have input into the solution. Raise issues and questions, but also provide support.

6. Agree to a timetable for improvement.

7. Document the meeting.

Follow-up meetings may be needed.

> **LO6** Describe the fundamental aspects of a reward system

6 | DESIGNING REWARD SYSTEMS

Another major set of HRM activities involves reward systems. This section emphasizes monetary rewards such as pay and fringe benefits.

6.1 | Pay Decisions Consider the Company, Position, and Individual

Reward systems can serve the strategic purposes of attracting, motivating, and retaining people. The wages paid to employees are based on a complex set of forces. Beyond the body of laws governing compensation, a number of basic decisions must be made in choosing an appropriate pay plan. The wage mix is influenced by a variety of factors:[46]

• *Internal factors* include the organization's compensation policy, the worth of each job, the employee's relative worth, and the employer's ability to pay.

• *External factors* include conditions of the labor market, area wage rates, the cost of living, the use of collective bargaining (union negotiations), and legal requirements.

Three types of decisions are crucial for designing an effective pay plan:

1. *Pay level*—the choice of whether to be a high-, average-, or low-paying company. Compensation is a major cost for any organization, so low wages can be justified on a short-term financial basis. But being the high-wage employer—the highest-paying company in the region—ensures that the company will attract many applicants. Being a wage leader may be important during times of low unemployment or intense competition.

2. *Pay structure*—the choice of how to price different jobs within the organization. Jobs that are similar in worth usually are grouped together into job families. A pay grade, with a floor and a ceiling, is established for each job family. Exhibit 8.7 illustrates a hypothetical pay structure.

3. *Individual pay decisions*—different pay rates for jobs of similar worth within the same family. Differences in pay within job families are decided in two ways. First, some jobs are occupied by individuals with more seniority than others. Second, some people may perform better and therefore deserve higher pay. Setting an individual's pay below that of coworkers—like choosing an overall low pay level—may become more difficult for employers to sustain in the future, as more employees use online resources such as Glassdoor.com, Salary.com, Vault.com, and PayScale.com to check whether their pay is above or below the average amount for similar job titles.[47]

Unlike many other types of decisions in organizations, decisions about pay, especially at the individual level, often are kept confidential. Is that practice advantageous for organizations? Surprisingly, there is little evidence about this practice, even though it affects almost every private sector employee.[48] Keeping pay decisions secret may help the organization by avoiding conflicts, protecting individuals' privacy, and reducing the likelihood that employees will leave to seek better pay

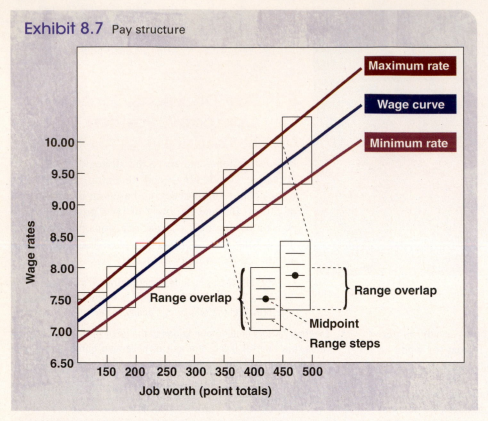

Exhibit 8.7 Pay structure

Maximum rate

Wage curve

Minimum rate

Wage rates

10.00

9.50

9.00

8.50

8.00

7.50

7.00

6.50

150 200 250 300 350 400 450 500

Job worth (point totals)

Range overlap

Range overlap

Midpoint

Range steps

Source: Bohlander/Snell/Sherman, *Managing Human Resources,* 11th ed., © 1998. Reprinted with permission of South-Western, a part of Cengage Learning, Inc. www.cengage.com/permissions.

if they are earning less than the average for their position. However, if decisions about pay are kept secret, employees may worry that decisions are unfair and may be less motivated because the link between performance and pay is unclear. Also, in an economic sense, labor markets are less efficient when information is unavailable, which can reduce organizations' ability to get the best workers at the optimum rate of pay. Given these possible pros and cons of pay secrecy, do you think this practice is wise? Is it ethical? And what about you—do you want to know how much your coworkers earn?

6.2 | Incentive Pay Encourages Employees to Do Their Best

Various incentive systems have been devised to motivate employees to be more productive.[49] The most common are *individual incentive plans,* which compare a worker's performance against an objective standard, with pay determined by the employee's performance. Examples include paying a salesperson extra for exceeding a sales target or awarding managers a bonus when their group meets a target. If effectively designed, individual incentive plans can be highly motivating. Some companies, including Boeing, are using them for nonmanagers. Boeing provides a cash bonus opportunity to nonmanagement employees when the company meets or exceeds its profit goals. Depending on the company's financial achievement, employees can earn from 1 to 20 days of additional pay.[50]

Several types of group incentive plans, in which pay is based on group performance, are increasingly used today. The plans aim to give employees a sense of participation and ownership in the firm's performance. *Gainsharing plans* reward employees for increasing productivity or saving money in areas under their direct control.[51] For example, if the usual waste allowance in a production line has been 5 percent and the company wants production employees to reduce that number, the company may offer to split any savings gained with the employees. *Profit-sharing plans* are usually implemented in the division or organization as a whole, although some incentives may still be tailored to unit performance. In most companies, the profit-sharing plan is based on a formula for allocating an annual amount to each employee if the company exceeds a specified profit target. Although profit-sharing plans do not reward individual performance, they do give all employees a stake in the company's success and motivate efforts to improve the company's profitability. Enterprise Rent-A-Car, which gives branch managers great latitude to address the needs of their local markets, uses an incentive pay system that allows local offices to share in the profits they have generated. The arrangement is especially attractive to employees with an entrepreneurial streak.[52]

When objective performance measures are unavailable but the company still wants to base pay on performance, it uses a *merit pay system.* Individuals' pay raises and bonuses are based on the merit rating they receive from their boss. Many organizations use merit pay systems to encourage higher levels of employee and organizational performance. However, not everyone agrees that this is the best approach. Stanford University Professor Jeffrey Pfeffer suggests that individual merit pay plans can undermine teamwork and the achievement of organizational goals; instead he recommends using group incentives like gain-sharing and profit-sharing.[53]

6.3 | Executive Pay Has Generated Controversy

In recent years the issue of executive pay has stirred controversy. One reason is that the gap between the pay of top executives and the average pay of employees has widened considerably. In the 1980s CEOs made less than 40 times the average worker's pay, but that multiple has now reached 343 times the average worker's pay. This gap is considerably wider in the United States than it is abroad.[54] Besides the difference between executive and average worker pay, the sheer size of CEO compensation also has been criticized. Top-earning CEOs can make tens of millions of dollars a year. Still, it's important to keep in

● Workers have begun to not only consider salary, but also environment, culture, and other compensation packages to help make employment decisions.

mind that the huge awards that make headlines are not necessarily typical. In 2012, CEOs of companies in the Standard & Poor's stock index earned on average $4.0 million, an increase of 19.7 percent over 2011;[55] this stands in stark contrast to the average wage of all U.S. workers, which was $46,400.[56]

The fastest-growing part of executive compensation comes from stock grants and *stock options*. Such options give the holder the right to purchase shares of stock at a specified price. For example, if the company's stock price is $8 a share, the company may award a manager the right to purchase a specific number of shares of company stock at that price. If the price of the stock rises to, say, $10 a share after a specified holding period—usually three years or more—the manager can *exercise* the option. He or she can purchase the shares from the company at $8 per share, sell the shares on the stock market at $10, and keep the difference. (Of course, if the stock price never rises above $8, the options will be worthless.) Companies issue options to managers to align their interests with those of the company's owners, the shareholders. The assumption is that managers will become even more focused on making the company successful, leading to a rise in its stock price. Assuming that the executives continue to own their stock year after year, the amount of their wealth

that is tied to the company's performance—and their incentive to work hard for the company—should continually increase.[57] However, many critics have suggested that excessive use of options encouraged executives to focus on short-term results to drive up the price of their stock, at the expense of their firm's long-run competitiveness. More recently, a plunging stock market highlighted another problem with stock options: many options became essentially worthless, so they failed to reward employees.[58] In the future, employees may be wary about accepting stock options in lieu of less risky forms of pay.

6.4 | Employees Get Benefits, Too

Although pay has traditionally been employees' primary monetary reward, benefits have been receiving increased attention. Benefits currently make up a far greater percentage of the total payroll than they did in past decades.[59] The typical employer today pays about 30 percent of payroll costs in benefits. Throughout most of the past two decades, benefits costs have risen faster than wages and salaries, fueled by the rapidly rising cost of medical care. Accordingly, employers are attempting to reduce benefits costs, even as their value to employees is rising. Benefits are also receiving more management attention because of their increased complexity. Many new types of benefits are now available, and tax laws affect myriad fringe benefits, such as health insurance and pension plans.

Like pay systems, employee benefit plans are subject to regulation. Employee benefits are divided into those required by law and those optional for an employer. Three basic benefits are required by law:

1. *Workers' compensation* provides financial support to employees suffering a work-related injury or illness.

2. *Social Security,* as established in the Social Security Act of 1935, provides financial support to retirees; in subsequent amendments, the act was expanded to cover disabled employees. The funds come from payments made by employers, employees, and self-employed workers.

3. *Unemployment insurance* provides financial support to employees laid off for reasons they cannot control. Companies that have terminated fewer employees pay less into the unemployment insurance fund, so organizations have an incentive to minimize terminations.

Many employers also offer benefits that are not required. The most common are pension plans and medical and hospital insurance. Both of these programs are undergoing significant change, partly because, in a global economy, they have put U.S. firms at a competitive disadvantage. For example, U.S. employers spend an average of $11,000 for each employee with health insurance.[60] Overseas firms generally do not bear these costs, which are usually government-funded, so they can compete more effectively on price. With U.S. medical costs rising rapidly, companies have reduced health benefits or asked employees to share more of their cost. A growing share of U.S. companies (more than one-third) offer no medical benefits at all, or they staff more positions with part-time workers and offer coverage only to full-time employees. At the same

Rapidly rising medical costs have made health care coverage an expensive part of employers' benefits packages.[62] Some employers—especially small ones—have coped by dropping health insurance altogether.

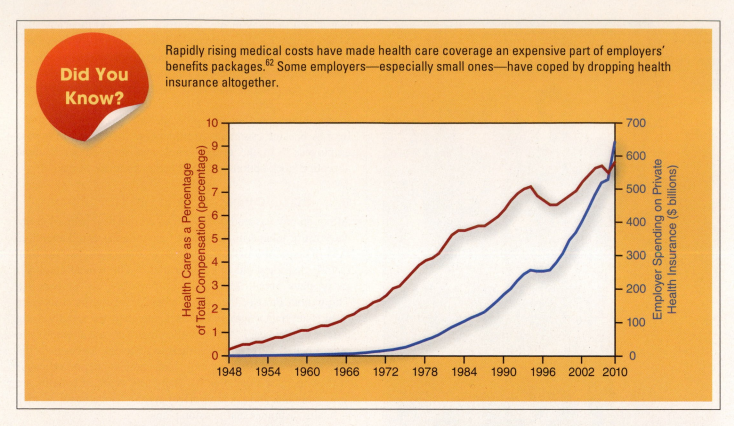

time, retirement benefits have been shifting away from guaranteed pensions. While a promised monthly pension used to be the norm, only about 18 percent of private company employees have one today (down from 36 percent two decades ago).[61] More often, the employee, the employer, or both contribute to an individual retirement account or 401(k) plan, which is invested. Upon retirement, the employee gets the balance that has accumulated in the account.

Because of the wide variety of possible benefits and the considerable differences in employee preferences and needs, companies often use **cafeteria** or **flexible benefit programs.** In this type of program, employees are given credits, which they "spend" by selecting individualized packages of benefits, including medical and dental insurance, dependent care, life insurance, and so on.

6.5 | Pay and Benefits Must Meet Legal Requirements

Several laws affect employee compensation and benefits. We have already mentioned the FLSA, which in addition to distinguishing between exempt and nonexempt employees also sets minimum wage, maximum hour, and child labor provisions.[63] The *Equal Pay Act (EPA)* of 1963 prohibits unequal pay for men and women who perform equal work. Equal work means jobs that require equal skill, effort, and responsibility and are performed under similar working conditions. The law does permit exceptions in which the difference in pay is due to a seniority system, merit system, incentive system based on quantity or quality of production, or any additional factor other than sex, such as market demand.

In contrast to the equal-pay-for-equal-work notion, **comparable worth** doctrine implies that women who perform *different* jobs of *equal* worth as those performed by men should be paid the same wage.[64] For example, nurses (predominantly female) were found to be paid considerably less than skilled craftworkers (predominantly male), even though the two jobs were found to be of equal value or worth.[65] Under the Equal Pay Act, this would not constitute pay discrimination because the jobs are very different. But under the comparable worth concept, these findings would indicate discrimination because the jobs are of equal worth. To date, no federal law requires comparable worth, and the Supreme Court has made no decisive rulings about it. However, some states have considered developing comparable worth laws, and others have raised the wages of female-dominated jobs. For example, Minnesota passed a comparable worth law for public sector employees after finding that women on average were paid 25 percent less than men. Iowa, Idaho, New Mexico, Washington, and South Dakota also have comparable worth laws for public sector employees.[66]

Some laws influence benefit practices. The *Pregnancy Discrimination Act* of 1978 states that pregnancy is a disability and qualifies a woman to receive the same benefits that she would with any other disability. The *Employee Retirement Income Security Act (ERISA)* of 1974 protects private pension programs from mismanagement. ERISA requires retirement benefits to be paid to those who vest or earn a right to draw benefits and ensures retirement benefits for employees whose companies go bankrupt or who otherwise cannot meet their pension obligations. The *Patient Protection and Affordable Care Act* (PPACA) of 2010 is requiring certain employers to provide health insurance to their employees (or pay $2,000 annually per employee for this purpose), insure employees with preexisting conditions, and provide coverage for employees' dependents until the age of 26.

6.6 | Employers Must Protect Health and Safety

The *Occupational Safety and Health Act (OSHA)* of 1970 requires employers to pursue workplace safety. Employers must maintain records of injuries and deaths caused by workplace accidents and submit to on-site inspections. Large-scale industrial accidents and nuclear power plant disasters worldwide have focused attention on the importance of workplace safety. Exhibit 8.8 presents several interesting facts about work-related injuries and illnesses in the United States.

Exhibit 8.8	Facts about work-related injuries and illnesses (2012)

Which jobs have the most lost work time associated with them due to injuries/illnesses?

1. Laborers and freight, stock, and material movers.
2. Nursing assistants.
3. Truck drivers, heavy and tractor–trailer.
4. Janitors and cleaners.
5. Police and sheriff's patrol officers.

When do most injuries and illnesses occur?

During the day (8–4 p.m.) shift, Monday–Friday, and between the second and fourth hours after arriving to work.

Which injuries/illnesses cause employees to miss the most workdays (and for how many days on average)?

1. Fractures (30 days).
2. Carpal tunnel syndrome (30 days).
3. Amputations (26 days).
4. Tendonitis (15 days).
5. Sprains, strains, and tears (10 days).

Do men or women miss more workdays due to injuries or illnesses?

Men do. They accounted for 62 percent of all missed days in 2012.

Do older workers have more days away from work due to injuries/illnesses?

Yes, but not by much. Workers aged 65 and older averaged 14 missed days of work due to injuries or illnesses, compared to 35- to 44-year-olds, who missed an average of 9 days per year.

Source: "Nonfatal Occupational Injuries and Illnesses Requiring Days Away from Work, 2012," economic news release, Bureau of Labor Statistics, www.bls.gov.

Another area of concern is the safety of young workers, who may lack the confidence to speak up if they see health or safety problems. A recent study of teenage workers found that many were exposed to hazards and used equipment that should have been off-limits to teens under federal regulations. For example, almost half of teenaged grocery store employees said they had performed prohibited tasks such as using box crushers and dough mixers.[67]

LO7 Summarize how unions and labor laws influence human resources management

7 | LABOR RELATIONS

Labor relations is the system of relations between workers and management. Labor unions recruit members, collect dues, and ensure that employees are treated fairly with respect to wages, working conditions, and other issues. When workers organize and negotiate with management, two processes are involved: unionization and collective bargaining. These processes have evolved since the 1930s in the United States to provide important employee rights.[68]

● Fast food workers and activists demonstrate outside the McDonald's corporate campus in Oak Brook, IL. They were calling on McDonald's to pay a minimum wage of $15-per-hour and offer better working conditions for their employees. Several protestors were arrested after they ignored police orders to leave the McDonald's campus. McDonald's, with over 35,000 restaurants around the world, is one of several companies at the center of the minimum wage debate. According to the Bureau of Labor Statistics, the median wage for fast-food and counter workers in the United States is $8.83/hour which is higher than the federally mandated minimum wage of $7.25/hour for all workers.

7.1 | What Labor Laws Exist?

Passed in 1935, the *National Labor Relations Act* (also called the *Wagner Act* after its legislative sponsor) ushered in an era of rapid unionization by declaring labor organizations legal, establishing five unfair employer labor practices, and creating the National Labor Relations Board (NLRB). Before the act, employers could fire workers who favored unions, and federal troops were often provided to put down strikes. Today the NLRB conducts unionization elections, hears complaints of unfair labor practices, and issues injunctions against offending employers. The Wagner Act greatly assisted the growth of unions by enabling workers to use the law and the courts to organize and collectively bargain for better wages, hours, and working conditions. Minimum wages, health benefits, maternity leave, the 40-hour workweek, and other worker protections were largely the result of collective bargaining over many years by unions.

Public policy began on the side of organized labor in 1935, but over the next 25 years, the pendulum swung toward management. The *Labor-Management Relations Act,* or *Taft-Hartley Act* (1947), protected employers' free speech rights, defined unfair labor practices by unions, and permitted workers to decertify (reject) a union as their representative.

Finally, the *Labor-Management Reporting and Disclosure Act,* or *Landrum-Griffin Act* (1959), swung the public policy pendulum midway between organized labor and management. By declaring a bill of rights for union members, establishing control over union dues increases, and imposing reporting requirements for unions, Landrum-Griffin was designed to curb abuses by union leadership and rid unions of corruption.

7.2 | How Do Employees Form Unions?

The effort to form a union begins when a union organizer or local union representative describes to workers the benefits they may receive by joining.[69] The union representative distributes authorization cards that permit workers to indicate whether they want an election to certify the union. The National Labor Relations Board will conduct an election if at least 30 percent

If an election is warranted, an NLRB representative conducts the election by secret ballot. A simple majority of those voting determines the winner, so apathetic workers who do not vote in effect support the union. If the union wins the election, it is certified as the bargaining unit representative. Management and the union are then legally required to bargain in good faith to obtain a collective bargaining agreement or contract.

Why do workers vote for or against a union? Four factors play a significant role:[70]

1. *Economic factors,* especially for workers in low-paying jobs—Unions attempt to raise the average wage rate for their members.

2. *Job dissatisfaction*—Poor supervisory practices, favoritism, lack of communication, and perceived unfair or arbitrary discipline and discharge are specific triggers of job dissatisfaction.

3. *Belief that the union has power* to obtain desired benefits can generate a pro-union vote.

4. The *image of the union*—Headline stories of union corruption and dishonesty can discourage workers from unionization.

7.3 | How Is Collective Bargaining Conducted?

In the United States, management and unions engage in a periodic ritual (typically every three years) of negotiating an agreement for wages, benefits, hours, and working conditions. Disputes can arise during this process, and sometimes the workers go on strike to compel agreement on their terms. Such an action, known as an *economic strike,* is permitted by law, but strikes are rare today. Strikers are not paid while they are on strike, and few workers want to undertake this hardship unnecessarily. In addition, managers may legally hire replacement workers during a strike, offsetting some of the strike's effect. Finally, workers are as aware as managers of the tougher competition companies face today; if treated fairly, they will usually share management's interest in coming to an agreement.

Once an agreement is signed, management and the union sometimes disagree over *interpretation* of the agreement. Usually they settle their disputes through **arbitration,** the use of a neutral third party, typically jointly selected, to resolve

> "Always treat your employees exactly as you want them to treat your best customers."
>
> —Stephen R. Covey

of the employees sign authorization cards. Management has several choices at this stage: to recognize the union without an election, to consent to an election, or to contest the number of cards signed and resist an election.

the dispute. The United States uses arbitration while an agreement is in effect to avoid *wildcat strikes* (in which workers walk off the job in violation of the contract) or unplanned work stoppages.

Certain clauses are common in a collective bargaining agreement:

- *Security clause*—In a **union shop,** the contract requires workers to join the union after a set period of time. **Right-to-work** states, through restrictive laws, do not permit union shops; workers have the right to work without being forced to join a union. The southern United States has many right-to-work states.

- *Wage component*—The contract spells out rates of pay, including premium pay for overtime and paid holidays.

- *Individual rights*—These include the use of seniority to determine pay increases, job bidding, and the order of layoffs.

- *Grievance procedure*—This procedure gives workers a voice in what goes on during contract negotiations and administration.[71] In about 50 percent of discharge cases that go to arbitration, the arbitrator overturns management's decision and reinstates the worker.[72]

Unions have a legal duty of fair representation, which means they must represent all workers in the bargaining unit and ensure that workers' rights are protected.

7.4 | What Does the Future Hold?

In recent years union membership has declined to about 12 percent of the U.S. labor force—down from a peak of over 33 percent at the end of World War II. Increased automation eliminated many of the manufacturing jobs that used to be union strongholds. Employees in today's white-collar office jobs are less interested in joining unions and are also more difficult to organize. Tough global competition has made managers much less willing to give in to union demands, so the benefits of unionization are less clear to many workers—particularly young, skilled workers who no longer expect to stay with one company all their lives. In addition, elimination of inefficient work rules, the introduction of profit sharing, and across-the-board salary reductions have been seen as steps toward a fundamentally different, cooperative long-term relationship.

When companies recognize that their success depends on the talents and energies of employees, the interests of unions and managers begin to converge. Rather than one side exploiting the other, unions and managers find common ground based on developing, valuing, and involving employees. Particularly in knowledge-based companies, the balance of power is shifting toward employees. Individuals, not companies, own their own human capital. This leaves poorly managed organizations in a particularly vulnerable position. To compete, organizations are searching for ways to obtain, retain, and engage their most valuable resources: human resources.

union shop an organization with a union and a union security clause specifying that workers must join the union after a set period of time

right-to-work legislation that allows employees to work without having to join a union

Study Checklist

- Did you tear out the perforated student review card at the back of the text to revisit learning objectives and key terms and definitions?

Connect® Management is available for M Management. Additional resources include:

- Interactive Applications:
  - Comprehension Case: Will the Union Get In?
  - Drag & Drop: Staffing the Organization
  - Sequencing/Timeline: Putting HR Planning in Perspective
  - Video Case: HRM at Best Buy

- LearnSmart—Multiple choice questions help you determine what you already know, are not sure about, or need to practice based on your score. And with SmartBook, you can read the relevant section in the eBook as well as practice and recharge what you've learned.

- Chapter Videos: SAS, Hollywood Labor Unions

- Young Manager Speaks Out: Blair Root, Nonprofit Director

9 chapter

Managing Diversity and Inclusion

Learning Objectives

After studying Chapter 9, you will be able to

LO1 Describe how changes in the U.S. workforce make diversity a critical organizational and managerial issue.

LO2 Explain how diversity, if well managed, can give organizations a competitive edge.

LO3 Identify challenges associated with managing a diverse workforce.

LO4 Define monolithic, pluralistic, and multicultural organizations.

LO5 List steps managers and their organizations can take to cultivate diversity.

LO6 Summarize the skills and knowledge about cultural differences needed to manage globally.

In the previous chapter, we described the laws that require equal opportunity and fair treatment in the workplace. But a proactive approach—of seeking and capitalizing on the benefits of a diverse workforce—is fundamental to the success of many organizations today. For example, by following a decades-long policy of hiring, developing, and utilizing the full potential of diverse employees, care provider Kaiser Permanente has created a competitive advantage in the health care industry.[1] In contrast, managers who lack the skills to lead men and women of different colors, cultures, ages, religions, abilities, and backgrounds will be at a significant disadvantage in their careers.

In the United States, the number of racial and ethnic minorities is increasing far faster than the growth rate in the white, nonminority population, and women make up a sizable share of the workforce. American workers, customers, and markets are highly diverse and becoming even more so. In addition, businesses are increasingly global, so managers must be much more aware of, and sensitive to, cultural differences. Also, the creativity and innovation that are vital for organizational success are fostered in an atmosphere that celebrates different perspectives and bright people from all walks of life. Few societies have access to the range of talents available in the United States, with its immigrant tradition and racially and ethnically diverse population. Yet getting people from divergent backgrounds to work together effectively is not easy. For this reason, managing diversity is one of America's biggest challenges—and opportunities.

Managing diversity and inclusion on the part of organizations have their roots in Equal Employment Opportunity (EEO), meaning "freedom from discrimination on the basis of sex, color, religion, national origin, disability and age."[2] Essentially, there are two distinctive (though related) sets of diversity and inclusion activities in which organizations engage: *diversity management*, which is proactive in nature, and *affirmative action* programs, which are more reactive and focus on compliance. Exhibit 9.1 highlights some of the differences between these two initiatives. Managing diversity involves, first, such basic activities as recruiting, training, promoting, and utilizing to full advantage individuals with different backgrounds,

Exhibit 9.1	Differences between affirmative action and diversity management programs	
Component	**Affirmative Action Program (AAP)**	**Diversity Management Program (DMP)**
Purpose	Correct historic wrongs and past/current discrimination against minorities, women, and other protected classes.	Value and leverage diversity of all stakeholders—from employees to customers—to achieve competitive advantage.
Origin	Executive Order 11246 and related to Title VII of the Civil Rights Act of 1964.	No precise date; however, DMPs have become an integral component of most employers' HR strategies.
Approach	Formally written plan to proactively recruit, hire, and promote minorities, women, and other protected classes.	Company-driven plan to foster an inclusive environment in which all stakeholders contribute to organizational objectives.
Required by law?	Yes. Federal, state, and local agencies, as well as certain federal contractors and subcontractors are required to have an AAP. It is voluntary for private employers to have one, unless it is court-ordered to correct discrimatory practices.	No. However, the majority of employers have DMPs because they believe that diversity equates to good business. Companies that align the diversity of their employees with that of their customers position themselves for success.
Enforcement	Office of Federal Contract Compliance Programs (OFCCP) in the U. S. Department of Labor.	An organization's HR department, with input from other internal stakeholders, including diversity councils or advisory groups.
Examples of organizations with program	U.S. Food & Drug Administration, Florida Department of Environmental Protection, Princeton University, Boeing, and the National Association of Basketball Coaches.	Johnson & Johnson, Procter & Gamble, Microsoft, Pepsi, Intel, Kraft Foods, General Electric, Ernst & Young, MasterCard Worldwide, and Kaiser Permanente.

Sources: U. S. Equal Employment Opportunity Commission website (online), "Diversity and Affirmative Action," www.eeoc.gov, accessed on May 18, 2014; Diversity Inc. Top 50 List (online), www.diversityinc.com, accessed on May 18, 2014; "Who Supports Affirmative Action?" American Civil Liberties Union (online), www.aclu.org, accessed on May 18, 2014; "When Would My Company Need to Have an Affirmative Action Program?" Society for Human Resource Management (online), December 4, 2012, www.shrm.org; "What is the Difference Between EEO, Affirmative Action, and Diversity?" Society for Human Resource Management (online), September 20, 2012, www.shrm.org; and H. J. Bernardin, *Human Resource Management: An Experiential Approach,* 5th ed. (Boston: McGraw-Hill, 2009), p. 71.

affirmative action
special efforts to recruit
and hire qualified members
of groups that have been
discriminated against in
the past

beliefs, capabilities, and cultures. But it means more than just hiring women and minorities and making sure they are treated equally and encouraged to succeed. It also means understanding and deeply valuing employee differences to build a more effective and profitable organization. Organizations that strive to foster the richness that a diverse workforce brings also work to build bridges between those employees to tap their potential. Such inclusion moves beyond valuing the differences of employees to valuing the connections that arise and develop between them.

Related to diversity management is **affirmative action**. Many organizations originally diversified their workforce out of concerns for social responsibility and legal necessity. To correct the past exclusion of women and minorities, companies introduced affirmative action—special efforts to recruit and hire qualified members of groups that have been discriminated against in the past. While many organizations do so voluntarily, contractors and subcontractors with 50 or more employees that receive more than $50,000 in government business are required to have an affirmative action program.[3] The intent is not to prefer these group members to the exclusion

of others, but to correct for the history of discriminatory practices and exclusion. For example, in Portland, Oregon, about one-fifth of the city's population consists of various ethnic minorities, but only 12 percent of new construction employees are minorities. The city government, Portland Development Commission, Port of Portland, and regional and state transportation departments established affirmative action programs to increase minority group members' participation in public contracts.[4]

Such efforts, along with legal remedies to end discrimination, have had a powerful impact. Today the immigrant nature of American society is virtually taken for granted—even seen as a source of pride. And women, African Americans, Hispanics, and other minorities routinely occupy positions that in years past would have been totally closed to them.

Yet employment discrimination persists, and despite upward mobility, some groups still lack full participation and opportunity in today's organizations. To move beyond correcting past wrongs and become truly inclusive requires a change in organizational culture—one in which diversity is seen as contributing directly to the attainment of organization goals.

Viewed in this way, affirmative action and diversity management are complementary, not the same. In contrast to equal employment opportunity (EEO) and affirmative action programs, managing diversity means moving beyond legislated mandates to embrace a proactive business philosophy that sees differences as positive. In this broader sense, managing diversity involves making changes in organizations' systems, structures, and practices to eliminate barriers that may keep people from reaching their full potential. It asks managers to recognize and value the uniqueness of each employee and to see the different ideas and perspectives each brings to the organization as a source of competitive advantage. In short, managing diversity goes beyond getting more minorities and women into the organization. It creates an environment in which employees from every background listen to each other and work better together

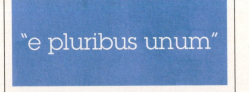

"e pluribus unum"

LISTEN & LEARN ○ ONLINE

YOUNG MANAGERS
Speak Out!

"One of the ways we encourage (diversity) is to make sure that we are educated . . . Also knowing how to handle different types of personalities or beliefs or backgrounds people come from."

—Stephanie Neubauer, Hair Salon Owner/Manager

so that the organization as a whole will become more effective. This emphasis on coming together to benefit the whole has led many companies to begin referring to their objective as diversity and inclusion.

This chapter examines the meaning of diversity and the management skills and organizational processes involved in managing the diverse workforce effectively. We begin by identifying the changes in society and the workplace that are creating this more diverse U.S. workforce. Next we consider challenges of diversity and ways to address those challenges. Then we explore the practices that support inclusion. Finally, because companies today have a global presence, we end by describing how to manage in environments with economic, cultural, and geographic differences.

> **LO1** Describe how changes in the U.S. workforce make diversity a critical organizational and managerial issue

1 | DIVERSITY IS DYNAMIC AND EVOLVING

Diversity is far from a new challenge for managers. However, over time, U.S. businesses have changed their approach to managing diversity.

1.1 | Diversity Shaped America's Past

From the late 1800s to the early 1900s, most of the immigrants to the United States came from Italy, Poland, Ireland, and Russia. Those people were considered outsiders because most did not speak English and had different customs and work styles. They struggled to gain acceptance in the steel, coal, automobile manufacturing, insurance, and finance industries. As late as the 1940s, and sometimes beyond, colleges routinely discriminated against immigrants, Catholics, and Jews, establishing strict quotas that limited their number, if any were admitted at all. This type of discrimination severely diminished the employment prospects of these groups until the 1960s.

Women's struggle for acceptance in the workplace was in some ways even more difficult. When the Women's Rights Movement was launched in Seneca Falls in 1848, most occupations were off-limits to women, and colleges and professional schools were closed to them. In the first part of the 20th century, when women began to be accepted into professional schools, they were subject to severe quotas. There was also a widespread assumption that certain jobs were done only by men, and other jobs only by women. As recently as the 1970s, classified-ad sections in newspapers listed jobs by sex, with sections headed "Help Wanted—Males" and "Help Wanted—Females." Women who wanted a bank loan needed a male cosigner, and married women were not issued credit cards in their own name.[5] This discrimination started to decline when the Civil Rights Act of 1964 and other legislation began to be enforced. Although women are still underrepresented at the most senior levels of corporate life, and their average pay rates still lag those of men, most jobs are now open to women.

The most difficult and wrenching struggle for equality involved America's nonwhite minorities. Rigid racial segregation of education, employment, and housing persisted for 100 years after the end of the Civil War. After years of courageous protest and struggle, the unanimous *Brown v. Board of Education* Supreme Court decision in 1954 declared segregation

● Freedom marchers in the 1960s were an important part of the American civil rights movement.

unconstitutional, setting the stage for laws we discussed in Chapter 8, including the Civil Rights Act of 1964. Although the struggle for equality is far from complete, many civil rights—equal opportunity, fair treatment in housing, and the illegality of religious, racial, and sex discrimination—received their greatest impetus from the Civil Rights movement.

With this background, the traditional American image of diversity emphasized assimilation. The United States was considered the "melting pot" of the world, a country where ethnic and racial differences were blended into an American purée. In real life, many ethnic and most racial groups retained their identities but did not express them at work. Deemphasizing their ethnic and cultural distinctions helped employees keep their jobs and get ahead.

1.2 | Diversity Is Growing in Today's Workforce

Today nearly half of the U.S. workforce consists of women, 16 percent of U.S. workers identify themselves as Hispanic or Latino, 11 percent are black, and 6 percent are Asian. One-third of all businesses in the United States are owned by women, employing about 20 percent of America's workers. Two-thirds of all global migration is into the United States.[6] U.S. businesses do not have a choice of whether to have a diverse

much diversity also exists within each category. Every group consists of individuals who are unique in personality, education, and life experiences. There may be more differences among, say, three Asians from Thailand, Hong Kong, and Korea than among a white, an African American, and an Asian all born in Chicago. And all individuals differ in their personal or professional goals and values.

Thus managing diversity may seem to be a contradiction. It means being acutely aware of characteristics *common* to a group of employees, while also managing these employees as *individuals*. Managing diversity means not just tolerating or accommodating all sorts of differences but supporting, nurturing, and utilizing these differences to the organization's advantage. A global survey of 546 senior executives from companies with more than $500 million in sales found that the top three methods used to promote diversity within their organizations include (1) expanding work/life balance (flexible hours and work-at-home) policies, (2) tapping wider applicant pools for recruitment, and (3) providing training to enhance respect for differences among colleagues.[7]

A sizable number of HR executives say their companies need to or plan to expand their diversity training programs. Although many companies initially instituted diversity programs to prevent discrimination, more are beginning to see the programs as a crucial way to expand their customer bases both

> "Leaders can use diversity strategically to create sustainable competitive advantages for their firms."
>
> —Martin N. Davidson, *University of Virginia*[8]

workforce; if they want to survive, they must learn to manage a diverse workforce sooner or better than their competitors do.

Today's immigrants are willing to be part of an integrated team, but they no longer are willing to sacrifice their cultural identities to get ahead. Nor do they have to do so. Companies are recognizing that accommodating employees' differences pays off in business. Managers are also realizing that their customers are becoming increasingly diverse, so retaining a diversified workforce can provide a significant competitive advantage in the marketplace.

Diversity today refers to far more than skin color and gender. The term broadly refers to a variety of differences, summarized in Exhibit 9.2. These differences include religious affiliation, age, disability status, military experience, sexual orientation, economic class, educational level, and lifestyle, as well as gender, race, ethnicity, and nationality.

Although members of different groups (white males, people born during the Depression, homosexuals, Iraq war veterans, Hispanics, Asians, women, African Americans, etc.) share within their groups many common values, attitudes, and perceptions,

domestically and worldwide. In fact, two out of three companies said they had broadened their diversity programs because of increasing globalization, according to a survey of 1,780 HR and training executives by the Boston-based consulting firm Novations/J. Howard and Associates.

Gender Issues One of the most important developments in the U.S. labor market has been the growing number of women working outside the home. Consider this:

- Women make up about 47 percent of the workforce.

- The overall labor force participation rate of women rose throughout the 1970s through the 1990s and is now holding steady even as the participation rate of men gradually declines.

- Almost 60 percent of marriages are dual-earner marriages.

- Nearly one of every three married women in two-income households earns more than her husband does.[9]

Balancing work life with family responsibilities presents an enormous challenge. Although men's roles in our society

Exhibit 9.2 Components of workforce diversity

Workforce diversity includes . . .
- Women
- Older employees
- Racial/ethnic minorities
- Immigrants
- Religious employees
- Physically/mentally disabled

. . . and these differences, too.
- Veteran status
- Sexual orientation
- Lifestyle
- Skill and educational level
- Economic class
- Function or position in firm

have been changing, women still carry the bulk of family responsibilities. That puts women at a disadvantage in companies that expect employees, particularly at the managerial level, to put in long hours and sacrifice their personal lives for the sake of their jobs, organizations, and careers. It also may cause those companies to lose valuable talent. Some companies therefore offer their employees ways to balance work and family commitments with such benefits as onsite child care, in-home care for elderly family members, flexible work schedules, and the use of newer technologies that permit more work from home.

Still, as managers weigh employees' needs for flexibility against the organization's need for productivity, they have to make complex decisions weighing job requirements and each employee's contributions and motivation. Michele Coleman Mayes, former senior vice president and general counsel of Pitney Bowes, agreed to let one attorney leave promptly at five o'clock each evening; the attorney works on her laptop at night as needed to meet her deadlines. But Mayes refused another employee's request to work part-time because the person in that position needed to be available each day to handle requests for other departments. Mayes told her employees that scheduling decisions "may not always be equal, but I will try to be fair."[10]

The desire for flexible scheduling is often cited as a reason why significant pay disparities remain between men and women.

glass ceiling metaphor for an invisible barrier that makes it difficult for women and minorities to rise above a certain level in the organization

sexual harassment conduct of a sexual nature that has negative consequences for employment

The average full-time working woman earns about 80 percent as much as men in the same job (recall the discussion in Chapter 8 about equal pay and comparable worth). This pay gap is closing faster for younger women. The women's-to-men's earnings ratio among 25- to 34-year-olds increased from 68 percent (in 1979) to 90 percent (in 2012). In comparison, this ratio for 45- to 54-year-olds rose from 57 percent to 75 percent.[11]

Another concern involving female workers is the low representation of women in top jobs. As women—along with minorities—move up the corporate ladder, they encounter a **glass ceiling**, a metaphor for an invisible barrier that makes it difficult for women and minorities to move beyond a certain level in the corporate hierarchy. For example, just 24 women are chief executives of *Fortune* 500 companies—that's 24 out of 500. Looking at all corporate officers of those companies, about 15 percent are women, and less than 2 percent are minority women.[12] Still, women's leadership is beginning to be seen at a broader range of companies. Today's well-known female CEOs include Indra Nooyi of PepsiCo, Virginia Rometty of IBM, Mary Barra of GM, Ursula Burns of Xerox, Pat Woertz of Archer Daniels Midland, Ellen Kullman of Dupont, and Marissa Mayer of Yahoo![13] Similarly, a small handful of minority CEOs are currently leading their *Fortune* 500 firms, including Otis Clarence Jr. of Darden Restaurants, Kenneth I. Chenault of American Express, Carlos Rodriguez of ADP, and Roger W. Ferguson Jr. of TIAA-CREF.[14]

Some companies are helping women break through the glass ceiling. Accenture sponsors monthly networking events for its female employees and offers flexible schedules and part-time arrangements. The following companies are among those the National Association of Female Executives recently identified as the "top 10" for executive women:[16]

AstraZeneca	KPMG
Ernst & Young	Marriott International
General Mills	Procter & Gamble
Grant Thornton	State Farm
IBM	Verizon

As women have gained more presence and power in the workforce, some have drawn attention to the problem of **sexual harassment** (discussed in Chapter 8), which is unwelcome

Did You Know?

According to the Society for Human Resource Management, the top five scoring countries on the Global Diversity Readiness Index are Sweden, Norway, New Zealand, Canada, and Finland. (Note: The United States was ranked 14th out of 47 countries.)[15]

sexual conduct that is a term or condition of employment. Sexual harassment falls into two categories:

1. *Quid pro quo harassment* occurs when "submission to or rejection of sexual conduct is used as a basis for employment decisions."

2. *Hostile environment* occurs when unwelcome sexual conduct "has the purpose or effect of unreasonably interfering with job performance or creating an intimidating, hostile, or offensive working environment." Behaviors that can cause a hostile work environment include persistent or pervasive displays of pornography, lewd or suggestive remarks, and demeaning taunts or jokes.

Both categories of harassment violate Title VII of the Civil Rights Act of 1964, regardless of the sex of the harasser and the victim (in a recent year, more than 16 percent of complaints filed with the federal government came from males). If an employee files a complaint of sexual harassment with the Equal Employment Opportunity Commission, the commission may investigate and, if it finds evidence for the complaint, may request mediation, seek a settlement, or file a lawsuit with the potential for stiff fines—and negative publicity that may damage the company's ability to recruit the best employees in the future.

Harassment by creating a hostile work environment is now more typical than quid pro quo harassment. Because it may involve more subjective standards of behavior, it puts an extra burden on managers to maintain an appropriate work environment by ensuring that all employees know what conduct is and is not appropriate and that there are serious consequences for this behavior. Even when managers do not themselves engage in harassment, if they fail to prevent it or to take appropriate action after receiving legitimate complaints about it, they may still be held liable, along with their companies, if a lawsuit is filed. Managers also need to know that the "hostile work environment" standard applies to same-sex harassment, as well as to non-gender-related cases, such as a pattern of racial or ethnic slurs.

One way managers can help their companies prevent harassment, or avoid punitive damages if a lawsuit is filed, is to make sure their organization has an effective and comprehensive policy on harassment. (See the six basic components in Exhibit 9.3.) Such a policy would have the following basic components:[17]

1. Develop a comprehensive organizationwide policy on sexual harassment and present it to all current and new employees. Stress that sexual harassment will not be tolerated under any circumstances. Emphasis is best achieved when the policy is publicized and supported by top management.

2. Hold training sessions with supervisors to explain Title VII requirements, their role in providing an environment free of sexual harassment, and proper investigative procedures when charges occur.

Exhibit 9.3 Basic Components of a Company's Policy to Prevent Harassment

Create organizationwide policy

Establish complaint procedure

Train supervisors

Act on complaints

Discipline offenders

Follow up and resolve cases

3. Establish a formal complaint procedure in which employees can discuss problems without fear of retaliation. The complaint procedure should spell out how charges will be investigated and resolved.

4. Act immediately when employees complain of sexual harassment. Communicate widely that investigations will be conducted objectively and with appreciation for the sensitivity of the issue.

5. When an investigation supports employee charges, discipline the offender at once. For extremely serious offenses, discipline should include penalties up to and including discharge. Discipline should be applied consistently across similar cases and among managers and hourly employees alike.

6. Follow up on all cases to ensure a satisfactory resolution of the problem.

Companies such as Avon, Corning, Infosys, and Metro-Goldwyn-Mayer have found that a strong commitment to diversity reduces problems with sexual harassment.[18]

Gender issues and the changing nature of work do not apply just to women. In some ways, the changing status of women has given men a chance to redefine their roles, expectations, and lifestyles. Some men are deciding that there is more to life than corporate success and are scaling back work hours and commitments to spend time with their families. Worker values are shifting toward personal time, quality of life, self-fulfillment, and family. Workers today, both men and women, are looking to achieve a balance between career and family.

Minorities and Immigrants Along with gender issues, the importance and scope of diversity are evident in the growth of racial minorities and immigrants in the workforce. Consider these facts:

- Black, Asian, and Hispanic workers hold more than one of every four U.S. jobs.

- Asian and Hispanic workforces are growing the fastest in the United States, followed by the African American workforce.

- Three in ten college enrollees are people of color.

- Foreign-born workers make up more than 16 percent of the U.S. civilian labor force. About half of these workers are Hispanic, and 24 percent are Asian.

● Yahoo! President and CEO Marissa Mayer delivers a keynote address at the 2014 International CES in Las Vegas, NV. CES, the world's largest annual consumer technology trade show, is featured 3,200 exhibitors showing off their latest products and services to about 150,000 attendees.

- The younger Americans are, the more likely they are to be persons of color.

- One in 66 people in the United States identifies himself or herself as multiracial, and the number could soar to 1 in 5 by 2050.[19]

These numbers indicate that the term *minority*, as it is used typically, may soon become outdated.

Particularly in regions of the country and urban areas where white males do not predominate, managing diversity means more than eliminating discrimination: it means capitalizing on the wide variety of skills available in the labor market. Organizations that do not take full advantage of the skills and capabilities of minorities and immigrants are severely limiting their potential talent pool and their ability to understand and capture minority markets. Those markets are growing rapidly, along with their share of purchasing power. And if you sell to businesses, you are likely to deal with some minority-owned companies because the number of businesses started by Asian American, African American, and Hispanic entrepreneurs is growing much faster than the overall growth in new companies in the United States. For example, more than half of the companies that started in California's high-tech Silicon Valley were founded by immigrants, and in a recent year, one-fourth of patent applications in the United States identified an immigrant as the inventor or a co-inventor.[20] Exhibit 9.4 lists some successful immigrant entrepreneurs.

Even so, the evidence shows some troubling disparities in employment and earnings. Unemployment rates are higher for black and Hispanic workers than for whites—twice as high in the case of black men. Earnings of black and Hispanic workers have consistently trailed those of white workers; recent figures put the median earnings for African American employees at 78 percent of median earnings for white workers and the median earnings of Hispanics at just 72 percent. African Americans and Hispanic Americans are also underrepresented in management and professional occupations.[21] This underrepresentation may itself help perpetuate the problem because it can leave many aspiring young minorities with fewer role models or mentors.

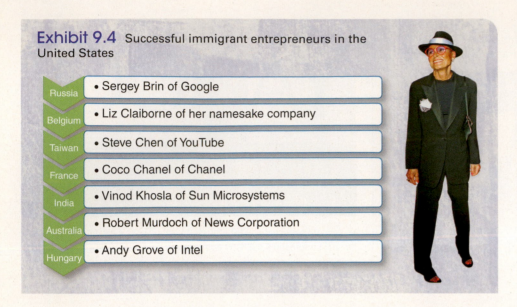

Exhibit 9.4 Successful immigrant entrepreneurs in the United States

Russia	• Sergey Brin of Google
Belgium	• Liz Claiborne of her namesake company
Taiwan	• Steve Chen of YouTube
France	• Coco Chanel of Chanel
India	• Vinod Khosla of Sun Microsystems
Australia	• Robert Murdoch of News Corporation
Hungary	• Andy Grove of Intel

There is considerable evidence that discrimination may account for at least some of the disparities in employment and earnings. For example, in one recent study, fictitious résumés were used to respond to help-wanted ads. Each résumé used either African American names like Lakisha and Jamal or white-sounding names like Emily and Greg. The résumés with white-sounding names were 50 percent more likely to get a callback for an interview than the same résumés with African American names. Despite equivalence in credentials, the often unconscious assumptions about different racial groups are very difficult to overcome.[22]

Nevertheless, significant progress has been made. Talented members of minority groups are contributing to organizational effectiveness in a wide variety of companies across multiple industries. A sample of companies that value diversity can be found on *Fortune*'s 2012 "Best Companies to Work For" ("most diverse") list, including Methodist Hospital, Cisco, Whole Foods Market, Marriott International, and Capital One.[23]

Virtually every large organization today has policies and programs for increasing minority representation, including compensation systems that reward managers for increasing the diversity of their operations. FedEx, Xerox, Motorola, Shell, Sun Microsystems, and other companies have corporate diversity officers who help managers attract, retain, and promote minority and women executives. Many organizations, including Lockheed Martin and Dun and Bradstreet, are also supporting minority internships and MBA programs. The internship programs help students and organizations learn about one another and, ideally, turn into full-time employment opportunities.

Mentally and Physically Disabled People The largest unemployed minority population in the United States is people with disabilities. The share of the population with a disability is growing as the average worker gets older and heavier.[24] According to the U.S. Census Bureau, 19 percent of the population reports having some degree of disability, and of only one in three individuals with disabilities are employed.[25] On average, disabled employees earn about $10,000 less than employees who are not disabled.[26] Still, more than half of people with a disability held jobs during the year in which they were surveyed. And among those who are unemployed, many would like to find work.

The Americans with Disabilities Act (ADA), mentioned in Chapter 8, defines a disability as a physical or mental impairment that substantially limits one or more major life activities. Examples of such physical or mental impairments include those resulting from orthopedic, visual, speech, and hearing impairments; cerebral palsy; epilepsy; multiple sclerosis; HIV infections; cancer; heart disease; diabetes; mental retardation; psychological illness; specific learning disabilities; drug addiction; and alcoholism.[27]

For most businesses, mentally and physically disabled people represent an unexplored but fruitful labor market. Frequently employers have found that disabled employees are more dependable than other employees, miss fewer days of work, and exhibit lower turnover. Tax credits are available to companies who hire disabled workers. In addition, managers who hire and support employees with disabilities are signaling to other employees and stakeholders their strong interest in creating an inclusive organization culture.

Education Levels When the United States was primarily an industrial economy, many jobs required physical strength, stamina, and skill in a trade, rather than college and professional degrees. In today's service and technology economy, more positions require a college education and even a graduate or professional degree. Today's prospective employees have responded by applying to college in record numbers. The proportion of the workforce with at least some college education has been growing steadily since the 1970s. The share of workers with a bachelor's degree has more than doubled since 1970. People with degrees in science and technology are in especially high demand. Employers often expand their search for scientists and computer professionals overseas, but visa requirements limit that supply.

At the other end of the spectrum, the share of workers with less than a high school diploma has tumbled from nearly 4 out of 10 in 1970 to below 1 out of 10 today. Among foreign-born workers, 24.6 percent have not completed high school.[28]

Age Groups By 2018, it is estimated that one out of four workers will be aged 55 or older.[29] As a result, entry-level workers for some positions are in short supply. Today's companies need to compete hard for a shrinking pool of young talent, preparing for applicants who know the job market and insist on the working conditions they value and the praise they were raised to expect. Bruce Tulgan, founder of Rainmaker Thinking, which specializes in researching generational differences, says Millennials (a.k.a., Gen Y) – today's young workers—tend to be "high-maintenance" but also "high-performing," having learned to process the flood of information that pours in over the Internet.[30] Many of these workers were raised by highly involved parents who filled their lives with "quality" experiences, so employers are designing work arrangements that are stimulating, involve teamwork, keep work hours reasonable to allow for outside activities, and provide for plenty of positive feedback. Employers are also updating their recruiting tactics to reach young workers where they are—online.

::::::::::::::::

Rackspace Hosting, the open cloud company known for its exceptional customer service, branded Fanatical Support, has more than 5,000 employees in nine data centers on four continents, most of whom are Millennials. The company does several unorthodox (by traditional thinking) things to keep the creative juices flowing among these younger employees. When Rackspace needed more office space to accommodate the fast-growing company, it bought a defunct 1.2 million square foot mall for $27 million in a suburb of San Antonio, Texas. Responding to employees' (known as Rackers) desire for a creative, inspiring space to work and engage one another, Rackspace renovated the inside and outside of the mall so that it would look and function like the Millennial-inspired campuses at Google, Amazon, and Microsoft. In 2014, The Castle, as the company's headquarters is known, is home to more than 3,000 Rackers who enjoy the following "quirky perqs": a stainless steel silver two-story slide, a life-sized chessboard, conference (getaway) rooms named after breakfast cereals and TV game shows, red bouncy balls to use for hallway races, a video arcade to hold Mortal Kombat competitions, and stationary gondolas in which to hold meetings. This Millennial-friendly approach is helping Rackspace earn considerable respect and success in the cloud space. Net revenue at the end of 2013 was $1.534 billion, an increase of 17.2 percent over that of 2012.[31]

::::::::::::::::

1.3 | Tomorrow's Workers Will Be More Varied Than Ever

Until recently, white American-born males dominated the U.S. workforce. This group still constitutes the largest percentage of workers—about 68 percent of U.S. workers are white, and more than half of them are male—but its share of the labor force is declining. As shown in Exhibit 9.5, by 2050 the percentage of whites in the labor force is projected to decrease to about 48.2 percent. By 2050 one of every three workers will be of Hispanic origin, the percentage of black workers will increase slightly to 12.4 percent, and Asians will make up 8.6 percent of all civilian workers.[32] This significant change in the workforce parallels trends in the overall U.S. population. Recently the Census Bureau announced that, for the first time, about one in three residents of the United States is a racial or ethnic minority. The largest and fastest-growing minority group is Hispanics. In several states—California, Hawaii, New Mexico, and Texas—and the District of Columbia, these minority groups plus Asians, Native Americans, and Pacific Islanders combine to make a population that is "majority minority."[33]

During most of its history, the United States experienced a surplus of workers. But that is expected to change. Lower birth rates in the United States and other developed countries are resulting in a smaller labor force. An even more substantial slowdown in the pace of growth of the labor force is projected between now and 2018, as the baby boom generation retires.[34]

Employers are likely to outsource some work to factories and firms in developing nations where birthrates are high and the labor supply is more plentiful. But they will have to compete for the best candidates from a relatively smaller and more diverse U.S. labor pool. Employers will need to know who these new workers are—and must be prepared to meet their needs.

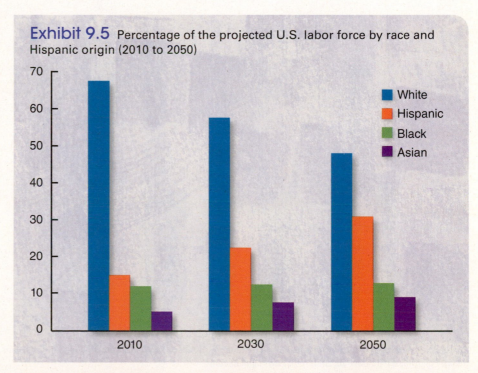

Exhibit 9.5 Percentage of the projected U.S. labor force by race and Hispanic origin (2010 to 2050)

Legend: White, Hispanic, Black, Asian

Source: Bureau of Labor Statistics, "Labor Force (Demographic) Data," news release, March 11, 2010, http://www.bls.gov.

In addition, the median age of America's workforce is rising as the number of older workers swells while the number of young workers grows only slightly. Industries such as nursing and manufacturing are already facing a tremendous loss of expertise as a result of downsizing and a rapidly aging workforce. Many other industries ranging from education to nuclear plant maintenance will soon be in a similar situation.[35] On the plus side, almost 70 percent of workers between the ages of 45 and 74 told researchers with AARP (formerly the American Association of Retired Persons) that they intend to work in retirement. Retirees often return to the workforce at the behest of their employers, who can't afford to lose the knowledge accumulated by longtime employees, their willingness to work nontraditional shifts, and their reliable work habits, which have a positive effect on the entire work group. As Exhibit 9.6 illustrates, recent research suggests that workers aged 65 or older are more engaged in their work than younger employees. Organizations benefit from having engaged or emotionally connected workers because they tend to be more enthusiastic and productive.[36]

To prevent an exodus of talent, employers need strategies to retain and attract skilled and knowledgeable older workers. Phased retirement plans that allow older employees to work fewer hours per week is one such strategy. Almost one-third of retiring faculty members at 16 University of North Carolina campuses take advantage of phased retirement, and the concept is catching on in many other public and private organizations. Other strategies include making workplace adaptations to help older workers cope with the physical problems they experience as they age, such as poorer vision, hearing, and mobility.

LO2 Explain how diversity, if well managed, can give organizations a competitive edge

2 | WELL-MANAGED DIVERSITY AND INCLUSION: A COMPETITIVE ADVANTAGE

Many organizations now view diversity from a more practical, business-oriented perspective, as a powerful tool for building competitive advantage. A study by the Department of Labor's Glass Ceiling Institute showed that the stock performance of firms that were high performers on diversity-related goals was over twice as high as that of other firms. In another recent study, companies with the highest percentage of women among senior managers had a significantly higher return to shareholders than companies with the lowest percentage. Conversely, announcements of damage awards from discrimination lawsuits frequently hurt stock returns.[37]

Managing a diverse workforce presents many advantages:

- *Ability to attract and retain motivated employees*—Companies with a reputation for providing opportunities for diverse employees will have a competitive advantage in the labor market. In addition, when employees believe their differences are not merely tolerated but valued, they may become more loyal, productive, and committed.

- *Better perspective on a differentiated market*—Just as women and minorities may prefer to work for an employer that values diversity, they may prefer

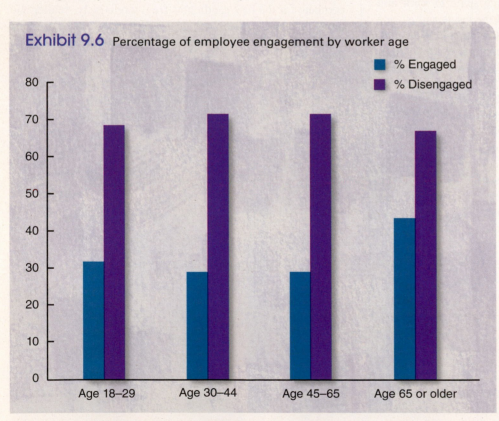

Exhibit 9.6 Percentage of employee engagement by worker age

Legend: ■ % Engaged ■ % Disengaged

Source: Adapted from N. Blacksmith and J. Harter, "Majority of American Workers Not Engaged in Their Jobs," Gallup Poll (Online), October 28, 2011, http://www.gallup.com.

to patronize such organizations. Similarly, each new generation has its own set of values and experiences, so diversity in ages can help the organization relate to more age groups of customers. A diverse workforce can give a company greater knowledge of the preferences and habits of this diversified marketplace, so it can design products and develop marketing campaigns to meet those consumers' needs, nationally and internationally.

- *Ability to leverage creativity and innovation in problem solving*—Work team diversity promotes creativity and innovation because people from different backgrounds hold different perspectives. With a broader base of experience from which to approach a problem, diverse teams, when effectively managed, invent more options and create more solutions than homogeneous groups do. They also are freer to deviate from traditional approaches and practices and are less likely to succumb to "groupthink."[39]

- *Enhancement of organizational flexibility*—A diverse workforce can make organizations more flexible because successfully managing diversity requires a corporate culture that tolerates many different styles and approaches. Less restrictive policies and procedures and less standardized operating methods enable organizations to be more flexible and better able to respond quickly to environmental changes.

Executives at Aetna, Denny's, and FedEx are so convinced of the competitive potential of a diverse workforce that they tie a portion of management compensation to success in recruiting and promoting minorities and women.[40]

3 | A DIVERSE AND INCLUSIVE WORKFORCE: CHALLENGING TO MANAGE

Despite the laws guaranteeing equal opportunity and the business advantages of diversity and inclusion, every year thousands of lawsuits are filed complaining of discrimination and unfair treatment, some involving large and well-respected firms.[41] Even in companies that are careful to avoid discrimination in hiring and pay, managing diversity can be difficult. Managers with all the goodwill in the world sometimes find it harder than they expected to get people from different backgrounds to work together for a common goal.[42]

Becoming an effective manager of a diverse organization requires identifying and overcoming several challenges:

- *Unexamined assumptions*—Seeing the world from someone else's perspective can be difficult because our own assumptions and viewpoints seem so normal and familiar. For example, heterosexuals may not even think before putting a picture of their loved ones on their desks because the practice is so common and accepted; but for lesbian, bisexual, gay, or transgender (LBGT) employees, displaying such a picture may cause considerable anxiety. Other unexamined assumptions involve the roles of men and women—for example, the assumption that women will shoulder the burden of caring for children, even if it conflicts with the demands of work. In a recent study, researchers sent employers résumés that were identical except that some bore a male name and others a female name, and half implied that the person submitting the résumé was a parent. Employers were less likely to invite the supposed parents for an interview—but only if the name was female.[43] Since the résumés were otherwise identical, it appears that people make assumptions about mothers that do not apply

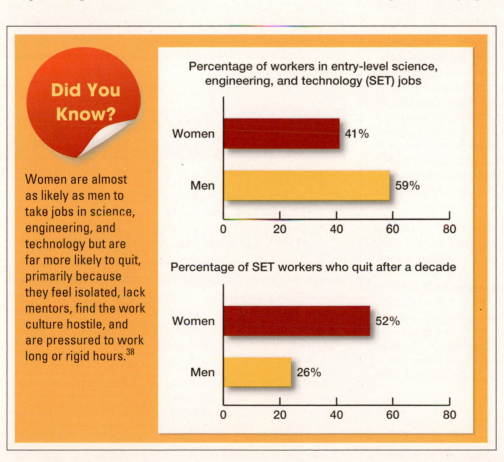

Did You Know?

Women are almost as likely as men to take jobs in science, engineering, and technology but are far more likely to quit, primarily because they feel isolated, lack mentors, find the work culture hostile, and are pressured to work long or rigid hours.[38]

Percentage of workers in entry-level science, engineering, and technology (SET) jobs

Women 41%
Men 59%

Percentage of SET workers who quit after a decade

Women 52%
Men 26%

to fathers or to childless women. In an organization that is oblivious to these different perspectives, managers may have more difficulty developing an enthusiastically shared sense of purpose.

- *Lower cohesiveness*—Diversity can decrease *cohesiveness,* defined as how tightly knit the group is and the degree to which group members act and think in similar ways. Cohesiveness is lower because of differences in language, culture, and/or experience. When mistrust, miscommunication, stress, and attitudinal differences reduce cohesiveness, productivity may decline. This may explain the results of a study showing greater turnover among store employees who feel they are greatly outnumbered by coworkers from other racial or

capabilities, aspirations, and motivations. Women may be stereotyped as not dedicated to their careers, older workers as unwilling to learn new skills, minority group members as less educated or capable. Stereotypes may cost the organization dearly by stifling employees' ambition so that they don't fully contribute. Research supports the idea that people perform better when they expect they can.[46] Unless managers are aware of their own and their employees' stereotypes, the stereotypes can shape important actions. For instance, employees labeled as unmotivated or emotional will be given less stress-provoking (and perhaps less important) jobs than their coworkers, perhaps resulting in lower commitment, higher turnover, and underused skills.[47]

> "Among CEOs of *Fortune* 500 companies, 58 percent are six feet or taller . . . Most of us, in ways we are not entirely aware of, automatically associate leadership with imposing physical stature."
>
> —Malcolm Gladwell

ethnic groups.[44] In a diverse group, managers need to build cohesiveness by establishing common goals and values.

- *Communication problems*—Perhaps the most common negative effect of diversity, communication problems include misunderstandings, inaccuracies, inefficiencies, and slowness. Speed is lost when not all group members are fluent in the same language or when additional time is required to explain things. Diversity can also lead to errors and misunderstandings. Group members may assume they interpret things similarly when they in fact do not, or they may disagree because of their different frames of reference.[45] For example, if managers do not actively encourage and accept the expression of different points of view, some employees may be afraid to speak up at meetings, giving the manager a false impression that consensus has been reached.

- *Mistrust and tension*—People prefer to associate with others who are like themselves. This normal, understandable tendency can lead to misunderstanding, mistrust, and even fear of those who are different. For example, if women and minority group members are routinely excluded from joining white male colleagues for lunch or at business gatherings, they may feel excluded by their colleagues. Similarly, tension often develops between people of different ages—for example, what one generation might see as a tasteless tattoo may be a creative example of body art for a member of another generation. Such misunderstandings can cause stress, tension, and even resentment, making it harder for people to work productively together.

- *Stereotyping*—We learn to interpret the world in a certain way based on our backgrounds and experiences. Our interests, values, and cultures filter, distort, block, and select what we perceive. We see and hear what we expect to see and hear. Group members often stereotype their "different" colleagues rather than accurately perceive and evaluate those persons' contributions,

For all these reasons and more, managing diversity is not easy. Yet managers must confront these issues. They need to develop the skills and strategies diversity requires if they and their organizations are to succeed in our increasingly multicultural business environment.

LO4 Define monolithic, pluralistic, and multicultural organizations

4 | MULTICULTURAL ORGANIZATIONS

To capitalize on the benefits and minimize the costs of a diverse workforce, managers can begin by examining their organization's prevailing assumptions about people and cultures. Exhibit 9.7 shows some of the fundamental assumptions that may exist. Based on these assumptions, we can classify organizations as one of three types and describe their implications for managers:

1. A **monolithic organization** has very little *cultural integration;* its employee population is highly homogeneous. For example, in hiring, an organization might favor alumni of the same college, perhaps targeting members of fraternities who are enthusiastic about the school's football team. When a monolithic organization does employ people from groups other than the norm, they primarily hold low-status jobs. Minority group members must adopt the norms of the majority to survive. This fact, coupled with small numbers, keeps conflicts among

groups low. Discrimination and prejudice typically prevail, informal integration is almost nonexistent, and minority group members do not identify strongly with the company.

2. **Pluralistic organizations** have a more diverse employee population and take steps to involve people from different backgrounds. These organizations use an affirmative action approach, actively trying to hire and train a diverse workforce and to prevent any discrimination against minority group members. They typically have much more integration than do monolithic organizations, but as in monolithic organizations, minority group members tend to be clustered at certain levels or in particular functions. Because of greater cultural integration, affirmative action programs, and training programs, the pluralistic organization has some acceptance of minority group members into the informal network, much less discrimination, and less prejudice. With improved employment opportunities, minority group members feel greater identification with the organization. However, resentment of majority group members, coupled with the greater number of women and minorities, creates more conflict.

● Wayne Embry became the first NBA African American general manager in 1972 when he was named to the post by the Milwaukee Bucks.

3. In **multicultural organizations**, diversity not only exists but is valued. In contrast to the pluralistic organization, which fails to address the cultural aspects of integration, these organizations fully integrate minority group members both formally and informally. But managers in such organizations do not focus primarily on employees' visible differences, like race or sex. Rather, managers value and draw on the *experience* and *knowledge* employees bring to the organization and help it achieve agreed-upon strategies and goals.[48] The multicultural organization is marked by an absence of prejudice and discrimination and by low levels of intergroup conflict. Such an organization creates a *synergistic* environment in which all members contribute to their maximum potential and the advantages of diversity can be fully realized.[49]

LO5 List steps managers and their organizations can take to cultivate diversity

5 | HOW ORGANIZATIONS CAN CULTIVATE A DIVERSE WORKFORCE

An organization's plans for becoming multicultural and making the most of its diverse workforce should include five components:

1. Securing top management's leadership and commitment.

2. Assessing the organization's progress toward goals.

Exhibit 9.7	Misleading and more accurate assumptions about diversity	
Dimension	**Misleading Assumption**	**More Accurate Assumption**
Homogeneity–heterogeneity	We are a melting pot; we are all the same.	We are more like a stew. Society consists of different groups.
Similarity–difference	"They" are all just like me. There are no real differences.	People exhibit both differences and similarities compared to me.
Parochialism–equifinality	Our way of living and working is the only way.	There are many distinct ways of reaching goals, living, and working.
Ethnocentrism–culture contingency	Our way is the best way; all other approaches are inferior versions of our way.	There are many different and equally good ways to reach goals; the best way depends on the people involved.

Source: Adapted from N. J. Adler, "Diversity Assumptions and Their Implications for Management," *Handbook of Organization,* 1996.

3. Attracting employees.

4. Training employees in diversity.

5. Retaining employees.

A recent study examining the performance of hundreds of companies over a 30-year period found that organizations in which responsibility for achieving diversity targets was assigned to particular individuals or groups made the most progress in increasing their share of female and black workers. Moderate change occurred in companies with mentoring and networking programs, but formal diversity training programs had little effect unless the organizations also used the other methods.[50] Thus cultivating diversity needs to be a well-planned organizationwide effort in which each element is supported by the personal commitment of individual managers,

Adequate funding must be allocated to the diversity effort to ensure its success. Also, top management can set an example for other organization members by participating in diversity programs and making participation mandatory for all managers.

As we mentioned earlier, some organizations have established corporate offices or committees to coordinate the companywide diversity effort and provide feedback to top management. Intel hired a chief diversity officer and Avon a director of multicultural planning and design. Other companies prefer to incorporate diversity management into the function of director of affirmative action or EEO.

The work of managing diversity cannot be done by top management or diversity directors alone. Many companies rely on minority advisory groups or task forces to monitor organiza-

---

> "Recognize yourself in he and she who are not like you and me."
>
> —Carlos Fuentes

---

who address this issue as seriously as they do other management challenges. These managers actively try to develop the skills, understanding, and practices that enable people of every background to do their best work in the common pursuit of the organization's goals.

∴∴∴∴∴∴∴∴∴∴

The National Basketball Association (NBA) has cultivated diversity throughout its history; in fact, it currently has the highest percentage of minority vice presidents and league office managers in the history of men's sports. Fifteen percent of NBA team vice presidents and 34 percent of the professionals who work in the league office are minorities. The NBA also has nine African American head coaches, and nearly half of the assistant coaches are minorities. NBA spokesperson Brian McIntyre reports that this is business as usual for the organization. He says NBA commissioner David Stern "has long felt that a diverse workplace is the only workplace."[51]

∴∴∴∴∴∴∴∴∴∴

5.1 | Start by Securing Top Managers' Commitment

Obtaining top management's leadership and commitment is critical for diversity programs to succeed. Otherwise the rest of the organization will not take the effort seriously. One way to communicate this commitment to all employees—and to the external environment—is to incorporate the organization's attitudes about diversity into the corporate mission statement and into strategic plans and objectives. Managers' compensation can be linked directly to accomplishing diversity goals.

tional policies, practices, and attitudes; assess their impact on the diverse groups within the organization; and provide feedback and suggestions to top management. At Equitable Life Assurance Society, employee groups meet regularly with the CEO to discuss issues pertaining to women, African Americans, and Hispanics and make recommendations for improvement. At Honeywell, disabled employees formed a council to discuss their needs. They proposed and accepted an accessibility program that went beyond federal regulations for accommodations of disabilities.

As you can see, progressive companies are moving from asking managers what they think minority employees need and toward asking the employees themselves what they need.

5.2 | Conduct an Organizational Assessment

The next step in managing diversity is to routinely assess the organization's workforce, culture, policies, and practices in areas such as recruitment, promotions, benefits, and compensation. Managers may evaluate whether they are attracting their share of diverse candidates from the labor pool and whether the needs of their customers are being addressed by the current composition of their workforce. The objective is to identify areas where there are problems or opportunities and to make recommendations when changes are needed. For example, Cisco measures several positive outcomes that it associates with being diverse and inclusive, including financial growth, employee engagement, and customer loyalty. The firm's managers believe that leveraging diversity is a critical ingredient as it grows into a global company.[52]

5.3 | Attract a Diverse Group of Qualified Employees

Companies can attract a diverse, qualified workforce by using effective recruiting practices, accommodating employees' work and family needs, and offering alternative work arrangements.

Recruitment A company's image can be a strong recruiting tool. Companies with reputations for hiring and promoting all types of people have a competitive advantage. Xerox gives prospective minority employees reprints of an article that rates the company as one of the best places for African Americans to work. Abbott, Deloitte, and Well Star Health System, after being named to *Working Mother* magazine's 2013 Best Companies list, issued news releases on their websites—a move partially aimed at attracting diverse job applicants.[53]

::::::::::::::

Diversity is built into the origins of the Philadelphia law firm of Caesar Rivise. The firm's founder was Abraham Caesar, an attorney specializing in intellectual property (such as patents and trademarks). In 1926 Caesar could not land a job at one of the local law firms because he was Jewish, so he founded his own firm, later adding partner Charles Rivise. The two attorneys wrote important reference books on patents, establishing a reputation as experts.

Given Caesar's early experiences, it's not surprising that his law firm committed itself to diversity in hiring. Stanley Cohen, now a partner, recalls that when he joined the firm in the 1960s, his secretary was a black man. Another Caesar Rivise employee since the 1960s, Bernice Mims, graduated at the top of her South Philadelphia High School class but lacked access to jobs because she was black and some employers stipulated "no Jews or Negroes." Caesar hired Mims as a law clerk, and she remained loyal to the firm, eventually working her way up to manager of human resources.

Today Caesar Rivise builds on its historical commitment to diversity by sponsoring diversity fellowships (tuition assistance and internships) at Drexel University's Earle Mack School of Law. Partnering with Drexel is a good strategic fit because the university emphasizes technology and science—backgrounds that are important for working with corporate clients on technical matters.[54]

::::::::::::::

Many disabled persons and economically disadvantaged people are physically isolated from job opportunities. Companies can bring information about job opportunities to the source of labor, or they can transport the labor to the jobs. Polycast Technology in Stamford, Connecticut, contracts with a private van company to transport workers from the Bronx in New York City to jobs in Stamford. Days Inn recruits homeless workers in Atlanta and houses them in a motel within walking distance of their jobs.

Accommodating Work and Family Needs More job seekers today are putting family needs first. Corporate work and family policies are now one of the most important recruiting tools. Employers that have adopted onsite child care report decreased turnover and absenteeism and improved morale. In addition to providing child care, many companies now assist with care for elderly dependents, offer time off to care for sick family members, provide parental leaves of absence, and offer various benefits that can be tailored to individual family needs. Some companies are accommodating the needs and concerns of dual-career couples by limiting relocation requirements or providing job search assistance to relocated spouses.

Alternative Work Arrangements Another way managers accommodate diversity is to offer flexible work schedules and arrangements. Stiff demand for talented employees is motivating companies to accommodate the needs of employees with family responsibilities. For example, Agilent Technologies offers its employees a variety of flexible work arrangements, including part-time, telecommuting, and job sharing. The firm's goal is to "be the best place to work for everyone."[55]

Other creative work arrangements include compressed workweeks (e.g., four 10-hour days) and job sharing, in which two part-time workers share one full-time job. Another option to accommodate working mothers and disabled employees is teleworking (working from home) or telecommuting (working from home via computer hookup to the main work site).

5.4 | Train Employees to Understand and Work with Diversity

As you learned earlier, employees can be developed in several ways. Traditionally, most management training was based on the unstated assumption that "managing" means managing a homogeneous, often white male, full-time workforce. But gender, race, culture, age, educational, and other differences create an additional layer of complexity.[56] Diversity training programs attempt to identify and reduce hidden biases and develop the skills needed to manage a diversified workforce effectively.

The majority of U.S. organizations sponsor some sort of diversity training. Typically diversity training has two components: awareness building and skill building.

Awareness Building *Awareness building* is designed to increase recognition of the meaning and importance of valuing diversity.[57] Its aim is not to teach specific skills but to sensitize employees to the assumptions they make about others and the way those assumptions affect their behaviors, decisions, and judgment. For example, male managers who have never reported to a female manager may feel awkward the first time they are required to do so. Awareness building can reveal this concern in advance and help the managers address it.

To build awareness, trainers teach people to become familiar with myths, stereotypes, and cultural differences as well as the organizational barriers that inhibit the full contributions of all employees. They develop a better understanding of

mentors higher-level managers who help ensure that high-potential people are introduced to top management and socialized into the norms and values of the organization

corporate culture, requirements for success, and career choices that affect opportunities for advancement.

In most companies, the "rules" for success are ambiguous, unwritten, and perhaps inconsistent with written policy. A common problem for women, minorities, immigrants, and young employees is that they are unaware of many of the unofficial rules that are obvious to people in the mainstream. For example, organizations often have informal networks and power structures that may not be apparent or readily available to everyone. As a result, some employees may not know where to go when they need to get an idea approved or want to build support and alliances. For managers, valuing diversity means teaching the unwritten "rules" or cultural values to those who need to know them and changing the rules when necessary to benefit employees and hence the organization. It also requires inviting "outsiders" in and giving them access to information and meaningful relationships with people in power.

Skill Building *Skill building* aims to develop the skills that employees and managers need to deal effectively with one another and with customers in a diverse environment. Most of the skills taught are interpersonal, such as active listening, coaching, and giving feedback. Ideally the organizational assessment is used to identify which skills should be taught, tailoring the training to the specific business issues that were identified. For example, if too many women and minorities believe they lack helpful feedback, the skill-building program can address that issue. Likewise, training in flexible scheduling can help managers meet the company's needs while accommodating and valuing workers who want to set aside time to advance their education, participate in community projects, or look after elderly parents. Tying the training to specific, measurable business goals increases its usefulness and makes it easier to assess.

:::::::::::::::

The Transportation Security Administration provided a combination of awareness training and skill building to prepare its airport security personnel to screen Muslim travelers without violating their civil rights. The TSA employees were taught that the religious customs of Islam include the hajj, an annual pilgrimage to Saudi Arabia. As a result, once a year air travelers include many groups of these pilgrims. The employees learned to recognize that, especially at the time of the hajj, women in head scarves traveling with men in beards may be devoutly religious Muslims engaging in a deeply personal religious journey. Besides teaching about the customs and practices of Islam, the training prepared TSA employees to perform their jobs without discriminating; for example, they learned how to effectively screen passengers who were wearing head coverings and what to do if passengers were transporting holy water.[58]

:::::::::::::::

5.5 | Retain Talented Employees

As replacing qualified and experienced workers becomes more difficult and costly, retaining good workers is becoming much more important. Several policies and strategies can help managers increase retention of all employees, especially those who are "different" from the norm.[59]

Support Groups Companies can form minority networks and other support groups to promote information exchange and social support. Support groups provide emotional and career support for members who traditionally have not been included in the majority's informal groups. They also can help diverse employees understand work norms and the corporate culture.

At Apple headquarters, support groups include a Jewish cultural group, a gay/lesbian group, an African American group, and a technical women's group. Avon encourages employees to organize into African American, Hispanic, and Asian networks by granting them official recognition and assigning a senior manager to provide advice. These groups help new employees adjust and give management feedback about problems that concern the groups.

:::::::::::::::

Coca-Cola believes in diversity. It has established several groups—known as diversity advisory councils and business resource groups—to provide feedback to upper management to ensure that employees feel included and valued. The diversity advisory councils have representatives from all functions and business units, and provide recommendations to senior management about how best to foster diversity within Coca-Cola. The goal of the business resource groups is to provide networking opportunities to employees who share similar interests and backgrounds.

Here is a sample of Coca-Cola's business resource (support) groups:

- *African American*—provides members with professional experiences through training and development and facilitates connections to support the community.

- *Asian/Pacific American*—encourages member development and community engagement to better connect with key customers.

- *Gay, lesbian, bisexual, and transgender (GLBT)*—fosters an equitable work environment where its members feel a sense of community within the company.

- *Latino*—provides opportunities for members to develop, engage in the organization, and be involved in the community.

- *Women*—facilitates members' careers by providing valuable opportunities for engagement and development, and helping support personal and career success.[60]

:::::::::::::::

Mentoring To help individuals enter the informal network that provides exposure to top management and access to information about organizational politics, many companies have implemented formal mentoring programs. **Mentors** are

Take Charge of Your Career

Find a mentor (Before they all retire)

Over the next couple of decades, hundreds of thousands of Baby Boomers will be retiring. Given the fact that there are about 80 million workers in this generational cohort, many experts are concerned that these retirees will take a great deal of organizational knowledge with them.

What can you do to help the organization as well as your own career? Find a mentor within the organization. If there is a formal procedure for matching mentors to mentees, sign up and try the program to see if it meets your needs and expectations. Unfortunately sometimes the match does not work out because the mentor is too busy, or there is no chemistry between the mentor and mentee. Another approach is for you to find your own mentor within the organization. Generally speaking, your immediate supervisor (and his or her immediate boss) is not the best choice because there may be things you want to share about your job that could reflect badly on him or her; so it may be prudent to look for someone else that is senior in the organization and not directly linked to your supervisor.

The right mentor can help you grow professionally and personally.

While it can be difficult to find the right mentor, one possible approach is to engage a few "mentor candidates" when you see them in the cafeteria, at a business function, in the hallways, or in the break room. You may want to ask them for their opinion about some project you are currently working on or a career tip regarding how to succeed in the organization; then listen carefully to how they respond. If they spend more than a couple of minutes with you giving meaningful and insightful feedback, this is usually a good sign that they may be taking an interest in you. If they seem rushed or slightly annoyed that you are asking for their opinion, they are unlikely to become a mentor.

Another approach is to offer to help a senior manager learn more about an area with which you are familiar. Some companies, like public relations firm Burson-Marsteller, sponsor "reverse mentoring" programs in which junior employees provide advice to senior executives on such topics as how to use social media to connect with customers. This program gives Millennial employees a chance to see another side of the organization by connecting with senior management.

Once you are reasonably sure that you have found someone from whom you can learn and who seems genuinely interested in mentoring you, cultivate your professional relationship by seeking and listening to her or his advice about additional work challenges or career issues. If the person turns out to be the right mentor, you will be amazed at how this relationship will benefit you personally and professionally.

Sources: J. M. Ivancevich and R. Konopaske, *Human Resource Management,* 12 ed. (New York: McGraw-Hill/Irwin, 2013); J. C. Meister and K. Willyerd, "Mentoring Millennials," *Harvard Business Review* 88, no. 5 (May 2010), pp. 68–72; and S. Banjo, "A Perfect Match? For Generation Y, A Good Workplace Environment Is Crucial," *The Wall Street Journal,* October 13, 2008, p. R9.

higher-level managers who help ensure that high-potential people are introduced to top management and socialized into the norms and values of the organization.

Aflac's efforts to develop a diverse workforce include programs aimed at retaining employees by offering them opportunities for development and advancement. The insurance company's mentoring program prepares employees from minority groups to move into management ranks. This program is part of a culture that demonstrates respect for all employees in a variety of ways, including forums where employees can share information about their ethnic customs. Abbott Laboratories operates a mentoring program where employees can find mentors online. Employees interested in having or being a mentor submit profiles about themselves, and software suggests possible matches based on experiences, skills, and interests. The advantage of the online relationships is that employees aren't limited by their geographic location or their likelihood of meeting in the course of their daily work.[61]

Career Development and Promotions To ensure that talented employees are not hitting a glass ceiling, companies such as Deloitte & Touche and Honeywell have established teams to evaluate the career progress of women, minorities, and employees with disabilities and to devise ways to move them up through the ranks. An extremely important step is to make sure deserving employees get a chance at line positions. Women in particular are often relegated to staff positions, like human resources, with less opportunity to demonstrate they can earn money for their employers. Career development programs that give exposure and experience in line jobs to a wide range of employees can make senior management positions more available to them.

Move Over Expatriates: Here Comes a New Breed of International Managers

For many decades, companies deployed expatriates (and their families) to a specific international location like Tokyo, London, or Mexico City for a multiyear assignment. The firm would usually provide expatriates with relocation assistance, cost of living adjustments, a foreign service premium, income tax assistance, private schooling for children, in-country housing, training, and other perquisites. However, there were some drawbacks associated with the use of long-term expatriates. The costs of sending an expatriate to another country for a few years often exceeded a million dollars. Also, the lack of language and cross-cultural skills, coupled with spouse or family adjustment issues, impeded some expatriates from performing to their full potential. Some even failed and returned early from their assignments. Once back, turnover was often an issue. After completing their overseas assignments, approximately 20 percent of repatriates left their employers within one year of their return. Not only was this an unacceptably low return on investment, but the combination of all of these factors contributed to fewer managers within the firm being willing to take an expatriate assignment.

These drawbacks to long-term expatriate assignments, combined with today's less expensive air travel and new communication technologies, have paved the way for a new type of international manager. Known by different names—flexpatriates, short-term assignees, extended business travelers, or virtual expatriates—these international managers travel to one or more countries for short-term projects or to meet with in-country stakeholders (such as customers, suppliers, government officials, managers of a joint venture, and alliance partners). Also, these international travelers do not relocate overseas, and they often have domestic job responsibilities in the home country.

These new international assignments can be quite varied. While doing your regular marketing job in the United States, you might be asked to staff your company's booth at trade shows in China, Russia, and Brazil for a week at a time at different points throughout the year. Or as a network analyst, you might be sent to Bangalore, India, for three months to help install a network in your company's new venture. Also, these assignments offer you the opportunity to gain some basic foreign language and cross-cultural skills, and develop your knowledge about how business is conducted in different countries. These skills and perspectives are valuable to employers as globalization and competition affect companies of all types and sizes.

Here are some ideas for how to increase your chances of landing one of these new types of international assignments:

1. *Let them know.* Discuss your interest in doing more international work with your supervisor and the human resource department. If your organization has a skills or career interests database, be sure to update it.

2. *Study a foreign language.* Find out into which countries your organization is planning to expand over the next few years. Choose the country with the largest market and then study its language. You will not become fluent overnight, but you will send a strong message to upper management that you are serious about helping your firm succeed overseas.

3. *Volunteer to be an "ambassador."* Whenever clients or suppliers from another country are planning on visiting your company in the United States, volunteer to pick them up at the airport, show them the local sights, and take them out to eat. While these activities probably fall outside your normal job duties, they will give you additional opportunities to develop your international skills and network. This extra effort could help you get the nod when the next international assignment becomes available.

Discussion Questions

- Why do you think shorter-term, traveling international assignments have become popular alternatives to multiyear expatriate assignments?

- To what degree will companies need employees with foreign language, cross-cultural experience, and other international skills in the next 5–10 years? How will these employees help firms compete globally?

SOURCES: E. Krell, "Taking Care of Business Abroad," *HRMagazine* 56, no. 12 (December 2011), pp. 44–49; B. Demel and W. Mayrhofer, "Frequent Business Travelers across Europe: Career Aspirations and Implications," *Thunderbird International Business Review* 52, no. 4 (July/August 2010), pp. 301–11; M. Harvey, L. Hartmann, H. Mayerhofer, and M. Moeller, "Corralling the 'Horses' to Staff the Global Organization," *Organizational Dynamics* 39, no. 3 (2010), pp. 258–68; and R. Konopaske, C. Robie, and J. M. Ivancevich, "Managerial Willingness to Assume Traveling Short-Term and Long-Term Global Assignments," *Management International Review* 49, no. 3 (2009), pp. 359–87.

Systems Accommodation Managers can support diversity by recognizing cultural and religious holidays, differing modes of dress, and dietary restrictions, as well as accommodating the needs of individuals with disabilities. Accommodations for disability may become more important in the future as the median age of the workforce continues to rise. In addition, the rise in the *weight* of the average U.S. worker may raise disability concerns. Not only are the familiar health consequences such as heart disease, joint problems, and diabetes associated with increased weight, but one study found that obese workers had many more workplace injury claims and absences related to injuries.[62] This pattern suggests that managers of the future will be even more concerned than in the past with keeping their workers of all sizes on the job by maintaining safe workplaces and offering benefits that encourage healthy lifestyles (possibly through company-sponsored fitness programs).

Accountability As we noted at the beginning of this section, one of the most effective ways to ensure that diversity efforts succeed is to hold managers accountable for hiring and developing a diverse workforce. Organizations must ensure that their performance appraisal and reward systems reinforce the importance of effective diversity management. At PepsiCo, each executive reporting to the CEO is assigned responsibility for employee development of a different group—for example, the company's women or Latinos or gay and lesbian employees. The executive responsible for that group must identify leadership talent, learn group members' concerns, identify areas where support is needed, and identify plans for addressing these issues.[63]

● Darden Restaurants' chairman of the board chief executive officer Clarence Otis is shown in Darden's offices in Orlando, Florida. Selling under such brands as Olive Garden, LongHorn Steakhouse, and Bahama Breeze, Darden Restaurants owns and operates 2,100 restaurants, has 200,000 employees, and serves 425 million meals per year.

the region (third-country national) to assist with the start-up.

While most corporations use some combination of all three types of employees, there are advantages and disadvantages of each. Colgate-Palmolive and Procter & Gamble use expatriates to get their products to international markets more quickly. AT&T and Toyota have used expatriates to transfer their corporate cultures and best practices to other countries—in Toyota's case, to its U.S. plants. But sending employees abroad can cost three to four times as much as employing host-country nationals, and in many countries, the personal security of expatriates is an issue. As a result, firms may send their expatriates on shorter assignments and communicate internationally via videoconferencing, phone, text, e-mail, and other electronic means. Local employees are more available, tend to be familiar with the culture and language, and usually cost less because they need not be relocated. At Kraft Foods, a policy of letting local marketing experts make decisions about local markets freed Chinese marketers to redesign the Oreo cookie so it would be more palatable to Chinese consumers' tastes (and easier on their wallets).[64] In addition, local governments often provide incentives to companies that create good jobs for their citizens, or they may restrict the use of expatriates. The trend away from using expatriates in top management positions is especially apparent in companies that truly want to create a multinational culture. In Honeywell's European division, many of the top executive positions are held by non-Americans.[65]

expatriates parent-company nationals who are sent to work at a foreign subsidiary

host-country nationals individuals from the country where an overseas subsidiary is located

third-country nationals individuals from a country other than the home country or the host country of an overseas subsidiary

---

LO6 Summarize the skills and knowledge about cultural differences needed to manage globally

6 | MANAGING ACROSS BORDERS

Adding to the challenges and opportunities of diversity, today's managers are increasingly responsible for managing employees from other countries or managing operations in other countries. When establishing operations overseas, headquarters executives have a choice among sending **expatriates** (individuals from the parent country), using **host-country nationals** (individuals from the host country), and deploying **third-country nationals** (individuals from a country other than the home country or the host country). For example, assume planners at Google headquarters in Mountain View, California, decide to establish a new office in Brazil. To get it up and running, they send an American executive (expatriate) who has international experience to be general manager of the new operation. Once there, the expatriate will likely hire several Brazilian employees (host-country nationals) and possibly an Argentinian or other experienced manager from

6.1 | Global Managers Need Cross-Cultural Skills

Working internationally can be stressful, even for experienced global managers. Stress can originate from a variety of sources, including culture shock, language barriers, and differences in work values.

Given the challenges, many overseas assignments fail. While conclusive information is lacking about how often expatriates underperform overseas or fail (defined as returning early from the international assignment), there is evidence that certain destinations like China are more challenging for expatriates.[67] Each failed assignment may cost tens of thousands to hundreds of thousands of dollars.[68] Typically the causes for failure extend beyond technical skills to include personal and social issues. In a recent survey of human resource managers around the globe, two-thirds said the main reason for failure is family issues, especially dissatisfaction of the employee's spouse or partner.[69] The problem may be compounded in this era of dual-career couples, in which one spouse may have to give up his or her job to accompany the expatriate manager to the new location. Complicating matters is the fact that it is difficult in most countries to obtain a work visa for the spouse of an expatriate. To ensure that an overseas posting will succeed, managers can encourage employees to talk to their spouses about what they will do in the foreign country.

For both the expatriate and the spouse, adjustment requires flexibility, emotional stability, empathy for the culture, communication skills, resourcefulness, initiative, and diplomatic skills.[70] When Kent Millington took the position of vice president of Asia operations for an Internet hosting company, his wife Linda quit her job to move with him to Japan. Especially for Linda Millington, the first three months were difficult because she didn't speak Japanese, found the transit system confusing, and even struggled to buy food because she couldn't translate the labels. But she persevered and participated in classes and volunteer activities. Eventually she and her husband learned to enjoy the experience and appreciated the chance to see just how well they could tackle a challenge.[71]

The following traits may be associated with candidates who are likely to succeed in a global environment:[72]

- *Sensitivity to cultural differences*—When working with people from other cultures, the candidate tries hard to understand their perspective.

- *Business knowledge*—The candidate has a solid understanding of the company's products and services.

- *Courage to take a stand*—The person is willing to take a stand on issues.

- *Bringing out the best in people*—He or she has a special talent for dealing with people.

- *Integrity*—The person can be depended on to tell the truth regardless of circumstances.

- *Insightfulness*—The candidate is good at identifying the most important part of a complex problem.

- *Commitment to success*—He or she clearly demonstrates commitment to seeing the organization succeed.

- *Risk taking*—The candidate takes personal as well as business risks.

- *Use of feedback*—The candidate has changed as a result of feedback.

- *Cultural adventurousness*—The person enjoys the challenge of working in countries other than his or her own.

- *Desire for opportunities to learn*—The candidate takes advantage of opportunities to do new things.

- *Openness to criticism*—The person does not appear brittle, as if criticism might cause him or her to break.

- *Desire for feedback*—He or she pursues feedback even when others are reluctant to give it.

- *Flexibility*—The candidate doesn't get so invested in things that he or she cannot change when something doesn't work.

Companies such as BP, Global Hyatt, and others with large international staffs have extensive training programs to prepare employees for international assignments. Other organizations, such as Coca-Cola, Motorola, Chevron, and Mattel, have extended this training to include employees located in the United States who deal in international markets. These programs focus on areas such as language, culture, and career development. As shown in Exhibit 9.8, companies can take several steps to prevent global assignees from failing.

Managers who are sent on an overseas assignment usually wonder about the effect such an assignment will have on their careers. Selection for a post overseas is usually an indication that they are being groomed to become more effective managers in an era of globalization. Also, they often have more responsibility, challenge, and operating leeway than they might have at home. Yet they may be concerned that they will be "out of the loop" on key developments back home. Good companies and managers address that issue with effective communication between subsidiaries and headquarters and by a program of visitations to and from the home office. Communication technology makes it easy for expatriates to keep in touch with colleagues in their

Exhibit 9.8	Ways to prevent failed global assignments
Structure the assignment clearly.	• Be clear about reporting relationships, job responsibilities, and job objectives.
Use valid selection methods.	• Methods should assess both technical skills and personal factors.
Prepare expatriates and their families.	• Send them on a "look-see" trip, and provide training and in-country support.
Assign mentors.	• Assign home office and in-country mentors.
Encourage communication.	• Connect with the expatriate via frequent texting, e-mailing, and videoconferencing.
Measure performance.	• Link performance measures to the objectives of the assignment.
Develop a reentry plan.	• Before the assignment ends, find the repatriate a job that utilizes newly acquired skills.

home country daily or even more often through e-mail, video-conferencing, and phone calls. Alan Paul, an American journalist working in China, says Internet phone service, a webcam, and podcasts of favorite radio programs enable him to stay in touch with family and friends back home, even to the extent that he has to work hard to have "a fully engaged existence in China."[74]

Cross-cultural management extends beyond U.S. employees going abroad and includes effective management of **inpatriates**—foreign nationals who are brought in to work at the parent company. These employees bring their employer extensive knowledge about how to operate effectively in their home countries. They are also better prepared to communicate their organization's products and values when they return. But they often have the same types of problems as expatriates and may be even more neglected because parent-company managers either are more focused on their expatriate program or unconsciously see the home country as normal—requiring no period of adjustment. Yet the language, customs, expense, and lack of local community support in the United States are at least as daunting to inpatriates as the experience of American nationals abroad.

6.2 | National Cultures Shape Values and Business Practices

In many ways, cultural issues are the most elusive aspect of international business. In an era when modern transportation and communication technologies have created a "global village," it is

our everyday behavior, so we tend to adapt poorly to situations that are unique or foreign to us. Without realizing it, some managers may even act out of **ethnocentrism**—a tendency to judge foreign people or groups by the standards of one's own culture or group, and to see one's own standards as superior. Such tendencies may be totally unconscious—for example, the assumption that "in England they drive on the *wrong* side of the road" rather than merely on the left. Or they may reflect a lack of awareness of the values underlying a local culture—for example, an assumption that a culture does not air American television programming because it is backward, when it is actually committed to maintaining its traditional values and norms.

Assumptions such as these are one reason why people traveling abroad frequently experience **culture shock**—the disorientation and stress associated with being in a foreign environment. Managers are better able to navigate this transition if they are sensitive to their surroundings, including social norms and customs, and readily able to adjust their behavior to such circumstances.[76] Employers can help by identifying some of the cultural norms to expect and by establishing performance measures for behaviors that contribute to success in the host

> "(Culture is) the collective programming of the mind distinguishing the members of one group or category of people from another.[73]"
>
> —Geert Hofstede

easy to forget how deep and enduring the differences can be. Even though people everywhere drink Coke, wear blue jeans, and drive Toyotas, we are not all becoming alike. Each country is unique for reasons rooted in history, culture, language, geography, social conditions, race, and religion. These differences complicate any international activity and guide how a company should conduct business across borders. For example, while working in Hong Kong, Geoffrey Fowler discovered that his coworkers chose topics for small talk—people's weight, salary, and the sizes of their apartments—that would horrify Americans. At the same time, Chinese workers are put off by the American custom of combining lunch with a business meeting at which junior employees are chewing away while a superior in the company is talking.[75]

Ironically, while most of us would guess that the trick to working abroad is learning about a foreign culture, in reality our problems often stem from our being oblivious to our own cultural conditioning. Most of us pay no attention to how culture influences

country (for example, the types of communication and direction employees will expect from their manager).

A wealth of cross-cultural research has been conducted on the differences and similarities among various countries. Geert Hofstede, for example, has identified four dimensions along which managers in multinational corporations tend to view cultural differences:

1. *Power distance*—the extent to which a society accepts the fact that power in organizations is distributed unequally.

2. *Individualism/collectivism*—the extent to which people act on their own or as a part of a group.

3. *Uncertainty avoidance*—the extent to which people in a society feel threatened by uncertain and ambiguous situations.

4. *Masculinity/femininity*—the extent to which a society values quantity of life (e.g., accomplishment, money) over quality of life (e.g., compassion, beauty).

Exhibit 9.9 graphs how 40 nations differ on the dimensions of individualism/collectivism and power distance. Countries like Australia, Great Britain, and the United States are individualistic and exhibit small power distance. In other words, employees from these cultures believe in individual achievement and rewards; and while they respect their superiors, they will disagree with and question orders if they feel such behavior is warranted. In contrast, Singapore, Colombia, and the Philippines are collectivist and are characterized by large power distance. Employees from these collectivist societies will often place the needs of their group and family ahead of individual needs. When attempting to motivate these individuals, expatriate managers should consider using group-based rewards and recognition programs. Also, employees from large power distance cultures will be less willing to openly question or provide feedback regarding their superiors' ideas and orders. Of course this depiction exaggerates the differences to some extent. Many Americans prefer to act as part of a group, just as many Taiwanese prefer to act individualistically. And globalization

may have already begun to blur some of these distinctions. Still, to suggest no cultural differences exist is equally simplistic. Clearly, cultures such as the United States, which emphasize "rugged individualism," differ significantly from collectivistic cultures such as those of Pakistan, Taiwan, and Colombia. And to be effective in cultures that exhibit a greater power distance, managers often must behave more autocratically, perhaps inviting less participation in decision making.

::::::::::::::::::::

In starting an insurance company in the United Arab Emirates, Texas native Michael Weinberg has learned a lot about that country's business culture. One surprise was the Arabs' far looser sense of time. On an early visit, Weinberg was doubtful when his partners—both Lebanese American and more familiar with the culture—assured him that showing up a few hours late for an appointment would be fine. As it turned out, their hosts were unruffled by their late arrival.

Traditionally, in Arabic culture, people's activities fit around the appointed times for prayer (related to the sun's position) and the climate's cycles of heating and cooling. In addition, participants in a meeting focus more on the relationships being built than on the next event on their calendar, so appointments often run longer than scheduled. These cultural norms result in a fluid understanding of time.

Still, visitors must be conscientious. They have to take into account the status of their host; a higher-status person expects visitors to be available as scheduled, even if that means a wait. Weinberg has learned to use waiting time to catch up on his e-mail. He also calls ahead to confirm meeting times and to notify his host if he'll be late.

Acknowledging the challenges of learning a culture, Weinberg has also experienced the joys, noting the "hospitality, warmth, love, education, and charity" of the Arab people he has met.[77]

::::::::::::::::::::

Effective managers are sensitive to these issues and consider them in dealing with people from other cultures. In contrast to people born in America, employees, coworkers, or customers from other countries might tend to communicate less directly, place more emphasis on hierarchy and authority, or make decisions more slowly. For example, an American manager working in Japan sent an e-mail message to her American supervisor and Japanese colleagues in which she pointed out flaws in the process they were working on. The supervisor appreciated the alert, but her colleagues were embarrassed by behavior they considered rude; she should have inquired indirectly—say, by wondering what might happen if such a problem did exist. In general, managers of international groups can manage such misunderstandings by acknowledging cultural differences frankly and finding ways to work around them, by modifying the group (e.g., assigning tasks to subgroups), by setting rules to correct problems that are upsetting group members, or by removing group members who demonstrate they cannot work effectively within a particular situation.[78]

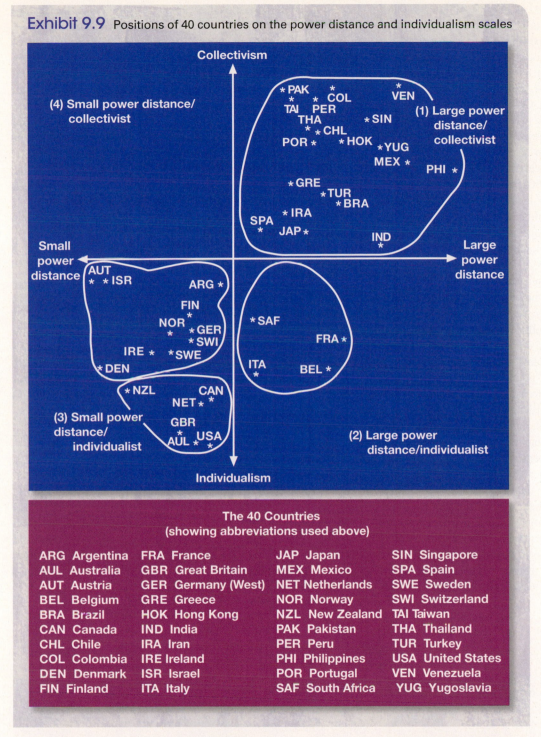

Exhibit 9.9 Positions of 40 countries on the power distance and individualism scales

Collectivism

(4) Small power distance/ collectivist

* PAK
TAI * * COL
THA PER
* CHL
POR * * HOK

* VEN
* SIN
* YUG
MEX *
PHI *

(1) Large power distance/ collectivist

* GRE
* TUR
* BRA
SPA * * IRA
JAP *
IND *

Small power distance

AUT
* * ISR
ARG *
FIN
*
NOR * GER
* * SWI
IRE * * SWE
* DEN

* SAF
FRA *
ITA
* BEL *

Large power distance

* NZL
CAN
NET * *
(3) Small power distance/ individualist
GBR
* USA
AUL * *

(2) Large power distance/individualist

Individualism

The 40 Countries
(showing abbreviations used above)

ARG Argentina	FRA France	JAP Japan	SIN Singapore
AUL Australia	GBR Great Britain	MEX Mexico	SPA Spain
AUT Austria	GER Germany (West)	NET Netherlands	SWE Sweden
BEL Belgium	GRE Greece	NOR Norway	SWI Switzerland
BRA Brazil	HOK Hong Kong	NZL New Zealand	TAI Taiwan
CAN Canada	IND India	PAK Pakistan	THA Thailand
CHL Chile	IRA Iran	PER Peru	TUR Turkey
COL Colombia	IRE Ireland	PHI Philippines	USA United States
DEN Denmark	ISR Israel	POR Portugal	VEN Venezuela
FIN Finland	ITA Italy	SAF South Africa	YUG Yugoslavia

Source: From G. Hofstede, G.J. Hofstede, and M. Minkov, *Cultures and Organizations, Software of the Mind,* Third Revised Edition, 2010. Reprinted with permission of the author.

In addition, when working in the United States, foreign nationals will encounter a number of work-related differences:

- *Meetings*—Americans and workers from some other countries may have different views about the purpose of meetings and how much time can be spent. Managers should make sure foreign nationals are comfortable with the American approach.

- *Work(aholic) schedules*—Workers in countries with strong labor organizations often get many more weeks of vacation than American workers. Europeans in particular may balk at working on weekends. Matters such as these are most helpfully raised and addressed at the beginning of the work assignment.

- *E-mail*—Parts of the world have not yet embraced e-mail and voice mail the way U.S. workers have. Often others prefer to communicate face to face. Particularly when language difficulties may exist, at the outset managers will probably want to avoid using e-mail for important matters.

- *Fast-trackers*—Although U.S. companies may take a young MBA graduate and put him or her on the fast track to management, most other cultures still see no substitute for the wisdom gained through experience. Experienced managers are often best for mentoring inpatriates.

- *Feedback*—Everyone appreciates praise, but other cultures tend to be less lavish in delivering positive feedback than the United States. U.S. managers should keep this point in mind when they give foreign nationals their performance reviews.[79]

6.3 | International Management Introduces Complex Ethical Challenges

If managers are to function effectively in a foreign setting, they must understand the ways culture influences how they are perceived and how others behave. One of the most sensitive issues in this regard is how culture plays out in terms of ethical behavior.[80] Issues of right and wrong get blurred as we move from one culture to another, and actions that may be customary in one setting may be unethical—even illegal—in another. The use of bribes, for example, is perceived as an accepted part of commercial transactions in many parts of the world. Transparency International publishes the "Bribe Payers' Index" that ranks 28 countries based on the likelihood that companies (from those countries) will pay bribes to win business abroad. Companies from the Netherlands, Switzerland, and Belgium were the least likely to pay bribes, while Russian, Chinese and Mexican companies were the most likely to engage in bribery abroad.[81]

What should a U.S. businessperson do? Failure to sweeten the deal with bribes can result in lost business. In the United States, the Foreign Corrupt Practices Act of 1977 prohibits U.S. employees from bribing foreign officials. (Small business gifts or payments to lower-level officials are permissible if the dollar amount of the payments would not influence the outcome of the negotiations.) Likewise, countries of the Organization for Economic Cooperation and Development, including the United States, have prohibited bribes since 1977. Even so, a study found that fewer than half of U.S. managers said bribes were unacceptable, and 20 percent actually said they were always acceptable.[82]

Enforcement of the antibribery law—if only in the United States—became more vigorous following high-profile financial scandals at Enron, WorldCom, and other corporations. Still, even in companies with a solid reputation for ethical conduct, bribery can occur. Alcoa recently agreed to pay $384 million to settle U.S. Security and Exchange Commission charges its subsidiaries repeatedly paid bribes to government officials in Bahrain to maintain business. In an unrelated case, Ralph Lauren Corporation agreed to pay more than $700,000 to settle charges that its Argentinian subsidiary profited by bribing government officials from 2005–2009.[83]

Without an understanding of local customs, ethical standards, and applicable laws, an expatriate may be woefully unprepared to work internationally. To safeguard against the problems and mitigate the punishment if an organization should be found guilty of bribery, the U.S. Sentencing Commission has deemed it essential for firms to establish effective ethics programs and see that they are enforced. To put teeth into the corporate ethics initiative, companies with global operations should be at least as engaged as domestic corporations in establishing and enforcing standards for ethical behavior. In Chapter 4, we identified a number of steps organizations should take. They include establishing and communicating the company's values, measuring performance in meeting ethical standards, rewarding employees at all levels for meeting those standards, and taking swift but fair action when violations occur. The primary difference in the international context is that these activities must be carried out with foreign business partners and employees in any subsidiary, franchise, or other company operation.

Interestingly, despite some obvious cultural differences, research suggests that regardless of nationality or religion, most people embrace a set of five core values:

1. Compassion.

2. Fairness.

3. Honesty.

4. Responsibility.

5. Respect for others.

These values lie at the heart of human rights issues and seem to transcend more superficial differences among cultures. Finding shared values allows companies to build more effective partnerships and alliances. As long as people understand that there is a set of core values, perhaps they can permit differences in strategy and tactics.[84]

To a large extent, the challenge of managing across borders comes down to the philosophies and systems used to manage people. In moving from domestic to international management, managers need to develop a wide portfolio of behaviors and the capacity to adjust their behavior for a particular situation. This adjustment, however, should not compromise the values, integrity, and strengths of their home country. When managers can transcend national borders and move among different cultures, they can leverage the strategic capabilities of their organization and take advantage of the opportunities that our global economy has to offer.

Study Checklist

Be heard!

Connect with other students, faculty, and McGraw-Hill professionals through the Student Ambassador Program.

Apply today: learnsmartadvantage.com/students/student-ambassadors

part four

10

chapter

Leadership

Learning Objectives

After studying Chapter 10, you will be able to

LO1 Explain how a good vision helps you be a better leader.

LO2 Discuss the similarities and differences between leading and managing.

LO3 Identify sources of power in organizations.

LO4 Know the three traditional approaches to understanding leadership.

LO5 Understand the important contemporary perspectives on leadership.

LO6 Identify types of opportunities to be a leader in an organization.

People get excited about the topic of leadership. They want to know what makes a great leader. Executives at all levels in all industries are also interested in this question. They believe the answer will bring improved organizational performance and personal career success. They hope to acquire the skills that will transform an "average" manager into a true leader.

One such leader is Marc Nager, an influential and charismatic figure in the entrepreneurial startup community. As the explore beyond this bare definition to capture the excitement and intrigue that devoted followers and students of leadership feel when they see a great leader in action, to understand what organizational leaders really do, and to learn what it really takes to become an outstanding leader.

Outstanding leaders combine good strategic substance and effective interpersonal processes to formulate and implement strategies that produce results and sustainable competitive advantage.[3] They may launch enterprises, build organization cultures,

> ## "People buy into the leader before they buy into the vision."
>
> —John C. Maxwell

CEO of UpGlobal, Nager has been the driving force behind the nonprofit's increasingly popular Startup Weekend aimed at "furthering human welfare through entrepreneurship." The how-to-start-your-own-business weekend events have been held more than 1,000 times in 400 cities in 100 countries. To date, these events have resulted in the creation of approximately 8,500 startup ventures.[1]

Of course you don't have to form a movement to acquire leadership skills. According to one source, "Leadership seems to be the marshaling of skills possessed by a majority but used by a minority. But it's something that can be learned by anyone, taught to everyone, denied to no one."[2]

What is leadership? To start, a leader is one who influences others to attain goals. The greater the number of followers, the greater the influence. And the more successful the attainment of worthy goals, the more evident the leadership. But we must

win wars, or otherwise change the course of events.[4] They are strategists who seize opportunities others overlook, but "they are also passionately concerned with detail—all the small, fundamental realities that can make or mar the grandest of plans."[5]

LISTEN & LEARN ◉ ONLINE

YOUNG MANAGERS
Speak Out

"When I come to work, I try and lead by example. So if there are qualities I want to see in my employees, I want to exhibit them myself."

—Brian Min, Kitchen Manager

What do people want from their leaders? Broadly speaking, they want help in achieving their goals.[6] Besides pay and promotions, these goals include support for personal development; clearing obstacles to high-level performance; and treatment that is respectful, fair, and ethical. Leaders serve people best by helping them develop their own initiative and good judgment, enabling them to grow, and helping them become better contributors. People want the kinds of things you will read about in this chapter and in other chapters of this book.

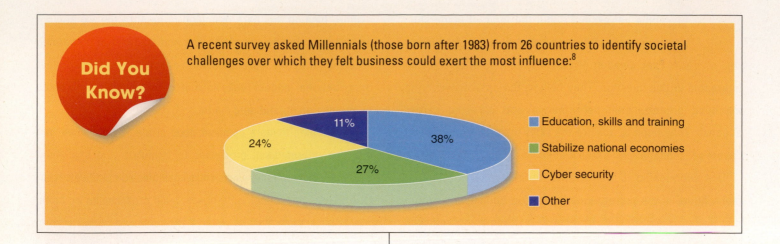

A recent survey asked Millennials (those born after 1983) from 26 countries to identify societal challenges over which they felt business could exert the most influence:[8]

- 38% Education, skills and training
- 27% Stabilize national economies
- 24% Cyber security
- 11% Other

What do organizations need? Organizations need people at all levels to be leaders. Leaders throughout the organization are needed to do the things that their people want but also to help create and implement strategic direction. Organizations place people in formal leadership roles so that they will achieve the organization's goals.

These two perspectives—what people want and what organizations need—are neatly combined in a set of five key behaviors identified by James Kouzes and Barry Posner, two well-known authors and consultants.[7] The best leaders, say Kouzes and Posner, do five things:

1. *Challenge the process*—They challenge conventional beliefs and practices, and they create change.

2. *Inspire a shared vision*—They appeal to people's values and motivate them to care about an important mission.

3. *Enable others to act*—They give people access to information and give them the power to perform to their full potential.

4. *Model the way*—They don't just tell people what to do; they are living examples of the ideals they believe in.

5. *Encourage the heart*—They show appreciation, provide rewards, and use various approaches to motivate people in positive ways.

You will read about these and other aspects of leadership in this chapter. The topics we discuss not only will help you become a better leader but also will give you benchmarks for assessing the competence and fairness with which your boss manages you.

LO1 Explain how a good vision helps you be a better leader

1 | VISION

Tony Hsieh, CEO of Zappos, believes the right vision "inspires employees to want to do things beyond expectations."[9] Until a few years ago, *vision* was not a word that managers uttered.

But today having a vision for the future and communicating that vision to others are known to be essential components of great leadership. "If there is no vision, there is no business," maintains entrepreneur Mark Leslie.[10] Joe Nevin, an MIS director, described leaders as "painters of the vision and architects of the journey."[11] Practicing businesspeople are not alone in this belief; academic research shows that a clear vision and communication of that vision lead to higher growth in entrepreneurial firms.[12]

A **vision** is a mental image of a possible and desirable future state of the organization. It expresses the leader's ambitions for the organization.[13] A leader can create a vision that describes high performance aspirations, the nature of corporate or business strategy, or even the kind of workplace worth building. The best visions are both ideal and unique.[14] If a vision conveys an *ideal*, it communicates a standard of excellence and a clear choice of positive values. If the vision is also *unique*, it communicates and inspires pride in being different from other organizations. The choice of language is important; the words should express realism and optimism, an action orientation, and resolution and confidence that the vision will be attained.[15]

Visions can be small or large and can exist throughout all organizational levels. The important points are that (1) a vision is necessary for effective leadership; (2) a person or team can develop a vision for any job, work unit, or organization; and (3) many people, including managers who do not develop into strong leaders, fail to develop a clear vision—instead they focus on performing or surviving day by day.

Put another way, leaders must know what they want.[16] And other people must understand what that is. The leader must be able to articulate the vision, clearly and often. Other people throughout the organization should understand the vision and be able to state it clearly themselves. That's a start. But the vision means nothing until the leader and followers take action to turn the vision into reality.[17]

Back in 1981, Narayana "N.R." Murthy quit his job and along with six colleagues (and just $250) decided to build

● Like with a jigsaw puzzle, a clear picture or vision of what needs to be accomplished provides direction and purpose.

- Although effective leaders maintain confidence and persevere despite obstacles, the facts may dictate that the vision must change. You will learn more about change and how to manage it later.

Where do visions come from?[21] Leaders should be sensitive to emerging opportunities, develop the right capabilities or worldviews, and not be overly invested in the status quo. You also can capitalize on networks of insightful individuals who have ideas about the future. Some visions are accidental; a company may stumble into an opportunity, and the leader may get credit for foresight. Some leaders and companies launch many new initiatives and, through trial and error, hit occasional home runs. If the company learns from these successes, the "vision" emerges.

∷∷∷∷∷∷∷∷∷∷

After a powerful tornado smashed through his town of Greensburg, Kansas, city administrator Steve Hewitt emerged from his basement to discover that the storm had destroyed the homes of most of the town's 1,400 residents. It also wiped out

---

> ## "Leadership is the capacity to translate vision into reality."
>
> —Warren G. Bennis

---

a company from scratch. Not just any company—N.R.'s vision was to create "India's most respected company." Fast-forward to today. The firm, Infosys, has evolved into a global leader of IT and consulting services with 160,000 employees in 30 countries and revenues of $8.25 billion. N.R. recently reflected on how transformative one's vision can be: "Posterity will not excuse you if you did not dream big. You owe it to your customers, your colleagues, your investors, and the society. Every major civilization, every great advance in science and technology, and every great company is built on a big dream."[18]

A metaphor reinforces the important concept of vision.[19] Putting a jigsaw puzzle together is much easier if you have the picture on the box cover in front of you. Without the picture, or vision, the lack of direction is likely to result in frustration and failure. That is what communicating a vision is all about: making clear where you are heading.

Not just any vision will do. Visions can be inappropriate, and even fail, for a variety of reasons:[20]

- An inappropriate vision may reflect only the leader's personal needs. Such a vision may be unethical or may fail to gain acceptance by the market or by those who must implement it.

- Related to the first reason, an inappropriate vision may ignore stakeholder needs.

Greensburg's hospital, fire station, elementary and high schools, water tower, and business district. Hewitt immediately contacted employees and assessed the extent of the damage. He found a safe place for his family to stay and then turned his full attention to rescue and recovery.

First, Hewitt dealt with the emergency at hand, directing the search and rescue, and then the cleanup, by crews of city workers and volunteers operating out of tents. Even as these activities continued, Hewitt began making decisions about the future. Determined to rebuild, he saw an opportunity in the town's tragic circumstances.

Hewitt envisioned a town that would model an energy-efficient and sustainable lifestyle. He persuaded the city council to pass a resolution that all new municipal buildings meet the stiff LEED platinum certification for "green" buildings, awarded by the U.S. Green Building Council's Leadership in Energy and Environmental Design, for major energy savings. Hewitt communicated his vision in radio broadcasts and flyers handed out at emergency checkpoints. He educated the community about the practical advantages of rebuilding homes to meet LEED standards, persuading many home owners and store owners to adopt the standards themselves. He developed plans for wind farms to supply electricity to the town. Besides inspiring the locals, these efforts drew publicity and donations, including an ecofriendly playground.[22]

∷∷∷∷∷∷∷∷∷∷

● An aerial view of the destruction caused by a tornado in Greensburg, KS, on May 5, 2007. During the rebuilding planning phase, tornado survivor and city administrator Steve Hewitt convinced city council members to pass a resolution that would require all new municipal buildings to be "green" and energy efficient.

2 | LEADING AND MANAGING

Effective managers are not necessarily true leaders. Many administrators, supervisors, and even top executives perform their responsibilities successfully without being great leaders. But these positions afford an opportunity for leadership. The ability to lead effectively, then, sets the excellent managers apart from the average ones.

2.1 | Comparing Leaders and Managers

Management must deal with the ongoing, day-to-day complexities of organizations, but true leadership includes effectively orchestrating important change.[23] While managing requires planning and budgeting routines, leading includes setting the direction—creating a vision—for the firm. Management requires structuring the organization, staffing it with capable people, and monitoring activities; leadership goes beyond these functions by inspiring people to attain the vision. Great leaders keep people focused on moving the organization toward its ideal future, motivating them to overcome any obstacles.

Good leadership, unfortunately, is all too rare. Managers may focus on the activities that earn them praise and rewards, such as actions that cause a rise in the company's stock price, rather than making tough ethical decisions or investing in long-term results. Some new managers, learning that "quick wins" will help them establish their credibility as leaders, push a pet project while neglecting the impact on the very people they were assigned to lead. This approach backfires because employees distrust this type of manager and lose any commitment they might have had to the team's long-term success. Successful leaders, in contrast, enlist the team in scoring *collective* quick wins that result from working together toward a shared vision.[24]

It is important to be clear that management and leadership are both vitally important. To highlight the need for more leadership is not to minimize the importance of management or managers. But leadership involves unique processes that are distinguishable from basic management processes.[25] Also, the requirement for different processes does not necessarily call for separate people. The same individual may manage and lead effectively—or may not.

Some people dislike the idea of distinguishing between management and leadership, maintaining that it is artificial or derogatory toward the managers and the management processes that make organizations run. Perhaps a more useful distinction is between supervisory and strategic leadership:[26]

- **Supervisory leadership** is behavior that provides guidance, support, and corrective feedback for day-to-day activities.

- **Strategic leadership** gives purpose and meaning to organizations by anticipating and envisioning a viable future for the organization and working with others to initiate changes that create such a future.[27]

:::::::::::::::::

Coach John Thompson III could be called a strategic leader. Formerly the head coach of the Princeton men's basketball team, Thompson is in his seventh season as head coach of Georgetown University's team. He has successfully revitalized Georgetown's faltering program. He knows how to develop discipline among his players and how to train them to choose their shots carefully and play a decisive game. And because he grew up on the Georgetown campus, watching his father coach, his sense of loyalty to the institution is ingrained. Georgetown University president John J. DeGioia credits Thompson for having successful experience plus "outstanding leadership and communication skills and . . . a deep commitment to the Georgetown tradition of academic excellence, integrity in competition, and basketball success." Proof of Thompson's leadership prowess can be seen from his overall record of 219-92 and conference record of 101–57 since coming to Georgetown.[28]

:::::::::::::::::

2.2 | Good Leaders Need Good Followers

Organizations succeed or fail not only because of how well they are led but also because of how well followers follow. Just as managers are not necessarily good leaders, employees are not always good followers. As one leadership scholar puts it, "Executives are given subordinates; they have to earn followers."[29] But it's also true that good followers help produce good leaders.

As a manager, you will be asked to play the roles of both leader and follower. As you lead the people who report to you, you will report to your boss. You will be a member of some teams and committees, and you may head others. While the leadership roles get the glamour and therefore are the coveted roles, followers must perform their responsibilities conscientiously. Good followership is not merely obeying orders, although some bosses may view it that way. The most effective followers can think independently while remaining actively committed to organizational goals.[30] Robert Townsend, who led a legendary turnaround at Avis, says the most important characteristic of a follower may be the willingness to tell the truth.[31]

Effective followers also distinguish themselves by their enthusiasm and commitment to the organization and to a person or purpose—an idea, a product—other than themselves or their own interests. They master skills that are useful to their organizations, and they hold performance standards that are higher than required. Effective followers may not get the glory, but they know their contributions to the organization are valuable. And as they make those contributions, they study leaders in preparation for their own leadership roles.[32]

LO3 Identify sources of power in organizations

3 | POWER AND LEADERSHIP

Central to effective leadership is **power**—the ability to influence other people. In organizations, this influence often means the ability to get things done or accomplish one's goals despite resistance from others.

One of the earliest and still most useful approaches to understanding power, offered by French and Raven, suggests that leaders have the five important potential sources of power shown in Exhibit 10.1:[33]

1. *Legitimate power*—A leader with legitimate power has the right, or the authority, to tell others what to do; employees are obligated to comply with legitimate orders. For example, a supervisor tells an employee to update the company's website, and the employee updates the website because he has to obey the boss's authority. In contrast, when a staff person lacks the authority to give an order to a line manager, the staff person has no legitimate power over the manager. As you might guess, managers have more legitimate power over their direct reports than they do over their peers, bosses, and others inside or outside their organizations.[34]

Exhibit 10.1	Sources of power in organizations
Source of Power	**Example of How Source of Power Is Used in Organizations**
Legitimate	Your supervisor asks you to work an extra shift and you comply.
Reward	The manager gives you a large bonus for exceptional performance.
Coercive	The sales director assigns you to the least profitable accounts.
Referent	Your boss is a really great person, so you're willing to work hard for her.
Expert	The marketing team leader is very experienced, so you listen to him.

Source: Adapted from J. R. P. French and B. Raven, "The Bases of Social Power," in *Studies in Social Power*, ed. D. Cartwright (Ann Arbor, MI: Institute for Social Research, 1959).

2. *Reward power*—The leader who has reward power influences others because she controls valued rewards; people comply with the leader's wishes to receive those rewards. For example, a manager works hard to achieve her performance goals and get a positive performance review and a big pay raise from her boss. In contrast, if company policy dictates that everyone receive the same salary increase, a leader's reward power decreases, because he or she is unable to give higher raises.

3. *Coercive power*—A leader with coercive power has control over punishments; people comply to avoid those punishments. For instance, a manager implements an absenteeism policy that administers disciplinary actions to offending employees. A manager has less coercive power if, say, a union contract limits her ability to punish.

4. *Referent power*—A leader with referent power has personal characteristics that appeal to others; people comply because of admiration, personal liking, a desire for approval, or a desire to be like the leader. For example, young, ambitious managers emulate the work habits and personal style of a successful, charismatic executive. An executive who is incompetent, disliked, and commands little respect has little referent power.

5. *Expert power*—A leader who has expert power has certain expertise or knowledge; people comply because they believe in, can learn from, or can otherwise gain from that expertise. For example, a sales manager gives his salespeople some tips on how to close a deal. The salespeople then alter their sales techniques because they respect the manager's expertise. However, this manager may lack expert power in other areas, such as finance, so his salespeople may ignore his advice concerning financial matters.

People who are in a position that gives them the right to tell others what to do, who can reward and punish, who are well liked and admired, and who have expertise on which other people can draw will be powerful members of the organization. All of these sources of power are potentially important. In general, lower-level managers have less

legitimate, coercive, and reward power than do middle- and higher-level managers.[35] But although it is easy to assume that the most powerful bosses are those who have high legitimate power and control major rewards and punishments, it is important not to underestimate the more "personal" sources like expert and referent power.[37]

● *Fortune's* 2013 Business Person of the Year, Elon Musk is making history. Since co-founding PayPal, he has achieved unprecedented success with Tesla Motors (an all-electric auto manufacturer) and Space Exploration Technologies (SpaceX). Next, Musk wants to build a "hyperloop" ultra-high-speed train between Los Angeles and San Francisco.[36]

4 | TRADITIONAL APPROACHES TO UNDERSTANDING LEADERSHIP

There are three traditional approaches to studying leadership: the trait approach, the behavioral approach, and the situational approach.

4.1 | Certain Traits May Set Leaders Apart

The **trait approach** is the oldest leadership perspective; it focuses on individual leaders and tries to determine the personal characteristics (traits) that great leaders share. What set Mahatma Gandhi, Margaret Thatcher, Theodore Roosevelt, and Martin Luther King Jr. apart from the crowd? The trait approach assumes the existence of a leadership personality and that leaders are born, not made.

From 1904 to 1948, researchers conducted more than 100 leadership trait studies.[38] At the end of that period, management scholars concluded that no particular set of traits is necessary for a person to become a successful leader. Enthusiasm for the trait approach diminished, but some research on traits continued. By the mid-1970s, a more balanced view emerged: although no traits *ensure* leadership

Traditional Thinking

Leaders are born, not made.

The Best Managers Today

Seek leadership experiences to develop their business knowledge, self-confidence, and leadership skills.

success, certain characteristics are potentially useful. The current perspective is that some personality characteristics—many of which a person need not be born with but can strive to acquire—do distinguish effective leaders from other people:[39]

1. *Drive*. Drive refers to a set of characteristics that reflect a high level of effort, including high need for achievement, constant striving for improvement, ambition, energy, tenacity (persistence in the face of obstacles), and initiative. In several countries, the achievement needs of top executives have been shown to be related to the growth rates of their organizations.[40] But the need to achieve can be a drawback if leaders focus on personal achievement and get so involved with the work that they do not delegate enough authority and responsibility. Also, while need for achievement predicts organizational effectiveness in entrepreneurial firms, it does not predict success for division heads in larger and more bureaucratic firms.[41]

● Shown here in 1982, Margaret Thatcher served as prime minister of the United Kingdom from 1979–1990. Known as the "Iron Lady," Thatcher is the only woman to have held that position.

2. *Leadership motivation*. Great leaders *want* to lead. So it helps to be *extraverted*—extraversion is consistently related to leadership emergence and leadership effectiveness.[42] Also important is a high need for power, a preference to be in leadership rather than follower positions.[43] A high power need induces people to try influencing others and sustains interest and satisfaction in the leadership process. When the power need is exercised in moral and socially constructive ways, leaders inspire more trust, respect, and commitment to their vision.

3. *Integrity*. Integrity is the correspondence between actions and words. Honesty and credibility, in addition to being desirable characteristics in their own right, are especially important for leaders because these traits inspire trust in others.

4. *Self-confidence*. Self-confidence is important because the leadership role is challenging, and setbacks are inevitable. A self-confident leader overcomes obstacles, makes decisions despite uncertainty, and instills confidence in others. Of course you don't want to overdo this; arrogance and cockiness have triggered more than one leader's downfall.

5. *Knowledge of the business*. Effective leaders have a high level of knowledge about their industries, companies, and technical matters. Leaders must have the intelligence to interpret vast quantities of information. Advanced degrees are useful in a career, but ultimately they are less important than acquired expertise in matters relevant to the organization.[44]

:::::::::::::::

While the best business leaders from China, India, and the United States exhibit many of these traits, their leadership styles are often heavily influenced by their cultures. Some American CEOs have been criticized for being more concerned about short-term financial and stock performance than long-term growth and internal employee management issues. For example, when CEOs announce a major layoff, there is usually a short-term bounce in their firms' stock prices. Longer-term consequences of drastic workforce reductions often include lower employee morale, high voluntary turnover of valued employees, and reduced organizational performance.

In contrast, many Indian business leaders focus less on short-term financial metrics and more on long-term growth and performance, and on maintaining stable employment. According to Rajesh Hukku, founder of financial services software firm i-flex Solutions (acquired by Oracle), ". . . Indian leaders do not ascribe to the 'hire and fire policy' which is prevalent in the U.S. Indian leaders look at their people as long-term assets . . . "and" . . . it is about taking a longer-term view versus a quarter-by-quarter view." This difference in leadership style is partly explained by the fact that laid-off workers lack a safety net (unemployment or Social Security system) in India.

Like their American and Indian counterparts, Chinese business leaders exhibit cultural tendencies common to their country. For example, Chinese leaders engage in *guanxi*, which is loosely defined as friendship with the expectation that favors will be continually exchanged ("who you know, not what you know"). While relationship building is important for American leaders, Chinese leaders tend to rely more heavily on the norm of reciprocity. Also, Chinese leaders operate from a position of national pride, careful to maintain their country's honor and reputation. Many seek and are comfortable exerting personal power. Ren Zhengfei, known as the "Telecom Titan," is founder and head of telecom equipment maker Huawei. A global firm with 87,500 employees, Huawei's goal is to build a culture with an aggressive "wolf spirit" in order to compete against global giants Alcatel-Lucent, Ericsson, and Nokia Siemens. Zhengfei follows a no-nonsense military style of leadership and asks each new Chinese employee who joins his firm to take an oath on "Duty, Honor, Company, and Country."

What is the bottom line? Leaders from different cultures share many traits but also exhibit attitudes, behaviors, and beliefs that have been shaped by their unique cultures.[46]

••••••••••••••••••

Finally, there is one personal skill that may be the most important: the ability to perceive the needs and goals of others and to adjust one's personal leadership approach accordingly.[47] Effective leaders do not rely on one leadership style; rather, they are capable of using different styles as the situation warrants.[48] This quality is the cornerstone of the situational approaches to leadership, which we will discuss shortly.

4.2 | Certain Behaviors May Make Leaders Effective

The **behavioral approach** to leadership tries to identify what good leaders do. Should leaders focus on getting the job done or on keeping their followers happy? Should they make decisions autocratically or democratically? The behavioral approach downplays personal characteristics in favor of the actual behaviors that leaders exhibit. Studies of leadership behavior have considered the degree to which leaders emphasize task performance versus group maintenance and the extent to which leaders invite employee participation in decision making.

Task Performance and Group Maintenance Leadership requires getting the job done. **Task performance behaviors** are the leader's efforts to ensure that the work unit or organization reaches its goals. This dimension is variously referred to as *concern for production, directive leadership, initiating*

● Effective leaders need to exhibit both task performance and group maintenance behaviors.

structure, or *closeness of supervision.* It includes a focus on work speed, quality and accuracy, quantity of output, and following the rules.[49] This type of leader behavior improves leader job performance and group and organizational performance.[50]

In exhibiting **group maintenance behaviors**, leaders take action to ensure the satisfaction of group members, develop and maintain harmonious work relationships, and preserve the group's social stability. This dimension is sometimes referred to as *concern for people, supportive leadership,* or *consideration.* It includes a focus on people's feelings and comfort, appreciation of them, and stress reduction.[51] This type of leader behavior has a strong positive impact on follower satisfaction and motivation and also on leader effectiveness.[52]

What *specific* behaviors do performance- and maintenance-oriented leadership imply? To help answer this question, assume you have been asked to rate your boss on these two dimensions. If a leadership study were conducted in your organization, you would be asked to fill out a questionnaire in which you answer questions like those listed in Exhibit 10.2.

Leader–member exchange (LMX) theory highlights the importance of leader behaviors not just toward the group as a whole but toward individuals on a personal basis.[53] The focus in the original formulation, which has since been expanded, is primarily on the leader behaviors historically considered group maintenance.[54] According to LMX theory, and as supported by research evidence, maintenance behaviors such as trust, open communication, mutual respect, mutual obligation, and mutual loyalty form the cornerstone of relationships that are satisfying and perhaps more productive.[55]

Remember, though, the potential for cross-cultural differences. Maintenance behaviors are important everywhere, but the specific behaviors can differ from one culture to another. For example, in the United States, maintenance behaviors include dealing with people face-to-face; in Japan, written memos are preferred over giving directions in person, thus avoiding confrontation and permitting face-saving in the event of disagreement.[57]

Exhibit 10.2 — Relating to your boss's leadership style

If your boss exhibits *task performance* leadership behaviors, then…

Be detailed and specific when providing verbal updates and written reports about the project.

Follow instructions and when there is a change to the original plan, clear it with your boss.

Expect your boss to closely monitor your work. Be responsive and don't take it personally.

Be prepared for constructive criticism and encouragement to do the best job possible.

Provide your boss with frequent updates about your progress on the project.

Deliver the finished project on time. Don't miss the deadline or ask for an extension.

If you boss displays *group maintenance* behaviors, then…

Share more freely about personal challenges you are facing at work.

Expect your boss to ask for your opinion about how to solve challenges at work.

Try to be a good team player and seek a consensus with others on key decisions.

Expect your boss to treat you and your co-workers in a fair and consistent manner.

Communicate in an open and transparent manner with others in the work environment.

Do not be surprised if your boss takes a personal interest in your growth and development.

Give credit to team members for helping with projects and problem solving.

Sources: Adapted from J. Misumi and M. Peterson, "The Performance-Maintenance (PM) Theory of Leadership: Review of a Japanese Research Program," *Administrative Science Quarterly* 30, June 1985, pp. 199–223; T. Judge, R. Piccolo, and R. Ilies, "The Forgotten Ones? The Validity of Consideration and Initiating Structure in Leadership Research," *Journal of Applied Psychology* 89 (2004), pp. 36–51; T. Hammer and J. Turk, "Organizational Determinants of Leader Behavior and Authority," *Journal of Applied Psychology* 72 (1987), pp. 674–683.

> "The reality is that leaders must, on the spur of the moment, be able to react rapidly and grasp opportunities."[56]
>
> —AnneMulcahy, Former CEO of Xerox

Participation in Decision Making How should a leader make decisions? More specifically, to what extent should leaders involve their people in making decisions?[58] As a dimension of leadership behavior, *participation in decision making* can range from autocratic to democratic:

- **Autocratic leadership** makes decisions and then announces them to the group.

- **Democratic leadership** solicits input from others. Democratic leadership seeks information, opinions, and preferences, sometimes to the point of meeting with the group, leading discussions, and using consensus or majority vote to make the final choice.

Effects of Leader Behavior How the leader behaves influences people's attitudes and performance. Studies of these effects focus on autocratic versus democratic decision styles or on performance- versus maintenance-oriented behaviors.

Decision styles. The classic study comparing autocratic and democratic styles found that a democratic approach resulted in the most positive attitudes, but an autocratic approach resulted in somewhat higher performance.[59] A **laissez-faire** style, in which the leader essentially made no decisions, led to more negative attitudes and lower performance. These results seem logical and probably represent the prevalent beliefs among managers about the general effects of these approaches.

Democratic styles, appealing though they may seem, are not always the most appropriate. When speed is of the essence, democratic decision making may be too slow, or people may want decisiveness from the leader.[60] Whether a decision should be made autocratically or democratically depends on the characteristics of the leader, the followers, and the situation.[61] Thus a situational approach to leader decision styles, discussed later in the chapter, is appropriate.

Performance and maintenance behaviors. The performance and maintenance dimensions of leadership are independent of each other. In other words, a leader can behave in ways that emphasize one, both, or neither of these dimensions. Some research indicates that the ideal combination is to engage in both types of leader behaviors.

A team of Ohio State University researchers investigated the effects of leader behaviors in a truck manufacturing plant of International Harvester.[62] Generally, supervisors scoring high on *maintenance behaviors* (which the researchers termed *consideration*) had fewer grievances and less turnover in their work units than supervisors who were low on this dimension. The opposite held for *task performance behaviors* (called

initiating structure). Supervisors high on this dimension had more grievances and higher turnover rates.

When maintenance and performance leadership behaviors were considered together, the results were more complex. But one conclusion was clear: when a leader rates high on performance-oriented behaviors, he or she should also be maintenance oriented. Otherwise the leader will face high levels of employee turnover and grievances.

At about the same time the Ohio State studies were being conducted, a research program at the University of Michigan was studying the impact of the same leader behaviors on groups' job performance.[63] Among other things, the researchers concluded that the most effective managers engaged in what they called *task-oriented behavior:* planning, scheduling, coordinating, providing resources, and setting performance goals. Effective managers also exhibited more *relationship-oriented behavior:* demonstrating trust and confidence, being friendly and considerate, showing appreciation, keeping people informed, and so on. As you can see, these dimensions of leader behavior are essentially the task performance and group maintenance dimensions.

After the Ohio State and Michigan findings were published, it became popular to talk about the ideal leader as one who is always both performance and maintenance oriented. The best-known leadership training model to follow this style is Blake and Mouton's Leadership Grid®.[64] In grid training, managers are rated on their performance-oriented behavior (called *concern for production*) and maintenance-oriented behavior *(concern for people).* Then their scores are plotted on the grid shown in Exhibit 10.3. The highest score is a 9 on both dimensions. Managers who score less than a 9,9—for example, those who are high on concern for people but low on concern for production—would then receive training on how to become a 9,9 leader.

For a long time, grid training was warmly received by U.S. business and industry. Later, however, it was criticized for embracing a simplistic, one-best-way style of leadership and ignoring the possibility that 9,9 is not best under all circumstances. For example, even 1,1 leadership can be appropriate if employees know their jobs (so they don't need to receive directions). Also, they may enjoy their jobs and coworkers enough that they do not care whether the boss shows personal concern for them. Still, if the manager is uncertain how to behave, it probably is best to exhibit behaviors that are related to both task performance and group maintenance.[65]

In fact, a wide range of effective leadership styles exists. Organizations that understand the need for diverse leadership styles will have a competitive advantage in the modern business environment over those in which managers believe there is only "one best way."

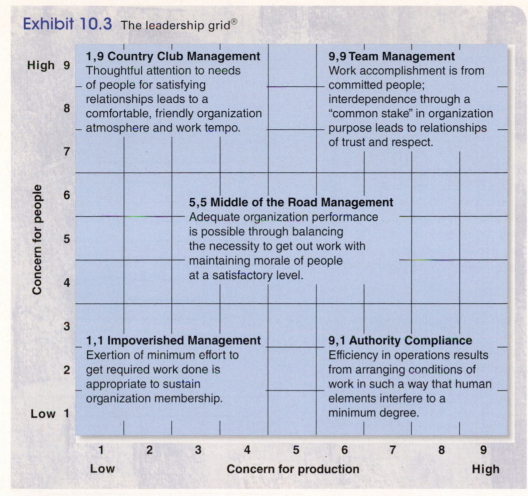

Exhibit 10.3 The leadership grid®

High 9 | **1,9 Country Club Management**
Thoughtful attention to needs of people for satisfying relationships leads to a comfortable, friendly organization atmosphere and work tempo.

9,9 Team Management
Work accomplishment is from committed people; interdependence through a "common stake" in organization purpose leads to relationships of trust and respect.

5,5 Middle of the Road Management
Adequate organization performance is possible through balancing the necessity to get out work with maintaining morale of people at a satisfactory level.

1,1 Impoverished Management
Exertion of minimum effort to get required work done is appropriate to sustain organization membership.

9,1 Authority Compliance
Efficiency in operations results from arranging conditions of work in such a way that human elements interfere to a minimum degree.

Concern for people

Low 1

1   2   3   4   5   6   7   8   9
Low   Concern for production   High

Source: The Blake Mouton Managerial Grid from MindTools.com. Reproduced with permission.

4.3 | The Best Way to Lead Depends on the Situation

According to proponents of the **situational approach** to leadership, universally important traits and behaviors don't exist. Rather, effective leader behaviors vary from situation to situation. *The leader should first analyze the situation and then decide what to do.* In other words, look before you lead.

A head nurse in a hospital described her situational approach to leadership this way: "My leadership style is a mix of all styles. In this environment I normally let people participate. But in a code blue situation where a patient is dying I automatically become very autocratic: 'You do this; you do that; you, out of the room; you all better be quiet; you, get Dr. Mansfield.' The staff tell me that's the only time they see me like that. In an emergency like that, you don't have time to vote, talk a lot, or yell at each other. It's time for someone to set up the order.

"I remember one time, one person saying, 'Wait a minute, I want to do this.' He wanted to do the mouth-to-mouth resuscitation. I knew the person behind him did it better, so I said, 'No, he does it.' This fellow told me later that I hurt him so badly to yell that in front of all the staff and doctors. It was like he wasn't good enough. So I explained it to him: that's the way it is. A life was on the line. I couldn't give you warm fuzzies. I couldn't make you look good because you didn't have the skills to give the very best to that patient who wasn't breathing anymore."[66] This nurse has her own intuitive situational approach to leadership. She knows the potential advantages of the participatory approach to decision making, but she also knows that in some circumstances she must make decisions herself.

The first situational model of leadership was proposed in 1958 by Tannenbaum and Schmidt. In their classic *Harvard Business Review* article, these authors described how managers should consider three factors before deciding how to lead:[67]

1. *Forces in the manager* include the manager's personal values, inclinations, feelings of security, and confidence in subordinates.

2. *Forces in the subordinate* include his or her knowledge and experience, readiness to assume responsibility for decision making, interest in the task or problem, and understanding and acceptance of the organization's goals.

3. *Forces in the situation* include the type of leadership style the organization values, the degree to which the group works effectively as a unit, the problem itself and the type of information needed to solve it, and the amount of time the leader has to make the decision.

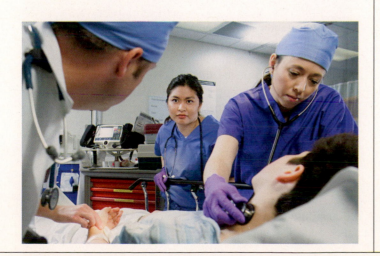

Vroom model a situational model that focuses on the participative dimension of leadership

Fiedler's contingency model of leadership effectiveness a situational approach to leadership postulating that effectiveness depends on the personal style of the leader and the degree to which the situation gives the leader power, control, and influence over the situation

Consider which of these forces makes an autocratic style most appropriate and which dictates a democratic, participative style. By engaging in this exercise, you are constructing a situational theory of leadership.

Although the Tannenbaum and Schmidt article was published a half century ago, most of its arguments remain valid. Since that time, other situational models have emerged. We will focus here on four: the Vroom model for decision making, Fiedler's contingency model, Hersey and Blanchard's situational theory, and path–goal theory.

The Vroom Model of Leadership

In the tradition of Tannenbaum and Schmidt, the **Vroom model** emphasizes the participative dimension of leadership: how leaders go about making decisions. The model uses the basic situational approach of assessing the situation before determining the best leadership style.[68] The following situational factors are used to analyze problems:[69]

- *Decision significance*—The significance of the decision to the success of the project or organization.

- *Importance of commitment*—The importance of team members' commitment to the decision.

- *Leader's expertise*—Your knowledge or expertise in relation to this problem.

- *Likelihood of commitment*—The likelihood that the team would commit itself to a decision that you might make on your own.

- *Group support for objectives*—The degree to which the team supports the organization's objectives at stake in this problem.

- *Group expertise*—Team members' knowledge or expertise in relation to this problem.

- *Team competence*—The ability of team members to work together in solving problems.

Each of these factors is based on an important attribute of the problem the leader faces and should be assessed as either high or low.

The Vroom model, shown in Exhibit 10.4, operates like a funnel. You answer the questions one at a time, choosing high or low for each, sometimes skipping questions as you follow the appropriate path. Eventually you reach one of 14 possible endpoints. For each endpoint, the model states which of five decision styles is most appropriate. Several different decision styles may work, but the style recommended is the one that takes the least time.

The five leader decision styles are defined in Exhibit 10.5.

Exhibit 10.4 Vroom's model of leadership

Time-Driven Model

Instructions: The matrix operates like a funnel. You start at the left with a specific decision problem in mind. The column headings denote situational factors which may or may not be present in that problem. You progress by selecting high or low (H or L) for each relevant situational factor. Proceed down from the funnel, judging only those situational factors for which a judgement is called for, until you reach the recommended process.

Left vertical label: **PROBLEM STATEMENT**

Decision Significance	Importance of Commitment	Leader Expertise	Likelihood of Commitment	Group Support	Group Expertise	Team Competence	
H	H	H	H	–	–	–	Decide
			L	H	H	H	Delegate
						L	Consult (Group)
					L	–	Consult (Group)
				L	–	–	Consult (Group)
		L	H	H	H	H	Facilitate
						L	Consult (Individually)
					L	–	Consult (Individually)
				L	–	–	Consult (Individually)
			L	H	H	H	Facilitate
						L	Consult (Group)
					L	–	Consult (Group)
				L	–	–	Consult (Group)
	L	H	–	–	–	–	Decide
		L		H	H	H	Facilitate
						L	Consult (Individually)
					L	–	Consult (Individually)
				L	–	–	Consult (Individually)
L	H	–	H	–	–	–	Decide
			L	–	–	H	Delegate
						L	Facilitate
	L	–	–	–	–	–	Decide

Source: Adapted from *Leadership and Decision-Making*, by Victori H. Vroom and Philip W. Yetton, © 1973. Reprinted by permission of the University of Pittsburgh Press.

The styles indicate that there are several shades of participation, not just autocratic or democratic.

Of course not every managerial decision warrants this complicated analysis. But the model becomes less complex after you work through it a couple of times. Also, using the model for major decisions ensures that you consider the important situational factors and alerts you to the most appropriate style to use.

Fiedler's Contingency Model

According to **Fiedler's contingency model of leadership effectiveness,** effectiveness depends on two factors: the personal style of the leader and the degree to which the situation gives the leader power, control, and influence over the situation.[70] Exhibit 10.6 illustrates this model. The upper half of the exhibit shows the situational

Exhibit 10.5 Vroom's leader decision styles

1. **Decide.** You make the decision alone and either announce or "sell" it to the group. You may collect information relevant to the problem from the group or others.

2. **One-on-one consultation.** You meet individually with group members, get their suggestions, and then make a decision.

3. **Consult the group.** You present the problem to the group members in a meeting, get their suggestions, and then make a decision.

4. **Facilitate.** You present the problem to the group at a meeting, provide boundaries within which the decision must be made, and facilitate the decision-making process in an unbiased manner until consensus is reached.

5. **Delegate.** You encourage the group to make the decision within prescribed limits. Members identify the problem, and develop and evaluate alternative solutions. Your role is behind the scenes, providing resources and encouragement.

Source: Adapted from V. H. Vroom, "Leadership and the Decision-Making Process," *Organizational Dynamics,* Spring 2000, pp. 82–93. Copyright © 2000 with permission from Elsevier Science.

analysis, and the lower half indicates the appropriate style. In the upper portion, three questions are used to analyze the situation:

1. Are leader–member relations good or poor? (To what extent is the leader accepted and supported by group members?)

2. Is the task structured or unstructured? (To what extent do group members know what their goals are and how to accomplish them?)

3. Is the leader's position power strong or weak (high or low)? (To what extent does the leader have the authority to reward and punish?)

These three sequential questions create a decision tree (from top to bottom in the exhibit) in which a situation is classified into one of eight categories. The lower the category number, the more favorable the situation is for the leader; the higher the number, the less favorable the situation. Fiedler originally called this variable "situational favorableness" but now it is "situational control." Situation 1 is the best: relations are good, task structure is high, and power is high. In the least favorable situation (8), in which the leader has very little situational control, relations are poor, tasks lack structure, and the leader's power is weak.

Different situations dictate different leadership styles. Fiedler measured leadership styles with an instrument assessing the leader's *least preferred coworker* (LPC)—that is, the attitude toward the follower the leader liked the least. This was considered an indication more generally of leaders' attitudes toward people. If a leader can single out the person she likes the least, but her attitude is not all that negative, she receives a high score on the LPC scale. Leaders with more negative attitudes toward others would receive low LPC scores. Based on the LPC score, Fiedler considered two leadership styles:

1. **Task-motivated leadership** places primary emphasis on completing the task and is more likely exhibited by leaders with low LPC scores.

2. **Relationship-motivated leadership** emphasizes maintaining good interpersonal relationships and is more likely from high-LPC leaders.

task-motivated leadership leadership that places primary emphasis on completing a task

relationship-motivated leadership leadership that places primary emphasis on maintaining good interpersonal relationships

Exhibit 10.6 Fiedler's analysis of situations in which the task- or relationship-motivated leader is more effective

Leader–member relations	Good				Poor			
Task structure	Structured		Unstructured		Structured		Unstructured	
Leader position power	High	Low	High	Low	High	Low	High	Low
	1	2	3	4	5	6	7	8

Favorable for leader →→→→→→ Unfavorable for leader

Type of leader most effective in the situation	Task-motivated	Task-motivated	Task-motivated	Relationship-motivated	Relationship-motivated	Relationship-motivated	Relationship-motivated	Task-motivated

Source: *From D. Organ and T. Bateman, Organizational Behavior 4E, McGraw-Hill. Copyright © 1990.*

Hersey and Blanchard's situational theory a life cycle theory of leadership postulating that a manager should consider an employee's psychological and job maturity before deciding whether task performance or maintenance behaviors are more important

job maturity the level of the employee's skills and technical knowledge relative to the task being performed

psychological maturity an employee's self-confidence and self-respect

path–goal theory a theory that concerns how leaders influence subordinates' perceptions of their work goals and the paths they follow toward attainment of those goals

These leadership styles correspond to task performance and group maintenance leader behaviors, respectively.

The lower part of Exhibit 10.6 indicates which style is situationally appropriate. For situations 1, 2, 3, and 8, a task-motivated leadership style is more effective. For situations 4 through 7, relationship-motivated leadership is more appropriate.

Fiedler's theory was not always supported by research. It is better supported if we replace the eight specific levels of situational control with three broad levels: low, medium, and high. The theory was controversial in academic circles, partly because it assumed leaders cannot change their styles but must be assigned to situations that suit their styles. However, the model has withstood the test of time and still receives attention. Most important, it brought a focus on the significance of finding a fit between the situation and the leader's style.

Hersey and Blanchard's Situational Theory

Hersey and Blanchard developed a situational model that added another factor the leader should take into account before deciding whether task performance or maintenance behaviors are more important. In their **situational theory,** originally called the *life-cycle theory of leadership,* the key situational factor is the maturity of the followers.[71] **Job maturity** is the level of the followers' skills and technical knowledge relative to the task being performed; **psychological maturity** is the followers' self-confidence and self-respect. High-maturity followers have the ability and the confidence to do a good job.

The theory proposes that the more mature the followers, the less the leader needs to engage in task performance behaviors. Maintenance behaviors are not important with followers with low or high maturity but are important for followers of moderate maturity. For low-maturity followers, the emphasis should be on performance-related leadership; for moderate-maturity followers, performance leadership is somewhat less important and maintenance behaviors become more important; and for high-maturity followers, neither dimension of leadership behavior is important.

Little academic research has been done on this situational theory, but the model is popular in management training seminars. Regardless of its scientific validity, Hersey and Blanchard's model provides a reminder that it is important to treat different people differently. Also, it suggests the importance of treating the same individual differently from time to time as he or she changes jobs or acquires more maturity in her or his particular job.[72]

Path–Goal Theory Perhaps the most comprehensive and generally useful situational model of leadership effectiveness is path–goal theory. Developed by Robert House, **path–goal theory** gets its name from its concern with how leaders influence followers' perceptions of their work goals and the paths they follow toward goal attainment.[73]

Path–goal theory has two key situational factors:

1. Personal characteristics of followers.

2. Environmental pressures and demands with which followers must cope to attain their work goals.

These factors determine which leadership behaviors are most appropriate.

The theory identifies four pertinent leadership behaviors:

1. *Directive leadership,* a form of task performance-oriented behavior.

2. *Supportive leadership,* a form of group maintenance-oriented behavior.

3. *Participative leadership,* or decision style.

4. *Achievement-oriented leadership,* or behaviors geared toward motivating people, such as setting challenging goals and rewarding good performance.

These situational factors and leader behaviors are merged in Exhibit 10.7. As you can see, appropriate leader behaviors—as determined by characteristics of followers and the work environment—lead to effective performance.

The theory also specifies *which* follower and environmental characteristics are important. Three key follower characteristics determine the appropriateness of various leadership styles:

1. *Authoritarianism* is the degree to which individuals respect, admire, and defer to authority. Path–goal theory suggests that leaders should use a directive leadership style with subordinates who are highly authoritarian because such people respect decisiveness.

2. *Locus of control* is the extent to which individuals see events as under their control. People with an internal locus of control believe that what happens to them is their own doing; people with an external locus of control believe that it is luck or fate. For subordinates who have an internal locus of control, a participative leadership style is appropriate because these individuals prefer to have more influence over their own lives.

3. *Ability* is people's beliefs about their own capabilities to do their assigned jobs. When subordinates' ability is low, a directive style will help them understand what has to be done.

Appropriate leadership style is also determined by three important environmental factors:

- *Tasks*—Directive leadership is inappropriate if tasks already are well structured.

- *Formal authority system*—If the task and the authority or rule system are dissatisfying, directive leadership will create greater dissatisfaction. If the task or authority system is dissatisfying, supportive leadership is especially appropriate because it offers one positive source of gratification in an otherwise negative situation.

- *Primary work group*—If the primary work group provides social support to its members, supportive leadership is less important.

Path–goal theory offers many more propositions. In general, the theory suggests that the functions of the leader are to (1) make the path to work goals easier to travel by providing coaching and direction, (2) reduce frustrating barriers to goal attainment, and (3) increase opportunities for personal satisfaction by increasing payoffs to people for achieving performance goals. The best way to do these things depends on your people and on the work situation. Again, analyze, and then adapt your style accordingly.

Substitutes for Leadership Sometimes leaders don't have to lead, or situations constrain their ability to lead effectively. The situation may be one in which leadership is unnecessary or has little impact. **Substitutes for leadership** can provide the same influence on people as leaders otherwise would have.

Certain follower, task, and organizational factors are substitutes for task performance and group maintenance leader behaviors.[74] For example, group maintenance behaviors are less important and have less impact if people already have a closely knit group, they have a professional orientation, the job is inherently satisfying, or there is great physical distance between leader and followers. So physicians who are strongly concerned with professional conduct, enjoy their work, and work independently do not need social support from hospital administrators.

Task performance leadership is less important and will have less of a positive effect if people have a lot of experience and ability, feedback is supplied to them directly from the task or by computer, or the rules and procedures are rigid. If these factors are operating, the leader does not have to tell people what to do or how well they are performing.

The concept of substitutes for leadership does more than indicate when a leader's attempts at influence will and will not work. It provides useful and practical prescriptions for how to manage more efficiently.[75] If the manager can develop the work situation to the point where a number of these substitutes for leadership are operating, the leader can spend less time attempting to influence people and will have more time for other important activities.

Research indicates that substitutes for leadership may be better predictors of commitment and satisfaction than of performance.[76] These substitutes are helpful, but you can't put substitutes in place and think you have completed your job as leader. And as a follower, consider this: If you're not getting good leadership, and if these substitutes are not in place, create your own "substitute" for leadership—self-leadership. Take the initiative to motivate yourself, lead yourself, create positive change, and lead others.

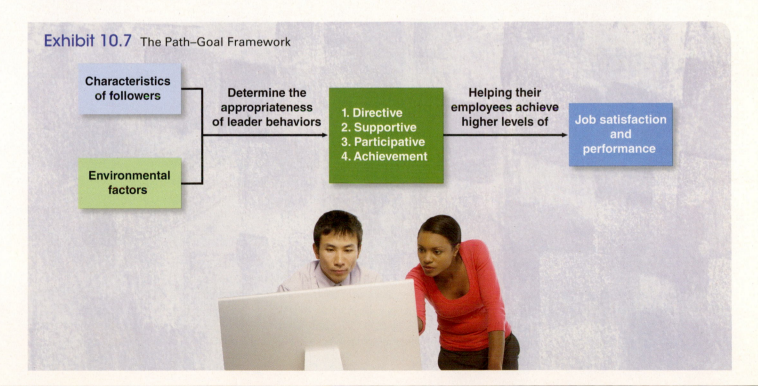

Exhibit 10.7 The Path–Goal Framework

Characteristics of followers / Environmental factors → Determine the appropriateness of leader behaviors → 1. Directive 2. Supportive 3. Participative 4. Achievement → Helping their employees achieve higher levels of → Job satisfaction and performance

5 | CONTEMPORARY PERSPECTIVES ON LEADERSHIP

So far, you have learned the major classic approaches to understanding leadership, all of which remain useful today. Several new developments are revolutionizing our understanding of this vital aspect of management.

5.1 | Charismatic Leaders Inspire Their Followers

Like many great leaders, Ronald Reagan had charisma. So does Barack Obama. In business, Oprah Winfrey, Thomas Watson, Indra Nooyi, Alexis Ohanian, and Richard Branson also have been charismatic leaders.

Charisma is an elusive concept—easy to spot but hard to define. What *is* charisma, and how does one acquire it?

According to one definition, "Charisma packs an emotional wallop for followers above and beyond ordinary esteem, affection, admiration, and trust . . . The charismatic is an idolized hero, a messiah and a savior."[77] Many people, particularly North Americans, value charisma in their leaders. But some people don't like the term *charisma;* it can be associated with the negative charisma of evil leaders whom people follow blindly.[78] Yet charismatic leaders who display appropriate values and use their charisma for appropriate purposes serve as ethical role models for others.[79]

Charismatic leaders are dominant and exceptionally self-confident, and they have a strong conviction in the moral righteousness of their beliefs.[80] They strive to create an aura of competence and success and communicate high expectations for and confidence in followers. Ultimately, charismatic leaders satisfy other people's needs.[81]

The charismatic leader articulates ideological goals and makes sacrifices in pursuit of those goals.[82] Martin Luther King Jr. had a dream for a better world, and John F. Kennedy spoke of landing a human on the moon. In other words, such leaders have a compelling vision. The charismatic leader also arouses a sense of excitement and adventure. He or she is an eloquent speaker who exhibits superior verbal skills, which help communicate the vision and motivate followers. Walt

Organizations Earn Prestigious Green Leadership Award

Each year, the U.S. Environmental Protection Agency (EPA) chooses a small number of organizations to receive the "Green Power Partner of the Year" award. This award recognizes organizations that distinguish themselves through their green power use, leadership, overall strategy, and impact on the green power market. The 2013 award winners were Cisco Systems, Georgetown University, Microsoft Corporation, and Ohio State University.

Cisco Systems, a worldwide leader in networking, realizes that green power plays a critical role in the company's environmental sustainability strategy. Not only has Cisco set aggressive emission reduction goals for the next three years, it has convinced more than 80 percent of its vendors, business partners, and supply chain to join in the green effort. Recently, the company launched a "Cisco Green" online community to boost employee enthusiasm for green initiatives and to recognize green champions within the company.

Committed to reducing its carbon footprint by 50 percent by 2020, Georgetown University cut emissions by 20 percent "through a combination of demand reduction, efficiency, and use of cleaner fuels." The university's goal is to be a leader in the use of green power, and it joined several universities from around the world when it signed the International Sustainable Campus Charter—a pledge to integrate sustainability into all buildings, operations, and planning.

Microsoft reduced its 2012 carbon emissions by 30 percent by increasing its "energy efficiency initiatives and investments in high-quality, externally-verified renewable energy and carbon reduction projects." In 2013, Microsoft used 73 percent more green power, earning

In 2012, Georgetown Energy secured $50,000 to be directed toward building "Solar Street" on a block of university-owned townhouses. The 18 kW worth of solar photo-voltaic panels reverts electricity savings back to students. Approximately $100,000 in savings is projected over the next 20 years.

it the number 2 spot on the EPA's Top 50 list. The company motivates its managers to be energy efficient by holding them financially accountable for their unit's

● Martin Luther King Jr. was a charismatic leader with a compelling vision: a dream for a better world.

Disney mesmerized people with his storytelling; had enormous creative talent; and instilled in his organization strong values of good taste, risk taking, and innovation.[83]

Leaders who possess these characteristics or do these things inspire in their followers trust, confidence, acceptance, obedience, emotional involvement, affection, admiration, and higher performance.[84] For example, having charisma not only helps CEOs inspire other employees in the organization but also may enable them to influence external stakeholders, including customers and investors.[85] Evidence for the positive effects of charismatic leadership has been found in a wide variety of groups, organizations, and management levels, and in countries including India, Singapore, the Netherlands, China, Nigeria, Japan, and Canada.[86]

Charisma has been shown to improve corporate financial performance, particularly under conditions of uncertainty—that is, in risky circumstances or when environments are changing and people have difficulty understanding what they should do.[87] Uncertainty is stressful, and it makes people more receptive to the ideas and actions of charismatic leaders. By the way, too, as an organization's (or team's) performance improves under a person's leadership, others see that person as increasingly charismatic as a result of the higher performance.[88]

5.2 | Transformational Leaders Revitalize Organizations

Charisma can contribute to transformational leadership. **Transformational leaders** get people to transcend their

charismatic leader a person who is dominant, self-confident, convinced of the moral righteousness of his or her beliefs, and able to arouse a sense of excitement and adventure in followers

transformational leaders leaders who motivate people to transcend their personal interests for the good of the group

emissions of carbon pollution. In this way, Microsoft "encourages employees to reduce emissions while raising funds for energy efficiency and renewable energy projects." Microsoft set the ambitious goal of achieving carbon neutrality for all of its data centers, software development labs, offices, and employee air travel.

Ohio State University, by signing the American College & University Presidents' Climate Commitment in 2008, declared its commitment to climate neutrality. Further, it adopted a Green Build and Energy Policy, which has led to (1) all new construction and major renovations will meet LEED Silver environmental standards and (2) the completion of a 450-well geothermal system to heat and cool residence halls. In addition, the university signed a 20-year agreement to buy 50 megawatts of wind power each year from the Blue Creek Wind Farm in northwestern Ohio. Not only will this help ensure the wind farm's survival, but it also allow the university's researchers to analyze data regarding rotor blade and wind energy markets, soil preservation, and noise optimization.

Discussion Questions

- It takes strong leadership to convince stakeholders to engage in the green initiatives under way at Cisco, Georgetown University, Microsoft, and Ohio State University. Based on your understanding of this chapter, how might leaders at these organizations have persuaded stakeholders to embrace these green initiatives?

- Can green energy eventually make up 100 percent of many organizations' energy usage? What obstacles or challenges do you think will need to be surmounted for this transformation to green energy to occur?

SOURCES: News release, "Green Power Partnership 2013 Award Winners," United States Environmental Protection Agency, www.epa.gov; Company website, www.cisco.com; L. Westergaard, "GU Earns EPA Green Award," *The Hoya* (online), October 1, 2013, www.thehoya.com; and News release, "Ohio State Receives Green Power Partner of the Year Award from U.S. EPA," Office of Energy and Environment, September 23, 2013, http://oee.osu.edu/green-power-partner-2013.html.

transactional leaders leaders who manage through transactions, using their legitimate, reward, and coercive powers to give commands and exchange rewards for services rendered

personal interests for the sake of the larger community.[89] They generate excitement and revitalize organizations. At Google, the ability to generate excitement is an explicit criterion for selecting managers. In the United Kingdom, Richard Branson of Virgin Group is a transformational leader who built a global business empire.[90]

The transformational process moves beyond the more traditional *transactional* approach to leadership. **Transactional leaders** view management as a series of transactions in which they use their legitimate, reward, and coercive powers to give commands and exchange rewards for services rendered. Unlike transformational leadership, transactional leadership is dispassionate; it does not excite, transform, empower, or inspire people to focus on the interests of the group or organization. However, transactional approaches may be more effective for individualists than for collectivists.[91] Also, some managers may use both approaches to leadership, depending on the situation.

Generating Excitement Transformational leaders generate excitement in several ways:[92]

- They are *charismatic,* as described earlier.

- They give their followers *individualized attention.* They delegate challenging work to deserving people, keep lines of communication open, and provide one-on-one mentoring to develop their people. They do not treat everyone alike because not everyone *is* alike.

- They are *intellectually stimulating.* They arouse in their followers an awareness of problems and potential solutions. They articulate the organization's opportunities, threats, strengths, and weaknesses. They stir the imagination and generate insights. As a result, problems are recognized, and high-quality solutions are identified and implemented with the followers' full commitment.

3. *Building trust*—Being consistent, dependable, and persistent, leaders position themselves clearly by choosing a direction and staying with it, thus projecting integrity.

4. *Having positive self-regard*—Leaders do not feel self-important or complacent, but rather recognize their personal strengths, compensate for their weaknesses, nurture and continually develop their talents, and know how to learn from failure. They strive for success rather than merely try to avoid failure.

Transformational leadership has been identified in industry, the military, and politics.[95] Examples of transformational leaders in business include Henry Ford (founder of Ford Motor Company), Herb Kelleher (former CEO of Southwest Airlines), Jeff Bezos (founder of Amazon.com), David Neeleman (in his former role as leader of JetBlue), and Lee Iacocca (who led Chrysler's turnaround during the 1980s).[96] As with studies of charisma, transformational leadership and its positive impact on follower satisfaction and performance have been demonstrated in countries the world over, including India, Egypt, Germany, China, England, and Japan.[97] A study in Korean companies found that transformational leadership predicted employee motivation, which in turn predicted creativity.[98] Under transformational leadership, people view their jobs as more intrinsically motivating (see Chapter 11 for more on this) and are more strongly committed to work goals.[99] And top management teams agree more clearly about important organizational goals, which translates into higher organizational performance.[100]

Transforming Leaders Importantly, transformational leadership is not the exclusive domain of presidents and chief executives. In the military, leaders who received transformational leadership training had a positive impact on followers' personal development. They also were successful as *indirect* leaders: military recruits under the transformational leaders' direct reports were stronger performers.[101] Don't forget, though: the best leaders are those who can display both transformational and transactional behaviors.[102]

> ## "Employees, especially young people, want more than a paycheck ... They want to feel as though their work has meaning."[93]
>
> —Marissa Mayer, CEO of Yahoo!

Skills and Strategies At least four skills or strategies contribute to transformational leadership:[94]

1. *Having a vision*—Leaders have a goal, an agenda, or a results orientation that grabs attention.

2. *Communicating their vision*—Through words, manner, or symbolism, leaders relate a compelling image of the ultimate goal.

Ford Motor Company, in collaboration with the University of Michigan School of Business, put thousands of middle managers through a program designed to stimulate transformational leadership.[103] The training included analysis of the changing business environment, company strategy, and personal reflection and discussion about the need to change. Participants assessed their own leadership styles and developed

● Jeff Bezos, CEO of Amazon, introduced Kindle Fire HD Family during a press conference in Santa Monica, CA.

Chapman's leadership but then plunged as demand dried up.

Chapman reacted by assembling his management team to evaluate what had gone wrong. The group determined that the earlier growth had been "undisciplined," not directed to areas where long-term success would be most likely. The team developed a company vision aimed at balanced and sustainable growth. Since then, says Chapman, the company has "never varied" from "executing our vision with discipline and passion."

The passion comes from a commitment to "people-centric leadership." Under Chapman, B-W managers must care about their employees, give them authority to make important decisions, and clarify how their contributions enhance the company's vision. An Organizational Empowerment Team develops leaders and applies methods such as lean manufacturing through which employees contribute to improved operations.

"We measure success by the way we touch the lives of people" captures Chapman's belief that companies can change the world through their impact on individual employees. "The usual corporate-culture buzzwords, like engagement, productivity, and performance, are self-serving to companies," says Bob Chapman. "We want to release human potential." Challenging employees to contribute to the corporate vision gives them a chance to feel that their efforts matter; recognition programs show them that they are appreciated. The result is what Chapman calls an "inspirational environment." With recent sales revenue of $1.7 billion, the company is realizing its potential, too.[106]

a specific change initiative to implement after the training—a change that would make a needed and lasting difference for the company.

Over the next six months, the managers implemented change on the job. Almost half of the initiatives resulted in transformational changes in the organization or work unit; the rest of the changes were smaller, more incremental, or more personal. Whether managers made small or transformational changes depended on their attitude going into the training, their level of self-esteem, and the amount of support they received from others on the job. Although some managers did not respond as hoped, almost half embraced the training, adopted a more transformational orientation, and tackled significant transformations for the company.

Level 5 leadership, a term well known among executives, is considered by some to be the ultimate leadership style. Level 5 leadership is a combination of strong professional will (determination) and personal humility that builds enduring greatness.[104] Thus a Level 5 leader is relentlessly focused on the organization's long-term success while behaving with modesty, directing attention toward the organization rather than him- or herself. Examples include John Chambers, CEO of Cisco Systems, Darwin E. Smith, ex-CEO of Kimberly Clark, and IBM's former chief executive, Louis Gerstner. Gerstner is widely credited for turning around a stodgy IBM by shifting its focus from computer hardware to business solutions. Following his retirement, Gerstner wrote a memoir that details what happened at the company but says little about himself. Although Level 5 leadership is seen as a way to transform organizations to make them great, it requires first that the leader exhibit a combination of transactional and transformational styles.[105]

Before his 30th birthday, Robert Chapman stepped into the job of chief executive of his family's business, Barry-Wehmiller Companies (B-W), following the sudden death of his father. Revenues at B-W, which makes packaging equipment and sells related services, grew rapidly during the early years of

5.3 | Authentic Leadership Adds an Ethical Dimension

In general, **authentic leadership** is rooted in the ancient Greek philosophy "To thine own self be true."[107] In your own leadership, you should strive for authenticity in the form of honesty, genuineness, reliability, integrity, and trustworthiness. Authentic transformational leaders care about public interests (community, organizational, or group), not just their own.[108] They are willing to sacrifice their own interests for others, and they can be trusted. They are ethically mature; people view leaders who exhibit moral reasoning as more transformational than leaders who do not.[109]

Pseudotransformational leaders are the opposite: they talk a good game, but they ignore followers' real needs as their own self-interests (power, prestige, control, wealth, fame) take precedence.[110]

6 | YOU CAN LEAD

Every organization has plenty of leadership opportunities available. Employees, team leaders, and higher-level managers alike can work with others within the organization to get things done.

6.1 | Today's Organizations Offer Many Opportunities to Lead

A common view of leaders is that they are superheroes acting alone, swooping in to save the day. But especially in these

study tip 10

Lead a Study Group

Study Tip 7 pointed out the benefits of forming a study group. One way to get more out of this experience is for you to take the lead in forming and managing the group, which should help you build servant–leadership and group maintenance leadership skills. The first step might be to recruit three or four students from your class to join the group. Next, ask them when and where they would like to meet. During the first meeting, ask the attendees in which areas of the course they are struggling and what topics they think the group should spend time reviewing. Be sure to make notes of the ideas so you can provide feedback to the members summarizing the group's needs and study objectives. Based on the newly defined direction of the group, ask members what they want to accomplish in the next meeting and then set a date, time, and place to meet.

complex times, leaders cannot and need not act alone. Business guru John Hersey advises today's leader to be a "SAGE." The letters in *sage* remind leaders to *seek out* other people, *ask* good questions that focus on the other person, *get involved* with other people, and *enrich* people's lives. That outward-looking approach helps leaders identify fresh solutions to vexing problems and invites followers to engage fully with the cause.[111]

Effective leadership must permeate the organization, not reside in one or two superstars at the top. The leader's job becomes one of spreading leadership abilities throughout the firm.[112] Make people responsible for their own performance. Create an environment in which each person can figure out what needs to be done and then do it well. Point the way and clear the path so that people can succeed. Give them the credit they deserve. Make heroes out of *them*. Thus what is now required of leaders is less the efficient management of resources and more the effective unleashing of people and their intellectual capital.

This perspective uncovers a variety of nontraditional leadership roles that are emerging as vitally important.[113] The term **servant–leader** was coined by Robert Greenleaf, a retired AT&T executive. The term is paradoxical in the sense that "leader" and "servant" are usually opposites; the servant–leader's relationship with employees is more like that of serving customers. For the humble and accepting individual who wants to both lead and serve others, servant–leadership is a way of relating to others to serve their needs and enhance their personal growth while strengthening the organization.[114] A first step is to ask your employees what problems they have or how you can help them. For example, when David Wolfskehl, founder of Action Fast Print, stopped telling his employees what to do and instead asked how he could help them solve their problems, productivity jumped 30 percent.[115]

A number of other nontraditional roles provide leadership opportunities. **Bridge leaders** are those who leave their cultures for a significant period of time.[116] They live, go to school, travel, or work in other cultures. Then they return home, become leaders, and through their expanded repertoire they serve as bridges between conflicting value systems within their own cultures or between their culture and other cultures.

With work often being team based, **shared leadership** occurs when leadership rotates to the person with the key knowledge, skills, and abilities for the issue facing the team at a particular time.[117] Shared leadership is most important when tasks are interdependent, are complex, and require creativity. High-performing teams engaged in such work exhibit more shared leadership than poor-performing teams. In consulting teams, the greater the shared leadership, the higher their clients rated the teams' performance.[118] The role of formal leader remains important—the formal leader still designs the team, manages its external boundaries, provides task direction, emphasizes the importance of the shared leadership approach, and engages in the transactional and transformational activities described here. But at the same time, the metaphor of geese in V-formation adds strength to the group: the lead goose periodically drops to the back, and another goose moves up and takes its place at the forefront.

Lateral leadership does not involve a hierarchical, superior–subordinate relationship but instead invites colleagues at the same level to solve problems together.[119] You alone can't provide a solution to every problem, but you can create processes through which people work collaboratively. If you can get people working to improve methods collaboratively, you can help create an endless stream of innovations. In other words, it's not about you providing solutions to problems; it's about creating better interpersonal processes for finding solutions. Strategies and tactics can be found throughout this book, including the chapters on decision making, organization structure, teams, communication, and change.

6.2 | Good Leaders Need Courage

To be a good leader, you need the courage to create a vision of greatness for your unit; identify and manage allies, adversaries, and fence sitters; and execute your vision, often against opposition. This does not mean you should commit career suicide by alienating too many powerful people; it does mean taking reasonable risks, with the good of the firm at heart, in order to produce constructive change.

For example, Charles Elachi needed courage when he took the position of director of NASA's Jet Propulsion Laboratories (JPL) at the beginning of the decade, when a series of budget cuts and efforts to cut corners had resulted in two failed attempts to gather data from Mars exploration projects. In that environment, morale was poor, and public support for JPL was weak. But rather than looking for people to blame,

carry out every procedure—and that the agency fund them. In the end, the mission actually exceeded expectations, including finding evidence that salt water had once been present on the planet.[120] Fast forward to today. The most recent phase of the Mars Exploration Program involves having the rover Curiosity explore the Red Planet to investigate whether conditions have been favorable for microbial life. After reaching the surface of Mars on August 6, 2012, via a complex landing procedure, the 10-foot-long robotic geologist has been working diligently to collect and analyze soil and rock samples. About 8 months into its mission, Curiosity fulfilled its major objective of finding evidence of a past environment well suited to supporting microbial life. From its first sample, the rover found "evidence of conditions favorable for life in Mars' early history: geological and mineralogical evidence for sustained liquid water, other key elemental ingredients for life, a chemical energy source, and water not too acidic or too salty."[121]

Specifically, fulfilling your vision will require some of the following acts of courage:[123]

● At the end of 2012, Curiosity's two-year mission was extended indefinitely. In June 2014, Curiosity completed a Martian year (687 Earth days) after finding that Mars once had environmental conditions favorable for microbial life.

servant–leader a leader who serves others' needs while strengthening the organization

bridge leaders leaders who bridge conflicting value systems or different cultures

shared leadership rotating leadership, in which people rotate through the leadership role based on which person has the most relevant skills at a particular time

lateral leadership style in which colleagues at the same hierarchical level are invited to collaborate and facilitate joint problem solving

> "When you connect with a purpose greater than yourself, you are fearless; you think big."
>
> —Nancy Barry, on leaving her executive position at the World Bank to become president of Women's World Banking, which makes microloans to impoverished women around the world.[122]

Elachi, a physicist and JPL veteran, got everyone focused on the ambitious next project, the Mars Exploration Program, that successfully landed two robotic geologists (rovers) named Spirit and Opportunity on Mars' surface in January of 2004. Undaunted by the two previous failures, Elachi clearly but politely communicated to everyone that another failure was out of the question. At the beginning of the project, he had team leaders list every test that would be necessary before the first spacecraft was sent into orbit. Two years later, he pulled out his "Incompressible Test List" and insisted that team members

- Seeing things as they are and facing them head-on, making no excuses and harboring no wishful illusions.

- Saying what needs to be said to those who need to hear it.

- Persisting despite resistance, criticism, abuse, and setbacks.

Courage includes stating the realities, even when they are harsh, and publicly stating what you will do to help and what you want from others. This means laying the cards on the table honestly: here is what I want from you . . . What do you want from me?[124]

Take Charge of Your Career

Develop your leadership skills

As with other things, you must work at actively developing your leadership abilities. Great musicians and great athletes don't become great on natural gifts alone. They also pay their dues by practicing, learning, and sacrificing. Leaders in a variety of fields, when asked how they became the best leader possible, offered the following comments:

- "I've observed methods and skills of my bosses that I respected."
- "By taking risks, trying, and learning from my mistakes."
- "Lots of practice."
- "By making mistakes myself and trying a different approach."
- "By purposely engaging with others to get things done."
- "By being put in positions of responsibility that other people counted on."
- "Reading autobiographies of leaders I admire to try to understand how they think."

How do you go about developing your leadership abilities? You don't have to wait until you land a management job or even finish your education. First, you can begin establishing credibility by practicing honesty, learning from your mistakes, and becoming competent in your chosen field. Second, you should learn to manage your time well so that you will set a good example for others and help them achieve your group's goals. Third, look for—and then seize—opportunities to take actions that will help the groups to which you already belong. Fourth, even before you are a supervisor, you can practice listening carefully when you are in a group and sharing what you know so that the whole group will be better informed. Finally, begin building a network of personal contacts by reaching out to others to offer help, not just to request it.

When you are searching for your next job, look for a position with an employer that is committed to developing leadership talent. Best practices include using self-assessments to identify specific areas for development and combining classroom training with individualized coaching. Ideally, leadership development is connected to opportunities to practice the skills you are learning about, so ask about chances to lead a project or a team, even for short periods of time.

More specifically, here are some developmental experiences you should seek:

- *Assignments:* building something from nothing; fixing or turning around a failing operation; taking on project or task force responsibilities; accepting international assignments.
- *People:* having exposure to positive role models; increasing visibility to others; working with people of diverse backgrounds.
- *Hardships:* overcoming ideas that fail and deals that collapse; confronting others' performance problems; breaking out of a career rut.
- *Other events:* formal courses; challenging job experiences; supervision of others; experiences outside work.

The most effective developmental experiences have three components: assessment, challenge, and support. *Assessment* includes information that helps you understand where you are now, what your strengths are, your current levels of performance and leadership effectiveness, and your primary development needs. You can think about your previous successes and failures, and your personal goals. You can seek answers from your peers at work, bosses, family, friends, customers, and anyone else who knows you and how you work. The information you collect will help clarify what you need to learn, improve, or change.

The most potent developmental experiences provide *challenge*—they stretch you. We all think and behave in habitual, comfortable ways. But you've probably heard people say how important it can be to get out of your comfort zone—to tackle situations that require new skills and abilities, that are confusing or ambiguous. Sometimes the challenge comes from lack of experience; other times, it requires changing old habits. It may be uncomfortable, but this is how great managers learn. Make sure you think about your experiences along the way and reflect on them afterward, introspectively and in discussion with others.

You receive *support* when others send the message that your efforts to learn and grow are valued. Without support, challenging developmental experiences can be overwhelming. With support, it is easier to handle the struggle, stay on course, open up to learning, and actually learn from experiences. Support can come informally from family members or friends, or more formally through the procedures of the organization and conversations with mentors or colleagues.

What results from leadership development? Through such experiences, you can acquire more self-awareness and self-confidence, a broader perspective on the organizational system, creative thinking, the ability to work more effectively in complex social systems, and the ability to learn from experience—not to mention leadership skills.

Sources: Adapted from S. Allen and M. Kusy, "Leaders Building Leaders," *Leadership Excellence* 28, 7 (July 2011), pp. 10–11; L. W. Boone and M. S. Peborde, "Developing Leadership Skills in College and Early Career Positions," *Review of Business,* Spring 2008; A. Gaines, "Straight to the Top," *American Executive,* August 2008; S. J. Allen and N. S. Hartman, "Leadership Development: An Exploration of Sources of Learning," *SAM Advanced Management Journal,* Winter 2008, pp. 10–19, 62–63; M. McCall, *High Flyers* (Boston: Harvard Business School Press, 1998); E. Van Velsor, C. D. McCauley, and R. Moxley, "Our View of Leadership Development," in *Center for Creative Leadership Handbook of Leadership Development,* ed. C. D. McCauley, R. Moxley, and E. Van Velsor (San Francisco: Jossey-Bass, 1998), pp. 1–25; and J. Kouzes and B. Posner, *The Leadership Challenge,* 2nd ed. (San Francisco: Jossey-Bass, 1995).

Study Checklist

- Did you tear out the perforated student review card at the back of the text to revisit learning objectives and key terms and definitions?

Connect® Management is available for M Management. Additional resources include:

- Interactive Applications:
  - Drag & Drop: Contemporary Leadership
  - Self-Assessment: Are You Ready for a Leadership Role?
  - Sequencing/Timeline: The Paths Leaders Take
  - Video Case: Leadership at Pike Place

- LearnSmart—Multiple choice questions help you determine what you already know, are not sure about, or need to practice based on your score. And with SmartBook, you can read the relevant section in the eBook as well as practice and recharge what you've learned.

- Chapter Video: Leadership at Japan Airlines

- Young Manager Speaks Out: Brian Min, Kitchen Manager

11 chapter

Motivating **People**

Learning Objectives

After studying Chapter 11, you will be able to

LO1 Understand principles for setting goals that motivate employees.

LO2 Give examples of how to reward good performance effectively.

LO3 Describe the key beliefs that affect people's motivation.

LO4 Explain ways in which people's individual needs affect their behavior.

LO5 Define ways to create jobs that motivate.

LO6 Summarize how people assess and achieve fairness.

LO7 Identify causes and consequences of a satisfied workforce.

This chapter tackles an age-old question: How can a manager motivate people to work hard and perform at their best levels? Tony Hsieh, CEO of online shoe seller Zappos (a subsidiary of Amazon), believes happy employees are the key to creating happy customers because they are motivated to deliver excellent customer service. Zappos selects employees with a passion for service and then sets them free to be themselves and use their best judgment, rather than constraining them with scripted responses and time limits on customer calls. How can Hsieh ensure a supply of such highly motivated employees? Inspired by the creative campuses of Google and Facebook, he is in the process of moving 2,000 employees to the company's new headquarters in the renovated old town hall building in downtown Las Vegas. Using $350 million of his own money, Hsieh is pursuing his dream of converting the depleted area of downtown Las Vegas into "a bustling retail and technology hub spanning 20 square blocks where residents walk to restaurants, bars, and gyms in a live-work community." By catering to employees who want to integrate work and play, Zappos and the tech hub will undoubtedly attract and motivate talent for the foreseeable future.[1]

A sales manager in one company had another unique approach to this question. Each month, the person with the worst sales performance took home a live goat for the weekend. The manager hoped the goat-of-the-month employee would be so embarrassed that he or she would work harder the next month to increase sales.[2] If this sales manager is graded by results, as he grades his salespeople, he will fail. He may succeed in motivating a few of his people to increase sales, but some good people will be motivated to quit the company.

Understanding why people do the things they do on the job is not an easy task for a manager. *Predicting* their response to management's latest productivity program is harder yet. Fortunately, enough is known about motivation to give the thoughtful manager practical, effective techniques for increasing people's effort and performance.

3. Come to work regularly.

4. Perform—that is, work hard to achieve high *output* (productivity) and high *quality.*

> ## "The reward of a thing well done is to have done it."
>
> —Ralph Waldo Emerson

Motivation refers to forces that energize, direct, and sustain a person's efforts. All behavior, except involuntary reflexes like eye blinks (which have little to do with management), is motivated. A highly motivated person will work hard to achieve performance goals. With adequate ability, understanding of the job, and access to the necessary resources, such a person will be highly productive.

To be effective motivators, managers must know what behaviors they want to motivate people to exhibit. Although productive people do a seemingly limitless number of things, most of the important activities can be grouped into five general categories:[3]

1. Join the organization.

2. Remain in the organization.

5. Exhibit good citizenship by being committed and performing above and beyond the call of duty to help the company.

On the first three points, you should reject the common recent notion that loyalty is dead and accept the challenge of creating an environment that will attract and energize people so that they commit to the organization.[4] The importance of citizenship behaviors may be less obvious than productivity, but these behaviors help the organization function smoothly. They also make managers' lives easier.

Many ideas have been proposed to help managers motivate people to engage in these constructive behaviors. The most useful of these ideas are described in the following pages. We start with the most fundamental *processes* that influence the motivation of all people. These processes—described by goal-setting, reinforcement, and expectancy theories—suggest actions for

goal-setting theory a motivation theory stating that people have conscious goals that energize them and direct their thoughts and behaviors toward a particular end

managers to take. Then we discuss the *content* of what people want and need from work, how individuals differ from one another, and how understanding people's needs leads to prescriptions for designing motivating jobs and empowering people to perform at the highest possible levels. Finally, we discuss the most important beliefs and perceptions about fairness that people hold toward their work, and the implications for motivation.

1 | SETTING GOALS

Providing work-related goals is an extremely effective way to stimulate motivation. In fact, it is perhaps the most important, valid, and useful approach to motivating performance.

Did You Know?

Approximately two-thirds of workers under the age of 25 are dissatisfied with their current jobs, and 44 percent are seriously considering leaving their organizations. Some of the reasons for their wanting to leave include boring work, flat pay, and escalating cost of health benefits.[5]

Goal-setting theory states that people have conscious goals that energize them and direct their thoughts and behaviors toward a particular end.[6] Keeping in mind the principle that goals matter, managers set goals for employees or collaborate with them on goal setting. For example, a satellite TV company might set goals for increasing the number of new subscribers, the number of current subscribers who pay for premium channels, or the timeliness of responses to customer inquiries.[7] Goal setting works for any job in which people have control over their performance.[8] You can set goals for performance quality and quantity, plus behavioral goals like cooperation or teamwork.[9] In fact, you can set goals for whatever is important.[10]

1.1 | Well-Crafted Goals are Highly Motivating

As illustrated in Exhibit 11.1, motivational goals share four characteristics. The most powerful goals are *meaningful;* noble purposes that appeal to people's "higher" values add extra motivating power.[11] TOMS pursues profit, but the company also donates one pair of shoes or glasses to the underprivileged for each pair that is purchased at regular prices. Madcap

LISTEN & LEARN ● ONLINE

YOUNG MANAGERS
Speak Out!

"You want to be able to affect their (employees) attitude towards their job in a positive way . . . You want to encourage them to do good work . . . It helps to make sure that they care about the specific things they are dealing with in their daily job."

—HerbSteward, Dock Foreman/Supervisor

Exhibit 11.1 Motivational goals possess four characteristics

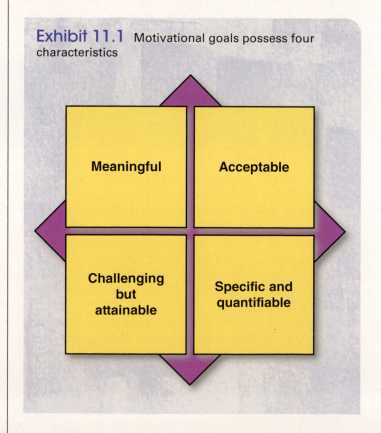

Meaningful

Acceptable

Challenging but attainable

Specific and quantifiable

Coffee works side-by-side with farmers in Colombia and El Salvador to grow and process high-quality coffee beans; higher quality beans means higher pay for the farmers.[12] Huntsman Chemical has goals of paying off corporate debt but also relieving human suffering—it sponsors cancer research and treatment through its Cancer Institute and hospitals. Meaningful goals also may be based on data about competitors; exceeding competitors' performance can stoke people's competitive spirit and desire to succeed in the marketplace.[13] This point is not just about the values companies espouse and the lofty goals they pursue; it's also about leadership at a more personal level. Compared with followers of transactional leaders, followers of transformational leaders (recall Chapter 10) view their work as more important and as highly congruent with their personal goals.[14]

Goals also should be *acceptable* to employees. This means, among other things, that they should not conflict with people's personal values and that people should have reasons to pursue the goals. Allowing people to participate in setting their work goals—as opposed to having the boss set goals for them— tends to generate goals that people accept and pursue willingly.

Acceptable, maximally motivating goals are *challenging but attainable.* In other words, they should be high enough to inspire better performance but not so high that people can never reach them. United Way has raised billions of dollars for thousands of nonprofits in local communities throughout the United States.[15] Each year leaders, staff, and volunteers from each local United Way carefully decide their fund-raising goal. If they make the goal too low, then there may be less funding available for good causes. A goal that is too challenging may overwhelm or turn off potential donors. Setting the right goal is important.

Founded in 2002, SpaceX designs, manufactures, and launches rockets and spacecraft. Guided by Elon Musk, the company's CEO, one of the company's key goals is to develop reusable and reliable rockets in order to make space exploration less costly. In 2012, one of SpaceX's spacecraft—Dragon—made history by being the first private vehicle to deliver a cargo payload to the International Space Station and return safely to Earth. Since then, the Dragon has resupplied the space station numerous times for NASA. SpaceX has another goal as it continues to revolutionize space technology: "to enable people to live on other planets."[16]

Ideal goals do not merely exhort employees in general terms to improve performance and start doing their best. Instead goals should be *specific and quantifiable,* more like GM's goal of selling 5 million four-door compact sedans in the fast-growing Chinese automotive market by 2016. The sedan, the Baojun 630, is a product of the SAIC-GM-Wuling joint venture.[17] Bringing these principles together, Microsoft uses the acronym SMART to create motivating goals: specific, measurable, achievable, results based, and time specific.[18]

**HOW TO LIVE UNITED:
JOIN HANDS.**
OPEN YOUR HEART.
**LEND YOUR MUSCLE.
FIND YOUR VOICE.**
GIVE 10%. GIVE 100%.
GIVE 110%.
GIVE AN HOUR.
GIVE A SATURDAY.
THINK OF WE BEFORE ME.
REACH OUT A HAND TO ONE AND
INFLUENCE
THE CONDITION OF ALL.
**GIVE. ADVOCATE. VOLUNTEER.
LIVE UNITED.** United Way

Want to make a difference? Help create opportunities for everyone in your community. United Way is creating real, lasting change where you live, by focusing on the building blocks of a better life— education, income and health. That's what it means to Live United. For more, visit LIVEUNITED.ORG.

1.2 | Stretch Goals Help Employees Reach New Heights

Some firms today set **stretch goals**—targets that are exceptionally demanding and novel, and that some people would never even think of.[19] There are two types of stretch goals:[20]

1. Vertical stretch goals are aligned with current activities, including productivity and financial results.

2. Horizontal stretch goals involve people's professional development, such as attempting and learning new, difficult things.

Impossible though stretch goals may seem to some, they often are in fact attainable.

Stretch goals can shift people away from mediocrity and toward major achievement. But if someone tries in good faith yet doesn't meet a stretch goal, don't punish—remember how difficult these goals are! Base your assessment on how much performance has improved, how the performance compares with that of others, and how much progress has been made.[21]

Stonyfield Farm Motivates through Its Mission

In 1979, Samuel and Louise Kaymen founded The Rural Education Center (TREC) at Stonyfield Farm in Wilton, New Hampshire. Relying on philanthropy for a significant part of its financial support, the nonprofit center taught rural and homesteading skills to hundreds of students. Meanwhile, Samuel, a diabetic, experimented with milk from the cows on the farm to produce wholesome, creamy, and delicious yogurt that didn't require added sugar. In 1982, as funds for TREC began to dry up, Samuel recruited Gary Hirshberg to join the board of directors to help implement a business strategy for TREC. Gary was an entrepreneur with experience in developing alternative technologies, including solar greenhouses, organic gardening, and a water-pumping windmill.

In order to earn revenue for the education center, Kaymen and Hirshberg decided to expand the dairy herd in order to produce and sell more yogurt. As demand for the organic yogurt exploded, the company began buying milk from local dairy farmers. In 1984, Hirshberg became Stonyfield's president and "CE-Yo" and four years later, Stonyfield built a modern plant in Londonderry, New Hampshire, where it continues to produce a variety of organic yogurts and smoothies. After initially investing in Stonyfield in 2001, French food company Groupe Danone now owns the company. Early in 2012, Hirshberg became chairman and passed his president and CE-Yo roles to Walt Freese, the former global CEO of Ben & Jerry's.

Stonyfield's mission is very motivational: "We're committed to healthy food, healthy people, a healthy planet and healthy business." An early pioneer of socially and environmentally responsible business, Stonyfield believes that "dedication to health and sustainability enhances shareholder value." Also, Stonyfield's mission has inspired the company to establish a "Profits for the Planet" program, which commits $2 million to organizations dedicated to restoring and protecting the environment. Stonyfield's plant engineers have reduced the energy used to make yogurt, and recycle as much waste as possible, keeping tens of millions of pounds of waste from being added to landfills. Stonyfield continues to support hundreds of organic farmers, and keeps over 200,000 agricultural acres free of persistent pesticides and other chemicals commonly used on nonorganic farms.

Given its mission, it comes as no surprise that Stonyfield Farm expects its employees to contribute to the company's environmental efforts. The company supports its employees with "education, training, and opportunities to merge the environmental knowledge they've gained at work with the decisions they make and actions they take in their personal lives." Some examples of training include general environmental,

Cofounder and Chairman of Stonyfield Farm, Gary Hirshberg, believes in socially and environmentally responsible business.

climate change, and organic farming orientations for new hires. And, ongoing environmental education is provided for all employees through regular "munch and learns" (informational presentations delivered over lunch hours) and bi-weekly "green tips" (an internal e-mail newsletter).

For the past 30 years, Stonyfield's founders, managers, and employees have been inspired by their entrepreneurial spirit and the mission of the company to do well by doing good.

DISCUSSION QUESTIONS

- What factors motivated Kaymen and Hirshberg to switch their focus from operating The Rural Education Center (TREC) to becoming full-time manufacturers of organic yogurt?
- Stonyfield's mission inspires and motivates the company's leaders, employees, and suppliers to behave in ways that support its socially and environmentally friendly business practices. What are some of the challenges the firm may face over the next several years with regard to maintaining this "green" business strategy?

SOURCES: Company website, http://www.stonyfield.com; and K. McCormack, "Stonyfield CEO Resigns to Focus on Food Policy," *Bloomberg Businessweek,* January 12, 2012, www.businessweek.com.

1.3 | Goal Setting Must Be Paired with Other Management Tools

Goal setting is an extraordinarily powerful management technique. But even specific, challenging, attainable goals work better under some conditions than others. For example, if people lack relevant ability and knowledge, managers might get better results from simply urging them to do their best or setting a goal to learn rather than a goal to achieve a specific performance level.[22] Individual performance goals can be dysfunctional if people work in a group and cooperation among team members is essential to team performance.[23] Individualized goals can create competition and reduce cooperation. If cooperation is important, performance goals should be established *for the team.*

Goals can generate manipulative game playing and unethical behavior. People sometimes find ingenious ways to set easy goals and convince their bosses that they are difficult.[24] Or they may find ways to meet goals simply to receive a reward, without necessarily contributing to the company's success. For example, one measure of an instructor's success is high ratings from participants when they fill out questionnaires after a training program. To meet the goal of achieving a high score, some instructors hand out treats or prizes or end sessions early—practices that are unlikely to add to what trainees actually learn. Even more perversely, when Rockford Acromatic Products Company promoted employee health by offering bonuses to employees who quit smoking for several months, several workers first *started* smoking so they could quit and earn the bonus.[25] In addition, people who don't meet their goals are more likely to engage in unethical behavior than are people who are trying to do their best but have no specific performance goals. This is true regardless of whether they have financial incentives, and it is particularly true when people fall just short of reaching their goals.[26]

Another familiar example comes from the pages of financial reports. Some executives have mastered the art of "earnings management"—precisely meeting Wall Street analysts' earnings estimates or beating them by a single penny.[27] The media trumpet, and investors reward, the company that meets or beats the estimates. People sometimes meet this goal by either manipulating the numbers or initiating whispering campaigns to persuade analysts to lower their estimates, making them more attainable. The marketplace wants short-term, quarterly performance, but long-term viability is ultimately more important to a company's success.

It is important *not* to establish a single productivity goal if there are other important dimensions of performance.[28] For instance, if the acquisition of knowledge and skills is important, you can also set a specific and challenging learning goal like "identify 10 ways to develop relationships with users of our products." Productivity goals will likely enhance productivity, but they may also cause employees to neglect other areas, such as learning, tackling new projects, or developing creative solutions to job-related problems. A manager who wants to motivate creativity can establish creativity goals along with productivity goals for individuals or for brainstorming teams.[29]

1.4 | Set Your Own Goals, Too

Goal setting works for yourself as well—it's a powerful tool for self-management. Set goals for yourself; don't just try hard or hope for the best. Create a statement of purpose for yourself comprising an inspiring distant vision, a mid-distant goal along the way, and near-term objectives to start working on immediately.[30] So if you are going into business, you might articulate your goal for the type of businessperson you want to be in five years, the types of jobs that could create the opportunities and teach you what you need to know to become that businessperson, and the specific schoolwork and job search activities that can get you moving in those directions. And on the job, apply this chapter's goal-setting advice to yourself.

LO2 Give examples of how to reward good performance effectively

2 | REINFORCING PERFORMANCE

Goals are universal motivators. So are the processes of reinforcement described in this section. In 1911 psychologist Edward Thorndike formulated the **law of effect**: behavior that is followed by positive consequences probably will be repeated.[31] This powerful law of behavior laid the foundation for countless investigations into the effects of the positive

study tip 11

Set mini-goals to study more efficiently

During this course, try setting mini-goals on a weekly basis to help you stay motivated and get your work done on time. Over the weekend, review the course syllabus and make a "to do" list of what needs to get done during the upcoming week. Update your planner with any important due dates. Next, each time you sit down for a study session, take a few goals from your list that you think you can complete, like finishing a homework assignment, reading a chapter, completing an online Connect assignment, and so forth. As you complete each task, place a checkmark next to it or cross it off the list. Setting specific, challenging, but attainable study goals (and keeping track of your progress) will help you stay motivated and perform better.

consequences, called **reinforcers**, that motivate behavior. **Organizational behavior modification** attempts to influence people's behavior and improve performance[32] by systematically managing work conditions and the consequences of people's actions.

2.1 | Behavior Has Consequences

Four key consequences of behavior either encourage or discourage people's behavior (see Exhibit 11.2):

1. **Positive reinforcement**—applying a consequence that increases the likelihood that the person will repeat the behavior that led to it. Examples of positive reinforcers include compliments, letters of commendation, favorable performance evaluations, and pay raises. Jim Goodnight, CEO of business analytics software company SAS, encourages employee retention by providing a great workplace culture with generous benefits, including a free on-site healthcare center (with doctors), a free 66,000-square-foot recreation and fitness center, subsidized Montessori childcare, a beauty salon, and an on-site pharmacy.[33]

2. **Negative reinforcement**—removing or withholding an undesirable consequence. For example, each team at Whole Foods votes to decide whether a new hire who has completed a 30- to 90-day probationary period can remain on the team. New hires require a two-thirds positive vote from team members.[34] For those new hires who earn their teammates' approval, the negative reinforcer (i.e., probationary status) is removed.

3. **Punishment**—administering an aversive consequence. Examples include criticizing or shouting at an employee, assigning an unappealing task, and sending a worker home without pay. Negative reinforcement can involve the *threat* of punishment by not delivering punishment when employees perform satisfactorily. Punishment is the actual delivery of the aversive consequence. Managers use punishment when they think it is warranted or when they believe others expect them to, and they usually concern themselves with following company policy and procedure.[35]

4. **Extinction**—withdrawing or failing to provide a reinforcing consequence. When this occurs, motivation is reduced, and the behavior is *extinguished,* or eliminated. Managers may unintentionally extinguish desired behaviors by not giving a compliment for a job well done, forgetting to say thanks for a favor, setting impossible performance goals so that the person never experiences success, and so on. Extinction may be used to end undesirable behaviors, too. The manager might ignore long-winded observations during a meeting or fail to acknowledge unimportant e-mail in the hope that the lack of feedback will discourage the employee from continuing.

The first two consequences, positive and negative reinforcement, are positive for the person receiving them—the person either gains something or avoids something negative. As a result, the person who experiences these consequences will be motivated to behave in the ways that led to the reinforcement. The last two consequences, punishment and extinction, are negative outcomes for the person receiving them: motivation to repeat the behavior that led to the undesirable results will be reduced.

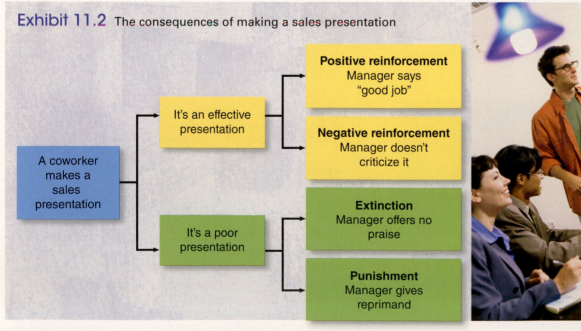

Exhibit 11.2 The consequences of making a sales presentation

A coworker makes a sales presentation

→ It's an effective presentation
- **Positive reinforcement** Manager says "good job"
- **Negative reinforcement** Manager doesn't criticize it

→ It's a poor presentation
- **Extinction** Manager offers no praise
- **Punishment** Manager gives reprimand

Managers should be careful to match consequences to what employees will actually find desirable or undesirable. At Staker & Parson, a supervisor once made the mistake of "punishing" an employee for tardiness by suspending him for three days during fishing season. The employee was delighted.[36]

2.2 | Be Careful What You Reinforce

You've learned about the positive effects of a transformational leadership style, but giving rewards to high-performing people is also essential.[37] Unfortunately, sometimes organizations and managers reinforce the wrong behaviors.[38] For example, compensation plans that include stock options are intended to reinforce behaviors that add to the company's value, but stock options also can reinforce decisions that artificially deliver short-term gains in stock prices, even if they hurt the company in the long run.

discourage. Michael LeBoeuf, a writer of popular business books, said the greatest management principle is "The things that get rewarded get done." LeBoeuf advises rewarding the kinds of activities illustrated in Exhibit 11.3.[40]

Also, the reward system has to support the firm's strategy, defining people's performance in ways that pursue strategic objectives.[41] Organizations should reward employees for developing themselves in strategically important ways—for building new skills that are critical to strengthening core capabilities and creating value.

Managers should use reinforcers creatively. California-based staffing agency Akraya Inc. helps its hardworking employees relax on the weekends by sending a cleaning service to employees' homes twice a month.[42] For Greg Dalmotte, vice president

> ### "I am not a product of my circumstances. I am a product of my decisions."
> —Stephen Covey

At some companies, employees are reinforced with admiration and positive performance evaluations for multitasking—say, typing e-mail while on the phone or checking text messages during meetings. This behavior may look efficient and send a signal that the employee is busy and valuable, but a growing body of research says multitasking actually slows the brain's efficiency and can contribute to mistakes.[39] Scans of brain activity show that the brain is not able to concentrate on two tasks at once; it needs time to switch among the multitasker's activities. So managers who praise the hard work of multitaskers may be unintentionally reinforcing inefficiency and failure to think deeply about problems.

To use reinforcement effectively, managers must identify which kinds of behaviors they reinforce and which they

Exhibit 11.3 Activities that should be rewarded

Solid solutions instead of quick fixes.

Risk taking instead of risk avoiding.

Applied creativity instead of mindless conformity.

Decisive action instead of paralysis by analysis.

Smart work instead of busywork.

Simplification instead of needless complication.

Quietly effective behavior instead of squeaky wheels.

Quality work instead of fast work.

Loyalty instead of turnover.

Working together instead of working against.

at Bank Atlantic, the challenge is to increase employees' engagement by "creating an environment where people like coming to work."[43] He oversees a program that encourages managers and associates to pass out "WOW! Bucks" to colleagues who have done something outstanding at work. The bucks can be used to buy DVD players, Coach handbags, and other items. Dalmotte says, "Words of encouragement have created associates who perform at a higher level."[44]

Innovative managers use nonmonetary rewards, including intellectual challenge, greater responsibility, autonomy, recognition, flexible benefits, and greater influence over decisions. Top-level managers at U.S. Bancorp invite young employees to form the "Dynamic Dozen." When they're not doing their regular jobs, these Gen Y employees help the bank figure out how to appeal to similarly aged customers, potential recruits, and other young employees in the bank. The "dozen" are rewarded by gaining exposure to senior managers and learning more about the bank's business.[45] These and other rewards for high-performing employees, when creatively devised and applied, can continue to motivate when pay and promotions are scarce. Managers at Cleveland Clinic are taking another approach to motivating many of its 29,000 employees. Employees who enroll in the company's Healthy Choice wellness program and engage in weight management, yoga classes, and so forth, pay less for insurance premiums than their less healthy coworkers.[46]

2.3 | Should You Punish Mistakes?

How a manager reacts to people's mistakes has a big impact on motivation. Punishment is sometimes appropriate, as when

● Mark Zuckerberg, CEO and cofounder of Facebook, encourages employees to request feedback about their performance and behavior from fellow employees on a regular basis. Facebook employees are expected to take the time to provide this feedback to their colleagues.

people violate the law, ethical standards, important safety rules, or standards of interpersonal treatment, or when they fail to attend or perform like a slacker. But sometimes managers punish people when they shouldn't—when poor performance isn't the person's fault or when managers take out their frustrations on the wrong people.

Managers who overuse punishment or use it inappropriately create a climate of fear in the workplace.[47] Fear causes people to focus on the short term, sometimes creating problems in the longer run. Fear also creates a focus on oneself, rather than on the group and the organization. B. Joseph White, president emeritus of the University of Illinois, recalls consulting for a high-tech entrepreneur who heard a manager present a proposal and responded with brutal criticism: "That's the . . . stupidest idea I ever heard in my life. I'm disappointed in you." According to White, this talented manager was so upset she never again felt fully able to contribute.[48]

For managers to avoid such damage, the key is how to think about and handle mistakes. Recognize that everyone makes mistakes and that mistakes can be dealt with constructively by discussing and learning from them. Don't punish, but praise people who deliver bad news to their bosses. Treat failure to act as a failure but don't punish unsuccessful, good-faith efforts. If you're a leader, talk about your failures with your people, and show how you learned from them. Give people second chances, and maybe third chances. Encourage people to try new things, and don't punish them if what they try doesn't work out.

2.4 | Feedback Is Essential Reinforcement

Most managers don't provide enough useful feedback, and most people don't receive or ask for feedback enough.[49] As a manager, you should consider all potential causes of poor performance, pay full attention when employees ask for feedback or want to discuss performance issues, and give feedback according to the guidelines you read about in Chapter 8.

Feedback can be offered in many ways.[50] Customers sometimes give feedback directly; you also can request customer feedback and give it to the employee. You can provide statistics on work that the person has directly influenced. A manufacturing firm can put the phone number or website of the production team on the product so that customers can contact the team directly. Performance reviews should be conducted regularly. And bosses should give regular, ongoing feedback—it helps correct problems immediately, provides immediate reinforcement for good work, and prevents surprises when the formal review comes.

For yourself, try not to be afraid of receiving feedback; instead, you should actively seek it. Paralleling the firm's online "status update" concept, employees at Facebook are encouraged to request and provide brief feedback to colleagues on a regular basis. According to Lori Goler, vice president of human resources, it should be a 45-second conversation where employees ask, "How did that go?" and "What could be done better?"[51] When you get feedback, don't ignore it. Try to avoid negative emotions like anger, hurt, defensiveness, or resignation. Think It's up to me to get the feedback I need; I need to know these things about my performance and behavior; learning about myself will help me identify needs and create new opportunities; it serves my interest best to know rather than not know; taking initiative on this gives me more power and influence over my career.[52]

LO3 Describe the key beliefs that affect people's motivation

3 | PERFORMANCE-RELATED BELIEFS

In contrast to reinforcement theory, which describes the processes by which factors in the work environment affect people's behavior, expectancy theory considers some of the cognitive processes that go on in people's heads. According to **expectancy theory**, the person's work *efforts* lead to some level of *performance*.[53] Then performance results in one or more *outcomes* for the person. This process is shown in Exhibit 11.4. People develop two important kinds of beliefs linking these three events:

1. *Expectancy,* which links effort to performance.

2. *Instrumentality,* which links performance to outcomes.

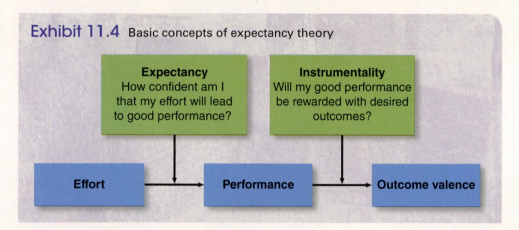

Exhibit 11.4 Basic concepts of expectancy theory

Expectancy How confident am I that my effort will lead to good performance?

Instrumentality Will my good performance be rewarded with desired outcomes?

Effort → Performance → Outcome valence

Source: D. Organ and T. Bateman, *Organizational Behavior* 4e, McGraw-Hill. Copyright © 1990. Used with permission.

3.1 | If You Try Hard, Will You Succeed?

The first belief, **expectancy**, is people's perceived likelihood that their efforts will enable them to attain their performance goals. An expectancy can be high (up to 100 percent), such as when a student is confident that if she studies hard, she can get a good grade on the final exam. An expectancy can also be low (down to a 0 percent likelihood), such as when a suitor is convinced that his dream date will never go out with him.

All else equal, high expectancies create higher motivation than do low expectancies. In the preceding examples, the student is more likely to study for the exam than the suitor is to pursue the dream date, even though both want their respective outcomes.

Expectancies can vary among individuals, even in the same situation. For example, a sales manager might initiate a competition in which the top salesperson wins a free trip to Hawaii. In such cases, the few top people, who have performed well in the past, will be more motivated by the contest than will the historically average and below-average performers. The top people will have higher expectancies—stronger beliefs that their efforts can help them turn in the top performance.

3.2 | If You Succeed, Will You Be Rewarded?

The example about the sales contest illustrates how performance results in some kind of **outcome**, or consequence, for the person. Actually, it often results in several outcomes. For example, turning in the best sales performance could lead to

(1) a competitive victory, (2) the free trip to Hawaii, (3) feelings of achievement, (4) recognition from the boss, (5) prestige throughout the company, and (6) resentment from other salespeople.

But how certain is it that performance will result in all of those outcomes? Will winning the contest really generate resentment? Will it really lead to increased prestige?

These questions address the second key belief described by expectancy theory: instrumentality.[54] **Instrumentality** is the perceived likelihood that performance will be followed by a particular outcome. Like expectancies, instrumentalities can be high (up to 100 percent) or low (approaching 0 percent). For example, you can be fully confident that if you get favorable customer reviews, you'll get a promotion, or you can feel that no matter what your customers say, the promotion will go to someone else.

Also, each outcome has an associated valence. **Valence** is the value the person places on the outcome. Valences can be positive, as a Hawaiian vacation would be for most people, or negative, as in the case of the other salespeople's resentment.

3.3 | All Three Beliefs Must Be High

For motivation to be high, expectancy, instrumentalities, and total valence of all outcomes must all be high. A person will *not* be highly motivated if any of the following conditions exist:

- He believes he can't perform well enough to achieve the positive outcomes that he knows the company provides to good performers (high valence and high instrumentality but low expectancy).

- He knows he can do the job and is fairly certain what the ultimate outcomes will be (say, a promotion and a transfer). However, he doesn't want those outcomes or believes other, negative outcomes outweigh the positive (high expectancy and high instrumentality but low valence).

- He knows he can do the job and wants several important outcomes (a favorable performance review, a raise, and a promotion). But he believes that no matter how well he performs, the outcomes will not be forthcoming (high expectancy and positive valences but low instrumentality).

3.4 | Expectancy Theory Identifies Leverage Points

Expectancy theory helps the manager zero in on key leverage points for influencing motivation. Three implications are crucial:

1. *Increase expectancies.* Provide a work environment that facilitates good performance, and set realistically attainable performance goals. Provide training, support, required resources, and encouragement so that people are confident they can perform at the expected levels. Recall that charismatic leaders excel at boosting their followers' confidence.

2. *Identify positively valent outcomes.* Understand what people want to get out of work. Think about what their jobs do and do not (but could) provide them. Consider how people may differ in the valences they assign to outcomes. Know the need theories of motivation, described in the next section, and their implications for identifying important outcomes.

3. *Make performance instrumental toward positive outcomes.* Make sure that good performance is followed by personal recognition and praise, favorable performance reviews, pay increases, and other positive results. Also, ensure that working hard and performing well will have as few negative results as possible. The way you emphasize instrumentality may need to be tailored to employees' locus of control. For people who have an external locus of control, tending to attribute results to luck or fate, you may need to reinforce behaviors (more than outcomes) frequently so that they see a connection between what they do and what you reward. It is useful to realize, too, that bosses usually provide (or withhold) rewards, but others do so as well.[55] Peers, direct reports, customers, and others can offer compliments, help, and praise. Organizations may set up formal reward systems as well. Umpqua Bank in Roseburg, Oregon, set up a link called "Brag Box" on its intranet, where employees can post comments about good deeds by their coworkers. Umpqua's vice president for rewards and recognition regularly checks the Brag Box and notifies managers when their employees have received a compliment, so the managers can further reinforce compliments with praise.[56]

Many companies, in an effort to manage rising health care costs, are using monetary incentives to motivate their employees to live healthier lives. Research suggests that, at least in the short run, incentives can motivate employees to take their medication, complete a health assessment, and participate in weight loss, smoking cessation, or cholesterol reduction programs. More companies are offering incentives. A survey found that in 2012, four out of five companies planned to offer financial rewards to employees who participated in their wellness or health management programs. David Hunnicutt, CEO of the Wellness Council of America, explains why incentives are effective: "Wellness incentives can significantly increase participation and improve the likelihood that employees will embrace, and ultimately adopt, healthier behaviors." This can be a win–win for employees, who become healthier, and their employers, who can use the savings in health-related costs to invest in their businesses.[57]

● Employees are increasingly participating in yoga classes and other wellness activities. In order to manage rising health care costs, companies are offering financial incentives to employees who live healthier lifestyles.

LO4 Explain ways in which people's individual needs affect their behavior

4 | UNDERSTANDING PEOPLE'S NEEDS

So far we have focused on *processes* underlying motivation. The manager who appropriately applies goal-setting, reinforcement, and expectancy theories is creating essential motivating elements in the work environment. But motivation also is affected by characteristics of the person. The second type of motivation theory, *content theories,* indicates the kinds of needs that people want to satisfy. People have different needs energizing and motivating them toward different goals and reinforcers. The extent to which and the ways in which a person's needs are met or not met at work affect his or her behavior on the job.

The most important theories describing the content of people's needs are Maslow's need hierarchy, Alderfer's ERG theory, and McClelland's needs.

4.1 | Maslow Arranged Needs in a Hierarchy

Abraham Maslow organized five major types of human needs into a hierarchy, as shown in Exhibit 11.5.[58] The **need hierarchy** illustrates Maslow's conception of people satisfying their needs in a specified order, from bottom to top. The needs, in ascending order, are as follows:

1. *Physiological*—food, water, sex, and shelter.

2. *Safety or security*—protection against threat and deprivation.

3. *Social*—friendship, affection, belonging, and love.

4. *Ego*—independence, achievement, freedom, status, recognition, and self-esteem.

5. *Self-actualization*—realizing one's full potential; becoming everything one is capable of being.

According to Maslow, people are motivated to satisfy the lower needs before they try to satisfy the higher needs. In today's workplace, physiological and safety needs generally are well satisfied, making social, ego, and self-actualization needs preeminent. But safety issues are still very important in manufacturing, mining, and other work environments. And for months after the terrorist attacks of September 2001, employees still

Maslow's need hierarchy a human needs theory postulating that people are motivated to satisfy unmet needs in a specific order

felt fear, denial, and anger—especially women, people with children, and those close to the events.[59] To deal with such safety issues, managers can show what the firm will do to improve security and manage employee risk, including crisis management plans.

Once a need is satisfied, it is no longer a powerful motivator. For example, labor unions negotiate for higher wages, benefits, safety standards, and job security. These bargaining issues relate directly to the satisfaction of Maslow's lower-level needs. Only after these needs are reasonably satisfied do the higher-level needs—social, ego, and self-actualization—become dominant concerns.

Maslow's hierarchy is a simplistic and not altogether accurate theory of human motivation.[60] For example, not everyone progresses through the five needs in hierarchical order. But Maslow made three important contributions. First, he identified important need categories, which can help managers create effective positive reinforcers. Second, it is helpful to think of two general levels of needs, in which lower-level needs must be satisfied before higher-level needs become important. Third, Maslow alerted managers to the importance of personal growth and self-actualization.

Self-actualization is the best-known concept arising from this theory. According to Maslow, the average person is only 10 percent self-actualized. In other words, most of us are living and working with a large untapped reservoir of potential. The implication is clear: managers should help create a work environment that provides training, resources, autonomy, responsibilities, and challenging assignments. This type of environment gives people a chance to use their skills and abilities creatively and allows them to achieve more of their full potential.

So treat people not merely as a cost to be controlled but as an asset to be developed. Many companies have embarked on programs that offer their people personal growth experiences. An employee at Federal Express said, "The best I can be is what I can be here. Federal Express . . . gave me the confidence

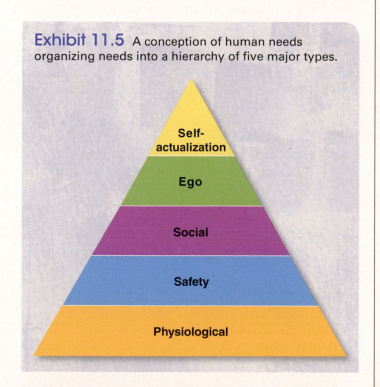

Exhibit 11.5 A conception of human needs organizing needs into a hierarchy of five major types.

Self-actualization

Ego

Social

Safety

Physiological

Source: J. Richard Hackman, et al., "A New Strategy for Job Enrichment," *California Management Review*, vol. 17, no. 4, Summer 1975. © 1975 by the Regents of the University of California. Republished by permission of the University of California Press.

● A FedEx worker unloads packages from his delivery truck in San Francisco, CA.

and self-esteem to become the person I had the potential to become."[61]

Individual managers also can promote employee growth. Senior faculty and leaders at M.D. Anderson Cancer Center believe that employee growth is best supported through a formal mentoring program. The program matches mentors to junior faculty from the Department of Cancer Biology until they are promoted to associate professor. After a settling-in period, the junior faculty member chooses a senior faculty member to chair and two additional faculty members to serve on the mentoring committee. The committee provides the junior faculty member with guidance and advice regarding academic challenges and research ideas.[62]

Organizations gain by fully using their human resources. Employees gain by capitalizing on opportunities to meet their higher-order needs on the job. At Campbell Soup Company, managers are rewarded for developing their employees, and Lisa Walker, business director of Campbell USA's wellness team, rises to the challenge. She helped one employee learn to collaborate better so that he would be seen as a team player with promotion potential. Walker's employee appreciated that her coaching gave him an opportunity for greater achievement, status, and self-esteem.[63]

4.2 | Alderfer Identified Three Work-Related Needs

A theory of human needs that is more advanced than Maslow's is Alderfer's ERG theory.[64] Maslow's theory has general applicability, but Alderfer aims expressly at understanding people's needs at work. **ERG theory** postulates three sets of needs can operate simultaneously:

1. *Existence* needs are all material and physiological desires.

2. *Relatedness* needs involve relationships with other people and are satisfied through the process of mutually sharing thoughts and feelings.

3. *Growth* needs motivate people to productively or creatively change themselves or their environment. Satisfaction of the growth needs comes from fully utilizing personal capacities and developing new capacities.

What similarities do you see between Alderfer's and Maslow's needs? Roughly speaking, existence needs subsume physiological and security needs, relatedness needs are similar to social and esteem needs, and growth needs correspond to self-actualization. ERG theory proposes that several different

needs can be operating at once. So while Maslow would say that self-actualization is important to people only after other sets of needs are satisfied, Alderfer maintains that people—particularly working people in our postindustrial society—can be motivated to satisfy existence, relatedness, and growth needs at the same time.

::::::::::::::::

Companies can use this knowledge as they design compensation or benefits programs. Kahler Slater Architects, a 150-employee architecture and design firm, faced economic pressures, causing a rollback of employee benefits, including health care coverage. But to tailor the cutbacks to its staff, company principals found out from employees exactly which benefits meant the most to them. Then the managers came up with a package that worked for all.

Employees reported that one of their most valued benefits was paid time off, but they gave up less important perks like free pastries in the company office. They also contributed more to their health care coverage. To boost morale and help build camaraderie, the owners reduced their own salaries by 25 percent, and began hosting after-work social gatherings. It also offered employees more options for working from home to help them manage their schedules and conflicts. Trusting their employees to get their jobs done from home or work has helped Kahler Slater earn a spot on Great Places to Work's list of Best Small Workplaces for 10 consecutive years.[65]

::::::::::::::::

Consider which theory best explains the motives identified by Diane Schumaker-Krieg to describe her successful career in the financial services industry. Schumaker-Krieg says she was "driven . . . by fear" in October 1987, when she was working for investment firm Dillon Read at the time of the stock market crash. Layoffs were spreading throughout the industry, jobs were scarce, and she was supporting her son following a divorce. Out of determination to take care of her son, Schumaker-Krieg reacted to being laid off by writing a business plan to adapt research for sale to small customers. She persuaded Dillon Read to fund the idea for a year, began building the business, moved it to Credit Suisse, and within years was earning $150 million in profits for her employer. During that time she remarried and earned enough to retire, but she continues working, now as global head of research and economics of Wells Fargo Securities. She sees her current motivation as enjoyment of her accomplishments, her business relationships, and opportunities to continue innovating.[67] Certainly, lower-level needs dominated the early years of Schumaker-Krieg's career, but did the basis for her motivation move one step at a time through all the levels of Maslow's hierarchy?

Did You Know?

Yarde Metals, a $500 million company with 700 employees spread across multiple manufacturing locations, encourages employees to use its napping rooms when they feel tired. The company's founder, Craig Yarde, believes: "Without a question, [naps] improve productivity." Evidence suggests that short power naps can help employees improve their focus and morale, while also reducing absences and health care costs.[66]

> "The degree to which you will find the right recognition [of employees' successes] is equal to the degree to which you know the employee[s], you know their wants and needs."
>
> —ErikaAnderson, *organizational development consultant*[70]

Maslow's theory is better known to American managers than Alderfer's, but ERG theory has more scientific support.[68] Both have practical value in that they remind managers of the types of reinforcers or rewards that can be used to motivate people. Regardless of whether a manager prefers the Maslow or the Alderfer theory of needs, he or she can motivate people by helping them satisfy their needs, particularly by offering opportunities for self-actualization and growth.

4.3 | McClelland Said Managers Seek Achievement, Affiliation, and Power

David McClelland also identified a number of basic needs that guide people. According to McClelland, three needs are most important for managers:[69]

1. The need for *achievement*—a strong orientation toward accomplishment and an obsession with success and goal attainment. Most managers and entrepreneurs in the United States have high levels of this need and like to see it in their employees.

2. The need for *affiliation*—a strong desire to be liked by other people. Individuals who have high levels of this need are oriented toward getting along with others and may be less concerned with performing at high levels.

3. The need for *power*—a desire to influence or control other people. This need can be a negative force (termed *personalized power*) if it is expressed through the aggressive manipulation and exploitation of others. People high on the personalized-power need want power purely for the pursuit of their own goals. But the need for power also can be a positive motive, called *socialized power,* which is channeled toward the constructive improvement of organizations and societies.

Different needs predominate for different people. Now that you have read about these needs, think about yourself—which one(s) are most and least important to you?

Low need for affiliation and moderate to high need for power are associated with managerial success for both higher- and lower-level managers.[71] One reason the need for affiliation is not necessary for leadership success is that managers high on this need have difficulty making tough but necessary decisions that will upset some people.

4.4 | Do Need Theories Apply Internationally?

How do the need theories apply abroad?[72] Although managers in the United States care most strongly about achievement, esteem, and self-actualization, managers in Greece and Japan are motivated more by security. Social needs are most important in Sweden, Norway, and Denmark. "Doing your own thing"—the phrase from the 1960s that describes an American culture oriented toward self-actualization—is not even translatable into Chinese. Being from a collectivist culture, the Chinese are more likely to value belongingness.[73] "Achievement," too, is difficult to translate into most other languages. Researchers in France, Japan, and Sweden would have been unlikely to even conceive of McClelland's achievement motive because people of those countries are more group-oriented than individually oriented.

Clearly achievement, growth, and self-actualization are profoundly important in the United States, Canada, and Great Britain. But these needs are not universally important. Every manager must remember that need importance varies from country to country and that people may not be motivated by the same needs. One study found that employees in many countries are highly engaged at companies that have strong leadership, work/life balance, a good reputation, and opportunities for employees to contribute, while another found variations from country to country:[74] employees in Canada were attracted by competitive pay, work/life balance, and opportunities for advancement; workers in Germany by autonomy; in Japan by high-quality coworkers; in the Netherlands by a collaborative work environment; and in the United States by competitive health benefits. Generally no single way is best, and managers can customize their approaches by considering how individuals differ.[75]

LO5 Define ways to create jobs that motivate

5 | DESIGNING JOBS THAT MOTIVATE

Here's an example of a company that gave a "reward" that didn't motivate. One of Mary Kay Ash's former employers gave her a sales award: a flounder fishing light. Unfortunately she doesn't

Traditional Thinking

Extrinsic rewards like pay are enough to motivate employees.

The Best Managers Today

Use both extrinsic and intrinsic rewards to energize, direct, and sustain employee effort.

---

extrinsic rewards rewards given to a person by the boss, the company, or some other person

intrinsic reward reward a worker derives directly from performing the job itself

job rotation changing from one routine task to another to alleviate boredom

job enlargement giving people additional tasks at the same time to alleviate boredom

---

fish. Fortunately she later was able to design her own organization, Mary Kay Cosmetics, around two kinds of motivators that *mattered* to her people:[76]

1. **Extrinsic rewards** are given to people by the boss, the company, or some other person. Examples include pay, benefits, business class airline travel, or a large office.

2. An **intrinsic reward** is a reward the person derives directly from performing the job itself. This occurs when you feel a sense of accomplishment after completing a challenging task.

An interesting project, an intriguing subject that is fun to study, a completed sale, and the discovery of the perfect solution to a difficult problem all can give people the feeling that they have done something well. This is the essence of the motivation that comes from intrinsic rewards.

Intrinsic rewards are essential to the motivation underlying creativity.[77] A challenging problem, a chance to create something new, and work that is exciting can provide intrinsic motivation that inspires people to devote time and energy to the task. So do managers who allow people some freedom to pursue the tasks that interest them most. The opposite situations result in routine, habitual behaviors that interfere with creativity.[78] A study in manufacturing facilities found that employees initiated more applications for patents, made more novel and useful suggestions, and were rated by their managers as more creative when their jobs were challenging and their managers did not control their activities closely.[79]

Conversely, some jobs and organizations create environments that quash creativity and motivation.[80] The classic example of a demotivating job is the highly specialized assembly-line job; each worker performs one boring operation before passing the work along to the next worker. Such specialization, or the "mechanistic" approach to job design, was the prevailing practice through most of the 20th century.[81] But jobs that are too

simple and routine result in employee dissatisfaction, absenteeism, and turnover.

Especially in industries that depend on highly motivated knowledge workers, keeping talented employees may require letting them design their own jobs so that their work is more interesting than it would be elsewhere.[82] Jobs can be designed in the following ways to increase intrinsic rewards and therefore motivation.

5.1 | Managers Can Make Work More Varied and Interesting

With **job rotation**, workers who spend all their time in one routine task can instead move from one task to another. Rather than dishing out the pasta in a cafeteria line all day, a person might work the pasta, then the salads, and then the vegetables or desserts. Job rotation is intended to alleviate boredom by giving people different things to do at different times.

As you may guess, job rotation may simply move the person from one boring job to another. But job rotation can benefit everyone when done properly, with people's input and career interests in mind. At General Electric, new hires and high-potential employees can rotate among jobs within a broad functional area of their choosing, including finance, engineering, operations management, or human resources. While completing these job rotations, they receive classroom training, mentoring, and performance feedback.[83] Austria-based Vienna Insurance Group (VIG) also uses job rotation for its high-potential employees. Program participants spend between 1 and 12 months working in their area of expertise in multiple VIG companies located in Austria and other countries in Europe. The goal of the program is for participants to develop practical know-how, international operations knowledge, and a professional network throughout the company's dispersed locations.[84]

Job enlargement is similar to job rotation in that people are given different tasks to do. But while job rotation involves doing one task at one time and changing to a different task at a different time, job enlargement assigns the worker multiple tasks at the same time. Thus an assembly worker's job is enlarged if he or she is given two tasks to perform rather than one. In a study of job enlargement in a financial services organization, enlarged jobs led to higher job satisfaction, better error detection by clerks, and improved customer service.[85]

Take Charge of Your Career

Will you be motivated in the new job?

Assume you are about to graduate from college and just received a job offer. Before accepting it, you decide to find out if the new job will offer you an appropriate level of extrinsic and intrinsic rewards. Most hiring managers will provide you with basic information during the interview process, or when they make you the offer. The essentials usually cover the starting salary, benefits, schedule, job description, working conditions, and so forth. What hiring managers typically do not tell you is their opinion about whether the starting salary is fair or whether after accepting the job, you will get to do work that is satisfying and intrinsically motivating.

You think about the job offer. The starting salary seems reasonable, but you suspect it may be a little lower than the going rate. You wonder if you should ask for a higher salary, but don't want to be perceived as pushy or unreasonable; after all, you have yet to work a single day for the company. Where should you turn for information on salaries?

There are websites available that can help you find current salary information for a variety of jobs worldwide. Glassdoor.com allows users to view salaries of actual positions at companies. Current and former employees of the companies, as well as other job applicants, can post salaries anonymously. Glassdoor.com has salary reports and company reviews from over 165,000 people working at approximately 19,000 companies in 100 countries. It also provides salary information for part-time jobs and

Glassdoor is a job and career site where employees anonymously dish on the pros and cons of their companies and bosses.

internships. Users can access this salary information for free as long as they submit (anonymously) their own salary to the website. Other websites that provide salary information are Salary.com and Payscale.com.

In contrast, it may prove more challenging for you to ascertain how intrinsically motivating the new job will be. However, websites like Glassdoor.com include detailed reviews (and photos) from company insiders that describe the positive aspects of the organization, areas for improvement, and advice for senior management. Another way to learn about whether you will feel motivated in the job is to talk with anyone you can who has dealt with the people from the organization, including professors who have consulted there, customers, vendors, current or former employees, and so forth. Ultimately you will never be 100 percent sure that you will be a happy, motivated employee for the next few years at the organization, but you can at least do enough homework to tilt the odds in your favor that it will be a good fit for the near term.

Sources: Adapted from www.glassdoor.com; www.salary.com; www.payscale.com; J. Eckle, "Peering through the Glass Door," *Computerworld* 43, no. 8, (February 23, 2009), pp. 36–37; and L. Wolgemuth, "Using What You Know about Coworker's Pay," *U.S. News & World Report* 145, no. 1 (July 7, 2008), pp. 69–70.

With job enlargement, the person's additional tasks are at the same level of responsibility. More profound changes occur when jobs are enriched. **Job enrichment** means that jobs are restructured or redesigned by adding higher levels of responsibility. This practice includes giving people not only more tasks but higher-level ones, such as when decisions are delegated downward and authority is decentralized. Efforts to redesign jobs by enriching them are now common in American industry. The first approach to job enrichment was Herzberg's two-factor theory, followed by the Hackman and Oldham model.

5.2 | Herzberg Proposed Two Important Job-Related Factors

Frederick Herzberg's **two-factor theory** distinguished between two broad categories of factors that affect people working on their jobs:[86]

1. **Hygiene factors** are *characteristics of the workplace:* company policies, working conditions, pay, coworkers, supervision, and so forth. These factors can make people unhappy if they are poorly managed. If they are well managed, and viewed as positive by employees, the employees will no longer be dissatisfied. However, no matter how good these factors are, they will not make people truly satisfied or motivated to do a good job.

job enrichment
changing a task to make it inherently more rewarding, motivating, and satisfying

two-factor theory
Herzberg's theory describing two factors affecting people's work motivation and satisfaction

hygiene factors
characteristics of the workplace, such as company policies, working conditions, pay, and supervision, that can make people dissatisfied

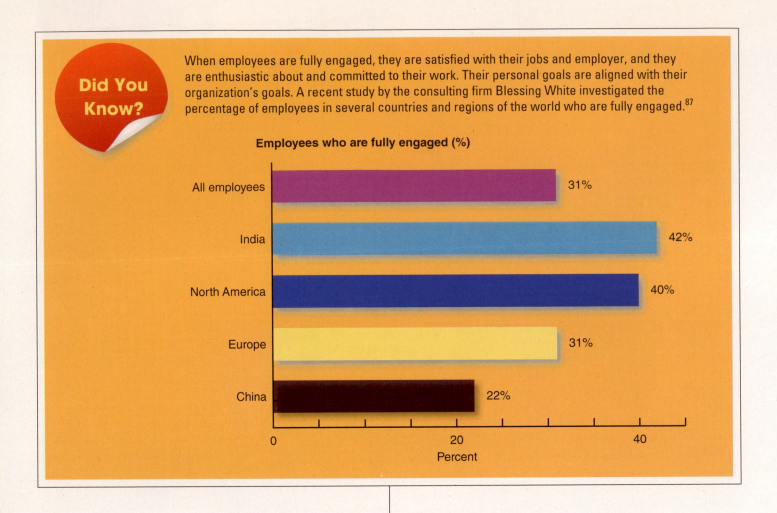

Did You Know?

When employees are fully engaged, they are satisfied with their jobs and employer, and they are enthusiastic about and committed to their work. Their personal goals are aligned with their organization's goals. A recent study by the consulting firm Blessing White investigated the percentage of employees in several countries and regions of the world who are fully engaged.[87]

Employees who are fully engaged (%)

All employees — 31%
India — 42%
North America — 40%
Europe — 31%
China — 22%

Percent

---

motivators factors that make a job more motivating, such as additional job responsibilities, opportunities for personal growth and recognition, and feelings of achievement

2. **Motivators** describe the *job itself*—that is, what people do at work. Motivators are the nature of the work itself, actual job responsibilities, opportunity for personal growth and recognition, and the feelings of achievement the job provides. According to Herzberg, the key to true job satisfaction and motivation to perform lies in this category of factors. When motivators are present, jobs are presumed to be satisfying and motivating for most people.

Herzberg's theory has been criticized by many scholars, so we will not go into more detail about his original theory. But Herzberg was a pioneer in the area of job design and still is a respected name among American managers. In addition, even if the specifics of his theory do not hold up to scientific scrutiny, he made several important contributions. Herzberg's theory highlights the important distinction between extrinsic rewards (from hygiene factors) and intrinsic rewards (from motivators). It also reminds managers not to count solely on extrinsic rewards to motivate workers but to focus on intrinsic rewards as well. Finally, it set the stage for later theories,

such as the Hackman and Oldham model, that explain more precisely how managers can enrich people's jobs.

5.3 | Hackman and Oldham: Meaning, Responsibility, and Feedback Provide Motivation

Following Herzberg's work, Hackman and Oldham proposed a more complete model of job design.[88] Exhibit 11.6 illustrates their model. As you can see, well-designed jobs lead to high motivation, high-quality performance, high satisfaction, and low absenteeism and turnover. These outcomes occur when people experience three critical psychological states (noted in the middle column of the figure):

1. They believe they are doing something meaningful because their work is important to other people.

2. They feel personally responsible for how the work turns out.

3. They learn how well they performed their jobs.

These psychological states occur when people are working on enriched jobs—that is, jobs that offer the following five core job dimensions:

Exhibit 11.6 The Hackman and Oldham model of job enrichment

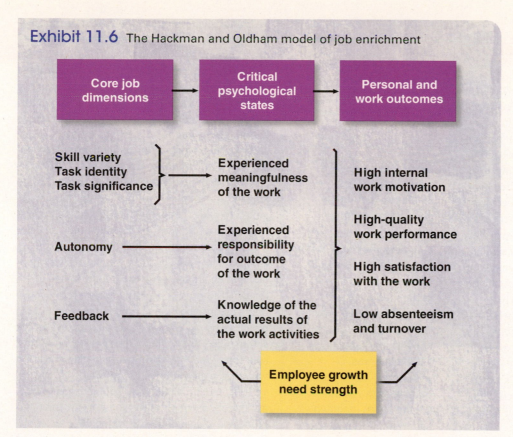

Source: From "A New Strategy for Job Enrichment" by J. Richard Hackman et al., *California Management Review.* Copyright © 1975 by the Regents of the University of California. Reprinted from the *California Management Review,* vol. 17, no. 4. By permission of The Regents.

"I love the outdoors and I love feeling that I have a part in protecting the public lands out there."[91]

4. *Autonomy*—independence and discretion in making decisions. In a research hospital, a department administrator told her people to do the kinds of research they wanted as long as it was within budget (and legal). With no other guidelines—that is, complete autonomy— productivity increased sixfold in a year.[92]

5. *Feedback*—information about job performance. Many companies post charts or provide computerized data indicating productivity, number of rejects, and other data. At Whole Foods Market, teams are responsible for hiring and scheduling in their area of the store. Team leaders get information about each month's payroll expense versus the budgeted amount. If the team comes in under budget, everyone knows because everyone gets a share of the savings. This practical feedback inspires teams to hire carefully and work hard.[93]

1. *Skill variety*—different job activities involving several skills and talents. For example, management trainees at Enterprise Rent-A-Car try their hands at every area of the business, including hiring employees, washing cars, waiting on customers, working with body shops, and ordering supplies. Assistant manager Sarah Ruddell defines the broad responsibilities as a plus: "You're not stuck doing the same thing over and over again."[89]

2. *Task identity*—the completion of a whole, identifiable piece of work. At State Farm Insurance, agents are independent contractors who sell and provide service for State Farm products exclusively. They have built and invested in their own businesses. As a result, agent retention and productivity are far better than industry norms.[90]

3. *Task significance*—an important, positive impact on the lives of others. Fire fighters have very hazardous jobs. In 2013, 19 members of Prescott's Granite Mountain Hotshots died while fighting a blaze on a ridge located near Yarnell, Arizona. In the aftermath of their tragic deaths, some people wondered why Hotshots take such extreme risks to battle fires and protect strangers' homes and businesses. As a relatively small group of highly qualified, rugged, and self-sufficient individuals employed by the U.S. Forest Service and its interagency partners, Hotshots do what they do because they feel their work matters. Brandon Hess, superintendent of the Tatanka Interagency Hotshot Crew out of Custer, South Dakota, does his job out of a sense of duty. Speaking from the front line of a wildfire in Colorado, Hess summarized his passion for the work:

The most effective job enrichment increases all five core dimensions.

A person's growth need strength will help determine just how effective a job enrichment program might be. **Growth need strength** is the degree to which individuals want personal and psychological development. Job enrichment would be more successful for people with high growth need strength. But very few people respond negatively to job enrichment.[95]

● Fulton hotshots (L-R) Daniel Hammond and Jake Cagle both of Bakersfield, CA set a back burn to help contain a fire in Glacier National Park, MT.

5.4 | To Motivate, Empowerment Must Be Done Right

Today many managers talk about "empowering" their people. Individuals may—or may not—feel empowered, and groups can have a "culture" of empowerment that enhances work unit performance.[96] **Empowerment** is the process of sharing power with employees, thereby enhancing their confidence in their ability to perform their jobs and their belief that they are influential contributors to the organization. Unfortunately empowerment doesn't always live up to its hype. One problem is that managers undermine it by sending mixed messages like "Do your own thing—the way we tell you."[97] But empowerment can be profoundly motivating when done properly.[98]

Empowerment changes employees' beliefs—from feeling powerless to believing strongly in their own personal effectiveness.[99] As a result, people take more initiative and persevere in achieving their goals and their leader's vision even in the face of obstacles.[100] Specifically, empowerment encourages the following beliefs among employees:[101]

- They perceive *meaning* in their work; their job fits their values.

- They feel *competent,* or capable of performing their jobs with skill.

- They have a sense of *self-determination,* of having some choice in regard to the tasks, methods, and pace of their work.

- They have an *impact*—that is, they have some influence over important strategic, administrative, or operating decisions or outcomes on the job.

Did You Know?

CareerBliss analyzed more than 100,000 employee-generated reviews to create a ranking of jobs in which employees are happiest. Respondents identified software quality assurance engineer as the "happiest" job, followed by executive chef, property manager, bank teller, and warehouse manager. Other jobs that made the top 20 list included electrician, HR manager, and financial analyst.[94] Do the most satisfying jobs have more of Hackman and Oldham's job characteristics?

Exhibit 11.7 includes comments from people when they were feeling empowered and disempowered.

To foster empowerment, management must create an environment in which all the employees feel they have real influence over performance standards and business effectiveness within their areas of responsibility.[102] An empowering work environment provides people with *information* necessary for them to perform at their best, *knowledge* about how to use the information and how to do their work, *power* to make decisions that give them control over their work, and the *rewards* they deserve for the contributions they make.[103] Such an environment reduces costs because fewer people are needed to supervise, monitor, and coordinate. It improves quality and service because high performance is inspired at the source—the people who do the work. It also allows quick action because people on the spot see problems, solutions, and opportunities for innovation on which they are empowered to act.

It is essential to give people clear strategic direction but to leave some room for flexibility and calculated risk taking. For example, Southwest Airlines' strategic principle of "meet customers' short-haul travel needs at fares competitive with the cost of automobile travel" helps employees keep strategic objectives in mind and use their discretion in making complicated decisions about service offerings, route selection, cabin design, ticketing procedures, and pricing.[104] More specific actions include increasing signature authority at all levels; reducing the number of rules and approval steps; assigning nonroutine jobs; allowing independent judgment, flexibility, and creativity; defining jobs

---

Exhibit 11.7   Reactions to feeling empowered and disempowered

When Feeling *Empowered,* People Had the Following Comments:

I was able to make a large financial decision on my own. I got to write a large check without being questioned.

After having received a memo that said, "Cut travel," I made my case about why it was necessary to travel for business reasons, and I was told to go ahead.

My president supported my idea without question.

All the financial data were shared with me.

When Feeling *Disempowered,* People Had the Following Comments:

I had no input into a hiring decision of someone who has to report directly to me. I didn't even get to speak to the candidate.

I worked extremely hard—long hours and late nights—on an urgent project, and then my manager took full credit for it.

My suggestions, whether good or bad, were either not solicited or, worse, ignored.

The project was reassigned without my knowledge or input.

Source: J. Kouzes and B. Posner, *The Leadership Challenge,* 2nd ed. Copyright © 1995 Jossey-Bass, Inc. This material is used by permission of Jossey-Bass, Inc., a subsidiary of John Wiley & Sons, Inc.

more broadly as projects rather than tasks; and providing more access to resources and people throughout the organization.[105]

Empowerment does not mean allowing people to decide trivial things like what color to paint the lunchroom. For empowerment to make a difference, people must have an impact on things they care about, such as quality and productivity.[106] Companies that have successfully used empowerment programs include Lord Corporation in Dayton, Ohio (which produces engine mounts for aircraft), and Herman Miller (the Michigan-based furniture manufacturer).[107]

:::::::::::::::::

Empowerment seems to be at the heart of motivation for employees of Google. Rather than just guessing what employees want, Google has applied its commitment to careful analysis. The company developed a computer algorithm (mathematical procedure) to see where its challenges lie in retaining its best talent. The algorithm evaluates data from employee surveys, performance reviews, pay histories, and peer reviews to identify which employees are most at risk of leaving the company.

A key lesson has already emerged: employees are most likely to leave Google if they believe the company is not fully tapping into their expertise. Most likely, this issue will continue to be significant. In Google's early years, employees enjoyed the thrill of being part of something new and rapidly expanding. The growth offered seemingly limitless possibilities, and employees had exceptional leeway to work on projects of their own invention. After more than a decade, the company has almost 25,000 employees and a greater need to coordinate their work and set priorities for allocating resources. To motivate employees to stay, Google will have to figure out how it can continue offering flexibility for learning and experimentation, perhaps coupled with more formal structures such as career paths.[108]

:::::::::::::::::

You should not be surprised when empowerment causes some problems, at least in the short term. Problems accompany virtually any change, including changes for the better. It's important to remember that empowerment brings responsibility, and employees don't necessarily like the accountability at first.[109] People may make mistakes, especially until they have had adequate training. Because more training is needed, costs are higher. Because people acquire new skills and make greater contributions, they may demand higher wages. But if they are well trained and truly empowered, they will deserve the pay—and they and the company will benefit.

LO6 Summarize how people assess and achieve fairness.

6 | ACHIEVING FAIRNESS

Ultimately one of the most important issues in motivation surrounds people's view of what they contribute to the organization and what they receive from it. Ideally they will view their relationship with their employer as a well-balanced, mutually beneficial exchange. As people work and realize the outcomes or consequences of their actions, they assess how fairly the organization treats them.

The starting point for understanding how people interpret their contributions and outcomes is equity theory.[110] **Equity theory** proposes that when people assess how fairly they are treated, they consider two key factors:

1. *Outcomes,* as in expectancy theory, refer to the various things the person receives on the job: recognition, pay, benefits, satisfaction, security, job assignments, punishments, and so forth.

2. *Inputs* refer to the contributions the person makes to the organization: effort, time, talent, performance, extra commitment, good citizenship, and so forth.

People generally expect that the outcomes they receive will reflect, or be proportionate to, the inputs they provide—a fair day's pay (and other outcomes) for a fair day's work (broadly defined by how people view all their contributions).

But this comparison of outcomes to inputs is not the whole story. People also pay attention to the outcomes and inputs others receive. At salary review time, for example, most people—from executives on down—try to pick up clues that will tell them who got the biggest raises. As described in the following section, they compare ratios, try to restore equity if necessary, and derive more or less satisfaction based on how fairly they believe they have been treated.

empowerment the process of sharing power with employees, thereby enhancing their confidence in their ability to perform their jobs and their belief that they are influential contributors to the organization.

equity theory a theory stating that people assess how fairly they have been treated according to two key factors: outcomes and inputs

● Employees who lack the power to do their jobs effectively are less likely to feel motivated at work.

6.1 | People Assess Equity by Making Comparisons

Equity theory suggests that people compare the ratio of their own outcomes to inputs against the outcome-to-input ratio of some comparison person. The comparison person can be a coworker, a boss, or an average industry pay scale. Stated more succinctly, people compare

$$\text{Their own } \frac{\text{Outcomes}}{\text{Inputs}} \text{ versus Other's } \frac{\text{Outcomes}}{\text{Inputs}}$$

If the ratios are equivalent, people believe the relationship is equitable, or fair. Equity causes people to be satisfied with their treatment. But the person who believes his or her ratio is lower than another's will feel inequitably treated. Inequity causes dissatisfaction and leads to an attempt to restore balance to the relationship.

Inequity and the negative feelings it creates may appear anywhere. As a student, perhaps you have been in the following situation. You stay up all night and get a C on the exam. Meanwhile, another student studies a couple of hours, goes out for the rest of the evening, gets a good night's sleep, and gets a B. You perceive your inputs (time spent studying) as much greater than the other student's, but your outcomes are lower. You are displeased at the seeming unfairness. In business, the same thing sometimes happens with pay raises. One manager puts in 60-hour weeks, earned a degree from a prestigious university, and believes she is destined for the top. When her archrival—whom she perceives as less deserving ("she never comes into the office on weekends, and all she does when she is here is butter up the boss")—gets the higher raise or the promotion, she experiences severe feelings of inequity. In the world of sports, motivation problems resulting from perceived pay inequities may be the reason major league baseball teams that have great differences in their player salaries tend to win fewer games.[111]

::::::::::::::::

Many people have felt inequity when they learn about large sums paid to high-profile CEOs. Ironically, one reason for rising CEO pay is an effort to set pay using a method that looks something like the equity comparison: the board of directors compares the CEO's pay with that of chief executives at organizations in a "peer group." Until 2006 companies did not have to disclose which companies were in the peer group, but one example exposed in the courtroom has suggested how inequity can arise. Richard A. Grasso received $140 million in compensation as chair of the New York Stock Exchange. A compensation expert hired by New York's attorney general learned that the companies of the peer group used as a basis for setting Grasso's pay had median revenues more than 25 times that of the NYSE, media assets 125 times the NYSE's, and a median number of employees that was about 30 times that of the NYSE.[112] Even when a company chooses an appropriate peer group, many boards try to pay their executives in the top one-fourth of the group. The drive to keep everyone's pay above average means the average keeps climbing.

::::::::::::::::

Assessments of equity are not made objectively. They are subjective perceptions or beliefs. In the preceding example of the two managers, the one who got the bigger raise probably felt she deserved it. Even if she admits to working fewer hours, she may convince herself she can because she is more efficient. In the example of the students, the one who scored higher may believe the outcome was equitable because (1) she worked harder over the course of the semester, and (2) she's smart (ability and experience, not just time and effort, can be seen as inputs).

6.2 | People Who Feel Inequitably Treated Try to Even the Balance

People who feel inequitably treated and dissatisfied are motivated to do something to restore equity. They have a number of options that they carry out to change the ratios or to reevaluate the situation and decide it is equitable after all.

The equity equation shown earlier indicates people's options for restoring equity when they feel inequitably treated:

- *Reducing their inputs*—giving less effort, performing at lower levels, or quitting: "Well, if that's the way things work around here, there's no way I'm going to work that hard (or stick around)."

- *Increasing their outcomes:* "My boss is going to hear about this. I deserve more; there must be some way I can get more."

- *Decreasing others' outcomes:* For example, an employee may sabotage work to create problems for his company or boss.[113] People can change their perceptions of an outcome, not just the outcome itself: "That promotion isn't as great a deal as she thinks. The pay is not that much better, and the headaches will be unbelievable."

- *Increasing others' inputs*—Here, too, the change may be in perceptions: "The more I think about it, the more I see he deserved it. He's worked hard all year, he's competent, and it's about time he got a break."

Thus a person can restore equity in a number of ways by behaviorally or perceptually changing inputs and outcomes. On the positive side, people may care about group equity and *may even increase their inputs* to keep a situation equitable for the group. In the first few months of each year, many accountants face a flood of work related to annual reports and tax preparation. At Gramkow, Carnevale, Seifert & Company, an accounting firm in Oradell, New Jersey, Kenneth Benkow works six days a week and many evenings during tax time. He explains, "What helps motivate me is that I look around the office and I see people who are working as hard or harder than I am. You feel guilty if you're not pulling your own weight."[114]

6.3 | Procedures—Not Just Outcomes—Should Be Fair

Inevitably managers make decisions that have outcomes more favorable for some than for others. Those with favorable outcomes will be pleased; those with worse outcomes, all else equal, will be more displeased. But managers desiring to put salve on the wounds—say, of people they like or respect or want to keep

● Former John Deere CEO Robert Lane stands next to an 8530 Row Crop Tractor in Moline, IL. Deere & Company is the world's leading manufacturer of agricultural machinery as well as a leading supplier of construction equipment and riding lawn mowers.

and motivate—still can reduce the dissatisfaction. They do this by demonstrating that they provide **procedural justice**—using a fair process in decision making and helping others know that the process was as fair as possible. When people perceive procedural fairness, they are more likely to support decisions and decision makers.[115] For example, one year after layoffs, managers' use of procedural justice (in the form of employee participation in decisions) still predicted survivors' organizational commitment, job satisfaction, and trust toward management.[116]

Even if people believe that their *outcome* was inequitable and unfair, they are more likely to view justice as having been served if the *process* was fair. You can increase people's beliefs that the process was fair by making the process open and visible, stating decision criteria in advance rather than after the fact, making sure that the most appropriate people—those who have valid information and are viewed as trustworthy—make the decisions, giving people a chance to participate in the process, and providing an appeal process that allows people to question decisions safely and receive complete answers.[117] This kind of treatment is expressed by Deere and Company's former chief executive, Bob Lane. Lane says that even when "we have to let people go" because the company is struggling, "each and every individual has inherent worth," so management must treat employees with dignity and help them understand the reasons behind the actions.[118]

In contrast, at an elevator plant in the United States, an army of consultants arrived one day, without explanation.[119] The rumor mill kicked in; employees guessed the plant would be shut down or some of them would be laid off. Three months later, management unveiled its new plan, involving a new method of manufacturing based on teams. But management did not adequately answer questions about the purpose of the changes, employees resisted, conflicts arose, and the formerly popular plant manager lost the trust of his people. Costs skyrocketed, and quality plummeted.

LO7 Identify causes and consequences of a satisfied workforce.

7 | JOB SATISFACTION

If people feel fairly treated from the outcomes they receive or the processes used, they will be satisfied. A satisfied worker is not necessarily more productive than a dissatisfied one; sometimes people are happy with their jobs because they don't have to work hard! But job dissatisfaction, aggregated across many individuals, creates a workforce that is more likely to exhibit the following characteristics:

- Higher turnover and absenteeism.

- Less good citizenship (going the "extra mile" and helping others at work) among employees.[120]

- More grievances and lawsuits.

- Strikes.

- Stealing, sabotage, and vandalism.

- Poorer mental and physical health (which can mean higher job stress, higher insurance costs, and more lawsuits).[121]

- More injuries.[122]

- Poor customer service.[123]

- Lower productivity and profits.[124]

All of these consequences of dissatisfaction, either directly or indirectly, are costly. Sadly, a recent survey reported that 74 percent of individuals would consider leaving their current jobs, while 32 percent are actively searching. A survey by Accenture found that the top contributors to employee dissatisfaction are (1) lack of recognition (43 percent), (2) internal politics (35 percent), (3) dislike of their boss (31 percent), and (4) lack of empowerment (31 percent).[125]

Job satisfaction is especially important for relationship-oriented service employees such as real estate agents, hair stylists, and stockbrokers. Customers develop (or don't develop) a commitment to a specific service provider. Satisfied service providers are less likely to quit the company and more likely to provide an enjoyable customer experience.[126]

7.1 | Companies Are Improving the Quality of Work Life

Quality of work life (QWL) programs create a workplace that enhances employee well-being and satisfaction. The general goal of QWL programs is to satisfy the full range of employee needs. People's needs apparently are well met at First Horizon National, which offers a flexible benefits package including health, dental, and vision insurance; paid vacation; tuition reimbursement; discounts for child care and financial products; a wellness program; and reimbursement for adoption-related expenses. More unusually, First Horizon extends those benefits to workers who telecommute and work part-time. The company has appeared on

psychological contract
a set of perceptions of what employees owe their employers, and what their employers owe them

Fortune's list of the 100 Best Companies to Work For, but more important is the impact on workers like Brenda Fung, a part-time designer of the company's intranet. Fung told a reporter, "This company has been so generous to me. There's no way I could even think of leaving."[127]

QWL addresses eight categories:[128]

1. Adequate and fair compensation.
2. A safe and healthy environment.
3. Jobs that develop human capacities.
4. A chance for personal growth and security.
5. A social environment that fosters personal identity, freedom from prejudice, a sense of community, and upward mobility.
6. Constitutionalism—the rights of personal privacy, dissent, and due process.
7. A work role that minimizes infringement on personal leisure and family needs.
8. Socially responsible organizational actions.

Organizations differ drastically in their attention to QWL. Critics claim that QWL programs don't necessarily inspire employees to work harder if the company does not tie rewards directly to individual performance. Advocates of QWL claim that it improves organizational effectiveness and productivity. The term *productivity,* as applied by QWL programs, means much more than each person's quantity of work output.[129] It also includes turnover, absenteeism, accidents, theft, sabotage, creativity, innovation, and especially the quality of work.

7.2 | Psychological Contracts Are Understandings of Give-and-Take

The relationship between individuals and employing organizations typically is formalized by a written contract. But in employees' minds there also exists a **psychological contract**—a set of perceptions of what they owe their employers and what their employers owe them.[130] This contract, whether it is seen as being upheld or violated—and whether the parties trust one another or not—has important implications for employee satisfaction and motivation and the effectiveness of the organization.

Historically, in many companies the employment relationship was stable and predictable. Now mergers, layoffs, outsourcing, and other disruptions have thrown asunder the "old deal."[131] In traditionally managed organizations, employees were expected to be loyal, and employers would provide secure employment. Today the implicit contract goes something like this:[132] if people stay, do their own job plus someone else's (who has been downsized), and do additional things like participating in task forces, the company will try to provide a job (if it can), provide gestures that it cares, and keep providing about the same pay (with periodic small increases). The likely result of this not-very-satisfying arrangement: uninspired people in a struggling business.

But a better deal is possible for both employers and employees.[133] Ideally your employer will provide continuous skill updating and an invigorating work environment in which you can use your skills and are motivated to stay even though you may have other job options.[134]

Consider how business coach Ram Charan assumed this new psychological contract in advising a frustrated HR manager.[135] The manager had asked Charan for guidance in coping with bureaucratic red tape that frustrated the entire group, including the manager himself. Charan encouraged the manager to reframe the situation as a need for learning, creativity, and leadership. The manager, said Charan, should investigate what the managers in other departments need from HR, so that his people would truly be serving business needs and helping to solve business problems. Charan also encouraged the manager to learn about his employees' career goals and interests so that he can focus on ways to develop his people's strengths through assignments and greater decision-making authority within the department. If the HR manager accepts Charan's guidance, he and his people will face more difficult yet more interesting challenges than they would by simply defining themselves as a static part of a bureaucracy.

Study Checklist

- Did you tear out the perforated student review card at the back of the text to revisit learning objectives and key terms and definitions?

Connect ® Management is available for M Management. Additional resources include:

- Interactive Applications:
  - Comprehension Case: The Electricity of Job Enrichment
  - Drag & Drop: What Motivation Theory Fits?
  - Self-Assessment: Your Personality and Goal Setting
  - Video Case: Passion for Hot Topic

- LearnSmart—Multiple choice questions help you determine what you already know, are not sure about, or need to practice based on your score. And with SmartBook, you can read the relevant section in the eBook as well as practice and recharge what you've learned.
- Chapter Video: The Container Store
- Young Manager Speaks Out: Herb Steward, Dock Foreman/Supervisor

Practice and Apply your Management knowledge through Connect

Go to: McGrawhillconnect.com

Teamwork

Learning Objectives

After studying Chapter 12, you should be able to

LO1 Discuss how teams can contribute to an organization's effectiveness.

LO2 Distinguish the new team environment from that of traditional work groups.

LO3 Summarize how groups become teams.

LO4 Explain why groups sometimes fail.

LO5 Describe how to build an effective team.

LO6 List methods for managing a team's relationships with other teams.

LO7 Give examples of ways to manage conflict.

A s Cisco Systems has grown, the computer networking giant has stayed nimble by delegating work to teams whose membership crosses functional, departmental, and national lines.[1] Sometimes—as in Cisco's case—teams "work," but sometimes they don't. The goal of this chapter is to help make sure that your management and work teams succeed rather than fail. Almost all companies now use teams to produce goods and services, to manage projects, and to make decisions and run the company.[2] For you this has two vital implications:

1. You *will* be working in and perhaps managing teams.

2. The *ability* to work in and lead teams is valuable to your employer and important to your career.

Fortunately coursework focusing on team training can enhance students' teamwork knowledge and skills.[3]

LO1 Discuss how teams can contribute to an organization's effectiveness

---

1 | THE CONTRIBUTIONS OF TEAMS

Team-based approaches to work have generated excitement. Used appropriately, teams can be powerfully effective as a *building block for organization structure*. Organizations like Semco, Whole Foods, and Kollmorgen (a manufacturer of printed circuits and electro-optic devices) are structured entirely around teams.[3M]'s breakthrough products emerge through the use of teams that are small entrepreneurial businesses within the larger corporation.

Teams also can increase *productivity*, improve *quality*, and reduce *costs*. By adopting a team structure and culture, Battle Creek, Michigan–based Summit Pointe, a mental health organization, has saved millions of dollars while improving patient care.[4] A 12-person team from a Ford plant in Saarlouis, Germany, solved a problem with its basecoat paint applications that resulted in annual costs savings of $2 million and a reduction of 70 kg of volatile organic compounds (environment-damaging solvents that are released into the air as paint dries).[5] At Nucor's steel plant in Decatur, Alabama, general manager Rex Query credits teamwork for high productivity and improved safety.[6]

Teams also can enhance *speed* and be powerful forces for *innovation* and *change*. To explore alternative forms of social connection and create new apps faster, Facebook recently launched Facebook Creative Labs (FCL). The initiative empowers small teams within the 6,000-employee company to self-organize and "build standalone apps or other projects that live outside the core Facebook experience." FCL's first offspring, a news feed reader app called Paper, promises to make the news feed experience more intuitive and meaningful for users.[7] General Mills uses a team approach to make decisions about the packaging for its products. For product divisions such as Big G cereals, Yoplait yogurt, or Green Giant vegetables, Packaging Partners teams bring together employees from brand design, engineering, production, research and development, and other relevant functions to figure out how packaging can reduce waste, cut costs, and send a clearer marketing message. In addition, Strategy Map teams convene employees from various product divisions to study packaging using a particular material and determine ways to work more efficiently with suppliers.[8]

Teams also provide many *benefits for their members*.[9] The team is a useful learning mechanism. Members learn about the company and themselves, and they acquire new skills and performance strategies. The team can satisfy important personal needs, such as affiliation and esteem. Team members may receive tangible organizational rewards that they could not have achieved working alone. After General Mills acquired Pillsbury, the managers of the meals division decided they needed to develop a common culture that would promote employee engagement, so they set up a Spirit Team of staff members to select activities. Realizing that just having fun together would not develop a deeper sense of purpose, the team decided to partner with a nonprofit organization, Perspectives Family Center, and support this organization with several events each year. Employees who participate feel great about what they do, and they connect the experience with a sense that their company cares about its local community.[10]

> "No one can whistle a symphony. It takes an orchestra to play it."
>
> —Halford E. Luccock

---

group a collection of people who interact to undertake a task but do not necessarily perform as a unit or achieve significant performance improvements

team a small number of people with complementary skills who are committed to a common purpose, set of performance goals, and approach for which they hold themselves mutually accountable

Team members can give one another feedback; identify opportunities for growth and development; and train, coach, and mentor.[11] A marketing representative can learn about financial modeling from a colleague on a new product development team, and a financial expert can learn about consumer marketing. Experience working together in a team, and developing strong problem-solving capabilities, is a vital supplement to specific job skills or functional expertise. And the skills are transferable to new positions.

2 | THE NEW TEAM ENVIRONMENT

The words *group* and *team* often are used interchangeably.[12] Modern managers sometimes use the word *teams* to the point that it has become cliché; they talk about teams while skeptics perceive no real teamwork. So making a distinction between groups and teams can be useful:

- A **group** is a collection of people who interact to undertake a task but do not necessarily perform as a unit or achieve significant performance improvements.

● At Google, software engineers have freedom and autonomy regarding which projects and teams to join. The firm invests heavily in training its newly hired software engineers, Nooglers, to work productively in teams.

- A **team** is formed of people (usually a small number) with complementary skills who trust one another and are committed to a common purpose, common performance goals, and a common approach for which they hold themselves mutually accountable.[13]

If you work for Google, chances are good that you will join one or more teams. Its software engineers, the ones who are responsible for developing new products and services like Chromebooks, Google Glass, and Google Hangouts. typically work in small three- or four-person product development teams. Even a large team of 20 or 30 engineers is broken into smaller teams that work on specific parts of the overall project, such as redesigning the Gmail website or making spam filters more effective. The role of leader shifts among members depending on the project's particular requirements. Engineers have the freedom to switch teams (without asking permission from management) and commit to work on projects to which they feel they can contribute. Shona Brown, Google's vice president for operations, comments, ". . . we want people to commit to things rather than be assigned to things." Google believes that this flexible and hands-off approach to team management spurs innovation and creativity at the firm.

Given the freedom and autonomy that employees have at Google, the firm invests heavily in training their newly hired software engineers, known as "Nooglers," to work productively in teams. The goal is to help new hires become fully productive as soon as possible. They undergo an orientation program and attend lectures about the firm's culture and practices delivered by senior engineers. Mentors are assigned to the new hires so Nooglers can learn more about how teams function and answer specific questions about the technical aspects of their jobs and projects. After completing a two-week starter project, Nooglers can organize or attend "Tech Talks," which are voluntary, self-organized events in which engineers get together to share knowledge with each other about a technical topic of interest.[14]

Organizations have been using groups for a long time, but today's workplaces are different.[15] Teams are used in many different ways, and to far greater effect, than in the past. Exhibit 12.1 highlights just a few of the differences between the traditional work environment and the way true teams work today. Ideally people are far more involved, they are better trained, cooperation is higher, and the culture is one of learning as well as producing.

2.1 | Organizations Have Different Types of Teams

Your organization may have hundreds of groups and teams, but they can be classified into just a few primary types.[16] **Work teams** make or do things such as manufacture, assemble, sell, or provide service. They typically are well defined,

work teams teams that make or do things like manufacture, assemble, sell, or provide service

project and development teams teams that work on long-term projects but disband once the work is completed

parallel teams teams that operate separately from the regular work structure, and exist temporarily

management teams teams that coordinate and give direction to the subunits under their jurisdiction and integrate work among subunits

transnational teams work groups composed of multinational members whose activities span multiple countries

Exhibit 12.1	Comparing traditional and new team work environments	
Activity	**Traditional Work Environment**	**New Team Work Environment**
Work planning	Managers do the planning.	Managers and team members plan together.
Job definition	Narrow set of tasks and duties.	Broad set of skills and knowledge.
Information	Mostly "management property."	Tends to be freely shared at all levels.
Risk taking	Discouraged and punished.	Measured risk taking is encouraged and supported.
Rewards	Based on individual performance.	Based on individual and team performance.
Work process	Managers determine "best methods."	Everyone continuously improves work processes.

Source: Adapted from *Leading Teams* by J. Zenger and Associates. *Reprinted by permission.*

a clear part of the formal organizational structure, and composed of a full-time, stable membership. Work teams are what most people think of when they think of teams in organizations.[17]

Project and development teams work on long-term projects, often over a period of years. They have specific assignments, such as research or new product development, and members usually must contribute expert knowledge and judgment. These teams work toward a one-time product, disbanding once their work is completed. Then new teams are formed for new projects.

Parallel teams operate separately from the regular work structure of the firm on a temporary basis. Members often come from different units or jobs and are asked to do work that is not normally done by the standard structure. Their charge is to recommend solutions to specific problems. They seldom have authority to act, however. Examples include task forces and quality or safety teams formed to study a particular problem. Whenever Baltimore's Bradford Bank acquires or starts up another operation, it assembles a team of employees drawn from various divisions to smooth the transition for customers. For example, when Bradford signed a deal to acquire deposits from American Bank, a team of employees from branch management, deposit services, and information technology studied American's products to make sure Bradford was ready to offer similar services to its new customers.[18]

Management teams coordinate and give direction to the subunits under their jurisdiction and integrate work among subunits.[19] The management team is based on authority stemming from hierarchical rank and is responsible for the overall performance of the business unit. Managers responsible for different subunits form a team together, and at the top of the organization resides the executive management team that establishes strategic direction and manages the firm's overall performance.

Transnational teams are work teams composed of multinational members whose activities span multiple countries.[20] Such teams differ from other work teams not only by being multicultural but also by often being geographically dispersed, being psychologically distant, and working on highly complex projects having considerable impact on company objectives.

YOUNG MANAGERS
Speak Out!

"Teamwork is very important to any company or any organization because one they are working together, you know, cohesively and they are happy with what they are doing, it really reflects upon you and your leadership capabilities."

—Alicia Catalano, Sales Team Leader

Teams Make Social Impact by Design

Companies are increasingly differentiating themselves by marketing new products and services that are designed with a social or environmental message. For example, rather than launching a new laundry detergent that would require hot water (and more energy usage), Procter & Gamble developed a surfactant that would clean clothes well in cold water; this led to the introduction of *Tide Coldwater.* Regarding the new product, Adam Werbach, CEO of advertising firm Saatchi & Saatchi, commented, "So there's a solution good for the climate, good for the consumer because it saved money and good for the business [Procter & Gamble] because it created a breakthrough product."

Who helps design such innovative products? Managers often call on creative cross-functional teams from design firms like IDEO.org and Continuum. In addition to serving corporate clients, these design teams are increasingly working with socially oriented organizations like foundations and nongovernmental organizations (NGOs) to help them more effectively fulfill their missions. The goal is to use design as a way to bring innovative solutions to complex problems, like providing the impoverished in developing countries with basic health services, sustainable agriculture, water, and sanitation.

Team members at IDEO.org combined forces with Hewlett-Packard, Unilever, the Rockefeller Foundation, VisionSpring (a New York–based social enterprise), and WSUP (a nonprofit working to improve safe, affordable water and sanitation) to design the following solutions for problems in developing world contexts:

1. In Uganda: Designed a handheld device to aid in microfinance banking transactions like making payments or withdrawing funds. By having the "bank come to them," borrowers in poor rural areas no longer have to make a day's journey to the city each week to visit a bank.

2. In India: Provided affordable, comprehensive eye care to children in rural villages by organizing "eye camps" for kids, screening and awareness programs in schools, and promotion campaigns through self-help groups. The IDEO.org team discovered that Indian children want to be treated like adults, so they trained children to administer some of the eye exams for their young peers.

3. In Ghana: Developed an in-home sanitation solution for many of the residents who do not have toilets. Those without toilets would either walk to the nearest public toilet or resort to "flying toilets" (plastic bags that are thrown out of the home after use). IDEO.org's idea also includes having local businesses make, supply, and service the portable toilets.

What's the bottom line? Teams from design firms like IDEO.org are applying their expertise to create innovations that meet people's needs and improve their lives.

IDEO.org team members like the one pictured above use design as a way to bring solutions to basic problems that affect the impoverished in developing countries.

DISCUSSION QUESTIONS

- Why do you think companies like Procter & Gamble are launching new products and services that are designed to have a social or environmental impact? Can you think of other examples of products and services that have used design in a similar fashion?

- In order to acquire a thorough understanding of the problems of the people in Uganda, India, and Ghana, the IDEO.org design team spends time getting to know the focal group, observing their daily behaviors, and interviewing them. How could the team use these same research techniques to design new products and services for companies here in the United States?

SOURCES: Company website, www.ideo.com; company website, http://continuuminnovation.com; A. Sklar and S. Madsen, "Design for Social Impact," *Ergonomics in Design* 18, no. 2 (2010), pp. 4–31; D. Woodward, "Winning By Design," *Director* 63, no. 5 (January 2010), pp. 50–54; and M. H. Meyer and T. J. Marion, "Innovating For Effectiveness: Lessons from Design Firms," *Research Technology Management* 53, no. 5 (September/October 2010), pp. 21–29.

Transnational teams tend to be **virtual teams**, communicating electronically more than face-to-face, although other types of teams may operate virtually as well. A virtual team encounters difficult challenges: building trust, cohesion, and team identity, and overcoming communication barriers and the isolation of virtual team members.[21] Ways that managers can overcome these challenges and improve the effectiveness of virtual teams include ensuring that team members understand how they are supposed to keep in touch, setting aside time at the beginning of virtual meetings to build relationships, ensuring that all participants in meetings and on message boards have a chance to communicate, sharing meeting minutes and progress reports, and recognizing and rewarding team members' contributions.[22]

virtual teams teams that are physically dispersed and communicate electronically more than face-to-face

traditional work groups groups that have no managerial responsibilities

quality circles voluntary groups of people drawn from various production teams who make suggestions about quality

autonomous work groups groups that control decisions about and execution of a complete range of tasks

semiautonomous work groups groups that make decisions about managing and carrying out major production activities but get outside support for quality control and maintenance

self-designing teams teams with the responsibilities of autonomous work groups, plus control over hiring, firing, and deciding what tasks members perform

self-managed teams autonomous work groups in which workers are trained to do all or most of the jobs in a unit, have no immediate supervisor, and make decisions previously made by first-line supervisors

2.2 | Self-Managed Teams Empower Employees

Today many different types of work teams exist, with many different labels. The terms can be confusing and sometimes are used interchangeably out of a lack of awareness of actual differences. Generally speaking, some teams are more traditional with little decision-making authority, being under the control of direct supervision. Other teams have more autonomy, decision-making power, and self-direction.[23] Let's define each category:

- **Traditional work groups** have no managerial responsibilities. The first-line manager plans, organizes, staffs, directs, and controls them, and other groups provide support activities, including quality control and maintenance.

- **Quality circles** are voluntary groups of people drawn from various production teams who make suggestions about quality but have no authority to make decisions or execute.

- **Semiautonomous work groups** make decisions about managing and carrying out major production activities but still get outside support for quality control and maintenance.

- **Autonomous work groups**, or *self-managing teams,* control decisions about and execution of a complete range of tasks—acquiring raw materials and performing operations, quality control, maintenance, and shipping. They are fully responsible for an entire product or an entire part of a production process.

- **Self-designing teams** do all of that and go one step further—they also have control over the design of the team. They decide themselves whom to hire, whom to fire, and what tasks the team will perform.

Movement from left to right on the continuum corresponds with more and more worker participation. Toward the right, the participation is not trivial and not merely advisory. It has real substance, going beyond suggestions to include action and impact.

The trend today is toward **self-managed teams**, in which workers are trained to do all or most of the jobs in the unit, they have no immediate supervisor, and they make decisions previously made by first-line supervisors.[24] Self-managed teams are most often found in manufacturing. People may resist self-managed work teams, in part because they don't want so much responsibility and the change is difficult.[25] In addition, many people don't like to do performance evaluation

of teammates or to fire people, and poorly managed conflict may be a particular problem in self-managed teams.[26] But when companies have introduced teams that reach the point of being truly self-managed, results have included lower costs and greater levels of team productivity, quality, and customer satisfaction.[27] Overall, semiautonomous and autonomous teams are known to improve the organization's financial and overall performance, at least in North America.[28]

At video-game maker Valve Corp., the firm's 300 employees recruit fellow employees to work on projects, but also decide on their pay and work hours. Eighty-three of General Electric's aviation-manufacturing facilities have no foreperson or shop floor boss. The plant manager acts as the only leader by setting production goals and helping resolve any problems that arise. Employee teams manage themselves by meeting before each shift to determine their own work schedules and workflow. The team-based system has boosted productivity at the GE plants.[29]

LO3 Summarize how groups become teams

3 | HOW GROUPS BECOME REAL TEAMS

As a manager, you will want your group to become an effective team. To accomplish this, you need to understand how groups can become true teams and why groups sometimes fail to become teams. Groups become true teams through basic group activities, the passage of time, and team development activities.

3.1 | Group Activities Shift as the Group Matures

Assume you are the leader of a newly formed group—actually a bunch of people. What will you face as you attempt to develop your group into a high-performing team? If groups are to develop successfully, they will typically progress through four broad stages as described in Exhibit 12.2.[30] Groups that deteriorate move to a *declining* stage, and temporary groups add an *adjourning* or terminating stage. Groups terminate when

Exhibit 12.2 Stages of team development

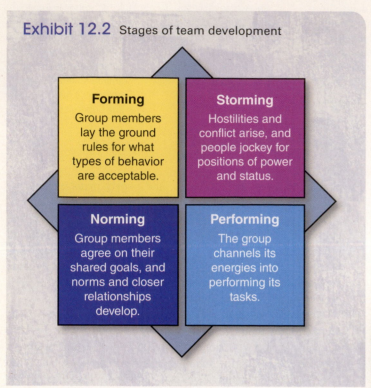

Forming
Group members lay the ground rules for what types of behavior are acceptable.

Storming
Hostilities and conflict arise, and people jockey for positions of power and status.

Norming
Group members agree on their shared goals, and norms and closer relationships develop.

Performing
The group channels its energies into performing its tasks.

In the initial meeting, the group should establish desired norms, roles, and other determinants of effectiveness, which are discussed throughout this chapter. At the second critical period (the midpoint), groups should renew or open lines of communication with outside constituencies. The group can use fresh information from its external environment to revise its approach to performing its task and ensure that it meets the needs of customers and clients. Without these activities, groups may get off on the wrong foot from the beginning, and members may never revise their behavior in the appropriate direction.[33]

3.3 | Some Groups Develop into Teams

As a manager or group member, you should expect the group to engage in all the activities just discussed at various times. But groups are not always successful. They do not

they complete their task or when they disband due to failure or loss of interest and new groups form, as the cycle continues.

Virtual teams also go through these stages of group development.[31] The forming stage is characterized by unbridled optimism: "I believe we have a great team and will work well together. We all understand the importance of the project and intend to take it seriously." Optimism turns into reality shock in the storming stage: "No one has taken a leadership role. We have not made the project the priority that it deserves." The norming stage comes at about the halfway point in the project life cycle, in which people refocus and recommit: "You must make firm commitments to a specific time schedule." The performing stage is the dash to the finish, as teammates show the discipline needed to meet the deadline.

3.2 | Over Time, Groups Enter Critical Periods

A key aspect of group development is the passage of time. Groups pass through critical periods, or times when they are particularly open to formative experiences.[32] The first such critical period is in the forming stage, at the first meeting, when rules and roles are established that set long-lasting precedents. A second critical period is the midway point between the initial meeting and a deadline (for instance, completing a project or making a presentation). At this point, the group has enough experience to understand its work; it comes to realize that time is becoming a scarce resource and the team must "get on with it"; and enough time remains to change its approach if necessary.

● Coworkers stand atop a post during a team building exercise at Outward Bound, an organization that teaches cooperation, problem solving, and decision making—for both in and out of the workplace—through various outdoor challenges.

always engage in the developmental activities that turn them into effective, high-performing teams.

A useful developmental sequence is depicted in Exhibit 12.3. The figure shows the various activities as the leadership of the group moves from traditional supervision, through a more participative approach, to true team leadership.[34] At the traditional *supervisory leadership* level, the team leader handles most (if not all) of the leadership duties, including assigning tasks, making and explaining decisions, training team members, managing members one-on-one, and so forth. As the group evolves to a more *participative leadership* approach, the team leader seeks input from group members for decisions, provides assignments and experiences to develop members' skills and abilities, coordinates group effort, and the like. At the *team leadership* level, the team leader's job focuses on building trust and inspiring teamwork, facilitating and supporting team decisions, broadening team capabilities through projects and assignments, creating a team identity, and so forth.

It is important to understand a couple of points about this model. Groups do not necessarily keep progressing from one "stage" to the next; they may remain permanently in the supervisory level or become more participative but never make it to true team leadership. As a result, progress on these dimensions must be a conscious goal of the leader and the members, and all should strive to meet these goals. Your group can meet these goals—and become a true team—by engaging in the activities in the figure.

4 | WHY DO GROUPS SOMETIMES FAIL?

Team building does not necessarily progress smoothly through such a sequence, culminating in a well-oiled team and superb performance.[35] Some groups never do work out. Such groups can be frustrating for managers and members, who may feel that teams are a waste of time and that the difficulties outweigh the benefits.

There are several potential barriers that can impede team success. Ineffective communication can occur between team members, or between the leader and members of the team. Some people overcommunicate while others rarely speak up, even when they have something important to contribute. The team leader can help by seeking all members' input. Another common barrier is when the team lacks a charter, vision, or goals. Early in the development process, the team leader and members should define the team's direction and the roles of each contributor. When teams experience a drop in morale and productivity, persistence, communication, and forward movement can help them return to previous levels of performance. A final barrier can occur if team members do not trust each other or their team leader. When trust is low, members may spend more time trying to influence team dynamics to protect their own interests than performing their actual jobs.[36] In contrast, when trust is present, teams achieve higher performance.[37]

It is not easy to build high-performance teams. *Teams* is often just a word used by management to describe merely putting people into groups. "Teams" sometimes are launched with little or no training or support systems. For example, both managers and group members need new skills to make a group work. These skills include learning the art of diplomacy, tackling "people issues" head on,

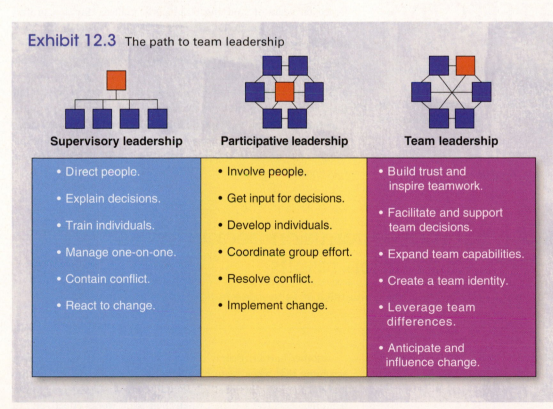

Exhibit 12.3 The path to team leadership

Supervisory leadership	Participative leadership	Team leadership
• Direct people.	• Involve people.	• Build trust and inspire teamwork.
• Explain decisions.	• Get input for decisions.	• Facilitate and support team decisions.
• Train individuals.	• Develop individuals.	• Expand team capabilities.
• Manage one-on-one.	• Coordinate group effort.	• Create a team identity.
• Contain conflict.	• Resolve conflict.	• Leverage team differences.
• React to change.	• Implement change.	• Anticipate and influence change.

Source: Adapted from *Leading Teams* by J. Zenger and Associates. Reprinted by permission.

and walking the fine line between encouraging autonomy and rewarding team innovations without letting the team get too independent and out of control.[38] Giving up some control is difficult for managers from traditional systems, but they have to realize they will gain control in the long run by creating stronger, better-performing units.

Teams should be truly empowered, as we discussed earlier. The benefits of teams are reduced when they are not allowed to make important decisions—in other words, when management doesn't trust them with important responsibilities. If teams must obtain permission for every innovative idea, they will revert to making safe, traditional decisions.[39]

Empowerment enhances team performance even among virtual teams. Empowerment for virtual teams includes thorough training in using the technologies and strong technical support from management. Some virtual teams have periodic face-to-face interactions, which help performance; empowerment is particularly helpful for virtual teams that don't often meet face-to-face.[40]

Failure lies in not knowing and doing what makes teams successful. To be successful, you must apply clear thinking and appropriate practices.[41] That is what the rest of the chapter is about.

LO5 Describe how to build an effective team

5 | BUILDING EFFECTIVE TEAMS

All the considerations just described form the building blocks of an effective work team. But what does it really mean for a team to be effective? What, precisely, can a manager do to design a truly effective team? Team effectiveness is defined by three criteria:[42]

1. The *productive output* of the team meets or exceeds the standards of quantity and quality; the team's output is acceptable to

the customers, inside or outside the organization, who receive the team's goods or services. At Lockheed Martin, Clarence L. "Kelly" Johnson's group designed, built, and flew the first U.S. tactical jet fighter, XP80, in 143 days.[43]

2. Team members realize *satisfaction* of their personal needs. Johnson gave his Lockheed teams the freedom to innovate and

stretch their skills. Team members were enthusiastic and realized great pride and satisfaction in their work.

3. Team members remain *committed* to working together again; that is, the group doesn't burn out and disintegrate after a grueling project. Looking back, the members are glad they were involved. In other words, effective teams remain viable and have good prospects for repeated success in the future.[44]

For help in developing these qualities, teams may use team-building activities or work with an outside coach. Team building usually involves activities focused on relationships among team members. Whether these activities are as simple as a group discussion or as elaborate as a weekend retreat with physical challenges, the team-building event should be followed by an opportunity for participants to evaluate what they learned and how they will apply those lessons at work.[45] Coaching a team should be different from coaching individual team members because it focuses on how the group as a whole operates and how it can improve interactions so that it will accomplish its goals.[46] The process doesn't have the confidentiality of one-on-one coaching, and the coach has to pace the process so that everyone is included. Team coaching addresses issues such as what the team is focused on, how it sets goals, and how it can improve communication and decision making. Ideally the coaching helps a team develop enough that it can begin to coach itself.

Based on years of studying team performance, Harvard professor Richard Hackman has identified principles of team effectiveness, including this simple rule: teams need to properly define their membership. However, many don't, perhaps because people hate to exclude someone. When a team problem came to light at a financial services company, the chief executive determined that the chief financial officer was unable to collaborate effectively with others on the executive team. So the CEO asked the financial executive to skip the "boring" team meetings, keeping their communications one-on-one. Without the CFO, the executive team began to function much better.

> ## "Teamwork is what makes common people capable of uncommon results."
>
> —Pat Summitt, former head coach of the University of Tennessee ladies' basketball team

Another barrier: People tend to focus too much on harmony, assuming that when team members feel good about their participation, the team is effective. Actually, effectiveness comes first: team members feel satisfied when their team works effectively. In a study of symphony orchestras, satisfaction came from how the musicians felt *after* a performance.

A third mistake Hackman encounters is the assumption that team members can be together too long, to the point that the team runs out of ideas. But aside from research and development teams, which should periodically add new members, Hackman has found that a more frequent problem is the opposite: team members haven't been together long enough to learn to work well together. Airplane cockpit crews, for example, perform much better when they have flown together previously.[47]

::::::::::::::::

5.1 | Effective Teams Focus on Performance

The key element of effective teamwork is commitment to a common purpose.[48] The best teams are those that have been given an important performance challenge by management and then have reached a common understanding and appreciation of their purpose. Without such understanding and commitment, a group will be just a bunch of individuals.

The best teams also work hard at developing a common understanding of how they will work together to achieve their purpose.[49] They discuss and agree on such details as how tasks and roles will be allocated and how team members will make decisions. The team should develop norms for examining its performance strategies and be amenable to changing them when appropriate. For example, work teams usually standardize at least some processes, but they should be willing to try creative new ideas if the situation calls for them.[50] With a clear, strong, motivating purpose and effective performance strategies, people will pull together into a powerful force that has a chance to achieve extraordinary things.

The team's general purpose should be translated into specific, measurable performance goals.[51] You already learned about how goals motivate individual performance. Performance can be defined by collective end products, instead of an accumulation of individual products.[52] Team-based performance goals help define and distinguish the team's product, encourage communication within the team, energize and motivate team members, provide feedback on progress, signal team victories (and defeats), and ensure that the team focuses clearly on results. Teams with both difficult goals and specific incentives to attain them achieve the highest performance levels.[53]

The best team-based measurement systems inform top management of the team's level of performance and help the team understand its own processes and gauge its own progress. Ideally the team plays the lead role in designing its own measurement system. This responsibility is a great indicator of whether the team is truly empowered.[54]

Teams, like individuals, need feedback on their performance. Feedback from customers is especially crucial. Some customers for the team's products are inside the organization. Teams should be responsible for satisfying them and should be given or should seek performance feedback. Better yet, wherever possible, teams should interact directly with external customers who make the ultimate buying decisions about their goods and services. External customers typically provide the most honest, and most crucial and useful, performance feedback.[55] When managers at Intuit, the software development company, noticed that customers were not posting positive recommendations on the web about the firm's new products, they took action. They assembled a team of nine coaches ("innovation catalysts") from across the company to help internal work groups create new prototypes and learn from customers. The goal of the new "Design for Delight" program is to create products that excite customers.[56]

5.2 | Managers Motivate Effective Teamwork

Sometimes individuals work less hard and are less productive when they are members of a group. Such **social loafing** occurs when individuals believe that their contributions are not important, others will do the work for them, their lack of effort will go undetected, or they will be the lone sucker if they work hard but others don't. Perhaps you have seen social loafing in some of your student teams.[57] Conversely, sometimes individuals work harder when they are members of a group than when they are working alone. This **social facilitation effect** occurs because individuals usually are more motivated in the presence of others, are concerned with what others think of them, and want to maintain a positive self-image.

A social facilitation effect is maintained—and a social loafing effect can be avoided—under the following conditions:[58]

- Group members know each other.

- They can observe and communicate with one another.

- Clear performance goals exist.

- The task is meaningful to the people working on it.

- Group members believe that their efforts matter and that others will not take advantage of them.

- The culture supports teamwork.

Under ideal circumstances, everyone works hard, contributes in concrete ways to the team's work, and is accountable to other team members. Accountability to one another, rather than just to "the boss," is an essential aspect of good teamwork. Accountability inspires mutual commitment and trust.[59] Trust in your teammates—and their trust in you—may be the ultimate key to effectiveness.

Team effort is also generated by designing the team's task to be motivating. Techniques for creating motivating tasks appear in the guidelines for job enrichment discussed in Chapter 11. Tasks are motivating when they use a variety of member skills and provide high task variety, identity, significance, autonomy, and performance feedback.

social loafing working less hard and being less productive when in a group

social facilitation effect working harder when in a group than when working alone

Ultimately teamwork is motivated by tying rewards to team performance.[60] If team performance can be measured validly, team-based rewards can be given accordingly. It is not easy to move from a system of rewards based on individual performance to one based on team performance and cooperation. It also may not be appropriate unless people are truly interdependent and must collaborate to attain true team goals.[61] Team-based rewards are often combined with regular salaries and rewards based on individual performance. At Nucor, where production employees work in teams of 12 to 20, team members earn bonuses based on the tons of steel shipped each week. To ensure high quality, the amount of any bad product is subtracted from total shipments—and if defective products reach the customer, the amount subtracted is multiplied by 3. On average, the amount of the team bonuses equals 170 to 180 percent of the team members' base salary. This type of motivation works because Nucor teams are empowered to make decisions aimed at improving their productivity, and the company actively shares performance data with its employees.[62]

If team performance is difficult to measure validly, then desired behaviors, activities, and processes that indicate good teamwork can be rewarded. Individuals within teams can be given differential rewards based on teamwork indicated by active participation, cooperation, leadership, and other contributions to the team.

If team members are to be rewarded differentially, such decisions are better *not* left only to the boss.[63] They should be made by the team itself, through peer ratings or multirater evaluation systems. Why? Team members are in a better position to observe, know, and make valid reward allocations. Finally, the more teams the organization has, and the more a full team orientation exists, the more valid and effective it will be to distribute rewards via gainsharing and other organizationwide incentives.

5.3 | Effective Teams Have Skilled Members

Team members should be selected and trained so that they become effective contributors to the team. The teams themselves often hire their new members.[64] MillerCoors Brewing Company and Eastman Chemical teams select members based on the results of tests designed to predict how well they will contribute to team success in an empowered environment.

Generally the skills required by teams include technical or functional expertise, problem-solving and decision-making skills, and interpersonal skills. Some managers and teams mistakenly overemphasize some skills, particularly technical or functional ones, and underemphasize the others. In fact, social skills can be critical to team functioning; one worker with a persistently negative attitude—for example, someone who bullies or constantly complains—can and often does put an entire team into a downward spiral.[66] It is vitally important that all three types of skills be represented, and developed, among team members.

5.4 | Norms Shape Team Behavior

Norms are shared beliefs about how people should think and behave. For example, some people like to keep information and knowledge to themselves, but teams should try to establish a norm of knowledge sharing because it can improve team performance.[67] From the organization's standpoint, norms can be positive or negative. In some teams, everyone works hard; in other groups, employees are opposed to management and do as little work as possible. Some groups develop norms of taking risks, others of being conservative.[68] A norm could dictate that employees speak of the company either favorably or critically. Team members may show concern about poor safety practices, drug and alcohol abuse, and employee theft,

norms shared beliefs about how people should think and behave

roles different sets of expectations for how different individuals should behave

task specialist an individual who has more advanced job-related skills and abilities than other group members possess

team maintenance specialist individual who develops and maintains team harmony

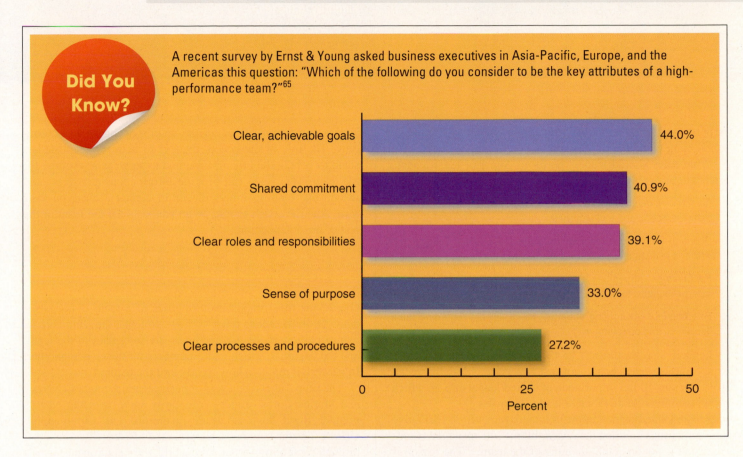

Did You Know?

A recent survey by Ernst & Young asked business executives in Asia-Pacific, Europe, and the Americas this question: "Which of the following do you consider to be the key attributes of a high-performance team?"[65]

Attribute	Percent
Clear, achievable goals	44.0%
Shared commitment	40.9%
Clear roles and responsibilities	39.1%
Sense of purpose	33.0%
Clear processes and procedures	27.2%

Percent

or they may not care about these issues (or may even condone such practices). Health consciousness is the norm among executives at some companies, but smoking is the norm at tobacco companies. Some groups have norms of distrust and of being closed toward one another, but as you might guess, norms of trust and open discussion about conflict can improve group performance.[69]

A professor described his consulting experiences at two companies that exhibited different norms in their management teams.[70] At Federal Express Corporation, a young manager interrupted the professor's talk by proclaiming that a recent decision by top management ran counter to the professor's point about corporate planning. He was challenging top management to defend its decision. A hot debate ensued, and after an hour everyone went to lunch without a trace of hard feelings. But at another corporation, the professor opened a meeting by asking a group of top managers to describe the company's culture. There was silence. He asked again. More silence. Then someone passed him an unsigned note that read, "Dummy, can't you see that we can't speak our minds? Ask for the input anonymously, in writing." As you can see, norms are important, and can vary greatly from one group to another.

5.5 | Team Members Must Fill Important Roles

Roles are different sets of expectations for how different individuals should behave. Although norms apply generally to all team members, different roles exist for different members within the norm structure.

Two important sets of roles must be performed:[71]

1. **Task specialist** roles are filled by individuals who have particular job-related skills and abilities. These employees keep the team moving toward accomplishment of the objectives.

2. **Team maintenance specialists** develop and maintain harmony within the team. They boost morale, give support, provide humor, soothe hurt feelings, and generally exhibit a concern with members' well-being.

Note the similarity between these roles and the important task performance and group maintenance leadership behaviors you learned about in Chapter 10. As suggested there, some of these roles will be more important than others at different times and under different circumstances. But these behaviors need not be carried out only by one or two leaders; any member of the team can assume them at any time. Both types of roles can

Traditional Thinking

Team leaders are directive, assign tasks, and monitor performance.

The Best Managers Today

Support team members, obtain external support, and delegate authority to the team.

be performed by different individuals to maintain an effectively functioning work team.

What roles should leaders perform? Superior team leaders are better at several things:[72] (as illustrated in Exhibit 12.4):

- *Relating*—exhibiting social and political awareness, caring for team members, and building trust.

- *Scouting*—seeking information from managers, peers, and specialists, and investigating problems systematically.

- *Persuading*—influencing team members, as well as obtaining external support for teams.

- *Empowering*—delegating authority, being flexible regarding team decisions, and coaching.

Leaders also should roll up their sleeves and do real work to accomplish team goals, not just supervise.[73] Finally, recall from Chapter 10 the importance of shared leadership, in which group members rotate or share leadership roles.[74]

Self-managed teams report to a management representative who sometimes is called the *coach*. In true self-managed teams, the coach is not an actual member of the team.[75] The reason is that the group is supposed to make its own decisions, and also the perceived power of the management representative could have a dampening effect on the team's openness and autonomy. The role of the coach, then, is to help the team understand its role in the organization and to serve as a resource for the team. The coach can provide information, resources, and insight that team members do not or cannot acquire on their own. And the coach should be an advocate for the team in the rest of the organization.

5.6 | Cohesiveness Affects Team Performance

One of the most important properties of a team is cohesiveness.[76] **Cohesiveness** refers to how attractive the team is to its members, how motivated members are to remain in the team, and the degree to which team members influence one another. In general, it refers to how tightly knit the team is.

The Blue Angels are a very cohesive team. A total of 16 Navy and Marine Corps officers voluntarily serve with the Navy's premier flight demonstration squadron. The Commanding Officer flies the Number 1 jet while the officers fly Numbers 2 through 7.[77] Touring around the world, the squadron performs a wide variety of aerial maneuvers that are tightly choreographed and delivered with the utmost precision.

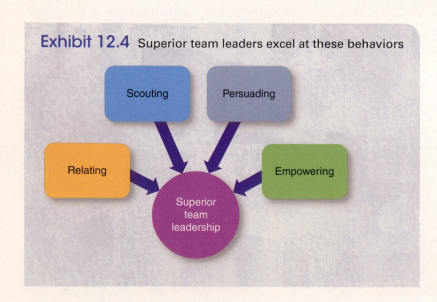

Exhibit 12.4 Superior team leaders excel at these behaviors

The Importance of Cohesiveness Cohesiveness is important for two primary reasons:

1. It contributes to *member satisfaction*. In a cohesive team, members communicate and get along well with one another. They feel good about being part of the team. Even if their jobs are unfulfilling or the organization is oppressive, people gain some satisfaction from enjoying their coworkers.

2. It has a major impact on *performance*.[78] A recent study of manufacturing teams led to a conclusion that performance improvements in both quality and productivity occurred in the most cohesive unit, whereas conflict within another team prevented any quality or productivity improvements.[79] Sports fans read about this all the time. When teams are winning, players talk about the team being close, getting along well, and knowing one another's games. In contrast, losing is attributed to infighting and divisiveness.

● The Blue Angels is the United States Navy's flight demonstration squadron. The Blue Angels' six demonstration pilots fly the F/A-18 Hornet in more than 70 shows at 34 locations throughout the United States annually. They still employ many of the same practices and techniques used in aerial displays from 1946.

But this interpretation is simplistic; exceptions to this intuitive relationship occur. Tightly knit work groups can also be disruptive to the organization, such as when they sabotage the assembly line, get their boss fired, or enforce low performance norms. When does high cohesiveness lead to good performance, and when does it result in poor performance? The ultimate outcome depends on two things:

1. The task.

2. Performance norms.

The Task If the task is to make a decision or solve a problem, cohesiveness can lead to poor performance. Groupthink occurs when a tightly knit group is so cooperative that agreeing with one another's opinions and refraining from criticizing others' ideas become norms. For a cohesive group to make good decisions, it should establish a norm of constructive disagreement. This type of debating is important for groups up to the level of boards of directors.[80] In top management teams it has been shown to improve the financial performance of companies.[81]

The effect of cohesiveness on performance, in contrast, can be positive, particularly if the task is to produce some tangible output. In day-to-day work groups for which decision making is not the primary task, cohesiveness can enhance performance. But that depends on the group's performance norms.[82]

Performance Norms Some groups are better than others at ensuring that their members behave the way the group prefers. Cohesive groups are more effective than noncohesive groups at norm enforcement. But the next question is, Do they have norms of high or low performance?

As Exhibit 12.5 shows, the highest performance occurs when a cohesive team has high-performance norms. But if a highly cohesive group has low-performance norms, that group will have the worst performance. In the group's eyes, it will have succeeded in achieving its goal of poor performance. Noncohesive groups with high-performance norms can be effective from the company's standpoint. However, they won't be as productive as they would be if they were more cohesive. Noncohesive groups with low-performance norms perform poorly, but they will not ruin things for management as effectively as cohesive groups with low-performance norms.

5.7 | Managers Can Build Cohesiveness and High-Performance Norms

Managers should build teams that are cohesive and have high-performance norms. The following actions (listed in Exhibit 12.6) can help create such teams:[83]

- *Recruit members with similar attitudes, values, and backgrounds. Similar individuals are more likely to get along with one another. Don't do this, though, if the team's task requires heterogeneous*

cohesiveness the degree to which a group is attractive to its members, members are motivated to remain in the group, and members influence one another

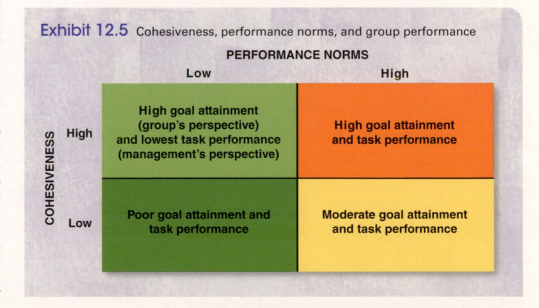

Exhibit 12.5 Cohesiveness, performance norms, and group performance

		PERFORMANCE NORMS	
		Low	**High**
COHESIVENESS	**High**	High goal attainment (group's perspective) and lowest task performance (management's perspective)	High goal attainment and task performance
	Low	Poor goal attainment and task performance	Moderate goal attainment and task performance

Take Charge of Your Career

Playing devil's advocate can help your team make better decisions

At some point in your career, you have probably witnessed how members of highly cohesive teams fall prey to groupthink when they always agree with one another and stop questioning each other's ideas. This phenomenon often leads groups to make suboptimal decisions. As a team member, you can help your team decrease the influence of groupthink, and thereby help it make better decisions by playing *devil's advocate*. In this role, your job is to point out the flaws in other's ideas.

Obviously this task requires good interpersonal skills and the ability to present your feedback as constructive in nature, not condescending or personally insulting. For example, you may want to preface your feedback with "Let me play devil's advocate for a moment" or "Let's consider some of the potential issues that may come up later." If successful, you can help your team explore and discuss additional perspectives regarding the problem at hand, which can ultimately produce more and better alternative decisions.

David Ogilvy, the legendary advertising executive, would play devil's advocate when his agency's staff created a new advertising campaign. Ogilvy would take on this role "to test his decision-making criteria about what constitutes a good campaign vs. what doesn't." Whenever a campaign that he originally considered to be ineffective, succeeded, Ogilvy would revise the framework for his original decision. Project managers of teams at firms like Agile software development (owned by Oracle) are advised to play devil's advocate to help improve the quality of the team's decision-making process.

Assuming the role of devil's advocate can help your team make better, more informed decisions.

How can you learn how to play devil's advocate? Use observation and practice. Observe how others perform this role, and note how the other people in the meeting or room react to the advocate's feedback. Try out your new role with a non-work-related group—perhaps an organization for which you volunteer or with a group of friends. Once you can deliver critical feedback in a constructive and even-handed manner, you can begin playing devil's advocate to help your work teams make better decisions. Your team leader or other managers in your organization are likely to appreciate your taking on this role.

Sources: H. Gregersen, "A.G. Lafley's Innovation Skills Will Weather P&G's Storm," *Bloomberg Businessweek* (online), June 3, 2013, www.businessweek.com; H. Greimel and M. Rechtin, "Toyota Adopts 'Devil's Advocate' in Quest to Restore Quality, Confidence," *Advertising Age* 82, no. 4 (January 24, 2011), p. 3; J. McAvoy and T. Butler, "The Role of Project Management in Ineffective Decision Making within Agile Software Development Projects," *European Journal of Information Systems*, no. 18 (2009), pp. 372–83; and R. Gandossy and J. Sonnenfeld, "'I See Nothing, I Hear Nothing': Culture, Corruption and Apathy," *International Journal of Disclosure and Governance* 2, no. 3 (September 2005), pp. 228–44.

---

skills and inputs—a homogeneous committee or board might make poor decisions because it will lack different information and viewpoints and may succumb to groupthink. Recent research has shown that educational diversity and national diversity provide more benefits than limitations to groups' use and application of information.[84]

- *Maintain high entrance and socialization standards.* Teams and organizations that are difficult to get into have more prestige. Individuals who survive a difficult interview, selection, or

Exhibit 12.6
Ways managers can build cohesive teams with high-performance norms

1. Recruit members with similar attitudes, values, and backgrounds.
2. Maintain high entrance and socialization standards.
3. Keep the team as small as possible.
4. Help the team succeed, and publicize its successes.
5. Be a participative leader.
6. Present a challenge from outside the team.
7. Tie rewards to team performance.

training process will be proud of their accomplishment and feel more attachment to the team.

- *Keep the team small* (but large enough to get the job done). The larger the group, the less important members may feel. Small teams make individuals feel like large contributors.

- *Help the team succeed, and publicize its successes.* You read about empowerment in the preceding chapter; you can empower teams as well as individuals.[85] Be a path–goal leader who facilitates success; the experience of winning brings teams closer together. Then, if you inform superiors of your team's successes, members will believe they are part of an important, prestigious unit. Teams that get into a good performance track continue to perform well as time goes on, but groups that don't often enter a downward spiral in which problems compound over time.[86]

- *Be a participative leader.* Participation in decisions gets team members more involved with one another and striving toward goal accomplishment. Too much autocratic decision making from above can alienate the group from management.

- *Present a challenge from outside the team.* Competition with other groups makes team members band together to defeat the enemy

Self-managed teams can have a positive impact on productivity. But people often resist self-managed teams, in part because they don't want to accept so much responsibility and it is difficult for them to adjust to the change in the decision-making process.

(witness what happens to school spirit before the big game against an archrival). Some of the greatest teams in business and in science have been completely focused on winning a competition.[87] But don't *you* become the outside threat. If team members dislike you as a boss, they will become more cohesive—but their performance norms will be against you, not with you.

- *Tie rewards to team performance.* To a large degree, teams are motivated just as individuals are: they do the activities that are rewarded. Make sure that high-performing teams get the rewards they deserve and that poorly performing groups get fewer rewards. You read about this earlier. Bear in mind that not just monetary rewards but also recognition for good work are powerful motivators. Recognize and celebrate team accomplishments. The team will become more cohesive and perform better to reap more rewards. Performance goals will be high, the organization will benefit from higher team motivation and productivity, and team members' individual needs will be better satisfied. Ideally, membership on a high-performing team that is recognized as such throughout the organization will become a badge of honor.[88]

But keep in mind that strong cohesiveness encouraging "agreeableness" can be dysfunctional. For problem solving and decision making, the team should establish norms promoting an open, constructive atmosphere including honest disagreement over issues without personal conflict and animosity.[89]

LO6 List methods for managing a team's relationships with other teams

6 | MANAGING LATERAL RELATIONSHIPS

Teams do not function in a vacuum; they are interdependent with other teams. For example, at Texas Instruments, teams are responsible for interfacing with other teams to eliminate production bottlenecks and implement new processes and also for working with suppliers on quality issues.[90] Thus some activities crucial to the team are those that entail dealing with people *outside* the group.

6.1 | Some Team Members Should Manage Outward

Several vital roles link teams to their external environments—that is, to other individuals and groups inside and outside the organization. A specific type of role that spans team boundaries is the **gatekeeper**, a team member who stays abreast of current information in scientific and other fields and tells the group about important developments. Information useful to the group can also include resources, trends, and political support throughout the corporation or the industry.[91]

The team's strategy dictates the team's mix of internally versus externally focused roles and the ways the mix changes over time. There are several general team strategies:[92]

- The **informing** strategy entails making decisions with the team and then telling outsiders of the team's intentions.

- **Parading** means the team's strategy is to simultaneously emphasize internal team building and achieve external visibility.

- **Probing** involves a focus on external relations. This strategy requires team members to interact frequently with outsiders; diagnose the needs of customers, clients, and higher-ups; and experiment with solutions before taking action.

The balance between an internal and external strategic focus and between internal and external roles depends on how much the team needs information, support, and resources from outside. When teams have a high degree of dependence on outsiders, probing is the best strategy. Parading teams perform at an intermediate level, and informing teams are likely to fail. They are too isolated from the outside groups on which they depend.

Informing or parading strategies may be more effective for teams that are less dependent on outside groups—for example, established teams working on routine tasks in stable external environments. But for most important work teams—task forces, new product teams, and strategic decision-making teams tackling unstructured problems in a rapidly changing external environment—effective performance in roles that involve interfacing with the outside will be vital.

gatekeeper a team member who keeps abreast of current developments and provides the team with relevant information

informing a team strategy that entails making decisions with the team and then informing outsiders of its intentions

parading a team strategy that entails simultaneously emphasizing internal team building and achieving external visibility

probing a team strategy that requires team members to interact frequently with outsiders, diagnose their needs, and experiment with solutions

6.2 | Some Relationships Help Teams Coordinate with Others in the Organization

Managing relationships with other groups and teams means engaging in a dynamic give-and-take that ensures proper coordination throughout the management system. To many managers, this process often seems like a free-for-all. To help understand the process and make it more productive, we can identify and examine the different types of lateral role relationships and take a strategic approach to building constructive relationships.

Different teams, like different individuals, have roles to perform. As teams carry out their roles, several distinct patterns of working relationships develop:[93]

- *Work flow relationships* emerge as materials are passed from one group to another. A group commonly receives work from one unit, processes it, and sends it to the next unit in the process. Your group, then, will come before some groups and after others in the process.

- *Service relationships* exist when top management centralizes an activity to which a large number of other units must gain access. Common examples are technology services, libraries, and clerical staff. Such units must assist other people to help them accomplish their goals.

- *Advisory relationships* are created when teams with problems call on centralized sources of expert knowledge. For example, staff members in the human resources or legal department advise work teams.

- *Audit relationships* develop when people not directly in the chain of command evaluate the methods and performances of other teams. Financial auditors check the books, and technical auditors assess the methods and technical quality of the work.

- *Stabilization relationships* involve auditing before the fact. In other words, teams sometimes must obtain clearance from others—for example, for large purchases—before they act.

- *Liaison relationships* involve intermediaries between teams. Managers often are called on to mediate conflict between two organizational units. Public relations people, sales managers, purchasing agents, and others who work across organizational boundaries serve in liaison roles as they maintain communications between the organization and the outside world.

Teams should assess each working relationship with another unit by asking basic questions: "From whom do we receive work, and to whom do we send work? What permissions do we control, and to whom must we go for authorizations?" In this way, teams can better understand whom to contact and when, where, why, and how to do so. Coordination throughout the working system improves, problems are avoided or short-circuited before they get too serious, and performance improves.[94]

7 | CONFLICT HAPPENS

Conflict is a normal part of life in organizations. Keep in mind there are many different ways to manage and resolve it.

7.1 | Conflicts Arise Both Within and Among Teams

The complex maze of interdependencies throughout organizations provides many opportunities for conflict to arise among groups and teams. **Conflict** is defined as a process in which one party perceives that its interests are being opposed or negatively affected by another party.[95] It can occur between individuals on the same team or among different teams. Many people's view of conflict is that it should be avoided at all costs. However, early management science contributor Mary Parker Follett was the first of many to note its potential advantages.[96] Typically conflict can foster creativity when it is about ideas rather than personalities. In contrast, at a nonprofit organization, team members were committed to maintaining harmony during meetings, but their unresolved differences spilled over into nasty remarks outside of the office.[97]

Many factors cause great potential for destructive conflict: the sheer number and variety of contacts, ambiguities in jurisdiction and responsibility, differences in goals, intergroup competition for scarce resources, different perspectives held by members of different units, varying time horizons in which some units attend to long-term considerations and others focus on short-term needs, and others. Tensions and anxieties are likely to arise in teams that are demographically diverse, include members from different parts of the organization, or are composed of contrasting personalities. Both demographic and cross-functional heterogeneity initially lead to problems such as stress, lower cooperation, and lower cohesiveness.[98]

Over time and with communication, diverse groups actually tend to become more cooperative and perform better than do homogeneous groups. Norms of cooperation can improve performance, as does the fact that cross-functional teams engage in more external communication with more areas of the organization.[99]

7.2 | Conflict Management Techniques

Teams inevitably face conflicts and must decide how to manage them. The aim should be to make the conflict productive—that is, to make those involved believe they have benefited rather than lost from the conflict.[100] People believe they have benefited from a conflict when they see the following outcomes:

- A new solution is implemented, the problem is solved, and it is unlikely to emerge again.

- Work relationships have been strengthened, and people believe they can work together productively in the future.

People handle conflict in different ways. You have your own style; others' styles may be similar or may differ. Their styles depend in part on their country's cultural norms. For example, the Chinese are more concerned with collective than with individual interests, and they are more likely than managers in the United States to turn to higher authorities to make decisions rather than resolve conflicts themselves.[101] But culture aside, any team or individual has several options regarding how they deal with conflicts.[102] These personal styles of dealing with conflict, shown in Exhibit 12.7, are distinguished based on how much people strive to satisfy their own concerns (the assertiveness dimension) and how much they focus on satisfying the other party's concerns (the cooperation dimension).

For example, a common reaction to conflict is **avoidance**. In this situation, people do nothing to satisfy themselves or others. They either ignore the problem by doing nothing at all or address it by merely smoothing over or deemphasizing the disagreement. This, of course, fails to solve the problem or clear the air. When Paul Forti was a middle manager in a management consulting firm, he was passed over for a promotion, and the organization brought in an outsider who was at first too busy to discuss his disappointment and future role in the firm. He handled the situation with avoidance, and as a result, their working relationship suffered for weeks.[103]

Accommodation means cooperating on behalf of the other party but not being assertive about one's own interests. **Compromise** involves moderate attention to both parties' concerns, being neither highly cooperative nor highly assertive. This style results in satisficing but not optimizing solutions. **Competing** is a strong response in which people focus strictly on their own wishes and are unwilling to recognize the other person's concerns. Finally, **collaboration** emphasizes both cooperation and assertiveness. The goal is to maximize satisfaction for both parties. Collaboration changed Paul Forti's relationship with his boss at the consulting firm. The new approach literally started by accident, when the senior manager slipped on some ice, Forti came to her aid, and she commented that she would like to get to know him better. Over lunch, she expressed her respect for Forti, and they developed a better working relationship in which she gave him interesting assignments and made sure clients knew about his expertise. Thus, although

Exhibit 12.7 Conflict management strategies

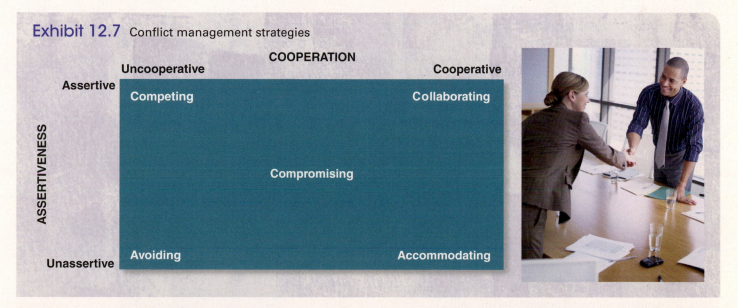

Source: K. Thomas, "Conflict and Conflict Management." In *Handbook of Industrial and Organizational Psychology,* ed. M. D. Dunnette. Copyright © 1976. Reprinted by permission of the Kenneth W. Thomas.

Forti hadn't gotten the promotion, he did get many opportunities to develop his career.[104]

Imagine that you and a friend want to go to a movie together, and you have different movies in mind. If he insists that you go to his movie, he is showing the competing style. If you agree, even though you prefer another movie, you are accommodating. If one of you mentions a third movie that neither of you is excited about but both of you are willing to live with, you are compromising. If you realize you don't know all the options, do some research, and find another movie that you're both enthusiastic about, you are collaborating.

Different approaches are necessary at different times.[105] For example, competing can be necessary when cutting costs or dealing with other scarce resources. Compromise may be useful when people are under time pressure, when they need to achieve a temporary solution, or when collaboration fails. People should accommodate when they learn they are wrong or to minimize loss when they are outmatched. Even avoiding may be appropriate if the issue is trivial or resolving the conflict should be someone else's responsibility.

But when the conflict concerns important issues, when both sets of concerns are valid and important, when a creative solution is needed, and when commitment to the solution is vital to implementation, collaboration is the ideal approach. Collaboration can be achieved by airing feelings and opinions, addressing all concerns, and avoiding goal displacement by not letting personal attacks interfere with problem solving. An important technique is to invoke **superordinate goals**—higher-level organizational goals toward which everyone should be striving and that ultimately need to take precedence over personal or unit preferences.[106] Collaboration offers the best chance of reaching mutually satisfactory solutions based on the ideas and interests of all parties, and of maintaining and strengthening work relationships.

7.3 | Mediating Can Help Resolve a Conflict

Managers spend a lot of time trying to resolve conflict between *other* people. You already may have served as a **mediator**, a "third party" intervening to help settle a conflict between other people. Third-party intervention, done well, can improve working relationships and help the parties improve their own conflict management, communication, and problem-solving skills.[107]

Some insight comes from a study of human resource (HR) managers and the conflicts with which they deal.[108] HR managers encounter every type of conflict imaginable: interpersonal difficulties from minor irritations to jealousy to fights; operations

Did You Know?

In 2013, the U.S. Equal Employment Opportunity Commission's private sector mediation program resolved approximately 9,000 complaints, resulting in $160.9 million in monetary benefits for complainants.[109]

issues, including union issues, work assignments, overtime, and sick leave; discipline over infractions ranging from drug use and theft to sleeping on the job; sexual harassment and racial bias; pay and promotion issues; and feuds or strategic conflicts among divisions or individuals at the highest organizational levels.

In the study, the HR managers successfully settled most of the disputes. As illustrated in Exhibit 12.8, these managers typically follow a four-stage strategy:

1. They *investigate* by interviewing the disputants and others and gathering more information. While talking with the disputants, they seek both parties' perspectives, remaining as neutral as possible. The discussion should stay issue-oriented, not personal.

2. They *decide* how to resolve the dispute, often in conjunction with the disputants' bosses. In preparing to decide what to do, blame should not be assigned prematurely; at this point they should be exploring solutions.

3. They *take action* by explaining their decisions and the reasoning, and advise or train the disputants to avoid future incidents.

4. They *follow up* by making sure everyone understands the solution, documenting the conflict and the resolution, and monitoring the results by checking back with the disputants and their bosses.

Throughout, the objectives of the HR people are to be fully informed so that they understand the conflict; to be active and assertive in trying to resolve it; to be as objective, neutral, and impartial as humanly possible; and to be flexible by modifying their approaches according to the situation.

Here are some other recommendations for more effective conflict management.[110] Don't allow dysfunctional conflict to build, or hope or assume that it will go away. Address it before it escalates. Try to resolve it, and if the first efforts don't work, try others. Even if disputants are not happy with your decisions, there are benefits

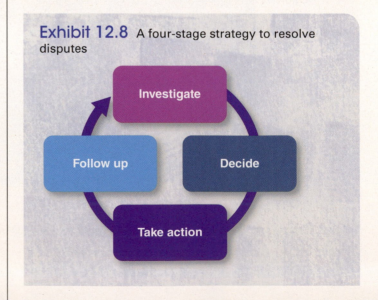

Exhibit 12.8 A four-stage strategy to resolve disputes

Investigate · Decide · Take action · Follow up

Pig Headed?

The best time to settle a dispute is before the mud starts flying – and knowing how to effectively minimize and manage conflict can be key. That's why education and training is such a vital part of the American Arbitration Association's mission.

As the world's leading provider of conflict management services, the AAA offers more than 75 years of experience in addressing the education and training needs of businesses, law firms and other professional associations. AAA educational offerings range from mediation and arbitration advocacy for legal professionals to training in negotiation and conflict management skills for executives, human resource managers and attorneys, all of which can be custom-tailored to your needs.

For more information about training programs or any of our conflict management services, call 1-800-311-3799 or visit us at www.adr.org.

American Arbitration Association
Dispute Resolution Services Worldwide

● Conflicts can arise for any team—the trick is to make them productive. This ad promotes the American Arbitration Association's mission to train professionals on how to effectively minimize and manage conflict—"before the mud starts flying."

to providing fair treatment, making a good-faith effort, and giving them a voice in the proceedings. Remember, too, that you may be able to ask HR specialists to help with difficult conflicts.

7.4 | Conflict Isn't Always Face-to-Face

When teams are geographically dispersed, as is often the case for virtual teams, team members tend to experience more conflict and less trust.[111] Conflict management affects the success of virtual teams.[112] In a recent study, avoidance hurt performance. Accommodation—conceding to others just to maintain

● Conflict between team members and coworkers is inevitable. There are several strategies that can help you get past the conflict and stay productive.

harmony rather than assertively attempting to negotiate integrative solutions—had no effect on performance. Collaboration had a positive effect on performance. The researchers also uncovered two surprises: compromise hurt performance, and competition helped performance. Compromises hurt because they often are watered-down, middle-of-the-road, suboptimal solutions. Competitive behavior was useful because the virtual teams were temporary and under time pressure, so having some individuals behave dominantly and impose decisions to achieve efficiency was useful rather than detrimental.

When people have problems in business-to-business e-commerce (e.g., costly delays), they tend to behave competitively and defensively rather than collaboratively.[113] Technical problems and recurring problems test people's patience. The conflict will escalate unless people use more cooperative, collaborative styles. Try to prevent conflicts before they arise; for example, make sure your information system is running smoothly before linking with others. Monitor and reduce or eliminate problems as soon as possible. When problems arise, express your willingness to cooperate, and then *actually be* cooperative. Even technical problems require the social skills of good management.

Study Checklist

☑ Did you tear out the perforated student review card at the back of the text to revisit learning objectives and key terms and definitions?

Connect® Management is available for M Management. Additional resources include:

☑ Interactive Applications:
- Case Analysis: Team Leadership
- Drag & Drop: How Do These Teams Perform?

- Drag & Drop: How Do We Manage Conflict?
- Video Case: Teams at One Smooth Stone

☑ LearnSmart—Multiple choice questions help you determine what you already know, are not sure about, or need to practice based on your score. And with SmartBook, you can read the relevant section in the eBook as well as practice and recharge what you've learned.

☑ Chapter Video: Zappos' Teams & Family Spirit

☑ Young Manager Speaks Out: Alicia Catalano, Sales Team Leader

13 chapter

Communicating

Learning Objectives

After studying Chapter 13, you will be able to

LO1 Discuss important advantages of two-way communication.

LO2 Identify communication problems to avoid.

LO3 Describe when and how to use the various communication channels.

LO4 Give examples of ways to become a better "sender" and "receiver" of information.

LO5 Explain how to improve downward, upward, and horizontal communication.

LO6 Summarize how to work with the company grapevine.

LO7 Describe the boundaryless organization and its advantages.

Effective communication is a fundamental aspect of job performance and managerial effectiveness.[1] It is a primary means by which managers carry out the responsibilities described throughout this book, such as making group decisions, sharing a vision, coordinating individuals and work groups within the organization's structure, hiring and motivating employees, and leading teams. In these and other areas of management, managers have to be able to share ideas clearly and convincingly, and they have to listen effectively to the ideas of others. Firms that use effective communication are four times more likely to report high levels of employee engagement as are firms using less effective communication.[2] In this chapter we present important communication concepts and practical guidelines for improving your effectiveness. We also discuss communication at the interpersonal and organizational levels.

1 | INTERPERSONAL COMMUNICATION

When people in an organization conduct a meeting, share stories in the cafeteria, or deliver presentations, they are making efforts to communicate. To understand why communication efforts sometimes break down and find ways to improve your communication skills, it helps to identify the elements of the communication process. **Communication** is the transmission of information and meaning from one party to another through the use of shared symbols. Exhibit 13.1 shows a general model of how one person communicates with another.

1.1 | One-Way Communication Is Common

The *sender* initiates the process by conveying information to the *receiver*—the person for whom the message is intended. The sender has a *meaning* he or she wishes to communicate and *encodes* the meaning into symbols (the words chosen for the message). Then the sender *transmits*, or sends, the message through some *channel*, such as a verbal or written medium.

The receiver *decodes* the message (e.g., reads it) and attempts to *interpret* the sender's meaning. The receiver may provide *feedback* to the sender by encoding a message in response to the sender's message.

In **one-way communication**, information flows in only one direction—from the sender to the receiver, with no feedback loop. A manager sends an e-mail to a subordinate without asking for a response. An employee phones the information technology (IT) department and leaves a message requesting repairs for her computer. A supervisor scolds a production worker about defects and then storms away.

The communication process often is hampered by *noise,* or interference in the system, that blocks perfect understanding. Noise could be anything that interferes with accurate communication: ringing telephones, thoughts about other things, or simple fatigue or stress. At times noise can derail your message. Imagine asking your boss for a raise on the same day that she received a below-average performance review. No matter how effectively you present your case, the likelihood of receiving an affirmative answer is low.

The model in Exhibit 13.1 is more than a theoretical treatment of the communication process: it points out the key ways in which communications can break down. Mistakes can be made at each stage of the model. A manager who is alert to potential problems can perform each step carefully to ensure more effective communication. The general model and two-way communication model exemplified in Exhibit 13.2 help explain the topics discussed next: the differences between one-way and two-way communication, communication pitfalls, misperception, and the various communication channels.

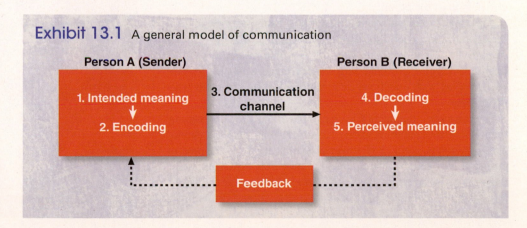

Exhibit 13.1 A general model of communication

Person A (Sender)
1. Intended meaning
2. Encoding

3. Communication channel

Person B (Receiver)
4. Decoding
5. Perceived meaning

Feedback

Exhibit 13.2 An illustration of a two-way communication model

The trainee (receiver) decodes the message and thinks to herself:

I need to be a better listener to earn more sales from customers.

A trainer (sender) encodes her message and delivers it via a presentation (communication channel):

"When dealing with customers, it's important to use active listening skills."

The trainee (now the sender) asks the trainer (now the receiver) a question:

"I agree, but how can I develop better listening skills?"

The trainer is receptive to the feedback and responds by saying:

"The company offers listening skills training seminars twice per year."

1.2 | Communication Should Flow in Two Directions

As shown in Exhibit 13.2, when a receiver (in this case, trainee) responds to a sender (here, trainer), **two-way communication** has occurred. One-way communication in situations like those just described can become two-way if the manager's e-mail invites the receiver to reply with any questions, the IT department returns the employee's call and asks for details about the computer problem, and the supervisor calms down and listens to the production worker's explanation of why defects are occurring.

True two-way communication means not only that the receiver provides feedback but also that the sender is receptive to the feedback. In these constructive exchanges, information is shared between both parties rather than merely delivered from one person to the other.

Because one-way communication is faster and easier for the sender, it is much more common than it should be. A busy executive finds it easier to dash off an e-mail message than to discuss a nagging problem with a subordinate. Also, he doesn't have to deal with questions or be challenged by someone who disagrees.

Two-way communication is more difficult and time-consuming than one-way communication. However, it is more accurate; fewer mistakes occur, and fewer problems arise. When receivers have a chance to ask questions, share concerns, and make suggestions or modifications, they understand more precisely what is being communicated and what they should do with the information.[3]

Consider what happened to Dick Nicholson when he was a sales manager attending a company reception for the sales department. Out of Nicholson's earshot, his company's chairman asked the vice president why a particular employee—a chronic underperformer—was "still a salesman." The vice president then told Nicholson what he thought the chairman meant: the chairman wanted to promote the salesperson. If communication were limited to one way, Nicholson could have simply carried out the chairman's apparent order, but instead he visited the chairman later and asked for an explanation. He was relieved when the chairman explained that he was wondering why the ineffective salesperson was still working for the company at all.[4]

2 | WATCH OUT FOR COMMUNICATION PITFALLS

As we know from personal experience, the sender's intended message does not always get across to the receiver. You are operating under an illusion if you think there is a perfect correlation between what you say and what people hear.[5] Errors can occur in all stages of the communication process. In the encoding stage, words can be misused, decimal points entered in the wrong places, facts left out, or ambiguous phrases perspectives—say, to really understand the viewpoints of customers or suppliers—can improve others' assessments of your performance.[8]

Filtering is the process of withholding, ignoring, or distorting information. Senders do this, for example, when they tell the boss what they think the boss wants to hear or give unwarranted compliments rather than honest criticism. Receivers also filter information; they may fail to recognize an important message or may attend to some aspects of the message but not others.

two-way communication a process in which information flows in two directions—the receiver provides feedback, and the sender is receptive to the feedback

perception the process of receiving and interpreting information

filtering the process of withholding, ignoring, or distorting information

---

> "The single biggest problem with communication is the illusion that it has taken place."
>
> —George Bernard Shaw

---

inserted. In the transmission stage, a report may get lost on a cluttered desk, the words on the slide may be too small to read from the back of the room, or words may be spoken with ambiguous inflections.

Decoding problems arise when the receiver doesn't listen carefully or reads too quickly and overlooks a key point. And of course receivers can misinterpret a message, as when a reader draws the wrong conclusion from an unclear text message, a listener takes a general statement by the boss too personally, or a an extended pause in a conversation is taken the wrong way.

2.1 | Everyone Uses Perceptual and Filtering Processes

More generally, people's perceptual and filtering processes create misinterpretations. **Perception** is the process of receiving and interpreting information. Such processes are not perfectly objective. They are subjective, because people's self-interested motives and attitudes toward the sender and the message bias their interpretations. People assume that others share their views, and naturally pay more attention to their own views than to the views of others.[6] But perceptual differences get in the way of consensus. To remedy this situation, it helps to remember that others' viewpoints are legitimate and to incorporate others' perspectives into your interpretation of issues.[7] Generally, adopting another person's viewpoint is fundamental to working collaboratively. And your ability to take others'

LISTEN & LEARN ● **ONLINE**

YOUNG MANAGERS
Speak Out!

"I prefer to receive performance feedback. That's how I find that I can grow better and be a better person. With daily feedback, there is a two-pronged approach. Identify a problem and something they are doing well. There is a direct link from communication to success."

—Timothy Paul, Store Manager

Filtering and subjective perception pervade one interesting aspect of the communications dynamic: how men and women differ in their communicating styles. A female manager at a magazine tended to phrase the assignments she gave her reporters as questions: "How would you like to do the X project with Y?" and "I was thinking of putting you on the X project; is that okay?" She was criticized by her male boss, who told her she did not assume the proper demeanor with her staff.[9] The female owner of a retail operation told one of her store managers to do something by saying, "The bookkeeper needs help with the billing. How would you feel about helping her out?" He said fine but didn't do it. Although the boss thought he meant he would do it, the store manager said he meant to indicate how he would feel about helping. He decided he had better things to do.[10]

Because of such filtering and perceptual differences, you cannot assume the other person means what you think he means, or understands the meanings you intend. Managers need to excel at reading interactions and adjusting their communication styles and perceptions to the people with whom they interact.[11] The human tendencies to filter and perceive subjectively underlie much of the ineffective communication, and the need for more effective communication practices, that you will read about in the rest of this chapter.

2.2 | Mistaken Perceptions Cause Misunderstandings

A common thread underlying the discussion so far is that people's perceptions can undermine attempts to communicate. People do not pay attention to everything going on around them. They inadvertently send mixed signals that can undermine the intended messages. Different people attend to

different things, and people interpret the same message in different ways. For example, a prospective customer may, at the end of a sales presentation, say, "I really like your product." One salesperson may leave the presentation thinking he won the customer's business, while a different salesperson may leave feeling less confident because she noticed that the customer did not sound very excited and avoided eye contact when he made the statement.

If the communication is between people from different cultures, these problems are magnified.[12] Communication breakdowns often occur when business transactions take place between people from different countries. Nancy J. Adler, an expert in international management, suggests the following tactics for communicating effectively with someone who speaks a different language:[13]

Verbal Behavior

- *Clear, slow speech.* Enunciate each word. Do not use colloquial expressions.

- *Repetition.* Repeat each important idea using different words to explain the same concept.

- *Simple sentences.* Avoid compound, long sentences.

- *Active verbs.* Avoid passive verbs.

Nonverbal Behavior[14]

- *Visual restatements.* Use as many visual restatements as possible, such as pictures, graphs, tables, and slides.

- *Gestures.* Use more facial and appropriate hand gestures to emphasize the meaning of words.

- *Demonstrations.* Act out as many themes as possible.

- *Pauses.* Pause more frequently.

- *Summaries.* Hand out written summaries of your verbal presentation.

Accurate Interpretation

- *Silence.* When there is a silence, wait. Do not jump in to fill the silence. The other person is probably just thinking more slowly in the nonnative language or translating.

- *Intelligence.* Do not equate poor grammar and mispronunciation with lack of intelligence; it is usually a sign of nonnative language use.

- *Differences.* If unsure, assume difference, not similarity.

Comprehension

- *Understanding.* Do not just assume that they understand; assume that they do not understand.

- *Checking comprehension.* Have colleagues repeat their understanding of the material back to you. Do not simply ask if they understand or not. Let them explain to you what they understand.

Design

- *Breaks.* Take more frequent breaks. Second language comprehension is exhausting.

- *Small modules.* Divide the material to be presented into smaller modules.

- *Longer time frame.* Allocate more time for each module than you usually need for presenting the same material to native speakers of your language.

Motivation

- *Encouragement.* Verbally and nonverbally encourage and reinforce speaking by nonnative language participants.

- *Drawing out.* Explicitly draw out marginal and passive participants.

- *Reinforcement.* Do not embarrass novice speakers.

An example highlights the operation of mixed signals and misperceptions. A bank CEO knew that he had to downsize his organization, and the employees who remained would have to commit to customer service, become more empowered, and really *earn* customer loyalty.[15] Knowing that his employees would have concerns about the coming reorganization, he decided to promise that he would do his best to guarantee employment to the survivors.

What signals did the CEO communicate to his people by his promises? One positive signal was that he cared about his people. But he also signaled that *he* would take care of *them,* thus undermining his goal of giving them more responsibility and empowering them. The employees wanted management to take responsibility for the market challenge that *they* needed to face by learning new ways of doing business. Inadvertently, the CEO spoke to their backward-looking desire for security, rather than conveying that the bank's future depended on *their* efforts. However, the CEO did avoid a common pitfall at companies that announce plans for downsizing or outsourcing: ignoring the emotional significance of their message.[16] Sometimes managers are so intent on delivering the business rationale for the changes that they fail to acknowledge the human cost of layoffs. When employees hear a message that neglects to address their feelings, they generally interpret the message to mean that managers don't care.

Another way people may undermine an intended message is when they are deceitful in their communication. Ethical communication is accurate, honest, sincere, and not deceptive in any way.[17] In contrast, unethical communicators may exaggerate or manipulate their message, omit negative information, or state opinions as facts to achieve personal gain.[18]

Consider how many problems can be avoided—and how much more effective communication can be—if people take the time to do four things:

1. Ensure that the receivers attend to the message they are sending.

2. Consider the other party's frame of reference and attempt to convey the message with that viewpoint in mind.

3. Take concrete steps to minimize perceptual errors and improper signals in sending and receiving.

4. Send consistent messages.

You should make an effort to predict people's interpretations of your messages and think in terms of how they could *misinterpret* your messages. It helps to say not only what you mean but also what you *don't* mean. Every time you say, "I am not saying *X,* I am saying *Y,*" you eliminate a possible misinterpretation.[19]

LO3 Describe when and how to use the various communication channels

3 | COMMUNICATIONS FLOW THROUGH DIFFERENT CHANNELS

Communication can be sent through a variety of channels (step 3 in Exhibit 13.1), including oral and written. As shown in Exhibit 13.3, the effectiveness of a communication channel depends on the situation.

Oral communication includes face-to-face discussion, telephone conversations, and formal presentations and speeches. Advantages are that questions can be asked and answered; feedback is immediate and direct; the receiver(s) can sense the sender's sincerity (or lack of it); and oral communication is more persuasive and sometimes less expensive than written. Yet oral communication also has disadvantages: it can lead to

● Face-to-face communication can be more effective than other channels when you want to exchange information, receive immediate feedback, or present your ideas in a persuasive manner.

Exhibit 13.3 Examples and tips related to the effective use of communication channels

Situation Asking your boss for a pay raise

Channel: Have a face-to-face discussion

Tips: Observe nonverbal communication, rehearse what you want to say and ask when s/he is in a good mood

Situation Reminding coworkers to attend a meeting

Channel: Send a succinct text message or e-mail

Tips: Provide date/time/location and why their attendance matters

Situation Introducing a new product to a key customer

Channel: Present the information via multiple channels

Tips: Relay information multiple times and review this chapter's Take Charge of Your career (see page 298)

spontaneous, ill-considered statements (and regret), and there is no permanent record of it (unless an effort is made to record it).

Written communication includes texts, e-mails, memos, letters, reports, computer files, and other written documents. Advantages to using written messages are that the message can be revised several times, it is a permanent record that can be saved, the message stays the same even if relayed through many people, and the receiver has more time to analyze the message. Disadvantages are that the sender has no control over where, when, or if the message is read; the sender lacks immediate feedback; the receiver may not understand parts of the message; and the message must be longer to contain enough information to answer anticipated questions.[20]

You should weigh these considerations when deciding whether to communicate orally or in writing. Also, sometimes it is wise to use both channels, such as following up a meeting with a confirming memo or writing a letter to prepare someone for your phone call.

3.1 | Electronic Media Offer Flexible, Efficient Channels

More and more of today's oral and written communication takes place through electronic media. Managers use computers, laptops, tablets, and smartphones, not only to gather and distribute quantitative data but also to "communicate" with others electronically. In electronic decision rooms, software supports simultaneous access to shared files, and allows people to share views and do work collectively.[21] Other means of electronic communication include *teleconferencing* and *videoconferencing*. Online meeting software that offers videoconferencing features, such as GoToMeeting (Citrix) and WebEx (Cisco),

is a common communication tool for mobile business professionals. While Skype is a popular choice for individuals who use video chat apps, other related apps are gaining in popularity. OoVoo is a free video chat app that displays the real-time images of up to four participants on a split screen (a group chat can include up to 11 users). Glide allows users to send out videos, fast, without uploading or downloading them. Recipients can view the videos live or offline and can chat in groups and send texts while other users are recording.[22] Also, you probably are intimately familiar with e-mail, instant messaging, text messaging, and blogging.

E-mail has become a fundamental tool of workplace communication with more than 100 billion business e-mails sent and received on a daily basis around the globe.[23] The number of mobile e-mail users is expected to double from 897 million users in 2013 to 1.8 billion users in 2017.[24] New versions of e-mail software may encourage workers to use a wider variety of electronic communication tools. IBM's recent update to IBM Notes (formerly Lotus Notes), called 9 Social Edition, helps you collaborate on business applications like word processing or spreadsheets, while staying socially connected with colleagues via e-mail, calendars, instant messaging, blogs, teamrooms, profiles, status updates, and file sharing.[25] Users can also let all project participants review the information and receive notifications when it changes. The latest version of Microsoft's Outlook e-mail program lets users make Internet phone calls, as well as manage documents and publish reports in a SharePoint collaborative workspace. The advantage of a collaborative workspace is that all participants can go directly to a central location and work directly on a project, without the intervening step of an e-mail.[26] These technology advances encourage collaboration along with communication.

web 2.0 a set of Internet-based applications that encourage user-provided content and collaboration

Blogging—posting text to a website—also has arrived in the business world. Some companies use blogs to communicate with the external environment—for example, by sharing information about product uses or corporate social responsibility efforts. Blogs also may foster communication within the organization.[27] A project team might have a blog where the team leader posts frequent updates along with relevant presentations and spreadsheets. Searching the blog site can be an easy way for team members to find information about the project. They also can post ideas and comments in response to the blogger's entries. Similarly, blogs can be used to encourage collaboration among employees with a shared interest in particular products, functions, or customers.

The most recently developed tools for electronic communication generally fall into a category called **Web 2.0**, a set of Internet-based applications that encourage user-provided content and collaboration. The most widely used Web 2.0 applications include social networking, podcasts, RSS (really simple syndication, where users subscribe to receive news, blogs, or other information they select), and wikis (online publications created with contributions from many authors/users). These tools became popular at such sites as Facebook, YouTube, and Wikipedia, but users have brought the experience to work, applying online collaboration to business needs. Unlike the first generation of Internet applications, introduced to organizations when information technology (IT) departments evaluated an application and made a purchase, employees typically begin using Web 2.0 tools on their own to meet a need. Rod Smith, IBM's vice president for emerging technologies, recalls a meeting at which he told Royal Bank of Scotland's IT head about wikis. The IT chief said the bank didn't use them, but when Smith asked the other participants, more than two dozen said *they* did.[28]

● Texting is a fast, convenient, and efficient form of communication for basic messages, but likely not the best medium for trying to solve more complex problems or when seeing nonverbal cues is essential.

Exhibit 13.4 summarizes advantages and disadvantages of electronic media.

Advantages The advantages of electronic communication are numerous and dramatic. Within firms, advantages include the sharing of more information and the speed and efficiency in delivering routine messages to large numbers of people across vast geographic areas. Business-related wikis such as Socialtext let project teams post their ideas in one forum for others to add contributions. Socialtext allows project leaders to grant users access based on their need to know and participate. Web Crossing uses wikis for product development. Michael Krieg, vice president of marketing, says the wikis save the company "untold amounts of paper, postage, meetings, travel budgets, conference calls, and the time required to coordinate it all."[29]

Communicating electronically can reduce time and expenses devoted to traveling while expanding participation to a larger number of people. In 2013, Provident New York Bancorp held its first virtual annual stockholder meeting. CEO William F. Helmer stated: "The virtual meeting gives better access to all of our shareholders to participate in the annual meeting, experience the full presentation, vote, and ask questions." Bancorp donated the savings gained from not having a large face-to-face meeting to the United Way.[30]

Some companies, including Boeing, use brainstorming software that allows anonymous contributions, presuming it will add more honesty to internal discussions. Research indicates more data sharing and critical argumentation, and higher-quality decisions, with a group decision support system than is found in face-to-face meetings.[31] But anonymity also offers potential for lies, gossip, insults, threats, harassment, and the release of confidential information.[32]

Exhibit 13.4	Advantages and disadvantages of using electronic media at work	
Advantages	**Disadvantages**
Allows information to be shared rapidly with large numbers of stakeholders.	May not be effective for solving some types of complex problems.
Enables routine messages to be delivered with speed and efficiency.	Prevents interpretation of subtle nonverbal cues conveyed by the sender.
Reduces time and expenses related to traveling, photocopying, and mailing.	Engenders less trust among users than does face-to-face communication.
Encourages more people to participate and share their ideas with others.	Messages can hurt feelings, be insensitively worded, or be intentionally hurtful.
Leaves a permanent record of communication for later reference.	Sensitive or private information can be leaked or sent to the wrong recipient.

Disadvantages The disadvantages of electronic communication include the difficulty of solving complex problems that require more extended, face-to-face interaction and the inability to pick up subtle, nonverbal, or inflectional clues about what the communicator is thinking or conveying. In online bargaining—even before it begins—negotiators distrust one another more than in face-to-face negotiations. After the negotiation (compared with face-to-face

Twitter as a Lifeline During Disasters

"What are you doing?"

It's a familiar question—particularly to legions of Twitter users worldwide. Social networking site Twitter provides a fast, easy way to stay close to friends, offering up the minutiae of life in real-time "bytes"—for example, "washing my sister's car," "catching a movie with friends," or "thinking about studying for econ midterm but need pizza first." With each tweet limited to 140 characters, Twitterers quickly learn to get their message across succinctly.

When Gen-Xers Jack Dorsey, Biz Stone, and Evan Williams founded Twitter in 2006, their idea was to enable users to access a communication network at what they called "the lowest common denominator." To access Twitter, users need nothing more than a cell phone with instant messaging capability. As a result, the site has grown exponentially. By 2014, Twitter reported having 255 million active users, with 77 percent of accounts registered outside of the United States. The company reports that approximately 500 million tweets are being sent each day!

Twitter quickly became something more than a casual conduit for staying in touch. The site is a valuable medium for reporting and tracking information during disasters and world events.

After earthquakes devastated China in May 2008, Twitter became the primary source of eyewitness accounts. It reported information even faster than the U.S. Geological Survey, the agency responsible for tracking quake readings worldwide. Just weeks later, when earthquakes hit Los Angeles, cell phone–delivered tweets flooded the Twitter network within seconds. In contrast, it was nine minutes before the Associated Press reported the story.

When a US Airways jet made an emergency landing on the Hudson River in 2009, it was a Twitter user who, with his cell phone, snapped a photo of the plane gliding into the river and posted it on a Twitter photo-sharing site. The surreal image appeared worldwide in minutes. Today the Federal Emergency Management Agency (FEMA) hosts a Twitter page and uses it to provide real-time information on disasters like the 2011 tornadoes that tore through Alabama and other southeastern states, killing 328 people over a two-day period.

A more recent tragic event occurred on April 15, 2013, when two bombs detonated near the finish line of the Boston marathon,

killing 3 people and injuring 260 others. Within minutes of the explosions, observers used Twitter and other social media to tweet and post news and images of the tragedy. The Pew Research Center found that approximately a quarter of Americans received information about the Boston marathon bombings and subsequent hunt for the perpetrators via social media sites like Twitter and Facebook.

Discussion Questions

- What are Twitter's advantages as an electronic communication medium? Its disadvantages?
- When might a manager find Twitter an appropriate communication channel? When might a manager want to discourage employees from using Twitter?

SOURCES: L. Petrecca, "After Bombings, Social Media Informs (and Misinforms)," *USA Today* (online), April 23, 2013, www.usatoday.com; P. Jonsson, "With Response to Tornadoes, FEMA Begins to Rebuild Its Reputation," *The Christian Science Monitor* (Online), May 6, 2011, www.csmonitor.com; Federal Emergency Management Agency, "Twitter FEMA Now: We Want to Hear from You," FEMA website, www.fema.gov; J. Diamond, "The Twitter Guys," *The New York Times*, May 8, 2009, http://nytimes.com; United Press International, "Don't Fight Twitter, Disaster Expert Says," UPI website, March 6, 2009, www.upi.com; C. Beaumont, "New York Plane Crash: Twitter Breaks the News, Again," *London Telegraph*, January 16, 2009, www.telegraph.co.uk; S. Ovide, "Twittering the USAirways Plane Crash," *The Wall Street Journal*, January 15, 2009, http://blogs.wsj.com; E. Noonan, "Life Is Tweet," *Boston Globe*, January 4, 2009, www.boston.com; J. Cox, "Tweets, Twits, and the California Earthquake," *Network World*, July 30, 2008, www.networkworld.com; and M. Ingram, "Twitter Breaks Chinese Earthquake News," *Toronto Globe and Mail*, May 12, 2008, www.theglobeandmail.com.

negotiators), people usually are less satisfied with their outcomes, even when the outcomes are economically equivalent.[33]

Although organizations rely heavily on computer-aided communication for group decision making, face-to-face groups generally take less time, make higher-quality decisions, and are more satisfying for members.[34] E-mail is most appropriate for routine messages that do not require the exchange of large quantities of complex information. It is less suitable for confidential information, resolving conflicts, or negotiating.[35]

Employees have reported being laid off via e-mail and even text messages.[36] These more impersonal forms of communication can hurt feelings, and an upset employee can easily forward messages, which often has a snowball effect that can embarrass everyone involved. Like e-mail, IMs can help people work together productively, but they can also leak sensitive information.

Companies are worried about leaks and negative portrayals, and they may require employees to agree to specific guidelines before starting blogs. Some general guidelines should guide corporate bloggers:[37]

- Remember that blogs posted on a company's website should avoid any content that could embarrass the company or disclose confidential information.
- Stick to the designated topic of any company-sponsored blog.
- If members of the media contact you about reporting on a blog you have written, get official approval before proceeding.

Most electronic communications are quick and easy, and some are anonymous. As a result, one inevitable consequence of electronic communication is "flaming": hurling insults, sending "nastygrams," venting frustration, snitching on coworkers to the boss, and otherwise breaching protocol. E-mail, blogs, and instant messaging liberate people to send messages they would not say to a person's face. Without nonverbal cues, "kidding" remarks may be taken seriously, causing resentment and regret. Some people try to clear up confusion with emoticons such as smiley faces, but those efforts can further muddy the intent.[38]

Also, confidential information, including government security and intelligence data, was recently leaked by ex-government contractor Edward Snowden. Currently taking refuge in Russia, Snowden is accused of releasing an untold number of classified National Security Agency documents. A governmental report assessed the extent of the leak: "The scope of the compromised knowledge related to U.S. intelligence capabilities is staggering."[39]

Other downsides to electronic communication are important.[40] Different people and sometimes different working units latch onto different channels as their media of choice. For example, an engineering division might use e-mail most, but a design group might rely primarily on instant messaging and neglect e-mail. Another disadvantage is that electronic messages sometimes are monitored or seen inadvertently by those for whom they are not intended. Be careful with your IMs: make sure you don't accidentally send them to the wrong person and that they don't pop up on the screen during a PowerPoint presentation.[41] One way to avoid sending to the wrong person is to close all IM windows except those you're currently using for active conversations. Deleting electronic messages—whether e-mail, IMs, or cell phone text messages—does not destroy them; they are saved elsewhere. Recipients can forward them to others without the original sender knowing it. Many companies use software to monitor e-mail and IMs. And the messages can be used in court cases to indict individuals or companies. Electronic messages sent from work and on company-provided devices are private property—but they are private property of the system's owner, not of the sender.

An e-mail golden rule (like the sunshine rule in the ethics chapter): don't hit "send" unless you'd be comfortable having the contents on the front page of a newspaper, being read by your mother or a competitor. And it's not a bad idea to have a colleague read nonroutine e-mails before you send them.

Did You Know?

E-mail overload costs businesses as much as $1 billion a year in lost employee productivity.[42]

3.2 | Managing the Electronic Load

Electronic communication media seem essential these days, and people wonder how they ever worked without them. But the sheer volume of communication can be overwhelming, especially when it doesn't let up during meetings or breaks after work.[43]

Fortunately, a few rules of thumb can help you manage your electronic communications.[44] For the problem of information overload, the challenge is to separate the truly important from the routine. Effective managers find time to think about bigger business issues and don't get too bogged down in responding to every message that seems urgent but may be trivial. Essential here is to think strategically about your goals, identify the items that are most important, and prioritize your time around those goals. This is easier said than done, of course, but it is essential, and it helps. Most communication software has tools that can help. For example, with instant messaging, set your "away" message when you want to concentrate on something else. Of course management also has a role to play. Some employees check messages constantly because they believe (perhaps correctly) that this is what their bosses expect of them. Managers can help employees by limiting and communicating the times during which they expect a prompt response.[45]

A few more specific suggestions: With e-mail, don't hit "reply to all" when you should hit just "reply." Get organized by creating folders sorted by subject, priority, or sender, and flag messages that require follow-up. If you receive a copy, you don't need to respond; it's just for your information.

Some companies are recognizing the downsides of electronic media overuse. In France, a recently signed labor agreement curtails electronic media overuse. The agreement requires employees, once they leave at the end of the work day (and over weekends), to disconnect and not respond to their managers' e-mails (even on their smartphones).[46] The agreement affects employees from the consulting and technology sectors, including the French groups of PricewaterhouseCoopers, Deloitte, Facebook, and Google.[47] Thierry Breton, CEO of tech firm Atos, implemented a "zero e-mail" policy that bans all employees of the firm from sending e-mails. He is replacing internal e-mail with collaborative and social media tools and an online chat system that allows videoconferencing.[48]

As overwhelming as electronic communications can be, you can take steps to simplify them. For example, a global customer account management team established two ground rules:

1. Whenever a member communicated with a customer, the member was to send a briefing to all team members.

2. They designated a primary contact on the team for each customer, with no one else on the team authorized to discuss or decide strategies or policies with the customer.

If contacted by a customer, team members would direct the customer to the appropriate contact person. These steps simplified communication channels and greatly reduced contradictory and confusing messages.[49]

3.3 | The Virtual Office

Many entrepreneurs conduct business via open "offices" on the Internet, working on their computers from wherever they happen to be. Similarly, major companies like IBM, GE, Deloitte LLP, and Prudential California Realty are slashing office space and giving people laptop or notebook computers, telecommunications software, voice mail, and other communications technologies so they can work virtually anywhere, anytime.[50] Based on the philosophy that management's focus should be on what people do, not where they are, the **virtual office** is a mobile office in which people can work anywhere—home, car, airport, customers' offices—as long as they have the tools to communicate with customers and colleagues.

In the short run at least, the benefits of virtual offices appear substantial. Saving money on rent and utilities is an obvious advantage. By offering most of its 45,000 employees the option to telecommute up to five days a week, Deloitte LLP reduced office space and energy costs by 30 percent.[51] A virtual office also gives employees access to whatever information they need from the company, whether they are in a meeting, visiting a client, or working from home.[52] Hiring and retaining talented people is easier because virtual offices support scheduling flexibility and even may make it possible to keep an employee who wants to relocate—for example, with a spouse taking a new job in another city.

But what will be the longer-term impact on productivity and morale? We may be in danger of losing too many "human moments"—those authentic encounters that happen only when two people are physically together.[53] Some people hate working at home. Some send faxes, e-mail, and voice mail in the middle of the night—and others receive them. Some work around the clock yet feel they are not doing enough. Long hours of being constantly close to the technical tools of work can cause burnout. And in some companies, direct supervision at the office is necessary to maintain the quality of work, especially when employees are inexperienced and need guidance. The virtual office requires changes in human beings and presents technical challenges, so although it is much hyped and useful, it will not completely replace real offices and face-to-face work.

Many of consulting giant Accenture's 290,000 employees spend most of their time at clients' workplaces. Under those conditions, cultivating teamwork is difficult for managers, and developing a career is challenging for consultants, who may have a client on one continent, a supervisor on another, and support staff in a third country.

To foster communication and maintain strong working relationships, Accenture assigns each new consultant to a career counselor, a senior employee in the same specialty who helps the employee develop his or her career. They communicate by phone monthly. Accenture trains its managers in how to lead virtual teams. They learn to schedule conference calls that respect time differences and to allow plenty of opportunity for casual conversation that maintains a sense of belonging to the team. Accenture also uses a web conferencing system for online meetings, as well as a company networking site called Accenture People, where employees can connect, share skills and interests, and collaborate.[54]

3.4 | Use "Richer" Media for Complex or Critical Messages

Some communication channels convey more information than others. The amount of information a medium conveys is called **media richness**.[55] The more information or cues a medium sends to the receiver, the "richer" the medium is.[56] The richest media are more personal than technological, provide quick feedback, allow lots of descriptive language, and send different types of cues. Face-to-face communication is the richest medium because it offers a variety of cues in addition to words: tone of voice, facial expression, body language, and other nonverbal signals. It also allows more descriptive language than, say, a memo does. In addition, it affords more opportunity for the receiver to give feedback to and ask questions of the sender, turning one-way into two-way communication.

The telephone is less rich than face-to-face communication, electronic mail is less rich yet, and memos are the least rich medium. In general, you should send difficult and unusual

---

study tip 13

When to use face-to-face communication

If you're like most students, you probably have a busy schedule and tend to rely on texting or e-mail for most of your communication. In the United States the average college student sends about 100 texts per day. When should you make the time to sit down for a face-to-face chat with a professor? You may want to use this rich communication medium when you have complex problems or concerns like reviewing the questions you missed on a recent exam, asking advice about how to handle a slacker on your student project team, or requesting a letter of recommendation for a scholarship. You are much more likely to understand better and resolve your problem faster by talking face-to-face than communicating electronically.

messages through richer media, transmit simple and routine messages through less rich media, and use multiple media for important messages that you want to ensure people attend to and understand.[57] You should also consider factors such as cost, which medium your receiver prefers, and the preferred communication style in your organization.[58] In the following situations, based on the message and the audience, which channel would you select?[59]

1. A midsize construction firm wants to announce a new employee benefit program.

2. A manager wishes to confirm a meeting time with 10 employees.

3. Increase enthusiasm in a midsize insurance company for a program that asks employees from different departments to work on the same project team.

4. A group of engineers who are geographically dispersed want to exchange design ideas with one another.

5. Describe a straightforward but somewhat detailed and updated version of a voice mail system to 1,000 employees who are geographically dispersed.

LO4 Give examples of ways to become a better "sender" and "receiver" of information

4 | IMPROVING COMMUNICATION SKILLS

In recent years, employers have been dismayed by college graduates' poor communication skills. A demonstrated ability to communicate effectively makes a job candidate more attractive and distinguishes him or her from others. You can do many things to improve your communication skills, both as a sender and as a receiver.

4.1 | Senders Can Improve Their Presentations, Writing, Word Choice, and Body Language

To start, be aware that honest, direct, straight talk is important but all too rare. CEOs are often coached on how to slant their messages for different audiences—the investment community, employees, or the board. That's not likely to be straight talk. The focus of the messages can differ, but they can't be inconsistent. People should be able to identify your perspective, your reasoning, and your intentions.[60] Beyond this basic point, senders

● Financial guru Suze Orman has been ranked as one of the best presenters by *Bloomberg Businessweek* magazine for her ability to relay information in easy-to-understand ways. She delivers financial information using clear, concise, and direct language. Great business communicators use simple language to discuss complex issues.

can improve their skills in making persuasive presentations, writing, language use, and sending nonverbal messages.

Presentation and Persuasion Skills Throughout your career, you will be called on to state your case on a variety of issues. You will have information and perhaps an opinion or proposal to present to others. Typically your goal will be to "sell" your idea. In other words, your challenge will be to persuade others to go along with your recommendation. As a leader, you will find that some of your toughest challenges arise when people do not want to do what has to be done. Leaders have to be persuasive to get people on board.[61]

Your attitude in presenting ideas and persuading others is very important. Persuasion is not what many people think: merely selling an idea or convincing others to see things your way. Don't assume that it takes a "my way or the highway" approach, with a one-shot effort to make a hard sell and resisting compromise.[62] It usually is more constructive to consider persuasion a process of learning from each other and negotiating a shared solution. Persuasive speakers are seen as authentic, which happens when speakers are open with the audience, make a connection, demonstrate passion, and show they are listening as well as speaking. Practice this kind of authenticity by noticing and adopting the type of body language you use when you're around people you're comfortable with, planning how to engage directly with your listeners, identifying the reasons why you care about your topic, and watching for nonverbal cues as well as fully engaging when you listen to audience comments and questions.[63]

The most powerful and persuasive messages are simple and informative, are told with stories and anecdotes, and convey excitement.[64] People are more likely to remember and buy into your message if you can express it as a story that is simple, unexpected, concrete, credible, and includes emotional content. For example, Nordstrom motivates employees by passing along stories of times when its people have provided extraordinary service, such as warming up customers' cars while they shopped or ironing a shirt so that a customer could wear it to a meeting. Trader Joe's shares similar stories of employees who have gone the extra mile for customers. One such employee received a phone call from a concerned daughter regarding

Take Charge of Your Career

Tips for making formal presentations more powerful!

Lynn Hamilton, from the University of Virginia, offers 10 useful tips for making formal presentations more powerful:

1. *Spend adequate time on the **content** of your presentation.* It's easy to get so distracted with PowerPoint slides or concern about delivery skills that the actual content of a presentation is neglected. Know your content inside and out; you'll be able to discuss it conversationally and won't be tempted to memorize. If you believe in what you're saying and own the material, you will convey enthusiasm and will be more relaxed.

2. *Clearly understand the **objective** of your presentation.* Answer this question with one sentence: "What do I want the audience to believe following this presentation?" Writing down your objective will help you focus on your bottom line. Everything else in a presentation—the structure, the words, the visuals—should support your objective.

3. ***Tell** the audience the **purpose** of the presentation.* As the saying goes, "Tell them what you're going to tell them, then tell them, then tell them what you've told them." Use a clear preview statement early on to help the audience know where you're taking them.

4. *Provide **meaning**, not just data.* Today information is widely available; you won't impress people by overloading them with data. People have limited attention spans and want presenters to help clarify the meaning of data.

5. ***Practice, practice, practice.*** Appearing polished and relaxed during a presentation requires rehearsal time. Practice making your points in a variety of ways. Above all, don't memorize a presentation's content.

6. *Remember that a presentation is more like a **conversation** than a speech.* Keep your tone conversational yet professional. Audience members will be much more engaged if they feel you are talking with them rather than at them. Rely on PowerPoint slides or a broad outline to jog your memory.

7. *Remember the incredible power of **eye contact**.* Look at individual people in the audience. Try to have a series of one-on-one conversations with people in the room. This will calm you and help you connect with your audience.

8. ***Allow imperfection.*** If you forget what you were going to say, simply pause, look at your notes, and go on. Don't "break character" and effusively apologize or giggle or look mortified. Remember that an audience doesn't know your material nearly as well as you do and won't notice many mistakes.

9. *Be prepared to **answer tough questions**.* Try to anticipate the toughest questions you might receive. Plan your answers in advance. If you don't have an answer, acknowledge the fact and offer to get the information later.

10. *Provide a **crisp wrap-up** to a question-and-answer session.* Whenever possible, follow the Q&A period with a brief summary statement. Set up the Q&A session by saying, "We'll take questions for 10 minutes and then have a few closing remarks." This prevents your presentation from just winding down to a weak ending. Also, if you receive hostile or hard-to-answer questions, you'll have a chance to have the final word.

Source: Reprinted with permission of Lynn A. Hamilton, University of Virginia.

---

her snowed-in 89-year-old father who needed food for his special low-sodium diet. The employee delivered the food to the elderly customer and did not charge for the food or the delivery.[65] To be credible, a communicator backs up the message with actions consistent with the words.

Writing Skills Effective writing is more than correct spelling, punctuation, and grammar (although these help). Good writing above all requires clear, logical thinking.[66] The act of writing can be a powerful aid to thinking because you have to think about what you really want to say and what the logic is behind your message.[67]

You want people to find your e-mail and reports readable and interesting. Strive for clarity, organization, readability, and brevity.[68] Brevity is much appreciated by readers who are overloaded with documents, including wordy memos. Use a dictionary and a thesaurus, and avoid fancy words.

Your first draft rarely is as good as it could be. If you have time, revise it. Take the reader into consideration. Go through your entire document, and delete all unnecessary words, sentences, and paragraphs. Use specific, concrete words rather than abstract phrases. Instead of saying, "A period of unfavorable weather set in," say, "It rained every day for a week."

Be critical of your own writing. If you want to improve, start by reading *The Elements of Style* by William Strunk and E. B. White and the most recent edition of *The Little, Brown Handbook*.[69]

Language Word choice can enhance or interfere with communication effectiveness. For example, jargon is actually a form of shorthand and can make communication more effective when both the sender and the receiver know the buzzwords. But when the receiver is unfamiliar with the jargon, misunderstandings result. When people from different functional areas or disciplines communicate with one another, misunderstandings often occur because of such language barriers. As in writing, simplicity usually helps.

Whether speaking or writing, you should consider the receiver's background—cultural as well as technical—and adjust your language accordingly. When you are receiving, don't assume

> "Good communication does not mean that you have to speak in perfectly formed sentences and paragraphs. It isn't about slickness. Simple and clear go a long way."
>
> —John Kotter

that your understanding is the same as the speaker's intentions. Cisco CEO John Chambers, whose background is in business, simply asks the engineering managers in his high-tech company to explain any jargon. He says, "They do it remarkably well."[70] At the same time, Chambers shows respect and enhances his credibility by being truly interested in their work. Whenever Chambers travels with or reviews engineers, he asks them to teach him a topic—and he listens.

The meaning of word choices also can vary by culture. Japanese people use the simple word *hai* (yes) to convey that they understand what is being said; it does not necessarily mean they agree. Asian businesspeople rarely use the direct "no," using more subtle ways of disagreeing.[71] Global teams fail when members have difficulties communicating because of language, cultural, and geographic barriers. Heterogeneity harms team functioning at first. But when they develop ways to interact and communicate, teams develop a common identity and perform well.[72]

When conducting business overseas, try to learn something about the other country's language and customs. Americans are less likely to do this than people from some other cultures; few Americans consider a foreign language necessary for doing business abroad, and a significant majority of U.S. firms do not require employees sent abroad to know the local language.[73] But those who do will have a big edge over competitors who do not.[74] Making the effort to learn the local language builds rapport, sets a proper tone for doing business, aids in adjustment to culture shock, and especially can help you "get inside" the other culture.[75] You will learn more about how people think, feel, and behave in their personal and business dealings.

4.2 | Nonverbal Signals Convey Meaning, Too

People send and interpret signals other than those that are spoken or written. These nonverbal messages can support or undermine the stated message. Often nonverbal cues make a greater impact than other signals. In employees' eyes, managers' actions often speak louder than the words managers choose. Project manager Steve Bailey had already given many presentations when he attended a presentation skills workshop. There a facilitator pointed out Bailey's habit of clasping and unclasping his hands as he spoke. The behavior was distracting and conveyed a lack of authority. When Bailey stopped making that gesture, he discovered that his audiences tended to be more convinced by his presentations.[76]

In conversation, except when you intend to convey a negative message, you should give nonverbal signals that express warmth, respect, concern, a feeling of equality, and a willingness to listen. Negative nonverbal signals show coolness, disrespect, lack of interest, and a feeling of superiority.[77] The following suggestions can help you send positive nonverbal signals:

- Use *time* appropriately. Avoid keeping your employees waiting to see you. Devote enough time to your meetings with them, and communicate frequently, which signals your interest in their concerns.

- Make your *office arrangement* conducive to open communication. A seating arrangement that avoids separating people helps establish a warm, cooperative atmosphere. In contrast, when you sit behind your desk and your subordinate sits before you, the environment is more intimidating and authoritative.[78]

- Remember your *body language*. Research indicates that facial expression and tone of voice can account for 90 percent of the communication between two people.[79] Several nonverbal body signals convey a positive attitude toward the other person: assuming a position close to the person; gesturing frequently; maintaining eye contact; smiling; having an open body orientation, such as facing the other person directly; uncrossing the arms; and leaning forward to convey interest in what the other person is saying.

● Learning to observe and interpret accurately people's nonverbal cues will help you become a more effective communicator.

Silence is an interesting nonverbal situation. The average American is said to spend about twice as many hours per day in conversation as the average Japanese.[80] North Americans tend to talk to fill silences. Japanese allow long silences to develop, believing they can get to know people better. Japanese believe that two people with good rapport will know each other's thoughts. The need to use words implies a lack of understanding.

Nonverbal Signals in Different Countries Here are just a few nonverbal mistakes that Americans might make in other countries.[81] Nodding the head up and down in Bulgaria means no. The American thumb-and-first-finger circular A-OK gesture is vulgar in Brazil, Singapore, Russia, and Paraguay. The head is sacred in Buddhist cultures, so you must never touch someone's head. In Muslim cultures, never touch or eat with the left hand, which is thought unclean. Crossing your ankle over your knee is rude in Indonesia, Thailand, and Syria. Don't point your finger toward yourself in Germany or Switzerland—it insults the other person.

You also must correctly interpret the nonverbal signals of others. Chinese scratch their ears and cheeks to show happiness.

assume that good listening is easy and natural, in fact it is difficult and far less common than needed. Catherine Coughlin practiced her listening skills as a customer service representative for Union Electric Company during the summers of the years she was earning her college degree. Whether an individual was calling about an unpaid bill or a power outage, or just looking for an excuse to talk to somebody, Coughlin found that "you've got to respect everyone and their story" and then decide how to respond. Over the following decades, Coughlin used that experience to build a successful career with Southwestern Bell Telephone and its successor companies. She is now senior executive vice president and global marketing officer of AT&T and is still committed to careful listening.[82]

A basic technique called *reflection* will help a manager listen effectively.[83] **Reflection** is a process by which a person states what he or she believes the other person is saying. This technique places greater emphasis on listening than on talking. When both parties actively engage in reflection, they get into each other's frame of reference rather than listening and responding from their own. The result is more accurate two-way communication. Besides using reflection, you can

---

> ## "You never learn anything while you're talking."
>
> —Catherine Coughlin, *senior executive vice president and global marketing officer, AT&T*[87]

Greeks puff air after they receive a compliment. Hondurans touch their fingers below their eyes to show disbelief or caution. Japanese indicate embarrassment or "no" by sucking in air and hissing through their teeth. Vietnamese look to the ground with their heads down to show respect. Compared with Americans, Russians use fewer facial expressions, and Scandinavians fewer hand gestures, whereas people in Mediterranean and Latin cultures may gesture and touch more. Brazilians are more likely than Americans to interrupt, Arabs to speak loudly, and Asians to respect silence.

Use these examples not to stereotype but to remember that people in other cultures have different styles and to aid in communication accuracy.

4.3 | Receivers Can Improve Their Listening, Reading, and Observational Skills

Once you become effective at sending oral, written, and nonverbal messages, you are halfway toward becoming a complete communicator. However, you must also develop adequate receiving capabilities. Receivers need good listening, reading, and observational skills.

Listening In today's demanding work environment, managers need excellent listening skills. Although it is easy to

improve how well you listen by practicing the following techniques:[84]

1. *Find an area of interest.* Even if you decide the topic is dull, ask yourself, "What is the speaker saying that I can use?"

2. *Judge content, not delivery.* Don't get caught up in the speaker's personality, mannerisms, speaking voice, or clothing. Instead try to learn what the speaker knows.

3. *Hold your fire.* Rather than getting immediately excited by what the speaker seems to be saying, withhold evaluation until you understand the speaker's message.

4. *Listen for ideas.* Don't get bogged down in all the facts and details; focus on central ideas.

5. *Be flexible.* Have several systems for note taking, and use the system best suited to the speaker's style. Don't take too many notes or try to force everything said by a disorganized speaker into a formal outline.

6. *Resist distraction.* Close the door, shut off the radio, move closer to the person talking, or ask him or her to speak louder. Don't look out the window or at papers on your desk.

7. *Exercise your mind.* Some people tune out when the material gets difficult. Develop an appetite for a good mental challenge.

8. *Keep your mind open.* Many people get overly emotional when they hear words referring to their most deeply held convictions—for

example, *union, subsidy, import, Republican* or *Democrat,* and *big business.* Try not to let your emotions interfere with comprehension.

9. *Capitalize on thought speed.* Take advantage of the fact that most people talk at a rate of about 125 words per minute, but most of us think at about four times that rate. Use those extra 400 words per minute to think about what the speaker is saying rather than turning your thoughts to something else.

10. *Work at listening.* Spend some energy. Don't just pretend you're paying attention. Show interest. Good listening is hard work, but the benefits outweigh the costs.

For managers, the stakes are high: failure to listen causes managers to miss good ideas and can even drive employees away. When Ben Berry was a senior systems analyst at a hospital, he was assigned to help lead a team charged with developing computer applications. The other team leader, a doctor, had little interest in hearing ideas from Berry and the team members. He was more focused on issuing directions. The team members and Berry felt discouraged from participating. Berry tried discussing the issue with his supervisor and with the doctor, but the doctor never saw a need to listen, so Berry left the organization to take another job.[86]

Listening begins with personal contact. Staying in the office, keeping the door closed, and eating lunch at your desk are sometimes necessary to get pressing work done, but that is no way to stay on top of what's going on. Better to walk the halls, initiate conversations and go to lunch even with people outside your area, have coffee in a popular gathering place, and maybe even move your desk onto the factory floor.[88]

When a manager takes time to really listen to and get to know people, they think, "She's showing an interest in me" or "He's letting me know that I matter" or "She values my ideas and contributions." Trust develops. Listening and learning from others are even more important for innovation than for routine work. Successful change and innovation come through lots of human contact.

Reading Illiteracy is a significant problem in the United States. Even if illiteracy is not a problem in your organization,

Did You Know?

An employee survey asked: "What is the most critical skill a leader can possess when working with others?" The three most frequent responses were (from most frequent): (1) communication/listening, (2) effective management skills, and (3) emotional intelligence and empathy.[85]

your reading materials, but read important messages, documents, and passages slowly and carefully. Note important points for later referral. Consider taking courses to increase your reading speed and comprehension skills. Finally, don't limit your reading to items about your particular job skill or technical expertise; read materials that fall outside your immediate concerns. You never know when a creative and useful idea will be inspired by a novel, a biography, a sports story, or an article about a problem in another business or industry.

Observing Effective communicators are also capable of observing and interpreting nonverbal communications. For example, by reading nonverbal cues, a presenter can determine how her talk is going and adjust her approach if necessary.

Some companies train their sales force to interpret the nonverbal signals of potential customers. People can also decode nonverbal signals to determine whether a sender is being truthful or deceitful. In the United States, deceitful communicators tend to maintain less eye contact, make either more or fewer body movements than usual, and smile either too much or too little. Verbally, they offer fewer specifics than do truthful senders.[89]

A vital source of useful observations comes from visiting people, plants, and other locations to get a firsthand view.[90] Many corporate executives rely heavily on reports from the field and don't travel to remote locations to observe what is going on. Reports are no substitute for actually seeing things happen in practice. Frequent visits to the field and careful observation can help a manager develop deep understanding of current operations, future prospects, and ideas for how to fully exploit capabilities.[91]

Of course you must *accurately interpret* what you observe. A Canadian conducting business with a high-ranking official in Kuwait was surprised that the meeting was held in an open office and was interrupted constantly.[92] He interpreted the lack of a big, private office and secretary to mean that the Kuwaiti was of low rank and uninterested in doing business, so he lost interest in the deal. The Canadian

> ## "You can observe a lot by watching."
> —Yogi Berra

reading mistakes are common and costly. As a receiver, for your own benefit, read memos and e-mail as soon as possible, before it's too late to respond. You may skim most of

observed the facts accurately, but his perceptual biases and limited awareness of cultural differences in norms caused him to misinterpret what he saw.

The Japanese are particularly skilled at interpreting every nuance of voice and gesture, putting most Westerners at a disadvantage.[93] When one is conducting business in Asian or other countries, local guides can be invaluable not only to interpret language but to "decode" behavior at meetings, what subtle hints and nonverbal cues mean, who the key people are, and how the decision-making process operates.

LO5 Explain how to improve downward, upward, and horizontal communication

5 | ORGANIZATIONAL COMMUNICATION

Being a skilled communicator is essential to being a good manager and team leader. But communication must also be managed throughout the organization. Every minute of every day, countless bits of information are transmitted through an organization. The flow of information affects how well people perform. When a group's success depends on discovering new information, individuals who independently tap information from a variety of sources help achieve that success. For evaluating information and arriving at decisions, people in the most effective groups communicate extensively with their team members (a richly connected network). The most productive teams switch back and forth between using centralized networks and richly connected networks.[94] These patterns of communication may include communications traveling downward, upward, horizontally, and informally within the organization.

5.1 | Downward Communication Directs, Motivates, Coaches, and Informs

Downward communication refers to the flow of information from higher to lower levels in the organization's hierarchy. Examples include a manager giving an assignment to an assistant, a supervisor making an announcement to his subordinates, and a company president delivering a talk to her management team. Downward communication that provides relevant information helps create employee identification with the company, supportive attitudes, and decisions consistent with the organization's objectives.[95]

People must receive the information they need to perform their jobs and become—and remain—loyal members of the organization. But they often lack adequate information.[96] Several problems underlie the lack of information:

- *Information overload*—Managers and employees are bombarded with so much information that they fail to absorb everything. Much of the information is not very important, but its volume causes a lot of relevant information to be lost.

- *Lack of openness between managers and employees*—Managers may believe "No news is good news," "I don't have time to keep them informed of everything they want to know," or "It's none of their business, anyway." Some managers withhold information even if sharing it would be useful.

- *Filtering*—As we discussed earlier in the chapter, when messages are passed from one person to another, some information is left out. When a message passes through many people, more information may be lost during each transmission. The message also can be distorted as people add words or interpretations. Filtering poses serious problems in organizations when messages are communicated downward through many organizational levels and much information is lost.

The data in Exhibit 13.5 suggest that by the time messages reach the people for whom they are intended, the receivers may get very little useful information. The fewer authority levels through which communications must pass, the less information will be lost or distorted. As a result, in flatter organizations, filtering is less of a problem with downward communication.

Managers can address some of these issues by fostering a culture that values communication. At a large telecommunications company, employees consistently rated the human resource

Exhibit 13.5 Information loss in downward communication

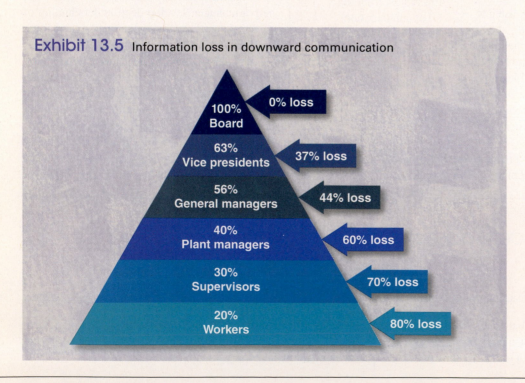

100% Board — 0% loss
63% Vice presidents — 37% loss
56% General managers — 44% loss
40% Plant managers — 60% loss
30% Supervisors — 70% loss
20% Workers — 80% loss

(HR) division best at communicating with them. The divisional president sent out monthly e-mail messages about new accounts, products in development, hiring trends, and individual employees' accomplishments. Employees and managers were also kept up-to-date through face-to-face communications at quarterly town hall meetings, monthly meetings of line managers, and weekly senior management meetings. And the president invited about 10 employees at a time to communicate informally at monthly breakfasts and lunches.[97]

Coaching

Some of the most important downward communications occur when managers give performance feedback to their direct reports. We discussed earlier the importance of giving feedback and positive reinforcement when it is deserved. It is also important to explicitly discuss poor performance and areas that can be improved.

Coaching is dialogue with a goal of helping another be more effective and achieve his or her full potential on the job.[98] Done properly, coaching develops executives and enhances performance.[99] According to a recent survey by the American Management Association, approximately half of responding companies use coaching to prepare individuals for a promotion or new role.[100] When people have performance problems or exhibit behaviors that need to be changed, coaching is often the best way to help them change and succeed. And coaching is not just for poor performers; as the greatest athletes know, it is for anyone who is good and aspires to excellence. Coaches for executives sometimes are hired from the outside, but a coach from outside your organization may not fully understand the context in which you work.[101] So don't take advice automatically. The best use of a coach is as a sounding board, helping you think through the potential impact of your ideas, generate new options, and learn from experience.

Companies including Coca-Cola use coaching as an essential part of their executive development process. When done well, coaching is true dialogue between two committed people engaged in joint problem solving. It is far more than an occasion for highlighting poor performance, delivering reprimands, or giving advice. Good coaching requires achieving real understanding of the problem, the person, and the situation; jointly generating ideas for what to do; and encouraging the person to improve. Good coaches ask a lot of questions, listen well, provide input, and encourage others to think for themselves. Effective coaching requires honesty, calmness, and supportiveness, all aided by a sincere desire to help. The ultimate and longest-lasting form of help is enabling people to think through and solve their own problems.

Downward Communication in Difficult Times

Adequate downward communication can be particularly valuable during difficult times. During corporate mergers and acquisitions, employees feel anxious and wonder how the changes will affect them. Ideally (and ethically), top management should communicate with employees about the change as early as possible.

But some argue against that approach, on the grounds that informing employees about the reorganization might cause them to quit too early. Then too, top management often cloisters itself, prompting rumors and anxiety. CEOs and other senior execs are surrounded by lawyers, investment bankers, and so on—people who are paid merely to make the deal happen, not to make it work. Yet with the people who are affected by the deal, you must increase, not decrease, communication.[102]

In a merger of two *Fortune* 500 companies, two plants received very different information.[103] All employees at both plants received the initial letter from the CEO announcing the merger. But after that, one plant was kept in the dark while the other was continually filled in on what was happening. Top management gave employees information about layoffs, transfers, promotions and demotions, and changes in pay, jobs, and benefits.

Which plant do you think fared better as the difficult transitional months unfolded? In both plants, the merger decreased employees' job satisfaction and commitment to the organization and increased their belief that the company was untrustworthy, dishonest, and uncaring. In the plant whose employees got little information, these problems persisted for a long time. But in the plant where employees received complete information, the situation stabilized, and attitudes improved toward their normal levels. Full communication not only helped employees survive an anxious period but also served a symbolic value by signaling care and concern for employees. Without such communications, employee reactions to a merger or acquisition may be so negative as to undermine the corporate strategy.

Open-Book Management

Executives often are proud of their newsletters, staff meetings, videos, and other vehicles of downward communication. More often than not, the information provided concerns company sports teams, birthdays, and new copy machines. But today a more unconventional philosophy is gathering steam. **Open-book management** is the practice of sharing with employees at all levels of the organization vital information previously meant for management's eyes only. This information includes financial goals, income statements, budgets, sales, forecasts, and other relevant data about company performance and prospects. This practice is dramatically different from the traditional closed-book approach in which people may or may not have a clue about how the company is doing, may or may not believe the things that management tells them, and may or may not believe that their personal performance makes a difference. Open-book management is controversial because many managers prefer to keep such information to themselves. Sharing strategic plans and financial information with employees could lead to leaks to competitors or to employee dissatisfaction with compensation. But

coaching dialogue with a goal of helping another be more effective and achieve his or her full potential on the job

open-book management practice of sharing with employees at all levels of the organization vital information previously meant for management's eyes only

upward communication
information that flows from lower to higher levels in the organization's hierarchy

the companies that share this information claim a favorable impact on motivation and productivity. Cecil Ursprung, former chair and CEO of Reflexite Corporation in New Britain, Connecticut, said, "Why would you tell 5 percent of the team what the score was and not the other 95 percent?"[104]

Father of scientific management Frederick Taylor early in the 20th century would have considered opening the books to all employees "idiotic."[105] But then Jack Stack tried it at Springfield ReManufacturing Corporation, which was on the brink of collapse.[106] The results? A reporter called Jack Stack's SRC "the most highly motivated and business-savvy workforce I ever encountered." In addition, "I met fuel-injection-pump rebuilders who knew the gross margins of every nozzle and pump they produced. I met crankshaft grinders and engine assemblers who could discuss the ROI of their machine tools." The rewards they deserve are part of the picture, too: "I met a

- Managers learn what's going on. Management gains a more accurate picture of subordinates' work, accomplishments, problems, plans, attitudes, and ideas.

- Employees gain from the opportunity to communicate upward. People can relieve some of their frustrations, achieve a stronger sense of participation in the enterprise, and improve morale.

- Effective upward communication facilitates downward communication as good listening becomes a two-way street.

A manufacturing company relied on upward communication as it prepared to operate shifts around the clock. Managers expected that the change would be challenging for some employees, so it assembled a focus group of factory workers to inform management about how the new work shifts would affect workers' families and other commitments, including night school. Discussing possibilities with the focus group members before the change had been formally announced posed the risk that employees would spread rumors, but management determined that this

> ## "Many people believe that if you are doing a good job and accomplishing something, your bosses necessarily know this, but they don't.
>
> —Jeffrey Pfeffer, *professor of organizational behavior, Stanford*[111]

guy who worked on turbochargers and ran his area as if it were his own small business. Then again, why shouldn't he? Like the other employees, he was an owner of SRC."[107] Worth only 10 cents per share in 1983, the company's current stock price is close to $200 per share.[108]

Other small companies joined the movement. Then bigger companies, including BP Canada, R. H. Donnelley, Wabash National, and Baxter Healthcare, began to use open-book management.

Opening the books, done properly, is a complete communications system that makes sense to people on the shop floor just as it does to the top executives. Moving toward open-book management includes these basic steps:[109]

1. Provide the information.

2. Teach basic finance and the basics of the business.

3. Empower people to make decisions based on what they know.

4. Make sure everyone shares directly in the company's success (and risks), such as through stock ownership and bonuses.

5.2 | Upward Communication Is Invaluable to Management

Upward communication travels from lower to higher ranks in the hierarchy. Adequate upward communication is important for several reasons:[110]

risk was less important than the risk of proceeding with ignorance of employees' concerns. The change to the new shifts took employees' concerns into account and proceeded smoothly.[112]

The problems common in upward communication resemble those for downward communication. Managers, like their subordinates, are bombarded with information and may neglect or miss information from below. In addition, some employees are not always open with their bosses; filtering occurs upward as well as downward. People tend to share only good news with their bosses and suppress bad news for several reasons:

- They want to appear competent.

- They mistrust their boss and fear that if he or she finds out about something they have done, they will be punished.

- They fear the boss will punish the messenger, even if the reported problem is not that person's fault.

- They believe they are helping their boss if they shield him or her from problems.

For these and other reasons, managers may not learn about important problems. As one leadership expert put it, "If the messages from below say you are doing a flawless job, send back for a more candid assessment."[113]

Managing Upward Communication Generating useful information from below requires managers to both *facilitate*

Traditional Thinking

Managers should ignore rumors because they are usually baseless and they think they will go away on their own.

The Best Managers Today

Neutralize potentially destructive rumors by providing factual information.

and *motivate* upward communication. For example, they can have an open-door policy and encourage people to use it, have lunch or coffee with employees, use surveys, institute a productivity program for suggestions, or have town hall meetings. They can ask for employee advice, make informal visits to plants, really think about and respond to employee suggestions, and distribute summaries of new ideas and practices inspired by employee suggestions and actions.[114]

Some executives practice MBWA (management by wandering around). That term, coined by Ed Carlson of United Airlines, refers simply to getting out of the office, walking around, and talking frequently and informally with employees.[115] Reed Hastings, CEO of Netflix, has taken MBWA to another level. He purposely doesn't have an office at the Netflix headquarters; he connects with managers and employees by working at random places around the buiding.[116]

At an aerospace company, management brought in consultants because trust and communications between management and employees were poor. The consultants assembled a team of employees to study the problem, and their top-priority recommendation was for managers to conduct informal walk-arounds, visiting employees in their work areas. The members of the problem-solving team told management they wanted these visits as a signal that managers cared to get to know them, spend time with them, and listen to them.[117]

Useful upward communication must be reinforced and not punished. Someone who tries to talk to a manager about a problem must not be consistently brushed off. An announced open-door policy must truly be open-door. Also, people must trust their supervisor and know that he or she will not hold a grudge if they deliver negative information. To get honesty, managers must truly listen, not punish the messenger for being honest, and act on valid comments.

5.3 | Horizontal Communication Fosters Collaboration

Much information needs to be shared among people on the same hierarchical level. Such **horizontal communication** can take place among people in the same work team or in different departments. For example, a purchasing agent discusses a problem with a production engineer, and a task force of department heads meets to discuss a particular concern. Horizontal communication also occurs with people outside the firm, including potential investors.[118]

Horizontal communication has several important functions:[119]

- It allows units to share information, coordinate work, and solve mutual problems.

- It helps resolve conflicts.

- By allowing interaction among peers, it provides social and emotional support.

horizontal communication
information shared among people on the same hierarchical level

All these factors contribute to morale and effectiveness. David Carere, vice president of finance, credit, and account settlement for Rich Products, emphasizes that his staff must collaborate with employees in other functions, especially sales and customer service. This horizontal collaboration helps the frozen dessert company ensure that its sales are profitable and that bad debt is kept to a minimum. To foster communication between his employees and those in other departments, Carere sets up meetings where the credit department explains its role to employees of other departments and learns more about what they do.[120]

Managing Horizontal Communication In complex environments, in which decisions in one unit affect another, information must be shared horizontally. An example of good horizontal communication is BluePages, IBM's internal social networking site. Accessed daily by about 6 million IBMers, the site invites employees to post information about who they are, how they can be contacted, what projects they work or worked on, and what

● Effective managers encourage and facilitate upward communication.

skills they possess.[121] NASA co-locates scientists from different disciplines. And Hewlett-Packard uses common databases for different product groups to share information and ideas.[122]

General Electric offers a great example of how to use productive horizontal communication as a competitive weapon.[123] GE's businesses could operate independently, but each is supposed to help the others. They transfer technical resources, people, information, ideas, and money among themselves. GE accomplishes this high level of communication and cooperation through easy access between divisions and to the CEO; a culture of openness, honesty, trust, and mutual obligation; and quarterly meetings in which all the top executives get together to share information and ideas. Similar activities take place at lower levels as well.

LO6 Summarize how to work with the company grapevine

6 | INFORMAL COMMUNICATION NEEDS ATTENTION

Organizational communications differ in formality:

- *Formal communications* are official, organization-sanctioned episodes of information transmission. They can move upward, downward, or horizontally and often are prearranged and necessary for performing some task.

- *Informal communication* is more unofficial. People gossip; employees complain about their boss; people talk about their favorite sports teams; work teams tell newcomers how to get by.[125]

The **grapevine** is the social network of informal communications. Informal networks provide people with information, help them solve problems, and teach them how to do their work successfully. You should develop a good network of people willing and able to help.[126] However, the grapevine can be destructive when irrelevant or erroneous gossip and rumors proliferate and harm operations.[127]

What does this mean for you personally? Don't engage in e-gossip. Embarrassing episodes become public, and lawsuits based on defamation of character and invasion of privacy have used e-mail evidence. But don't avoid the grapevine, either.[128] Listen, but evaluate before believing what you hear. Who is the source? How credible is he or she? Does the rumor make sense? Is it consistent or inconsistent with other things you know or have heard? Seek more information. Don't stir the pot.

6.1 | Managing Informal Communication

Rumors start over any number of topics, including salaries, job security, costly mistakes, and the identity of people who are

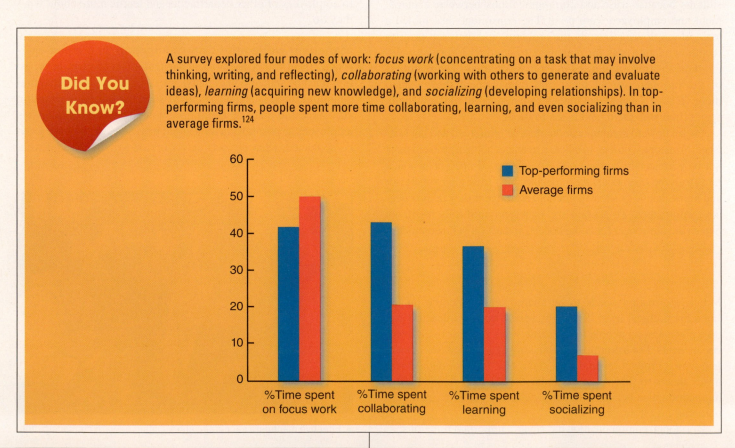

Did You Know?

A survey explored four modes of work: *focus work* (concentrating on a task that may involve thinking, writing, and reflecting), *collaborating* (working with others to generate and evaluate ideas), *learning* (acquiring new knowledge), and *socializing* (developing relationships). In top-performing firms, people spent more time collaborating, learning, and even socializing than in average firms.[124]

■ Top-performing firms
■ Average firms

%Time spent on focus work
%Time spent collaborating
%Time spent learning
%Time spent socializing

leaving or being promoted. Rumors can destroy people's faith and trust in the company—and in each other. But the grapevine cannot be eliminated. So managers need to *work with* the grapevine. The grapevine can be managed in several ways:[129]

- If a manager hears a story that could get out of hand, he or she should *talk to the key people* involved to get the facts and their perspectives. Don't allow malicious gossip.

- To *prevent* rumors from starting, managers can explain events that are important but have not been explained; dispel uncertainties by providing facts; and establish open communications and trust over time.[130] These efforts are especially important during times of uncertainty, such as after a merger or layoff or when sales slow down, because rumors increase along with anxiety. For example, when advertising revenues fell at R. H. Donnelley, which publishes yellow pages directories, management stepped up efforts to make sure employees heard any company news straight from management, rather than on the news. Donnelley also encouraged its managers to make regular visits to salespeople to answer their questions.[131]

- The manager should *neutralize* rumors once they have started. Disregard the rumor if it is ridiculous; openly confirm any parts that are true; make public comments (no comment is seen as a confirmation of the rumor); deny the rumor, if the denial is based in truth (don't make false denials); make sure communications about the issue are consistent; select a spokesperson of appropriate rank and knowledge; and hold town meetings if needed.[132]

Some companies use informal rumors to create buzz and excitement in advance of a new product launch. In 2014, rumors abound regarding Amazon's purported soon-to-be launched smartphone that is expected to feature 3-D graphics (without users having to wear special glasses) and six cameras that will track eye movement to enable touchless commands.[133] Numerous tech and business blogs, journals, and websites are tracking this "next big thing."

> **LO7** Describe the boundaryless organization and its advantages

7 | BOUNDARYLESS ORGANIZATIONS HAVE NO BARRIERS TO INFORMATION FLOW

Many executives and management scholars today believe organizations need to ensure free access to information in all directions. Jack Welch, when he was CEO of General Electric, coined the term *boundarylessness*. A **boundaryless organization** is one without any barriers to information flow. If no boundaries separate people, jobs, processes, and places, then ideas, information, decisions, and actions can move to where they are most needed.[134] This free flow does not imply a random free-for-all of unlimited communication and information overload. It implies information available *as needed*, moving quickly and easily enough that the organization functions far better as a whole than as separate parts.

GE's chief learning officer uses the metaphor of the organization as a house with three kinds of boundaries: the floors and ceilings, the walls separating the rooms, and the outside walls. In organizations, these barriers correspond to the boundaries between different organizational levels, between different units and departments, and between the organization and its external stakeholders, such as suppliers and customers. GE also identifies a fourth wall: global boundaries separating domestic from global operations.[135]

A method of breaking down boundaries is GE's famous Workout program, a series of meetings for business members across multiple hierarchical levels, characterized by extremely frank, tough discussions that break down vertical boundaries. Workout has involved over hundreds of thousands of GE people; in any given week, thousands may be participating in a Workout program.[136] Workout is also done with customers and suppliers, breaking down outside boundaries. GE has reached out to the community by sharing this expertise with nonprofits, such as CommonBond Communities, a provider of affordable housing. A GE employee led a Workout session in which CommonBond employees identified how to improve processes and horizontal communication.[137]

GE uses plenty of other techniques to break down boundaries, too. It relentlessly benchmarks competitors and companies in other industries to learn best practices all over the world. GE places different functions together physically, such as engineering and manufacturing. It shares services across units. And it sometimes shares physical locations with its customers.

Boundaryless organizations intentionally create dialogue across boundaries, turning barriers into permeable membranes. As the GE people put it, people from different parts of the organization need to learn "how to talk."[138] They must also learn "how to walk." That is, dialogue is essential, but it must be followed by commensurate action.

As GE's Workout program and the rest of this chapter demonstrates, effective communication is an essential tool for all leaders, managers, and employees. As you continue reading, consider how being an effective communicator can help you achieve managerial control (Chapter 14) and innovation and change (Chapter 15).

boundaryless organization
organization in which there are no barriers to information flow

Study Checklist

- Did you tear out the perforated student review card at the back of the text to revisit learning objectives and key terms and definitions?

Connect® Management is available for M Management. Additional resources include:

- Interactive Applications:
  - Comprehension Case: Have We Changed the Channel?
  - Drag & Drop: Communication at Cupcake Kingdom
  - Self-Assessment: Your Communication Style Under Stress
  - Video Case: Is This Effective Communication?

- LearnSmart—Multiple choice questions help you determine what you already know, are not sure about, or need to practice based on your score. And with SmartBook, you can read the relevant section in the eBook as well as practice and recharge what you've learned.

- Chapter Video: Google, The Digital Age, and Your Memory

- Young Manager Speaks Out: Timothy Paul, Store Manager

part five

14 chapter

Managerial Control

Learning Objectives

After studying Chapter 14, you should be able to

LO1 Explain why companies develop control systems for employees.

LO2 Summarize how to design a basic bureaucratic control system.

LO3 Describe the purposes for using budgets as a control device.

LO4 Recognize basic types of financial statements and financial ratios used as controls.

LO5 List procedures for implementing effective control systems.

LO6 Discuss ways in which market and clan control influence performance.

As seen in Chapter 3, macroenvironments and competition can influence business opportunities and control strategies. Take pharmaceutical companies. The weak economy and downward price pressure from generic drug manufacturers have caused pharmaceutical companies to look for ways to reduce costs. Adding additional pressure to the industry is the recent increase in governmental regulations and laws, both in the United States and when shipping certain drugs to some foreign countries. To address these external pressures, some pharmaceutical companies are controlling costs by outsourcing logistics—the storage, shipping, and delivery of drugs and related products to customers. By outsourcing nonessential value chain activities, these drug makers can focus on R&D for product development and other core competency activities.

What companies are poised to take over the logistics of these and other health care companies? Efficient and control-oriented shipping companies like United Parcel Service (UPS). Over the past eight years, UPS has built 41 dedicated health care facilities around the world. Not only do these warehouses have temperature-controlled storage and freezer capabilities to keep drugs from losing efficacy, but they also meet quality assurance and geographic regulatory requirements (e.g., Food and Drug Administration, Health Canada, European Medicines Agency, and so forth). UPS also has its own team of 4,000 pharmacists to expedite orders made by hospitals and other customers of pharmaceutical companies.

Walgreens picked UPS to ship $9 million (375,000 doses) of flu vaccine from UPS's headquarters in Kentucky to Laos, a trip of 8,500 miles. Using two refrigerated airfreight containers and 50 logisticians, UPS successfully delivered the vaccines. Medtronic is a Minneapolis-based medical technology company that provides, among other products, an FDA-approved integrated diabetes management system. While the company doesn't make insulin, it sells the equipment patients need to manage their diabetes: insulin pump, continuous glucose monitor, and therapy management software. UPS pharmacists at the firm's headquarters in Louisville, Kentucky, fill the orders and ship them (via UPS) to Medtronic's patients. As a result of outsourcing their medical device shipping needs to UPS, Medtronic was able to reduce costs by closing its own distribution warehouse and decreasing the cost of processing each order.[1]

LO1 Explain why companies develop control systems for employees

1 | SPINNING OUT OF CONTROL?

Control is one of the fundamental forces that keep the organization together and heading in the right direction. **Control** is any process that directs the activities of individuals toward the achievement of organizational goals. It is how effective managers make sure that activities are going as planned. During challenging economic times when resources are limited and budgets need to be stretched, managerial control becomes even more important for survival. Some managers don't want to admit it, but control problems—the lack of controls or the wrong kinds of controls—frequently cause irreparable damage to organizations. Here are some signs that a company lacks controls:

- *Lax top management*—Senior managers do not emphasize or value the need for controls, or they set a bad example.

- *Absence of policies*—The firm's expectations are not established in writing.

- *Lack of agreed-upon standards*—Organization members are unclear about what needs to be achieved.

- *"Shoot the messenger" management*—Employees feel their careers would be at risk if they reported bad news.

- *Lack of periodic reviews*—Managers do not assess performance on a regular, timely basis.

- *Bad information systems*—Key data are not measured and reported in a timely and easily accessible way.

- *Lack of ethics in the culture*—Organization members have not internalized a commitment to integrity.

Employees simply wasting time cost U.S. employers billions of dollars each year![2] Ineffective control systems result

control any process that directs the activities of individuals toward the achievement of organizational goals

> "More than at any time in the past, companies will not be able to hold themselves together with the traditional methods of control: hierarchy, systems, budgets, and the like. . . . The bonding glue will increasingly become ideological."
>
> — Collins & Porras[5]

bureaucratic control the use of rules, regulations, and authority to guide performance

market control control based on the use of pricing mechanisms and economic information to regulate activities within organizations

in problems ranging from employee theft to lead in the paint of children's toys. Large auto makers are not immune. Mary Barra, CEO of General Motors, was questioned by members of Congress as to why it took GM more than 10 years to recall and fix vehicles with faulty ignition switches. Barra responded that she did not know why the recall took so long and announced that an internal investigation was under way. Evidence suggested that the faulty switches in some GM models led to the engine shutting off and subsequent loss of power steering, power brakes, and air bags, causing 13 deaths and 31 accidents. In 2014, GM recalled 2.6 million vehicles to replace the ignition switches. Barra suggested that the 10-year delay was partly attributable to GM's "cost culture" (where reducing costs is the top priority) but added that the auto giant is currently moving toward a more "customer-focused culture."[3]

Control has been called one of the Siamese twins of management. The other twin is planning. Some means of control are necessary because once managers form plans and strategies, they must ensure that the plans are carried out. They must make sure that other people are doing what needs to be done and not doing inappropriate things. Control provides managers with continuous feedback so that when plans are not carried out properly, managers can take steps to correct the problem. This process is the primary control function of management. By ensuring creativity, enhancing quality, and reducing cost, managers must figure out ways to control the activities in their organizations.

Not surprisingly, effective planning facilitates control, and control facilitates planning. Planning lays out a framework for the future and, in this sense, provides a blueprint for control. Control systems, in turn, regulate the allocation and use of resources and, in so doing, facilitate the next phases of planning. In today's complex organizational environment, both functions have become more difficult to implement while they have become more important in every department of the organization. Managers today must control their people, inventories, quality, and costs, to mention just a few of their responsibilities.

According to William Ouchi of the University of California at Los Angeles, managers can apply three broad strategies for achieving organizational control:[4]

1. **Bureaucratic control** is the use of rules, standards, regulations, hierarchy, and legitimate authority to guide performance. It includes such items as budgets, statistical reports, and performance appraisals to regulate behavior and results. It works best where tasks are certain and workers are independent.

2. **Market control** involves the use of prices, competition, and exchange relationships to regulate activities in organizations as though they were economic transactions. Business units may be treated as profit centers and trade resources (services or goods) with one another via such mechanisms. Managers who run these units may be evaluated on the basis of profit and loss. Market control is most effective where tangible output can be identified and a market can be established between the parties to be controlled.

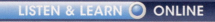

LISTEN & LEARN ⊙ ONLINE

YOUNG MANAGERS
Speak Out!

"Keep an open mind in terms of the experiences that you will encounter as a manager, have confidence in yourself that you can make decisions, don't be afraid to ask questions, and be willing to learn, and learn from your mistakes."

—Jeremy Partacz, Customer Experience Manager

Take Charge of Your Career

Learn how to control without being too controlling!

Control is one of the most misunderstood areas in management. For many employees, the term can conjure up images of the scene in the movie, *The Internship,* when the authoritarian boss (actor John Goodman) yells "You're dinosaurs!" as justification for firing watch salesmen Billy McMahon (actor Vince Vaughn) and Nick Campbell (actor Owen Wilson).

Fortunately there are many managers who create and maintain high-morale environments in which employees know what is expected of them and are trusted to deliver results. These managers have learned, often through trial and error, or observing more experienced managers, that exerting the correct amount of control over employees is an important skill. Different employees respond in different ways to control. Some employees like knowing exactly what needs to be done and appreciate you asking them how their work is progressing, while others prefer to be left alone so they can get their work done.

Managers who learn what each employee requires in terms of guidance and control will be more effective.

How can you develop your control management skills? Assume that three of your employees are about to begin a lengthy, complex project. Here are some tips regarding how to exert control without being too controlling:

- Spend time helping your employees develop a detailed project plan, including key milestones and due dates. By exerting control

Vince Vaughn as Billy McMahon and Owen Wilson as Nick Campbell in *The Internship,* 2013. This scene shows the duo seeking internships from Google after being laid off from their current jobs.

during the planning stage of a project, you are less likely to have to be heavy-handed later on.

- When an employee makes a mistake, ask what he could have done differently to avoid the error. Use a neutral and professional tone. You may even want to share a quick story about a previous error you made and how you fixed it. This signals to the employee that it's okay to make a mistake, but it needs to be corrected.

- After the project is finished, ask your employees what could be done to improve the process for next time. This is where controlling leads to better planning, organizing, and leading. No matter how well your employees' performance met the standards of the project, there is always room for continuous improvement.

You can learn how to exert the right amount of control over your employees. Give yourself some time to develop this skill, and be sure to observe how your employees react to your guidance, questions, and directives. This is another feedback loop that will help you continuously improve your managerial control skills.

---

3. **Clan control**, unlike the first two types, does not assume that the interests of the organization and individuals naturally diverge. Instead it is based on the idea that employees may share the values, expectations, and goals of the organization and act in accordance with them. When members of an organization have common values and goals—and trust one another—formal controls may be less necessary. Clan control is based on interpersonal processes of organization culture, leadership, and groups and teams. It works best where there is no "one best way" to do a job and employees are empowered to make decisions.

> **LO2** Summarize how to design a basic bureaucratic control system

2 | BUREAUCRATIC CONTROL SYSTEMS

Bureaucratic (or formal) control systems are designed to measure progress toward set performance goals and, if necessary, to apply corrective measures to ensure that performance achieves managers' objectives. Control systems detect and correct significant variations, or discrepancies, in the results of planned activities.

2.1 | Control Systems Have Four Steps

As Exhibit 14.1 shows, a typical control system has four major steps:

1. Setting performance standards.

2. Measuring performance.

3. Comparing performance against the standards and determining deviations.

4. Taking action to correct problems and reinforce successes.

Step 1: Setting Performance Standards Every organization has goals: profitability, innovation, satisfaction of customers

> **clan control** control based on the norms, values, shared goals, and trust among group members

● When Google cofounder Larry Page replaced his mentor Eric Schmidt as Google's CEO in 2012, Page insisted that the company had to be more aggressive about countering the threat posed by Facebook's ever-growing popularity. Over the past year, Page responded with a social networking crusade that is reshaping Google.

you learned in an earlier chapter, benchmarking is the process of comparing your firm's practices and technologies with those of other organizations. Standards can be set for any activity—financial activities, operating activities, legal compliance, charitable contributions, and so on.[6]

We have discussed principles of setting performance standards in other chapters. For example, employees tend to be motivated by specific, measurable performance standards that are challenging and aim for improvement over past performance. Typically performance standards are derived from job requirements, such as increasing market share by 10 percent, reducing costs 20 percent, and answering customer complaints within 24 hours. But performance standards don't apply just to people in isolation; they frequently integrate human and system performance. With more than 4,500 employees, Blue Cross Blue Shield (BCBS) of North Carolina provides 3.8 million customers with health insurance. During the recent economic recession, the organization realized that many of its managers lacked several important leadership skills. The situation was described in the following manner: "Managers were not fully prepared to achieve corporate goals or lead emerging business opportunities." In response, BCBS developed an organizationwide set of competencies and performance standards, and assessed their 600 managers' current capabilities against those standards. Managers who did not initially meet the standards were given additional training and team assignments to increase their leadership skills and competencies. As a result of the initiative, BCBS was able to reduce operating costs by more than $1 million, reengineer business processes, and reduce employee turnover. The new standards also resulted in an 18 percent increase in promotions and manager quality scores that surpassed the 80 percent benchmark.[7]

As illustrated in Exhibit 14.2, there are several metrics against which performance standards can be compared. For example, production activities include volume of output (quantity), defects (quality), on-time availability of finished goods (time use), and dollar expenditures for raw materials and direct labor (cost). Many important aspects of performance, such as customer service, can be measured by the same standards—adequate supply and availability of products, quality of service, speed of delivery, and so forth.

Exhibit 14.1 The control process

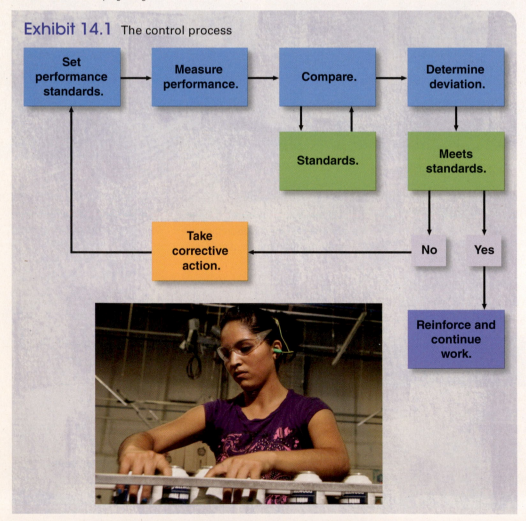

Exhibit 14.2 Common measures of performance standards

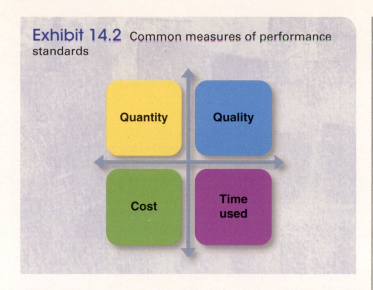

Quantity

Quality

Cost

Time used

One word of caution: the downside of establishing performance targets and standards is that they may not be supported by other elements of the control system. Each piece of the system is important and depends on the others. Otherwise the system can get out of balance.

Step 2: Measuring Performance The second step in the control process is to measure performance levels. For example, managers can count units produced, days absent, papers filed, samples distributed, and dollars earned. Performance data commonly are obtained from three sources:

1. *Written reports* include computer printouts and on-screen reports. Thanks to computers' data-gathering and analysis capabilities and decreasing costs, companies of any size can gather huge amounts of performance data.

2. *Oral reports* allow two-way communication. When a salesperson contacts his or her supervisor each evening to report the day's accomplishments, problems, and customer reactions, the manager can ask questions to gain additional information or clear up any misunderstandings. When necessary, tentative corrective actions can be worked out during the discussion.

3. *Personal observation* involves going to the area where activities take place and watching what is occurring. The manager can directly observe work methods, employees' nonverbal signals, and the general operation. Personal observation gives a detailed picture of what is going on, but it also has some disadvantages. It does not provide accurate quantitative data; the information usually is general and subjective. Also, employees can misunderstand the purpose of personal observation as mistrust or lack of confidence. Still, many managers believe in the value of firsthand observation. As you learned in earlier chapters, personal contact can increase leadership visibility and upward communication. It also provides valuable information about performance to supplement written and oral reports.

Regardless of the performance measure used, the information must be provided to managers on a timely basis. For example, consumer goods companies like General Foods carefully track new product sales in selected local markets first so that they can make any necessary adjustments before a national rollout. Information that is not available is of little or no use to managers.

Step 3: Comparing Performance with the Standard

The third step in the control process is comparing performance with the standard. In this process, the manager evaluates the performance. For some activities, relatively small deviations from the standard are acceptable, while in others a slight deviation may be serious. In many manufacturing processes, a significant deviation in either direction (e.g., drilling a hole that is too small or too large) is unacceptable. In other cases, a deviation in one direction, such as sales or customer satisfaction below the target level, is a problem, but a deviation in the other—exceeding the sales target or customer expectations—is a sign employees are getting better-than-expected results. Therefore, managers who perform the oversight must analyze and evaluate the results carefully.

The managerial **principle of exception** states that control is enhanced by concentrating on the exceptions to, or significant deviations from, the expected result or standard. In other words, in comparing performance with the standard, managers need to direct their attention to the exception—for example, a handful of defective components produced on an assembly line or the feedback from customers who are upset or delighted with a service. Atlanta-based US Security Associates uses information technology to gather performance data on its uniformed security guards and dispatches supervisors to investigate any variances from performance norms, such as a failure of a guard to sign in at a client's location on time.[8]

With the principle of exception, only exceptional cases require corrective action. This principle is important in controlling. The manager is not concerned with performance that equals or closely approximates the expected results. Managers can save much time and effort if they apply the principle of exception.

::::::::::::::::

The accounting and consulting firm of Moody, Famiglietti & Andronico (MFA) uses a formal control process to ensure that it provides exceptional service tailored to each client's needs and preferences. The Tewksbury, Massachusetts, firm adopted the U.S. Army's practice of conducting before-action reviews and after-action reviews to learn from experience and apply those lessons in the future.

When employees are preparing to handle an assignment, they call a short meeting with everyone who has worked with that client during the previous year, as well as employees who have handled similar assignments for other clients. During this before-action review, participants trade experiences with and knowledge about

standard expected performance for a given goal: a target that establishes a desired performance level, motivates performance, and serves as a benchmark against which actual performance is assessed

principle of exception a managerial principle stating that control is enhanced by concentrating on the exceptions to or significant deviations from the expected result or standard

study tip 14

"Controlling" your grades

Most students monitor how their grades are progressing during the semester. However, some students don't realize until it is too late that they're not going to earn their desired grade. You can stay on top of your progress and make adjustments by following the steps in the control process in Exhibit 14.1:

1. Set your performance standard or desired grade.
2. Measure your performance by calculating your grade average after every assignment, quiz, or exam.
3. Compare your running grade average against your standard.
4. If your grade average is lower than desired, take corrective action like studying harder or asking the professor for study advice. Alternatively, if your grade average meets your standard, continue your current study approach.

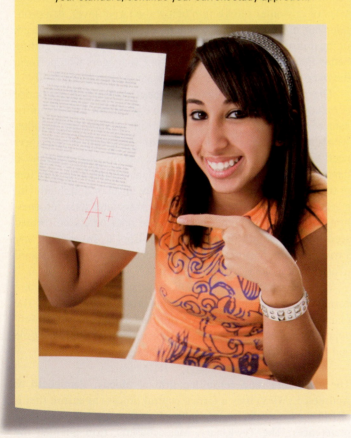

the client—say, questions that are likely to arise or existing tools for handling common problems. The input from this meeting helps the team establish goals.

During the assignment, team members meet periodically to assess progress and identify any adjustments needed. Soon after the project's completion, the team reassembles to compare outcomes with goals. Participants identify successful actions to recommend

in the future, as well as mistakes to avoid next time. Besides noting whether they helped the client meet goals, they also record what they learned about serving the client. Because lessons they learn will come up at future before-action reviews, MFA employees are motivated to fix mistakes and improve methods.[9]

Step 4: Taking Action to Correct Problems and Reinforce Successes The last step in the control process is to take appropriate action when there are significant deviations. This step ensures that operations are adjusted to achieve the planned results—or to continue exceeding the plan if the manager determines that is possible. If significant variances are discovered, the manager usually takes immediate and vigorous action.

An alternative approach is for the corrective action to be taken, not by higher-ups, but by the operator at the point of the problem. In computer-controlled production technology, two basic types of control are feasible:

1. *Specialist control*—Operators of computer numerical control (CNC) machines must notify engineering specialists of malfunctions. With this traditional division of labor, the specialist takes corrective action.

2. *Operator control*—Multiskilled operators can rectify their own problems as they occur. This strategy is more efficient because deviations are controlled closer to their source. It is also more satisfying because operators benefit by having a more enriched job.

The selection of the corrective action depends on the nature of the problem. The corrective action may involve a shift in marketing strategy (if, say, the problem is lower-than-expected sales), a disciplinary action, a new way to check the accuracy of manufactured parts, or a major modification to a process or system. Sometimes managers learn they can get better results if they adjust their own practices. Yum Brands, whose franchise restaurants include KFC, Taco Bell, Pizza Hut, and Long John Silver's, conducts regular surveys to learn whether employees feel strong commitment to their jobs. These data are shared with managers to help them measure their performance as leaders and motivators. Jonathan McDaniel, a Houston KFC manager, once learned that his employees were unhappy with their work hours. He began asking them ahead of time whether they wanted particular days off each month—information that helped him create better schedules and end a cause of employee dissatisfaction.[11]

2.2 | Bureaucratic Control Occurs Before, During, and After Operations

Bureaucratic control combines three approaches, defined according to their timing:

1. **Feedforward control** takes place before operations begin and includes policies, procedures, and rules designed to ensure that planned activities are carried out properly. Examples include inspection of raw materials and proper selection and training of employees.

2. **Concurrent control** takes place while plans are being carried out. It includes directing, monitoring, and fine-tuning activities as they occur.

3. **Feedback control** focuses on the use of information about results to correct deviations from the acceptable standard after they arise.

Feedforward Control Feedforward control (sometimes called *preliminary control*) is future oriented; its aim is to prevent problems before they arise. Instead of waiting for results and comparing them with goals, a manager or employees can exert control by limiting activities in advance. For example, companies have policies defining the scope within which decisions are made. As in the example of Coca-Cola's Code of Business Conduct,[12] a company may dictate that managers must adhere to clear ethical and legal guidelines when making decisions. Formal rules and procedures also prescribe people's actions before they occur. For example, legal experts advise companies to establish policies forbidding disclosure of proprietary information or making clear that employees are not speaking for the company when they post messages on blogs, microblogging sites such as Twitter, or social networking sites such as Facebook. Human resource policies defining what forms of body art are acceptable to display at work can avoid awkward case-by-case conversations about a tattoo that offends coworkers or piercings that are incompatible with the company's image.[13]

::::::::::::::::::

At Donnelly Custom Manufacturing in Alexandria, Minnesota, all 225 employees of this short run, close tolerance injection mold manufacturer participated in "error proofing" workshops that taught them to identify and correct errors before they occur. After potential problems are identified, employees develop and then rank order solutions according to the speed, complexity, and cost of implementing them. The employees also consider the effectiveness of each alternative solution. Since applying these "error proofing" techniques to several molding jobs with a long-time customer, 75 percent fewer parts were rejected due to human error, and parts-per-million defects were lowered by two-thirds.[14]

::::::::::::::::::

Recently more managers have grown concerned about the organizational pitfalls of workplace romances, and some have sought a solution in feedforward controls. As wonderful as it is to find love, problems can arise if romantic activities between a supervisor and subordinate create a conflict of interest or charges of sexual harassment. Other employees might interpret the relationship wrongly—that the company sanctions personal relationships as a path to advancement. In addition, romantic ups-and-downs can spill over into the workplace and affect everyone's mood and motivation. Controls aimed at preventing such problems in an organization include training in appropriate behavior (including how to avoid sexual harassment) and creating and enforcing workplace policies. According to a 2013 survey by the Society for Human Resource Management, 42 percent of companies used verbal and written policies to exert control over workplace romances. Nearly all (99 percent) of the policies prohibited romances between a supervisor and a subordinate. The most common consequence of being discovered in an office romance was a transfer of one of the participants to another department.[15]

Concurrent Control Concurrent control, which takes place while plans are carried out, is the heart of any control system. On a manufacturing floor, all efforts are directed toward producing the correct quantity and quality of the right products in the specified amount of time. In an airline terminal, the baggage must get to the right airplanes before flights depart. And in many settings, supervisors watch employees to ensure they work efficiently and avoid mistakes.

Advances in information technology have created powerful concurrent controls. Computerized systems give managers immediate access to data from the remotest corners of their companies. For example, managers can update budgets instantly from a continuous flow of performance data. In production facilities, monitoring systems that track errors per hour, machine speeds, and other measures let managers correct small production problems before they become disasters. Point-of-sale terminals in store checkout lines send sales data back to a retailer's headquarters to show which products are selling in which locations.

For Ronald M. Shaich, CEO of Panera Bread, paying attention to what is happening in the restaurants in critical. Recently, the company experienced a decrease in sales as some customers, frustrated with long lines and inconsistent service, opted to purchase their sandwiches and salads elsewhere. Simply put, customer demand for the restaurant chain's products has outgrown the company's ability to consistently deliver a high-quality in-store experience. Shaich is addressing these problems by implementing the following

Did You Know?

In his book, *Drive,* Dan Pink states: "A Cornell University study of 320 small businesses, half of which granted workers autonomy and half of which relied on top-down direction, found that the businesses that offered autonomy grew at four times the rates of the control-oriented firms and had one-third the turnover."[10]

feedforward control the control process used before operations begin, including policies, procedures, and rules designed to ensure that planned activities are carried out properly

concurrent control the control process used while plans are being carried out, including directing, monitoring, and fine-tuning activities as they are performed

feedback control control that focuses on the use of information about previous results to correct deviations from the acceptable standard

Traditional Thinking

Managers should rely on feedback control to correct deviations from acceptable standards.

The Best Managers Today

Use feedforward control to ensure that planned activities are executed properly.

changes: (1) adding 35 extra hours of labor per week to each store (adding $15 million in annual labor costs), (2) redesigning workflows and retraining employees, and (3) moving many of the phone orders (10 percent of sales) to the Web to free-up employees to serve in-store customers.[16]

Feedback Control Feedback control is involved when performance data have been gathered and analyzed and the results have been returned to someone (or something) in the process to make corrections. When supervisors monitor behavior, they are exercising concurrent control. When they point out and correct improper performance, they are using feedback as a means of control.

Timing is an important aspect of feedback control. Long time lags often occur between performance and feedback, such as when actual spending is compared with the quarterly budget, instead of weekly or monthly, or when some aspect of performance is compared with the projection made a year earlier. Yet if feedback on performance is not timely, managers cannot quickly identify and eliminate the problem and prevent more serious harm.[17]

organization's "innovation catalysts"—people who actively participate in information sharing. Managers can use the social network analysis to reward innovation catalysts; give them important assignments; and, in areas where not enough collaboration is occurring, train and motivate employees to share knowledge.[18]

The Role of Six Sigma One of the most important quality control tools to emerge is six sigma, which we mentioned in Chapter 7. It is a particularly robust and powerful application of feedback control. Six sigma is designed to reduce defects in all organization processes—not just product defects but anything that may result in customer dissatisfaction, such as inadequate service, delayed delivery, and excessively high prices due to high costs or inefficiency. The system was developed at Motorola in the late 1980s, when the company found it was being beaten consistently in the competitive marketplace by foreign firms that were able to produce higher-quality products at a lower cost. Since then, the technique has been widely adopted and even improved on by many companies, such as GE, Allied Signal, Ford, Xerox, 3M, Dell, and Bechtel.

> "Mistakes and problems are inevitable in complex enterprises. . . . We shouldn't expect heads of established organizations to be perfect, but we should expect them to catch and correct their mistakes quickly."
>
> —Rosabeth Moss Kanter, professor, Harvard Business School[19]

Some feedback processes are under real-time (concurrent) control, such as a computer-controlled robot on an assembly line. Such units have sensors that continually determine whether they are in the correct position to perform their functions. If they are not, a built-in control device makes immediate corrections.

In other situations, feedback processes require more time. Some companies that value innovation are applying social network analysis, which uses data from surveys to create diagrams showing which employees collaborate with which colleagues. Employees who are at a hub of information sharing are the

Sigma is the Greek letter used in statistics to designate the estimated standard deviation, or variation in a process. It indicates how often defects in a process are likely to occur. The lower the sigma number, the higher the level of variation or defects; the higher the sigma number, the lower the level of variation or defects. For example, as illustrated in Exhibit 14.3, a two-sigma-level process has more than 300,000 defects per million opportunities (DPMO)—not a very well-controlled process. A three-sigma-level process has 66,807 DPMO, which is roughly a 93 percent level of accuracy. Many organizations operate at this level, which on its face does not sound too bad, until we consider its implications—for example, 7 items of airline baggage lost for every 100 processed. The additional costs to organizations of such inaccuracy are enormous. Even at just above a 99 percent defect-free rate, or 6,210 DPMO, the accuracy level is often unacceptable—the statistical equivalent of about 50 dropped newborn babies a day.[20]

At six sigma level, a process is producing fewer than 3.4 defects per million, which means it is operating at a 99.99966 percent level of accuracy. Six sigma companies have not only close to zero product or service defects but also substantially lower production costs and cycle times and much higher levels of customer satisfaction. The methodology isn't just for the factory floor, either. Accountants have used six sigma to improve the quality of their audits investigating risks faced by their clients.[21]

The six sigma approach is based on an intense statistical analysis of business processes that contribute to customer satisfaction.[22] For example, a process GE measured when it began using the method was product delivery time. Once the defects or variations are measured, their causes are analyzed. Teams of employees work on designing and testing new processes that will reduce the causes of the variations. For example, if the team finds that delivery delays are caused by production bottlenecks, it will work on eliminating those. When an improved process is installed, it is analyzed again for remaining defects, and employees then work on reducing those. This cycle continues until the desired quality level is achieved. In this way, the six sigma process leads to continuous improvement in an organization's operations.

Six sigma has come under some criticism for not always delivering business results.[23] One likely reason why six sigma doesn't always improve the bottom line is that it focuses only on how to eliminate defects in a process, not whether the process is the best one for the organization. So, for example, at 3M, a drive to improve efficiency through six sigma has been blamed for slowing the flow of innovative ideas. At Home Depot, six sigma has been credited with improving such processes as customer checkout and deciding where to place products in stores, but some say the effort took store workers away from customers. One way managers can apply the strengths of six sigma and minimize the drawbacks is by setting different goals and control processes for the company's mature products than for its areas of innovation.

2.3 | Management Audits Control Various Systems

Over the years, **management audits** have developed as a means of evaluating the effectiveness and efficiency of various systems within an organization, from social responsibility programs to accounting control. Management audits may be external or internal. Managers conduct external audits of other companies and internal audits of their own companies. Some of the same tools and approaches are used for both types of audit.[24]

External Audits An **external audit** occurs when one organization evaluates another organization. Typically an external body such as a certified public accountant (CPA) firm conducts financial audits of an organization (discussed later in the chapter). But any company can conduct external audits of competitors or other companies for its own strategic decision-making purposes. This type of analysis investigates other organizations for possible merger or acquisition, determines the soundness of a company that will be used as a major supplier, or discovers the strengths and weaknesses of a competitor to maintain or better exploit the competitive advantage of the investigating organization. Publicly available data usually are used for these evaluations.[25]

External audits provide essential feedback control when they identify legal and ethical lapses that could harm the organization and its reputation. They also are useful for preliminary control because they can prevent problems from occurring. If a company seeking to acquire other businesses gathers adequate, accurate information about possible candidates, it is more likely to acquire the most appropriate companies and avoid unsound acquisitions.

Internal Audits An organization may assign a group to conduct an **internal audit** to assess what the company has done for itself and what it has done for its customers or other recipients of its goods or services. The company can be evaluated on a number of factors, including financial stability, production efficiency, sales effectiveness, human resources development, earnings growth, energy use, public relations, civic responsibility, and other criteria of organizational effectiveness. The audit

management audit an evaluation of the effectiveness and efficiency of various systems within an organization

external audit an evaluation conducted by one organization, such as a CPA firm, on another

internal audit a periodic assessment of a company's own planning, organizing, leading, and controlling processes

Exhibit 14.3		Relationship between sigma level and defects per million opportunities
Sigma Level	**DPMO**	**Is Four Sigma Good Enough?**
2σ	308,537	Consider these everyday examples of four sigma quality . . .
3σ	66,807	• 20,000 lost articles of mail per hour.
4σ	**6,210**	• Unsafe drinking water 15 minutes per day.
5σ	233	• 5,000 incorrect surgical operations per week.
6σ	3.4	• 200,000 wrong prescriptions each year.
		• No electricity for 7 hours each month.

Source: T. Rancour and M. McCracken, "Applying 6 Sigma Methods for Breakthrough Safety Performance," *Professional Safety* 45. no. 10 (October 2000). pp. 29–32. Reprinted with permission of American Society of Safety Engineers. Permission conveyed through Copyright Clearance Center.

budgeting the process of investigating what is being done and comparing the results with the corresponding budget data to verify accomplishments or remedy differences; also called *budgetary controlling*.

accounting audits procedures used to verify accounting reports and statements

activity-based costing (ABC) a method of cost accounting designed to identify streams of activity and then to allocate costs across particular business processes according to the amount of time employees devote to particular activities

reviews the company's past, present, and future, including any risks the organization should be prepared to face.[26] A recent study found that the stock prices of companies with highly rated audit committees tended to rise faster than shares of companies with lower-rated internal auditors. The higher-rated audit committees probably do a better job of finding and eliminating undesirable practices.[27]

To perform a management audit, auditors list desired qualifications and assign a weight to each qualification. Among the most common undesirable practices uncovered by a management audit are the performance of unnecessary work, duplication of work, poor inventory control, uneconomical use of equipment and machines, procedures that are more costly than necessary, and wasted resources. At Capital One Financial Corporation, the human resource (HR) department performed an audit of facilities usage. Over several months, staff members walked through headquarters, noting which desks were occupied. The audit determined that more than 4 out of 10 desks were unused each day, and another 3 out of 10 were unused at least part of the day. Employees were away at meetings, visiting clients, or working flexible schedules. The HR staff developed a plan for Capital One to operate more efficiently in one-third of its space. Now most employees keep their work items in a cart, which they take to a desk when they need one. The change saves the company $3 million a year.[28]

3 | BUDGETARY CONTROLS

Budgetary control is one of the most widely recognized and commonly used methods of managerial control. It ties together feedforward control, concurrent control, and feedback control, depending on the point at which it is applied. *Budgetary control* is the process of finding out what's being done and comparing the results with the corresponding budget data to verify accomplishments or remedy differences. Budgetary control commonly is called **budgeting**.

3.1 | Fundamental Budgetary Considerations

In private industry, budgetary control begins with an estimate of sales and expected income. Exhibit 14.4 shows a budget with a forecast of expected sales (the *sales budget*) on the top row, followed by several categories of estimated expenses for the first three months of the year. In the bottom row, the profit estimate is determined by subtracting each month's budgeted expenses from the sales in that month's sales budget. Columns next to each month's budget provide space to enter the actual accomplishments so managers can readily compare expected amounts and actual results.

Although this discussion of budgeting focuses on the flow of money into and out of the organization, budgeting information is not confined to finances. The entire enterprise and any of its units can create budgets for their activities, using units other than dollars, if appropriate. For example, many organizations use production budgets forecasting physical units produced and shipped, and labor can be budgeted in skill levels or hours of work required.

A primary consideration of budgeting is the length of the budget period. All budgets are prepared for a specific time period. Many budgets cover one, three, or six months or one year. The length of time selected depends on the primary purpose of the budgeting. The period should include the enterprise's complete normal cycle of activity. For example, seasonal variations should be included for production and for sales. The budget period commonly coincides with other control devices, such as managerial reports, balance sheets, and statements of profit and loss. Selection of the budget period also should consider the extent to which reasonable forecasts can be made.

| **Exhibit 14.4** | A sales-expense budget |

	January		February		March	
	Estimate	**Actual**	**Estimate**	**Actual**	**Estimate**	**Actual**
Sales	$1,200,000		$1,350,000		$1,400,000	
Expenses						
General overhead	$ 310,000		$ 310,000		$ 310,000	
Selling	242,000		275,000		288,000	
Producing	327,000		430,500		456,800	
Research	118,400		118,400		115,000	
Office	90,000		91,200		91,500	
Advertising	32,500		27,000		25,800	
Estimated gross profit	$ 80,100		$ 97,900		$ 112,900	

As shown in Exhibit 14.5, the budgetary control process proceeds through three stages.

Although practices differ widely, a member of top management often serves as the chief coordinator for formulating and using the budget. Usually the chief financial officer (CFO) has these duties. He or she needs to be less concerned with the details than with resolving conflicting interests, recommending adjustments when needed, and giving official sanction to the budgetary procedures. In a small company, budgeting responsibility generally rests with the owner.

3.2 | Types of Budgets

There are many types of budgets. Several are frequently used:

- *Sales budget.* Usually data for the sales budget include forecasts of sales by month, sales area, and product.

- *Production budget.* The production budget commonly is expressed in physical units. Required information for preparing this budget includes types and capacities of machines, economic quantities to produce, and availability of materials.

- *Cost budget.* The cost budget is used for areas of the organization that incur expenses but no revenue, such as human resources and other support departments. Cost budgets may also be included in the production budget. Costs may be fixed (independent of the immediate level of activity), like rent, or variable (rising or falling with the level of activity), like raw materials.

- *Cash budget.* The cash budget is essential to every business. It should be prepared after all other budget estimates are completed. The cash budget shows the anticipated receipts and expenditures, the amount of working capital available, the extent to which outside financing may be required, and the periods and amounts of cash available.

- *Capital budget.* The capital budget is used for the cost of fixed assets like plants and equipment. Such costs are usually treated not as regular expenses but as investments because of their long-term nature and importance to the organization's productivity.

- *Master budget.* The master budget includes all the major activities of the business. It brings together and coordinates all the activities of the other budgets and can be thought of as a "budget of budgets."

Traditionally, budgets were imposed *top-down*, with senior management setting specific targets for the entire organization at the beginning of the budget process. In today's more complex organizations, the budget process is more likely to be *bottom-up*, with top management setting the general direction, while lower-level and midlevel managers actually develop the budgets and submit them for approval. When the budgets are consolidated, senior managers

Exhibit 14.5 Three stages of budgetary control

| Stage 1: Establish expectancies |
| Starts with the broad plan for the company and estimate of sales, and ends with budget approval and publication. |

| Stage 2: Perform budgetary operations |
| Deals with identifying what is being accomplished and comparing the results with expectancies. |

| Stage 3: Take action |
| Involves responding appropriately with some combination of reinforcing successes and correcting problems. |

can determine whether the organization's budget objectives are being met. Then the budget is either approved or sent back down the hierarchy for additional refinement.

Accounting records must be inspected periodically to ensure they were properly prepared and are correct. **Accounting audits,** which are designed to verify accounting reports and statements, are essential to the control process. This audit is performed by members of an outside firm of public accountants. Knowing that accounting records are accurate, true, and in keeping with generally accepted accounting practices (GAAP) creates confidence that a reliable base exists for sound overall controlling purposes.

3.3 | Activity-Based Costing

Traditional methods of cost accounting may be inappropriate in today's business environment because they are based on outdated methods of rigid hierarchical organization. Instead of assuming that organizations are bureaucratic "machines" that can be separated into component functions such as human resources, purchasing, and maintenance, companies such as Hewlett-Packard and GE have used **activity-based costing (ABC)** to allocate costs across business processes.

ABC starts with the assumption that organizations are collections of people performing many different but related activities to satisfy customer needs. The ABC system is designed to identify those streams of activity and then allocate costs across particular business processes. The basic procedure, outlined in Exhibit 14.6, works as follows: First, employees are asked to break down what they do each day in order to define their *basic activities*. For example, employees in Dana Corporation's material control department engage in a number of activities that range from processing

TerraCycle's Cost Control Formula Is Garbage

Many products today are made from various types of waste—old tires, scrap metal, plastic bottles. Companies look for ways to recycle and reuse just about every material imaginable. But the founder of one company looked to the ground for his business inspiration and came up with a unique idea for plant fertilizer: worm poop. About 13 years ago, Tom Szaky was a student when he entered his university's annual business plan competition. He used an old high school science project as its basis. Using the worms to generate fertilizer was cheap, simple, and organic. Best of all, his business idea won the prize. In fact, the company he eventually started—TerraCycle—was largely funded by various business competition winnings.

Despite the fact that his organic plant food, TerraCycle, is now sold in such stores as Home Depot and Walmart, Szaky still thinks the way a student does when it comes to budgets. That means cheap. The company is located not far from his alma mater, Princeton. He hosts college interns each summer in a rambling old house furnished with cast-off dorm furniture and used computers that have been discarded by larger companies but still have more than enough computing power for TerraCycle. The furnishings are eclectic but free. "No entrepreneur should ever buy furniture or mediocre computer equipment," advises Szaky. "Everything here is garbage. Princeton renovates one dorm a year, so we get all that." Gesturing toward a huge fan and a 52-inch TV, he says, "That's all student waste. You find it in dumpsters on move-out day." The interns work for peanuts, but they love the job.

One reason TerraCycle is so successful is that its plant fertilizer product is inexpensive to produce. TerraCycle is made from the waste of red worms that eat garbage. The worms don't incur labor costs and never stop producing waste. The compost of waste is brewed into a kind of tea on which plants seem to thrive. It is packed in reused soda bottles outfitted with spray

tops that have been discarded by manufacturers of other spray products. And the boxes in which all the bottles are shipped are the misprinted cast-offs from other companies. Because everything that Szaky uses has already been used before, the whole operation is a bargain. This means he can offer the same bargain to retailers—who can earn gross margins that are double or triple what they'd earn on the more familiar chemically produced fertilizers.

Major retailers have noticed TerraCycle. In recent years, the firm has expanded its green business model well beyond plant fertilizer. The company converts traditionally hard-to-recycle waste (including drink pouches, chip bags, toothbrushes, and many more) into a large variety of consumer products including flip-flops, backpacks, office supplies, park benches, and playgrounds. Expecting 2014 revenues to be approximately $20 million, Terracycle's products are currently sold through Target, Home Depot, Walmart, Whole Foods, and other retailers. During the past couple of years, TerraCycle launched operations in Norway, Spain, Germany, Ireland, Switzerland, Denmark, Israel, Belgium, Argentina, and the Netherlands. The company has created more than 30 new waste collection programs and expanded its global staff to more than 100 employees.

Tom Szaky, CEO of TerraCycle, dropped out of Princeton University to launch his eco-friendly company whose original product, plant fertilizer, was made from worm waste and packaged in used plastic bottles and jugs. Today, the company collects waste and converts it into a variety of new products that it sells through major retailers.

Szaky's long-term objective is ambitious: "Our goal is to eliminate the idea of waste by creating collection and solution systems for anything that today must be sent to a landfill." Given the pace at which TerraCycle is growing, the millions of people from various countries sending him tons of waste, and the expanding number of partnerships with major retailers, he's not just talking trash.

Discussion Questions

- Identify some criteria that you think Szaky would use in establishing performance standards for TerraCycle. What methods might he use to measure performance?

- What elements of budgetary control does Szaky use to help his business develop and grow?

SOURCES: Company website, www.terracycle.com; H. Bradford, "TerraCycle Recycles The 'Non-Recyclable'—Cigarette Butts, Candy Wrappers And Its Own Profits," *Huffington Post* (online), July 30, 2013, www.huffingtonpost.com; J. Neff, "How Little Brands Land Big Bang for Their Buck," *Advertising Age* 82, no. 40 (November 7, 2011), p. 36; D. Flaum, "Here's the Real Poop on Recycling," Memphis Commercial Appeal, August 7, 2007, www.terracycle.net; "Waste, Worms, and Wealth: The Story of TerraCycle," U.S. Environmental Protection Agency, May 15, 2007, www.epa.gov; K. Walsh, "How TerraCycle Built a Corporate Network with Discarded Hardware and Open Source Software," *CIO,* April 5, 2007, www.cio.com; "Worm Poo in Plastic Bottles: Get Rich and Save the World," CNN, January 26, 2007, www.cnn.com; and B. Burlingham, "The Coolest Little Start-Up in America," *Inc.*, July 2006, www.inc.com.

sales orders and sourcing parts to requesting engineering changes and solving problems. These activities form the basis for ABC. Second, managers look at total expenses computed by traditional accounting—fixed costs, supplies, salaries, fringe benefits, and so on—and spread total amounts over the activities according to the amount of time spent on each activity. At Dana, customer service employees spend nearly 25 percent of their time processing sales orders and only about 3 percent scheduling parts. Thus 25 percent of the total cost ($144,846) goes to order processing, and 3 percent ($15,390) goes to scheduling parts. As can be seen in Exhibit 14.6, both the traditional and ABC systems reach the same bottom line. However, because the ABC method allocates costs across business processes, it provides a more accurate picture of how costs should be charged to products and services.[29]

This heightened accuracy can give managers a more realistic picture of how the organization is actually allocating its resources. It can highlight where wasted activities are occurring or whether activities cost too much relative to the benefits provided. Managers can then act to correct the problem. For example, Dana's most expensive activity is sales order processing. Its managers might try to find ways to lower that cost, freeing up resources for other tasks. By providing this type of information, ABC has become a valuable method for streamlining business processes.

> **LO4** Recognize basic types of financial statements and financial ratios used as controls

4 | FINANCIAL CONTROLS

In addition to budgets, businesses commonly use other statements for financial control. Two financial statements that help control overall organizational performance are the balance sheet and the profit and loss statement.

4.1 | Balance Sheet

The **balance sheet** shows the financial picture of a company at a given time. This statement itemizes three elements:

1. **Assets** are the values of the various items the corporation owns.

2. **Liabilities** are the amounts the corporation owes to various creditors.

3. **Stockholders' equity** is the amount accruing to the corporation's owners.

The relationship among these three elements is as follows:

Assets = Liabilities + Stockholders' equity

Exhibit 14.7 shows an example of a balance sheet. During the year, the company grew because it enlarged its building and acquired more machinery and equipment by means of long-term debt in the form of a first mortgage. Additional stock was sold to help finance the expansion. At the same time, accounts receivable were increased, and work in process was reduced. Observe that Total assets ($3,053,367) = Total liabilities ($677,204 + $618,600) + Stockholders' equity ($700,000 + $981,943 + $75,620).

Summarizing balance sheet items over a long period of time uncovers important trends and gives a manager further insight into overall performance and areas in which adjustments are needed. For example, at some point, the company might decide that it would be prudent to slow down its expansion plans.

4.2 | Profit and Loss Statement

The **profit and loss statement** is an itemized financial statement of the income and expenses of a company's operations.

balance sheet a report that shows the financial picture of a company at a given time and itemizes assets, liabilities, and stockholders' equity

assets the values of the various items the corporation owns

liabilities the amounts a corporation owes to various creditors

stockholders' equity the amount accruing to the corporation's owners

profit and loss statement an itemized financial statement of the income and expenses of a company's operations

Exhibit 14.6 How Dana discovers what its true costs are

Old way

Old-style accounting identifies costs according to the category of expense. The new math tells you that your real costs are what you pay for the different tasks your employees perform. Find that out and you will manage better.

Salaries	$371,917
Fringes	$118,069
Supplies	$76,745
Fixed costs	$23,614
Total	**$590,345**

New way — Activity-based costing

	Salaries	Fringes	Supplies	Fixed costs	
Process sales order.					$144,846
Source parts.					$136,320
Expedite supplier orders.					$ 72,143
Expedite internal processing.					$ 49,945
Receive supplier quality.					$ 47,599
Reissue purchase orders.					$ 45,235
Expedite customer orders.					$ 27,747
Schedule intracompany sales.					$ 17,768
Request engineering change.					$ 16,704
Resolve problems.					$ 16,648
Schedule parts.					$ 15,390
				Total	**$590,345**

Source: Courtesy Dana Holding Corporation.

Exhibit 14.7 — A comparative balance sheet

Comparative Balance Sheet for the Years Ending December 31

	This Year	Last Year
Assets		
Current assets:		
Cash	$ 161,870	$ 119,200
U.S. Treasury bills	250,400	30,760
Accounts receivable	825,595	458,762
Inventories:		
Work in process and finished products	429,250	770,800
Raw materials and supplies	251,340	231,010
Total current assets	1,918,455	1,610,532
Other assets:		
Land	157,570	155,250
Building	740,135	91,784
Machinery and equipment	172,688	63,673
Furniture and fixtures	132,494	57,110
Total other assets before depreciation	1,202,887	367,817
Less: Accumulated depreciation and amortization	67,975	63,786
Total other assets	1,134,912	304,031
Total assets	$3,053,367	$1,914,563
Liabilities and stockholders' equity		
Current liabilities:		
Accounts payable	$287,564	$ 441,685
Payrolls and withholdings from employees	44,055	49,580
Commissions and sundry accruals	83,260	41,362
Federal taxes on income	176,340	50,770
Current installment on long-term debt	85,985	38,624
Total current liabilities	667,204	622,021
Long-term liabilities:		
15-year, 9 percent loan, payable in each of the years 2002–2015	210,000	225,000
5 percent first mortgage	408,600	
Registered 9 percent notes payable	_____	275,000
Total long-term liabilities	618,600	500,000
Stockholders' equity:		
Common stock: authorized 1,000,000 shares, outstanding last year 492,000 shares, outstanding this year 700,000 shares at $1 par value	700,000	492,000
Capital surplus	981,943	248,836
Earned surplus	75,620	51,706
Total stockholders' equity	1,757,563	792,542
Total liabilities and stockholders' equity	$3,053,367	$1,914,563

Exhibit 14.8 shows a comparative statement of profit and loss for two consecutive years. In this illustration, the enterprise's operating revenue has increased. Expense also has increased, but at a lower rate, resulting in a higher net income. Some managers draw up tentative profit and loss statements and use them as goals. Then they measure performance against these goals or standards. From comparative statements of this type, a manager can identify trouble areas and correct them.

Controlling by profit and loss is most commonly used for the entire enterprise and, in the case of a diversified corporation, its divisions. However, controlling can be by departments, as in a decentralized organization in which department managers have control over both revenue and expense. In that case, each department has its own profit and loss statement. Each department's output is measured, and a cost, including overhead, is charged to each department's operation. Expected net income is the standard for measuring a department's performance.

4.3 | Financial Ratios

An effective approach for checking an enterprise's overall performance is to use key financial ratios, which suggest strengths and weaknesses. Key ratios are calculated from selected items on the profit and loss statement and the balance sheet:

1. *Liquidity ratios* indicate a company's ability to pay short-term debts. The most common liquidity ratio is *current assets to current liabilities*, called the **current ratio** or *net working capital ratio*. This ratio indicates the extent to which current assets can decline and still be adequate to pay current liabilities. Some analysts set a ratio of 2 to 1, or 2.00, as the desirable minimum. For example, if you refer back to Exhibit 14.7, the liquidity ratio there is about 2.86 ($1,918,455/$667,204). The company's current assets are more than capable of supporting its current liabilities.

2. *Leverage ratios* show the relative amount of funds in the business supplied by creditors and shareholders. An important example is the **debt–equity ratio**, which indicates the company's ability to meet its long-term financial obligations. If this ratio is less than 1.5, the amount of debt is not considered excessive. In Exhibit 14.7, the debt–equity ratio is only 0.35 ($618,600/$1,757,563). The company has financed its expansion almost entirely by issuing stock rather than by incurring significant long-term debt.

3. *Profitability ratios* indicate management's ability to generate a financial return on sales or investment. For example, **return on investment (ROI)** is a ratio of profit to capital used, or a rate of return from capital (equity plus long-term debt). This ratio lets managers and shareholders assess how well the firm is doing compared with other investments. For example, in Exhibit 14.7,

if the company's net income were $300,000 this year, its return on capital would be 12.6 percent ($300,000/ ($1,757,563 + $618,600)), normally a reasonable rate of return.

Using Financial Ratios

Although ratios provide performance standards and indicators of what has occurred, exclusive reliance on financial ratios can have negative consequences. Ratios usually are expressed in limited time horizons (monthly, quarterly, or yearly), so they often cause **management myopia**—managers focus on short-term earnings and profits at the expense of their longer-term strategic obligations.[30] To reduce management myopia and focus attention further into the future, control systems can use long-term (say, three- to six-year) targets.

A second negative outcome of ratios is that they relegate other important considerations to a secondary position. Managers focused on ratios may not pay enough attention to research and development, management development, progressive human resource practices, environmental sustainability, and other considerations.

current ratio a liquidity ratio that indicates the extent to which short-term assets can decline and still be adequate to pay short-term liabilities

debt–equity ratio a leverage ratio that indicates the company's ability to meet its long-term financial obligations

return on investment (ROI) a ratio of profit to capital used, or a rate of return from capital

management myopia focusing on short-term earnings and profits at the expense of longer-term strategic obligations

---

Exhibit 14.8 A comparative statement of profit and loss

Comparative Statement of Profit and Loss for the Years Ending June 30			
	This Year	Last Year	Increase or Decrease
Income:			
Net sales	$253,218	$257,636	$4,418*
Dividends from investments	480	430	50
Other	1,741	1,773	32
Total	255,439	259,839	4,400*
Deductions:			
Cost of goods sold	180,481	178,866	1,615
Selling and administrative expenses	39,218	34,019	5,199
Interest expense	2,483	2,604	121*
Other	1,941	1,139	802
Total	224,123	216,628	7,495
Income before taxes	31,316	43,211	11,895*
Provision for taxes	3,300	9,500	6,200*
Net income	$ 28,016	$ 33,711	$5,695*

*Decrease.

As a result, the use of ratios should be supplemented with other control measures. Organizations can hold managers accountable for market share, number of patents granted, sales of new products, human resource development, energy efficiency, waste reduction, and other performance indicators.

4.4 | Bureaucratic Control has a Downside

So far you have learned about control from a mechanical viewpoint. But organizations are not strictly mechanical; they are composed of people. While control systems are used to constrain people's behavior and make their future behavior predictable, people are not machines that automatically fall into line as the designers of control systems intend. In fact, control systems can lead to dysfunctional behavior. To set up an effective control system, managers need to consider how people will react to it, including three potential negative responses:[31]

1. Rigid bureaucratic behavior.

2. Tactical behavior.

3. Resistance.

Rigid Bureaucratic Behavior Often people act in ways that will look good on the control system's measures. This tendency is useful when it focuses people on required behaviors. But it can result in rigid, inflexible behavior geared toward doing *only* what the system requires. For example, in the earlier discussion of the six sigma control process, we noted that it emphasizes efficiency over innovation. After 3M began using six sigma extensively, it slipped from its goal of having at least one-third of sales come

employees must keep their desks neat. Of course a chaotic workplace has its problems, but one survey found that people who said their desks were "very neat" spent more of their day looking for items than people who said their desks were "fairly messy."[34] By that measure, controlling neatness actually makes employees less efficient. Likewise, trying to control your own productivity by limiting phone calls and e-mail to certain times of day is beneficial only if ignoring the phone or e-mail won't cause you to annoy customers or miss important problems.

We have all been victimized at some time by rigid bureaucratic behavior and veterans are no exception.

> Take the recent discovery that administrators falsified medical records and appointment times at the Phoenix Veterans Administration (VA) Medical Center. The falsification was done to "comply" with a VA policy that veteran patients would see a doctor within 14 days of making an appointment. According to an employee who worked at the medical center, administrators were waiting "6 to 20 weeks" to create the appointment. In the wake of these revelations, the VA's bureaucracy and leadership received much of the blame, culminating in the resignation of Eric Shinseki, the Secretary of the Department of Veteran Affairs. Blame has also been leveled at the underfunded VA budget that contributes to shortages of medical centers (1,700 nationwide) and primary care physicians (5,100 total) who are currently caring for 85 million veterans.[35]

Stories such as these have, of course, given bureaucracy a bad name. Some managers will not even use the term *bureaucratic control* because of its potentially negative connotation. However, the control system itself is not the problem. The problems occur when the systems are no longer viewed as tools for running the business but instead as rules for dictating rigid behavior.

> "The disease which inflicts bureaucracy and what they usually die from is routine."
>
> —John Stuart Mill

from newly released products. When George Buckley took the CEO post, only one-fourth of sales were coming from new products. Buckley began relying less extensively on efficiency controls because, as he explained to a reporter, "Invention is by its very nature a disorderly process."[32] This shift to innovation is paying off for 3M. Several new products, like ultrathin solar panels, are expected to help the company's growth double to 7–8 percent per year over the next several years.[33] The control challenge, of course, is for 3M to be both efficient and creative.

Rigid bureaucratic behavior occurs when control systems prompt employees to stay out of trouble by following the rules. Unfortunately such systems often lead to poor customer service and make the entire organization slow to act. Some companies, including General Motors and UPS, enforce rules that

Tactical Behavior Control systems will be ineffective if employees engage in tactics aimed at "beating the system." The most common type of tactical behavior is to manipulate information or report false performance data. People may produce invalid data about what *has* been done and about what *can* be done. False reporting about the past is less common because it is easier to identify someone who misreports what happened than someone who incorrectly predicts or estimates what might happen. Still, managers sometimes change their accounting systems to "smooth out" the numbers. Also, people may intentionally feed false information into a management information system to cover up errors or poor performance. New York City prosecutors indicted the owner and five employees of American Standard Testing & Consulting Laboratories

Inc., a concrete-testing company, for falsifying testing results on major construction projects. The indictment accuses the six individuals of systematically skipping safety tests and writing false reports about the "quality and strength of concrete used in building projects around the city." Tests were allegedly faked at several locations, including Yankee Stadium, Memorial Sloan Kettering Cancer Center, and the Fulton Street subway station. The owners of the affected sites were notified and have taken steps to fix the problem.[36]

More commonly, people falsify predictions or requests for the future. When asked to give budgetary estimates, employees usually ask for more than they need. Or if they believe a low estimate will help them get a budget or a project approved, they may submit unrealistically *low* estimates. Budget-setting sessions can become tugs-of-war between subordinates trying to get slack in the budget and superiors attempting to minimize slack. Similar tactics are exhibited when managers negotiate unrealistically low performance standards so that subordinates will have little trouble meeting them, when salespeople project low forecasts so they will look good by exceeding them, and when workers slow down the work pace while time study analysts are setting work pace standards. The people in these examples are concerned only with their own performance figures, not with the overall performance of their department or company.

Resistance to Control Often people strongly resist control systems. They do so for several reasons:

- Comprehensive control systems increase the accuracy of performance data and make employees more accountable for their actions. Control systems uncover mistakes, threaten people's job security and status, and decrease people's autonomy.

- Control systems can change expertise and power structures. For example, management information systems can speed up the costing, purchasing, and production decisions previously made by managers. Those individuals may fear a loss of expertise, power, and decision-making authority as a result.

- Control systems can change an organization's social structure. They can create competition and disrupt social groups and friendships. People may end up competing against those with whom they formerly had comfortable, cooperative relationships. People's social needs are important, so they will resist control systems that reduce satisfaction of those needs.

● Many companies administer pre-hire and random drug tests as a way to control illicit drug use among employees.

- Control systems may be seen as an invasion of privacy, lead to lawsuits, and cause low morale.

LO5 List procedures for implementing effective control systems

5 | MORE EFFECTIVE CONTROL SYSTEMS

Effective control systems maximize potential benefits and minimize dysfunctional behaviors. To achieve this, management needs to design control systems that meet several criteria:

- The systems are based on valid performance standards.
- They communicate adequate information to employees.
- They are acceptable to employees.
- They use multiple approaches.
- They recognize the relationship between empowerment and control.

5.1 | Establish Valid Performance Standards

An effective control system must be based on valid and accurate performance standards. The most effective standards, as discussed earlier, tend to be expressed in quantitative terms; they are objective rather than subjective. Also, the measures should be difficult to sabotage or fake. Moreover, the system must incorporate all important aspects of performance. For example, a company that focused only on sales volume without also looking at profitability might soon go out of business. As you learned earlier, unmeasured behaviors get neglected. Consider performance standards for delivering training and other HR programs, which often emphasize trainee satisfaction as reported on surveys. In contrast, the Philadelphia Department of Licenses and Inspections verified that its training improved employee performance. The department, notorious for long lines and rude workers, sought help from the Philadelphia Ritz-Carlton Hotel (the chain is known for its superb customer service). The hotel's area general manager trained 40 department workers in how to improve their service skills. Afterward, the department checked wait times for license applicants, which dropped from 82 minutes to

14 minutes. The department is continuing its partnership with Ritz-Carlton through additional employee training.[37]

Management also must defend against another problem: too many measures that create overcontrol and employee resistance. To make many controls tolerable, managers can emphasize a few key areas while setting "satisfactory" performance standards in others. Or they can set simple priorities, such as directing a purchasing agent to meet targets in the following order: quality, availability, cost, inventory level. Finally, managers can set tolerance ranges, as when financial budgets include optimistic, expected, and minimum levels.

Many companies' budgets set cost targets only. This causes managers to control spending but also to neglect earnings. At Emerson Electric, profit and growth are key measures. If an unanticipated opportunity to increase market share arises, managers can spend what they need to go after it. The phrase "it's not in the budget" is less likely to stifle people at Emerson than it is at most other companies.

This principle applies to nonfinancial aspects of performance as well. At many customer service call centers, control aims to maximize efficiency by focusing on the average amount of time each agent spends handling each phone call. But the business objectives of call centers should also include other measures such as cross-selling products or improving customer satisfaction and repeat business. Online commerce site eBay Enterprise is using voice analytics technology by Interaction Analytics to mine business insights from the 20 million customer calls it receives each year. The data are analyzed by employees of the company's new Consumer Insight Department, who look for variables that can promote increased sales for the company's clients. Since implementing the Big Data program, eBay Enterprise has experienced a 9 percent increase in customer satisfaction and a 19 percent bump in average order value over the past two years.[38]

As illustrated in Exhibit 14.9, business consultant Michael Hammer has identified seven "deadly sins" of performance measurement to avoid.[39] The following examples suggest how these sins might manifest in organization:

1. *Vanity*—A company might measure order fulfillment in terms of whether products are delivered by the latest date promised by the organization rather than by the tougher and more meaningful measure of when the customers request to receive the products.

2. *Provincialism*—If a company's transportation department measures only shipping costs, it won't have an incentive to consider that shipping reliability (delivery on a given date) will affect performance at the company's stores or distribution centers.

3. *Narcissism*—A maker of computer systems measured on-time shipping of each component; if 90 percent of the system's components arrived at the customer on time, it was 90 percent on time. But from the customer's point of view, the system wasn't on time at all because the customer needed *all* the components to use the system.

4. *Laziness*—An electric power company simply assumed customers cared about installation speed, but in fact customers really cared more about receiving an accurate installation schedule.

5. *Pettiness*— An example would be clothing manufacturers that assume they should consider just manufacturing cost rather than the overall costs of making exactly the right products available in stores when customers demand them.

6. *Inanity*— A fast-food restaurant targeted waste reduction and was surprised when restaurant managers began slowing down operations by directing their employees to hold off on cooking anything until orders were placed.

7. *Frivolity*— In some organizations, more effort goes to blaming others than to correcting problems.

According to Hammer, the basic correction to these "sins" is to carefully select standards that look at entire business processes, such as product development or order fulfillment, and identify which actions make those processes succeed. Then managers should measure performance against these standards precisely, accurately, and practically, making individuals responsible for their achievement and rewarding success.

5.2 | Provide Adequate Information

Management must communicate to employees the importance and nature of the control system. Then people must receive feedback

Exhibit 14.9	The seven "deadly sins" of performance measurement
Vanity	Using measures that make managers and the organization look good.
Provincialism	Limiting measures to functional/departmental responsibilities rather than the organization's overall objectives.
Narcissism	Measuring from the employee's, manager's, or company's point of view rather than the customer's.
Laziness	Neglecting to expend the effort to analyze what is important to measure.
Pettiness	Measuring just one component of what affects business performance.
Inanity	Failing to consider the way standards will affect real-world human behavior and company performance.
Frivolity	Making excuses for poor performance rather than taking performance standards seriously.

Source: Adapted from M. Hammer, "The Seven Deadly Sins of Performance Measurement and How to Avoid Them," *MIT Sloan Management Review* 48, no. 3 (Spring 2007), pp. 19–28.

about their performance. Feedback motivates people and provides information that enables them to correct their own deviations from performance standards. Allowing people to initiate their own corrective action encourages self-control and reduces the need for outside supervision. *Open-book management,* described in an earlier chapter, is a powerful use of this control principle.

Information should be as accessible as possible, particularly when people must make decisions quickly and frequently. For example, a national food company with its own truck fleet had a difficult problem. The company wanted drivers to go through customer sales records every night, insert new prices from headquarters every morning, and still make their rounds—an impossible set of demands. To solve this control problem, the company installed personal computers in more than 1,000 delivery trucks. Now drivers use their PCs for constant communication with headquarters. Each night drivers send information about the stores, and each morning headquarters sends prices and recommended stock mixes.

In general, a manager designing a control system should evaluate the information system in terms of the following questions:[40]

- Does it provide people with data relevant to the decisions they need to make?

- Does it provide the right amount of information to decision makers throughout the organization?

- Does it provide enough information to each part of the organization about how other, related parts of the organization are functioning?

::::::::::::::::

Ritz-Carlton sets performance measures for maintaining its impressive reputation and ensures that employees see how they contribute. The measures are based on the key factors behind the hotel chain's success: its mystique, employee engagement, customer engagement, product service excellence, community involvement, and financial performance. For each success factor, cross-functional teams identify targets as detailed as the number of scuff marks on elevator doors or the percentage of satisfied employees at a location. Because these teams include frontline employees, employees believe that their input matters.

At each location, at the beginning of every shift, all employees meet to discuss activities, issues, and Ritz-Carlton's business philosophy. They compare recent performance against the targets in each area. These conversations reinforce the key performance factors and help employees appreciate the importance of what they do.

● Cross-functional teams of employees at The Ritz-Carlton Hotel set specific performance measures, including customer engagement and product service excellence, in order to maintain its outstanding reputation.

Each business unit focuses on up to three priorities, with each employee working to improve customer, employee, or financial results. Employees appreciate their role in giving guests a special experience. They take to heart the hotel's first service value: "I build strong relationships and create Ritz-Carlton guests for life." When Joanne Hanna checked into a Ritz-Carlton after a grueling

> "I've learned that mistakes can often be as good a teacher as success."
>
> —Jack Welch, former CEO, General Electric

series of airport delays, a hotel employee carried her bags and listened to her frustration. After learning she didn't have time for a spa visit or a masseuse, he brought her a scented candle—and had the information entered into Ritz-Carlton's database. Now, on every visit, a candle in Hanna's room reminds her of the employee's empathy.[41]

::::::::::::::

5.3 | Ensure Acceptability to Employees

Employees are less likely to resist a control system and exhibit dysfunctional behaviors if they accept the system. They are more likely to accept systems that have useful performance standards but are not overcontrolling. Employees also will find systems more acceptable if they believe the standards are possible to achieve.

The control system should emphasize positive behavior rather than focusing on simply controlling negative behavior. McBride Electric, an electrical contracting company, uses an electronic monitoring system called DriveCam to encourage its drivers to behave responsibly in terms of safety and fuel consumption. A DriveCam video monitor in each truck records activity inside and outside the cab; it saves that recording only if the truck is involved in a specified "trigger event" such as braking hard or swerving. Management explained the system to the drivers, emphasizing that it would help the company improve profits (a relevant message in a company that practices open-book management) and would protect the workers if they were ever accused falsely of unsafe practices. Not only did McBride immediately begin seeing improvements in safety and vehicle wear and tear, but it was also able to make good on its promise to defend employees. An anonymous phone caller complained that poor driving by a McBride driver had caused him to wreck his car. The McBride manager who took the call explained that he would be able to review a video taken from the truck that day—and the caller quickly hung up.[42] This approach exhibits the motivational quality of "procedural justice," described in Chapter 11. It gave employees the feeling that they were being evaluated by a fair process, so they were more likely to accept it.

5.4 | Maintain Open Communication

When deviations from standards occur, it is important that employees feel able to report the deviations so the problem can be addressed. If employees believe their managers want to hear only good news, or worse, if they fear reprisal for reporting bad news, even if it is not their fault, then any controls in place are much less likely to be effective. Problems may go unreported or even reach the point where solutions are much more expensive or difficult. But if managers create an environment of openness and honesty, where employees feel comfortable sharing even negative information and are appreciated for doing so in a timely fashion, then the control system is much more likely to work effectively.

Still, managers sometimes need to discipline employees who are failing to meet important standards. In such cases, an approach called *progressive discipline* is usually most effective. In this approach, clear standards are established, but failure to meet them is dealt with in a progressive, or step-by-step, process. The first time an employee's sales performance has been worse than it should have been, the supervising manager may offer verbal counseling or coaching. If problems persist, the next step might be a written reprimand. This type of reasonable and considered approach signals to all employees that the manager is interested in improving their performance, not in punishing them.

5.5 | Use Multiple Approaches

Multiple controls are necessary. For example, banks need controls on risk so they don't lose a lot of money from defaulting borrowers, as well as profit controls including sales budgets that aim for growth in accounts and customers.

As you learned earlier in this chapter, control systems generally should include both financial and nonfinancial performance targets and incorporate aspects of preliminary, concurrent, and feedback control. In recent years, a growing number of companies have combined targets for managers into a **balanced scorecard**, a combination of four sets of performance measures:[43]

1. Financial.

2. Customer satisfaction.

3. Business processes (quality and efficiency).

4. Learning and growth.

The goal is generally to broaden management's horizon beyond short-term financial results so that the company's long-term success is more likely. For example, J.P. Morgan Chase uses a balanced scorecard approach that extends beyond earnings to address such questions as (1) Are we recruiting and developing great people? (2) Are we innovating better products? (3) Are we relentlessly improving our core processes? (4) Are we making good returns on capital?[44] The balanced scorecard also is adaptable to nonprofit settings. Ocean-Monmouth Legal Services, which provides legal services to poor people in New Jersey, uses a balanced scorecard to track progress in meeting strategic, operational, financial, and client satisfaction goals. The organization's executive director, Harold E. Creacy, credits the approach with helping to cope with the rising costs and tight resources that so often plague nonprofits.[45]

Effective control also requires managers and organizations to use many of the other techniques and practices of good management. For example, compensation systems grant rewards for meeting standards and impose consequences if they are not met. And to gain employee acceptance, managers may rely on many of the other communication and motivational tools that we discussed in earlier chapters, such as persuasion and positive reinforcement.

6 | THE OTHER CONTROLS: MARKETS AND CLANS

Although the concept of control has always been a central feature of organizations, the principles and philosophies underlying its use are changing. In the past, control was focused almost exclusively on bureaucratic (and market) mechanisms. Generations of managers were taught that they could maximize productivity by regulating what employees did on the job—through standard operating procedures, rules, regulations, and close supervision. To increase output on an assembly line, for example, managers in the past tried to identify the "one best way" to approach the work and then to monitor employees' activities to make certain that they followed standard operating procedures. In short, they controlled work by dividing and simplifying tasks, a process referred to as *scientific management*.

Although formal bureaucratic control systems are perhaps the most pervasive in organizations (and the most talked about in management textbooks), they are not always the most effective. *Market controls* and *clan controls* may represent more flexible, though no less potent, approaches to regulating performance.

6.1 | Market Controls Let Supply and Demand Determine Prices and Profits

Market controls involve the use of economic forces—and the pricing mechanisms that accompany them—to regulate performance. The system works like this: When output from an individual, department, or business unit has value to other people, a price can be negotiated for its exchange. As a market for these transactions becomes established, two effects occur:

- Price becomes an indicator of the value of the good or service.

- Price competition has the effect of controlling productivity and performance.

The basic principles that underlie market controls can operate at the level of the corporation, the business unit (or department), and the individual. Exhibit 14.10 shows a few ways in which market controls are used in an organization.

Market Controls at the Corporate Level In large, diversified companies, market controls often are used to regulate independent business units. Particularly in large conglomerate firms that act as holding companies, business units typically are treated as profit centers that compete with one another. Top executives may place few bureaucratic controls on business unit managers but evaluate performance in terms of profit and loss data. While decision making and power are decentralized to the business units, market controls ensure that business unit performance is in line with corporate objectives.

This use of market control mechanisms has been criticized by those who insist that economic measures do not adequately reflect environmental sustainability or the complete value of an organization. Employees often suffer as diversified companies are repeatedly bought and sold based on market controls.

balanced scorecard control system combining four sets of performance measures: financial, customer, business process, and learning and growth

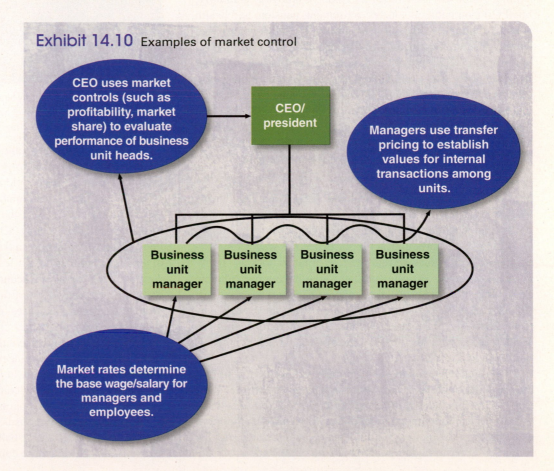

Exhibit 14.10 Examples of market control

CEO uses market controls (such as profitability, market share) to evaluate performance of business unit heads.

CEO/president

Managers use transfer pricing to establish values for internal transactions among units.

Business unit manager

Business unit manager

Business unit manager

Business unit manager

Market rates determine the base wage/salary for managers and employees.

transfer price price charged by one unit for a good or service provided to another unit within the organization

Market Controls at the Business Unit Level Market control also can be used within business units to regulate exchanges among departments and functions. One way organizations try to apply market forces to internal transactions is through transfer pricing. A **transfer price** is the charge by one unit in the organization for a good or service that it supplies to another unit of the same organization. For example, in automobile manufacturing, transfer prices may be affixed to components and subassemblies before they are shipped to subsequent business units for final assembly. Ideally the transfer price reflects what the receiving business unit would have to pay for that good or service in the marketplace.

As organizations have more options to outsource goods and services to external partners, market controls such as transfer prices provide natural incentives to keep costs down and quality up. Managers stay in close touch with prices in the marketplace to make sure their own costs are in line, and they try to improve the service they provide to increase their department's value to the organization. Consider the situation in which human resources activities can be done internally or outsourced to a consulting firm. If the human resources department cannot supply services at a reasonable price, there may be no reason for that department to exist inside the firm. For example, California-based Agilent Technologies outsourced benefits administration and payroll for its 20,000 employees. Similarly, Shell Oil Company outsourced retirement, pension, and health administration to an HR service provider.[46] Philadelphia-based Buzz Marketing Group, a family-run research and viral marketing firm, found itself about to double in size after landing some large accounts like Dell. Tina Wells, the firm's founder, was spending too much time on HR issues and not enough time on managing the business. She turned to Paychex—a $2.3 billion firm that specializes in meeting the HR needs of companies—to manage payroll, revamp company policies and procedures, write job descriptions, and track employee performance.[47]

Market Controls at the Individual Level Market controls also are used at the individual level. For example, in situations where organizations are trying to hire employees, the supply and demand for particular skills influence the wages employees can expect to receive and the rate organizations are likely to pay. Employees or job candidates who have more valuable skills tend to be paid a higher wage. Of course wages don't always reflect market rates—sometimes they are based (perhaps arbitrarily) on internal resource considerations—but the market rate is often the best indicator of an employee's potential worth to a firm.

Market-based controls such as these are important in that they provide a natural incentive for employees to enhance their skills and offer them to potential employers. Even after individuals gain employment, market-based wages are important as controls in that people with higher economic value may be promoted faster to higher positions in the organization.

● Are the sometimes ridiculously high salaries that today's professional athletes are paid truly indicative of the players' skills?

Market controls often are used by boards of directors to manage CEOs of major corporations. Although many people think of CEOs as the people controlling everyone else in the company, a CEO is accountable to the board of directors, and the board must ensure that the CEO acts in its interest. Absent board control, CEOs may act in ways that make them look good personally (such as making the company bigger or more diversified) but that do not lead to higher profits for the firm. And as recent corporate scandals have shown, without board control, CEOs may also artificially inflate the firm's earnings or not fully declare expenses, making the firm look much more successful than it really is.

Traditionally, boards have tried to control CEO performance mainly through the use of incentive pay, including bonuses tied to short-term profit targets. In large U.S. companies, most CEO compensation is tied to the company's performance. In addition to short-term incentives, boards use long-term incentives linked to the firm's share price, usually through stock options, which we discussed earlier. Also, balanced scorecards are intended to keep CEOs focused on the company's longer-term health. And under the Sarbanes-Oxley Act, board members are expected to exercise careful control over the company's financial performance, including oversight of the CEO's compensation package.

6.2 | Clan Control Relies on Empowerment and Culture

Managers are discovering that control systems based solely on bureaucratic and market mechanisms are insufficient for directing today's workforce. There are several reasons:

- *Employees' jobs have changed.* Employees working with computers, for example, have more variable jobs, and much of their work is intellectual and therefore invisible. Because of this, there is no one best way to perform a task, and programming or standardizing jobs is extremely difficult. Close supervision also is unrealistic because it is nearly impossible to supervise activities such as reasoning and problem solving.

- *The nature of management has changed.* Managers used to know more about the job than employees did. Today, with the shift to knowledge work, employees typically know more about their jobs than anyone else does. When real expertise in organizations exists at the very lowest levels, hierarchical control becomes impractical.[48]

● In order to enhance their agility, speed, and responsiveness, some companies are moving to a clan control approach that is based on employee empowerment, trust, and organizational culture.

act in accordance with them, then clan control can be very effective.[49] As we noted at the beginning of this chapter, *clan control* involves creating relationships built on mutual respect and encouraging each individual to take responsibility for his

> "Use good judgment in all situations. There will be no additional rules."
>
> — Nordstrom's employee manual

- *The employment relationship has changed.* The social contract at work is being renegotiated. Employees once were most concerned about pay, job security, and the hours of work. Today, however, more and more employees want to be more fully engaged in their work, taking part in decision making, devising solutions to unique problems, and receiving assignments that are challenging and involving. They want to use their brains.

For these three reasons, the concept of *empowerment* not only has become more popular in organizations but also has become a necessary aspect of a manager's repertoire of control. With no "one best way" to approach a job and no way to scrutinize what employees do every day, managers must empower employees to make decisions and trust that they will act in the firm's best interests. But this does not mean giving up control. It means creating a strong culture of high standards and integrity so that employees will exercise effective control on their own.

Recall our discussion of organization culture in Chapter 3. An organization culture that encourages the wrong behaviors will severely hinder an effort to impose effective controls. But if managers create and reinforce a strong culture that encourages correct behavior, one in which everyone understands management's values and expectations and is motivated to

or her actions. Employees work within a guiding framework of values, and they are expected to use good judgment. For example, at NetApp, an IT company specializing in data storage and protection, a commitment to employee empowerment prompted the switch from a 12-page travel policy to some simple guidelines for employees who need to go on a business trip: "We are a frugal company. But don't show up dog-tired to save a few bucks. Use your common sense."[50] An empowered organization emphasizes satisfying customers rather than pleasing the boss. Mistakes are tolerated as the unavoidable by-product of dealing with change and uncertainty and are viewed as opportunities to learn. And team members learn together.

Here are a few practical guidelines for managing in an empowered world:[51]

- *Put control where the operation is.* Layers of hierarchy, close supervision, and checks and balances are quickly disappearing and being replaced with self-guided teams. For centuries even the British Empire—as large as it was—never had more than six levels of management, including the Queen.

- *Use real-time rather than after-the-fact controls.* Issues and problems must be solved at the source by the people doing the actual work. Managers become a resource to help out the team.

- *Rebuild the assumptions underlying management control to build on trust rather than distrust.* Today's "high-flex" organizations are based on empowerment, not obedience. Information must facilitate decision making, not police it.

- *Move to control based on peer norms.* Clan control is a powerful thing. Workers in Japan, for example, have been known to commit suicide rather than disappoint or lose face within their team. Although this is extreme, it underlines the power of peer influence. The Japanese have a far more homogeneous culture and set of values than we do. In North America, we must build peer norms systematically and put much less emphasis on managing by the numbers.

- *Rebuild the incentive systems to reinforce responsiveness and teamwork.* The twin goals of adding value to the customer and team performance must become the dominant raison d'être of the measurement systems.

The resilience and time investment of clan control are a double-edged sword. Clan control takes a long time to develop and an even longer time to change. This gives an organization stability and direction during periods of upheaval in the environment or the organization (e.g., during changes in top management). Yet if managers want to establish a new culture—a new form of clan control—they must help employees unlearn the old values and embrace the new. We will talk more about this transition process in the next chapter of this book.

Study Checklist

- Did you tear out the perforated student review card at the back of the text to revisit learning objectives and key terms and definitions?

Connect® Management is available for M Management. Additional resources include:

Interactive Applications:
- Case Analysis: How Legal Sea Foods Uses Control
- Drag & Drop: Engaging Employees at the Ritz Carlton
- Drag & Drop: The Right Ratio for the Job
- Video Case: From Race Cars to Airplanes

- LearnSmart—Multiple choice questions help you determine what you already know, are not sure about, or need to practice based on your score. And with SmartBook, you can read the relevant section in the eBook as well as practice and recharge what you've learned.
- Chapter Video: Tom and Eddies
- Young Manager Speaks Out: Jeremy Partacz, Customer Experience Manager

What have other students found to help them study?

15 chapter

Innovating and **Changing**

Learning Objectives

After studying Chapter 15, you should be able to

LO1 Summarize how to assess technology needs.

LO2 Identify the criteria on which to base technology decisions.

LO3 Compare key ways of acquiring new technologies.

LO4 Evaluate the elements of an innovative organization.

LO5 Discuss what it takes to be world-class.

LO6 Describe how to manage change effectively.

LO7 List tactics for creating a successful future.

Technological innovation is complex, moving fast—and vital for a firm's competitive advantage. Today's organizations depend on their managers' ability to capitalize on new technologies and other changes not only to carry out their basic tasks more efficiently and effectively but also to retain an edge over their competitors. Because technology and rapid innovation are critical for success, managers must understand how technologies can change the ways organizations compete and the ways people work.

Earlier in the text, we defined *technology* as the methods, processes, systems, and skills used to transform resources into products. More generally, we can think of technology as the commercialization of science: the systematic application of scientific knowledge to a new product, process, or service. In this sense, technology is embedded in every product, service, and procedure used or produced.[1] But if we find a better way to accomplish our task, we have an innovation. *Innovation* is a change in method or technology—a positive, useful departure from previous ways of doing things.

There are two fundamental types of innovation:

1. *Process innovations* are changes that affect the way outputs are produced. Examples from Chapter 7 include flexible manufacturing practices such as just-in-time, mass customization, and simultaneous engineering.

2. *Product or service innovations* are changes in the actual outputs (goods and services) produced.[2]

These two categories cover a multitude of creative new ideas. They can change product offerings, the basic "platforms" or features and processes used to create products, the customer problems the organization can solve, the types of customers the organization serves, the nature of the experience provided by the organization, the way the organization earns money from what it does, the efficiency and effectiveness of its processes, the structure of the organization, the supply chain through which it delivers goods and services, the physical or virtual points at which it interacts with customers, the ways the organization communicates, and the brand associated with the organization and its products.[3]

Critical forces converge to create new technologies. Understanding the forces driving technological development can help a manager anticipate, monitor, and manage technologies more effectively.

- There must be a *need*, or *demand*, for the technology. Without this need driving the process, there is no reason for technological innovation to occur.

- Meeting the need must be theoretically possible, and the *knowledge* to do so must be available from basic science.

- We must be able to *convert* the scientific knowledge into practice in engineering and economic terms. If doing something is theoretically possible but economically impractical, the technology cannot be expected to emerge.

- The *funding, skilled labor, time, space,* and *other resources* needed to develop the technology must be available.

- *Entrepreneurial initiative* must identify and pull all the necessary elements together.

This chapter discusses how technology can affect an organization's competitiveness and how managers identify which technologies an organization should adopt. Then we assess the primary ways in which organizations develop or acquire those technologies, including the leadership and management decisions that help new technology succeed. Of course technology is not the only way organizations innovate and change. The remainder of the chapter looks more broadly at innovation, including change efforts aimed at achieving world-class status, the process of managing change, and efforts you can make to shape your own career.

LO1 Summarize how to assess technology needs

1 | DECIDING TO ADOPT NEW TECHNOLOGY

Decisions about technology and innovation are strategic, and managers need to approach them systematically. In Chapter 5 we discussed two generic strategies a company can use to position itself in the market:[4]

1. *Low cost*—The company has an advantage from maintaining a lower cost than its competitors.

2. *Differentiation*—The advantage comes from offering a unique good or service for which customers are willing to pay a premium price.

For either strategy, managers must assess technology needs, decide whether to adopt a new technology, and if they adopt the technology, determine the best method for developing or acquiring it.

In today's increasingly competitive environment, failure to correctly assess the organization's technology needs can fundamentally impair the organization's effectiveness. Consider the biggest industry sector in the U.S. economy: health care services, where spending is soaring. One reason that health care costs so much is that the industry has been slow to adopt technology that can make operations more efficient. According to a RAND Corporation study, Americans could save $162 billion a year if health care providers made better investments in information technology. For example, fewer medication errors is an exceptional achievement considering the St. Louis-based health care network administers 12 million doses of medicine per year to 154,000 hospital patients and 1.3 million outpatients.[6]

To assess technology needs, managers measure current technologies and look for trends affecting the industry.

1.1 | Measuring Current Technologies

To assist managers in understanding their current technology base, a **technology audit** helps clarify the key technologies on

> "An organization's ability to learn, and translate that learning into action rapidly, is the ultimate competitive advantage."
>
> —Jack Welch, former CEO of General Electric

than one-fifth of hospitals use a complete bar code system for dispensing medicine, which could save money and reduce medication errors.[5] For example, SSM Health Care reported barcode scanning rates of near 100 percent in 2012, resulting in zero wrong-patient medication errors. Having no which an organization depends. One technique for measuring competitive value sorts technologies into several categories (see Exhibit 15.1 for examples) according to their competitive value:[7]

- *Emerging technologies* are still under development but may significantly alter the rules of competition in the future. Managers should monitor the development of emerging technologies but may not need to invest in them until they have been more fully developed.

- *Pacing technologies* have yet to prove their full value but have the potential to provide a significant advantage that alters the rules of competition. Managers should develop or invest in pacing technologies because of the competitive advantages they can provide.

- *Key technologies* have proved effective but offer a strategic advantage because not everyone uses them. Eventually alternatives to key technologies can emerge. But until then, key technologies can give organizations a significant competitive edge and make it harder for new entrants to threaten the organization.

- *Base technologies* are commonplace in the industry; everyone must have them. They provide little competitive advantage, but managers have to invest to ensure their organization's continued competence in the technology.

Technologies can evolve rapidly through these categories. For example, electronic word processing was an emerging technology in the late 1970s. By the early 1980s, it could have been considered pacing because its cost and capabilities restricted its usefulness to a few applications. With continued improvements and more powerful computer chips, electronic word processing

LISTEN & LEARN ⊙ ONLINE

YOUNG MANAGERS
Speak Out!

"I am encouraged to be creative, innovative, and proactive in my position. Have you thought about the pros and cons? What are they? Move forward with it."

—Keisha Heard, Financial Aid Program Coordinator

Exhibit 15.1 Four technology categories and example

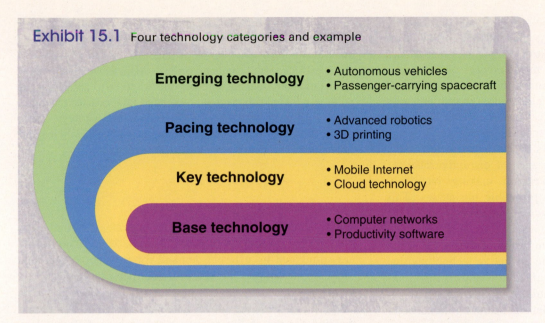

Emerging technology	• Autonomous vehicles • Passenger-carrying spacecraft
Pacing technology	• Advanced robotics • 3D printing
Key technology	• Mobile Internet • Cloud technology
Base technology	• Computer networks • Productivity software

Sources: Adapted from R. E. Oligney and M. I. Economides, "Technology as an Asset," *Hart's Petroleum Engineer International* 71, no. 9 (September 1998), p. 27; C. MacKechnie, "What Are the Types of Business Techology," *Chron* (online), http://smallbusiness.chron.com, accessed on June 15, 2014; and J. Manyika, M. Chul, J. Bughin, R. Dobbs, P. Bisson, and A. Marrs, "Disruptive Technologies: Advances That Will Transform Life, Business, and the Global Economy," *McKinsey & Company Report,* May 2013, www.mckinsey.com.

quickly became a key technology. Its costs dropped, its usage spread, and it demonstrated the capacity to enhance productivity. By the late 1980s, it was a base technology in most applications, and now it is used so widely that it is routine in almost every office.

1.2 | Assessing External Technological Trends

As with any planning, decisions about technology must balance internal capabilities (strengths and weaknesses) with external opportunities and threats. To understand how technology is changing within an industry, managers can use techniques we introduced in previous chapters:

- *Benchmarking* compares the organization's practices and technologies with those of other companies. Harley-Davidson recovered its reputation for manufacturing quality motorcycles after company executives toured Honda's plant and witnessed firsthand the relative weaknesses of Harley's manufacturing technologies and the vast potential for improvement. Competitors understandably are reluctant to share their secrets, but companies may be more willing to share their knowledge if they are not direct competitors and if the exchange of information might benefit both companies.

- *Environmental scanning* focuses on what can be done and what is being developed. It emphasizes identifying and monitoring the sources of new technologies for an industry. It also may include reading cutting-edge research journals and attending conferences and seminars. Organizations that operate closer to the cutting edge of technology rely more on scanning.

1.3 | Engaging in Disruptive Innovation

Measuring current technologies and assessing external technological trends through benchmarking and scanning may not be enough to stay ahead of the innovation curve. Periodically, major technological shifts occur even in relatively stable industries that can dramatically change the competitive landscape. **Disruptive innovation** refers to a process by which a product, service, or business model takes root initially in simple applications at the bottom of a market and then moves "up market", eventually displacing established competitors.[8] Some examples of how disruptive innovations have transformed entire industries include the following: MP3 file technology and

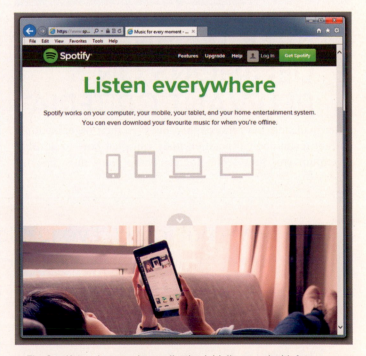

● The Spotify music streaming application initially started with free accounts. However, as of August 2012 Time reported that four million people were paid subscribers.

digital music platforms like Apple's iTunes have dramatically changed the music industry; tablets and other handheld Internet devices are replacing many desktop computers; smartphones have replaced many stand-alone music devices and cameras; online retailer Amazon revolutionized how people shop and encouraged bricks-and-mortar retailers to follow suit; and low-cost airlines like Southwest Airlines have consistently outperformed many traditional hub-and-spoke carriers.[9]

As these transformative shifts occur in industries, many good managers miss the significance of disruptive changes because they are more focused on making incremental improvements to their core profitable businesses. This tendency, known as *the innovator's dilemma,* poses the following challenge: "How can executives simultaneously do what is right for the near-term health of their established businesses, while focusing on the disruptive technology that ultimately could lead to their downfall?"[10] Many organizations seem to be faced with this dilemma—for example, Microsoft (desktop vs. cloud computing), General Motors (internal combustion vs. electric/hybrid), and British Petroleum (conventional oil vs. renewable energy). Organizations and managers that wrestle with and successfully balance these two objectives—to sustain and grow the current core businesses while identifying and investing in high-potential disruptive innovations—will increase their chances of remaining competitive and successful in the long run.[11]

> **LO2** Identify the criteria on which to base technology decisions

2 | BASE TECHNOLOGY DECISIONS ON RELEVANT CRITERIA

After managers have thoroughly analyzed their organization's current technological position, they can plan how to develop or exploit emerging technologies. These plans must balance

the risks and ambiguities of adopting a new technology. All of these considerations jointly influence managers' decisions about technology innovations. A lack in even one of them can derail an otherwise promising project. Also, as we discuss later in this chapter, decisions go beyond whether to adopt a technology to include changes in the related factors—for example, improving the organization's capabilities and strategies, hiring or training employees, and changing internal policies and procedures.

2.1 | Anticipated Market Receptiveness

The first consideration in developing a strategy around technological innovation is market potential. Many innovations are stimulated by external demand for new goods and services. For example, the share of Internet users who use a language other than English has been growing rapidly. This trend, along with the globalization of business, has fueled demand for the ability to search the web in different languages. Companies are creating a variety of software innovations to meet this demand. Microsoft's Bing Translator translates text and web pages between any of the supported languages like Russian, Arabic, and Portuguese, automatically detecting the language when needed.[12] Yahoo! Answers will send queries to a native speaker of the user's language. It indexes those responses so they can be searched by future users in that language.[13]

In assessing market receptiveness, executives need to make two determinations:

1. In the short run, the new technology should have an immediate, valuable application.

2. In the long run, the technology must be able to satisfy a market need or needs.

For example, when prescribing medicine, physicians view the traditional method of scribbling on a pad and handing the prescription to a patient or nurse as very simple to use. For the physicians to learn to use new technology for that purpose, it must be worthwhile to them. Hospitals that move to electronic

> "I have not failed. I've just found 10,000 ways that don't work."
>
> —Thomas Edison

many interrelated factors, including the organization's competitive strategy, the technical abilities of its employees to deal with the new technology, the fit of the technology with the company's operations, and the company's ability to deal with

management of drug distribution need to roll out entire systems, but those systems let doctors tap into information networks where they can look up drug interactions, side effects, and so on. When doctors see how the system helps them deliver better care and reduce errors, most are quick to embrace the new technology.[14]

2.2 | Technological Feasibility

Managers also must consider whether technological innovations are feasible. Technical obstacles may represent barriers to progress. For example, the makers of computer chips face continual hurdles in developing newer and faster models. Since Intel brought the first microprocessor to market in 1971, chip makers have made dramatic advances in computing. The number of transistors on a chip, and its resulting performance, has doubled nearly every 18 to 24 months. But the frontier of microprocessor technology is restricted by the combined forces of physics and economics. The wires that run between transistors are 400 times thinner than a human hair, and the task of continually doubling the speed of electrons passing wires of near-zero width is tricky—and may become impossible at some point. To continue boosting processor speed economically, developers have had to be creative, using techniques such as shrinking components and embedding multiple processors cores on one microchip to shorten the distance data must travel between processors.[15] For example, Intel recently announced the release of a new X99 chip and DDR4 memory. The processor will be the company's first 8-core desktop model.[16]

Other industries face similar technological hurdles. In the sustainable energy industry—such as solar cell and wind turbine production—explosive growth is constrained by the lack of an economical storage system that can make renewable energy available whenever and wherever it is needed.[17] In medicine, scientists and doctors work continuously to identify the causes of and cures for diseases such as cancer and AIDS. Automakers' efforts to develop electric cars have been constrained by the difficulty of designing a battery that can power the long trips Americans love to take.

2.3 | Economic Viability

Apart from whether a firm can "pull off" a technological innovation, executives must consider whether there is a good financial incentive for doing so. The use of hydrogen-powered fuel cell technology for automobiles is almost feasible technically, but its costs are still too high. Even if those costs were brought down to more acceptable levels, the absence of a supporting infrastructure—such as hydrogen refueling stations—represents another barrier to economic viability.

On a more practical level of economic feasibility, new technologies often require long-term commitment of substantial resources. And integrating them effectively in an organization can require a great deal of management time. For these reasons, managers must objectively analyze technology costs versus benefits. Of course technology's benefits can be substantial. The IQ Business Group (IQBG), an information management company, uses cloud technology to help private companies and governmental agencies reduce the costs related to organizing and storing the massive amount of information and data that flows within organizations on a daily basis. Recently, IQBG signed a $53 million contract to help the United States Department of the Interior (DOI) manage its record and e-mail flows. The new system will capture and classify 100 percent of the 75 million e-mails the agency sends and receives per month. By moving the on-premise IT system to a cloud-based system, the DOI may save roughly 7 percent of its IT budget annually.[18]

Patents and copyrights can help organizations recoup the costs of their investments in technological innovations. Without such protection, the investments in research and development might not be justifiable. Unfortunately the growth in piracy and fakery of patented pharmaceuticals, software, and other products adds barriers to economic viability. Globalization has created a worldwide market for goods produced by low-cost counterfeiters and pirates. Pfizer's anti-impotence drug Viagra, Hewlett-Packard inkjet cartridges, Intel computer chips, GM car designs, Nokia mobile phones, Coach handbags, Nike Air Jordan shoes, and countless music and movie recordings—all these and many more have been counterfeited or illegally copied and sold. Worldwide lost sales as a result of the theft of *intellectual property* have been estimated at more than $500 billion a year.

Some companies have taken action on this problem. Auto parts maker Bendix set up a team charged with enforcing intellectual property rights, used packaging that is harder to counterfeit, and educates customers by setting up trade show displays with side-by-side comparisons of its product and knock-offs. Other companies, including Pfizer, are using radio-frequency tags on their packages to track products more accurately during distribution. These measures are designed to help organizations maintain the economic viability of their innovations.[19]

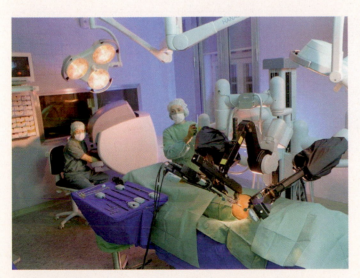

● The da Vinci Surgical System is a robotic surgical system designed to facilitate complex surgery using a minimally invasive approach and is controlled by a surgeon from a console. An estimated 200,000 surgeries were conducted with the system in 2012.

● Bureau of Customs (BOC) officials inspect counterfeit designer bags at their headquarters in Manila. Illegally imported fake medicines, cellphone batteries and chargers, and counterfeit designer bags valued in the millions of dollars are confiscated annually.

2.4 | Anticipated Capability Development

Our advice that organizations base strategies on their core capabilities applies to technology and innovation strategies. At Merck and Intel, core capabilities in research and development lead to new technological innovations. By contrast, firms that are not technology oriented must develop new capabilities to survive. For example, when Amazon.com changed the face of e-retailing in the 1990s, traditional brick-and-mortar bookstores had to adapt quickly. To regain competitiveness, they had to bolster their information technology capabilities, which wasn't always easy for them to do.

of managers, and the expectations of stakeholders. With regard to technology adoption, we can consider three broad types of organizations:

- *Prospector firms*—These proactive "technology-push" innovators have cultures that are outward-looking and opportunistic. Examples include 3M, Apple, Amazon, Samsung, IBM, Microsoft, and Google. Executives in these organizations give priority to developing and exploiting technological expertise, and decision makers have bold, intuitive visions of the future. Typically they have technology champions who articulate competitively aggressive, first-mover technological strategies. Executives tend to be more concerned about the opportunity costs of not taking action than they are about the potential to fail.

- *Defender firms*—These companies adopt a more circumspect posture toward innovation. They tend to operate in stable environments, so their strategies focus on deepening their capabilities through technologies that extend rather than replace their current ones. Strategic decisions are likely to be based on careful analysis and experience in the industry setting. In the United States, supermarkets have competed for decades by emphasizing low-cost distribution over large distances. That strategy has helped the companies survive low-cost pressure from Walmart but has not always translated well when U.S.-based supermarket chains have tried to expand into other parts of the world.[20]

- *Analyzer firms*—These hybrid organizations need to stay technologically competitive but tend to let others demonstrate solid demand in new arenas before responding. Such companies often adopt an early-follower strategy to grab a dominant position more from their strengths in marketing and manufacturing than from technological innovation. For example, Microsoft's Xbox game console, Office software, and Zune music player all contain innovations, but other companies pioneered the original path-breaking product concepts.

Every company has different capabilities to deal with new technology. *Early adopters* of new technologies tend to be

> "Almost everyone is more enthusiastic about change when the change is their own idea, and less enthusiastic if they feel the change is being imposed on them."
>
> —Maggie Bayless, *managing partner, ZingTrain*[21]

The upshot is that while certain technologies may have tremendous market applicability, managers must have (or develop) the internal capabilities to execute their technology strategies. In organizations without the skills needed to implement an innovation, even promising technological advances may prove disastrous.

2.5 | Organizational Suitability

The decision to adopt technological innovations also should take into account the culture of the organization, the interests

larger, more profitable, and more specialized. As a result, they can absorb the risks associated with early adoption while profiting more from its advantages. In addition, the people involved in early adoption are more highly educated, have greater ability to deal with abstraction, can cope with uncertainty more effectively, and have strong problem-solving capabilities. Thus early adopters can more effectively manage the difficulties and uncertainty of a less fully developed technology.[22]

Managers evaluating new technology also should consider its impact on employees. Often new technology brings process changes that directly affect the organization's work environment. These changes may create anxiety and resistance among employees, making integration of the technology more difficult. But employees' cooperation is often a major factor in determining how difficult and costly the introduction of new technology will be. We discuss the issue of managing change in more detail later in this chapter.

LO3 Compare key ways of acquiring new technologies

3 | KNOW WHERE TO GET NEW TECHNOLOGIES

Developing new technology may conjure up visions of scientists and product developers working in research and development (R&D) laboratories. In many industries, the primary sources of new technology are the organizations that use it. More than three-fourths of scientific innovations are developed by the users of the scientific instruments being improved and subsequently may be licensed or sold to manufacturers or suppliers.[23] However, new technology can come from many sources, including suppliers, manufacturers, users, other industries, universities, the government, and overseas companies.

In 1984, Charles Hull invented a printing process that used materials (instead of ink) to create a 3D model from a digital image or picture. The original purpose of 3D printing was to make and test a model of a part or product prior to investing large sums in manufacturing it.[24] Now, 3D printing is being used to make a wide range of finished products such as unmanned robotic aircraft, military weapons, compact electronic circuit boards, necklaces, and children's dolls.[25]

Also, this printing technology is being used for advanced biomedical research. Dr. Jennifer Lewis, a materials scientist at Harvard University, and her team recently printed biological tissue with blood vessels. It is believed that this research could someday result in the creation of artificial organs for drug testing or for use as replacement parts.[26] Other universities are also exploring the myriad possibilities of 3D printing. Researchers at Princeton University combined biological tissue and electronics to print a bionic ear, while a research team at Cambridge University printed retinal cells to form eye tissue.[27]

make-or-buy decision the question an organization asks itself about whether to acquire new technology from an outside source or develop it itself

Essentially, the question of how to acquire new technology is a **make-or-buy decision.** In other words, should the organization develop the technology itself or acquire it from an outside source? That decision is not simple. As illustrated in Exhibit 15.2, there are many alternatives, and each has advantages and disadvantages. Here are some of the most common options:

- *Internal development*—Developing a new technology within the company can keep the technology proprietary—exclusive to the organization. However, internal development usually requires additional staff and funding for long periods. Even if the development succeeds, considerable time may elapse before practical benefits are realized. Intel balances these risks and benefits by operating research and development laboratories in several locations, including Israel, India, Poland, and China. Engineers in these labs have come up with breakthrough ideas, and labs in offshore locations can get around legal restrictions on technology imports, as well as save money relative to the cost of hiring talent in the United States.[28]

Exhibit 15.2	Advantages and disadvantages of alternative make-or-buy technology decisions	
Alternatives	**Advantage(s)**	**Disadvantage(s)**
Internal development	Technology is proprietary and provides competitive advantage.	Expensive, time-consuming to develop.
Purchase	Simple to implement and cost-effective.	Does not provide competitive advantage.
Contracted development	Allows a firm without internal development capabilities to acquire technology.	Higher monitoring costs and risk that technology eventually appears in marketplace.
Licensing	Permits firms to access unique technology for a fee; more economical than development.	Firm does not own or control the unique technology; it depends on another firm.
Technology trading	Speeds learning curve and reduces costly trial-and-error approach to using technologies.	Some information is not directly applicable, and not all industries are willing to share information.
Research partnerships and joint ventures	Two or more firms share costs associated with new technology development.	Coordination costs can be high and organizational cultures can clash, limiting the outcomes.
Acquisition of a technology owner	Firm gains control and ownership over desired technology.	Purchase of company can be expensive. ent.

- *Purchase*—Most technology already is available in products or processes that can be purchased. A bank that needs sophisticated information-processing equipment need not develop the technology itself. It can buy it from suppliers. In most situations, this is the simplest, easiest, and most cost-effective way to acquire new technology. However, the technology itself will not offer a competitive advantage.

- *Contracted development*—If the technology is not available and a company lacks the resources or time to develop it internally, it may contract the development from outside sources, such as other companies, independent research laboratories, and university and government institutions. Usually outside contracting involves an agreed-upon series of objectives and timetables for the project, with payments for completion of each.

- *Licensing*—Certain technologies that are not easily purchased can be licensed for a fee. For example, companies that develop video games often license technology, including the software that models the physics behind the activities depicted in the game. The artwork, characters, and music for a particular game may be unique, but the basic laws of real-world physics apply to the action shown in most of today's sophisticated games, so there is no advantage to programming that aspect of each game. Licensing is more economical.[29]

- *Technology trading*—Some companies are willing to share ideas. Mary Jo Cartwright, a director of manufacturing operations for Batesville Casket Company, toured a John Deere farm equipment plant and noted a technology called *visual management screens,* which display how-to information for production workers. Some time later, when Batesville became involved in more customization, the company introduced visual management screens to give workers detailed and understandable assembly instructions.[30] Not all industries are amenable to this kind of sharing, but technology trading is becoming increasingly common because of the high cost of developing advanced technologies independently.[31]

- *Research partnerships and joint ventures*—Research partnerships are arrangements for jointly pursuing specific new technology development. Typically each member contributes a different set of skills or resources, as when an established company contributes money and management know-how, and a start-up contributes technological expertise. Boeing is opening a joint research center with Embraer to advance the aviation biofuel industry in Brazil.[32] Joint ventures are similar to research partnerships but generally are aimed at establishing entirely new companies.[33] An example is the strategic alliance formed by Volvo Group, the Swedish automaker, and Dongfeng Motor Group, a Chinese commerical truck manufacturer, to produce medium- and heavy-duty trucks for the Chinese market. This alliance combines Volvo's technological expertise and global reach with Dongfeng's knowledge of the Chinese truck market.[34]

- *Acquisition of a technology owner*—If a company lacks a technology but wishes to acquire ownership, it might purchase the company that owns the technology. This transaction can be an outright purchase of the entire company or a minority interest sufficient to gain access to the technology. For example, Motorola bought shares of Global Locate, which developed the technology for fast-working global positioning systems (GPSs). Customers are increasingly interested in GPS applications in cell phones and other mobile devices. A semiconductor supplier called Broadcom acquired Global Locate outright, so it could supply semiconductors featuring GPS navigation without having to license that technology or depend on an outside supplier.[35]

Choosing among these alternatives is simpler if managers ask a few basic questions:

1. Is it important (and possible) in terms of competitive advantage that the technology remain proprietary?

2. Are the time, skills, and resources for internal development available?

3. Is the technology readily available outside the company?

As Exhibit 15.3 illustrates, the answers to these questions guide the manager to the most appropriate technology acquisition option.

If the preferred decision is to acquire a company, managers take additional steps to ensure the acquisition will make sense for the long term. For example, they try to make sure that key employees will remain with the firm, instead of leaving

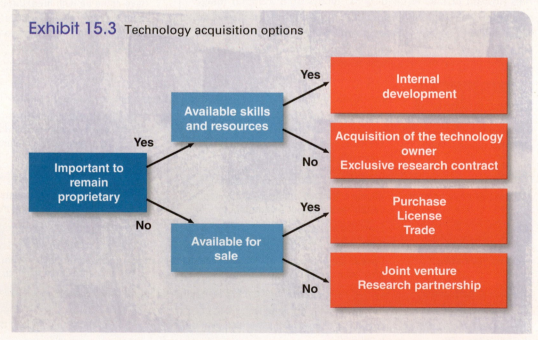

Exhibit 15.3 Technology acquisition options

and perhaps taking essential technical expertise with them. Similarly, as with any large investment, managers carefully assess whether the financial benefits of the acquisition will justify the purchase price.

LO4 Evaluate the elements of an innovative organization

4 | ORGANIZING FOR INNOVATION

Successful innovation is a lot more than a great idea. A study by the Boston Consulting Group found that lack of good ideas is hardly ever the obstacle to profitable innovation. More often, ideas fail to generate financial returns because the organization isn't set up to innovate. The culture is risk averse, projects get bogged down, efforts aren't coordinated, and management can't figure out where to direct the company's money.[36]

In Chapter 7 we introduced the concept of *learning organizations*—companies that excel at solving problems, seeking and finding new approaches, and sharing new knowledge with all members of an organization. Learning organizations are particularly well positioned to carry out the two basic kinds of innovation:[37]

1. *Exploiting* existing capabilities, such as improving production speed or product quality.

2. *Exploring* new knowledge—that is, seeking to develop new goods or services.

Both innovation processes are necessary. Innovative learning organizations use their existing strengths to improve their operations—and their bottom lines. They also unleash people's creative energies and capabilities to develop new products and processes that will ensure their long-term competitiveness. In this section we discuss some ways that managers organize for innovation.

4.1 | Who Is Responsible for New Technology Innovations?

In organizations, technology was traditionally the responsibility of vice presidents for research and development, who oversaw corporate and divisional R&D laboratories. But companies today usually have the position of *chief information officer (CIO)* or *chief technology officer (CTO).* The CIO is a corporate-level senior executive with broad responsibilities: coordinating the technological efforts of the business units, representing technology in the top management team, identifying ways that technology can support the company's strategy, supervising new technology development, and assessing the technological implications of major strategic initiatives such as acquisitions, new ventures, and strategic alliances. CIOs also manage their organization's *information technology (IT)* group.[38]

Without the CIO's integrative role, an organization's departments could easily adopt different technology tools and standards, leading to much higher equipment and maintenance expense and difficulties in connecting the different parts of the organization. Their technical skills prepare them to supervise the organization's technology experts and help managers ensure that technology is aligned with the strategic goals of the organization.

Other people play critical roles in developing new technology. The *entrepreneur,* in an effort to exploit untried technologies, invents new products or finds new ways to produce old products. The entrepreneur opens up new possibilities that can change entire industries. For example, Steve Jobs started Apple Computer in his garage, helping to popularize the personal computer and years later the MP3 music player.

In organizations, managers and employees may play key roles in acquiring and developing new technologies:[39]

- The *technical innovator* develops the new technology or has the skills needed to install and operate the technology. This person possesses technical skills but may lack the managerial skills needed to advance the idea and secure acceptance within the organization.

- The *product champion*—often at the risk of his or her position and reputation—promotes the idea throughout the organization, searching for support and acceptance. The champion can be a high-level manager but often is not. If the champion lacks the power and financial resources to make the required changes independently, she or he must convince people in authority to support the innovation. In other words, product champions must get sponsorship.

- Sponsorship comes from the *executive champion,* who has the status, authority, and financial resources to support the project and protect the product champion. This person's support and protection enable the new technology by making available the resources needed to develop the innovation and promoting the change.

4.2 | To Innovate, Unleash Creativity

Merck, 3M, Hewlett-Packard, and Rubbermaid have long histories of producing many successful new technologies and products. What sets these and other continuous innovators apart is an organizational culture that encourages innovation.[40]

Consider the 3M legend about inventor Francis G. Okie. In the early 1920s, Okie dreamed up the idea of using sandpaper instead of razor blades for shaving. The aim was to reduce the risk of nicks and avoid sharp instruments. The idea failed, but rather than punishing Okie for the failure, 3M encouraged him to champion other ideas, which included 3M's first blockbuster success: waterproof sandpaper. A culture that permits failure is crucial for fostering the creative thinking and risk taking required for innovation.

Traditional Thinking

Innovative ideas should come from employees of specialized departments like R&D labs.

The Best Managers Today

Seek creative ideas from many sources, including employees from anywhere in the organization, customers, suppliers, and even competitors.

As strange as it may seem, *celebrating* failure can be vital to the innovation process.[41] Failure is the essence of learning, growing, and succeeding. In innovative companies, many people are trying many new ideas. A majority of the ideas fail, but the few big hits that emerge can make a company an innovative star. Grey Advertising, winner of Ad Age's 2014 Agency of the Year award, believes in encouraging failure even if on an epic scale. Grey instituted a "Heroic Failure Award," which is given to an employee whose advertising idea or approach ended in an epic fail. The award is a large trophy that remains in the possession of the winner until the next failure.[42] This type of attitude from a manager can foster creative thinking throughout the ranks.

Thus, although 3M has been admired for its culture of innovation, it became inefficient, with unpredictable profits and an unimpressive stock price. Recently that's been changing as new product launches and international sales have revitalized 3M's profits.[45]

To balance innovation with other business goals, companies often establish special temporary project structures that are isolated from the rest of the organization and allowed to operate under different rules. These units go by many names, including "skunkworks," "greenhouses," and "reserves."

To foster a culture that values innovation, software maker Intuit set up a program called Innovation Lab. Adopting a policy that Google made famous, the company allows employees

> *"Failure is the best way to clear the fog to see a path to success."*
>
> —Diego Rodriguez and Ryan Jacoby of *IDEO, an innovative design firm*[43]

To foster innovation, 3M uses a simple set of rules:[44]

- Set goals for innovation.
- Commit to research and development.
- Inspire intrapreneurship.
- Facilitate, don't obstruct.
- Focus on the customer.
- Tolerate failure.

These rules can be—and are—copied by other companies. But 3M has an advantage in that it has followed these rules since its inception and ingrained them in its culture.

4.3 | Don't Let Bureaucracy Squelch Innovation

Bureaucracy is an enemy of innovation. Its main purpose is maintaining orderliness and efficiency, not pushing the creative envelope. Developing radically different technologies requires a fluid and flexible (organic) structure that does not restrict thought and action. However, such a structure can be chaotic and disruptive.

to spend 10 percent of their time on unstructured activities aimed at generating and developing new ideas. They can choose an idea they feel passionate about or can devote the time to learning about new technologies. Intuit also sponsors "idea jams"—days set aside for employees with an idea to assemble a team to develop the idea. Idea jams are one-day events that take place every three months. Employees also have access to workgroup software called Brainstorm, which helps them share ideas and recruit team members to work on the ideas during the idea jams and their unstructured time. Review groups and mentors ensure that ideas are practical and successful. Intuit provides cash awards for winning ideas, but the excitement of Innovation Lab and idea jams is what really motivates Intuit employees to contribute to innovations such as the mobile version of QuickBooks Online.[46]

4.4 | Development Projects Can Drive Innovation

A powerful tool for managing technology and innovations is the **development project**.[47] A development project is a focused organizational effort to create a new product or process via technological advances. For example, when MTV launched MTV World, whose channels are aimed at various Asian American markets, the company used development projects embedded in a culture that values innovation. Nusrat Durrani, senior vice president and general manager of MTV World, was among a group of employees drawn from various parts of the company. The development team members brought together a wide variety of backgrounds and experiences to create a successful plan for MTV World.[48]

Development projects typically feature a special cross-functional team that works together on an overall concept or idea. Like most cross-functional teams, its success depends on how well individuals work together to pursue a common vision. These teams interact with suppliers and customers, making their task more complex. Because of their urgency and strategic importance, most development projects are conducted under intense time and budget pressures.

Development projects have multiple benefits. Not only do they create new products and processes, but they also may cultivate skills and knowledge useful for future endeavors. Thus the capabilities derived from a development project often can be turned into a source of competitive advantage. When Ford created a development project to design an air-conditioning compressor to outperform its Japanese rival, executives also discovered they had laid the foundation for new processes that Ford could use in future projects. Their new capability in integrated design and manufacturing helped Ford reduce the costs and lead times for other product developments. Thus *organizational learning* became equally important as a measure of the project's success.

For development projects to achieve their fullest benefit, they should build on core capabilities, have a guiding vision about what must be accomplished and why, have a committed team, instill a philosophy of continuous improvement, and coordinate efforts across all units.

4.5 | Job Design and Human Resources Make Innovation Possible

Adopting a new technology may require changes in the design of jobs. Often tasks are redefined to fit people to the demands of the technology. But this may fail to maximize total productivity because it ignores the human part of the equation. Social relationships and human aspects of the task may suffer, lowering overall productivity.

The sociotechnical systems approach to work redesign specifically addresses this problem. As mentioned in Chapter 2, this approach redesigns tasks in a way that jointly optimizes the social and technical efficiency of work. Beginning with studies on the introduction of new coal-mining technologies in 1949, the sociotechnical systems approach to work design focused on small, self-regulating work groups.[49] Later it was found that such work arrangements operated effectively only in an environment where bureaucracy was limited.

development project a focused organizational effort to create a new product or process via technological advances

Today's trends in bureaucracy bashing, lean and flat organizations, work teams, and workforce empowerment are logical extensions of the sociotechnical philosophy of work design. At the same time, the technologies of the information age—in which people at all organizational levels have access to vast amounts of information—make these leaner and less bureaucratic organizations possible.

Managers face choices in how to apply a new technology. Technology can be used to limit the tasks and responsibilities of workers and "de-skill" the workforce, turning workers into servants of the technology. Or managers can select and train workers to master the technology, using it to achieve great accomplishments and improve the quality of their lives. Technology, when managed effectively, can empower workers as it improves the organization's competitiveness.

As managers decide how to design jobs and manage employees, they need to consider how human resource systems can complement the introduction of new technology. For example, advanced manufacturing technology usually requires people with high levels of skill, a commitment to continuous learning, and ability to work in teams. Organizations can help this technology succeed by using pay systems that attract and reward people with the necessary qualities.[50] Examples include group incentives and skill-based pay. If a company's pay system is not aligned with the new technologies, it may not reward behavior that makes the changes work. Even worse, existing reward systems may reinforce counterproductive behaviors.

Taken as a whole, these ideas provide guidelines for managing the strategic and organizational issues associated with technology and innovation. To adapt to a dynamic marketplace, organizations may need to reshape themselves. Managing change and organizational learning are central elements of what it takes to become a world-class organization.

LO5 Discuss what it takes to be world-class

5 | BECOMING WORLD-CLASS

Managers today want, or *should* want, their organizations to become world-class.[51] Being *world-class* requires applying the best and latest knowledge and ideas and having the ability to operate at the highest standards of any place anywhere.[52] Becoming world-class is more than merely improving. It means becoming one of the very best in the world at what you do. To some people, world-class excellence seems a lofty, impossible, unnecessary goal. But this goal is essential to success in today's intensely competitive business world.

World-class companies create high-value products and earn superior profits over the long run. They demolish the obsolete methods, systems, and cultures of the past that impede progress and apply more effective and competitive organizational strategies, structures, processes, and management of human resources. The result is an organization that can compete successfully on a global basis.[53]

5.1 | Build Organizations for Sustainable, Long-Term Greatness

Two Stanford professors, James Collins and Jerry Porras, studied 18 corporations that had achieved and maintained greatness for half a century or more.[54] The companies included Sony, American Express, Motorola, Marriott, Johnson & Johnson, Disney, 3M, Hewlett-Packard, Citicorp, and Walmart. Over the years, these companies have been widely admired as premier institutions in their industries and have made a real impact. Although every company experiences downturns, these companies have consistently prevailed across the decades. They turn in extraordinary performance over the long run rather than fleeting greatness. This study is reported in the book called *Built to Last*—which is what these great organizations are.

The researchers sought to identify the essential characteristics of enduringly great companies. These great companies have strong core values in which they believe deeply, and they express and live the values consistently. They are driven by

● *Project FROG (Flexible Response to Ongoing Growth) wants to revolutionize the construction industry. The San Francisco-based company designs and sells modular components that are easily assembled into energy efficient, green buildings for a variety of uses, including retail, healthcare, and overflow classrooms for K-12.*

goals—not just incremental improvements or business-as-usual goals, but stretch goals (recall Chapter 11). They change continuously, driving for progress via adaptability, experimentation, trial and error, entrepreneurial thinking, and fast action. And they do not focus on beating the competition; they focus primarily on beating themselves. They continually ask, "How can we improve ourselves to do better tomorrow than we did today?"

Underneath the action and the changes, the companies' core values and vision remain steadfast. For example, American Express's core values and mission include facilitating commerce and enabling its customers to do and achieve more in life. Walt Disney's values and mission include fanatical attention to detail, continuous progress through creativity, commitment to preserving Disney's "magic" image, delivery of happiness and "wholesome American values," and a lack of cynicism. Note that the values are not all the same. In fact, no set of common values consistently predicts success. Instead the critical factor is that the great companies *have* core values, *know* what they are and what they mean, and *live* by them—year after year.

5.2 | Replace the "Tyranny of the *Or*" with the "Genius of the *And*"

Many companies, and individuals, are plagued by what the authors of *Built to Last* call the "tyranny of the *or*"—the belief that things must be either A or B and cannot be both. The authors provide many common examples: beliefs that you must choose either change or stability, be conservative or bold, have control and consistency or creative freedom, do well in the short term or invest for the future, plan methodically or be opportunistic, create shareholder wealth or do good for the world, be pragmatic or idealistic.[55] However, beliefs that only one goal can be attained often are invalid.

An alternative to the "tyranny of the *or*" is the "genius of the *and*"—the ability to achieve multiple objectives at the same time.[56] It develops via the actions of many individuals throughout the organization. In earlier chapters we discussed the importance of delivering multiple competitive values to customers, performing all the management functions, reconciling hard-nosed business logic with ethics, and leading and empowering. Authors Collins and Porras have their own list:[57]

- Purpose beyond profit *and* pragmatic pursuit of profit.
- Relatively fixed core values *and* vigorous change and movement.
- Conservatism with the core values *and* bold business moves.
- Clear vision and direction *and* experimentation.
- Stretch goals *and* incremental progress.
- Control based on values *and* operational freedom.
- Long-term thinking and investment *and* demand for short-term results.
- Visionary, futuristic thinking *and* daily, nuts-and-bolts execution.

You have learned about all of these concepts throughout this course and should not lose sight of any—in your mind or in your actions. To achieve them requires the continuous and effective management of change.

5.3 | Organization Development Systematically Shapes Success

How do organizations apply the "genius of the *and*" and move in the other positive directions described throughout this book? Several general approaches create positive change, and many of them can be incorporated into a formal process of organization development.

Organization development (OD) is a systemwide application of behavioral science knowledge to develop, improve, and reinforce the strategies, structures, and processes that lead to organization effectiveness.[58] Throughout this course, you have acquired knowledge about behavioral science and the strategies, structures, and processes that help organizations become more effective. The "systemwide" component of the definition means OD is not a narrow improvement in technology or operations but a broader approach to changing organizations, units, or people. The "behavioral science" component means OD is not focused directly on economic, financial, or technical aspects of the organization—although they may benefit through changes in the behavior of the people in the organization. The other key part of the definition—to develop, improve, and reinforce—refers to the actual process of changing for the better and for the long term.

Two features of organization development are important.[59] First, it aims to increase organizational effectiveness—improving the organization's ability to respond to customers, stockholders, governments, employees, and other stakeholders, which results in better-quality products, higher financial returns, and high quality of work life. Second, OD has an important underlying value orientation: it supports human potential, development, and participation in addition to performance and competitive advantage.

As illustrated in Exhibit 15.4, many OD techniques fit under this philosophical umbrella. You have learned about these topics throughout your management course. You also will learn more about the process of creating change in the rest of this chapter.

5.4 | Certain Management Practices Make Organizations Great

A study of 200 management techniques employed by 160 companies over 10 years identified the specific management practices that lead to sustained, superior performance.[60] The authors boiled their findings down to four key factors:

1. *Strategy* that is focused on customers, continually fine-tuned based on marketplace changes, and clearly communicated to employees.

2. *Execution* by good people, given decision-making authority on the front lines, who are doing quality work and cutting costs.

> **organization development (OD)** the systemwide application of behavioral science knowledge to develop, improve, and reinforce the strategies, structures, and processes that lead to organizational effectiveness

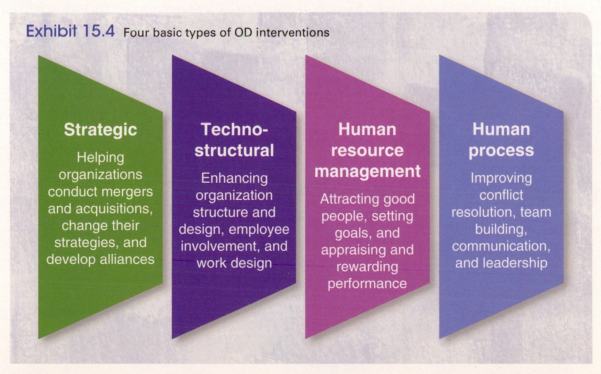

Exhibit 15.4 Four basic types of OD interventions

Strategic — Helping organizations conduct mergers and acquisitions, change their strategies, and develop alliances

Techno-structural — Enhancing organization structure and design, employee involvement, and work design

Human resource management — Attracting good people, setting goals, and appraising and rewarding performance

Human process — Improving conflict resolution, team building, communication, and leadership

Source: Adapted from T. Cummings and C. Worley, *Organization Development and Change,* 8th ed. (Mason, OH: Thomson/South-Western, 2005).

3. *Culture* that motivates, empowers people to innovate, rewards people appropriately (psychologically as well as economically), entails strong values, challenges people, and provides a satisfying work environment.

4. *Structure* that makes the organization easy to work in and easy to work with, characterized by cooperation and the exchange of information and knowledge throughout the organization.

You have been learning about these concepts throughout this course.

People are the key to successful change.[61] For an organization to be great, people have to care about its fate and know how they can contribute. But typically leadership lies with a few people at the top. Too few take on the burden of change; too few care deeply and make innovative contributions. People throughout the organization need to take a greater interest and a more active role in helping the business as a whole. They have to identify with the entire organization, not just with their unit and close colleagues.

<table>
<tr><td>LO6</td><td>Describe how to manage change effectively</td></tr>
</table>

6 | MANAGING CHANGE

Change happens, constantly and unpredictably. Any competitive advantage you may have depends on particular circumstances at a particular time, but circumstances change.[62] New competitors appear, new markets emerge, and the economic environment shifts. While the recent global recession has devastated countless organizations from companies to

state governments to nonprofit agencies, it has forced many managers to see innovation as a key to organizational survival. The business as usual mind-set has given way to a "change to survive" mentality. However, the challenge for organizations is not just to produce innovative new products but to balance a culture that is innovative and builds a sustainable business.[64] For individuals, the ability to cope with change is related to their job performance and the rewards they receive.[65]

The success of most change efforts requires *shared leadership;* people must be not just *supporters* of change but also *implementers.*[66] This shared responsibility for change is not unusual in start-ups and very small organizations, but it often is lost with growth and over time. In large, traditional corporations, it is rare. Organizations must rekindle individual creativity and responsibility, instituting true change in the behavior of people throughout the ranks. The essential task is to motivate people to keep changing in response to new business challenges.

6.1 | Motivate People to Change

People must be *motivated* to change. But often they resist changing. Some people resist change more than others, but managers tend to underestimate the amount of resistance they will encounter.[67]

People at all levels of their organizations, from entry-level workers to top executives, resist change. There are many examples where this resistance led to dire consequences for companies. Kodak, once the dominant player in photography and film, was slow to adapt to the explosion of digital photography. Similarly, Blockbuster relied for too long on bricks-and-mortar video rental outlets and underestimated the potential popularity of online video streaming that goes directly to people's homes.[68]

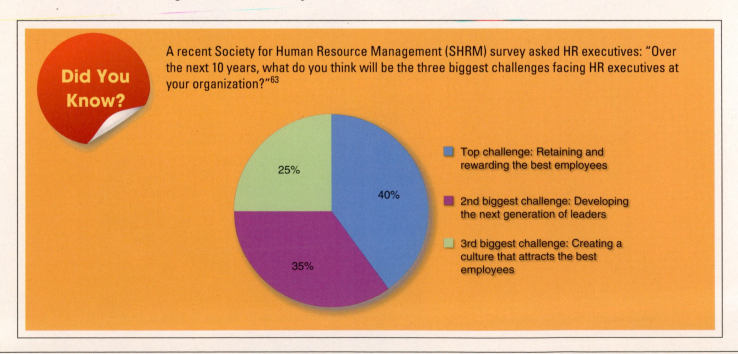

Did You Know?

A recent Society for Human Resource Management (SHRM) survey asked HR executives: "Over the next 10 years, what do you think will be the three biggest challenges facing HR executives at your organization?"[63]

- 40% / 35% / 25%

■ Top challenge: Retaining and rewarding the best employees

■ 2nd biggest challenge: Developing the next generation of leaders

■ 3rd biggest challenge: Creating a culture that attracts the best employees

At IBM many changes have been necessary to keep bureaucracy from stifling innovation, and all of them have been challenging. At one point executives learned that lower-level managers were getting bogged down because they had to invest too much time and effort in obtaining approval from higher-ups. Chair of the Board Sam Palmisano announced that he would give first-level managers authority to spend $5,000 without prior approval—a daring move considering that the authority applied to 30,000 managers. However, the managers felt uncomfortable with their new authority, and in the first year of the new program, they spent only $100,000 of the $150 million Palmisano had entrusted to them.[69] In other words, they were reluctant to change the way they worked, even though it could make their jobs easier.

To deal with such reactions and successfully implement positive change, managers must understand why people often resist change. Some reasons for resistance arise regardless of the actual content of the change:[70]

- *Inertia.* Usually people don't want to disturb the status quo. The old ways of doing things are comfortable and easy, so people don't want to try something new. For example, it is easier for some managers to provide performance feedback to employees once a year than on a real-time, frequent basis.

- *Timing.* People often resist change because of poor timing. If managers or employees are unusually busy or under stress, or if relations between management and workers are strained, the timing is wrong for introducing new proposals. Where possible, managers should introduce change when people are receptive.

- *Surprise.* If a change is sudden, unexpected, or extreme, resistance may be the initial—almost reflexive—reaction. Managers or others initiating a change often forget that others haven't given the matter much thought; the change leaders need to allow time for others to think about the change and prepare for it.

- *Peer pressure.* Sometimes work teams resist new ideas. If a group is highly cohesive and has anti-management norms, peer pressure will cause individuals to resist even reasonable changes. Of course peer pressure can be a positive force, too. Change leaders who invite—and listen to—ideas from team members may find that peer pressure becomes a driving force behind the change's success.

Other causes of resistance arise from the specific nature of a proposed change:[71]

- *Self-interest.* Most people will resist a change if they think it will cause them to lose something of value. What could people fear to lose? At worst their jobs if management is considering closing down a plant. A merger, reorganization, or technological change could create the same fear. Other possible fears include loss of the feeling of being competent in a familiar job, expectations that the job will become more difficult or time-consuming, uncertainty about whether enough training or other resources will be provided for succeeding at the change, and doubts about the organization's future success, given that management wasn't satisfied with the status quo.

- *Misunderstanding.* Even when management proposes a change that will benefit everyone, people may resist because they don't fully understand it. People may not see how the change fits with

● Not able to keep up with the competition of both Netflix and RedBox, Blockbuster filed for bankruptcy in September 2010. Ironically 10 years earlier they turned down a chance to purchase the still fledgling Netflix for $50 million.

the firm's strategy, or they simply may not see the change's advantage over current practices.[72] One company met resistance to the idea of introducing flexible working hours. A false rumor circulated among plant employees that people would have to work evenings, weekends, or whenever their supervisors wanted. The employees' union demanded that management drop the idea. The president, caught off guard by this unexpected resistance, complied with the union's demand.

- *Different assessments.* Employees receive different—and usually less—information than management receives. Such discrepancies cause people to develop different assessments of proposed changes. Some may be aware that the benefits outweigh the costs, while others may see only the costs. This is a common problem when management announces a change in work procedures and doesn't explain to employees why the change is needed. Management expects increased efficiency, but workers may see the change as another arbitrary, ill-informed management rule that simply causes headaches for them.

- *Management tactics.* Sometimes a change that succeeds elsewhere is undertaken in a new location, and problems may arise during the transfer.[73] Management may try to force the change and fail to address concerns in order to develop employee commitment. Or it may not provide enough resources, knowledge, or leadership to help the change succeed. Managers who overpromise what they—or the change—can deliver may discover that the next time they want to introduce a change, they have lost credibility, so employees resist.

It is important to recognize that employees' assessments can be more accurate than management's; employees may know a change won't work even if management doesn't. In

unfreezing realizing that current practices are inappropriate and that new behavior is necessary

performance gap the difference between actual performance and desired performance

moving Instituting the change

force-field analysis an approach to implementing Lewin's unfreezing/moving/

refreezing model by involving identifying the forces that prevent people from changing and those that will drive people toward change

this case, resistance to change benefits the organization. Thus, even though management typically considers resistance a challenge to overcome, it may actually represent an important signal that a proposed change requires further, more open-minded scrutiny.[74]

6.2 | A Three-Stage Model Suggests Ways to Manage Resistance

Motivating people to change often requires three basic stages, shown in Exhibit 15.5: unfreezing, moving to institute the change, and refreezing.[75]

Unfreezing During the **unfreezing** stage, management realizes that its current practices are no longer appropriate and the company must break out of (unfreeze) its present mold by doing things differently. People must come to recognize that some of the past ways of thinking, feeling, and doing things are obsolete.[76] A direct and sometimes effective way to do this is to communicate the negative consequences of the old ways by comparing the organization's performance with that of its competitors. Management can also share with employees data about costs, quality, and profits.[77] Sometimes employees just need to understand the rationale for changing.

When managers communicate a problem, they must take care not to arouse people's defensiveness. Managers tend to place employees on the defensive when they pin the blame for shortcomings directly and entirely on the workers[78] and when they

bombard employees with facts aimed at inducing fear. When a problem seems huge, people often decide it is hopeless and withdraw from facing it. In *Change or Die,* journalist Alan Deutschman uses that pattern of behavior to explain why heart attack victims often fail to follow diet and exercise plans, even though doctors tell them they will literally die if they don't take care of themselves.[79] Deutschman sees a similar pattern playing out in companies where executives rely on threats of layoffs and corporate bankruptcy to motivate employees to adopt new work practices. In these difficult situations, leaders more effectively unfreeze negative behavior with a message of hope and a commitment to collaborate with others so that they can effect change together.

An important contributor to unfreezing is the recognition of a performance gap, which can precipitate major change. A **performance gap** is the difference between actual performance and the performance that should or could exist.[80] A gap typically implies poor performance, as when sales, profits, stock price, or other financial indicators are down. This situation attracts management's attention, and management introduces changes to try to correct things.

Another very important form of performance gap occurs when performance is good but someone realizes it could be better. Thus the gap is between what is and what *could be*. This realization is where entrepreneurs seize opportunities and companies gain a competitive edge. In the realm of change management, employees are best motivated by situations that combine the sense of urgency that comes from identifying a problem with the sense of excitement that comes from identifying an opportunity. Also, employees care about more than market share and revenues; they want to know how making a change can help them have a positive impact on their work group, their customers, their company, their community, and themselves. For example, a financial services company struggled to persuade employees that a change would enhance the company's competitive position. Employees got on board only after the change leaders started talking about how the change would help employees reduce errors, avoid duplication of effort, make jobs more interesting, and fulfill the organization's mission to deliver affordable housing.[81]

Moving The next step, **moving** to institute the change, begins with establishing a vision of where the company is heading. You learned about vision in the leadership chapter. The vision can be realized through strategic, structural, cultural, and individual change.

A technique that helps to manage the change process, **force-field analysis,** involves identifying the specific forces that prevent people from changing and the specific forces that will drive people toward change.[82] In other words, managers

Exhibit 15.5 Motivating people to change

Unfreezing	**Moving**	**Refreezing**
Breaking from the old ways of doing things.	Instituting the change.	Reinforcing and supporting the new ways.
Example A company decides to switch to the cloud for data storage.	**Example** The IT department transfers data to the cloud.	**Example** Employees are trained on using the new storage system.

investigate forces acting in opposite directions at a particular time. Change leaders assess organizational strengths and select forces to add or remove in order to create change. Eliminating the restraining forces helps people unfreeze, and increasing the driving forces helps and motivates them to move forward.

Use of force-field analysis demonstrates that often a range of forces are pressing on an organization and its people at a particular time. This analysis can increase people's optimism that it is possible to strategize and plan for change. Kurt Lewin, who developed force-field analysis, theorized that although driving forces may be more easily affected, shifting them may increase opposition (tension and/or conflict) within the organization and add restraining forces. So to create change, it may be more effective to remove restraining forces.

Refreezing Finally, **refreezing** means strengthening the new behaviors that support the change. The changes must be diffused and stabilized throughout the company. Refreezing involves implementing control systems that support the change, applying corrective action when necessary, and reinforcing behaviors and performance that support the agenda. Management should consistently support and reward all evidence of movement in the right direction.[83]

In today's organizations, refreezing may not be the best third step if it creates new behaviors that are as rigid as the old ones. The ideal new culture is one of continuous change. Refreezing is appropriate when it permanently installs behaviors that maintain essential core values, such as a focus on important business results and the values maintained by companies that are "built to last." But refreezing should not create new rigidities that might become dysfunctional as the business environment continues to change.[84] The refrozen behaviors should promote continued adaptability, flexibility, experimentation, assessment of results, and continuous improvement. In other words, lock in key values, capabilities, and strategic mission, but not necessarily specific management practices and procedures.

6.3 | Specific Approaches Can Encourage Cooperation

You can try to command people to change, but the key to long-term success is to use other approaches.[85] Developing true support is better than "driving" a program forward.[86] How, specifically, can managers motivate people to change?

Most managers underestimate the variety of ways they can influence people during a period of change.[87] Several effective approaches to managing resistance and enlisting cooperation are available, as summarized in Exhibit 15.6.

- *Education and communication*—Management should educate people about upcoming changes before they occur. It should communicate the *nature* of the change and its *logic*. This process can include reports, e-mails, one-on-one discussions, and presentations to groups. Effective communication includes feedback and listening. Whenever Round Table Pizza introduces a new project or process, managers set up meetings with their employees to discuss the change and bring up any concerns they have.[88] That provides an environment in which management can explain the rationale for the change—and perhaps improve it.

Exhibit 15.6 Methods for managing resistance to change

Approach	Situations Where Commonly Used	Advantages	Drawbacks
Education and communication	Where there is a lack of information or inaccurate information and analysis.	Once persuaded, people will often help with the implementation of the change.	Can be very time-consuming if lots of people are involved.
Participation and involvement	Where the initiators do not have all the information they need to design the change, and where others have considerable power to resist.	People who participate will be committed to implementing change, and any relevant information they have will be integrated into the change plan.	Can be very time-consuming if participators design an inappropriate change.
Facilitation and support	Where people are resisting because of adjustment problems.	No other approach works as well with adjustment problems.	Can be time-consuming and expensive, and still fail.
Negotiation and rewards	Where someone or some group will clearly lose out in a change, and where that group has considerable power to resist.	Sometimes it is a relatively easy way to avoid major resistance.	Can be too expensive in many cases if it alerts others to negotiate for compliance.
Manipulation and cooptation	Where other tactics will not work, or are too expensive.	It can be a relatively quick and inexpensive solution to resistance problems.	Can lead to future problems if people feel manipulated.
Explicit and implicit coercion	Where speed is essential, and the change initiators possess considerable power.	It is speedy and can overcome any kind of resistance.	Can be risky if it leaves people angry at the initiators.

Source: Reprinted by permission of the *Harvard Business Review*. An exhibit from "Choosing Strategies for Change" by J. P. Kotter and L. A. Schlesinger (March–April 1979). Copyright © 1979 by the Harvard Business School Publishing Corporation; all rights reserved.

How "Big Data" Contributes to Sustainable Farming

By the middle of the 21st century, the world's population is expected to reach 9 billion people, a 30 percent increase over today's population. In order to stave off hunger in the future, global food production will have to increase by 70 percent over current levels, and more efficient methods for producing crops, dairy products, and meat will need to be developed. Waste, which can occur at any point during the agricultural value chain, claims about half, or 2 billion tons, of the food produced in the world. Animal health is also a concern. Brian Walsh, CEO of Vital Herd, observes: "Forty percent of dairy cows get ill each year." The U.S. Department of Agriculture estimates total economic loss from animal sickness and death is more than $5 billion, with worldwide losses reaching 12 times this amount. With agriculture consuming 70 percent of the world's freshwater supply, methods need to be developed to conserve this precious resource.

Big Data and technology can help address these challenges and support the trend toward sustainable farming. Big Data refers to the analysis of massive amounts of data companies collect from customers, social media sites, blogs, and other sources in order to improve products, reduce costs, and attract and retain customers. In an agricultural context, the use of real-time data gathering and analysis about such variables as weather, moisture levels in the soil, air quality, wind speed and direction, temperature, humidity, and crop maturity can lead to the development and use of "precision agriculture" technologies. According to Ulisses Mello, who heads a team of scientists from IBM Research-Brazil, such technologies "can maximize food production, minimize environmental impact and reduce costs."

Here are some examples of how companies and growers are using Big Data to be more efficient and productive with regard to farming:

- Climate Corporation (founded by two ex-Google executives) operates a cloud-based farming information system that combines millions of weather measurements and soil observations to predict temperature, rain, and wind forecasts for 24-hour and 7-day periods. Accurate weather forecasts help farmers know when to irrigate their crops, apply fertilizer, and so forth.

- Agribusiness Monsanto markets a "prescription" to farmers that provides detailed suggestions regarding which seeds to plant based on the farm's soil type, disease history, and pests. The company is also testing a technology that uses computer logarithms to analyze data to identify which fields are likely to support corn seeds planted closer together. Both of these innovations can lead to greater yields in food production.

- DuPont Pioneer is launching Encirca, a data platform to help farmers mine their data to improve crop production and use seed, nitrogen, and water more efficiently. The platform can also provide

---

- *Participation and involvement*—The people who are affected by a change should be involved in its design and implementation. For major, organizationwide change, participation in the process can extend from the top to the very bottom of the organization.[89] People who are involved in decisions understand them more fully and are more committed to them. Participation also allows for education and communication. Kate Peck, an administrative assistant with ZingTrain, engaged others when she saw a need for change in the haphazard way office supplies were stored. Peck decided they should be arranged according to which items were used most often. Peck sent an e-mail to the staff explaining what she planned to change and why, inviting feedback, and asking who else might need to be informed. One employee suggested that Peck create a diagram for the cabinets to help employees learn what each one contains. When Peck implemented the changes, her coworkers agreed she had improved the situation, and they found whatever they needed more quickly.[90]

- *Facilitation and support*—Management should make the change as easy as possible for employees and support their efforts. Facilitation involves providing the training and other resources people need to carry out the change and perform their jobs under the new circumstances. This step often includes decentralizing authority and empowering people. For many employees, change can be stressful.[91] Managers can help employees cope with their stress by listening patiently to problems, being understanding if performance drops temporarily or the change is not perfected immediately, and generally being on the employees' side and showing consideration during a difficult period.

● The Bar Lamar Tap Room in Whole Foods Market® in Austin, TX. Whole Foods hopes that the tap rooms become community-gathering spots.

growers with field-specific weather forecasts. Given that 90 percent of all crop losses are attributable to weather, this forecast feature can help growers make better decisions.

Other data-sensing products are available to help prevent spoilage and waste during the transportation stages of the agricultural logistics chain. Some estimates suggest that between 10 and 15 percent of chilled food spoils during transport, costing approximately $25 billion. Tech Mahindra, an IT service company based in Bangalore, India, provides a system called Farm-to-Fork, "which aims to monitor containers centrally, sending alerts out whenever the conditions in a container deviate from the ideal ones." Sensors, located in each container, monitor and transmit temperature and other information via mobile data networks. Problems are fixed either automatically or when the ship arrives at port.

Big Data is changing the way food is grown in the world. Using real-time data and cloud computing technologies, agribusinesses and growers are tapping more precise information to inform their decision making, ultimately resulting in more efficient crop yields and reduced waste during all stages of the value chain.

SOURCES: "Precision Agriculture: Using Predictive Weather Analytics to Feed Future Generations," company website, www.research.ibm.com; A. Connelly, "Farming's 'Green Revolution' Uses New Technologies," Kentucky.com, June 9, 2014, www.kentucky.com; C. Doering, "Big Data Means Big Profits, Risks for Farmers," *USA Today* (online), May 11, 2014, www.usatoday.com; "American Farmers Confront 'Big Data' Revolution," Fox News (online), March 29, 2014, www.foxnews.com; P. Rubens, "Can Big Data Crunching Help Feed the World?" BBC (online), www.bbc.com, accessed on June 18, 2014; S. Freidman, "Farmers Embrace Big Data to Reduce Pollution," GreenBiz.com, October 4, 2013, www.greenbiz.com; and S. Rosenbush and M. Totty, "How Big Data Is Changing the Whole Equation for Business," *The Wall Street Journal* (online), March 10, 2013, www.wsj.com.

- *Negotiation and rewards*—When necessary, management can offer concrete incentives for cooperating with the change. Perhaps job enrichment is acceptable only with a higher wage rate, or a work rule change is resisted until management agrees to a concession on some other rule (say, about taking breaks). Rewards such as bonuses, wages and salaries, recognition, job assignments, and perks can be examined and perhaps restructured to reinforce the direction of the change.[92] Change is further facilitated by demonstrating that the change itself benefits people.[93] John Mackey, founder of Whole

- *Manipulation and cooptation*—Sometimes managers use more subtle, covert tactics to implement change. One form of manipulation is cooptation, which involves giving a resisting individual a desirable role in the change process. The leader of a resisting group often is co-opted. For example, management might invite a union leader to be a member of an executive committee or ask a key member of an outside organization to join the company's board of directors. As a person becomes involved in the change, he or she may become less resistant to the actions of the co-opting group or organization.

> ## "People don't resist change. They resist being changed!"
> —Peter Senge

Foods, encourages continuous innovation by decentralizing decision making to managers and employees at the store level. One recent idea that germinated from this approach was the "tap room—an in-store beer and wine bar that lets customers nibble on food while sampling local wine and beers by the glass." So far, tap rooms are showing a lot of promise and have been rolled out to approximately 100 stores.[94]

- *Explicit and implicit coercion*—Some managers apply punishment or the threat of punishment to those who resist change. With this approach, managers use force to make people comply with their wishes. A manager might insist that subordinates cooperate with the change and threaten them with job loss, denial of a promotion, or an unattractive work assignment. Sometimes you just have to lay down the law.

Each approach to managing resistance has advantages and drawbacks and, like many of the other situational management approaches described in this book, each is useful in certain situations. Exhibit 15.6 summarizes advantages, drawbacks, and appropriate circumstances for these approaches to managing resistance to change. Effective change managers are familiar with the various approaches and apply them according to the situation.

:::::::::::::::::

In the 1990s, when advertisers were wary of using the Internet, Yahoo! management hired someone it could trust as head of its sales force: Wenda Harris Millard. Millard was a 50-year-old veteran of the magazine industry. She taught her young and brash salespeople to work respectfully with their older ad agency clients, and she showed those clients that online ads could benefit them. Agency creative types loved TV ads but thought of Internet advertising as mainly boring pop-ups with a box saying "Click here." Yahoo! under Millard brought them together at educational summits and established the Yahoo Big Idea Chair award for the most creative online advertising. Seeing what innovative companies were doing, ad agency people became able to envision online advertising as a medium that allowed plenty of room for creativity—and Yahoo! began selling ads to big companies, reaching millions of web visitors every day.[96]

:::::::::::::::::

Throughout the process, change leaders need to build in stability. Recall from the companies that were "built to last" that they share essential core characteristics and keep focused on them. In the midst of change, turmoil, and uncertainty, people need anchors onto which they can latch.[97] Making an organization's values and mission constant and visible can often serve this stabilizing function. In addition, strategic principles can be important anchors during change.[98] Managers also should maintain the visibility of key people, continue key assignments and projects, and make announcements about which organizational components will *not* change. Such anchors will reduce anxiety and help overcome resistance.

6.4 | Managers Have to Harmonize Multiple Changes

There are no single-shot methods of changing organizations successfully. Single shots rarely hit a challenging target. Usually many issues need simultaneous attention, and any single small change will be absorbed by the prevailing culture and disappear. *Total organization change* involves introducing and sustaining multiple policies, practices, and procedures across multiple units and levels.[99] Such change affects the thinking and behavior of everyone in the organization, can enhance the organization's culture and success, and can be sustained over time.

A survey at a Harvard Business School conference found that the average attendee's company had five major change efforts going on at once.[100] The most common change programs were practices you have studied in this course: continuous improvement, quality programs, time-based competition, and creation of a learning organization, a team-based organization, a network organization, core capabilities, and strategic alliances. The problem is, these efforts usually are simultaneous but not coordinated. As a result, changes get muddled; people lose focus.[101] The people involved suffer from confusion, frustration, low morale, and low motivation.

Because companies introduce new changes constantly, people complain about their companies' "flavor of the month" approach to change. Employees often see change efforts as just the company's jumping on the latest bandwagon or fad. The more these fads come and go, the more cynical people become, and the harder it is to get them committed to making the change a success.[102]

One solution is to identify which change efforts are really worthwhile. Here are some specific questions to ask before embarking on a change project:[103]

- What is the evidence that the approach really can produce positive results?

- Is the approach relevant to your company's strategies and priorities?

- What are the costs and potential benefits?

- Does it really help people add value through their work?

- Does it help the company focus better on customers and what they value?

- Can you go through the decision-making process described in Chapter 5, understand what you're facing, and feel that you are taking the right approach?

Management also needs to integrate the various efforts into a coherent picture that people can see, understand, and get behind.[104] You do this by understanding each change program and its goals, identifying similarities and differences of the programs, and dropping programs that don't meet priority goals or demonstrate clear results. Most important, you do it by communicating to everyone concerned the common themes of the various programs: their common rationales, objectives, and methods. You show them how the parts fit the strategic big picture and how the changes will improve things for the company and its people. You must communicate these benefits thoroughly, honestly, and frequently.[105]

6.5 | Managers Must Lead Change

Successful change requires managers to actively lead it. The essential activities of leading change are summarized in Exhibit 15.7.

> "Change is a verb."
>
> — *Mimi Silbert, founder,* Delancey Street Foundation[95]

The companies that lead change most effectively *establish a sense of urgency*.[106] To do so, managers must examine current realities and pressures in the marketplace and the competitive arena, identify crises and opportunities, and be frank and honest about them. In this sense, urgency is a reality-based sense of determination, not just fear-based busyness. The immediacy of the need for change is important partly because so many large companies grow complacent. Complacency can arise from various sources:[107]

- Absence of a major and visible crisis.

- Too many visible resources.

- Organizational structures that focus employees on narrow functional goals.

- Internal measurement systems that focus on the wrong performance indexes.

- Lack of sufficient performance feedback from external sources.

- Low-candor, low-confrontation culture ("kill the messenger of bad news").

- Human nature, with its capacity for denial, especially if people are already busy or stressed.

- Too much happy talk from senior management.

To stop complacency and create urgency, a manager can talk candidly about the organization's weaknesses relative to competitors, making a point to back up statements with data. Other tactics include setting stretch goals, putting employees in direct contact with unhappy customers and shareholders, distributing worrisome information to all employees instead of merely engaging in management "happy talk," eliminating excessive perks, and highlighting the future opportunities that the organization so far has failed to pursue.

Ultimately, urgency is driven by compelling business reasons for change. Survival, competition, and winning in the marketplace are compelling; they provide a sense of direction and energy around change. Change becomes a business necessity.[108]

To *create a guiding coalition* means putting together a group with enough power to lead the change. Change efforts fail for lack of a powerful coalition.[109] Major organization change requires leadership from top management, working as a team. But over time, the support must expand outward and downward throughout the organization. Middle managers and supervisors are essential. Groups at all levels can hold change efforts together, communicate information about the changes, and provide the means for enacting new behaviors.[110]

Developing a vision and strategy, as discussed in earlier chapters, directs the change effort. This process involves determining the idealized, expected state of affairs after the change is implemented. Because confusion is common during major organizational change, this image of the future state must be as clear as possible and must be communicated to everyone.[111] This image, or vision, can clarify expectations, dispel rumors, and mobilize energies. Communication about it should include how the transition will occur, why the change is being implemented, and how people will be affected.

Communicating the change vision requires using every possible channel and opportunity to reinforce the vision and required new behaviors. It is said that aspiring change leaders undercommunicate the vision by a factor of 10, 100, or even 1,000, seriously undermining the chances of success.[112] In contrast, when Virginia Blood Services (VBS) launched an effort to improve its organizational culture in order to lower employee turnover and accident rates, communication was central to the change effort. The communication program at VBS includes employee meetings every three months, an employee newsletter distributed every two weeks, and messages from the president. In each site's break room, the organization replaced

Exhibit 15.7 Leading change

1. **Establishing a sense of urgency**

2. **Creating the guiding coalition**

3. **Developing a vision and strategy**

4. **Communicating the change vision**

5. **Empowering broad-based action**

6. **Generating short-term wins**

7. **Consolidating gains and producing more change**

8. **Anchoring new approaches in the culture**

bulletin boards—where no one bothered to read the memos and government posters—with wall-mounted display cases featuring colorful posters and motivational, sometimes humorous messages about safety, quality, and teamwork. The items in the displays are changed every week to maintain interest. The communication program, which supports practical measures like safety training and new scheduling procedures, has helped to build support for the new organizational culture, motivating employees to stay safe and on the job.[113]

Empowering broad-based action means removing obstacles to success, including systems and structures that constrain rather than facilitate. Encourage risk taking and experimentation, and empower people by providing information, knowledge, authority, and rewards.

means anticipating and preparing for an uncertain future. It implies being a leader and *creating* the future you want.

7.1 | Think About the Future

If you think only about the present or wallow in the uncertainties of the future, your future is just a roll of the dice. It is far better to exercise foresight, set an agenda for the future, and pursue it with everything you've got. So contemplate and envision the future.

BusinessWeek predicts that dramatic change will continue: "The global economy could be on the cusp of an age of innovation equal to that of the past 75 years. All the right factors are in place: Science is advancing rapidly, more countries are willing to devote resources to research and development and

> ## "If your actions inspire others to dream more, learn more, do more and become more, you are a leader."
>
> —John Quincy Adams

Generate short-term wins. Don't wait for the ultimate grand realization of the vision. You need results. As small victories accumulate, you make the transition from an isolated initiative to an integral part of the business.[114] Plan for and create small victories that show everyone that progress is being made. Recognize and reward the people who made the wins possible, doing it as visibly as you can so that people notice and the positive message permeates the organization.

Consolidate gains and produce more change. With the well-earned credibility of previous successes, keep changing things in ways that support the vision. Hire, promote, and develop people who will further the vision. Reinvigorate the organization and your change efforts with new projects and change agents.

Finally, *anchor new approaches in the culture.*[115] Highlight positive results, communicate the connections between the new behaviors and the improved results, and keep developing new change agents and leaders. Continually increase the number of people joining you in taking responsibility for change.[116]

LO7 List tactics for creating a successful future

7 | SHAPING THE FUTURE

Most change is reactive. A better way to change is to be proactive. *Reactive change* means responding to pressure after a problem has arisen. It implies being a follower. *Proactive change*

education, and corporate managers, too, are convinced of the importance of embracing change."[117]

Shoshana Zuboff and Jim Maxim, authors of *The Support Economy,* claim that the era of industrial capitalism is over, traditional business enterprises are disappearing, vast new markets exist, new kinds of companies are ready to be created, and the new business model hasn't yet emerged.[118] But new business concepts are always interesting to contemplate.

::::::::::::::::::

Uber is a fast-growing car service located across 70 cities in 38 countries. Its mission is to open up more possibilities for riders and more business for drivers. Urbanites and visitors (e.g., businesspeople in town for a day or two) alike use an app on their smartphones to view fares and easily connect with Uber's drivers, who promptly arrive in one of five styles of black company vehicles (fares vary based on which model a customer chooses) to shuttle them to and from their destination—whether that be a business meeting, wedding reception, or weekend getaway. All drivers undergo a three-step (county, federal, and state) background check and ongoing reviews of their motor vehicle records. Also, Uber collects and posts anonymous customer feedback and driver profiles on the company's website.

Uber has set a lofty goal for itself. Currently valued at $3.5 billion, the company wants to be for logistics, delivery, and travel what Amazon is for retail; namely, the ubiquitous first choice. To that end, the company recently changed its tagline from "Everyone's private driver" to the much broader "Where lifestyle meets logistics." Looking to the future, Uber wants to radically alter the way the world moves and seems to be progressing toward this lofty goal as it rapidly expands its presence in more than 70 cities and 38 countries.[119]

::::::::::::::::::

7.2 | Create the Future

As companies prepare to compete in an uncertain future, they can try different strategic postures. **Adapters** take the current industry structure and its future evolution as givens and choose where to compete. Most companies take this posture by conducting standard strategic analysis and choosing how to compete within given environments. In contrast, **shapers** try to change the structure of their industries, creating a future competitive landscape of their own design.[120]

Researchers studying corporate performance over a 10-year period found that 17 companies in the *Fortune* 1000 increased total shareholder return by 35 percent or more per year.[121] How? They completely reinvented industries. Harley-Davidson turned around by selling not just motorcycles, but nostalgia. Amgen broke the rules of the biotech industry by focusing not on what customers wanted, but on great science. Starbucks took a commodity and began selling it in trendy stores. CarMax and other companies reinvented the auto industry.

You need to create advantages. Rather than maintaining your position in the current competitive arena, the challenge is to create new competitive arenas, transform your industry, and imagine a future that others don't see. Creating advantage is better than playing catch-up. At best, working to catch up buys time; it cannot get you ahead of the pack or buy world-class excellence.[122] To create new markets or transform industries—these are perhaps the ultimate forms of proactive change.[123]

Exhibit 15.8 illustrates the vast opportunity to create new markets. Articulated needs are those that customers acknowledge and try to satisfy. Unarticulated needs are those that customers have not yet experienced. Served customers are those to whom your company is now selling, and unserved customers are untapped markets.

While business as usual concentrates on the lower left quadrant, the leaders who recreate the game are constantly trying to create new opportunities in the other three quadrants.[124] For example, you can pursue the upper left quadrant by imagining how you can satisfy a larger proportion of your customers' total needs. Caterpillar appreciates that its customers want more than its heavy equipment; they also need excellent service so they can use that equipment to meet their own customers' needs. As a result, if a customer anywhere in the world needs a Caterpillar part, the company will ship it there within 24 hours. And Lands' End expanded both its product offerings and number of served customers by offering customization—the ability to specify exact measurements when ordering jeans and other selected items of clothing.[125]

Other companies hope to meet unarticulated needs by developing and exploiting cutting-edge technology. The nanometer—one-billionth of a meter, 1/100,000 the width of a human hair, or about the size of 10 hydrogen atoms in a row—is the building block of a new industry, nanotechnology. Why is the nanometer so important?[126] Because matter of this size often behaves differently—transmitting light or electricity, or becoming harder than diamonds, or becoming powerful chemical catalysts. Early applications include coatings and light-emitting dots for more efficient semiconductors and nanoparticles that clean up polluted water by forming chemical bonds with contaminants.[127] Applications under development include 50-nanometer capsules containing vitamins and other nutrients that can be added to beverages without changing their taste or that can be activated by microwaves.[128]

As you've read, technological change is a central part of the changing landscape, and competition often arises between newcomers and established companies. All things considered, which should you and your firm do?

- Preserve old advantages or create new advantages?
- Lock in old markets or create new markets?
- Take the path of greatest familiarity or the path of greatest opportunity?

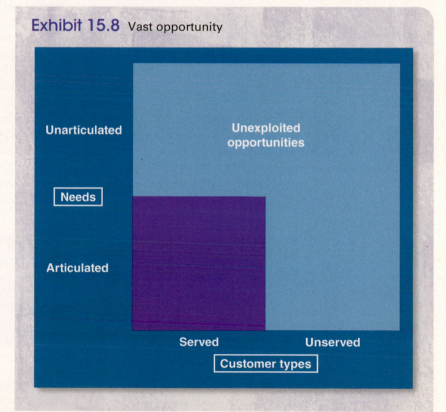

Exhibit 15.8 Vast opportunity

Unarticulated

Unexploited opportunities

Needs

Articulated

Served   Unserved

Customer types

Source: Reprinted by permission of *Harvard Business Review.* From *Competing for the Future,* by Gary Hamel and C. K. Prahalad, Harvard School Press. Copyright © 1994 by the Harvard Business School Publishing Corporation; all rights reserved.

Take Charge of your Career

The "New" job security: Continually add value at work

While working for an established company a few decades ago, as long as you were reliable and did your job well, chances are good that you would have had job security. These days, it's a different story. Due to fluctuating economic conditions, intense global competition, changing technology, and changing philosophies toward employment, most companies no longer provide their employees with job security. Layoffs and outsourcing have become commonplace. Sounds bleak, doesn't it? Well, companies still need good employees who continually go the extra mile and look for ways to add value at work. Here are some methods that can help you add value and, in so doing, increase your job security:

- Go beyond your job description: volunteer for projects, identify problems, and initiate solutions.
- Seek out others and share ideas and advice.
- Offer your opinions and respect those of others.
- Take an inventory of your skills every few months.
- Learn something new every week.
- Discover new ways to make a contribution.
- Engage in active thought and deliberate action.
- Take risks based on what you know and believe.
- Recognize, research, and pursue opportunity.
- Differentiate yourself.

A common theme here and throughout this entire book is that you are responsible for creating your own "luck" and career successes. Now more than ever, you need to rely on your self-motivation, interpersonal skills, strong and trusted network of colleagues and mentors, and hard work to be successful. Take charge of your career!

Source: List compiled from C. Hakim, *We Are All Self-Employed* (San Francisco: Barrett-Koehler, 1994).

- Be only a benchmarker or a pathbreaker?
- Place priority on short-term financial returns or on making a real, long-term impact?
- Do only what seems doable or what is difficult and worthwhile?
- Change what is or create what isn't?
- Look to the past or live for the future?[129]

7.3 | Shape Your Own Future

If you are an organizational leader and your organization operates in traditional ways, your key goal should be to create a revolution, reengineering your company before it becomes a dinosaur of the modern era.[130] What should be the goals of the revolution? You've been learning about them throughout this course.

for mediocrity; don't assume that "good" is necessarily good enough—for yourself or for your employer. Think about how to exceed, not just meet, expectations; how to break free of apparent constraints that are unimportant, arbitrary, or imagined; and how to seize opportunities instead of letting them pass by.[132]

You can continually add value to your employer—and also to yourself—as you upgrade your skills, ability to contribute, security with your current employer, and ability to find alternative employment if necessary. The most successful individuals take charge of their own development the way an entrepreneur takes charge of a business.[133]

More advice from the leading authors on career management:[134] Consciously and actively manage your own career. Develop marketable skills, and keep developing more. Make career choices based on personal growth, development, and

---

> "There is nothing wrong with change, if it is in the right direction."
>
> —*Winston Churchill*

But maybe you are not going to lead a revolution. Maybe you just want a successful career and a good life. You still must deal with an economic environment that is increasingly competitive and fast-moving.[131] To create the future you want for yourself, you have to set high personal standards. Don't settle

learning opportunities. Look for positions that stretch you, and for bosses who develop their protégés. Seek environments that provide training and the opportunity to experiment and innovate. And know yourself—assess your strengths and weaknesses, your true interests, and ethical standards. If you are

not already thinking in these terms and taking commensurate action, you should start now.

Additionally, become indispensable to your organization. Be happy and enthusiastic in your job and committed to doing great work, but don't be blindly loyal to one company. Be prepared to leave, if necessary. View your job as an opportunity to prove what you can do and increase what you can do, not as a comfortable niche for the long term.[135] Go out on your own if it meets your skills and temperament.

You need to maintain your options. More and more, contemporary careers include leaving a large organization and going entrepreneurial, becoming self-employed in the "postcorporate world."[136] In such a career, independent individuals make their own choices, responding quickly to demands and opportunities. Developing start-up ventures, consulting, accepting temporary employment, doing project work for one organization and then another, working in professional partnerships, being a constant deal maker—these can be the elements of a successful career. Ideally, this self-employed model balances working with life at home and with family because people have more control over their work activities and schedules.

This go-it-alone approach can sound ideal, but it also has downsides. Independence can be frightening, the future unpredictable. It can isolate "road warriors" who are always on the go, working from their cars and airports, and interfere with social and family life.[137] Effective self-management is needed to keep career and family obligations in perspective and in control. Coping with uncertainty and change is also easier if you develop resilience. To become more resilient, practice thinking of the world as complex but full of opportunities; expect change, but see it as interesting and potentially rewarding, even if changing is difficult. Also, keep a sense of purpose, set priorities for your time, be flexible when facing uncertainty or a need to change, and take an active role in the face of change, rather than waiting for change to happen to you.[138]

7.4 | Learn and Lead the Way to Your Goals

Continuous learning is a vital route to renewable competitive advantage.[139] People in your organization—and you, personally—should constantly explore, discover, and take action, repeating this cycle as you progress in your career:[140]

1. *Explore* your current reality, being as honest and open as possible about what is happening. Identify your problems and areas of opportunity. Gather data. Check with customers, suppliers, and other key stakeholders. Reveal hidden issues, and look for root causes. Rethink the issue based on what you have learned.

2. *Discover* a deeper understanding of the current reality. The issues and choices should become clearer. Identify possible solutions or ways to take advantage of opportunities. Plan what to do, anticipating problems that may arise.

3. *Act* by testing solutions, implementing your plan, and evaluating the results. Recognize problems; that will prepare you for repeating the cycle. And be sure to celebrate your successes, too.

With this approach, you can learn what is effective and what is not and then adjust and improve accordingly. Continuous learning helps your company achieve lower cost, higher quality, better service, superior innovation, and greater speed—and helps you develop on a personal level.

Commit to lifelong learning. Be willing to seek new challenges, and reflect honestly on successes and failures.[141] Lifelong learning requires occasional risk taking. Move outside your comfort zone, honestly assess the reasons behind your successes and failures, ask for and listen to other people's information and opinions, and stay open to new ideas.

A leader—and this could include you—should be able to create an environment in which "others are willing to learn and change so their organizations can adapt and innovate [and] inspire diverse others to embark on a collective journey of continual learning and leading."[142] *Learning leaders* exchange knowledge freely; commit to their own continuous learning as well as to others'; commit to examining their own behaviors and defensiveness that may inhibit their learning; devote time to their colleagues, suspending their own beliefs while they listen thoughtfully; and develop a broad perspective, recognizing that organizations are an integrated system of relationships.[143]

Honored as one of the best management books of the year in Europe, *Leaning into the Future* gets its title from a combination of the words *leading* and *learning*.[144] The two perspectives, which may appear very different, are powerful and synergistic when pursued in complementary ways. A successful future derives from adapting to the world *and* shaping the future, being responsive to others' perspectives *and* being clear about what you want to change, encouraging others to change *while* recognizing what you need to change about yourself, understanding current realities *and* passionately pursuing your vision, learning *and* leading.

This is another example of an important concept from the beginning of the chapter. For yourself, as well as for your organization, live the genius of the *and*.

Study Checklist

- Did you tear out the perforated student review card at the back of the text to revisit learning objectives and key terms and definitions?

Connect® Management is available for M Management. Additional resources include:

- Interactive Applications:
  - Drag & Drop: Innovation at MTV
  - Drag & Drop: Which Products Create New Markets?
  - Sequencing/Timeline: Leading the Charge for Change
  - Video Case: Should the Space Shuttle Continue?

- LearnSmart—Multiple choice questions help you determine what you already know, are not sure about, or need to practice based on your score. And with SmartBook, you can read the relevant section in the eBook as well as practice and recharge what you've learned.

- Chapter Video: Johnson & Johnson eUniversity

- Young Manager Speaks Out: Keisha Heard, Financial Aid Program Coordinator

Notes

Chapter 1

1. See www.starbucks.com; "Moments of Connection—A Look Back at Starbucks 2013 Milestones," December 23, 2013, http://news.starbucks.com.

2. H. Schultz, "How Starbucks Got Its Mojo Back," *Newsweek* 157, no. 12 (March 21, 2011), pp. 1–7.

3. S. Bertoni, "How Do You Win the Mobile Wallet War? Be Like Starbucks," *Forbes,* February 21, 2014, www.forbes.com.

4. M. Hamblen, "Starbucks Hits $1B in Mobile Payment Revenues in 2013, Analysis Says," *Computerworld,* February 5, 2014, www.computerworld.com.

5. V. Wong, "Starbucks $2.7 Billion Decision to 'Control Its Own Destiny,'" *Businessweek,* November 11–17, 2013, www.businessweek.com.

6. P. Sellers, "MPW Global Edition Car Talk (And More!) With GM's New Chief," *Fortune,* February 24, 2014, www.fortune.com.

7. "Shift Change," *Bloomberg Businessweek,* December 16–22, 2013, pp. 50–55.

8. G. Vasilash, "Introducing the 2014 Cadillac ELR, *Automotive Design & Production,* January 2014, pp. 34–40.

9. Sellers, "MPW Global Edition.

10. D. Lepak, K. Smith, and M. S. Taylor, "Value Creation and Value Capture: A Multilevel Perspective," *Academy of Management Review* 23 (2007), pp. 180–94.

11. K. Palmer, "The Secrets to Zappos' Success," *U.S. News and World Report,* August 10, 2010, www.usnews.com.

12. See www.zappos.com/c/code-of-conduct.

13. C. Palmeri, "Zappos Retails Its Culture," *Bloomberg Businessweek,* December 30, 2009, www.businessweek.com.

14. Ibid.

15. See www.xerox.com.

16. D. Mattioli, "Boss Talk/Ursula Burns: Xerox Chief Looks beyond Photocopiers toward Services," *The Wall Street Journal,* June 13, 2011, p. B9.

17. N. Kolakowski, "Ursula Burns: Focused on the Core," *eWeek* 29, no. 3 (February 13, 2012), pp. 10–13.

18. D. Mattioli, "Boss Talk/Ursula Burns."

19. A. Gonzalez, "New Gulf-Spill Reports Points to Missed Signs," *The Wall Street Journal,* August 18, 2011, http://online.wsj.com.

20. J. Ball, "Lessons from the Gulf: William Reilly on Why the Oil Spill Happened, and Where the Industry Goes from Here," *The Wall Street Journal,* March 7, 2011, p. R5.

21. Ibid.

22. See www.Teslamotors.com; A. Ohnsman, "Tesla Rises After Model S Sales in 2013 Exceed Forecast," *Bloomberg News,* January 15, 2014, www.bloomberg.com; D. R. Baker, "Electric Car Startup Downshifts for Rough Road," *San Francisco Chronicle,* December 28, 2008, www.sfgate.com; R. Buckman, "Tesla Cuts 20% of Workforce," *Forbes* (online), December 24, 2008, http://www.forbes.com; C. C. Miller, "Musk Unplugged: Tesla CEO Discusses Car Troubles," *The New York Times,* October 24, 2008, http://bits.blogs.nytimes.com; M. LaMonica, "Tesla Motors Replaces CEO, Plans Layoff," *CNET News,* October 15, 2008, http://news.cnet.com; and M. V. Copeland, "Tesla's Wild Ride," *Fortune,* July 11, 2008, http://money.cnn.com.

23. T. Cappellen and M. Janssens, "Characteristics of International Work: Narratives of the Global Manager," *Thunderbird International Business Review* 52, no. 4 (July/August 2010), pp. 337–48.

24. E. Ofek and L. Wathieu, "Are You Ignoring Trends That Could Shake Up Your Business? *Harvard Business Review* 88, no. 7 (July/August 2010), pp. 124–31; and M. Branscombe, "Tools That Will Discreetly Tap a Shoulder to Offer Help," *Financial Times,* October 8, 2008, p. 4.

25. Randstad USA, "Focusing on Employees Can Pay Future Dividends," news release, October 20, 2008, http://us.randstad.com/about/mediaRoom.html.

26. See www.kathleenedmond.com; and B. Penzer, "Profile: Kathleen Edmond Chief Ethics Officer, Best Buy," *AFP Exchange* 26, no. 6 (July/August 2006), pp. 34–38.

27. "Business: In Praise of David Brent, Middle Managers," *The Economist* 400, no. 8748 (August 27, 2011), p. 56.

28. Q. N. Huy, "In Praise of Middle Managers," *Harvard Business Review,* September 2001, pp. 72–79.

29. L. A. Hill, "New Manager Development for the 21st Century," *Academy of Management Executive,* August 2004, pp. 121–26.

30. F. Hassan, "The Frontline Advantage," *Harvard Business Review* 89, no. 5 (May 2011), pp. 106–14.

31. J. R. Hackman and R. Wageman, "A Theory of Team Coaching," *Academy of Management Review* 30, no. 2 (April 2005), pp. 269–87.

32. S. E. Humphrey, J. R. Hollenbeck, C. J. Meyer, and D. R. Ilgen, "Trait Configurations in Self-Managed Teams: A Conceptual Examination of the Use of Seeding for Maximizing and Minimizing Trait Variance in Teams," *Journal of Applied Psychology,* 92, no. 3 (2007), pp. 885–92.

33. Hackman and Wageman, "A Theory of Team Coaching."

34. F. P. Morgeson, D. S. DeRue, and E. P. Karam, "Leadership in Teams: A Functional Approach to Understanding Leadership Structures and Processes," *Journal of Management* 36, no. 1 (January 2010), pp. 5–34.

35. B. Joiner and S. Josephs, "Leadership Agility," *Leadership Excellence* 24, no. 6 (June 2007), p. 16; and L. R. Sayles, "Doing Things Right: A New Imperative for Middle Managers," *Organizational Dynamics,* Spring 1993, pp. 5–14.

36. H. Mintzberg, *The Nature of Managerial Work* (New York: Harper & Row, 1973).

37. R. L. Katz, "Skills of an Effective Administrator," *Harvard Business Review* 52 (September–October, 1974), pp. 90–102.

38. Hill, "New Manager Development for the 21st Century."

39. S. J. Hysong, "The Role of Technical Skill in Perceptions of Managerial Performance," *Journal of Management Development* 27, no. 3 (2008), pp. 275–90.

40. J. Samuelson, "The New Rigor: Beyond the Right Answer," *Academy of Management Learning & Education* 5, no. 3 (September 2006), pp. 356–65.

41. H. Mintzberg, "The Manager's Job: Folklore and Fact," *Harvard Business Review* 53 (July–August 1975), pp. 49–61.

42. F. Di Meglio, "Columbia Gets Personal," *Bloomberg Businessweek Online,* October 18, 2006, www.businessweek.com.

43. "To Get That Job, Bring on the Charm," *InformationWeek,* August 23, 2006, www.informationweek.com.

44. Di Meglio, "Columbia Gets Personal."

45. D. Coleman, R. Boyatzis, and A. McKee, *Primal Leadership: Realizing the Power of Emotional Intelligence* (Boston: Harvard Business School Press, 2002).

46. J. Christoffersen, "Global Ambition: GE Looks Outside U.S. for Growth," *Cincinnati Post,* January 18, 2007, http://news .cincinnati.com.

47. Ibid.

48. S. John, "We Are Involved in Revitalization of Cities: Wim Elfrink, Cisco's Chief Globalization Officer," *The Economic Times* (Online), June 16, 2011, http://economictimes.indiatimes.com.

49. M. Jayashankar, "Cisco's Second Place," *Forbes India,* May 4, 2012, www.forbesindia.com.

50. N. Lakshman, "Cisco's Grand India Ambitions," *Bloomberg Businessweek,* January 3, 2007, www.businessweek.com.

51. John, "We Are Involved in Revitalization of Cities."

52. R. Soderbery, "How Many Things Are Currently Connected to the 'Internet of Things,'" *Forbes,* January 7, 2013, www.forbes.com.

53. G. T. Huang, "Over the Border," *New Scientist,* January 20, 2007, www.newscientist.com.

54. See Johnson & Johnson's 2010 Annual Report at www.jnl.com; and W. Armbruster, "Outsourcing a Key Element in Dell's Strategy," *Journal of Commerce* (April 26, 2010), www.joc.com.

55. K. Hille, "Functionality Remains Top Priority for Chinese Group," *Financial Times* (September 3, 2010), p. 15.

56. S. Shellenbarger, "Time-Zoned: Working around the Round-the-Clock Workday," *The Wall Street Journal,* February 15, 2007, http://online.wsj.com.

57. S. Clifford, "How to Get Ahead in China," *Inc.,* May 2008, pp. 96–104.

58. T. Bisoux, "Corporate Counter Culture," *BizEd,* November/ December 2004, pp. 16–20, quoted on p. 19.

59. G. Huber, *The Necessary Nature of Future Firms* (Thousand Oaks, CA: Sage, 2004).

60. J. Greene and C. Edwards, "Desktops Are So Twentieth Century," *BusinessWeek,* December 8, 2006, www.businessweek.com.

61. F. Cairncross, *The Company of the Future* (Cambridge, MA: Harvard Business School Press, 2002).

62. M. Hamblen, "Update: More Than 1B Smartphones Were Shipped in 2013," *Computerworld,* January 28, 2014, www .computerworld.com.

63. S. DeCarlo, "Billionaire Scorecard: Zuckerberg Up, Bezos Down," *Forbes,* February 12, 2012, www.forbes.com.

64. P. Adler and S. Kwon, "Social Capital: Prospects for a New Concept," *Academy of Management Review* 27 (2002), pp. 17–40.

65. G.Avalos, "Shackled to Technology," *Contra Costa Times* (Walnut Creek, CA), January 14, 2007, www.contracostatimes.com.

66. J. Chatzky, "Confessions of an E-Mail Addict," *Money,* March 2007, www.money.cnn.com.

67. Ibid.

68. R. Austin, "Managing Knowledge Workers," *Science,* July 21, 2006, http://sciencecareers.sciencemag.org.

69. D. Raths, "Hospital IT Departments Prescribe Portals for Physicians," *KMWorld,* February 2007, www.kmworld.com.

70. M. Hansen and B. von Oetinger, "Introducing T-Shaped Managers: Knowledge Management's Next Generation," *Harvard Business Review,* March 2001, pp. 106–16; and A. Birchall, "T-Shaped People: The New Employees of the Digital Age," *Management Today,* August 29, 2012, www.mtmag.com.

71. J. Teresko, "Toyota's Real Secret," *Industry Week,* February 2007, www.industryweek.com.

72. B. Morrissey, "AT&T, IBM Fuel Web Presence with Outsourced Content," *Brandweek* 50, no. 35 (October 5, 2009), p. 8.

73. Ibid.

74. L. Willcocks and R. Plant, "Pathways to E-Business Leadership: Getting from Bricks to Clicks," *Sloan Management Review,* Spring 2001, pp. 50–59.

75. S. Vranica, "P&G Boosts Social-Networking Efforts," *The Wall Street Journal,* January 8, 2007, http://online.wsj.com.

76. M. Tossi, "Labor Force Projections to 2020: A More Slowly Growing Workforce," *Monthly Labor Review,* Bureau of Labor Statistics (2012), pp. 43–64.

77. S. Golnaz and T. Hoa, "Managing Your Diverse Workforce through Improved Communication," *Journal of Management Development* 21, no. 3–4 (2002), pp. 227–38.

78. See Deloitte's 2011 Diversity & Inclusion Annual Report at www.deloitte.com.

79. R. Newman, "10 Great Companies That Lost Their Edge," *U.S. News & World Reports,* August 19, 2010, http://money .usnews.com.

80. R. Newman, "10 Innovative Companies You Should Copy," *U.S. News & World Reports,* August 19, 2010, http://money .usnews.com.

81. Ibid.

82. The World's Most Innovative Companies in 2013, *Forbes,* www .forbes.com, accessed on March 12, 2014.

83. "Board Sheds Light on Dark Dining," *The Wall Street Journal,* August 18, 2010, www.wsj.com; A. Sage, "Love Is Blind in Pitch Black Restaurant," *Reuters,* December 8, 2006, http://news .yahoo.com; Opaque–Dining in the Dark, "What Is Opaque?" www.opaque-events.com; and Opaque–Dining in the Dark, "First Ever 'Dining in the Dark' Experience Coming to Los Angeles July 23," www.opaque-events.com.

84. R. I. Sutton, "The Weird Rules of Creativity," *Harvard Business Review,* September 2001, pp. 94–103.

85. L. Landro, "Hospitals Take Consumers' Advice," *The Wall Street Journal*, February 7, 2007, http://online.wsj.com.

86. O. Port, "The Kings of Quality," *BusinessWeek*, August 30, 2004, p. 20.

87. K. Ward, "Attracting Opposites," *Lexington Herald-Leader*, December 12, 2006; and L. M. Pierce, "How to Do It 'My Way,'" *Food & Drug Packaging*, January 2007.

88. D. A. Garvin, "Manufacturing Strategic Planning," *California Management Review*, Summer 1993, pp. 85–106.

89. Reported in "Hospital Ratings May Not Be True Quality Measure," *Washington Post*, December 13, 2006, www.washingtonpost.com.

90. U.S. Bureau of Labor Statistics, *Occupational Outlook Quarterly* 53, no. 4 (Winter 2009–10), www.bls.gov/opub/2009/winter/art5fullp1.htm.

91. See www.bls.gov/emp/ep_table_203.htm.

92. M. Fetterman, "Best Buy Gets in Touch with Its Feminine Side," *USA Today*, December 20, 2006, www.usatoday.com.

93. A. Lashinsky, "Chaos By Design," *Fortune*, October 2, 2006, http://money.cnn.com.

94. Teresko, "Toyota's Real Secret."

95. Ibid.

96. R. Ford, "Improving Efficiency by Maximizing Technology," *Retailing Today*, October/November 2008, p. 7.

97. K. Maher, "Wal-Mart Seeks New Flexibility in Worker Shifts," *The Wall Street Journal*, January 3, 2007, http://online.wsj.com.

98. J. C. Anselmo and W. Garvey, "Sporting Chance," Aviation *Week & Space Technology* 173, no. 5 (February 7, 2011), p. 41.

99. V. Fuhrmans, "A Novel Plan Helps Hospital Wean Itself Off Pricey Tests," *The Wall Street Journal*, January 12, 2007, http://online.wsj.com.

100. See www.columbiahm.com.

101. M. Yager, "Outsource to Gain Human Resources Expertise," *Hotel and Motel Management* 223, no. 7 (April 21, 2008), p. 14.

Chapter 2

1. "Sumerian Dictionary to Decipher Ancient Texts," National Geographic Society, July 23, 2002, http://news.nationalgeographic.com; and C. S. George, *The History of Management Thought* (Englewood Cliffs, NJ: Prentice-Hall, 1968).

2. George, *The History of Management Thought.*

3. P. M. Deane, *The First Industrial Revolution* (Cambridge: Cambridge University Press, 1980).

4. A. D. Chandler, *Scale and Scope: The Dynamic of Capitalism* (Cambridge, MA: Belknap Press of Harvard University Press, 1990).

5. Ibid.

6. See www.ge.com/company/history/edison.html and http://inventors.about.com/library/inventors/bledison.htm.

7. George, *The History of Management Thought.*

8. J. Baughman, *The History of American Management* (Englewood Cliffs, NJ: Prentice-Hall, 1969), Chap.1.

9. George, *The History of Management Thought,* chaps. 5–7; and F. Taylor, *The Principles of Scientific Management* (New York: Harper & Row, 1911).

10. J. Case, "A Company of Businesspeople," *Inc.,* April 1993, pp. 70–93.

11. D. A. Wren, *The History of Management Thought,* 5th ed. (Upper Saddle River, NJ: Wiley, 2005), chap. 8.

12. Ibid.

13. J. Stoller, "The World According to Gantt," *CMA Management* 84, no. 5 (August/September 2010), pp. 33–34.

14. Wren, *The History of Management Thought,* chap. 8.

15. Ibid.

16. Ibid.

17. Ibid.

18. See www.sdsc.edu/sciencewomen/gilbreth.html.

19. J. Schlosser and E. Florian, "Fortune 500 Amazing Facts!" *Fortune,* April 5, 2004, pp. 152–59.

20. M. Weber, *The Theory of Social and Economic Organizations,* trans. T. Parsons and A. Henderson (New York: Free Press, 1947).

21. H. Fayol, *General and Industrial Management,* trans. C. Storrs (Marshfield, MA: Pitman Publishing, 1949).

22. George, *The History of Management Thought,* chap. 9; and J. Massie, "Management Theory," in *Handbook of Organizations,* ed. J. March (Chicago: Rand McNally, 1965), pp. 387–422.

23. C. Barnard, *The Functions of the Executive* (Cambridge, MA: Harvard University Press, 1938).

24. George, *The History of Management Thought;* Massie, "Management Theory."

25. E. Mayo, *The Human Problems of Industrial Civilization* (New York: Macmillan, 1933); and F. Roethlisberger and W. Dickson, *Management and the Worker* (Cambridge, MA: Harvard University Press, 1939).

26. A. Maslow, "A Theory of Human Motivation," *Psychological Review* 50 (July 1943), pp. 370–96.

27. A. Carey, "The Hawthorne Studies: A Radical Criticism," *American Sociological Review* 32, no. 3 (1967), pp. 403–16.

28. G. Liu, R. Shah, and R. Schroeder, "Linking Work Design to Mass Customization: A Sociotechnical Systems Perspective," *Decision Sciences* 37, no. 4 (2006).

29. E. L. Trist, "The Sociotechnical Perspective: The Evolution of Sociotechnical Systems as a Conceptual Framework and as Action Research Program," in *Perspectives on Organization Design and Behavior,* eds. A Van de Ven and W. F. Joyce (New York: John Wiley, 1981); and E. L. Trist and K. W. Bamworth, "Some Social and Psychological Consequences of the Longwall Methods of Coal-Getting," *Human Relations* 4 (1951), pp. 6–24.

30. See www.tavinstitute.org/about/our_history.

31. R. R. Rehder, "Japanese Transplants a New Model for Detroit," *Business Horizons* 31, no. 1, pp. 52–62.

32. Ibid.

33. George, *The History of Management Thought,* chap. 11.

34. D. Fogerty and P. Bell, "Should You Outsource Analytics?" *MIT Management Review* 55, no. 2 (2014), 41–45.

35. See www.sas.com/en_us/insights/big-data/what-is-big-data.html.

36. D. McGregor, *The Human Side of Enterprise* (New York: McGraw-Hill, 1960).

37. C. Argyris, *Personality and Organization* (New York: Harper and Row, 1957).

38. R. Likert, *The Human Organization* (New York: McGraw-Hill, 1967).

39. L. von Bertalanffy, "The History and Status of General Systems Theory," Academy of Management Journal 15 (1972), pp. 407–26; and D. Katz and R. Kahn, *The Social Psychology of Organizations,* 2nd ed. (New York: John Wiley & Sons, 1978).

40. J. Thompson, *Organizations in Action* (New York: McGraw-Hill 1967); J. Galbraith, Organization Design (Reading, MA: Addison-Wesley, 1977); and D. Miller and P. Friesen, *Organizations: A Quantum View* (Englewood Cliffs, NJ: Prentice-Hall, 1984).

41. J. Collins, *Good to Great* (New York: Harper Collins, 2001).

42. Ibid.

43. J. Krames, "Too Early to Consign Jack Welch to History," *Financial Times,* June 26, 2001, p. 12.

44. D. Organ, "Talent versus Experience," *Business Horizons* 45, no. 1 (January/February 2002), p. 1.

45. Krames, "Too Early to Consign Jack Welch to History."

46. See www.hbs.edu.

47. See www.garyhamel.com.

48. Wren, *The History of Management Thought,* chap. 19.

49. Ibid.

50. "The Man Who Invented Management," *Bloomberg Businessweek,* November 28, 2005, www.businessweek.com.

51. See http://mitsloan.mit.edu.

52. See www.hbs.edu.

53. Ibid.

54. See www.stephencovey.com.

55. See www.tompeters.com.

56. J. Pellegrino and M. Hilton, "Education for Life and Work: Developing Transferable Knowledge and Skills in the 21st Century," National Academies Press (2012), http://www.nap.edu; A. Schleicher, "OECD Skills Strategy: The Pathway of Choice," Organisation for Economic Cooperation and Development (2012), pp. 43–44.

Chapter 3

1. Company website and "Brewing a Better World—Transformation," *Corporate Social Responsibility Report,* Fiscal Year 2009, www.greenmountaincoffee.com; R. A. Munarriz, "Warm Up to Green Mountain Coffee Roasters," *The Motley Fool,* January 29, 2009, www.fool.com; "Green Mountain Coffee Roasters, Inc. Releases 'Brewing a Better World' Corporate Social Responsibility Report," *CSR Wire,* January 12, 2009, www.csrwire.com; K. Marquardt, "Brewing Profits, a Cup at a Time," *U.S. News & World Report,* November 17/24, 2008, pp. 55–58; P. Rolfes, "Green Mountain Coffee Roasters: Grounds for Growth," Smallcapinvestor.com, July 23, 2008, www.smallcapinvestor.com; A. Ackerman, "Retail Coffee Favored in Volatile Economy," *Consumer Goods Technology,* July 22, 2008, www.consumer-goods.com; and "Green Mountain Coffee Roasters Founder Bob Stiller Will Step Down," *Automatic Merchandiser,* July 8, 2008, www.amonline.com.

2. "Sales of Single-Serve Coffee Have Tripled Since 2011," *Money,* November 21, 2013, www.money.msn.com; L. Pollock, "Starbucks Coffee to Be Offered in Keurig K-Cup Packs in November," *The Wall Street Journal* (online), August 30, 2011, http://online.wsj.com; and B. Jopson, "Coffee Chains See Future in Single Cups," *Financial Times,* April 8, 2011, p. 17.

3. See www.keuriggreenmountain.com, press release "Keurig Green Mountain and Peet's Coffee & Tea Announce Partnership," March 14, 2014; B. Rubin, "Starbucks to End Exclusivity Deal with Keuring," *The Wall Street Journal* (online), March 14, 2014, www.wsj.com; and J. Jacobsen, "Partnerships Holding Strong in Beverage Market," *Beverage Industry* (May 2013), p. 6.

4. S. Ante, "Government Extends HealthCare.gov Contract for Verizon's Terremark," *The Wall Street Journal* (online), March 7, 2014, www.wsj.com.

5. See www.justice.gov/criminal/fraud/fcpa/.

6. J. Weil, "JPMorgan Wrestles with Sons, Daughters and Corruption," *Bloomberg View,* January 22, 2014, www.bloombergview.com; and J. Palzallolo, "Nepotism: Is It a Crime?" *The Wall Street Journal* (online), August 19, 2013.

7. Weil, "JP Morgan Wrestles with Sons, Daughters and Corruption."

8. "SEC Charges Hewlett-Packard with FCPA Violations," Press release, April 9, 2014, U.S. Securities and Exchange Commission, http://www.sec.gov.

9. M. Trottman and K. Maher, "Plan to Ease Way for Unions: Labor Board Proposes Speeding Up Organizing Votes," *The Wall Street Journal* (online), http://online.wsj.com.

10. K. Evans, "Economy Dives as Goods Pile Up," *The Wall Street Journal,* January 31, 2009, http://online.wsj.com.

11. J. Fuller and M. C. Jensen, "Just Say No to Wall Street," *Journal of Applied Corporate Finance* 14, no. 4 (Winter 2002), pp. 41–46.

12. B. Lefebvre, "Shale-Oil Boom Spurs Refining Binge," *The Wall Street Journal,* March 2, 2014, http://online.wsj.com.

13. J. Mouawad, "Oil Innovations Pump New Life into Old Wells," *The New York Times,* March 5, 2007, www.nytimes.com.

14. Y. Ellis, B. Daniels, and A. Jauregui, "The Effects of Multitasking on the Grade Performance of Business Students," *Research in Higher Education Journal,* no. 8 (August 2010), pp. 1–10.

15. B. Leubsdorf, "Recession's Lingering Scars Could Include Lower Labor Force Participation," *The Wall Street Journal* blog (online), April 16, 2014, http://blogs.wsj.com.

16. "Employment Projections: 2012–2022 Summary," *Economic News Release,* December 19, 2013, Bureau of Labor Statistics, www.bls.gov.

17. M. M. Hamilton, "Age 65 and Not Ready or Able to Go," *Washington Post,* January 14, 2007, www.washingtonpost.com.

18. Table A-4, "Employment Status of the Civilian Population 25 Years and Over by Educational Attainment," Bureau of Labor Statistics, www.bls.gov/news.release/empsit.t04.htm.

19. See, for example, B. Arnoldy, "Too Prosperous, Massachusetts Is Losing Its Labor Force," *Christian Science Monitor,* January 9, 2007, www.csmonitor.com.

20. T. R. McLean and E. P. Richards, "Teleradiology: A Case Study of the Economic and Legal Considerations in International Trade in Telemedicine," *Health Affairs* 25, no. 5 (September/October 2006), pp. 1378–86.

21. M. Toossi, "Labor Force Projections to 2020: A More Slowly Growing Workforce," *Monthly Labor Review,* January 2012, pp. 43–64.

22. M. J. Kim, "Is Supreme Court Right to OK Arizona's 'Business Death Penalty,'" *U.S. News & World Reports,* May 26, 2011, http://www.usnews.com.

23. Bureau of Labor Statistics, "Women in the Labor Force, 1970–2009," January 5, 2011, www.bls.gov/opud/ted/2011/ted_20110105.htm.

24. "2011 Working Mother 100 Best Companies Survey," *Working Mother Magazine,* www.workingmother.com.

25. Ibid.

26. A. Kloos, N. Fritz, S. Kostyk, G. Young, and D. Kegelmeyer, "Video Game Play (Dance Dance Revolution) as a Potential Exercise Therapy in Huntington's Disease: A Controlled Clinical Trial," *Clinic Rehabilitation,* no. 11 (November 2013), pp. 972–82.

27. "Gaming Goes for the Burn," *PR Week,* February 19, 2007.

28. A. Das, "More Wii Warriors Are Playing Hurt," *The New York Times,* April 21, 2009, www.nytimes.com; and M. Zitz, "Nintendo Winning Game System Red Hot," *Free Lance–Star* (Fredericksburg, VA), February 23, 2007.

29. M. E. Porter, "How Competitive Forces Shape Strategy," *Harvard Business Review* 57, no. 2 (March/April 1979), pp. 137–45.

30. "Apple Reinvents the Phone with iPhone," Press Release January 1, 2007, www.apple.com.

31. "50 Greatest Business Rivalries of all Time," *Money* (online), March 21, 2013, http://money.cnn.com.

32. Ibid.

33. D. J. Collis and C. A. Montgomery, *Corporate Strategy: Resources and Scope of the Firm* (New York: McGraw-Hill/Irwin, 1997).

34. I. Lunden, "Gartner: 102B App Store Downloads Globally in 2013, $26 B in Sales, 17% from In-App Purchases," *TechCrunch* (online), September 19, 2013, www.techcrunch.com.

35. "Top Global Apps—June 2013," *Distimo,* July 8, 2013, www.distimo.com.

36. A Smith, "Pfizer Plan Fails to Wow Wall Street," *CNN Money* (online), January 17, 2007, http://money.cnn.com.

37. P. Sanders and D. Michaels, "Boeing Courts American with Upgraded 737," *The Wall Street Journal* (online), July 20, 2011, www.wsj.com.

38. D. Henschen, "Office 365 vs. Google Apps: Advantage Microsoft," *InformationWeek* 1305, pp. 10–12; and R. D. Hof, "Google Steps into Microsoft's Office," *Businessweek,* February 12, 2007, www.businessweek.com.

39. G. Bounds, "The Rise of Holiday Me-tailers—Technology Fuels Hyper-Customized Vanity Purchases," *The Wall Street Journal,* December 8, 2010, p. D1.

40. D. Terdiman, "How Oreo's Brilliant Blackout Tweet Won the Super Bowl," *CNET,* February 3, 2013, http://news.cnet.com.

41. "Top 10 Influential Social Media Marketing Campaigns of 2013," *Adhere Creative,* December 12, 2013, http://www.adherecreative.com; "Super Bowl 2013: Ravens Withstand 49ers Rally and Power Outage, Surge to Championship," *CBS News* (online), February 4, 2013, http://www.cbsnews.com.

42. A. Porterfield, "Companies Doing Social Media Right and Why," *Social Media Examiner* (online), April 12, 2011, http://www.socialmediaexaminer.com.

43. M. Tran, "Singer Gets His Revenge on United Airlines and Soars to Fame," *The Guardian News Blog* (online), July 23, 2009, http://www.the guardian.com.

44. P. Kotler, *Marketing Management: Analysis, Planning, Implementation and Control*, 9th ed. (Engelwood Cliffs, NJ: Prentice Hall, 1990).

45. See www.wholefoodsmarket.com/company-info.

46. C. Albanesius, "Is the Amazon Phone on Tap for June 18 Launch Event? PCMag (online), June 4, 2014, http://www.pcmag.com.

47. Y. Kane, "Look It's Mii-on Wii," *The Wall Street Journal* (online), March 16, 2007, http://www.wsj.com.

48. D. Clark, "IBM Gets Allies to Chip Away at Intel," *The Wall Street Journal* (online), August 6, 2013, www.wsj.com.

49. Adapted from H. L. Lee and C. Billington, "The Evolution of Supply-Chain-Management Models and Practice at Hewlett-Packard," *Interfaces* 25, no. 5 (September–October 1995), pp. 42–63.

50. T. Maylett and K. Vitasek, "For Closer Collaboration, Try Education," *Supply Chain Management Review,* January–February 2007.

51. A. A. Buchko, "Conceptualization and Measurement of Environmental Uncertainty: An Assessment of the Miles and Snow Perceived Environmental Uncertainty Scale," *Academy of Management Journal* 37, no. 2 (April 1994), pp. 410–25.

52. A. F. Hagen, "Corporate Executives and Environmental Scanning Activities: An Empirical Investigation," *SAM Advanced Management Journal* 60, no. 2 (Spring 1995), pp. 41–47; R. L. Daft, "Chief Executive Scanning, Environmental Characteristics, and Company Performance: An Empirical Study," *Strategic Management Journal* 9, no. 2 (March/April 1988), pp. 123–39; and M. Yasai-Ardekani, "Designs for Environmental Scanning Systems: Tests of a Contingency Theory," *Management Science* 42, no. 2 (February 1996), pp. 187–204.

53. S. Ghoshal, "Building Effective Intelligence Systems for Competitive Advantage," *Sloan Management Review* 28, no. 1 (Fall 1986), pp. 49–58; and K. D. Cory, "Can Competitive Intelligence Lead to a Sustainable Competitive Advantage?" *Competitive Intelligence Review* 7, no. 3 (Fall 1996), pp. 45–55.

54. V. Luckerson, "5 Reasons the Samsung Galaxy S5 Will Crush the iPhone," *Time* (online), February 25, 2014, www.time.com.

55. S. K. Evans, "Connecting Adaptation and Strategy: The Role of Evolutionary Theory in Scenario Planning," *Futures* 43, no. 4 (May 2011), pp. 460–68; and P. J. H. Schoemaker, "Multiple Scenario Development: Its Conceptual and Behavioral Foundation," *Strategic Management Journal* 14, no. 3 (March 1993), pp. 193–213.

56. R. R. Peterson, "An Analysis of Contemporary Forecasting in Small Business," *Journal of Business Forecasting Methods & Systems* 15, no. 2 (Summer 1996), pp. 10–12; and S. Makridakis, "Business Forecasting for Management: Strategic Business Forecasting," *International Journal of Forecasting* 12, no. 3 (September 1996), pp. 435–447.

57. See www.perscholas.org/aboutus.html; M. Sledge, "Per Scholas, Bronx Job-training Non-profit with Record of Success, Expands to Ohio," *Huffington Post* (online), August 5, 2012, www.huffingtonpost.com; and D. Russakoff, "Building a Career Path Where There Was Just a Dead End," *Washington Post,* February 26, 2007, www.washingtonpost.com.

58. Bureau of Labor Statistics, "Contingent and Alternative Employment Arrangements, February 2005," news release, July 27, 2005, www.bls.gov/cps/.

59. M. B. Meznar, "Buffer or Bridge? Environmental and Organizational Determinants of Public Affairs Activities in American Firms," *Academy of Management Journal* 38, no. 4 (August 1995), pp. 975–96.

60. See www.ford.com/cars/mustang/customizer/.

61. D. Lei, "Advanced Manufacturing Technology: Organizational Design and Strategic Flexibility," *Organization Studies* 17, no. 3 (1996), pp. 501–23; and J. W. Dean Jr. and S. A. Snell, "The Strategic Use of Integrated Manufacturing: An Empirical Examination," *Strategic Management Journal* 17, no. 6 (June 1996), pp. 459–80.

62. C. Zeithaml and V. Zeithaml, "Environmental Management: Revising the Marketing Perspective," *Journal of Marketing* 48 (Spring 1984), pp. 46–53.

63. Center for Responsive Politics, "PACs by Industry," *OpenSecrets,* www.opensecrets.org (based on data from the Federal Election Commission, released February 18, 2014).

64. Ibid.

65. W. P. Burgers, "Cooperative Strategy in High Technology Industries," *International Journal of Management* 13, no. 2 (June 1996), pp. 127–34; and J. E. McGee, "Cooperative Strategy and New Venture Performance: The Role of Business Strategy and Management Experience," *Strategic Management Journal* 16, no. 7 (October 1995), pp. 565–80.

66. Zeithaml and Zeithaml, "Environmental Management."

67. A. Bluestein, L. Buchanan, M. Chafkin, J. Del Rey, A. Joyner, and R. McCarthy, "The Ultimate Business Tune-Up for Times Like These," *Inc.,* January 2009, www.inc.com.

68. R. A. D'Aveni, *Hypercompetition—Managing the Dynamics of Strategic Maneuvering* (New York: Free Press 1994); and M. A. Cusumano, "Strategic Maneuvering and Mass-Market Dynamics: The Triumph of VHS over Beta," *Business History Review* 66, no. 1 (Spring 1992), pp. 51–94.

69. Model adapted from Zeithaml and Zeithaml, "Environmental Management."

70. R. Winkler, "Google and LG to Release Smartwatch," *The Wall Street Journal* (online), March 18, 2014, http://online.wsj.com; B. Stone, "Google's Smoking-Fast Fiber Network," *Businessweek* (online), July 23, 2012, www.businessweek.com.

71. N. Shirouzu, "Chinese Begin Volvo Overhaul," *The Wall Street Journal,* June 7, 2011, p. B.1.

72. "Devolving Volvo: For Both Buyer and Seller, The Deal Is Worth the Risks," *The Economist* (Online), March 28, 2010, www.economist.com; and "Ford Is Driven to Cut Debt," *The Wall Street Journal* (online), August 20, 2010, http://online.wsj.com.

73. R. Miles and C. Snow, *Organizational Strategy, Structure, and Process* (New York: McGraw-Hill, 1978).

74. S.E. Needleman, "Restaurateur Fights Online Mudslinging," *Startup Journal,* www.startupjournal.com.

75. E. H. Schein, "Coming to a New Awareness of Organizational Culture," *Sloan Management Review* 25, no. 2 (Winter 1984), pp. 3–16.

76. R. H. Kilmann, M. J. Saxton, and R. Serpa, *Gaining Control of the Corporate Culture* (San Francisco: Jossey-Bass, 1985); and K. S. Cameron and R. E. Quinn, *Diagnosing and Changing Organizational Culture: Based on the Competing Values Framework* (Englewood Cliffs, NJ: Addison-Wesley, 1998).

77. Schein, "Coming to a New Awareness of Organizational Culture."

78. J. E. Vascellaro and S. Morrison, "Google Gears Down for Tougher Times," *The Wall Street Journal,* December 3, 2008, http://online.wsj.com.

79. Cameron and Quinn, *Diagnosing and Changing Organizational Culture.*

80. S. Desmidt and A. Heene, "Mission Statement Perception: Are We All on the Same Wavelength? A Case Study in a Flemish Hospital," *Health Care Management Review,* January–March 2007.

81. C. Gallo, "How Ritz-Carlton Maintains Its Mystique," *Businessweek,* February 13, 2007, www.businessweek.com.

82. R. Leifer and P. K. Mills, "An Information Processing Approach for Deciding upon Control Strategies and Reducing Control Loss in Emerging Organizations," *Journal of Management* 22, no. 1 (1996), pp. 113–37; S. A. Dellana and R. D. Hauser, "Toward Defining the Quality Culture," *Engineering Management Journal* 11, no. 2 (June 1999), pp. 11–15; and D. Cohen and L. Prusak, *In Good Company: How Social Capital Makes Organizations Work* (Cambridge, MA: Harvard Business School Press, 2001).

83. J. Koob, "Early Warnings on Culture Clash," *Mergers & Acquisitions,* July 1, 2006.

84. www.coca-colacompany.com/our-company/mission-vision-values.

Chapter 4

1. A. Guerrero, "7 Tips for Checking Facebook at Work," *U.S. News & World Report* (online), April 2, 2014, www.money.usnews.com.

2. L. Conway, "Virgin Atlantic Sacks 13 Staff for Calling Its Flyers 'Chavs,'" *The Independent* (online), November 1, 2008, www.independent.co.uk/.

3. Guerrero, "7 Tips for Checking Facebook at Work."

4. "A Tongal-Produced Ad Scores a Super Bowl Touchdown," *Huffington Post* (online), March 4, 2013, www.huffintonpost. com; S. Elliott, "Building a Buzz in Social Media Ahead of Traditional Marketing," *The New York Times* (online), June 22, 2011, www.nytimes.com.

5. R. E. Freeman, *Strategic Management: A Stakeholder Approach* (Boston: Pitman, 1984); R. E. Freeman, J. Harrison, A. Wicks, B. Parmar, and S. de Colle, *Stakeholder Theory: The State of the Art* (Cambridge, UK: Cambridge University Press, 2010); R. E. Freeman, J. Harrison, and A. Wicks, *Managing for Stakeholders: Business in the 21st Century* (New Haven, CT: Yale University Press, 2007).

6. See the Business Roundtable Institute for Corporate Ethics at www.corporate-ethics.org/.

7. "Inside Information: See Some Recent and Infamous Cases Involving Inside Trading," *The Wall Street Journal* (online), October 13, 2011, www.wsj.com.

8. "Disaster at Rana Plaza: Corporate Social Responsibility," *The Economist* (online), May 4, 2013, www.theeconomist.com.

9. See http://topics.wsj.com/person/M/bernard-madoff/1077.

10. Edelman, "2014 Edelman Trust Barometer Executive Summary," *Trust Barometer 2014* pages of Edelman website, www.edelman. com; Edelman, "Business More Trusted Than Media and Government in Every Region of the Globe," news release, January 22, 2007, *Trust Barometer 2007* pages of Edelman website, www .edelman.com/trust/2007/.

11. T. Hays, "Prosecutors Take on Powerful NYC Police Union," *Bloomberg Businessweek,* October 28, 2011, http:// businessweek.com.

12. Ibid.

13. "Jury Convicts Jerry Sandusky," June 23, 2012, http://espn.go.com.

14. "Jerry Sandusky Found Guilty in Child Sex Abuse Trial," June 22, 2012, www.cbsnews.com.

15. J. Miller and R. Bachman, "Paterno Ousted at Penn State," *The Wall Street Journal* (online), November 10, 2011, http://online. wsj.com.

16. "Penn State to Pay $59.7 Million Over Sandusky Claims," *The Wall Street Journal* (online), October 28, 2013, www.wsj.com.

17. "United States: Low Marks All Round: Atlanta's Public Schools," *The Economist* 400, no. 8742 (July 16, 2011), p. 32.

18. R. Albergotti and V. O'Connell, "Armstrong Admits to 'One Big Lie'," *The Wall Street Journal* (online), January 18, 2013, www .wsj.com; "Lance Armstrong Stripped of Tour de France Titles," *U.S. News & World Report* (online), October 1, 2012, www .usnews.com.

19. K. Gurchiek, "U.S. Workers Unlikely to Report Office Misconduct," *HRMagazine,* 51, no. 5 (May 2006), pp. 29–31.

20. T. Zucco, "Ethics Issues? Check Goals," *Tampa Bay Times,* January 28, 2006.

21. M. Banaji, M. Bazerman, and D. Chugh, "How (Un)Ethical Are You?" *Harvard Business Review,* December 2003, pp. 56–64.

22. S. L. Grover, "The Truth, the Whole Truth, and Nothing but the Truth: The Causes and Management of Workplace Lying," *Academy of Management Executive* 19 (May 2005), pp. 148–57.

23. D. Gelles, "Blogs That Spin a Web of Deception," *Financial Times,* February 12, 2009.

24. M. E. Guy, *Ethical Decision Making in Everyday Work Situations* (New York: Quorum Books, 1990).

25. O. C. Ferrell, J. Fraedrich, and L. Ferrell, *Business Ethics: Ethical Decision Making and Cases,* 8th ed. (Cincinnati, OH: South-Western College Publishing, 2010).

26. Ibid.

27. Guy, *Ethical Decision Making.*

28. Caux Round Table, "Principles for Business," www.cauxround-table.org/index.cfm?&menuid58.PDF, adopted 1994.

29. See www.globalethics.org/mission-and-values.php.

30. Ethics Resource Center, "2012 National Business Ethics Survey of Fortune 500 Companies," www.ethics.org/.

31. O. C. Ferrell and J. Fraedrich, *Business Ethics: Ethical Decision Making and Cases,* 3rd ed. (Boston: Houghton Mifflin, 1997).

32. J. B. Kau, D. C. Keenan, C. Lyubinov, and V. C. Slawson, "Subprime Mortgage Default," *Journal of Urban Economics* 70, no. 2–3 (September/November 2011), pp. 75–86.

33. S. N. Robinson and D. P. Nantz, "Lessons to Be Learned from the Financial Crisis," *Journal of Private Enterprise* 25, no. 1 (Fall 2009), pp. 5–23.

34. O. C. Ferrell, J. Fraedrich, and L. Ferrell, *Business Ethics: Ethical Decision Making and Cases 2009 Update,* 7th ed. (Mason, OH: South-Western Cengage Learning, 2010), p. vii.

35. M. I. Mazumder and N. Ahmad, "Greed, Financial Innovation or Laxity of Regulation? A Close Look into the 2007–2009 Financial Crisis and Stock Market Volatility," *Studies in Economics and Finance* 27, no. 2 (2010), pp. 110–44.

36. Ibid.

37. Ibid, p. 116.

38. Ferrell, Fraedrich, and Ferrell, *Business Ethics,* 7th ed. p. iii.

39. J. Ydstie, "SEC Charges Ex-Fannie Mae, Freddie Mac CEOs," NPR, December 16, 2011, www.npr.org.

40. Mazumder and Ahmad, "Greed, Financial Innovation or Laxity."

41. J. L. Bierstaker, "Differences in Attitudes about Fraud and Corruption across Cultures: Theories, Examples and Recommendations," *Cross Cultural Management* 16, no. 3 (2009), pp. 241–50.

42. Ibid.

43. L. Kohlberg and D. Candee, "The Relationship of Moral Judgment to Moral Action" in *Morality, Moral Behavior, and Moral Development,* ed. W. M. Kurtines and J. L. Gerwitz (New York: John Wiley & Sons, 1984).

44. L. K. Trevino, "Ethical Decision Making in Organizations: A Person–Situation Interactionist Model," *Academy of Management Review* 11, no. 3 (July 1986), pp. 601–17.

45. Ferrell and Fraedrich, *Business Ethics.*

46. Transparency International, Corruption Perceptions Index 2013 Results, http://cpi.transparency.org/cpi2013/results/.

47. J. Badarocco Jr. and A. Webb, "Business Ethics: A View from the Trenches," *California Management Review,* Winter 1995, pp. 8–28; G. Laczniak, M. Berkowitz, R. Brookes, and J. Hale, "The Business of Ethics: Improving or Deteriorating?" *Business Horizons,* January–February 1995, pp. 39–47.

48. B. Kallestad, "Survey: Bad Bosses Common, Problematic," Associated Press, January 1, 2007, http://news.yahoo.com.

49. M. Gunther, "God and Business," *Fortune,* July 9, 2001, pp. 58–80.

50. V. Anand, B. Ashworth, and M. Joshi, "Business as Usual," *Academy of Management Executive* 18, no. 2 (2004), pp. 39–53; A. Bernstein, "Too Much Corporate Power?" *BusinessWeek,* September 11, 2000, pp. 146–47.

51. "The JetBlue Saga: A Model Response to a Media Crisis," *PR News* 63, no. 8 (February 26, 2007), p. 1.

52. D. Kaufman, "Problem Flight? Tell Me about It," *Financial Times,* December 6, 2008, p. 30.

53. D. Michaels, "Corporate News: EU to Clarify Air Passengers' Rights," *The Wall Street Journal,* April 11, 2011, p. B.2.

54. Jonathan Allard, "Ethics at Work," *CA Magazine* (Canadian Institute of Chartered Accountants), August 2006.

55. D. M. Thorne, O. C. Ferrell, and L. Ferrell, *Business & Society,* 4th ed. (Cincinnati, OH: South-Western College Publishing, 2011); R. T. De George, *Business Ethics,* 3rd ed. (New York: Macmillan, 1990).

56. B. W. Heineman Jr., "Avoiding Integrity Land Mines," *Harvard Business Review,* April 2007, pp. 100–8.

57. R. E. Allinson, "A Call for Ethically Centered Management," *Academy of Management Executive,* February 1995, pp. 73–76.

58. C. W. L. Hill, *International Business,* 8th ed. (New York: McGraw-Hill/Irwin, 2011), pp. 122–23.

59. R. A. Cooke, "Danger Signs of Unethical Behavior: How to Determine If Your Firm Is at Ethical Risk," *Journal of Business Ethics,* April 1991, pp. 249–53.

60. L. K. Trevino and M. Brown, "Managing to Be Ethical: Debunking Five Business Ethics Myths," *Academy of Management Executive,* May 2004, pp. 69–81.

61. L. Brewer, "Decisions: Lynn Brewer, Enron Whistleblower," *Management Today,* August 2006.

62. Trevino and Brown, "Managing to Be Ethical."

63. "2010 Ethics & Workplace Survey: Trust in the Workplace," www.deloitte.com; S. Allen, "Visible Hands," *Leadership Excellence* 28, no. 1 (January 2011), p. 13.

64. Trevino and Brown, "Managing to Be Ethical."

65. D. Messick and M. Bazerman, "Ethical Leadership and the Psychology of Decision Making," *Sloan Management Review,* Winter 1996, pp. 9–22.

66. C. Handy, *Beyond Uncertainty: The Changing Worlds of Organizations* (Boston: Harvard Business School Press, 1996).

67. J. Stevens, H. Steensma, D. Harrison, and P. Cochran, "Symbolic or Substantive Document? The Influence of Ethics Codes on Financial Executives' Decisions," *Strategic Management Journal* 26 (2005), pp. 181–95; J. Weber, "Does It Take an Economic Village to Raise an Ethical Company?" *Academy of Management Executive* 19 (May 2005), pp. 158–59.

68. See www.thecoca-colacompany.com/ourcompany/pdf/COBC_English.pdf.

69. See www.ethics.org/.

70. R. Zablow, "Creating and Sustaining an Ethical Workplace," *Risk Management Magazine* (online), September 2006, pp. 26–30, http://www.rmmag.com. Ethics Resource Center (ERC), "Code Construction and Content," The Ethics Resource Center Toolkit, www.ethics.org; J. Brown, "Ten Writing Tips for Creating an Effective Code of Conduct," Ethics Resource Center, www.ethics.org.

71. Ethics Resource Center, "Performance Reviews Often Skip Ethics, HR Professionals Say," news release, June 12, 2008, www.ethics.org.

72. G. R. Weaver, L. K. Trevino, and P. L. Cochran, "Corporate Ethics Programs as Control Systems: Influences of Executive Commitment and Environmental Factors," *Academy of Management Journal* 42 (1999), pp. 41–57.

73. L. S. Paine, "Managing for Organizational Integrity," *Harvard Business Review,* March–April 1994, pp. 106–17.

74. L. O'Brien, "'Yahoo Betrayed My Husband," *Wired News,* March 15, 2007. www.wired.com.

75. G. R. Weaver, L. K. Trevino, and P. L. Cochran, "Integrated and Decoupled Corporate Social Performance: Management Commitments, External Pressures, and Corporate Ethics Practices" *Academy of Management Journal* 42 (1999), pp. 539–52.

76. "Forswearing Greed: A Hippocratic Oath for Managers," *The Economist* 391, no. 8634 (June 6, 2009), p. 66.

77. Trevino and Brown, "Managing to Be Ethical," p. 70.

78. Ibid.

79. Banaji, Bazerman, and Chugh, "How (Un)Ethical Are You?"

80. Anand, Ashforth, and Joshi, "Business as Usual."

81. A. Taylor, "Execs' Posh Retreat after Bailout Angers Lawmakers," *Yahoo News,* October 7, 2008, http://news.yahoo.com.

82. T. Thomas, J. Schermerhorn Jr., and J. Dienhart, "Strategic Leadership of Ethical Behavior in Business," *Academy of Management Executive,* May 2004, pp. 56–66.

83. L. T. Hosmer, *The Ethics of Management,* 4th ed. (New York: McGraw-Hill/Irwin, 2003).

84. Trevino and Brown, "Managing to Be Ethical."

85. "Ex-Aide at Coke Is Guilty in Plot to Steal Secrets," *The Wall Street Journal,* February 5, 2007, http://online.wsj.com.

86. "2012 Report to the Nations on Occupational Fraud and Abuse," Association of Certified Fraud Examiners, www.acfe.com/.

87. D. Dahl, "Learning to Love Whistleblowers," *Inc.,* March 2006.

88. M. E. Schreiber and D. R. Marshall, "Reducing the Risk of Whistleblower Complaints," *Risk Management* 53, no. 11 (November 2006).

89. A. Lendez and N. Sliger, "Listen Closely: Is That a Whistle Blowing or a Slot Machine Ringing?" *Directorship* 36, no. 6 (December 2010/January 2011), pp. 64–68.

90. L. Preston and J. Post, eds., *Private Management and Public Policy* (Englewood Cliffs, NJ: Prentice-Hall, 1975).

91. Ferrel and Fraedrich, *Business Ethics.*

92. A. Carroll, "Managing Ethically with Global Stakeholders: A Present and Future Challenge," *Academy of Management Executive,* May 2004, pp. 114–20.

93. L. Etter, "Smithfield to Phase Out Crates," *The Wall Street Journal,* January 25, 2007, http://online.wsj.com.

94. P. C. Godfrey, "The Relationship between Corporate Philanthropy and Shareholder Wealth: A Risk Management Perspective," *Academy of Management Review* 30 (2005), pp. 777–98.

95. R. Giacalone, "A Transcendent Business Education for the 21st Century," *Academy of Management Learning & Education,* 2004, pp. 415–20.

96. M. Witzel, "Not for Wealth Alone: The Rise of Business Ethics," *Financial Times Mastering Management Review,* November 1999, pp. 14–19.

97. Y. Fassin, "The Stakeholder Model Refined," *Journal of Business Ethics,* no. 84 (2009), pp. 113–35; R. K. Mitchell, B. R. Agle, and D. J. Wood, "Toward a Theory of Stakeholder Identification and Salience: Defining The Principle of Who and What Really Counts," *Academy of Management Review* 4, no. 22 (1997), pp. 853–86; R. E. Freeman, *Strategic Management: A Stakeholder Approach* (Boston: Pittman).

98. Freeman, *Strategic Management.*

99. D. Roberts and P. Engardio, "Secrets, Lies, and Sweatshops," *BusinessWeek,* November 17, 2006, www.businessweek.com.

100. D. Quinn and T. Jones, "An Agent Morality View of Business Policy," *Academy of Management Review* 20 (1995), pp. 22–42.

101. B. McKay, "Why Coke Aims to Slake Global Thirst for Safe Water," *The Wall Street Journal,* March 15, 2007, http://online.wsj.com.

102. N. Varchaver, "Chemical Reaction," *Fortune,* April 2, 2007.

103. P. Schreck, "Reviewing the Business Case for Corporate Social Responsibility: New Evidence and Analysis," *Journal of Business Ethics* 103 (2011), pp. 167–88; D. Schuler and M. Cording, "A Corporate Social Performance-Corporate Financial Performance Behavioral Model for Consumers," *Academy of Management Review* 31 (2006), pp. 540–58.

104. D. Turban and D. Greening, "Corporate Social Performance and Organizational Attractiveness to Prospective Employees," *Academy of Management Journal* 40 (1997), pp. 658–72.

105. A. McWilliams and D. Siegel, "Corporate Social Responsibility: A Theory of the Firm Perspective," *Academy of Management Review* 26 (2001), pp. 117–27.

106. M. E. Porter and M. R. Kramer, "Strategy and Society: The Link between Competitive Advantage and Corporate Social Responsibility," *Harvard Business Review,* December 2006, pp. 78–92.

107. Ibid, p. 84.

108. S. L. Hart and M. B. Milstein, "Global Sustainability and the Creative Destructions of Industries," *Sloan Management Review,* Fall 1999, pp. 23–33.

109. P. M. Senge and G. Carstedt, "Innovating Our Way to the Next Industrial Revolution," *Sloan Management Review,* Winter 2001, pp. 24–38.

110. C. Holliday, "Sustainable Growth, the DuPont Way," *Harvard Business Review,* September 2001, pp. 129–34.

111. A. Back, "GE's China Ideas Bank-Conglomerate Launches $100 Million Contest to Spur Gas-Energy Innovation," *The Wall Street Journal,* September 29, 2011, p. B 4.

112. P. Shrivastava, "Ecocentric Management for a Risk Society," *Academy of Management Review* 20 (1995), pp. 118–37.

113. Ibid.

114. Ibid.

115. M. Gunther, "Green Is Good," *Fortune* 155 (April 2, 2007), pp. 42–44.

116. J. O'Toole, "Do Good, Do Well: The Business Enterprise Trust Awards," *California Management Review* (Spring 1991), pp. 9–24.

117. A. Alter, "Yet Another 'Footprint' to Worry About: Water," *The Wall Street Journal,* February 17, 2009, www.online.wsj.com.

118. Ibid.; Shrivastava, "Ecocentric Management."

119. M. Russo and P. Fouts, "A Resource-Based Perspective on Corporate Environmental Performance and Profitability," *Academy of Management Journal* 40 (1997), pp. 534–59; R. D. Klassen and D. Clay Whybark, "The Impact of Environmental Technologies on Manufacturing Performance," *Academy of Management Journal* 42 (1999), pp. 599–615.

120. M. LaMonica, "IBM Sees Green in Environmental Tech," C/Net News.com, March 6, 2007, http://news.com.com.

121. J. Ball, "Green Goal of 'Carbon Neutrality' Hits Limit," *The Wall Street Journal,* December 30, 2008, http://online.wsj.com; Google Inc., "Going Green at Google," Corporate Overview: Green Initiatives, Google Corporate home page, www.google.com/corporate/green/.

122. G. Pinchot and E. Pinchot, *The Intelligent Organization* (San Francisco: Berrett-Koehler, 1996).

123. S. L. Hart, "Beyond Greening: Strategies for a Sustainable World," *Harvard Business Review,* January–February 1997, pp. 66–76.

Chapter 5

1. S. Reed and D. Roberts, "What's Doing in China," *Bloomberg Businessweek,* November 21–27, 2011, pp. 88–93.

2. W. M. Bulkeley, "How an IBM Lifer Built Software Unit into a Rising Star," *The Wall Street Journal,* April 2, 2007, http://online.wsj.com.

3. B. Bowers, "In Tough Times, Tackle Anxiety First," *The New York Times,* November 13, 2008.

4. G. Farrell, "CEO Profile: Wells Fargo's Kovacevich Banks on Success as a One-Stop Shop," *USA Today,* March 26, 2007, www.usatoday.com.

5. "Riding High; Wells Fargo," *The Economist* (online), September 14, 2013, www.theeconomist.com.

6. D. C. Hambrick and J. W. Fredrickson, "Are You Sure You Have a Strategy?" *Academy of Management Executive* 19, no. 4 (2005), pp. 51–62.

7. J. L. Bower and C. G. Gilbert, "How Managers' Everyday Decisions Create or Destroy Your Company's Strategy," *Harvard Business Review,* February 2007, pp. 72–79.

8. See http://honda.com; J. Salerno and W. Garvey, "FAA Certifies the HF120," *Business & Commercial Aviation* 11, no. 1 (January 2014), p. 13; K. Lynch, "HondaJet Flies Fifth Aircraft, Certification Pushed to 2014," *Aviation Week* (online), May 20, 2013, www.aviationweek.com; "GM, Honda to Collaborate on Next-Generation Fuel Cell Technologies," Press release on July 2, 2013, http://media.gm.com; A. Richardson, "Lessons from Honda's Early Adaptive Strategy," *Harvard Business Review* (online blog), February 1, 2011, http://blogs.hbr.org.

9. S. W. Floyd and P. J. Lane, "Strategizing throughout the Organization: Management Role Conflict in Strategic Renewal," *Academy of Management Review* 25, no. 1 (January 2000), pp. 154–77.

10. Mission statements quoted from the corporate websites: IDEO, "About IDEO," www.ideo.com/about/; Unilever, "About Us," www.unileverme.com/aboutus/; Google, "About the Company," www.google.com/about/company/.

11. Vision statements quoted from the organizations' websites: DuPont, "Our Company: DuPont Vision," www2.dupont.com; City of Redmond, "City of Redmond Vision Statement," www.ci.redmond.wa.us; Smithsonian, "Vision Statement," www.si.edu/About/Mission.

12. A. Martin, "The Happiest Meal: Hot Profits," *The New York Times,* January 11, 2009, www.nytimes.com.

13. A. A. Thompson and A. J. Strickland III, *Strategic Management: Concepts and Cases,* 8th ed. (Burr Ridge, IL: Richard D. Irwin, 1995), p. 23.

14. R. Gobel, "Inspiring Innovation," *Success,* April 2009, pp. 24–26; Intuit, "About Intuit-Executive Profiles," http://about.intuit.com/about_intuit/executives/brad_smith.jsp.

15. S. Solar, www.us.schott.com/photovoltaic/english/index.html; M. Kanelios, "Full Steam Ahead for Nevada Solar Project," CNet News.com, March 20, 2007, http://news.com.com.

16. D. Porter, "One Man's Garbage Becomes Another's Power Plant," *Yahoo! News,* October 28, 2008, www.news.yahoo.com.

17. D. J. Collis and C. A. Montgomery, *Corporate Strategy: A Resource-Based Approach,* 2nd ed. (New York, McGraw-Hill/Irwin, 2005).

18. R. L. Priem, "A Consumer Perspective on Value Creation," *Academy of Management Review* 32, no. 1 (2007), pp. 219–35.

19. Farrell, "CEO Profile."

20. A. W. King, "Disentangling Interfirm and Intrafirm Causal Ambiguity: A Conceptual Model of Causal Ambiguity and Sustainable Competitive Advantage," *Academy of Management Review* 32, no. 1 (2007), pp. 156–78.

21. www.ibm.com; K. Maddox, "IBM's 'Smarter Planet' Evolves: New TV Spots Aim to Make Complex Concepts Easier to Understand," *B to B* 97 (February 13, 2012), p. 8; J. R. Galbraith, "The Multi-Dimensional and Reconfigurable Organization," *Organizational Dynamics* 39 (June 2010), pp. 115–25.

22. H. Min and H. Min, "Benchmarking the Service Quality of Fast-Food Restaurant Franchises in the USA," *Benchmarking* 18, no. 2 (2011), pp. 282–300.

23. See www.sony.com/SCA/bios/stringer.shtml; B. Gruley and C. Edwards, "Sony Needs a Hit," *Bloomberg Businessweek,* November 21–27, 2011, pp. 72–77.

24. P. Haspeslagh, "Portfolio Planning: Uses and Limits," *Harvard Business Review* 60, no. 1 (1982), pp. 58–67; R. Hamermesh, *Making Strategy Work* (New York: John Wiley & Sons, 1986); R. A. Proctor, "Toward a New Model for Product Portfolio Analysis," *Management Decision* 28, no. 3 (1990), pp. 14–17.

25. A. Johnson, "Abbott's Makeover Attracts Investors," *The Wall Street Journal,* January 19, 2007, http://online.wsj.com.

26. M. Porter, *Competitive Advantage* (New York: Free Press, 1985), pp. 11–14.

27. J. Ewers, "Making It Stick," *U.S. News & World Report,* February 5, 2007, pp. EE3–EE8.

28. K. Palmer, "The Secrets to Zappos' Success," *U.S. News and World Reports,* August 10, 2010, http://money.usnews.com.

29. R. Varadarajan, "Think Small," *The Wall Street Journal,* February 14, 2007, http://online.wsj.com.

30. A. M. Franco, M. B. Sarkar, R. Agarwal, and R. Echambadi, "Swift and Smart: The Moderating Effects of Technological Capabilities on the Market Pioneering-Firm Survival Relationship," *Management Science* 55, no. 11 (November 2009), pp. 1842–61; S. A. Zahra, S. Nash, and D. J. Bickford, "Transforming Technological Pioneering in Competitive Advantage," *Academy of Management Executive* 9, no. 1 (1995), pp. 17–31; M. Sadowski and A. Roth, "Technology Leadership Can Pay Off," *Research Technology Management* 42, no. 6 (November/December 1999), pp. 32–33.

31. A. G. Shilling, "First-Mover Disadvantage," *Forbes,* June 18, 2007.

32. F. F. Suarez and G. Lanzolla, "The Role of Environmental Dynamics in Building a First Mover Advantage Theory," *Academy of Management Review* 32, no. 2 (2007), pp. 377–92.

33. Bulkeley, "How an IBM Lifer Built Software Unit into a Rising Star"; Farrell, "CEO Profile."

34. J. Scheck and P. Glader, "R&D Spending Holds Steady in Slump," *The Wall Street Journal,* April 6, 2009, http://online.wsj.com.

35. G. Norris, "GE Honda Targets Year-End for HF120 Certification," *Aviation Week* (online), October 22, 2013, www.aviationweek.com.

36. B. Smith, "Maybe I Will, Maybe I Won't: What the Connected Perspectives of Motivation Theory and Organisational Commitment May Contribute to Our Understanding of Strategy Implementation," *Journal of Strategic Marketing* 17, no. 6 (2009), pp. 473–85; M. Beer and R. A. Eisenstat, "The Silent Killers of Strategy Implementation and Learning," *MIT Sloan Management Review* 4 (Summer 2000), pp. 29–40.

37. R. A. Eisenstat, "Implementing Strategy: Developing a Partnership for Change," *Planning Review,* September–October 1993, pp. 33–36.

38. W. Garvey, "HondaJet Progresses," *Aviation Week & Space Technology,* no. 173.1 (January 3, 2011), p. 32.

39. M. Magasin and F. L. Gehlen, "Unwise Decisions and Unanticipated Consequences," *Sloan Management Review* 41 (1999), pp. 47–60; M. McCall and R. Kaplan, *Whatever It Takes: Decision Makers at Work* (Englewood Cliffs, NJ: Prentice-Hall, 1985); L. Kopeikina, "The Elements of a Clear Decision," *MIT Sloan Management Review* 47 (Winter 2006), pp. 19–20.

40. B. Bass, *Organizational Decision Making* (Homewood, IL: Richard D. Irwin, 1983).

41. J. Gibson, J. Ivancevich, J. Donnelly Jr., and R. Konopaske, *Organizations: Behavior, Structure, Processes,* 14th ed. (Burr Ridge, IL: McGraw-Hill, 2012), p. 464. Copyright © 2012 by The McGraw-Hill Companies. Reproduced with permission of The McGraw-Hill Companies.

42. J. March, "Bounded Rationality, Ambiguity, and the Engineering of Choice," *Bell Journal of Economics* 9 (1978), pp. 587–608.

43. H. Kuchler and T. Bradshaw, "Facebook Buys WhatsApp in $19 Billion Deal," *Financial Times* (online), February 19, 2014, www.ft.com.

44. McCall and Kaplan, *Whatever It Takes.*

45. M. Chafkin, "Case Study: When the Bank Called in a Loan, Larry Cohen Had to Act Fast to Save the Family Business," *Inc.,* June 2006, pp. 58–60.

46. D. Jones, "Cisco CEO Sees Tech as Integral to Success," *USA Today,* March 19, 2007, p. 4B (interview of John Chambers).

47. K. MacCrimmon and R. Taylor, "Decision Making and Problem Solving," in *Handbook of Industrial and Organizational Psychology,* ed. M. D. Dunnette (Chicago: Rand McNally, 1976).

48. Chafkin, "Case Study," p. 58.

49. Q. Spitzer and R. Evans, *Heads, You Win! How the Best Companies Think* (New York: Simon & Schuster, 1997).

50. C. Gettys and S. Fisher, "Hypothesis Plausibility and Hypotheses Generation," *Organizational Behavior and Human Performance* 24 (1979), pp. 93–110.

51. E. R. Alexander, "The Design of Alternatives in Organizational Contexts: A Pilot Study," *Administrative Science Quarterly* 24 (1979), pp. 382–404.

52. A. R. Rao, M. E. Bergen, and S. Davis, "How to Fight a Price War," *Harvard Business Review,* March–April 2000, pp. 107–16.

53. Chafkin, "Case Study."

54. Ibid.

55. J. L. Bower and C. G. Gilbert, "How Managers' Everyday Decisions Create or Destroy Your Company's Strategy," *Harvard Business Review,* February 2007, pp. 72–79.

56. A. Fox, "Avoiding Furlough Fallout," *HRMagazine* 54, no. 9 (September 2009), pp. 37–41.

57. D. Mattioli and S. Murray, "Employers Hit Salaried Staff with Furloughs," *The Wall Street Journal,* February 24, 2009, http://online.wsj.com.

58. "Is Executive Hubris Ruining Companies?" *Industry Week,* January 31, 2007, www.industryweek.com (interview of Matthew Hayward).

59. Spitzer and Evans, *Heads, You Win!*

60. McCall and Kaplan, *Whatever It Takes.*

61. "Is Executive Hubris Ruining Companies?"

62. J. Pfeffer and R. Sutton, *The Knowing-Doing Gap* (Boston: Harvard Business School Press, 2000).

63. D. Drickhamer, "By the Numbers," *Material Handling Management,* January 2006.

64. D. Siebold, "Making Meetings More Successful," *Journal of Business Communication* 16 (Summer 1979), pp. 3–20.

65. Chafkin, "Case Study."

66. J. W. Dean Jr. and M. Sharfman, "Does Decision Process Matter? A Study of Strategic Decision-Making Effectiveness," *Academy of Management Journal* 39 (1996), pp. 368–96.

67. R. Nisbett and L. Ross, *Human Inference: Strategies and Shortcomings* (Englewood Cliffs, NJ: Prentice-Hall, 1980).

68. D. Messick and M. Bazerman, "Ethical Leadership and the Psychology of Decision Making," *Sloan Management Review,* Winter 1996, pp. 9–22.

69. P. Dvorak, "Dangers of Clinging to Solutions of the Past," *The Wall Street Journal,* March 2, 2009, http://online.wsj.com.

70. T. Bateman and C. Zeithaml, "The Psychological Context of Strategic Decisions: A Model and Convergent Experimental Findings," *Strategic Management Journal* 10 (1989), pp. 59–74.

71. E. White, "Why Good Managers Make Bad Decisions," *The Wall Street Journal,* February 12, 2009, http://online.wsj.com.

72. Messick and Bazerman, "Ethical Leadership."

73. P. A. F. Fraser-Mackenzie and I. E. Dror, "Dynamic Reasoning and Time Pressure: Transition from Analytical Operations to Experiential Responses," *Theory and Decision* 71, no. 2 (August 2011), pp. 211–25; D. Malhotra, G. Ku, and J. K. Murnigham, "When Winning Is Everything," *Harvard Business Review* 86, no. 5 (May 2008), pp. 78–86.

74. J. S. Lublin, "Recall the Mistakes of Your Past Bosses, So You Can Do Better," *The Wall Street Journal,* January 2, 2007, http://online.wsj.com.

75. K. M. Esenhardt, "Speed and Strategic Choice: How Managers Accelerate Decision Making," *California Management Review* 32 (Spring 1990), pp. 39–54.

76. Q. Spitzer and R. Evans, "New Problems in Problem Solving," *Across the Board,* April 1997, pp. 36–40.

77. G. W. Hill, "Group versus Individual Performance: Are N + 1? Heads Better Than 1?" *Psychological Bulletin* 91 (1982), pp. 517–39.

78. N. R. F. Maier, "Assets and Liabilities in Group Problem Solving: The Need for an Integrative Function," *Psychological Review* 74 (1967), pp. 239–49.

79. Ibid.

80. D. A. Garvin and M. A. Roberto, "What You Don't Know about Making Decisions," *Harvard Business Review,* September 2001, pp. 108–16.

81. A. Amason, "Distinguishing the Effects of Functional and Dysfunctional Conflict on Strategic Decision Making: Resolving a Paradox for Top Management Teams," *Academy of Management Journal* 39 (1996), pp. 123–48; R. Dooley and G. Fyxell, "Attaining Decision Quality and Commitment from Dissent: The Moderating Effects of Loyalty and Competence in Strategic Decision-Making Teams," *Academy of Management Journal,* August 1999, pp. 389–402.

82. C. De Dreu and L. Weingart, "Task versus Relationship Conflict, Team Performance, and Team Member Satisfaction: A Meta-Analysis," *Journal of Applied Psychology* 88 (2003), pp. 741–49.

83. K. Eisenhardt, J. Kahwajy, and L. J. Bourgeois III, "Conflict and Strategic Choice: How Top Management Teams Disagree," *California Management Review,* Winter 1997, pp. 42–62.

84. Ibid.

85. "Innovation from the Ground Up," *Industry Week,* March 7, 2007, www.industryweek.com (interview of Erika Andersen); A. Farnham, "How to Nurture Creative Sparks," *Fortune,* January 10, 1994, pp. 94–100; T. M. Amabile, "A Model of Creativity and Innovation in Organizations," in *Research in Organizational Behavior,* ed. B. Straw and L. Cummings, vol. 10 (Greenwich, CT: JAI Press, 1988), pp. 123–68.

86. T. Amabile, C. Hadley, and S. Kramer, "Creativity under the Gun," *Harvard Business Review,* August 2002, pp. 52–61.

87. S. Farmer, P. Tierney, and K. Kung-McIntyre, "Employee Creativity in Taiwan: An Application of Role Identity Theory," *Academy of Management Journal* 46 (2003), pp. 618–30.

Chapter 6

1. See Company websites, www.oprah.com, www.marthastewart.com, http://www.marykay.com, www.esteelauder.com, www.google.com, www.verawang.com, www.infosys.com; J. Timmons and S. Spinelli, *New Venture Creation: Entrepreneurship for the 21st Century,* 6th ed. (New York: McGraw-Hill/Irwin, 2004), p. 7; J. Gangemi, "Where Are Last Year's Winners Now?" *BusinessWeek,* October 30, 2006, www.businessweek.com.

2. D. Harper, "Towards a Theory of Entrepreneurial Teams," *Journal of Business Venturing* 23, no. 6 (2008), pp. 613–26; S. Shane and S. Venkataraman, "The Promise of Entrepreneurship as a Field of Research," *Academy of Management Review* 25 (2000), pp. 217–26.

3. J. A. Timmons, *New Venture Creation* (Burr Ridge, IL: Richard D. Irwin, 1994).

4. G. T. Lumpkin and G. G. Dess, "Clarifying the Entrepreneurial Orientation Construct and Linking It to Performance," *Academy of Management Review* 21 (1996), pp. 135–72.

5. Company website, www.virgin.com; P. K. Jayadvan and J. Harsimran, "Virgin Galactic Is Offering Low-Cost Space Flights," *The Economic Times* (Online), February 12, 2011, http://economictimes.indiatimes.com/; S. Wilson, "Branson," *Entrepreneur,* November 2008, pp. 58–62; E. Benammar, "Richard Branson Forced to Abandon Transatlantic Record Attempt," *Telegraph,* October 24, 2008, www.telegraph.co.uk; J. Thottam, "Richard Branson's Flight Plan," *Time,* April 17, 2008, www.time.com; A. Deutschman, "The Enlightenment of Richard Branson," *Fast Company,* December 19, 2007, www.fastcompany.com; K. Farabaugh, "Virgin Group Founder Commits Billions of Dollars to Help Environment," *Voice of America,* March 19, 2007, http://voanews.com; M. Specter, "Branson's Luck," *New Yorker,* May 14, 2007, www.newyorker.com.

6. R. W. Smilor, "Entrepreneurship: Reflections on a Subversive Activity," *Journal of Business Venturing* 12 (1997), pp. 341–46.

7. W. Megginson, M. J. Byrd, S. R. Scott Jr., and L. Megginson, *Small Business Management: An Entrepreneur's Guide to Success,* 2nd ed. (Boston: Irwin/McGraw-Hill, 1997).

8. Timmons and Spinelli, *New Venture Creation,* p. 3.

9. Ibid.

10. Angus Loten, "Start-Ups Key to States' Economic Success," *Inc.,* February 7, 2007, http://www.inc.com.

11. Timmons and Spinelli, *New Venture Creation.*

12. Ibid.

13. Ibid.

14. Adapted from J. A. Timmons and S. Spinelli, *New Venture Creation,* 6th ed., pp. 67–68. Copyright © 2004. Reproduced with permission of the authors.

15. K. Hellman and R. S. Siegel, "Achieving Entrepreneurial Success," *Marketing Management* 20, no. 2, pp. 24–37; D. Bricklin, "Natural-Born Entrepreneur," *Harvard Business Review,* September 2001, pp. 53–59, quoting p. 58.

16. A. Levit, " 'Insider' Entrepreners," *The Wall Street Journal,* April 6, 2009, http://online.wsj.com.

17. K. Palmer, "The Secrets of Zappos' Success," *U.S. News & World Reports* (online), August 10, 2010, http://money.usnews.com; "For Zappos, the Next Trend Is More Customized Pages for Customers," *Internet Retailer,* February 12, 2009, www.internetretailer.com.

18. L. Blakely, "The Queen of Social Media," *Inc.* (online), May 28, 2013, www.inc.com.

19. Ibid.

20. See www.marketingzen.com; "Young Millionaires," *Entrepreneur* (online), November 30, 2011, www.entrepreneur.com; "2009 Finalists: America's Best Young Entrepreneurs," *Businessweek* (online), September 10, 2009, www.businessweek.com.

21. Company website, www.idealab.com; "Announcing UberAds: Deriving Consumer Intent from Social Signals and Tripling Ad Performance," *Marketing Weekly News* (online), June 8, 2013, p. 26; A. Marsh, "Promiscuous Breeding," *Forbes,* April 7, 1997, pp. 74–77; J. Nocera, "Fewer Eggs, More Baskets in the Incubator," *The New York Times,* October 28, 2006.

22. Company website, www.naturalawn.com; L. Kanter, "The Eco-Advantage," *Inc.,* November 2006, pp. 78–103 (NaturaLawn example on p. 84).

23. H. Aldrich, *Ethnic Entrepreneurs: Immigrant Business in Industrial Societies* (Newbury Park, CA: Sage, 1990).

24. Company website, www.dbhealthcare.com/services-and-solutions/; R. Flandez, "Immigrants Gain Edge Doing Business Back Home," *The Wall Street Journal,* March 20, 2007, http://online.wsj.com.

25. See company websites, www.elcompanies.com, www.esteelauder.com, and www.thebiographychannel.com.uk/biographies/estee-lauder.com.

26. L. Buchanan, "Create Jobs, Eliminate Waste, Preserve Value," *Inc.,* December 2006, pp. 94–106.

27. Ibid.

28. Ibid., pp. 99–100.

29. Timmons and Spinelli, *New Venture Creation.*

30. Company website, www.debbieffields.com.

31. J. Collins and J. Porras, *Built to Last* (London: Century, 1996).

32. Ibid., www.esteelauder.com; www.oprah.com.

33. K. H. Vesper, *New Venture Mechanics* (Englewood Cliffs, NJ: Prentice Hall, 1993).

34. Company website, www.voltaicsystems.com; Kanter, "The Eco-Advantage," p. 87.

35. Company website, www.touchbionics.com; G. Brumfeil, "The Insane and Exciting Future of the Bionic Body," *Smithsonian Magazine* (online), September 2013, www.smithsonianmag.com.

36. "10 Must-Have iPad Apps for Seniors," *U.S. News & World Reports* (online), November 8, 2010, www.money.usnews.com; J. Berg, "Entrepreneurs Develop Errand Service," *Patriot-News* (Harrisburg, PA), January 23, 2007, http://galenet.galegroup.com.

37. Kanter, "The Eco-Advantage," p. 87; company website, www.aiso.net.

38. Ibid., p. 84.

39. Americas Heroes at Work website, www.americasheroesheroes .gov; "Invisible Wounds: Mental Health and Cognitive Care Needs of America's Returning Veterans," Rand Center for Military Health Policy Research (2008), www.randcorp.org; K. Gurchiek, "Initiative Links Employers, Wounded Vets," *HRMagazine* 53, no. 10 (October 2008), pp. 115–16.

40. Company website, www.sambazon.com; E. Watson, "Surfing, Super Fruits and Social Justice: Sambazon and the Genesis of an Amazonian Super Food Empire," *Food Navigator* (online), January 3, 2013, www.foodnavigator.com; G. Bounds, "The Perils of Being First," *The Wall Street Journal,* March 19, 2007, http://online.wsj.com.

41. Timmons and Spinelli, *New Venture Creation.*

42. International Franchise Association, "The State of the Franchise Economy in 2013," news release, www.franchise.org.

43. Company website, www.noodles.com; B. Kowitt, "Can Noodles & Company Sate Outsize Investor Hunger?" *Fortune* (online), August 9, 2013, www.fortune.com.

44. K. Spors, "Franchised versus Nonfranchised Businesses," *The Wall Street Journal,* February 27, 2007, http://online.wsj.com.

45. Timmons and Spinelli, *New Venture Creation.*

46. M. V. Copeland and S. Hamner, "The 20 Smartest Companies to Start Now," *Business 2.0,* September 2006.

47. P. Shapira and J. Youtie, "Introduction to the Symposium Issue: Nanotechnology Innovation and Policy-Current Strategies and Future Trajectories," *Journal of Technology Transfer* 36, no. 6 (December 2011), pp. 581–86.

48. Company website, www.gozerog.com; A. Pasztor, "Sharper Image Sells New Toy: Zero Gravity's Spacey Flights," *The Wall Street Journal,* March 28, 2007, http://online.wsj.com; B. Spillman, "Nothing to These Flights," *Las Vegas Review-Journal,* March 5, 2007.

49. Company website, www.virgingalactic.com; A. Pasztor, "Virgin Galactic's Flights Seen Delayed Yet Again," *The Wall Street Journal,* October 26, 2011, p. B2; "Space Adventure for $200,000 a Seat," *The Wall Street Journal* (online), September 30, 2011, www.wsj.com; "Virgin Galactic's White Knight Two Lands in San Francisco," *Forbes* (online), April 6, 2011, www.forbes.com.

50. J. E. Lange, "Entrepreneurs and the Continuing Internet: The Expanding Frontier," in Timmons and Spinelli, *New Venture Creation,* pp. 183–220.

51. Ibid.

52. Nielsen//NetRatings, "Resources: Free Data and Rankings," February 2007, www.nielsen-netratings.com.

53. Company website, www.zazzle.com; "J. Graham, "Zazzle Aims to Dazzle with On-demand Merchandise," *ABC News* (online), April 19, 2014, http://abcnews.com; A. Ha, "Zazzle Instant Brings Custom Product Creation to Your iPhone," *Techcrunch* (online), September 7, 2012, http://techcruch.com; J. E. Vascellaro, "Selling Your Designs Online," *The Wall Street Journal,* April 5, 2007, http://online.wsj.com.

54. Vesper, *New Venture Mechanics.*

55. Timmons, *New Venture Creation.*

56. J. R. Baum and E. A. Locke, "The Relationship of Entrepreneurial Traits, Skill, and Motivation to Subsequent Venture Growth," *Journal of Applied Psychology* 89 (2004), pp. 587–98.

57. "Top 32 Quotes Every Entrepreneur Should Live By," *Forbes* (online), May 2, 2013, www.forbes.com.

58. Nocera, "Fewer Eggs, More Baskets."

59. M. Sonfield and R. Lussier, "The Entrepreneurial Strategy Matrix: A Model for New and Ongoing Ventures," *Business Horizons,* May–June 1997, pp. 73–77.

60. "Just the Facts," *Inc.,* September 2008, www.inc.com; "Start-Up Capital," Inc., September 2008, www.inc.com.

61. Company website, www.oprah.com; C. Suddath, "An Aha Moment: Oprah Winfrey's OWN Is Finally Profitable," *Bloomberg Businessweek* (online), July 31, 2013, www.businessweek.com; B. Stelter, "Oprah Winfrey's Cable Channel Is Starting to Pay, Discovery Says," *The New York Times* (online), July 30, 2013, www.nytimes.com; S. Schechner, "TV Networks See Key Audience Erode," *The Wall Street Journal,* May 27, 2011, p. B.5; J. Goudreau, "Will Oprah Winfrey Spin OWN Into Network Gold?" *Forbes* (online), September 21, 2011, www.forbes.com.

62. Lange, "Entrepreneurs and the Continuing Internet."

63. S. Venkataraman and M. Low, "On the Nature of Critical Relationships: A Test of the Liabilities and Size Hypothesis," in *Frontiers of Entrepreneurship Research* (Babson Park, MA: Babson College, 1991), p. 97.

64. Timmons and Spinelli, *New Venture Creation.*

65. P. Hoy, "Most Small Businesses Start without Outside Capital," *Inc.,* October 3, 2006, www.inc.com.

66. "Annual Venture Investment Dollars Rise 7% and Exceed 2012 Totals, According to the MoneyTree Report," press release from PricewaterhouseCoopers, January 17, 2014, www.pwc.com.

67. C. Tuna, "Tough Call: Deciding to Start a Business," *The Wall Street Journal,* January 8, 2009, http://online.wsj.com.

68. Buchanan, "Create Jobs."

69. Company website, National Business Incubator Association, www.nbia.org.

70. M. V. Copeland, "A Studio System for Startups," *Business 2.0,* May 2007.

71. Company website, The Dartmouth Regional Technology Center www.thedrtc.com.

72. N. Brodsky, "Street Smarts: Our Irrational Fear of Numbers," *Inc.,* January 2009, www.inc.com.

73. M. Chafkin, "How I Did It," *Inc.,* September 1, 2006.

74. "Best Industries for Starting a Business in 2013," *Inc.* (online), www.inc.com/ss/best-industries-for-starting-a-business#1.

75. A. Cordeiro, "Sweet Returns," *The Wall Street Journal,* April 23, 2009, http://online.wsj.com.

76. Gibson, " 'Learning from Others' Mistakes."

77. D. McGinn, "Why Size Matters," *Inc.,* Fall 2004, pp. 32–36.

78. L. Buchanan, "Six Ways to Open an Office Overseas," *Inc.,* April 2007, pp. 120–21.

79. H. Sapienza, E. Autio, G. George, and S. Zahra, "A Capabilities Perspective on the Effects of Early Internationalization on Firm Survival and Growth," *Academy of Management Review* 31, no. 4 (2006), pp. 914–33.

80. B. Burlingham, "How Big Is Big Enough?" *Inc.,* Fall 2004, pp. 40–43.

81. Ibid.

82. S. Finkelstein, "The Myth of Managerial Superiority in Internet Start-ups: An Autopsy," *Organizational Dynamics,* Fall 2001, pp. 172–85.

83. J. Gangemi, "Young, Fearless, and Smart," *BusinessWeek,* October 30, 2006.

84. R. Weisman, "Bootstrappers Avoid Outside Money Ties," *Boston Globe,* February 5, 2007.

85. Cordeiro, "Sweet Returns."

86. P. F. Drucker, "How to Save the Family Business," *The Wall Street Journal,* August 19, 1994, p. A10.

87. D. Gamer, R. Owen, and R. Conway, *The Ernst & Young Guide to Raising Capital* (New York: John Wiley & Sons, 1991).

88. Ibid.

89. A. Lustgarten, "Warm, Fuzzy, and Highly Profitable," *Fortune,* November 15, 2004, p. 194.

90. A. McKee, *Management: A Focus on Leaders* (Upper Saddle River, NJ: Prentice Hall, 2011).

91. R. D. Hisrich and M. P. Peters, *Entrepreneurship: Starting, Developing, and Managing a New Enterprise* (Burr Ridge, IL: Irwin, 1994).

92. R. Hisrich and M. Peters, *Entrepreneurship: Starting, Developing, and Managing a New Enterprise,* p. 41. Copyright © 1998 by The McGraw-Hill Companies. Reproduced with permission of The McGraw-Hill Companies.

93. Ibid.

94. W. A. Sahlman, "How to Write a Great Business Plan," *Harvard Business Review,* July–August 1997, pp. 98–108.

95. Ibid.

96. Ibid.

97. M. Copeland, "Start Last, Finish First," *Business 2.0* 7 (2006), p. 41.

98. Sahlman, "How to Write a Great Business Plan."

99. R. D. Atkinson and L. A. Stewart, *The 2012 State New Economy Index* (The Information Technology and Innovation Foundation, 2012), www.itif.org.

100. Sahlman, "How to Write a Great Business Plan."

101. M. Zimmerman and G. Zeitz, "Beyond Survival: Achieving New Venture Growth by Building Legitimacy," *Academy of Management Review* 27 (2002), pp. 414–21.

102. A. L. Stinchcombe, "Social Structure and Organizations," in J. G. March, ed., *Handbook of Organizations* (Chicago: Rand McNally, 1965), pp. 142–93.

103. L. Taylor, "Want Your Start-Up to Be Successful? Appearance Is Everything," *Inc.,* February 23, 2007, www.inc.com.

104. Ibid.

105. R. A. Baron and G. D. Markman, "Beyond Social Capital: How Social Skills Can Enhance Entrepreneurs' Success," *Academy of Management Executive,* February 2000, pp. 106–16.

106. J. Florin, M. Lubatkin, and W. Schulze, "A Social Capital Model of High-Growth Ventures," *Academy of Management Journal* 46 (2003), pp. 374–84.

107. E. Ramstad, "In the Land of Conglomerates, Brian Ko Goes His Own Way," CareerJournal.com, January 4, 2007, www.careerjournal.com.

108. Company website, Ladies Who Launch, www.ladieswholaunch.com; "Ladies Who Launch Awards Contract for Franchise Social Media Strategy to Supreme Social Media LLC," *Marketing Weekly News,* February 13, 2010, p. 61.

109. Gangemi, "Young, Fearless, and Smart."

110. Company website, www.tpo-inc.com; J. Martin, "Free Advice," *Fortune Small Business* 19, no. 3 (April 2009), p. 37.

111. "Building a Business Partnership That Lasts," *Entrepreneur* (online), August 16, 2011, www.entrepreneur.com.

112. M. Eisner, " 'Working Together': Why Successful Business Partnerships Are As Important As Successful Marriages," *Huffington Post* (online), September 14, 2010, www.huffingtonpost.com.

113. Company website, www.berkshirehathaway.com.

114. J. Markoff, "Searching for Michael Jordan? Microsoft Wants a Better Way," *The New York Times,* March 7, 2007; "Microsoft Researchers Collaborate to Change the World," Agence France Presse, March 6, 2007, www.afp.com.

115. R. M. Kanter, *The Change Masters* (New York: Simon & Schuster, 1983).

116. S. Dumenco, "Is Google's Larry Page Already Turning Out to Be a Truly Great CEO?" *Advertising Age* 82, no. 34 (September 26, 2011), pp. 20–23.

117. D. Kiley, "Ford's New Powerstroke: A Design Breakthrough," *Bloomberg Businessweek* (online), October 14, 2009, www.businessweek.com.

118. Collins and Porras, *Built to Last.*

119. R. M. Kanter, C. Ingols, E. Morgan, and T. K. Seggerman, "Driving Corporate Entrepreneurship," *Management Review* 76 (April 1987), pp. 14–16.

120. J. Argenti, *Corporate Collapse: The Causes and Symptoms* (New York: John Wiley & Sons, 1979).

121. Kanter et al., "Driving Corporate Entrepreneurship."

122. Y. Ling, Z. Simsek, M. Lubatkin, and J. Veiga, "Transformational Leadership's Role in Promoting Corporate Entrepreneurship: Examining the CEO–TMT Interface," *Academy of Management Journal,* 2008, pp. 557–76.

123. G. T. Lumpkin and G. G. Dess, "Clarifying the Entrepreneurial Orientation Construct and Linking It to Performance," *Academy of Management Review* 21 (1996), pp. 135–72.

124. T. Due, *The Black Rose: The Dramatic Story of Madam C. J. Walker, America's First Black Female Millionaire* (New York: One World/Ballantine, 2001).

125. T. Bateman and J. M. Crant, "The Proactive Dimension of Organizational Behavior," *Journal of Organizational Behavior,* 1993, pp. 103–18.

126. Sapienza et al., "A Capabilities Perspective."

127. Lumpkin and Dess, "Clarifying the Entrepreneurial Orientation Construct."

128. C. Pinchot and E. Pinchot, *The Intelligent Organization* (San Francisco: Barrett-Koehler, 1996).

CHAPTER 7

1. Company press release: "Gartner Says Worldwide Video Game Market to Total $93 Billion in 2013," October 29, 2013, www.gartner.com.

2. Company website, www.appdata.com.

3. D. Trainer, "Investors Play Dangerous Game With Zynga Stock," *Forbes* (online), October 1, 2013, www.forbes.com.

4. Ibid.

5. S. Reyburn, "EA Reports $1.04B Net Revenue in Q4 2013, Generates $104M from Mobile," *Inside Social Games* (online), May 7, 2013, www.insidesocialgames.com.

6. "The Listless Feeling Down on the Virtual Farm," *Bloomberg Businessweek,* November 28–December 4, 2011, pp. 43–44.

7. T. Burns and G. Stalker, *The Management of Innovation* (London: Tavistock, 1961).

8. D. Krackhardt and J. R. Hanson, "Information Networks: The Company behind the Chart," *Harvard Business Review,* July–August 1993, pp. 104–11.

9. R. N. Ashkenas and S. C. Francis, "Integration Managers: Special Leaders for Special Times," *Harvard Business Review* 78, no. 6 (November–December 2000), pp. 108–16.

10. A. West, "The Flute Factory: An Empirical Measurement of the Effect of the Division of Labor on Productivity and Production Cost," *American Economist* 43, no. 1 (Spring 1999), pp. 82–87.

11. P. Lawrence and J. Lorsch, *Organization and Environment* (Homewood, IL: Richard D. Irwin, 1969).

12. Ibid.; and B. L. Thompson, *The New Manager's Handbook* (New York: McGraw-Hill, 1994). See also S. Sharifi and K. S. Pawar, "Product Design as a Means of Integrating Differentiation," *Technovation* 16, no. 5 (May 1996), pp. 255–64; and W. B. Stevenson and J. M. Bartunek, "Power, Interaction, Position, and the Generation of Cultural Agreement in Organizations," *Human Relations* 49, no. 1 (January 1996), pp. 75–104.

13. P. Puranam, H. Singh, and M. Zollo, "Organizing for Innovation: Managing the Coordination–Autonomy Dilemma in Technology Acquisitions," *Academy of Management Journal* 49, no. 2 (2006), pp. 263–80.

14. *Corporate Director's Guidebook,* 6th ed. (Washington, DC: American Bar Association, 2012); S. F. Shultz, *Board Book: Making Your Corporate Board a Strategic Force in Your Company's Success* (New York: AMACOM, 2000); and R. D. Ward, *Improving Corporate Boards: The Boardroom Insider Guidebook* (New York: John Wiley & Sons, 2000).

15. "The Korn/Ferry Market Cap 100: Board Leadership at America's Most Valuable Public Companies," April 24, 2014, www.kornferryinstitute.com.

16. C. M. Daily and D. R. Dalton, "CEO and Board Chair Roles Held Jointly or Separately: Much Ado about Nothing?" *Academy of Management Executive* 11, no. 3 (August 1997), pp. 11–20.

17. D. Goldsmith, "Creating Master Decision Makers," *Leadership in Action* 28, no. 5 (2008), 22–23; Company websites, www.conocophillips.com, www.infosys.com; www.shutterfly.com, http://www.disney.com.

18. A. Chilcote and S. Reece, *"Power Paradox," Leadership Excellence* 26, no. 6 (June 2009), pp. 8–9; A. J. Ali, R. C. Camp, and M. Gibbs, "The Ten Commandments Perspective on Power and Authority in Organizations," *Journal of Business Ethics* 26, no. 4 (August 2000), pp. 351–61; and R. F. Pearse, "Understanding Organizational Power and Influence Systems," *Compensation & Benefits Management* 16, no. 4 (Autumn 2000), pp. 28–38.

19. S. Vickery, C. Droge, and R. Germain, "The Relationship between Product Customization and Organizational Structure," *Journal of Operations Management* 17, no. 4 (June 1999), pp. 377–91.

20. J. Spolsky, "How Hard Could It Be? How I Learned to Love Middle Managers," *Inc.,* September 2008, www.inc.com.

21. P. Jehiel, "Information Aggregation and Communication in Organizations," *Management Science* 45, no. 5 (May 1999), pp. 659–69; and A. Altaffer, "First-Line Managers: Measuring Their Span of Control," *Nursing Management* 29, no. 7 (July 1998), pp. 36–40.

22. "Span of Control vs. Span of Support," *Journal for Quality and Participation* 23, no. 4 (Fall 2000), p. 15; J. Gallo and P. R. Thompson, "Goals, Measures, and Beyond: In Search of Accountability in Federal HRM," *Public Personnel Management* 29, no. 2 (Summer 2000), pp. 237–48; and C. O. Longenecker and T. C. Stansfield, "Why Plant Managers Fail: Causes and Consequences," *Industrial Management* 42, no. 1 (January/February 2000), pp. 24–32.

23. Z. X. Chen and S. Aryee, "Delegation and Employee Work Outcomes: An Examination of the Cultural Context of Mediating Processes in China," *Academy of Management Journal* 50, no. 1 (2007), pp. 226–38.

24. P. Labarre, "What Does Fulfillment at Work Really Look Like?" *Fortune* (online), May 1, 2012, http://fortune.cnn.com.

25. P. Labarre, "Forget Empowerment-Aim for Exhilaration," *Management Exchange* (online), April 25, 2012, www.managementexchange.com.

26. R. Semler, "Set Them Free: Want a Nimble, Motivated Workforce?" *CIO Insight* 1, no. 38 (April 2004), p. 30.

27. R. Semler, *Maverick: The Success Story Behind the World's Most Unusual Workplace* (New York: Grand Central Publishing, April 1, 1995).

28. "How to Delegate More Effectively," *Community Banker,* February 2009, p. 14; B. Nefer, "Don't Be Delegation-Phobic," *Supervision,* December 2008; J. Mahoney, "Delegating Effectively," *Nursing Management* 28, no. 6 (June 1997), p. 62; and J. Lagges, "The Role of Delegation in Improving Productivity," *Personnel Journal,* November 1979, pp. 776–79.

29. G. Matthews, "Run Your Business or Build an Organization?" *Harvard Management Review,* March–April 1984, pp. 34–44.

30. N. Siggelkow and J.W. Rivkin, "When Exploration Backfires: Unintended Consequences of Multi-level Organizational Search," *Academy of Management Proceedings* (2006), pp. BB1–BB6.

31. Company website, www.burgerville.com; and S. Smith, "Jeff Harvey's Innovative Instincts," *Restaurant Business* 109, no. 12 (December 2010), pp. 28–34.

32. Smith, "Jeff Harvey's Innovation Instincts."

33. R. Forrester, "Empowerment: Rejuvenating a Potent Idea," *Academy of Management Executive* 14, no. 3 (August 2000), pp. 67–80; and M. L. Perry, C. L. Pearce, and H. P. Sims Jr., "Empowered Selling Teams: How Shared Leadership Can Contribute to Selling Team Outcomes," *Journal of Personal Selling & Sales Management* 19, no. 3 (Summer 1999), pp. 35–51.

34. L. Gard, "Growth Trifecta," *Construction Today,* January 2009; and Environmental Systems Design, "About ESD," corporate website, www.esdesign.com.

35. E. E. Lawler III, "New Roles for the Staff Function: Strategic Support and Services," in *Organizing for the Future*, J. Galbraith, E. E. Lawler III, and Associates (San Francisco: Jossey-Bass, 1993).

36. D. Ulrich, J. Younger, and W. Brockbank, "The Twenty-First-Century HR Organization," *Human Resource Management* 47, no. 4 (2008), pp. 829–50.

37. R. Cross and L. Baird, "Technology Is Not Enough: Improving Performance by Building Organizational Memory," *Sloan Management Review* 41, no. 3 (Spring 2000), pp. 69–78; and R. Duncan, "What Is the Right Organizational Structure?" *Organizational Dynamics* 7 (Winter 1979), pp. 59–80.

38. G. S. Day, "Creating a Market-Driven Organization," *Sloan Management Review* 41, no. 1 (Fall 1999), pp. 11–22.

39. G. Strauss and L. R. Sayles, *Strauss and Sayles's Behavioral Strategies for Managers,* © 1980, p. 221. Reprinted by permission of Prentice-Hall, Inc., Englewood Cliffs, New Jersey.

40. R. Boehm and C. Phipps, "Flatness Forays," *McKinsey Quarterly* 3 (1996), pp. 128–43.

41. B. T. Lamont, V. Sambamurthy, K. M. Ellis, and P. G. Simmonds, "The Influence of Organizational Structure on the Information Received by Corporate Strategists of Multinational Enterprises," *Management International Review* 40, no. 3 (2000), pp. 231–52.

42. L. A. Johnson, "Pfizer Planning to Redraw Its Battle Lines," *America's Intelligence Wire,* October 8, 2008.

43. Company website, www.deere.com.

44. M. Derven, "Managing the Matrix in the New Normal," *T + D* 64, no. 7 (July 2010), pp. 42–29; H. Kolodny, "Managing in a Matrix," *Business Horizons,* March–April 1981, pp. 17–24.

45. Ibid.

46. D. Cackowski, M. K. Najdawi, and Q. B. Chung, "Object Analysis in Organizational Design: A Solution for Matrix Organizations," *Project Management Journal* 31, no. 3 (September 2000), pp. 44–51; J. Barker, "Conflict Approaches of Effective and Ineffective Project Managers: A Field Study in a Matrix Organization," *Journal of Management Studies* 25, no. 2 (March 1988), pp. 167–78; G. J. Chambers, "The Individual in a Matrix Organization," *Project Management Journal* 20, no. 4 (December 1989), pp. 37–42, 50; and S. Davis and P. Lawrence, "Problems of Matrix Organizations," *Harvard Business Review,* May–June 1978, pp. 131–42.

47. A. Ferner, "Being Local Worldwide: ABB and the Challenge of Global Management Relations," *Industrielles* 55, no. 3 (Summer 2000), pp. 527–29; and C. Bartlett and S. Ghoshal, "Matrix Management: Not a Structure, a Frame of Mind," *Harvard Business Review* 68 (July–August 1990), pp. 138–45.

48. Derven, "Managing the Matrix in the New Normal."

49. J. Tata, S. Prasad, and R. Thorn, "The Influence of Organizational Structure on the Effectiveness of TQM Programs," *Journal of Managerial Issues* 11, no. 4 (Winter 1999), pp. 440–53; and Davis and Lawrence, "Problems of Matrix Organizations."

50. R. E. Miles and C. C. Snow, *Fit, Failure, and the Hall of Fame* (New York: Free Press, 1994); and G. Symon, "Information and Communication Technologies and Network Organization: A Critical Analysis," *Journal of Occupational and Organizational Psychology* 73, no. 4 (December 2000), pp. 389–95.

51. Company website, www.bombardier.com; and N. Anand and R. L. Daft, "What Is the Right Organization Design?" *Organizational Design* 36, no 4 (2007), pp. 329–344.

52. Miles and Snow, *Fit, Failure, and the Hall of Fame.*

53. S.-C. Kang, S. S. Morris, and S. A. Snell, "Relational Archetypes, Organizational Learning, and Value Creation: Extending the Human Resource Architecture," *Academy of Management Review* 32, no. 1 (2007), pp. 236–56.

54. J. G. March and H. A. Simon, *Organizations* (New York: John Wiley & Sons, 1958); and J. D. Thompson, *Organizations in Action* (New York: McGraw-Hill, 1967).

55. P. S. Adler, "Building Better Bureaucracies," *Academy of Management Executive* 13, no. 4 (November 1999), pp. 36–49.

56. "2013 China Motorcycle Output and Sales Analysis," *China Motor World* (online), January 25, 2014, www.chinamotorworld.com; and D. Tapscott, "The Global Plant Floor," *BusinessWeek,* March 20, 2007.

57. J. Galbraith, "Organization Design: An Information Processing View," *Interfaces* 4 (Fall 1974), pp. 28–36. See also S. A. Mohrman, "Integrating Roles and Structure in the Lateral Organization," in *Organizing for the Future,* ed. J. Galbraith, E. E. Lawler III, and Associates (San Francisco: Jossey-Bass, 1993); and B. B. Flynn and F. J. Flynn, "Information-Processing Alternatives for Coping with Manufacturing Environment Complexity," *Decision Sciences* 30, no. 4 (Fall 1999), pp. 1021–52.

58. Galbraith, "Organization Design"; and Mohrman, "Integrating Roles and Structure."

59. A. McMains, "Agency of the Year mcgarrybowen," *Adweek* 52, no. 44 (December 12, 2011–January 8, 2012), pp. 30–32; A. Keevil, *mcgarrybowen,* case study (Charlottesville, VA: Darden Business Publishing, 2011); and R. Parekh, "Why Verizon Dropped McCann for McGarry on Wireless Business," *Advertising Age* 81, no. 15 (April 12, 2010), pp. 2–4.

60. G. Hamel and C. K. Prahalad, "Competing for the Future," *Harvard Business Review,* July–August 1994, pp. 122–28.

61. G. Hamel and C. K. Prahalad, *Competing for the Future* (Boston: Harvard Business School Press, 1994).

62. D. G. Sirmon, M. A. Hitt, and R. D. Ireland, "Managing Firm Resources in Dynamic Environments to Create Value: Looking inside the Black Box," *Academy of Management Review* 32, no. 1 (2007), pp. 273–92.

63. A. Loten, "Online Reputations Lost as Yahoo Switches to Yelp," *The Wall Street Journal* (online), April 10, 2014, www.wsj.com; D. MacMillan, and "Yahoo to Partner with Yelp on Local Search; Partnership Is Part of Effort to Differentiate Yahoo from Google and Microsoft's Bing," *The Wall Street Journal* (online), February 10, 2014, www.wsj.com.

64. G. Slowinski, E. Hummel, A. Gupta, and E. R. Gilmont, "Effective Practices for Sourcing Innovation," *Research-Technology Management,* January–February 2009, pp. 27–34.

65. R. M. Kanter, "Collaborative Advantage: The Art of Alliances," *Harvard Business Review,* July–August 1994, pp. 96–108; J. B. Cullen, J. L. Johnson, and T. Sakano, "Success through Commitment and Trust: The Soft Side of Strategic Alliance Management," *Journal of World Business* 35, no. 3 (Fall 2000), pp. 223–40; and P. Kale, H. Singh, and H. Perlmutter, "Learning

and Protection of Proprietary Assets in Strategic Alliances: Building Relational Capital," *Strategic Management Journal* 21, no. 3 (March 2000), pp. 217–37.

66. P. Senge, *The Fifth Discipline* (New York: Doubleday Currency, 1990).

67. D. A. Garvin, "Building a Learning Organization," *Harvard Business Review,* July–August 1993, pp. 78–91; D. A. Garvin, *Learning in Action: A Guide to Putting the Learning Organization to Work* (Boston: Harvard Business School Press, 2000); and V. J. Marsick and K. E. Watkins, *Facilitating Learning Organizations: Making Learning Count* (Aldershot, Hampshire: Gower, 1999).

68. Ibid.; and N. Anand, H. K. Gardner, and T. Morris, "Knowledge-Based Innovation: Emergence and Embedding of New Practice Areas in Management Consulting Firms," *Academy of Management Journal* 50, no. 2 (2007), pp. 406–28.

69. R. J. Vandenberg, H. A. Richardson, and L. J. Eastman, "The Impact of High Involvement Work Process on Organizational Effectiveness: A Second-Order Latent Variable Approach," *Group & Organization Management* 24, no. 3 (September 1999), pp. 300–39; G. M. Spreitzer and A. K. Mishra, "Giving Up Control without Losing Control: Trust and Its Substitutes' Effects on Managers' Involving Employees in Decision Making," *Group & Organization Management* 24, no. 2 (June 1999), pp. 155–87; and S. Albers Mohrman, G. E. Ledford, and E. E. Lawler III, *Strategies for High Performance Organizations—The CEO Report: Employee Involvement, TQM, and Reengineering Programs in Fortune 1000 Corporations* (San Francisco: Jossey-Bass, 1998).

70. W. F. Cascio, "Downsizing: What Do We Know? What Have We Learned?" *Academy of Management Executive* 7 (February 1993), pp. 95–104; and S. J. Freeman, "The Gestalt of Organizational Downsizing: Downsizing Strategies as Package of Change," *Human Relations* 52, no. 12 (December 1999), pp. 1505–41.

71. A. Vance, "Microsoft Slashes Jobs as Sales Fall," *The New York Times,* January 23, 2009, www.nytimes.com; A. Vance, "Microsoft Profit Falls for First Time in 23 Years," *The New York Times,* April 24, 2009, www.nytimes.com; and P. Kafka, "Microsoft Starts the Layoff Machine Again with Thousands of Cuts," *All Things Digital,* May 5, 2009, http://mediamemo.allthingsd.com.

72. "Layoff 'Survivor' Stress: How to Manage the Guilt and the Workload," *HR Focus,* 86, no. 8 (August 2009), pp. 4–6; W. F. Cascio, "Strategies for Responsible Restructuring," *Academy of Management Executive* 19, no. 4 (2005), pp. 39–50; Cascio, "Downsizing"; and J. Ciancio, "Survivor's Syndrome," *Nursing Management* 31, no. 5 (May 2000), pp. 43–45.

73. Cascio, "Strategies for Responsible Restructuring"; Cascio, "Downsizing"; Freeman, "The Gestalt of Organizational Downsizing"; and M. Hitt, B. Keats, H. Harback, and R. Nixon, "Rightsizing: Building and Maintaining Strategic Leadership and Long-Term Competitiveness," *Organizational Dynamics,* Fall 1994, pp. 18–31.

74. B. Creech, *The Five Pillars of TQM: How to Make Total Quality Management Work for You* (New York: Plume Publishing, 1995); and J. R. Evans and W. M. Lindsay, *Management and Control of Quality* (Cincinnati, OH: Southwestern College Publishing, 1998).

75. T. S. Bateman and S. A. Snell, *Management: Leading & Collaborating in the Competitive World,* 9th ed. (New York: McGraw-Hill/Irwin, 2011), p. 558; and D. Brandt, "Lean Six Sigma and the City," *Industrial Engineer* 43, no. 7 (July 2011), pp. 50–52.

76. International Organization for Standardization, "ISO 9000/ISO 14000: Understand the Basics," www.iso.org.

77. "UniFirst Manufacturing Facilities Awarded ISO 9001: 2000 Certification," *Modern Uniforms,* February–March 2006.

78. J. Woodward, *Industrial Organization: Theory and Practice* (London: Oxford University Press, 1965).

79. G. Liu and G. D. Deitz, "Linking Supply Chain Management with Mass Customization Capability," *International Journal of Physical Distribution & Logistics Management* 41, no. 7 (2011), pp. 668–83; J. H. Gilmore and B. J. Pine, eds., *Markets of One: Creating Customer-Unique Value through Mass Customization* (Cambridge, MA: Harvard Business Review Press, 2000); and B. J. Pine, *Mass Customization: The New Frontier in Business Competition* (Cambridge, MA: Harvard Business School Press, 1992).

80. F. Sahin, "Manufacturing Competitiveness: Different Systems to Achieve the Same Results," *Production and Inventory Management Journal* 41, no. 1 (First Quarter 2000), pp. 56–65.

81. S. Wadhwa and K. S. Rao, "Flexibility: An Emerging Meta-Competence for Managing High Technology," *International Journal of Technology Management* 19, no. 7–8 (2000), pp. 820–45.

82. B. A. Peters and L. F. McGinnis, "Strategic Configuration of Flexible Assembly Systems: A Single Period Approximation," *IIE Transaction* 31, no. 4 (April 1999), pp. 379–90.

83. J. K. Liker and J. M. Morgan, "The Toyota Way in Services: The Case of Lean Product Development," *Academy of Management Perspectives* 20, no. 2 (May 2006), pp. 5–20; "Strategic Reconfiguration: Manufacturing's Key Role in Innovation," *Production and Inventory Management Journal,* Summer–Fall 2001, pp. 9–17; S. R. Morrey, "Learning to Think Lean: A Roadmap and Toolbox for the Lean Journey," *Automotive Manufacturing & Production* 112, no. 8 (August 2000), p. 147; and F. Sahin, "Manufacturing Competitiveness: Different Systems to Achieve the Same Results," *Production and Inventory Management Journal* 41, no. 1 (First Quarter 2000), pp. 56–65.

84. Liker and Morgan, "The Toyota Way in Services"; and H. Cho, "Squeezing the Fat from Health Care," *Baltimore Sun,* September 17, 2006.

85. Sahin, "Manufacturing Competitiveness"; and G. S. Vasilash, "Flexible Thinking: How Need, Innovation, Teamwork & a Whole Bunch of Machining Centers Have Transformed TRW Tillsonburg into a Model of Lean Manufacturing," *Automotive Manufacturing & Production* 111, no. 10 (October 1999), pp. 64–65.

86. C. H. Chung, "Balancing the Two Dimensions of Time for Time-Based Competition," *Journal of Managerial Issues* 11, no. 3 (Fall 1999), pp. 299–314; and D. R. Towill and P. McCullen, "The Impact of Agile Manufacturing on Supply Chain Dynamics," *International Journal of Logistics Management* 10, no. 1 (1999), pp. 83–96. See also G. Stalk and T. M. Hout, *Competing against Time: How Time-Based Competition Is Reshaping Global Markets* (New York: Free Press, 1990).

87. M. Tucker and D. Davis, "Key Ingredients for Successful Implementation of Just-in-Time: A System for All Business Sizes,"

Business Horizons, May-June 1993, pp. 59–65; and H. L. Richardson, "Tame Supply Chain Bottlenecks," *Transportation & Distribution* 41, no. 3 (March 2000), pp. 23–28.

88. See, for example, "Just-in-Time: Has Its Time Passed?" *Baseline,* September 11, 2006.

89. J. E. Ettlie, "Product Development—Beyond Simultaneous Engineering," *Automotive Manufacturing & Production* 112, no. 7 (July 2000), p. 18; U. Roy, J. M. Usher, and H. R. Parsaei, eds. *Simultaneous Engineering: Methodologies and Applications* (Newark, NJ: Gordon and Breach, 1999); and M. M. Helms and L. P. Ettkin, "Time-Based Competitiveness: A Strategic Perspective," *Competitiveness Review* 10, no. 2 (2000), pp. 1–14.

90. J. Zygmont, "Detroit Faster on Its Feet," *Ward's Auto World,* July 1, 2006.

CHAPTER 8

1. G. Welderman, "Pam Nicholson: Enterprise's $15 Billion CEO," *BizJournal* (online), July 12, 2013; "Breaking Barriers: Enterprise Rent-A-Car's Pam Nicholson," *The Wall Street Journal,* August 4, 2008, www.wsj.com; A. S. Wellner, "Nothing but Green Skies," *Inc.,* November 2007, www.inc.com; and "Mentoring Is a Mission at Enterprise Rent-A-Car," *Diversity in Action,* April/May 2007, www.diversitycareers.com.

2. "HR That Means Business: Focusing on Value Creation," company website, www.deloitte.com; and "HR That Means Business: Focusing on Value Creation," "HR's Impact on Shareholder Value," *Workforce Management,* December 11, 2006.

3. P. M. Wright and S. A. Snell, "Partner or Guardian? HR's Challenge in Balancing Value and Values," *Human Resource Management* 44, no. 2 (2005), pp. 177–82.

4. R. J. Grossman, "11 Initiatives for 2011," *HRMagazine* 56, no. 1 (January 2011), p. 24; E. Pofeldt, "Empty Desk Syndrome: How to Handle a Hiring Freeze," *Inc.,* May 2008, pp. 39–40; and C. Tuna, "Some Employers See Hiring Opportunity," *The Wall Street Journal,* April 3, 2009, http://online.wsj.com.

5. "An Interview with HR & Leadership Icon, Dave Ulrich," Juniper.net (online), September 12, 2012.

6. P. Coy and J. Ewing, "Where Are All the Workers?" *Businessweek,* April 9, 2007, www.businessweek.com.

7. J. Hopkins, "Small Employers Struggle to Fill Jobs," *USA Today,* January 4, 2007, www.usatoday.com; "Most Employers Unprepared for Baby Boomer Retirements," *CCH Pension,* November 9, 2006, http://hr.cch.com; and D. Ellwood, *Grow Faster Together, or Grow Slowly Apart* (Washington, DC: Aspen Institute, 2003), www.aspeninstitute.org.

8. P. S. Budhwar and A. Varma, "Emerging HR Management Trends in India and the Way Forward," *Organizational Dynamics* 40, no. 4 (October–December 2011), pp. 317–25; A. Kazmin, S. Pearson, G. Robinson, and H. Weitzman, "Talent Shortage Adds to Growth Strains," *Financial Times,* May 19, 2011, p. 9; and Manpower's "2010 Talent Shortage Survey Results," company website, www.manpower.com.

9. M. T. Brannick, E. L. Levine, and F. P. Morgeson, *Job and Work Analysis: Methods, Research, and Applications for Human Resource Management,* 2nd ed. (Thousand Oaks, CA: Sage Publications, 2007); F. P. Morgeson and M. A. Campion, "Accuracy in Job Analysis: Toward an Inference-Based Model,"

Journal of Organizational Behavior 21, no. 7 (November 2000), pp. 819–27; and J. S. Shippmann, R. A. Ash, L. Carr, and B. Hesketh, "The Practice of Competency Modeling," *Personnel Psychology* 53, no. 3 (Autumn 2000), pp. 703–40.

10. J. S. Schippmann, *Strategic Job Modeling: Working at the Core of Integrated Human Resources* (Mahwah, NJ: Lawrence Erlbaum Associates, 1999).

11. D. E. Terpstra, "The Search for Effective Methods," *HR Focus,* May 1996, pp. 16–17; H. G. Heneman III and R. A. Berkley, "Applicant Attraction Practices and Outcomes among Small Businesses," *Journal of Small Business Management* 37, no. 1 (January 1999), pp. 53–74; and J.-M. Hiltrop, "The Quest for the Best: Human Resource Practices to Attract and Retain Talent," *European Management Journal* 17, no. 4 (August 1999), pp. 422–30.

12. G. Ruiz, "Print Ads See Resurgence as Hiring Source," *Workforce Management,* March 26, 2007; and G. Ruiz, "Recruiters Cite Referrals as Top Hiring Tool," *Workforce Management,* October 23, 2006.

13. F. Hansen, "Employee Referral Programs, Selective Campus Recruitment Could Touch Off Bias Charges," *Workforce Management,* June 26, 2006.

14. Company website, www.veteranjobsmission.com/about-the-mission, "Our Nation's Military Members and Veterans Represent the Best this Country Has to Offer."

15. "The 2011/2012 Talent Management and Rewards Study, North America," Towers Watson, www.towerswatson.com.

16. R. Myers, "Interviewing Techniques: Tips from the Pros," *Journal of Accountancy,* August 2006; M. McDaniel, D. L. Whetzel, F. L. Schmidt, and S. D. Maurer, "The Validity of Employment Interviews: A Comprehensive Review and Meta-Analysis," *Journal of Applied Psychology* 79, no. 4 (August 1994), pp. 599–616; M. A. Campion, J. E. Campion, and P. J. Hudson Jr., "Structured Interviewing: A Note on Incremental Validity and Alternative Question Types," *Journal of Applied Psychology* 79, no. 6 (December 1994), pp. 998–1002; and R. A. Fear, *The Evaluation Interview* (New York: McGraw-Hill, 1984).

17. Myers, "Interviewing Techniques."

18. T. Macan, "The Employment Interview: A Review of Current Studies and Directions for Future Research," *Human Resource Management Review* 19, no. 3 (September 2009), pp. 201–19.

19. T. Lewin, "Dean at M.I.T. Resigns, Ending a 28-Year Lie," *The New York Times,* April 27, 2007, www.nytimes.com.

20. C. E. Stenberg, "The Role of Pre-Employment Background Investigations in Hiring," *Human Resource Professional* 9, no. 1 (January/February 1996), pp. 19–21; P. Taylor, "Providing Structure to Interviews and Reference Checks," *Workforce,* May 1999, Supplement, pp. 7–10; "Fear of Lawsuits Complicates Reference Checks," *InfoWorld* 21, no. 5 (February 1, 1999), p. 73; and D. E. Terpstra, R. B. Kethley, R. T. Foley, and W. Limpaphayom, "The Nature of Litigation Surrounding Five Screening Devices," *Public Personnel Management* 29, no. 1 (Spring 2000), pp. 43–54.

21. C. Bigda, "Web Widens Job-Search Connections," *Chicago Tribune,* March 4, 2007, www.chicagotribune.com.

22. "The Trouble with Background Checks," *Bloomberg Businessweek* (Online), May 29, 2008, www.businessweek.com.

23. See also M. R. Barrick and M. K. Mount, "The Big Five Personality Dimensions and Job Performance: A Meta-Analysis," *Personnel Psychology* 44 (1991), pp. 1–26; D. P. O'Meara, "Personality Tests Raise Questions of Legality and Effectiveness," *HRMagazine,* January 1994, pp. 97–100; and L. A. McFarland and A. M. Ryan, "Variance in Faking across Noncognitive Measures," *Journal of Applied Psychology* 85, no. 5 (October 2000), pp. 812–21.

24. R. E. Ployhart, J. A. Weekley, and K. Baughman, "The Structure and Function of Human Capital Emergence: A Multilevel Examination of the Attraction-Selection-Attrition Model," *Academy of Management Journal* 49, no. 4 (2006), pp. 661–77.

25. P. M. Wright, M. K. Kacmar, G. C. McMahan, and K. Deleeuw, "P 5 f (M 3 A): Cognitive Ability as a Moderator of the Relationship between Personality and Job Performance," *Journal of Management* 21, no. 6 (1995), pp. 1129–2063; P. R. Sackett and D. J. Ostgaard, "Job-Specific Applicant Pools and National Norms for Cognitive Ability Tests: Implications for Range Restriction Corrections in Validation Research," *Journal of Applied Psychology* 79, no. 5 (October 1994), pp. 680–84; F. L. Schmidt and J. E. Hunter, "Tacit Knowledge, Practical Intelligence, General Mental Ability, and Job Knowledge," *Current Directions in Psychological Science* 2, no. 1 (1993), pp. 3–13; M. Roznowski, D. N. Dickter, L. L. Sawin, V. J. Shute, and S. Hong, "The Validity of Measures of Cognitive Processes and Generability for Learning and Performance on Highly Complex Computerized Tutors: Is the G Factor of Intelligence Even More General?" *Journal of Applied Psychology* 85, no. 6 (December 2000), pp. 940–55; and J. M. Cortina, N. B. Goldstein, S. C. Payne, H. K. Davison, and S. W. Gilliland, "The Incremental Validity of Interview Scores over and above Cognitive Ability and Conscientiousness Scores," *Personnel Psychology* 53, no. 2 (Summer 2000), pp. 325–51.

26. F. Lievens and F. Patterson, "The Validity and Incremental Validity of Knowledge Tests, Low-Fidelity Simulations, and High-Fidelity Simulations for Predicting Job Performance in Advanced-Level High-Stakes Selection," *Journal of Applied Psychology* 96, no. 5 (2011), pp. 927–40; W. Arthur Jr., D. J. Woehr, and R. Maldegen, "Convergent and Discriminant Validity of Assessment Center Dimensions: A Conceptual and Empirical Reexamination of the Assessment Center Construct-Related Validity Paradox," *Journal of Management* 26, no. 4 (2000), pp. 813–35; and R. Randall, E. Ferguson, and F. Patterson, "Self-Assessment Accuracy and Assessment Center Decisions," *Journal of Occupational and Organizational Psychology* 73, no. 4 (December 2000), p. 443.

27. U.S. Department of Labor website, www.dol.gov/compliance/laws/comp-eppa.htm; McFarland and Ryan, "Variance in Faking across Noncognitive Measures"; and Terpstra et al., "The Nature of Litigation Surrounding Five Screening Devices."

28. D. S. Ones, C. Viswesvaran, and F. L. Schmidt, "Comprehensive Meta-Analysis of Integrity Test Validities: Findings and Implications for Personnel Selection and Theories of Job Performance," *Journal of Applied Psychology* 78 (August 1993), pp. 679–703.

29. J. A. Oxman, "The Hidden Leverage of Human Capital," *MIT Sloan Management Review* 43, no. 4 (Summer 2002), pp. 78–83; R.-L. DeWitt, "The Structural Consequences of Downsizing," *Organization Science* 4, no. 1 (February 1993), pp. 30–40; and P. P. Shah, "Network Destruction: The Structural Implications of Downsizing," *Academy of Management Journal* 43, no. 1 (February 2000), pp. 101–12.

30. See *Adair v. United States,* 2078 U.S. 161 (1908); and D. A. Ballam, "Employment-at-Will; The Impending Death of a Doctrine," *American Business Law Journal* 37, no. 4 (Summer 2000), pp. 653–87.

31. P. Falcone, "Employee Separations: Layoffs vs. Terminations for Cause," *HRMagazine* 45, no. 10 (October 2000), pp. 189–96; and P. Falcone, "A Blueprint for Progressive Discipline and Terminations," *HR Focus* 77, no. 8 (August 2000), pp. 3–5.

32. "J. W. Bucking, "Employee Terminations: Ten Must-Do Steps When Letting Someone Go," *Supervision,* May 2008; and M. Price, "Employee Termination Process Is Tough for Those on Both Sides," *Journal Record* (Oklahoma City, OK), October 23, 2008. Bullet points taken from S. Alexander, "Firms Get Plenty of Practice at Layoffs, but They Often Bungle the Firing Process," *The Wall Street Journal,* November 14, 1991, p. 31. Copyright © 1991 Dow Jones & Co., Inc. Reproduced with permission of Dow Jones & Co., Inc. via Copyright Clearance Center.

33. J. Deschenaux, "Train Managers and Supervisors to Limit EEO Liability," *HRMagazine* (online), June 21, 2013, www.shrm.org.

34. *Employer EEO Responsibilities* (Washington, DC: Equal Employment Opportunity Commission, U.S. Government Printing Office, 1996); and N. J. Edman and M. D. Levin-Epstein, *Primer of Equal Employment Opportunity,* 6th ed. (Washington, DC: Bureau of National Affairs, 1994).

35. Equal Employment Opportunity Commission website, www.eeoc.gov/facts/fs-sex.html.

36. R. Gatewood and H. Field, *Human Resource Selection,* 3rd ed. (Chicago: Dryden Press, 1994), pp. 36–49; and R. A. Baysinger, "Disparate Treatment and Disparate Impact Theories of Discrimination: The Continuing Evolution of Title VII of the 1964 Civil Rights Act," in *Readings in Personnel and Human Resource Management,* ed. R. S. Schuler, S. A. Youngblood, and V. L. Huber (St. Paul, MN: West Publishing, 1987).

37. M. C. Fisk and G. Stohr, "Wal-Mart Ruling Hurts Bias Cases, May Spare Other Class Actions," *Bloomberg News* (Online), June 20, 2011, www.bloomberg.com.

38. "2010 Training Industry Report," *Training* 47, no. 6 (November/December 2010), pp. 18–32.

39. G. Anders, "Companies Find Online Training Has Its Limits," *The Wall Street Journal,* March 26, 2007, http://online.wsj.com.

40. Ibid.

41. J. Gordon, "Building Brand Champions: How Training Helps Drive a Core Business Process at General Mills," *Training,* January–February 2007.

42. P. Dvorak, "Simulation Shows What It's Like to Be Boss," *The Wall Street Journal,* March 31, 2008, http://online.wsj.com.

43. For more information, see K. Wexley and G. Latham, *Increasing Productivity through Performance Appraisal* (Reading, MA: Addison-Wesley, 1994).

44. G. Toegel and J. Conger, "360 Degree Assessment: Time for Reinvention," *Academy of Management Learning and Education* 2, no. 3 (September 2003), p. 297; and L. K. Johnson, "Retooling 360s for Better Performance," *Harvard Business School Working Knowledge,* February 23, 2004, online.

45. M. Edwards and A. J. Ewen, "How to Manage Performance and Pay with 360-Degree Feedback," *Compensation and Benefits Review* 28, no. 3 (May/June 1996), pp. 41–46. See also M. N. Vinson, "The Pros and Cons of 360-Degree Feedback: Making It Work," *Training and Development* 50, no. 4 (April 1996), pp. 11–12; and R. S. Schuler, *Personnel and Human Resource Management* (St. Paul, MN: West Publishing, 1984).

46. G. Bohlander, S. Snell, and A. Sherman, *Managing Human Resources,* 12th ed. (Cincinnati, OH: South-Western, 2001).

47. Company website, www.glassdoor.com; company website, http://vault.com; J. Eckle, "Peering through the Glass Door," *Computerworld* 43, no. 8 (February 23, 2009), pp. 36–37; and D. Darlin, "Using the Web to Get the Boss to Pay More," *The New York Times,* March 3, 2007, www.nytimes.com.

48. A. Colella, R. L. Paetzold, A. Zardkoohi, and M. J. Wesson, "Exposing Pay Secrecy," *Academy of Management Review* 32, no. 1 (2007), pp. 55–71.

49. L. A. Rozycki, "Incentive Plans: A Motivational Tool That Works," *CPA Practice Management Forum* 4, no. 10 (October 2008), pp. 12–16; G. M. Ritzky, "Incentive Pay Programs That Help the Bottom Line," *HRMagazine* 40, no. 4 (April 1995), pp. 68–74; S. Gross and J. Bacher, "The New Variable Pay Programs: How Some Succeed, Why Some Don't," *Compensation and Benefits Review* 25, no. 1 (January–February 1993), p. 51; and G. T. Milkovich and J. M. Newman, *Compensation* (New York: McGraw-Hill/Irwin, 1999).

50. Company website, www.boeing.com.

51. T. Welbourne and L. Gomez-Mejia, "Gainsharing: A Critical Review and a Future Research Agenda," *Journal of Management* 21, no. 3 (1995), pp. 559–609; L. P. Gomez-Mejia, T. M. Welbourne, and R. M. Wiseman, "The Role of Risk Sharing and Risk Taking under Gainsharing," *Academy of Management Review* 25, no. 3 (July 2000), pp. 492–507; D. Collins, *Gainsharing and Power: Lessons from Six Scanlon Plans* (Ithaca, NY: ILR Press, 1998); and P. K. Zingheim and J. R. Schuster, *Pay People Right!* (San Francisco: Jossey-Bass, 2000).

52. "Top Entry Level Employers," CollegeGrad.com, www.collegegrad.com; D. LaGesse, "A 'Stealth Company' No Longer," *U.S. News & World Report,* October 27, 2008, www.usnews.com; P. Sellers, "A Powerful Woman Revs Ahead at Enterprise," *Fortune,* August 4, 2008, www.fortune.com; L. E. Wickman, "Enterprise Rent-A-Car: Ahead of the Curve with Personalized Recruitment," *Talent Management* [no date], www.talentmgt.com; "Mentoring Is a Mission."

53. F. Hansen, "Merit-Pay Payoff?" *Workforce Management* 87, no. 18 (November 3, 2008), pp. 33–38.

54. S. Greenhouse, "Labor Puts Executive Pay in the Spotlight," *The New York Times Economix* (April 19, 2011), http://economix.blogs.nytimes.com; R. Kirkland, "The Real CEO Pay Problem," *Fortune,* July 10, 2006; K. Drawbaugh, "Soaring Executive Pay Meets Reforms," Reuters, March 9, 2007, http://news.yahoo.com; R. Watts and D. Roberts, "FTSE Pay Spirals out of Control," *Sunday Telegraph* (London), September 24, 2006; "Study: Australian Execs Outstrip Workers," *UPI NewsTrack,* January 28, 2006; and M. Fackler and D. Barboza, "In Asia, Executives Earn Much Less," *The New York Times,* June 16, 2006.

55. "GMI's 2013 CEO Pay Survey," http://gmiratings.com.

56. "May 2013 National Occupational Employment and Wage Estimates," news release from the Bureau of Labor Statistics, www.bls.gov.

57. M. J. Conyon, "Executive Compensation and Incentives," *Academy of Management Perspectives* 20, no. 1 (February 2006), pp. 25–44.

58. J. D. Glater, "Stock Options Are Adjusted after Many Share Prices Fall," *The New York Times,* March 27, 2009, www.nytimes.com; and D. Nicklaus, "Worthless Options Worry Companies," *St. Louis Post-Dispatch,* April 3, 2009.

59. U.S. Census Bureau, *Statistical Abstract of the United States,* 2007, p. 418; and Bureau of Labor Statistics, *Charting the U.S. Labor Market in 2005,* June 2006, www.bls.gov.

60. J. Geisel, "Group Health Plan Costs Rising More Slowly: Average Increase Falls to 6.1% in 2011, Mercer Survey Shows," *Business Insurance* 45, no. 45 (November 21, 2011), p. 3.

61. M. Koba, "New Rule Signals Kiss of Death for Pensions," *CNBC Personal Finance* (online), May 3, 2013, www.cnbc.com.

62. Employee Benefit Research Institute, "Finances of the Employee Benefit System," in *EBRI Databook on Employee Benefits,* updated December 2011, www.ebri.org.

63. E. C. Kearns and M. Gallagher, eds., *The Fair Labor Standards Act* (Washington, DC: Bureau of National Affairs, 1999).

64. C. Fay and H. W. Risher, "Contractors, Comparable Worth and the New OFCCP: Deja Vu and More," *Compensation and Benefits Review* 32, no. 5 (September/October 2000), pp. 23–33; and G. Flynn, "Protect Yourself from an Equal-Pay Audit," *Workforce* 78, no. 6 (June 1999), pp. 144–46.

65. Bohlander et al., *Managing Human Resources.*

66. E. Henry, "Wage-Bias Bill: Study Panel Proposed," *Arizona Business Gazette,* February 28, 2002, pp. 2–4; and S. E. Gardner and C. Daniel, "Implementing Comparable Worth/Pay Equity: Experiences of Cutting-Edge States," *Public Personnel Management* 27, no. 4 (Winter 1998), pp. 475–89.

67. "U.S. Teens Work Late, Long and in Danger, Study," *Reuters,* March 5, 2007, http://news.yahoo.com; and C. K. Johnson, "Teens Tell about On-the-Job Dangers," *Chicago Tribune,* March 5, 2007, www.chicagotribune.com.

68. L. Kahn, *Primer of Labor Relations,* 25th ed. (Washington, DC: Bureau of National Affairs Books, 1994); and A. Sloane and F. Witney, *Labor Relations* (Englewood Cliffs, NJ: Prentice Hall, 1985).

69. S. Premack and J. E. Hunter; "Individual Unionization Decisions," *Psychological Bulletin* 103 (1988), pp. 223–34; L. Troy, *Beyond Unions and Collective Bargaining* (Armonk, NY: M. E. Sharpe, 1999); and J. A. McClendon, "Members and Nonmembers: Determinants of Dues-Paying Membership in a Bargaining Unit," *Relations Industrielles* 55, no. 2 (Spring 2000), pp. 332–47.

70. R. Sinclair and L. Tetrick, "Social Exchange and Union Commitment: A Comparison of Union Instrumentality and Union Support Perceptions," *Journal of Organizational Behavior* 16, no. 6 (November 1995), pp. 669–79. See also Premack and Hunter, "Individual Unionization Decisions."

71. D. Lewin and R. B. Peterson, *The Modern Grievance Procedure in the United States* (Westport, CT: Quorum Books, 1998).

72. G. Bohlander and D. Blancero, "A Study of Reversal Determinants in Discipline and Discharge Arbitration Awards: The Impact of Just Cause Standards," *Labor Studies Journal* 21, no. 3 (Fall 1996), pp. 3–18.

Chapter 9

1. "No. 1: Kaiser Permanente," *DiversityInc.,* www.diversityinc.com; company website, www.kaiserpermanente.org; and R. Ridge, "Practicing to Potential," *Nursing Management* 42, no. 6 (June 2011), pp. 33–37.

2. "What Is the Difference Between EEO, Affirmative Action, and Diversity?" Society for Human Resource Management (online), September 20, 2012, www.shrm.org.

3. U.S. Department of Labor, Office of Federal Contract Compliance Programs (OFCCP), www.dol.gov/ofccp/regs/compliance/fs11246.htm.

4. L. Tucker, "Portland Local and Oregon State Organizations Have Instituted Affirmative Action Programs," *Daily Journal of Commerce,* Portland, January 23, 2006.

5. B. Eisenberg and M. Ruthsdotter, "Living the Legacy: The Women's Rights Movement 1848–1998," National Women's History Project, www.legacy98.org/move-hist.html.

6. Ibid.; and Bureau of Labor Statistics, "Employed Persons by Detailed Occupation, Sex, Race, and Hispanic or Latino Ethnicity" (Washington, DC: U.S. Department of Labor), www.bls.gov/cps/cpsaat11.pdf.

7. "Global Diversity and Inclusion: Perceptions, Practices, and Attitudes," A Study for the Society of Human Resource Management (SHRM) by the Economist Intelligence Unit, released on June 18, 2009, www.shrm.org.

8. M. N. Davidson, *The End of Diversity As We Know It: Why Diversity Efforts Fail and How Leveraging Difference Can Succeed* (San Francisco: Berrett-Koehler Publishers, 2011).

9. Bureau of Labor Statistics, "Household Data: Annual Averages," Labor Force Statistics from the Current Population Survey, www.bls.gov/cps/demographics.htm; and Bureau of Labor Statistics, "Labor Force Statistics from the Current Population Survey," December 2012, www.bls.gov/cps/wives_earn_more.htm.

10. C. Hymowitz, "Bend without Breaking: Women Executives Discuss the Art of Flex Schedules," *The Wall Street Journal,* March 6, 2007, http://online.wsj.com.

11. Bureau of Labor Statistics, "Highlights of Women's Earnings in 2012" (Washington, DC: U.S. Department of Labor, October 2013), www.bls.gov.

12. R. Soares, M. Bartkiewicz, and L. Mulligan-Ferry, "2013 Catalyst Census: Fortune 500 Women Executive Officers and Top Earners," *Catalyst,* www.catalyst.org.

13. "The 2014 World's Most 100 Powerful Women," *Forbes,* www.forbes.com.

14. "Where's the Diversity in Fortune 500 CEOs?" *DiversityInc* (online), www.DiversityInc.com, accessed on May 19, 2014.

15. "Global Diversity and Inclusion: Perceptions, Practices, and Attitudes."

16. "NAFE 2013 Top 50 Companies for Executive Women," National Association of Female Executives, www.nafe.com.

17. G. Bohlander, S. Snell, and A. Sherman, *Managing Human Resources,* 12th ed. (Cincinnati, OH: South-Western Publishing, 2001) Copyright © 2001. Reprinted by permission of South-Western, a division of Thomson Learning, http://www.thomsonrights.com.

18. S. Bhattacharya and P. Mehra, "In Good Company," *Business Today* (online), October 17, 2010, http://businesstoday.intoday.in; Bohlander et al., *Managing Human Resources;* and W. Petrocelli and B. K. Repa, *Sexual Harassment on the Job: What It Is and How to Stop It* (Berkeley, CA: Nolo Press, 1998).

19. Bureau of Labor Statistics, "Foreign-Born Workers: Labor Force Characteristics-2012," news release, May 22, 2013, www.bls.gov; and J. Lee and F. D. Bean, "America's Changing Color Lines," *Annual Review of Sociology,* 2004, pp. 221–43.

20. "The United States of Entrepreneurs," *The Economist,* March 14, 2009, www.kauffman.org.

21. Bureau of Labor Statistics, "Labor Force Characteristics by Race and Ethnicity, 2012," October 2013, Report 1044, Table 16: Median Usual Weekly Earnings of Full-time Wage and Salary Workers by Gender, Race, and Hispanic or Latino Ethnicity, 1979-2012 Annual Averages," www.bls.gov.

22. M. Bertrand and S. Mullainathan, "Are Emily and Greg More Employable Than Lakisha and Jamal?" NBER Working Paper No. 9873, July 2003, www.nber.org.

23. *Fortune*'s "100 Best Companies to Work for—Most Diverse," http://money.cnn.com.

24. M. Brault, "Americans with Disabilities: 2010," United States Census Bureau, Current Population Reports, Issued July 2012, www.census.gov.

25. Census Bureau, "Anniversary of Americans with Disabilities Act, July 26," news release, May 29, 2013, www.census.gov.

26. Ibid.

27. Equal Employment Opportunity Commission (EEOC), "Disability Discrimination," www.eeoc.gov; EEOC, "Notice Concerning the Americans with Disabilities Act (ADA) Amendments Act of 2008," www.eeoc.gov; and EEOC, "ADA Charge Data by Impairments/Bases: Resolutions, FY1997–FY2008," www.eeoc.gov.

28. "Fast Facts: Back to School Statistics for 2013," National Center for Education Statistics, http://nces.ed.gov, accessed May 20, 2014; Bureau of Labor Statistics, "Labor Force Characteristics of Foreign-Born Workers Summary," news release, May 22, 2013, www.bls.gov.

29. Bureau of Labor Statistics, "Labor Force Characteristics of Foreign-Born Workers Summary," news release, May 27, 2011, www.bls.gov.

30. M. Toosi, "Labor Force Projections to 2018: Older Workers Staying More Active," *Monthly Labor Review,* Bureau of Labor Statistics, November 2009, pp. 30–51.

31. Company website, www.rackspace.com; E. Bamforth, "Most Quirky S.A. Office Perks," *San Antonio Express-News, My San Antonio* (online), May 20, 2014, www.mysantonio.com; S. Tressler, "Best S.A. Office Perks," *San Antonio Express-News, My San Antonio* (online), July 30, 2013, www.mysantonio.com; "Rackspace Hosting Reports Fourth Quarter 2013 Results," *The Wall Street Journal* (online), February 10, 2014, www.wsj.com; K. Murphy, "Revitalizing a Dead Mall (Don't Expect

Shoppers)," *The New York Times,* October 30, 2012, (online), www.nytimes.com.

32. Bureau of Labor Statistics, "Labor Force Projections to 2018: Older Workers Staying More Active," *Monthly Labor Review,* November 2009, www.bls.gov.

33. Census Bureau, "Minority Population Tops 100 Million," news release, May 17, 2007, www.census.gov.

34. Ibid.

35. J. Johnsson, "A Labor Shortage for U.S. Nuclear Plants," *Bloomberg Businessweek* (Online), July 7, 2011, http://businessweek.com; and Bureau of Labor Statistics, "The Labor Market for Teachers," *Monthly Labor Review* (Online) 133, no. 1, January 2010, www.bls.gov.

36. N. Blacksmith and J. Harter, "Majority of American Workers Not Engaged in Their Jobs," Gallup Poll (Online), October 28, 2011, www.gallup.com.

37. L. M. Roth, "Women on Wall Street: Despite Diversity Measures, Wall Street Remains Vulnerable to Sex Discrimination Charges," *The Academy of Management Perspectives* 21, no. 1 (February 2007), pp. 24–35; N. D. Ursel and M. Armstrong-Stassen, "How Age Discrimination in Employment Affects Stockholders," *Journal of Labor Research* 27, no. 1 (Winter 2006), pp. 89–99; and K. Weisul, "The Bottom Line on Women at the Top," *Businessweek,* January 26, 2004, www.businessweek.com.

38. L. Belkin, "Diversity Isn't Rocket Science, Is It?" *The New York Times,* May 15, 2008, www.nytimes.com; T. Weiss, "Science and the Glass Ceiling," *Forbes,* May 12, 2008, www.forbes.com; and Center for Work-Life Policy, "The Athena Factor: Reversing the Brain Drain in Science, Engineering, and Technology," news release, May 21, 2008, www.worklifepolicy.org.

39. N. Adler, *International Dimensions of Organizational Behavior,* 3rd ed. (Boston: PWS-Kent, 1997); and T. Cox and S. Blake, "Managing Cultural Diversity: Implications for Organizational Competitiveness," *Academy of Management Executive* 5 (August 1991), pp. 45–56.

40. C. Larsen, "Top Companies 2007: Meet the Top Companies," National Association of Female Executives, www.nafe.com; and Alleyne, "The 40 Best Companies for Diversity."

41. See, for example, F. Hansen, "Payback Time," *Workforce Management* 89, no. 3 (March 2010), pp. 14–15; "3M Agrees to Pay $3 Million to Settle EEOC Age Bias Case," *HR Focus* 88, no. 10 (October 2011), pp. 8–9; "Verizon Agrees to $20 Million Payment to Settle ADA Case," *HR Focus* 88, no. 8 (August 2011), pp. 6–7; and M. Bustillo, "Best Buy Settles Lawsuit on Hiring," *The Wall Street Journal,* June 18, 2011, p. B3.

42. R. Roosevelt Thomas Jr., "From Affirmative Action to Affirming Diversity," *Harvard Business Review,* March–April 1990.

43. K. Jesella, "Mom's Mad, and She's Organized," *The New York Times,* February 22, 2007, www.nytimes.com.

44. G. Avalos, "Study Looks at Diversity, Turnover," *Contra Costa Times* (Walnut Creek, CA), October 13, 2006.

45. Adler, *International Dimensions of Organizational Behavior;* and Cox and Blake, "Managing Cultural Diversity."

46. T. Inamori and F. Analoui, "Beyond Pygmalion Effect: The Role of Managerial Perception," *The Journal of Management Development* 29, no. 4 (2010), pp. 306–21; and J. D. Nordell, "Positions of Power: How Female Ambition Is Shaped," *Slate,* November 21, 2006, www.slate.com.

47. Adler, *International Dimensions of Organizational Behavior.*

48. K. A. Jehn, "Workplace Diversity, Conflict, and Productivity: Managing in the 21st Century," *SEI Center for Advanced Studies in Management,* Wharton School, University of Pennsylvania, Diversity, http://mktgsun.wharton.upenn.edu/SEI/diversity.html.

49. A. J. Murrell, F. J. Crosby, and R. J. Ely, *Mentoring Dilemmas: Developmental Relationships within Multicultural Organizations* (Mahwah, NJ: Lawrence Erlbaum Associates, 1999). See a review of this book by M. L. Lengnick-Hall, "Mentoring Dilemmas: Developmental Relationships within Multicultural Organizations," *Personnel Psychology* 53, no. 1 (Spring 2000), pp. 224–27.

50. A. Kalev, F. Dobbin, and E. Kelly, "Best Practices or Best Guesses? Assessing the Efficacy of Corporate Affirmative Action and Diversity Policies," *American Sociological Review* 71 (2006), pp. 589–617.

51. "NBA Gets 'A' Grade, Remains Leader in Sports Diversity," *USA Today* (online), June 16, 2011, www.usatoday.com; and T. Reed, "NBA Has the Most Diverse Workforce," Associated Press, May 9, 2007, http://news.yahoo.com.

52. S. Hoffman, R. Lane, and M. Nagel, "Measurement: Proving the ROI of Global Diversity and Inclusion Efforts," Cisco's Global Diversity Primer (online), www.cisco.com.

53. "Top Ten of Working Mother 100 Best Companies 2013," *Working Mother Magazine* (online), www.workingmother.com.

54. M. Y. Kinney, "Firm Makes a Case for Loyalty," *Philadelphia Inquirer,* April 5, 2009; R. Hightower, "Law Firm to Celebrate Employee's 50-Year Mark," *Philadelphia Tribune,* April 9, 2009, www.phillytrib.com; Caesar, Rivise, Bernstein, Cohen & Pokotilow, "About Us," www.crbcp.com; Drexel University, "Drexel at a Glance," www.drexel.edu; and Drexel University Earle Mack School of Law, "Diversity Initiatives," www.drexel.edu/law/diversity.asp.

55. M. Stanger, "Companies That Offer Flexible Schedules Get More Out of Their Employees," *Business Insider* (online), February 14, 2013, www.businessinsider.com.

56. A. Pace, "Diversity Is Driving the Bus," *T + D* 65, no. 2 (February 2011), pp. 18–19; L. E. Overmyer Day, "The Pitfalls of Diversity Training," *Training and Development* 49, no. 12 (December 1995), pp. 24–29; S. Rynes and B. Rosen, "A Field Survey of Factors Affecting the Adoption and Perceived Success of Diversity Training," *Personnel Psychology* 48, no. 2 (Summer 1995), pp. 247–70; L. Ford, "Diversity: From Cartoons to Confrontations," *Training & Development* 54, no. 8 (August 2000), pp. 70–71; and J. M. Ivancevich and J. A. Gilbert, "Diversity Management: Time for a New Approach," *Public Personnel Management* 29, no. 1 (Spring 2000), pp. 75–92.

57. R. S. Badhesha, J. M. Schmidtke, A. Cummings, and S. D. Moore, "The Effects of Diversity Training on Specific and General Attitudes toward Diversity," *Multicultural Education & Technology Journal* 2, no. 2 (2008), pp. 87–106; and M. Burkart, "The Role of Training in Advancing a Diversity Initiative," *Diversity Factor* 8, no. 1 (Fall 1999), pp. 2–5.

58. A. Marks, "For Airport Screeners, More Training about Muslims," *Christian Science Monitor,* January 9, 2007, www.csmonitor.com.

59. E. McKeown, "Quantifiable Inclusion Strategies," *T + D* 64, no. 10 (October 2010), pp. 16–17; "How Bad Is the Turnover Problem?" *HR Focus,* March 2007; B. Thomas, "Black Entrepreneurs Win, Corporations Lose," *BusinessWeek,* September 20, 2006; and P. Shurn-Hannah, "Solving the Minority Retention Mystery," *The Human Resource Professional* 13, no. 3 (May/June 2000), pp. 22–27.

60. "Diversity Councils and Business Resource Groups," www.thecoca-colacompany.com.

61. Alleyne, "The 40 Best Companies for Diversity"; and M. E. Podmolik, "Mentor Match Found Online," *Chicago Tribune,* May 14, 2007, www.chicagotribune.com.

62. C. K. Johnson, "Study: Fat Workers Cost Employers More," Associated Press, April 23, 2007, http://news.yahoo.com.

63. Rodriguez, "Diversity Finds Its Place."

64. J. Jargon, "Kraft Reformulates Oreo, Scores in China," *The Wall Street Journal,* May 1, 2008, http://online.wsj.com.

65. N. J. Adler and S. Bartholomew, "Managing Globally Competent People," *Academy of Management Executive* 6, no. 3 (1992), pp. 52–65; and C. G. Howard, "Profile of the 21st-Century Expatriate Manager," *HRMagazine,* June 1992, pp. 93–100.

66. J. Byrne, "IBM Now Employs More Workers in India than US," New York Post (online), October 5, 2013, www.nypost.com.

67. L. S. Paine, "The China Rules," *Harvard Business Review* 88, no. 6 (June 2010), pp. 103–108.

68. C. Csizmar, "Does Your Expatriate Program Follow the Rules of the Road?" *Compensation and Benefits Review* 40, no. 1 (January 2008), pp. 61–65; and A. W. Andreason, "Expatriate Adjustment to Foreign Assignments," *International Journal of Commerce and Management* 13, no. 1 (Spring 2003), pp. 42–61.

69. P. Capell, "Know before You Go: Expats' Advice to Couples," *Career Journal Europe,* May 2, 2006, www.careerjournaleurope.com.

70. R. A. Swaak, "Expatriate Failures: Too Many, Too Much Cost, Too Little Planning," *Compensation & Benefits Review,* November/December 1995, pp. 50–52.

71. Capell, "Know before You Go."

72. G. M. Sprietzer, M. W. McCall, and J. D. Mahoney, "Early Identification of International Executive Potential," *Journal of Applied Psychology* 82, no. 1 (1997), pp. 6–29; R. Mortensen, "Beyond the Fence Line," *HRMagazine,* November 1997, pp. 100–9; "Expatriate Games," *Journal of Business Strategy,* July/August 1997, pp. 4–5; and "Building a Global Workforce Starts with Recruitment," *Personnel Journal* (special supplement), March 1996, pp. 9–11.

73. See Geert Hofstede's website, www.geerthofstede.nl.

74. A. Paul, "How the Internet Shrinks the Distance between Us," *The Wall Street Journal,* March 16, 2007, http://online.wsj.com.

75. G. A. Fowler, "In China's Offices, Foreign Colleagues Might Get an Earful," *The Wall Street Journal,* February 13, 2007, http://online.wsj.com.

76. J. Slocum, "Coming to America," *Human Resource Executive,* October 2, 2008, www.hrexecutive.com.

77. E. Flitter, "Time Runs Differently in the Emirates," *The Wall Street Journal,* April 16, 2008, http://online.wsj.com.

78. J. Brett, K. Behfar, and M. C. Kern, "Managing Multicultural Teams," *Harvard Business Review,* November 2006, pp. 84–91.

79. D. Stamps, "Welcome to America," *Training,* November 1996, pp. 23–30.

80. A. Ardichvili, D. Jondle, and B. Kowske, "Dimensions of Ethical Business Cultures: Comparing Data from 13 Countries of Europe, Asia, and the Americas," *Human Resource Development International* 13, no. 3 (2010), pp. 299–315; and L. K. Trevino and K. A. Nelson, *Managing Business Ethics: Straight Talk about How to Do It Right* (New York: John Wiley & Sons, 1995).

81. Transparency International, "Bribe Payers Index Report, 2011," www.transparency.org.

82. J. G. Longnecker, J. A. McKinney, and C. W. Moore, "The Ethical Issues of International Bribery: A Study of Attitudes among U.S. Business Professionals," *Journal of Business Ethics* 7 (1988), pp. 341–46.

83. SEC Enforcement Actions: FCPA Cases, U.S. Securities and Exchange Commission (online), www.sec.gov, accessed May 21, 2014.

84. A. B. Desai and T. Rittenburg, "Global Ethics: An Integrative Framework for MNEs," *Journal of Business Ethics* 16 (1997), pp. 791–800; and P. Buller, J. Kohls, and K. Anderson, "A Model for Addressing Cross-Cultural Ethical Conflicts," *Business & Society* 36, no. 2 (June 1997), pp. 169–93.

Chapter 10

1. Company website, www.up.co/; Blog by Marc Nager on *Huffington Post* (online), www.huffingtonpost.com/marc-nager/, accessed May 23, 2014.

2. W. Bennis and B. Nanus, *Leaders* (New York: Harper & Row, 1985), p. 27.

3. J. Petrick, R. Schere, J. Brodzinski, J. Quinn, and M. Fall Ainina, "Global Leadership Skills and Reputational Capital: Intangible Resources for Sustainable Competitive Advantage," *Academy of Management Executive,* February 1999, pp. 58–69.

4. Bennis and Nanus, *Leaders.*

5. Ibid., p. 144.

6. E. E. Lawler III, Treat People Right! *How Organizations and Individuals Can Propel Each Other into a Virtual Spiral of Success* (San Francisco: Jossey-Bass, 2003).

7. J. Kouzes and B. Posner, *The Leadership Challenge,* 2nd ed. (San Francisco: Jossey-Bass, 1995).

8. "Big Demands and High Expectations: The Deloitte Millennial Survey," Deloitte's January 2014 Executive Survey, www2.deloitte.com.

9. "Zappos.com CEO Tony Hsieh: Vision, Values and the Pursuit of Happiness," http://theexecutiveroundtable.wordpress.com.

10. Kouzes and Posner, *The Leadership Challenge.*

11. Ibid.

12. J. Baum, E. A. Locke, and S. Kirkpatrick, "A Longitudinal Study of the Relation of Vision and Vision Communication to Venture Growth in Entrepreneurial Firms," *Journal of Applied Psychology* 83 (1998), pp. 43–54.

13. E. C. Shapiro, *Fad Surfing in the Boardroom* (Reading, MA: Addison-Wesley, 1995).

14. Kouzes and Posner, *The Leadership Challenge.*

15. Ibid.

16. W. Bennis and R. Townsend, *Reinventing Leadership* (New York: William Morrow, 1995).

17. Ibid.

18. Company website and Infosys Annual Report 2010–2011, www .infosys.com; and A. P. Raman, "Why Don't We Try to Be India's Most Respected Company?" *Harvard Business Review* 89, no. 11 (November 2011), pp. 80–85.

19. Kouzes and Posner, *The Leadership Challenge.*

20. J. A. Conger, "The Dark Side of Leadership," *Organizational Dynamics* 19 (Autumn 1990), pp. 44–55.

21. J. Conger, "The Vision Thing: Explorations into Visionary Leadership," in *Cutting Edge Leadership* 2000, ed. B. Kellerman and L. Matusak (College Park, MD: James MacGregor Burns Academy of Leadership, 2000).

22. S. Hewitt, "How We Rebuilt Tornado-Destroyed Town," CNN.com, May 26, 2011; B. Wolpin, "The Tough Get Going," *American City and County,* November 1, 2008; M. Jackson, "Come-Back Kid," *American City and County,* November 1, 2008, and B. Zongker, "Museum Features Kansas Town That Went Green," Associated Press, *Yahoo News,* October 26, 2008, http://news.yahoo.com.

23. J. P. Kotter, "What Leaders Really Do," *Harvard Business Review* 68 (May–June 1990) pp. 103–11.

24. M. E. Van Buren and T. Safferstone, "Collective Quick Wins," *Computerworld,* January 26, 2009, pp. 24–25.

25. G. Yukl, *Leadership in Organizations,* 3rd ed. (Englewood Cliffs, NJ: Prentice Hall, 1994).

26. R. House and R. Aditya, "The Social Scientific Study of Leadership: Quo Vadis?" *Journal of Management* 23 (1997), pp. 409–73.

27. R. D. Ireland and M. A. Hitt. "Achieving and Maintaining Strategic Competitiveness in the 21st Century. The Role of Strategic Leadership," *Academy of Management Executive* (February 1999), pp. 43–57.

28. John Thompson III Foundation website, www.jtiiifoundation. org; J. Wood, "John Thompson III Named New Head Coach," *The Hoya,* www.thehoya.com; and D Vitale, "Meet the Next Generation of Great Hoops Coaches, According to Dickie V," *USA Today,* February 13, 2007, www.usatoday.com.

29. J. Gardner, "The Heart of the Matter: Leader–Constituent Interaction," in *Leading & Leadership,* ed. T. Fuller (Notre Dame, IN: University of Notre Dame Press, 2000), pp. 239–44, quote on p. 240.

30. R. E. Kelly, "In Praise of Followers," *Harvard Business Review* 66 (November–December 1988), pp. 142–48.

31. Bennis and Townsend, *Reinventing Leadership.*

32. Kelly, "In Praise of Followers."

33. J. R. P. French and B. Raven, "The Bases of Social Power," in *Studies in Social Power,* ed. D. Cartwright (Ann Arbor, MI: Institute for Social Research, 1959).

34. G. Yukl and C. Falbe, "Importance of Different Power Sources in Downward and Lateral Relations," *Journal of Applied Psychology* 76 (1991), pp. 416–23.

35. Ibid.

36. "2013's Top People in Business," *CNNMoney* (online), http:// money.cnn.com, accessed on May 23, 2014.

37. Yukl and Falbe, "Importance of Different Power Sources."

38. R. M. Stogdill, "Personal Factors Associated with Leadership: A Survey of the Literature," *Journal of Psychology* 25 (1948), pp. 35–71.

39. S. Kirkpatrick and E. Locke, "Leadership: Do Traits Matter?" *The Executive* 5 (May 1991), pp. 48–60.

40. G. A. Yukl, *Leadership in Organizations,* 2nd ed. (Englewood Cliffs, NJ: Prentice Hall, 1989).

41. R. Heifetz and D. Laurie, "The Work of Leadership," *Harvard Business Review,* January–February 1997, pp. 124–34.

42. T. Judge, J. Bono, R. Ilies, and M. Gerhardt, "Personality and Leadership: A Qualitative and Quantitative Review," *Journal of Applied Psychology* 87 (2002), pp. 765–80.

43. R. Foti and N. M. A. Hauenstein, "Pattern and Variable Approaches in Leadership Emergence and Effectiveness," *Journal of Applied Psychology* 92 (2007), pp. 347–55.

44. J. P. Kotter, *The General Managers* (New York: Free Press, 1982).

45. See http://womenshistory.about.com.

46. P. McDonald, "Maoism Versus Confucianism: Ideological Influences on Chinese Business Leaders," *Journal of Management Development* 30, no. 7/8 (2011), pp. 632–46; P. Galagan, "The Biggest Losers: The Perils of Extreme Downsizing," *T & D* 64, no. 11 (November 2010), pp. 27–30; G. Hofstede, "Asian Management in the 21st Century," *Asia Pacific Journal of Management* 24 (May 16, 2007), pp. 411–20; "Are Indian Business Leaders Different?" Knowledge@Wharton, November 1, 2007, http://knowledge.wharton.upenn.edu; and E. Wood, A. Whiteley, and S. Zhang, "The Cross Model of Guanxi Usage in Chinese Leadership," *The Journal of Management Development* 21, no. 3/4 (2002), pp. 263–72.

47. S. Zaccaro, R. Foti, and D. Kenny, "Self-Monitoring and Trait-Based Variance in Leadership: An Investigation of Leader Flexibility across Multiple Group Situations," *Journal of Applied Psychology* 76 (1991), pp. 308–15.

48. M. D. Watkins, "Picking the Right Transition Strategy," *Harvard Business Review* 87, no. 1 (January 2009), pp. 47–53; and D. Goleman, "Leadership That Gets Results," *Harvard Business Review,* March–April 2000, pp. 78–90.

49. J. Misumi and M. Peterson, "The Performance-Maintenance (PM) Theory of Leadership: Review of a Japanese Research Program," *Administrative Science Quarterly* 30 (June 1985), pp. 198–223.

50. T. Judge, R. Piccolo, and R. Ilies, "The Forgotten Ones? The Validity of Consideration and Initiating Structure in Leadership Research," *Journal of Applied Psychology* 89 (2004), pp. 36–51.

51. Misumi and Peterson, "The Performance-Maintenance (PM) Theory."

52. Judge, Piccolo, and Ilies, "The Forgotten Ones?"

53. G. Graen and M. Uhl-Bien, "Relationship-Based Approach to Leadership: Development of Leader-Member Exchange (LMX) Theory of Leadership over 25 Years: Applying a Multi-Level Multidomain Perspective," *Leadership Quarterly* 6, no. 2 (1995), pp. 219–47.

54. House and Aditya, "The Social Scientific Study of Leadership."

55. G. Han, "Trust and Career Satisfaction: The Role of LMX," *Career Development International* 15, no. 5 (2010), pp. 437–58; and C. R. Gerstner and D. V. Day, "Meta-Analytic Review of Leader-Member Exchange-Theory: Correlates and Construct Issues," *Journal of Applied Psychology* 82 (1997), pp. 827–44.

56. A. Mulcahy, "Timeliness Trumps Perfection," *The McKinsey Quarterly* 2 (2010), pp. 56-57.

57. House and Aditya, "The Social Scientific Study of Leadership."

58. T. L. Russ, "Theory X/Y Assumptions as Predictors of Managers' Propensity for Participative Decision Making," *Management Decision* 49, no. 5 (XXXX), pp. 823–36; and J. Wagner III, "Participation's Effect on Performance and Satisfaction: A Reconsideration of Research," *Academy of Management Review,* April 1994, pp. 312–30.

59. R. White and R. Lippitt, *Autocracy and Democracy: An Experimental Inquiry* (New York: Harper & Brothers, 1960).

60. D. Carey, M. Patsalos, and M. Useem, "Leadership Lessons for Hard Times," *The McKinsey Quarterly* 4 (2009), pp. 52–61; and J. Muczyk and R. Steel, "Leadership Style and the Turnaround Executive," *Business Horizons,* March–April 1999, pp. 39–46.

61. A. Tannenbaum and W. Schmidt, "How to Choose a Leadership Pattern," *Harvard Business Review* 36 (March–April 1958), pp. 95–101.

62. E. Fleishman and E. Harris, "Patterns of Leadership Behavior Related to Employee Grievances and Turnover," *Personnel Psychology* 15 (1962), pp. 43–56.

63. R. Likert, *The Human Organization: Its Management and Value* (New York: McGraw-Hill, 1967).

64. R. Blake and J. Mouton, *The Managerial Grid* (Houston: Gulf, 1964).

65. Misumi and Peterson, "The Performance-Maintenance (PM) Theory."

66. J. Wall, *Bosses* (Lexington, MA: Lexington Books, 1986), p. 103.

67. Tannenbaum and Schmidt, "How to Choose a Leadership Pattern."

68. V. H. Vroom, "Leadership and the Decision-Making Process," *Organizational Dynamics,* Spring 2000, pp. 82–93.

69. V. H. Vroom, "Leadership and the Decision-Making Process." Copyright © 2000 with permission from Elsevier Science.

70. F. E. Fiedler, *A Theory of Leadership Effectiveness* (New York: McGraw-Hill, 1967).

71. P. Hersey and K. Blanchard, *The Management of Organizational Behavior* (Englewood Cliffs, NJ: Prentice Hall, 1984).

72. Yukl, *Leadership in Organizations.*

73. R. J. House, "A Path Goal Theory of Leader Effectiveness," *Administrative Science Quarterly* 16 (1971), pp. 321–39.

74. J. Howell, D. Bowen, P. Dorfman, S. Kerr, and P. Podsakoff, "Substitutes for Leadership: Effective Alternatives to Ineffective Leadership," *Organizational Dynamics* 19 (Summer 1990), pp. 21–38.

75. R. G. Lord and W. Gradwohl Smith, "Leadership and the Changing Nature of Performance," in *The Changing Nature of Performance,* ed. D. R. Ilgen and E. D. Pulakos (San Francisco: Jossey-Bass, 1999).

76. S. Dionne, F. Yammarino, L. Atwater, and L. James, "Neutralizing Substitutes for Leadership Theory: Leadership Effects and Common-Source Bias," *Journal of Applied Psychology* 87 (2002), pp. 454–64.

77. B. M. Bass, *Leadership and Performance beyond Expectations* (New York: Free Press, 1985).

78. Y. A. Nur, "Charisma and Managerial Leadership: The Gift That Never Was," *Business Horizons,* July–August 1998, pp. 19–26; and R. J. House, "A 1976 Theory of Charismatic Leadership," in *Leadership: The Cutting Edge,* ed. J. G. Hunt and L. L. Larson (Carbondale, IL: Southern Illinois University Press, 1977).

79. R. Nielsen, J. A. Marrone, and H. S. Slay, "A New Look at Humility: Exploring the Humility Concept and Its Role in Socialized Charismatic Leadership," *Journal of Leadership & Organizational Studies* 17, no. 1 (February 2010), pp. 33–43; and M. Brown and L. Trevino, "Socialized Charismatic Leadership, Values Congruence, and Deviance in Work Groups," *Journal of Applied Psychology* 91 (2006), pp. 954–62.

80. M. Potts and P. Behr, *The Leading Edge* (New York: McGraw-Hill, 1987).

81. J. Howell and B. Shamir, "The Role of Followers in the Charismatic Leadership Process: Relationships and Their Consequences," *Academy of Management Review* 30 (2005), pp. 96–112.

82. S. Yorges, H. Weiss, and O. Strickland, "The Effect of Leader Outcomes on Influence, Attributions, and Perceptions of Charisma," *Journal of Applied Psychology* 84 (1999), pp. 428–36.

83. Potts and Behr, *The Leading Edge.*

84. D. A. Waldman and F. J. Yammarino, "CEO Charismatic Leadership: Levels-of-Management and Levels-of-Analysis Effects," *Academy of Management Review* 24 (1999), pp. 266–85.

85. A. Fanelli and V. Misangyi, "Bringing Out Charisma: CEO Charisma and External Stakeholders," *Academy of Management Review* 31 (2006), pp. 1049–61.

86. House and Aditya, "The Social Scientific Study of Leadership"; and I. Wanasika, J. P. Howell, R. Littrell, and P. Dorfman, "Managerial Leadership and Culture in Sub-Saharan Africa," *Journal of World Business* 46, no. 2 (April 2011), pp. 234–41.

87. D. A. Waldman, G. G. Ramirez, R. J. House, and P. Puranam, "Does Leadership Matter? CEO Leadership Attributes and Profitability under Conditions of Perceived Environmental Uncertainty," *Academy of Management Journal* 44 (2001), pp. 134–43.

88. N. Paulsen, D. Maldonado, V. J. Callan, and O. Ayoko, "Charismatic Leadership, Change and Innovation in an R & D Organization," *Journal of Organizational Change Management* 22, no. 5 (2009), pp. 511–23; and B. Agle, N. Nagarajan, J. Sonnenfeld, and D. Srinivasan, "Does CEO Charisma Matter? An Empirical Analysis of the Relationships among Organizational Performance, Environmental Uncertainty, and Top Management Team Perceptions of CEO Charisma," *Academy of Management Journal* 49 (2006), pp. 161–74.

89. J. M. Howell and K. E. Hall-Merenda, "The Ties that Bind: The Impact of Leader-Member Exchange, Transformational and Transactional Leadership, and Distance on Predicting Follower Performance," *Journal of Applied Psychology* 84 (1999), pp. 680–94; and B. M. Bass, "Leadership: Good, Better, Best," *Organizational Dynamics,* Winter 1985, pp. 26–40.

90. F. J. Yammarino, F. Dansereau, and C. J. Kennedy, "A Multiple-Level Multidimensional Approach to Leadership: Viewing Leadership through an Elephant's Eye," *Organizational Dynamics,* Winter 2001, pp. 149–63.

91. D. I. Jung and B. J. Avolio, "Effects of Leadership Style and Followers' Cultural Orientation on Performance in Group and Individual Task Conditions," *Academy of Management Journal* 42 (1999), pp. 208–18.

92. Bass, *Leadership and Performance.*

93. C. Gallo, "Google's Marissa Mayer: 3 Leadership Traits She'll Bring to Yahoo," *Forbes* (online), July 17, 2012, www.forbes.com.

94. Bennis and Nanus, *Leaders.*

95. B. Bass, B. Avolio, and L. Goodheim, "Biography and the Assessment of Transformational Leadership at the World-Class Level," *Journal of Management* 13 (1987), pp. 7–20.

96. K. Albrecht and R. Zemke, *Service America* (Homewood, IL: Dow Jones Irwin, 1985).

97. S. Biswas and A. Varma, "Antecedents of Employee Performance: An Empirical Investigation in India," *Employee Relations* 34, no. 2 (2012), pp. 177–92; B. L. Kirkman, G. Chen, J. L., Farh, Z. X. Chen, and K. B. Lowe, "Individual Power Distance Orientation and Follower Reactions to Transformational Leaders: A Cross-level, Cross-cultural Examination," *Academy of Management Journal* 52, no. 4 (August 2009), pp. 744–64; T. A. Judge and J. E. Bono, "Five-Factor Model of Personality and Transformational Leadership," *Journal of Applied Psychology* 85 (2000), pp. 751–65; and B. Bass, "Does the Transactional-Transformational Paradigm Transcend Organizational and National Boundaries?" *American Psychologist* 22 (1997), pp. 130–42.

98. S. J. Shin and J. Zhou, "Transformational Leadership, Conservation, and Creativity: Evidence from Korea," *Academy of Management Journal* 46 (2003), pp. 703–14.

99. R. Piccolo and J. Colquitt, "Transformational Leadership and Job Behaviors: The Mediating Role of Core Job Characteristics," *Academy of Management Journal* 49 (2006), pp. 327–40.

100. A. Colbert, A. Kristof-Brown, B. Bradley, and M. Barrick, "CEO Transformational Leadership: The Role of Goal Importance Congruence in Top Management Teams," *Academy of Management Journal* 51 (2008), pp. 81–96.

101. T. Dvir, D. Eden, B. Avolio, and B. Shamir, "Impact of Transformational Leadership on Follower Development and Performance: A Field Experiment," *Academy of Management Journal* 45 (2002), pp. 735–44.

102. B. M. Bass, *Transformational Leadership: Industry, Military, and Educational Impact* (Mahwah, NJ: Lawrence Erlbaum Associates, 1998).

103. G. Spreitzer and R. Quinn, "Empowering Middle Managers to Be Transformational Leaders," *Journal of Applied Behavioral Science* 32 (1996), pp. 237–61.

104. J. Collins, "Level 5 Leadership: The Triumph of Humility and Fierce Resolve," *Harvard Business Review* 1 (2005), pp. 136–46; J. Collins, "Level 5 Leadership," *Harvard Business Review* 1 (2001), pp. 66–76; and J. Kline Harrison and M. William Clough, "Characteristics of 'State of the Art' Leaders: Productive Narcissism versus Emotional Intelligence and Level 5 Capabilities," *Social Science Journal* 43 (2006), pp. 287–92.

105. D. Vera and M. Crossan, "Strategic Leadership and Organizational Learning," *Academy of Management Review* 29 (2004), pp. 222–40.

106. Company website, www.barry-wehmiller.com; S. Leibs, "Putting People Before the Bottom Line (and Still Making Money)," *Inc.* (online), May 2014, www.inc.com; E. Herlzfeld, "Leadership Leads to Growth," *Official Board Markets,* April 11, 2009; and Barry-Wehmiller website, www.barry-wehmiller.com.

107. F. Luthans, *Organizational Behavior,* 10th ed. (New York: McGraw-Hill/Irwin, 2005).

108. B. M. Bass, "Thoughts and Plans," in *Cutting Edge Leadership* 2000, ed. B. Kellerman and L. R. Matusak (College Park, MD: James MacGregor Burns Academy of Leadership, 2000), pp. 5–9.

109. N. Turner, J. Barling, O. Epitropaki, V. Butcher, and C. Milner, "Transformational Leadership and Moral Reasoning," *Journal of Applied Psychology* 87 (2002), pp. 304–311.

110. Bass, "Thoughts and Plans."

111. Company website, "The 6 Actions That Will Make You Succeed in Tough Times," September 7, 2010, http://johnhersey.com; and J. Hersey, "Some SAGE Advice," *Hardware Retailing,* May 2009.

112. W. Bennis, "The End of Leadership: Exemplary Leadership Is Impossible without Full Inclusion, Initiatives, and Cooperation of Followers," *Organizational Dynamics,* Summer 1999, pp. 71–79.

113. L. Spears, "Emerging Characteristics of Servant Leadership," in *Cutting Edge Leadership 2000,* ed. B. Kellerman and L. Matusak (College Park, MD: James MacGregor Burns Academy of Leadership, 2000); and L. Buchanan, "In Praise of Selflessness: Why the Best Leaders Are Servants," *Inc.,* May 2007, pp. 33–35.

114. D. van Dierendonck, "Servant Leadership: A Review and Synthesis," *Journal of Management* 37, no. 4 (July 2011), pp. 1228–61.

115. Buchanan, "In Praise of Selflessness," p. 34.

116. J. Ciulla, "Bridge Leaders," in *Cutting Edge Leadership 2000,* ed. B. Kellerman and L. Matusak (College Park, MD: James MacGregor Burns Academy of Leadership, 2000), pp. 25–28.

117. C. L. Pearce, "The Future of Leadership: Combining Vertical and Shared Leadership to Transform Knowledge Work," *Academy of Management Executive,* February 2004, pp. 47–57.

118. J. Carson, P. Tesluk, and J. Marrone, "Shared Leadership in Teams: An Investigation of Antecedent Conditions and Performance," *Academy of Management Journal* 50 (2007), pp. 1217–34.

119. R. Fisher and A. Sharp, *Getting It Done* (New York: HarperCollins, 1998).

120. NASA website, http://marsrovers.jpl.nasa.gov; J. Achenbach, "NASA Curiosity Rover Discovers Evidence of Freshwater Mars Lake," *The Washington Post* (online), December 9, 2013, www.washingtonpost.com.

121. E. Howell, "Mars Curiosity: Facts and Information," *Space* (online), March 13, 2013, www.space.com.

122. M. Useem, "Thinking Big, Lending Small," *U.S. News and World Report,* October 22, 2006, www.usnews.com. Note: In 2006 Nancy Barry founded and became president of NBA-Enterprise Solutions to Poverty.

123. P. Block, *The Empowered Manager* (San Francisco: Jossey-Bass, 1991).

124. Ibid.

CHAPTER 11

1. J. Glionna, "Las Vegas Plan Steps on Some Toes," *Los Angeles Times* (online), February 28, 2014, www.latimes.com; "Got Talent? Companies' Concerns," *The Economist* 400, no. 8750 (September 10, 2011), p. 12; M. Chafkin, "Everybody Loves Zappos," *Inc.,* May 2009, pp. 66–73; L. Rockwell, "Zappos Chief Speaks," *Austin American-Statesman,* March 13, 2009, www.austin360.com; J. M. O'Brien, "Zappos Knows How to Kick It," *Fortune,* January 22, 2009, http://money.cnn.com; C. C. Miller, "Making Sure the Shoe Fits at Zappos.com," *The New York Times,* November 6, 2008, http://bits.blogs.nytimes.com; and H. Coster, "A Step Ahead," *Forbes,* June 2, 2008, www.forbes.com.

2. R. Kreitner and F. Luthans, "A Social Learning Approach to Behavioral Management: Radical Behaviorists 'Mellowing Out,'" *Organizational Dynamics,* Autumn 1984, pp. 47–65.

3. D. Katz and R. L. Kahn, *The Social Psychology of Organizations* (New York: John Wiley & Sons, 1966).

4. C. A. Bartlett and S. Ghoshal, "Building Competitive Advantage through People," *Sloan Management Review,* Winter 2002, pp. 34–41.

5. G. M. Jarvis, "Employee Morale Ebbs Along with Workforce," *Chicago Tribune* (online), July 1, 2011, www.chicagotribune.com; and "Americans' Job Satisfaction Falls to Record Low," *USA Today* (online), January 6, 2010, www.usatoday.com.

6. E. Locke, "Toward a Theory of Task Motivation and Incentives," *Organizational Behavior and Human Performance* 3 (1968), pp. 157–89.

7. W. F. Cascio, "Managing a Virtual Workplace," *Academy of Management Executive,* August 2000, pp. 81–90.

8. E. A. Locke, "Guest Editor's Introduction: Goal-Setting Theory and Its Applications to the World of Business," *Academy of Management Executive* 4 (November 2004), pp. 124–25.

9. G. P. Latham, "The Motivational Benefits of Goal-Setting," *Academy of Management Executive* 4 (November 2004), pp. 126–29.

10. E. A. Locke, "Linking Goals to Monetary Incentives," *Academy of Management Executive* 4 (November 2004), pp. 130–33.

11. E. E. Lawler III, *Treat People Right!* (San Francisco: Jossey-Bass, 2003).

12. D. Brodwin, "How Companies Can Do Well Doing Good," *U.S. News & World Report* (online), June 3, 2013, www.usnews.com.

13. Lawler, *Treat People Right!*

14. J. Bono and T. Judge, "Self-Concordance at Work: Toward Understanding the Motivational Effects of Transformational Leaders," *Academy of Management Journal* 46 (2003), pp. 554–71.

15. Nonprofit Organization website, http://liveunited.org.

16. Company website, www.spacex.com; T. Agan, "What SpaceX Can Teach Us About Cost Innovation," *Bloomberg* (online), April 25, 2013, www.bloomberg.com.

17. T. Higgins, "GM Said to Seek Deals in China to Reach 5 Million Goal," *Bloomberg* (online), February 5, 2013, www.bloomberg.com; L. Lin, "Foreign Carmakers Try Brands Just for China," *Bloomberg Businessweek* (online), March 3, 2011, www.businessweek.com.

18. K. N. Shaw, "Changing the Goal-Setting Process at Microsoft," *Academy of Management Executive* 4 (November 2004), pp. 139–43.

19. S. B. Sitkin, K. E. See, C. C. Miller, M. W. Lawless, and A. M. Carton, "The Paradox of Stretch Goals: Organizations in Pursuit of the Seemingly Impossible," *Academy of Management Review* 36, no. 3 (2011), pp. 544–66.

20. S. Kerr and S. Laundauer, "Using Stretch Goals to Promote Organizational Effectiveness and Personal Growth: General Electric and Goldman Sachs," *Academy of Management Executive* 4 (November 2004), pp. 134–38.

21. Ibid.

22. Latham, "Motivational Benefits of Goal-Setting."

23. T. Mitchell and W. Silver, "Individual and Group Goals When Workers Are Interdependent: Effects on Task Strategies and Performance," *Journal of Applied Psychology* 75 (1990), pp. 185–93.

24. Latham, "Motivational Benefits of Goal-Setting."

25. S. Boehle, "The Games Trainers Play," *Training,* August 1, 2006, www.trainingmag.com; and M. P. McQueen, "Wellness Plans Reach Out to the Healthy," *The Wall Street Journal,* March 28, 2007, http://online.wsj.com.

26. L. D. Ordonez, M. E. Scheitzer, A. D. Galinsky, and M. H. Bazerman, "Goals Gone Wild: The Systematic Side Effects of Overprescribing Goal Setting," *Academy of Management Perspectives* 23, no. 1 (February 2009), pp. 6–16; and M. Schweitzer, L. Ordonez, and B. Douma, "Goal Setting as a Motivator of Unethical Behavior," *Academy of Management Journal* 47 (2004), pp. 422–32.

27. M. A. Duran, "Norm-Based Behavior and Corporate Malpractice," *Journal of Economic Issues* 41, no. 1 (March 2007); and D. Durfee, "Management or Manipulation?" *CFO,* December 2006.

28. G. Seijts and G. Latham, "Learning versus Performance Goals: When Should Each Be Used?" *Academy of Management Executive* 19 (February 2005), pp. 124–31; P. C. Early, T. Connolly, and G. Ekegren, "Goals, Strategy Development, and Task Performance: Some Limits on the Efficacy of Goal Setting," *Journal of Applied Psychology* 74 (1989), pp. 24–33; and C. E. Shalley, "Effects of Productivity Goals, Creativity Goals, and Personal Discretion on Individual Creativity," *Journal of Applied Psychology* 76 (1991), pp. 179–85.

29. R. C. Litchfield, "Brainstorming Reconsidered: A Goal-Based View," *Academy of Management Review* 33 (2008), pp. 649–68.

30. R. Fisher and A. Sharp, *Getting It Done* (New York: HarperCollins, 1998).

31. E. Thorndike, *Animal Intelligence* (New York: Macmillan, 1911).

32. A. D. Stajkovic and F. Luthans, "Differential Effects of Incentive Motivators on Work Performance," *Academy of Management Journal* 44 (2001), pp. 580–90.

33. "SAS: No. 1," *Fortune,* "100 Best Companies to Work for 2011," http://money.cnn.com.

34. J. Mackey and R. Sisodia, "Want to Hire Great People? Hire Consciously," *CNN Money* (online), January 17, 2013, www.fortune.cnn.com.

35. K. Butterfield, L. K. Trevino, and G. Ball, "Punishment from the Manager's Perspective: A Grounded Investigation and Inductive Model," *Academy of Management Review* 39 (1996), pp. 1479–512.

36. Adam Madison, "Positive Results," *Rock Products,* September 1, 2008, downloaded from Business & Company Resource Center, http://galenet.galegroup.com.

37. T. Judge and R. Piccolo, "Transformational and Transactional Leadership: A Meta-Analytic Test of Their Relative Ability," *Journal of Applied Psychology* 89 (2004), pp. 755–68.

38. S. Kerr, "On the Folly of Rewarding A While Hoping for B," *Academy of Management Journal* 18 (1975), pp. 769–83.

39. See S. Lohr, "Science Finds Advantage in Focusing, Not Multitasking," *Chicago Tribune,* March 25, 2007, sec.1, p. 10.

40. M. LeBoeuf, *The Greatest Management Principle in the World* (New York: Berkley Books, 1985).

41. E. E. Lawler III, *Rewarding Excellence* (San Francisco: Jossey-Bass, 2000).

42. R. J. Alsop, "Perks Do Exist in a Vacuum," *Workforce Management* 90, no. 9 (September 2011), pp. 42–46.

43. M. H. Pounds, "Too Much Pixie Dust Can Spoil a Job Title," *Sun-Sentinel* (online), January 24, 2008, www.sun-sentinel.com.

44. "25 Ways to Reward Employees Without Spending a Dime," *HR World* (Online), January 7, 2012, www.hrworld.com.

45. "U.S. Bancorp's CEO Hosts 2013 Investor Day Conference," Yahoo! Finance (online), May 27, 2014, http://finance.yahoo.com; and S. Cocheo, "U.S. Bancorp's 'Dynamic Dozen' and How They Help the Bank Serve Gen Y," *ABA Banking Journal* (online), May 13, 2011, www.ababj.com.

46. R. Beals, "Employees Get Paid to Exercise, While Some Pay to Sit Out," *U.S. News & World Report* (online), February 14, 2012.

47. J. Pfeffer and R. Sutton, *The Knowing-Doing Gap* (Boston: Harvard Business School Press, 2000).

48. J. S. Lublin, "Recall the Mistakes of Your Past Bosses, So You Can Do Better," *The Wall Street Journal,* January 2, 2007, http://online.wsj.com.

49. S. Moss and J. Sanchez, "Are Your Employees Avoiding You? Managerial Strategies for Closing the Feedback Gap," *Academy of Management Executive* 18, no. 1 (February 2004), pp. 32–44.

50. Lawler, *Treat People Right!*

51. R. E. Silverman, "Yearly Reviews? Try Weekly; Accustomed to Updates, New Generation of Workers Craves Regular Feedback," *The Wall Street Journal* (online), Septmber 6, 2011, http://online.wsj.com.

52. S. B. Silverman, C. E. Pogson, and A. B. Cober, "When Employees at Work Don't Get It: A Model for Enhancing Individual Employee Change in Response to Performance Feedback," *Academy of Management Executive* 19, no. 2 (May 2005), pp. 135–47; and J. Jackman and M. Strober, "Fear of Feedback," *Harvard Business Review,* April 2003, pp. 101–7.

53. V. H. Vroom, *Work and Motivation* (New York: John Wiley & Sons, 1964).

54. R. E. Wood, P. W. B. Atkins, and J. E. H. Bright, "Bonuses, Goals, and Instrumentality Effects," *Journal of Applied Psychology* 84 (1999), pp. 703–20.

55. S. Kerr, "Organizational Rewards: Practical, Cost-neutral Alternatives That You May Know, But Don't Practice," *Organizational Dynamics* 28, no. 1 (1999), pp. 61–70.

56. M. Scarborough, "The Rewards of Recognition: Six Strategies for Successful Employee Programs," *Community Banker,* January 2009, pp. 24–27.

57. E. Emerman, "Use of Rewards and Penalties to Drive Employee Health Jumps during 2012," National Business Group on Health, press release, October 25, 2011; and S. J. Wells, "Getting Paid for Staying Well," *HRMagazine* 55, no. 2 (February 2010), pp. 59–63.

58. A. H. Maslow, "A Theory of Human Motivation," *Psychological Review,* July 1943, pp. 370–96.

59. L. Mainicro and D. Gibson, "Managing Employee Trauma: Dealing with the Emotional Fallout from 9–11," *Academy of Management Executive,* August 2003, pp. 130–43.

60. M. Wahba and L. Birdwell, "Maslow Reconsidered: A Review of Research on the Need Hierarchy Theory," *Organizational Behavior and Human Performance* 15 (1976), pp. 212–40.

61. G. Dessler, "How to Earn Your Employees' Commitment," *Academy of Management Executive,* May 1999, pp. 58–67, quoted on p. 63.

62. Organization's website, www.mdanderson.org.

63. C. Hymowitz, "Managers Lose Talent When They Neglect to Coach Their Staffs," *The Wall Street Journal,* March 19, 2007, http://online.wsj.com.

64. C. Alderfer, *Existence, Relatedness, and Growth: Human Needs in Organizational Settings* (Glencoe, IL: Free Press, 1972).

65. Great Place to Work's 2013 List of Best Small Workplaces, www.greatplacetowork.com, accessed on May 28, 2014; S. Covel, "Picking the Perks That Employees Value," *The Wall Street Journal,* April 9, 2007, http://online.wsj.com.

66. E. Markowitz, "Should Your Employees Take Naps?" Inc. (online), August 12, 2011, www.inc.com; and L. Tanner, "Study: Napping Might Help Heart," *Yahoo News,* February 12, 2007, http://news.yahoo.com.

67. C. Hymowitz, "When the Paycheck Isn't Optional, Ambition Is Less Complicated," *The Wall Street Journal,* April 26, 2007, http://online.wsj.com.

68. C. Pinder, *Work Motivation* (Glenview, IL: Scott, Foresman, 1984).

69. D. McClelland, *The Achieving Society* (New York: Van Nostrand Reinhold, 1961).

70. Quoted in Cho, "Lessons in Employee Appreciation."

71. D. McClelland and R. Boyatzis, "Leadership Motive Pattern and Long-Term Success in Management," *Journal of Applied Psychology* 67 (1982), pp. 737–43.

72. N. Adler, *International Dimensions of Organizational Behavior,* 2nd ed. (Boston: Kent, 1991); and G. Hofstede, *Cultures and Organizations* (London: McGraw-Hill, 1991).

73. P. A. Gambrel and R. Cianci, "Maslow's Hierarchy of Needs: Does It Apply in a Collectivist Culture," *Journal of Applied Management and Entrepreneurship* 8, no. 2 (April 2003), pp. 143–62.

74. N. R. Lockwood, "Leveraging Employee Engagement for Competitive Advantage: HR's Strategic Role," *HRMagazine,* March 2007.

75. E. E. Lawler III and D. Finegold, "Individualizing the Organization: Past, Present, and Future," *Organizational Dynamics,* Summer 2000, pp. 1–15.

76. Ibid.

77. A. M. Grant and J. W. Berry, "The Necessity of Others Is the Mother of Invention: Intrinsic and Prosocial Motivations, Perspective Taking, and Creativity," *Academy of Management Journal* 54, no. 1 (2011), pp. 73–96; and T. M. Amabile, "A Model of Creativity and Innovation in Organizations," in *Research in Organizational Behavior,* ed. B. M. Staw and L. L. Cummings (Greenwich, CT: JAI Press, 1988), pp. 10, 123–67.

78. C. M. Ford, "A Theory of Individual Creative Action in Multiple Social Domains," *Academy of Management Review* 21 (1996), pp. 1112–42.

79. G. Oldham and A. Cummings, "Employee Creativity: Personal and Contextual Factors at Work," *Academy of Management Journal* 39 (1996), pp. 607–34.

80. T. Amabile, R. Conti, H. Coon, J. Lazenby, and M. Herron, "Assessing the Work Environment for Creativity," *Academy of Management Journal* 39 (1996), pp. 1154–84.

81. M. Campion and G. Sanborn, "Job Design," in *Handbook of Industrial Engineering,* ed. G. Salvendy (New York: John Wiley & Sons, 1991).

82. Lawler and Finegold, "Individualizing the Organization."

83. S. Dobson, "Rotating Roles Put Workers on Fast Track," *Canadian HR Reporter* 22, no. 18 (October 19, 2009), pp. 21–23.

84. Company website, www.vig.com.

85. M. Campion and D. McClelland, "Interdisciplinary Examination of the Costs and Benefits of Enlarged Jobs: A Job Design Quasi-Experiment," *Journal of Applied Psychology* 76 (1991), pp. 186–98.

86. F. Herzberg, *Work and the Nature of Men* (Cleveland: World, 1966).

87. BlessingWhite, *Employee Engagement Report, 2011: Beyond the Numbers: A Practical Approach for Individuals, Managers, and Executives,* www.blessingwhite.com.

88. J. R. Hackman, G. Oldham, R. Janson, and K. Purdy, "A New Strategy for Job Enrichment," *California Management Review* 16 (Fall 1975), pp. 57–71.

89. P. Lehman, "No. 5 Enterprise: A Clear Road to the Top," *BusinessWeek,* September 18, 2006.

90. Company website, www.statefarm.com; and R. Rechheld, "Loyalty-Based Management" *Harvard Business Review,* March–April 1993, pp. 64–73.

91. Agency website, www.fs.fed.us/fire/people/hotshots/; and A. Breed, "For Most Wildland Firefighters, Motivation Goes Way Beyond an Adrenaline Rush, Travel, Good Pay," Fox News (online), July 8, 2013, www.foxnews.com.

92. T. Peters and N. Austin, *A Passion for Excellence* (New York: Random House, 1985).

93. P. Kaihla, "Best-Kept Secrets of the World's Best Companies," *Business 2.0,* April 2006, http://galenet.galegroup.com.

94. J. Smith, "The Happiest Jobs in America," *Forbes* (online), March 23, 2012, www.forbes.com.

95. Campion and Sanborn, "Job Design."

96. S. Seibert, S. Silver, and W. A. Randolph, "Taking Empowerment to the Next Level: A Multiple-Level Model of Empowerment, Performance, and Satisfaction," *Academy of Management Journal* 47 (2004), pp. 332–49.

97. C. Argyris, "Empowerment: The Emperor's New Clothes," *Harvard Business Review,* May–June 1998, pp. 98–105.

98. X. Zhang and K. M. Bartol, "Linking Empowering Leadership and Employee Creativity: The Influence of Psychological Empowerment, Intrinsic Motivation, and Creative Process Engagement," *Academy of Management Journal* 53, no. 1 (February 2010), pp. 107–128; and R. Forrester, "Empowerment: Rejuvenating a Potent Idea," *Academy of Management Executive,* August 2000, pp. 67–80.

99. R. C. Liden, S. J. Wayne, and R. T. Sparrowe, "An Examination of the Mediating Role of Psychological Empowerment on the Relations between the Job, Interpersonal Relationships, and Work Outcomes," *Journal of Applied Psychology* 85 (2000), pp. 407–16.

100. Peters and Austin, *A Passion for Excellence.*

101. K. Thomas and B. Velthouse, "Cognitive Elements of Empowerment: An 'Interpretive' Model of Intrinsic Task Motivation," *Academy of Management Review* 15 (1990), pp. 666–81.

102. Price Waterhouse Change Integration Team, *Better Change* (Burr Ridge, IL: Richard D. Irwin, 1995).

103. E. E. Lawler III, *The Ultimate Advantage: Creating the High Involvement Organization* (San Francisco: Jossey-Bass, 1992).

104. O. Gadiesh and J. L. Gilbert, "Transforming Corner-Office Strategy into Frontline Action," *Harvard Business Review,* May 2001, pp. 72–79.

105. J. Kouzes and B. Posner, *The Leadership Challenge* (San Francisco: Jossey-Bass, 1995).

106. Price Waterhouse, *Better Change.*

107. J. Jasinowski and R. Hamrin, *Making It in America* (New York: Simon & Schuster, 1995).

108. D. Goldman, "Google Plans Biggest Hiring Year in Company History," *CNN Money* (online), January 25, 2011, http://money.cnn.com; S. Morrison, "Google Searches for Staffing Answers," *The Wall Street Journal,* May 19, 2009, http://online.wsj.com; M. Liedtke, "Ambitions Enough for Another 10 Years," *Houston Chronicle,* September 6, 2008; and "Google's Lessons for Employers: Put Your Employees First," *HR Focus,* September 2008.

109. W. A. Randolph and M. Sashkin, "Can Organizational Empowerment Work in Multinational Settings?" *Academy of Management Executive* 16 (2002), pp. 102–15.

110. J. Adams, "Inequality in Social Exchange," in *Advances in Experimental Social Psychology,* ed. L. Berkowitz (New York: Academic Press, 1965).

111. M. Bloom, "The Performance Effects of Pay Dispersion of Individuals and Organizations," *Academy of Management Journal* 42 (1999), pp. 25–40.

112. G. Morgenson, "Peer Pressure: Inflating Executive Pay," *The New York Times,* November 26, 2006, www.nytimes.com.

113. D. Skarlicki, R. Folger, and P. Tesluk, "Personality as a Moderator in the Relationships between Fairness and Retaliation," *Academy of Management Journal* 42 (1999), pp. 100–108.

114. D. Prial, "Crunch Time for CPAs," *The Record* (Bergen County, NJ), April 17, 2007.

115. J. Brockner, "Making Sense of Procedural Fairness: How High Procedural Fairness Can Reduce or Heighten the Influence of Outcome Favorability," *Academy of Management Review* 27 (2002), pp. 58–76; and D. De Cremer and D. van Knippenberg, "How Do Leaders Promote Cooperation? The Effects of Charisma and Procedural Fairness," *Journal of Applied Psychology* 87 (2002), pp. 858–66.

116. M. Kernan and P. Hanges, "Survivor Reactions to Reorganization: Antecedents and Consequences of Procedural, Interpersonal, and Informational Justice," *Journal of Applied Psychology* 87 (2002), pp. 916–28.

117. Lawler, *Treat People Right!*

118. A. Pomeroy, "Company Is a Team, Not a Family," *HRMagazine,* April 2007.

119. W. C. Kim and R. Mauborgne, "Fair Process: Managing in the Knowledge Economy," *Harvard Business Review,* July–August 1997, pp. 65–75.

120. T. Bateman and D. Organ, "Job Satisfaction and the Good Sold: The Relationship between Affect and Employee 'Citizenship,'" *Academy of Management Journal,* 1983, pp. 587–95.

121. D. Henne and E. Locke, "Job Dissatisfaction: What Are the Consequences?" *International Journal of Psychology* 20 (1985), pp. 221–40.

122. J. Barling, E. K. Kelloway, and R. Iverson, "High-Quality Work, Job Satisfaction, and Occupational Injuries," *Journal of Applied Psychology* 88 (2003), pp. 276–83.

123. D. Bowen, S. Gilliland, and R. Folger, "HRM and Service Fairness: How Being Fair with Employees Spills Over to Customers," *Organizational Dynamics,* Winter 1999, pp. 7–23.

124. J. Harter, F. Schmidt, and T. Hayes, "Business-Unit-Level Relationship between Employee Satisfaction, Employee Engagement, and Business Outcomes: A Meta-Analysis," *Journal of Applied Psychology* 87 (2002), pp. 268–79.

125. A. Hall, "'I'm Outta Here!' Why 2 Million Americans Quit Every Month (And 5 Steps to Turn the Epidemic Around)," *Forbes* (online), March 11, 2013, www.forbes.com.

126. T. Bisoux, "Corporate CounterCulture," *BizEd,* November/December 2004, pp. 16–20.

127. A. Fisher, "Playing For Keeps," 100 Best Companies to Work For 2007, *Fortune* Rankings, January 29, 2007, http://money.cnn.com; and First Horizon National Corp., "Careers" and "Our Benefits," www.firsthorizon.com.

128. R. E. Walton, "Improving the Quality of Work Life," *Harvard Business Review,* May–June 1974, pp. 12, 16, 155.

129. E. E. Lawler III, "Strategies for Improving the Quality of Work Life," *American Psychologist* 37 (1982), pp. 486–93; and J. L. Suttle, "Improving Life at Work: Problems and Prospects," in *Improving Life at Work,* ed. J. R. Hackman and J. L. Suttle (Santa Monica, CA: Goodyear, 1977).

130. S. L. Robinson, "Trust and Breach of the Psychological Contract," *Administrative Science Quarterly* 41 (1996), pp. 574–99.

131. D. Rousseau, "Changing the Deal While Keeping the People," *Academy of Management Executive* 10 (1996), pp. 50–58.

132. E. E. Lawler III, *From the Ground Up* (San Francisco: Jossey-Bass 1996).

133. Ibid.

134. S. Ghoshal, C. Bartlett, and P. Moran, "Value Creation: The New Management Manifesto," *Financial Times Mastering Management Review,* November 1999, pp. 34–37.

135. R. Charan, "Stop Whining, Start Thinking," *BusinessWeek,* August 14, 2008, www.businessweek.com.

CHAPTER 12

1. R. Linden, "Developing a Collaborative Mindset," *Leader to Leader* 58 (Fall 2010), pp. 57–62; O. Marks, "From Command and Control to Collaboration and Teamwork," ZDNet.com, February 9, 2009, http://blogs.zdnet.com; S. Lawson, "Cisco to Shift Resources to Consumer Push," *PC World,* December 9, 2008, www.pcworld.com; E. McGirt, "How Cisco's CEO John Chambers Is Turning the Tech Giant Socialist," *Fast Company,* November 25, 2008, www.fastcompany.com; B. Fryer, "Cisco CEO John Chambers on Teamwork and Collaboration," *Harvard Business Review,* October 24, 2008, www.discussionleader.hbsp.com; "Reinventing Cisco Systems," *redOrbit,* January 27, 2008, www.redorbit.com; and J. Chambers, "Commentary," *Forbes,* January 23, 2008, www.forbes.com.

2. S. Cohen and D. Bailey, "What Makes Teams Work: Group Effectiveness Research from the Shop Floor to the Executive Suite," *Journal of Management* 23 (1997), pp. 239–90.

3. L. Riebe, D. Roepen, B. Santarelli, and G. Marchioro, "Teamwork: Effectively Teaching an Employability Skill," *Education and Training* 52, no. 6/7 (2010), pp. 528–539; and G. Chen, L. Donahue, and R. Klimoski, "Training Undergraduates to Work in Organizational Teams," *Academy of Management Learning and Education* 3 (2004), pp. 27–40.

4. Ken Blanchard Companies, "Client Spotlight: Summit Pointe," *Ignite!* March 2007, www.kenblanchard.com/ignite.

5. J. Jacobsen, "Ford Team Uses Six Sigma to Reduce Costs While Improving Environmental Impact," American Society for Quality (online), December 2011, www.asq.org; and "What Are VOCs in Paint, and Is More or Less of Them Better?" *Consumer Reports News* (online), April 28, 2008, www.consumerreports.org.

6. E. Fleischauer, "Nucor Manager Says Teamwork Key to Success; Q1 Earnings Up," *Decatur (AL) Daily,* April 20, 2007, www.decaturdaily.com.

7. J. Constine, "Facebook's New 'Creative Labs' Lets the 6,000-employee Giant Move Fast Like a Startup," *Tech Crunch* (online), January 30, 2014, www.techcrunch.com.

8. K. Holland, "How to Build Teamwork after an Awful Season," *The New York Times,* December 28, 2008.

9. D. Nadler, J. R. Hackman, and E. E. Lawler III, *Managing Organizational Behavior* (Boston: Little, Brown, 1979).

10. Holland, "How to Build Teamwork."

11. M. Cianni and D. Wnuck, "Individual Growth and Team Enhancement: Moving toward a New Model of Career Development," *Academy of Management Executive* 11 (1997), pp. 105–15.

12. Cohen and Bailey, "What Makes Teams Work"; and S. Huovinen and M. Pasanen, "Entrepreneurial and Management Teams: What Makes the Difference," *Journal of Management and Organization* 16, no. 3 (July 2010), pp. 436–54.

13. J. Katzenbach and D. Smith, "The Discipline of Teams," *Harvard Business Review,* March–April 1993, pp. 111–20.

14. N. Summer, "Google's 2013: The Evolution of Android, Chromebooks, Google + , YouTube, Google Glass and More," *The Next Web* (online), December 17, 2013, www.thenextweb.com; "Nooglers Get to Grips with the Google Way," *Human Resource Management International Digest,"* 19, no. 3 (2011), pp. 6–9; M. Johnson and M. Senges, "Learning to Be a Programmer in a Complex Organization," *Journal of Workplace Learning* 22, no. 3 (2010), pp. 180–94; and G. Hamel, "Break Free!" *Fortune* (Online), September 19, 2007, www.cnnmoney.com.

15. J. Zenger et al., *Leading Teams* (Burr Ridge, IL: Business One Irwin, 1994).

16. S. Cohen, "New Approaches to Teams and Teamwork," in J. Galbraith, E. E. Lawler III, and Associates, *Organizing for the Future* (San Francisco: Jossey-Bass, 1993).

17. Cohen and Bailey, "What Makes Teams Work."

18. L. Mullins, "Integration Crew for Maryland Bank," *American Banker,* February 13, 2007.

19. Ibid.

20. C. Snow, S. Snell, S. Davison, and D. Hambrick, "Use Transnational Teams to Globalize Your Company," *Organizational Dynamics,* Spring 1996, pp. 50–67.

21. F. Siebdrat, M. Hoegl, and H. Ernst, "How to Manage Virtual Teams," *MIT Sloan Management Review* 50, no. 4 (Summer 2009), pp. 63–68; and B. Kirkman, B. Rosen, C. Gibson, P. Tesluk, and S. McPherson, "Five Challenges to Virtual Team Success: Lessons from Sabre, Inc.," *Academy of Management Executive* 16 (2002), pp. 67–80.

22. A. Malhotra, A. Majchrzak, and B. Rosen, "Leading Virtual Teams," *Academy of Management Perspectives,* February 2007, pp. 60–70, table 1.

23. R. Banker, J. Field, R. Schroeder, and K. Sinha, "Impact of Work Teams on Manufacturing Performance: A Longitudinal Field Study," *Academy of Management Journal* 39 (1996), pp. 867–90.

24. D. Yeatts, M. Hipskind, and D. Barnes, "Lessons Learned from Self-Managed Work Teams," *Business Horizons,* July–August 1994, pp. 11–18.

25. B. Kirkman and D. Shapiro, "The Impact of Cultural Values on Job Satisfaction and Organizational Commitment in Self- Managing Work Teams: The Mediating Role of Employee Resistance," *Academy of Management Journal* 44 (2001), pp. 557–69.

26. Ibid.

27. B. Kirkman and D. Shapiro, "The Impact of Cultural Values on Employee Resistance to Teams: Toward a Model of Globalized Self-Managing Work Team Effectiveness," *Academy of Management Review* 22 (1997), pp. 730–57.

28. B. Macy and H. Isumi, "Organizational Change, Design, and Work Innovation: A Meta-Analysis of 131 North American Field Studies—1961–1991," *Research in Organizational Change and Development* 7 (1993), pp. 235–313.

29. R. Silverman, "Who's the Boss? There Isn't One," *Wall Street Journal* (online), June 19, 2012, www.wsj.com.

30. B. W. Tuckman, "Developmental Sequence in Small Groups," *Psychological Bulletin* 63 (1965), pp. 384–99.

31. S. Furst, M. Reeves, B. Rosen, and R. Blackburn, "Managing the Life Cycle of Virtual Teams," *Academy of Management Executive,* May 2004, pp. 6–20. Quotes in this paragraph are from pp. 11 and 12.

32. C. J. G. Gersick, "Time and Transition in Work Teams: Toward a New Model of Group Development," *Academy of Management Journal* 31 (1988), pp. 9–41.

33. J. R. Hackman, *Groups That Work (and Those That Don't)* (San Francisco: Jossey-Bass, 1990).

34. Zenger et al., *Leading Teams.*

35. R. Cross, "Looking before You Leap: Assessing the Jump to Teams in Knowledge-Based Work," *Business Horizons,* September–October 2000, pp. 29–36.

36. M. E. Palanski, S. S. Kahai, and F. J. Yammarino, "Team Virtues and Performance: An Examination of Transparency, Behavioral Integrity, and Trust," *Journal of Business Ethics* 99, no. 2 (2011), pp. 201–216.

37. Ibid.

38. J. Case, "What the Experts Forgot to Mention," *Inc.,* September 1993, pp. 66–78.

39. A. Nahavandi and E. Aranda, "Restructuring Teams for the Reengineered Organization," *Academy of Management Executive,* November 1994, pp. 58–68.

40. B. Kirkman, B. Rosen, P. Tesluk, and C. Gibson, "The Impact of Team Empowerment on Virtual Team Performance: The Moderating Role of Face-to-Face Interaction," *Academy of Management Journal* 47 (2004), pp. 175–92.

41. J. R. Katzenbach and D. K. Smith, *The Wisdom of Teams* (Boston: Harvard Business School Press, 1993).

42. Nadler et al., *Managing Organizational Behavior.*

43. T. Peters and N. Austin, *A Passion for Excellence* (New York: Random House, 1985).

44. Nadler et al., *Managing Organizational Behavior.*

45. S. Adams, "Making All Your Teams into A-Teams," *Training Journal,* August 2008.

46. D. Clutterbuck, "How to Coach a Team in the Field: What Is Involved in Team Coaching and What Skills Are Required?" *Training Journal,* February 2007.

47. D. Coutu, "Why Teams Don't Work," *Harvard Business Review,* May 2009, pp. 99–105 (interview of J. Richard Hackman).

48. Katzenbach and Smith, "The Discipline of Teams."

49. Ibid.

50. L. Gibson, J. Mathieu, C. Shalley, and T. Ruddy, "Creativity and Standardization: Complementary or Conflicting Drivers of Team Effectiveness?" *Academy of Management Journal* 48 (2005), pp. 521–31.

51. C. Meyer, "How the Right Measures Help Teams Excel," *Harvard Business Review,* May–June 1994, pp. 95–103.

52. J. R. Katzenbach and J. A. Santamaria, "Firing Up the Front Line," *Harvard Business Review,* May–June 1999, pp. 107–17.

53. D. Knight, C. Durham, and E. Locke, "The Relationship of Team Goals, Incentives, and Efficacy to Strategic Risk, Tactical Implementation, and Performance," *Academy of Management Journal* 44 (2001), pp. 326–38.

54. B. L. Kirkman and B. Rosen, "Powering Up Teams," *Organizational Dynamics,* Winter 2000, pp. 48–66.

55. E. E. Lawler, *From the Ground Up.* (San Francisco: Jossey-Bass, 1996).

56. R. L. Martin, "The Innovation Catalysts," *Harvard Business Review* 89, no. 6 (June 2011), pp. 82–90.

57. A. Jassawalla, H. Sashittal, and A. Maishe, "Students' Perceptions of Social Loafing: Its Antecedents and Consequences in Undergraduate Business Classroom Teams," *Academy of Management Learning and Education,* 2009, pp. 42–54.

58. M. Erez, "Is Group Productivity Loss the Rule or the Exception? Effects of Culture and Group-Based Motivation," *Academy of Management Journal* 39 (1996), pp. 1513–37.

59. Katzenbach and Smith, "The Discipline of Teams."

60. C. M. Barnes, J. R. Hellenbeck, D. K. Jundt, D. S. DeRue, and S. J. Harmon, "Mixing Individual Incentives and Group Incentives: Best of Both Worlds or Social Dilemma?" *Journal of Management* 37, no. 6 (November 2011), pp. 1611–35; M. Bolch, "Rewarding the Team," *HRMagazine,* February 2007; and P. Pascarelloa, "Compensating Teams," *Across the Board,* February 1997, pp. 16–22.

61. R. Wageman, "Interdependence and Group Effectiveness," *Administrative Science Quarterly* 40 (1995), pp. 145–80.

62. Bolch, "Rewarding the Team."

63. Lawler, *From the Ground Up.*

64. R. Wellins, R. Byham, and G. Dixon, *Inside Teams* (San Francisco: Jossey-Bass, 1994).

65. "Characteristics of High Performance Teams," Ernst & Young Report (online), www.ey.com, accessed on June 1, 2014.

66. B. Leichtling, "One Bad Apple Spoils Whole Team," *Charlotte Business Journal* (Online), December 16, 2011, www.bizjournals.com; J. Allen, "One 'Bad Apple' Does Spoil the Whole Office," Reuters, February 12, 2007, http://news.yahoo.com; and J. Wardy, "Don't Let One with Bad Attitude Infect Others," *Daily Record* (Morris County, NJ), April 23, 2007, www.dailyrecord.com.

67. A. Srivastava, K. Bartol, and E. Locke, "Empowering Leadership in Management Teams: Effects on Knowledge Sharing, Efficacy, and Performance," *Academy of Management Journal,* 2006, pp. 1239–51.

68. J. M. Levine, E. T. Higgins, and H. Choi, "Development of Strategic Norms in Groups," *Organizational Behavior and Human Decision Processes* 82 (2000), pp. 88–101.

69. K. Jehn and E. Mannix, "The Dynamic Nature of Conflict: A Longitudinal Study of Intragroup Conflict and Group Performance," *Academy of Management Journal* 44 (2001), pp. 238–51.

70. J. O'Toole, *Vanguard Management: Redesigning the Corporate Future* (New York: Doubleday, 1985).

71. R. F. Bales, *Interaction Process Analysis: A Method for the Study of Small Groups* (Reading, MA: Addison-Wesley, 1950).

72. V. U. Druskat and J. Wheeler, "Managing from the Boundary: The Effective Leadership of Self-Managing Work Teams," *Academy of Management Journal* 46 (2003), pp. 435–57.

73. Katzenbach and Smith, *The Wisdom of Teams.*

74. J. Carson, P. Tesluk, and J. Marrone, "Shared Leadership in Teams: An Investigation of Antecedent Conditions and Performance," *Academy of Management Journal,* 2007, pp. 1217–34.

75. C. Stoner and R. Hartman, "Team Building: Answering the Tough Questions," *Business Horizons,* September–October 1993, pp. 70–78.

76. S. E. Seashore, *Group Cohesiveness in the Industrial Work Group* (Ann Arbor: University of Michigan Press, 1954).

77. Blue Angels website, www.blueangels.navy.mil/team/officers.aspx.

78. A. G. Tekleab, N. R. Quigley, and P. E. Tesluk, "A Longitudinal Study of Team Conflict, Conflict Management, Cohesion, and Team Effectiveness," *Group & Organization Management* 34, no. 2 (April 2009), pp. 170–205; and B. Mullen and C. Cooper, "The Relation between Group Cohesiveness and Performance: An Integration," *Psychological Bulletin* 115 (1994), pp. 210–27.

79. Banker et al., "Impact of Work Teams on Manufacturing Performance."

80. D. P. Forbes and F. J. Milliken, "Cognition and Corporate Governance: Understanding Boards of Directors as Strategic Decision-Making Groups," *Academy of Management Review* 24 (1999), pp. 489–505.

81. T. Simons, L. H. Pelled, and K. A. Smith, "Making Use of Difference: Diversity, Debate, and Decision Comprehensiveness in Top Management Teams," *Academy of Management Journal* 42 (1999), pp. 662–73.

82. Seashore, *Group Cohesiveness in the Industrial Work Group.*

83. B. Lott and A. Lott, "Group Cohesiveness as Interpersonal Attraction: A Review of Relationships with Antecedent and Consequent Variables," *Psychological Bulletin,* October 1965, pp. 259–309.

84. K. Dahlin, L. Weingart, and P. Hinds, "Team Diversity and Information Use," *Academy of Management Journal* 48 (2005), pp. 1107–23.

85. B. L. Kirkman and B. Rosen, "Beyond Self-Management: Antecedents and Consequences of Team Empowerment," *Academy of Management Journal* 42 (1999), pp. 58–74.

86. Hackman, *Groups That Work.*

87. W. Bennis, *Organizing Genius* (Reading, MA: Addison-Wesley, 1997).

88. Cianni and Wnuck, "Individual Growth and Team Enhancement."

89. K. Jehn, "A Multimethod Examination of the Benefits and Detriments of Intragroup Conflict," *Administrative Science Quarterly* 40 (1995), pp. 245–82.

90. Wellins et al., *Inside Teams.*

91. D. G. Ancona, "Outward Bound: Strategies for Team Survival in an Organization," *Academy of Management Journal* 33 (1990), pp. 334–65.

92. Ibid.

93. L. Sayles, *Leadership: What Effective Managers Really Do, and How They Do It* (New York: McGraw-Hill, 1979).

94. Ibid.

95. J. A. Wall Jr. and R. R. Callister, "Conflict and Its Management," *Journal of Management* 21, no. 3 (1995), pp. 515–58.

96. B. R. Fry and T. L. Thomas, "Mary Parker Follett: Assessing the Contribution and Impact of Her Writings," *Journal of Management History* 2, no. 2 (1996), pp. 11–19.

97. P. Lencioni, "How to Foster Good Conflict," *The Wall Street Journal,* November 13, 2008, http://online.wsj.com; and D. Schachter, "Learn to Embrace Opposition for Improved Decision Making," *Information Outlook,* October 2008.

98. J. Chatman and F. Flynn, "The Influence of Demographic Heterogeneity on the Emergence and Consequences of Cooperative Norms in Work Teams," *Academy of Management Journal* 44 (2001), pp. 956–74; and R. T. Keller, "Cross-Functional Project Groups in Research and New Product Development: Diversity, Communications, Job Stress, and Outcomes," *Academy of Management Journal* 44 (2001), pp. 547–55.

99. "Managing Multicultural Teams: Winning Strategies from Teams around the World," *Computerworld,* November 20, 2006, http://find.galegroup.com.

100. D. Tjosvold, *Working Together to Get Things Done* (Lexington, MA: Lexington Books, 1986).

101. C. Tinsley and J. Brett, "Managing Workplace Conflict in the United States and Hong Kong," *Organizational Behavior and Human Decision Processes* 85 (2001), pp. 360–81.

102. K. W. Thomas, "Conflict and Conflict Management," in *Handbook of Industrial and Organizational Psychology,* ed. M. D. Dunnette (Chicago: Rand McNally, 1976).

103. J. S. Lublin, "How Best to Supervise Internal Runner-Up for the Job You Got," *The Wall Street Journal,* January 30, 2007, http://online.wsj.com.

104. Ibid.

105. K. W. Thomas, "Toward Multi-Dimensional Values in Teaching: The Example of Conflict Behaviors," *Academy of Management Review,* 1977, pp. 484–89.

106. C. O. Longenecker and M. Neubert, "Barriers and Gateways to Management Cooperation and Teamwork," *Business Horizons,* September–October 2000, pp. 37–44.

107. P. S. Nugent, "Managing Conflict: Third-Party Interventions for Managers," *Academy of Management Executive* 16 (2002), pp. 139–54.

108. M. Blum and J. A. Wall Jr., "HRM: Managing Conflicts in the Firm," *Business Horizons,* May–June 1997, pp. 84–87.

109. Agency website, www.eeoc.gov, Press release "EEOC Issues FY 2013 Performance Report," December 16, 2013.

110. J. A. Wall Jr. and R. R. Callister, "Conflict and Its Management," *Journal of Management* 21 (1995), pp. 515–58.

111. J. Polzer, C. B. Crisp, S. Jarvenpaa, and J. Kim, "Extending the Faultline Model to Geographically Dispersed Teams: How Collocated Subgroups Can Impair Group Functioning," *Academy of Management Journal* 49 (2006), pp. 679–92.

112. M. Montoya-Weiss, A. Massey, and M. Song, "Getting It Together: Temporal Coordination and Conflict Management in Global Virtual Teams," *Academy of Management Journal* 44 (2001), pp. 1251–62.

113. R. Standifer and J. A. Wall Jr., "Managing Conflict in B2B Commerce," *Business Horizons,* March–April 2003, pp. 65–70.

CHAPTER 13

1. L. Penley, E. Alexander, I. E. Jernigan, and C. Henwood, "Communication Abilities of Managers: The Relationship to Performance," *Journal of Management* 17 (1991), pp. 57–76.

2. D. Robb, "From the Top," *HRMagazine* 54, no. 2 (February 2009), pp. 61–64.

3. W. V. Haney, "A Comparative Study of Unilateral and Bilateral Communication," *Academy of Management Journal* 7 (1964), pp. 128–36.

4. J. Sandberg, "What Exactly Was It That the Boss Said? You Can Only Imagine," *The Wall Street Journal,* September 19, 2006, http://online.wsj.com.

5. M. McCormack, "The Illusion of Communication," *Financial Times Mastering Management Review,* July 1999, pp. 8–9.

6. R. Cross and S. Brodt, "How Assumptions of Consensus Undermine Decision Making," *Sloan Management Review* 42 (2001), pp. 86–94.

7. S. Mohammed and E. Ringseis, "Cognitive Diversity and Consensus in Group Decision Making: The Role of Inputs, Processes, and Outcomes," *Organizational Behavior and Human Decision Processes* 85 (2001), pp. 310–35.

8. S. Parker and C. Axtell, "Seeing Another Viewpoint: Antecedents and Outcomes of Employee Perspective Taking," *Academy of Management Journal* 44 (2001), pp. 1085–1100.

9. D. Tannen, "The Power of Talk: Who Gets Heard and Why," *Harvard Business Review,* September–October 1995, pp. 138–48.

10. Ibid.

11. Ibid.

12. L. K. Larkey, "Toward a Theory of Communicative Interactions in Culturally Diverse Workgroups," *Academy of Management Review,* April 1996, pp. 463–91.

13. N. J. Adler, *International Dimensions of Organizational Behavior.* Copyright © 1986. Reprinted with permission of South-Western College Publishing, a division of Thomson Learning.

14. For more information about cross-cultural body language, see www.bodylanguageexpert.co.uk/questionnaire-cross-cultural-body-language.html.

15. C. Argyris, "Good Communication That Blocks Learning," *Harvard Business Review,* July-August 1994, pp. 77–85.

16. E. Krell, "The Unintended Word," *HRMagazine,* August 2006.

17. J. V. Thill and C. L. Bovee, *Business Communication Version* 2.0 (Upper Saddle River, NJ: Prentice-Hall, 2005), p. 17.

18. Ibid.

19. C. Deutsch, "The Multimedia Benefits Kit," *The New York Times,* October 14, 1990, sec. 3, p. 25.

20. T. W. Comstock, *Communicating in Business and Industry* (Albany, NY: Delmar, 1985).

21. J. Taylor and W. Wacker, *The 500 Year Delta: What Happens after What Comes Next* (New York: HarperCollins, 1997).

22. A. Koganova, "Don't Just Stop at Skype: Alternative Video Conferencing Apps for Businesses," *TMCnet* (online), July 25, 2013,

www.tmcnet.com; and Y. Arar, "Web Conferencing Showdown: What's the Best Software for Online Meetings?" *PC World* (online), September 24, 2012, www.pcworld.com.

23. S. Radicati and J. Levenstein, "Email Statistics Report, 2013–2017," press release, April 2013, The Radicati Group Inc., www.radicati.com.

24. Ibid.

25. Company website, www.ibm.com.

26. M. Totty, "Rethinking the Inbox," *The Wall Street Journal* (online), March 26, 2007, http://www.online.wsj.com. "Rethinking the Inbox"; company website, http://sharepoint.microsoft.com.

27. M. Rodier, "A Simple Plan," *Wall Street & Technology* 28 (August 2010), pp. 22–23; and S. J. Leandri, "Five Ways to Improve Your Corporate Blogs," *Information Outlook,* January 2007.

28. R. D. Hof, "Web 2.0: The New Guy at Work," *BusinessWeek,* June 19, 2006.

29. J. Dye, "Collaboration 2.0: Make the Web Your Workspace," *EContent,* January–February 2007.

30. "Virtual Shareholders Meeting for Provident New York Bancorp," *The Wall Street Journal* (online), January 16, 2013, www.wsj.com.

31. S. S. K. Lam and J. Schaubroeck, "Improving Group Decisions by Better Pooling Information: A Comparative Advantage of Group Decision Support Systems," *Journal of Applied Psychology* 85 (2000), pp. 565–73.

32. M. Schrage, "If You Can't Say Anything Nice, Say It Anonymously," *Fortune,* December 6, 1999, p. 352; and B. Stone, "A Call for Manners in the World of Nasty Blogs," *The New York Times,* April 9, 2007, www.nytimes.com.

33. C. Naquin and G. Paulson, "Online Bargaining and Interpersonal Trust," *Journal of Applied Psychology* 88 (2003), pp. 113–20.

34. B. Baltes, M. Dickson, M. Sherman, C. Bauer, and J. LaGanke, "Computer-Mediated Communication and Group Decision Making: A Meta-Analysis," *Organizational Behavior and Human Decision Processes* 87 (2002), pp. 156–79.

35. R. Rice and D. Case, "Electronic Message Systems in the University: A Description of Use and Utility," *Journal of Communication* 33 (1983), pp. 131–52; and C. Steinfield, "Dimensions of Electronic Mail Use in an Organizational Setting," *Proceedings of the Academy of Management,* San Diego, 1985.

36. M. Gardner, "You've Got Mail: 'We're Letting You Go," *Christian Science Monitor,* September 18, 2006, www.csmonitor.com; and L. Weeks, "Read the Blog: You're Fired," National Public Radio, December 8, 2008, www.npr.org.

37. Leandri, "Five Ways to Improve Your Corporate Blogs."

38. Reuters, "Is That Really What Your E-mail Meant to Say?" *Yahoo News,* February 14, 2007, http://news.yahoo.com.

39. J. Leopold, "Pentagon Report: Scope of Intelligence Compromised by Snowden 'Staggering'," *The Guardian* (online), May 22, 2014, www.theguardian.com.

40. B. Glassberg, W. Kettinger, and J. Logan, "Electronic Communication: An Ounce of Policy Is Worth a Pound of Cure," *Business Horizons,* July–August 1996, pp. 74–80.

41. A. Joyce, "Never Out of IM Reach," *The Washington Post,* December 26, 2004, p. F5; and G. Hughes, "Quick Guide to IM-ing at Work," *Yahoo Tech,* January 24, 2007, http://tech.yahoo.com.

42. J. Robinson, "Tame the E-Mail Beast," *Entrepreneur Magazine* (online), February 12, 2010, www.entrepreneur.com.

43. Robinson, "Tame the E-Mail Beast"; Totty, "Rethinking the Inbox"; Reuters, "BlackBerrys, Laptops Blur Work/Home Balance: Poll," *Yahoo News,* April 5, 2007, http://news.yahoo.com; and M. Locher, "BlackBerry Addiction Starts at the Top," *PC World,* March 6, 2007, www.pcworld.com.

44. Taylor and Wacker, *The 500 Year Delta;* Locher, "BlackBerry Addiction"; and Hughes, "Quick Guide to IM-ing."

45. Locher, "BlackBerry Addiction."

46. "When the French Clock Off at 6 pm, They Really Mean It," *The Guardian* (online), April 9, 2014, www.theguardian.com.

47. Ibid.

48. S. Kim, "Tech Firm Implements Employee 'Zero Email' Policy," *ABC News,* November 29, 2011, http://abcnews.go.com.

49. V. Govindarajan and A. Gupta, "Building an Effective Global Team," *Organizational Dynamics* 42 (2001), pp. 63–71.

50. D. Meinert, "Make Telecommuting Pay Off," *HRMagazine* 56, no. 6 (June 2011), pp. 33–38; N. B. Kurland and D. E. Bailey, "Telework: The Advantages and Challenges of Working Here, There, Anywhere, Anytime," *Organizational Dynamics,* Autumn 1999, pp. 53–68; and B. Van Der Meer, "Realty Companies Making Internet Home," *Modesto (CA) Bee,* December 15, 2006.

51. Meinert, "Make Telecommuting Pay Off."

52. B. Leonard, "Managing Virtual Teams," *HRMagazine* 56, no. 6 (June 2011), pp. 39–43; and T. Mackintosh, "Is This the Year You Move to a Virtual Office?" *Accounting Technology,* May 2007.

53. E. M. Hallowell, "The Human Moment at Work," *Harvard Business Review,* January–February 1999, pp. 58–66.

54. Company website, www.accenture.com; and J. Marquez, "Connecting a Virtual Workforce," *Workforce Management,* September 22, 2008.

55. R. Lengel and R. Daft, "The Selection of Communication Media as an Executive Skill," *Academy of Management Executive* 2 (1988), pp. 225–32.

56. J. R. Carlson and R. W. Zmud, "Channel Expansion Theory and the Experiential Nature of Media Richness Perceptions," *Academy of Management Journal* 42 (1999), pp. 153–70.

57. L. Trevino, R. Daft, and R. Lengel, "Understanding Managers' Media Choices: A Symbolic Interactionist Perspective," in *Organizations and Communication Technology,* ed. J. Fulk and C. Steinfield (London: Sage, 1990).

58. J. Fulk and B. Boyd, "Emerging Theories of Communication in Organizations," *Journal of Management* 17 (1991), pp. 407–46.

59. From *Communicating for Managerial Effectiveness* by P. G. Clampitt. Copyright © 1991 by Sage Publications, Inc. Reprinted by permission of Sage Publications, Inc.

60. L. Bossidy and R. Charan, *Confronting Reality: Doing What Matters to Get Things Right* (New York: Crown Business, 2004).

61. J. Guterman, "How to Become a Better Manager by Thinking Like a Designer," *MIT Sloan Management Review* 50, no. 4 (Summer 2009), pp. 39–42; and M. McCall, M. Lombardo, and

A. Morrison, *The Lessons of Experience: How Successful Executives Develop on the Job* (Lexington, MA: Lexington, 1988).

62. J. A. Conger, "The Necessary Art of Persuasion," *Harvard Business Review,* May–June 1998, pp. 84–95.

63. N. Morgan, "How to Become an Authentic Speaker," *Harvard Business Review,* November 2008, pp. 115–19.

64. N. Nohria and B. Harrington, *Six Principles of Successful Persuasion* (Boston: Harvard Business School Publishing Division, 1993).

65. B. Gaille, "6 Examples of Shockingly Excellent Customer Service," ByReptutation (online), www.byreptutation.com, accessed on June 6, 2014.

66. H. K. Mintz, "Business Writing Styles for the 70's," *Business Horizons,* August 1972. Cited in *Readings in Interpersonal and Organizational Communication,* ed. R. C. Huseman, C. M. Logue, and D. L. Freshley (Boston: Allyn & Bacon, 1977).

67. C. D. Decker, "Writing to Teach Thinking," *Across the Board,* March 1996, pp. 19–20.

68. M. Forbes, "Exorcising Demons from Important Business Letters," *Marketing Times,* March–April 1981, pp. 36–38.

69. W. Strunk Jr. and E. B. White, *The Elements of Style,* 3rd ed. (New York: Macmillan, 1979); and H. R. Fowler and J. E Aaron, *The Little, Brown Handbook,* 12th ed. (New York: Longman, 2011).

70. D. Jones, "Cisco CEO Sees Tech as Integral to Success," *USA Today,* March 19, 2007, p. 4B (interview with John Chambers).

71. G. Ferraro, "The Need for Linguistic Proficiency in Global Business," *Business Horizons,* May–June 1996, pp. 39–46.

72. P. C. Early and E. Mosakowski, "Creating Hybrid Team Cultures: An Empirical Test of Transnational Team Functioning," *Academy of Management Journal* 43 (2000), pp. 26–49.

73. Ferraro, "The Need for Linguistic Proficiency."

74. C. Chu, *The Asian Mind Game* (New York: Rawson Associates, 1991).

75. Ferraro, "The Need for Linguistic Proficiency"; and J. F. Puck, M. G. Kittler, and C. Wright, "Does It Really Work? Re-assessing the Impact of Pre-departure Cross-cultural Training on Expatriate Adjustment," *The International Journal of Human Resource Management* 19, no. 12 (December 2008), pp. 2182–97.

76. J. S. Lublin, "Improv Troupe Teaches Managers How to Give Better Presentations," *Career Journal,* February 7, 2007, www.careerjournal.com.

77. Comstock, *Communicating in Business and Industry.*

78. M. Korda, *Power: How to Get It, How to Use It* (New York: Random House, 1975).

79. A. Mehrabian, "Communication without Words," *Psychology Today,* September 1968, p. 52. Cited in M. B. McCaskey, "The Hidden Message Managers Send," *Harvard Business Review,* November–December 1979, pp. 135–48.

80. Ferraro, "The Need for Linguistic Proficiency."

81. M. Munter, "Cross-cultural Communication for Managers," *Business Horizons* 36, no. 3 (May–June 1993), pp. 69–78.

82. A. T. Palmer, "Art of Listening Picked Up Young," *Chicago Tribune,* April 29, 2007, sec. 5, p. 3.

83. A. Athos and J. Gabarro, *Interpersonal Behavior* (Englewood Cliffs, NJ: Prentice-Hall, 1978).

84. R. G. Nichols, "Listening Is a 10-Part Skill," *Nation's Business* 45 (July 1957), pp. 56–60. Cited in R. C. Huseman, C. M. Logue, and D. L. Freshley, eds., *Readings in Interpersonal and Organizational Communication* (Boston: Allyn & Bacon, 1977).

85. Research report: "Critical Leadership Skills: Key Traits that can Make or Break Today's Leaders," The Ken Blanchard Companies, www.kenblanchard.com, accessed on June 6, 2014.

86. M. K. Pratt, "Five Ways to Drive Your Best Workers out the Door," *Computerworld,* August 25, 2008, pp. 26–27, 30.

87. Palmer, "The Art of Listening Picked Up Young."

88. J. Kouzes and B. Posner, *The Leadership Challenge* (San Francisco: Jossey-Bass, 1995).

89. G. Graham, J. Unruh, and P. Jennings, "The Impact of Nonverbal Communication in Organizations: A Survey of Perceptions," *Journal of Business Communications* 28 (1991), pp. 45–62.

90. Ibid.

91. D. Upton and S. Macadam, "Why (and How) to Take a Plant Tour," *Harvard Business Review,* May–June 1997, pp. 97–106.

92. N. Adler, *International Dimensions of Organizational Behavior,* 2nd ed. (Boston: Kent, 1991).

93. Chu, *The Asian Mind Game.*

94. A. Pentland, "How Social Networks Network Best," *Harvard Business Review,* February 2009, p. 37.

95. A. Smidts, A. T. H. Pruyn, and C. B. M. van Riel, "The Impact of Employee Communication and Perceived External Prestige on Organizational Identification," *Academy of Management Journal* 49 (2001), pp. 1051–62.

96. J. W. Koehler, K. W. E. Anatol, and R. L. Applebaum, *Organizational Communication: Behavioral Perspectives* (Orlando, FL: Holt, Rinehart & Winston, 1981).

97. Krell, "The Unintended Word."

98. J. Waldroop and T. Butler, "The Executive as Coach," *Harvard Business Review,* November–December 1996, pp. 111–17.

99. P. Coate and K. R. Hill, "Why Smart Companies Hire Performance Coaches to Turn Managers Into Leaders," *Employment Relations Today* 38, no. 1 (Spring 2011), pp. 35–43; and D. T. Hall, K. L. Otazo, and G. P. Hollenbeck, "Behind Closed Doors: What Really Happens in Executive Coaching," *Organizational Dynamics,* Winter 1999, pp. 39–53.

100. V. Elmer, "Coaching is Hot. Is it Right for You?" *Fortune* (online), August 29, 2011, www.fortune.com.

101. T. Judge and J. Cowell, "The Brave New World of Coaching," *Business Horizons,* July–August 1997, pp. 71–77; E. E. Lawler III, *Treat People Right!* (San Francisco: Jossey-Bass, 2003); and L. A. Hill, "New Manager Development for the 21st Century," *Academy of Management Executive,* August 2004, pp. 121–26.

102. J. Gutknecht and J. B. Keys, "Mergers, Acquisitions, and Takeovers: Maintaining Morale of Survivors and Protecting Employees," *Academy of Management Executive,* August 1993, pp. 26–36.

103. D. Schweiger and A. DeNisi, "Communication with Employees Following a Merger: A Longitudinal Field Experiment," *Academy of Management Journal* 34 (1991), pp. 110–35.

104. J. Case, "The Open-Book Managers," *Inc.,* September 1990, pp. 104–13.

105. J. Case, "Opening the Books," *Harvard Business Review,* March–April 1997, pp. 118–27.

106. T. R. V. Davis, "Open-Book Management: Its Promise and Pitfalls," *Organization Dynamics,* Winter 1997, pp. 7–20.

107. B. Burlingham, "Jack Stack, SRC Holdings," *Inc.,* April 2004, pp. 134–35.

108. Company website, www.srcholdings.com.

109. R. Aggarwal and B. Simkins, "Open Book Management: Optimizing Human Capital," *Business Horizons* 44 (2001), pp. 5–13.

110. W. V. Ruch, *Corporate Communications* (Westport, CT: Quorum, 1984).

111. J. Sandberg, "Working for a Boss Who Only Manages Up Can Be a Real Downer," *The Wall Street Journal,* May 16, 2006, http://online.wsj.com.

112. Krell, "The Unintended Word."

113. J. Gardner, "The Heart of the Matter: Leader–Constituent Interaction," in *Leading and Leadership,* ed. T. Fuller (Notre Dame, IN: Notre Dame University Press, 2000), pp. 239–44.

114. R. Ashkenas, D. Ulrich, T. Jick, and S. Kerr, *The Boundaryless Organization* (San Francisco: Jossey-Bass, 1995).

115. Ruch, *Corporate Communications.*

116. A. Vance, "At HP, Meg Whitman Wants People to Show Up for Work," *Businessweek* (online), October 9, 2013, www.businessweek.com.

117. L. Dulye, "Get Out of Your Office," *HRMagazine,* July 2006.

118. A. Hutton, "Four Rules for Taking Your Message to Wall Street," *Harvard Business Review,* May 2001, pp. 125–32.

119. Koehler et al., *Organizational Communication.*

120. W. Atkinson, "Let's Work Together Right Now," *Collections & Credit Risk,* May 2006.

121. "How Social Networking Increases Collaboration at IBM," *Strategic Communication Management* 14, no. 1 (December 2009/January 2010), pp. 32–36.

122. Ashkenas et al., *The Boundaryless Organization.*

123. D. K. Denton, "Open Communication," *Business Horizons,* September–October 1993, pp. 64–69.

124. J. Pogue, "Working around the Water Cooler," *Employee Benefit News,* February 1, 2009; Gensler, "Gensler Survey Measures Connection between Workplace Design and Business Performance," news release, October 23, 2008, www.gensler.com; and Gensler, 2008 Workplace Survey: United States, 2008, www.gensler.com.

125. N. B. Kurland and L. H. Pelled, "Passing the Word: Toward a Model of Gossip and Power in the Workplace," *Academy of Management Review* 25 (2000), pp. 428–38.

126. R. Cross, P. Gray, S. Cunningham, M. Showers, and R. Thomas, "The Collaborative Organization: How to Make Employee Networks Really Work," *MIT Sloan Management Review* 52, no. 1 (Fall 2010), pp. 83–90; and L. Abrams, R. Cross, E. Lesser, and D. Levin, "Nurturing Interpersonal Trust in Knowledge-Sharing Networks," *Academy of Management Executive* 17 (November 2003), pp. 64–77.

127. R. L. Rosnow, "Rumor as Communication: A Contextual Approach," *Journal of Communication* 38 (1988), pp. 12–28.

128. L. Burke and J. M. Wise, "The Effective Care, Handling, and Pruning of the Office Grapevine," *Business Horizons,* May–June 2003, pp. 71–76.

129. K. Davis, "The Care and Cultivation of the Corporate Grapevine," *Dun's Review,* July 1973, pp. 44–47.

130. N. Difonzo, P. Bordia, and R. Rosnow, "Reining in Rumors," *Organizational Dynamics,* Summer 1994, pp. 47–62.

131. "Office Politics Is on the Rise According to a Survey by Accountemps," *Bradenton (FL) Herald,* October 25, 2008; and A. M. Wolf, "A Morale Boost," *Raleigh (NC) News & Observer,* March 15, 2009, http://galenet.galegroup.com.

132. Difonzo et al., "Reining in Rumors."

133. J. O'Toole, "Amazon's 3D Smartphone May Finally Be Set for Release," *CNN Money* (online), June 4, 2014, www.money.cnn.com.

134. Ashkenas et al., *The Boundaryless Organization.*

135. R. M. Hodgetts, "A Conversation with Steve Kerr," *Organizational Dynamics,* Spring 1996, pp. 68–79.

136. R. M. Fulmer, "The Evolving Paradigm of Leadership Development," *Organizational Dynamics,* Spring 1997, pp. 59–72.

137. General Electric, "GE Shares Skills, Intellectual Capital with CommonBond Communities," news release, December 4, 2006, www.genewscenter.com.

138. Ashkenas et al., *The Boundaryless Organization.*

Chapter 14

1. Company website, www.ups.com; company website, www.medtronic.com; and J. Levitz and T. Martin, "UPS, Other Big Shippers Carve Health-Care Niches," *The Wall Street Journal* (online), June 27, 2012www.online.wsj.com.

2. W. G. Ouchi, "Markets, Bureaucracies, and Clans," *Administrative Science Quarterly* 25 (1980), pp. 129–41.

3. J. Muller, "Exclusive: Inside New CEO Mary Barra's Urgent Mission to Fix GM," *Forbes* (online), May 28, 2014; T. Krisher and M. Gordon, "New CEO Barra Faces Tough Task in Shedding Old GM," *Businessweek* (online), April 2, 2014, www.businessweek.com; P. Barrett, "The One Important Thing GM CEO Mary Barra Told Congress," *Businessweek* (online), April 1, 2014, www.businessweek.com.

4. R. Simons, A. Davila, and R. S. Kaplan, *Performance Measurement & Control Systems for Implementing Strategy* (Englewood Cliffs, NJ: Prentice Hall, 2000); W. G. Ouchi, "A Conceptual Framework for the Design of Organizational Control Mechanisms," *Management Science* 25 (1979), pp. 833–48; W. G. Ouchi, "Markets, Bureaucracies, and Clans," *Administrative Science Quarterly* 25 (1980), pp. 129–41; and R. D. Robey and C. A. Sales, *Designing Organizations* (Burr Ridge, IL: Richard D. Irwin, 1994).

5. J. C. Collins and J. I. Porras, *Built to Last: Successful Habits of Visionary Companies* (New York: HarperBusiness, 1994).

6. E. D. Pulakos, S. Arad, M. A. Donovan, and K. E. Plamondon, "Adaptability in the Workplace: Development of a Taxonomy of Adaptive Performance," *Journal of Applied Psychology* 85, no. 4 (August 2000), pp. 12–24; and J. H. Sheridan, "Lean Sigma Synergy," *Industry Week* 249, no. 17 (October 16, 2000), pp. 81–82.

7. Company website, www.bcbsnc.com; and "Blue Cross Blue Shield of North Carolina," *T 1 D* 64, no. 10 (October 2010), pp. 72–73.

8. J. T. Burr, "Keys to a Successful Internal Audit," *Quality Progress* 30, no. 4 (April 1997), pp. 75–77; and J. Zorabedian, "Uniform Security," *American Executive,* June 2008.

9. L. Buchanan, "Leadership: Armed with Data," *Inc.,* March 2009, www.inc.com.

10. D. H. Pink, *Drive: The Surprising Truth About What Motivates Us* (New York: Riverhead Books, 2011), p. 89.

11. E. White, "How Surveying Workers Can Pay Off," *The Wall Street Journal,* June 18, 2007, http://online.wsj.com.

12. Coca-Cola's Code of Business Conduct, www.thecoca-colacompany.com/ourcompany/pdf/COBC_English.pdf.

13. J. D. Bible, "Tattoos and Body Piercings: New Terrain for Employers and Courts," *Labor Law Journal* 61, no. 3 (Fall 2010), pp. 109–23; B. Roberts, "Stay Ahead of the Technology Use Curve," *HRMagazine,* October 2008; and K. A. Carr, "Broaching Body Art," *Crain's Cleveland Business,* September 29, 2008, http://galenet.galegroup.com.

14. Company website, www.donnmfg.com; "Error Proofing Your Staff," *Quality* 50, no. 3 (March 2011), pp. 54–55.

15. "SHRM Survey Findings: Workplace Romance," Society for Human Resource Management (online presentation), September 24, 2013, www.shrm.org.

16. T. Gara, "Panera Bread's Problem: Customers are Walking Away from Long Lines," *The Wall Street Journal* (online), October 23, 2013, www.wsjonline.com.

17. V. U. Druskat, "Effects and Timing of Developmental Peer Appraisals in Self-Managing Work Groups," *Journal of Applied Psychology* 84, no. 1 (February 1999), p. 58.

18. T. Cox, "Finding the Real MVPs in the Business," *Industry Week,* January 17, 2007, www.industryweek.com.

19. R. M. Kanter, "The Matter with the Mainstream," *U.S. News & World Report,* October 30, 2006.

20. S. Waddock and N. Smith, "Corporate Responsibility Audits: Doing Well by Doing Good," *Sloan Management Review* 41, no. 2 (Winter 2000), pp. 75–83; L. L. Bergeson, "OSHA Gives Incentives for Voluntary Self-Audits," *Pollution Engineering* 32, no. 10 (October 2000), pp. 33–34; and T. Rancour and M. McCracken, "Applying 6 Sigma Methods for Breakthrough Safety Performance," *Professional Safety* 45, no. 10 (October 2000), pp. 29–32.

21. S. Aghili, "A Six Sigma Approach to Internal Audits," *Strategic Finance,* February 2009.

22. A. Dehghann, A. Shahin, and B. Zenouzi, "Service Quality Gaps & Six Sigma," *Journal of Management Research* 4, no. 1 (2012), pp. 11–12; and A. Laureani, J. Antony, and A. Douglas, "Lean Six Sigma in a Call Centre: A Case Study," *International Journal of Productivity and Performance Management* 59, no. 8 (2010), pp. 757–68.

23. See, for example, B. Hindo, "At 3M, a Struggle between Efficiency and Creativity," *BusinessWeek,* June 11, 2007; B. Hindo and B. Grow, "Six Sigma; So Yesterday?" *BusinessWeek,* June 11, 2007, http://find.galegroup.com; and J. Rae, "Viewpoint: Have It Both Ways," *BusinessWeek,* June 11, 2007, http://find.galegroup.com.

24. Rancour and McCracken, "Applying 6 Sigma Methods for Breakthrough Safety Performance;" and G. Eckes, "Making Six Sigma Last," *Ivey Business Journal,* January–February 2002, p. 77.

25. J. L. Colbert, "The Impact of the New External Auditing Standards," *Internal Auditor* 5, no. 6 (December 2000), pp. 46–50.

26. Aghili, "A Six Sigma Approach"; Y. Giard and Y. Nadeau, "Improving the Processes," *CA Magazine,* December 2008; and G. Cheney, "Connecting the Dots to the Next Crisis," *Financial Executive,* April 2009, pp. 30–33.

27. J. D. Glater, "The Better the Audit Panel, the Higher the Stock Price," *The New York Times,* April 8, 2005, p. C4.

28. B. Roberts, "Data-Driven Human Capital Decisions," *HRMagazine,* March 2007.

29. P. C. Brewer and L. A. Vulinec, "Harris Corporation's Experiences with Using Activity-Based Costing," *Information Strategy: The Executive's Journal* 13, no. 2 (Winter 1997), pp. 6–16; and T. P. Pare, "A New Tool for Managing Costs," *Fortune,* June 14, 1993, pp. 124–29.

30. K. Merchant, *Control in Business Organizations* (Boston: Pitman, 1985); C. W. Chow, Y. Kato, and K. A. Merchant, "The Use of Organizational Controls and Their Effects on Data Manipulation and Management Myopia," *Accounting, Organizations, and Society* 21, nos. 2/3 (February/April 1996), pp. 175–92.

31. E. E. Lawler III and J. Rhode, *Information and Control in Organizations* (Pacific Palisades, CA: Goodyear, 1976); A. Ferner, "The Underpinnings of 'Bureaucratic' Control Systems: HRM in European Multinationals," *Journal of Management Studies* 37, no. 4 (June 2000), pp. 521–39; and M. S. Fenwick, "Cultural and Bureaucratic Control in MNEs: The Role of Expatriate Performance Management," *Management International Review* 39 (1999), pp. 107–25.

32. Hindo, "At 3M, a Struggle between Efficiency and Creativity."

33. "3M: A Hot U.S. Innovator Nowhere Near Silicon Valley," *The Wall Street Journal* (online), March 5, 2011, http://online.wsj.com.

34. D. H. Freedman, "Go Ahead, Make a Mess," *Inc.,* December 2006, pp. 120–25.

35. J. Craig, "VA Medical Scandal Presents Opportunity to Right a Wrong," *The Pitt News* (online), June 10, 2014, http://www.pittnews.com; and M. Shear and R. Oppel, "V.A. Chief Resigns in Face of Furor on Delayed Care," *The New York Times* (online), May 31, 2014, www.nytimes.com.

36. M. Rothfeld and C. Bray, "Crackdown Targets Tests On Concrete," *The Wall Street Journal,* August 5, 2011, p. A15.

37. M. Gelbart, "L&I Gets Ritz-Carlton Image Tips," *Philadelphia Inquirer,* March 10, 2009, www.philly.com.

38. W. Atkinson, "eBay Uses Voice Analytics to Increase Client Sales," *CIO Insight* (online), September 26, 2013, www.cioinsight.com.

39. M. Hammer, "The Seven Deadly Sins of Performance Measurement and How to Avoid Them," *MIT Sloan Management Review* 48, no. 3 (Spring 2007), pp. 19–28.

40. Lawler and Rhode, *Information and Control in Organizations;* and J. A. Gowan Jr. and R. G. Mathieu, "Critical Factors in Information System Development for a Flexible Manufacturing System," *Computers in Industry* 28, no. 3 (June 1996), pp. 173–83.

41. M. Bush, "Why You Should Be Putting On the Ritz," *Advertising Age* 81, no. 25 (June 21, 2010), pp. 1–2; and J. Robison, "How the Ritz-Carlton Manages the Mystique," *Gallup Management Journal,* December 11, 2008.

42. W. Leavitt, "Twenty-First Century Driver Training," *Fleet Owner,* January 1, 2006.

43. R. S. Kaplan and D. P. Norton, *The Balanced Scorecard: Translating Strategy into Action* (Boston: Harvard Business School Press, 1996); and A. Gumbus and R. N. Lussier, "Entrepreneurs Use a Balanced Scorecard to Translate Strategy into Performance Measures," *Journal of Small Business Management* 44, no. 3 (July 2006).

44. Company website, www.jpmorgan.com.

45. M. A. Reed-Woodard, "The Business of Nonprofit," *Black Enterprise,* June 2007.

46. B. Roberts, "Let's Make a Deal," *HRMagazine* 53, no. 11 (November 2008), pp. 85–91.

47. Company website, www.paychex.com; A. Choi, "When a Family Business Should Outsource Human Resources," *Entrepreneur* (online), May 7, 2013, www.entrepreneur.com.

48. K. Moores and J. Mula, "The Salience of Market, Bureaucratic, and Clan Controls in the Management of Family Firm Transitions: Some Tentative Australian Evidence," *Family Business Review* 13, no. 2 (June 2000), pp. 91–106; and A. Walker and R. Newcombe, "The Positive Use of Power on a Major-Construction Project," *Construction Management and Economics* 18, no. 1 (January/February 2000), pp. 37–44.

49. P. H. Fuchs, K. E. Mifflin, D. Miller, and J. O. Whitney, "Strategic Integration: Competing in the Age of Capabilities," *California Management Review* 42, no. 3 (Spring 2000), pp. 118–47; M. A. Lando, "Making Compliance Part of Your Organization's Culture," *Healthcare Executive* 15, no. 5 (September/October 1999), pp. 18–22; and K. A. Frank and K. Fahrbach, "Organization Culture as a Complex System: Balance and Information in Models of Influence and Selection," *Organization Science* 10, no. 3 (May/June 1999), pp. 253–77.

50. "100 Best Companies to Work For, 2009," *Fortune,* February 2, 2009, http://money.cnn.com.

51. G. H. B. Ross, "Revolution in Management Control," *Management Accounting,* November 1990, pp. 23–27. Reprinted with permission.

Chapter 15

1. R. A. Burgelman, M. A. Maidique, and S. C. Wheelwright, *Strategic Management of Technology and Innovation* (New York: McGraw-Hill, 2000).

2. D. C. L. Prestwood and P. A. Schumann Jr., "Revitalize Your Organization," *Executive Excellence* 15, no. 2 (February 1998), p. 16; C. Y. Baldwin and K. B. Clark, "Managing in an Age of Modularity," *Harvard Business Review* 75, no. 5 (September–October 1997), pp. 84–93; S. Gopalakrishnan, P. Bierly, and E. H. Kessler, "A Reexamination of Product and Process Innovations Using a Knowledge-Based View," *Journal of High Technology Management Research* 10, no. 1 (Spring 1999), pp. 147–66; and J. Pullin, "Bombardier Commands Top Marks," *Professional Engineering* 13, no. 3 (July 5, 2000), pp. 40–46.

3. M. Sawhney, R. C. Wolcott, and I. Arroniz, "The 12 Different Ways for Companies to Innovate," *MIT Sloan Management Review* 47, no. 3 (Spring 2006), pp. 75–81.

4. M. E. Porter, *Competitive Strategy* (New York: Free Press, 1980).

5. "AHRQ Study Shows Using Bar-Code Technology with eMar Reduces Medication Administration and Transcription Errors," *Agency for Healthcare Research and Quality,* press release (May 5, 2010), pp. 1–2; and G. Colvin, "McKesson: Wiring the Medical World," *Fortune,* February 5, 2007, http://money.cnn.com.

6. Organization website, www.ssmhc.com.

7. R. E. Oligney and M. I. Economides, "Technology as an Asset," *Hart's Petroleum Engineer International* 71, no. 9 (September 1998), p. 27.

8. See www.claytonchristensen.com/disruptive_innovation.html (accessed February 9, 2012).

9. "The Lask Kodak Moment?" *The Economist* 402, no. 8767 (January 14, 2012), p. 63; and M. E. Raynor, "Getting to New and Improved," *The Conference Board Review* 48, no. 4 (Fall 2011), pp. 61–67.

10. C. M. Christensen, *The Innovator's Dilemma: The Revolutionary Book That Will Change the Way You Do Business* (New York: Harper Paperbacks, 2003), p. xvi.

11. Ibid.

12. Company website, www.bing.com/translator/.

13. J. E. Vascellaro, "Found in Translation," *The Wall Street Journal,* May 24, 2007, http://online.wsj.com.

14. Colvin, "McKesson."

15. See, for example, B. Ames, "IBM Speeds Chips with DRAM Memory," *PC World,* February 12, 2007, http://www.pcworld.com; S. Ferguson, "Intel Plans Push Into Mobility, Emerging Markets," *eWeek,* May 3, 2007, http://www.eweek.com; and S. Ferguson, "AMD's Next Gen Mobile Chip, Platform to Conserve Power," *eWeek,* May 18, 2007, http://www.eweek.com.

16. A. Leather, "Intel Unveils 2014 Roadmap: 4 Fantastic New Processors For PC Enthusiasts," *Forbes* (online), March 19, 2014, www.forbes.com.

17. M. Kanellos, "The Most Important Man in Energy Storage? Try Archimedes," *Forbes* (online), March 26, 2013, www.forbes.com.

18. Company website, http://iqbginc.com/company/about-us/; H. Kramer, "Washington Moves Into The Cloud: Saving Money And Securing Data," *Forbes* (online), July 8, 2013, www.forbes.com.

19. J. Jusko, "Foiling Fakes," *Industry Week,* May 2007.

20. "Fresh, but Far from Easy," *The Economist,* June 23, 2007.

21. M. Bayless, "A Recipe for Effective Change," *Gourmet Retailer,* January 2007.

22. R. Dewan, B. Jing, and A. Seidmann, "Adoption of Internet-Based Product Customization and Pricing Strategies," *Journal of Management Information Systems* 17, no. 2 (Fall 2000), pp. 9–28; P. A. Geroski, "Models of Technology Diffusion," *Research Policy* 29, no. 4/5 (April 2000), pp. 603–25; and E. M. Rogers, *Diffusion of Innovations* (New York: Free Press, 1995).

23. E. Von Hippel, *The Sources of Innovation* (Oxford, UK: Oxford University Press, 1994); and D. Leonard, *Wellsprings of Knowledge: Building and Sustaining the Sources of Innovation* (Cambridge, MA: Harvard Business School Press, 1998).

24. K. Maxey, "Infographic: The History of 3D Printing," *Engineering* (online), September 3, 2013, www.engineering.com.

25. T. Ehrlich and E. Fu, "Our Future with 3D Printers: 7 Disrupted Industries," *Forbes* (online), October 29, 2013, www.forbes.com.

26. D. Rotman, "Ten Breakthrough Technologies 2014—Microscale 3-D Printing," *MIT Technology Review* (online), www.technologyreview.com, accessed on June 16, 2014.

27. Ibid.

28. Company website, www.intel.com; and T. Krazit, "Intel R&D on Slow Boat to China," *CNet News,* April 16, 2007, http://news.com.com.

29. K. MacQueen, "Cashing in His V-Chips," *Maclean's,* June 11, 2007; and "Online Gaming's Netscape Moment?" *The Economist,* June 9, 2007, http://find.galegroup.com.

30. T. Purdum, "Benchmarking Outside the Box: Best Practices Can Rise from Where You Least Expect Them," *Industry Week,* March 2007.

31. Von Hippel, *The Sources of Innovation;* and Leonard, *Wellsprings of Knowledge.*

32. Company website, www.boeing.com; "Boeing, Embraer to Open Joint Research Center for Sustainable Aviation Biofuel," *PR Newswire* (online), May 12, 2014, www.finance.yahoo.com.

33. J. Hagedoorn, A. N. Link, and N. S. Vonortas, "Research Partnerships," *Research Policy* 29, no. 4/5 (April 2000), pp. 567–86; and S.-S. Yi, "Entry, Licensing and Research Joint Ventures," *International Journal of Industrial Organization* 17, no. 1 (January 1999), pp. 1–24.

34. "Volvo in Strategic Alliance with Chinese Company Dongfeng Motor Group," Press release, January 26, 2013, http://newsvolvogroup.com.

35. "Broadcom Acquires GPS Specialist Global Locate for $146 Million," *Information Week,* June 12, 2007.

36. Andrew et al., *Innovation 2009,* p. 11.

37. J. G. March, "Exploration and Exploitation in Organizational Learning," *Organization Science* 2, no. 1 (1991), pp. 71–87.

38. T. Hoffman, "Change Agents," *ComputerWorld,* April 23, 2007; Center for CIO Leadership, "Center for CIO Leadership Unveils 2008 Survey Results," news release, November 18, 2008, www.marketwire.com; Center for CIO Leadership, "CIO Leadership Survey Executive Summary," abstract, 2008, www.cioleadershipcenter.com; and G. H. Anthes, "The CIO/CTO Balancing Act," *ComputerWorld* 34, no. 25 (June 19, 2000), pp. 50–51.

39. D. L. Day, "Raising Radicals: Different Processes for Championing Innovative Corporate Ventures," *Organization Science* 5, no. 2 (May 1994), pp. 148–72; C. Siporin, "Want Speedy FDA Approval? Hire a 'Product Champion,'" *Medical Marketing & Media,* October 1993, pp. 22–28; C. Siporin, "How You Can Capitalize on Phase 3B," *Medical Marketing & Media,* October 1994, p. 72; and E. H. Kessler, "Tightening the Belt: Methods for Reducing Development Costs Associated with New Product Innovation," *Journal of Engineering and Technology Management* 17, no. 1 (March 2000), pp. 59–92.

40. B. Hindo, "At 3M, a Struggle between Efficiency and Creativity," *BusinessWeek,* June 11, 2007, www.businessweek.com; Palmer, "Creativity on Demand"; E. Figueroa and P. Conceicao, "Rethinking the Innovation Process in Large Organizations: A Case Study of 3M," *Journal of Engineering and Technology Management* 17, no. 1 (March 2000), pp. 93–109; and D. Howell, "No Such Thing as a Daft Idea," *Professional Engineering* 13, no. 4 (February 23, 2000), pp. 28–29.

41. S. Shellenbarger, "Better Ideas through Failure: Companies Reward Employee Mistakes to Spur Innovation, Get Back Their Edge," *The Wall Street Journal* (September 27, 2011), p. D1; D. A. Fields, "How to Stop the Dumbing Down of Your Company," *Industry Week,* March 7, 2007, www.industryweek.com; L. K. Gundry, J. R. Kickul, and C. W. Prather, "Building the Creative Organization," *Organizational Dynamics* 22, no. 2 (Spring 1994), pp. 22–36; and T. Kuczmarski, "Inspiring and Implementing the Innovation Mind-Set," *Planning Review,* September–October 1994, pp. 37–48.

42. G. Moran, "Fostering Greater Creativity by Celebrating Failure, *Fast Company* (online), April 4, 2014, www.fastcompany.com.

43. D. Rodriguez and R. Jacoby, "Embracing Risk to Grow and Innovate," *BusinessWeek,* May 16, 2007, www.businessweek.com.

44. Company reports; R. Mitchell, "Masters of Innovation: How 3M Keeps Its New Products Coming," *BusinessWeek,* April 10, 1989, pp. 58–63; T. Katauskas, "Follow-Through: 3M's Formula for Success," *R&D,* November 1990; and T. J. Martin, "Ten Commandments for Managing Creative People," *Fortune,* January 16, 1995, pp. 135–36.

45. L. P. Norton, "3M: A Hot U.S. Innovator Nowhere Near Silicon Valley," *The Wall Street Journal* (Eastern edition), March 6, 2011, p. 2.

46. D. Tsuruoka, "Intuit Innovation Lab, 'Idea Jams' Aim to Spur Creativity," *Investor's Business Daily,* April 14, 2009.

47. H. Kent Bowen, Kim B. Clark, Charles A. Holloway, and Steven C. Wheelwright, "Development Projects: The Engine of Renewal," *Harvard Business Review,* September–October 1994, pp. 110–20; C. Eden, T. Williams, and F. Ackermann, "Dismantling the Learning Curve: The Role of Disruptions on the Planning of Development Projects," *International Journal of Project Management* 16, no. 3 (June 1998), pp. 131–38; and M. V. Tatikonda and S. R. Rosenthal, "Technology Novelty, Project Complexity, and Product Development Project Execution Success: A Deeper Look at Task Uncertainty in Product Innovation," *IEEE Transactions on Engineering Management* 47, no. 1 (February 2000), pp. 74–87.

48. L. Dishman, "MTV's Nusrat Durrani Introduces Global Beats to U.S. Audiences," *Fast Company* (Online), November 7, 2011, www.fastcompany.com; and B. Nemer, "How MTV Channels Innovation," *BusinessWeek,* November 6, 2006.

49. E. Trist, "The Evolution of Sociotechnical Systems as a Conceptual Framework and as an Action Research Program," in *Perspectives on Organizational Design and Behavior,* ed. A. Van de Ven and W. F. Joyce, pp. 19–75 (New York: John Wiley & Sons, 1981); and A. Molina, "Insights into the Nature of Technology Diffusion and Implementation: The Perspective of Sociotechnical

Alignment," *Technovation* 17, nos. 11/12 (November/December 1997), pp. 601–26.

50. S. A. Snell and J. W. Dean Jr., "Strategic Compensation for Integrated Manufacturing: The Moderating Effects of Jobs and Organizational Inertia," *Academy of Management Journal* 37 (1994), pp. 1109–40.

51. C. Giffi, A. Roth, and G. Seal, *Competing in World-Class Manufacturing: America's 21st Century Challenge* (Homewood, IL: Business One Irwin, 1990).

52. R. M. Kanter, *World Class: Thriving Locally in the Global Economy* (New York: Touchstone, 1995).

53. Giffi, Roth, and Seal, *Competing in World-Class Manufacturing*.

54. J. Collins and J. Porras, *Built to Last* (London: Century, 1996).

55. Ibid.

56. C. Gibson and J. Birkinshaw, "The Antecedents, Consequences, and Mediating Role of Organizational Ambidexterity," *Academy of Management Journal* 47 (2004), pp. 209–26.

57. Collins and Porras, *Built to Last*.

58. T. Cummings and C. Worley, *Organization Development and Change,* 8th ed. (Mason, OH: Thomson/South-Western, 2005).

59. Ibid.

60. N. Nohria, W. Joyce, and B. Roberson, "What Really Works," *Harvard Business Review,* July 2003, pp. 42–52.

61. D. R. Conner, *Managing at the Speed of Change* (New York: Random House, 2006); and R. Teerlink, "Harley's Leadership U-Turn," *Harvard Business Review,* July–August 2000, pp. 43–48.

62. C. M. Christensen, "The Past and Future of Competitive Advantage," *Sloan Management Review,* Winter 2001, pp. 105–9.

63. "SHRM Research Spotlight: Future HR Challenges and Talent Management Tactics," Society for *Human Resource Management* (online), November 2012, www.shrm.org.

64. M. Schrage, "Getting Beyond the Innovation Fetish," *Fortune,* November 13, 2000, pp. 225–32.

65. T. A. Judge, C. J. Thoresen, V. Pucik, and T. M. Welbourne, "Managerial Coping with Organizational Change: A Dispositional Perspective," *Journal of Applied Psychology* 84 (1999), pp. 107–22.

66. E. E. Lawler III, *Treat People Right!* (San Francisco: Jossey-Bass, 2003).

67. Conner, *Managing at the Speed of Change;* E. Lamm and J. R. Gordon, "Empowerment, Predisposition to Resist Change, and Support for Organizational Change," *Journal of Leadership & Organizational Studies* 17, no. 4 (November 2010), pp. 426–37; and S. Oreg, "Resistance to Change: Developing an Individual Differences Measure," *Journal of Applied Psychology* (2003), pp. 680–93.

68. G. Satell, "How to Create a Culture of Change," *Forbes* (online), June 13, 2014, www.forbes.com; and M. McArdle, "Why Companies Fail," *The Atlantic* (online), February 6, 2012, www.theatlantic.com.

69. A. Deutschman, *Change or Die* (Los Angeles: Regan, 2007), pp. 164–78.

70. J. Stanislao and B. C. Stanislao, "Dealing with Resistance to Change," *Business Horizons,* July–August 1983, pp. 74–78.

71. J. P. Kotter and L. A. Schlesinger, "Choosing Strategies for Change," *Harvard Business Review,* March–April 1979, pp. 106–14.

72. D. Zell, "Overcoming Barriers to Work Innovations: Lessons Learned at Hewlett-Packard," *Organizational Dynamics,* Summer 2001, pp. 77–85.

73. Ibid.

74. E. B. Dent and S. Galloway Goldberg, "Challenging Resistance to Change," *Journal of Applied Behavioral Science,* March 1999, pp. 25–41.

75. G. Johnson, *Strategic Change and the Management Process* (New York: Basil Blackwell, 1987); and K. Lewin, "Frontiers in Group Dynamics," *Human Relations* 1 (1947), pp. 5–41.

76. E. H. Schein, "Organizational Culture: What It Is and How to Change It," in *Human Resource Management in International Firms,* ed. P. Evans, Y. Doz, and A. Laurent (New York: St. Martin's Press, 1990).

77. M. Beer, R. Eisenstat, and B. Spector, *The Critical Path to Corporate Renewal* (Cambridge, MA: Harvard Business School Press, 1990).

78. E. E. Lawler III, "Transformation from Control to Involvement," in *Corporate Transformation,* ed. R. Kilmann and T. Covin (San Francisco: Jossey-Bass, 1988).

79. Deutschman, *Change or Die,* pp. 1–15.

80. D. Hellriegel and J. W. Slocum Jr., *Management,* 4th ed. (Reading, MA: Addison-Wesley, 1986).

81. C. Aiken and S. Keller, "The Irrational Side of Change Management," *McKinsey Quarterly,* April 2009, www.mckinseyquarterly.com.

82. Lewin, "Frontiers in Group Dynamics."

83. Schein, "Organizational Culture."

84. E. E. Lawler III, *From the Ground Up* (San Francisco: Jossey-Bass, 1995).

85. Q. Nguyen Huy, "Time, Temporal Capability, and Planned Change," *Academy of Management Review* 26 (2001), pp. 601–23.

86. B. Sugarman, "A Learning-Based Approach to Organizational Change: Some Results and Guidelines," *Organizational Dynamics,* Summer 2001, pp. 62–75.

87. Kotter and Schlesinger, "Choosing Strategies for Change."

88. N. H. Woodward, "To Make Changes, Manage Them," *HRMagazine,* May 2007.

89. R. H. Miles, "Beyond the Age of Dilbert: Accelerating Corporate Transformations by Rapidly Engaging All Employees," *Organizational Dynamics,* Spring 2001, pp. 313–21.

90. Bayless, "A Recipe for Effective Change."

91. M. S. Dahl, "Organizational Change and Employee Stress," *Management Science* 57, no. 2 (February 2011), pp. 240–56; J. R. Darling and V. L. Heller, "The Key for Effective Stress Management: Importance of Responsive Leadership in *Organizational Development Journal* 29, no. 1 (Spring 2011), pp. 9–26; and O. Robinson and A. Griffiths, "Coping with the Stress of Transformational Change in a Governmental Department," *The Journal of Applied Behavioral Science* 41, no. 2 (June 2005), pp. 204–21.

92. D. A. Nadler, "Managing Organizational Change: An Integrative Approach," *Journal of Applied Behavioral Science* 17 (1981), pp. 191–211.

93. D. Rousseau and S. A. Tijoriwala, "What's a Good Reason to Change? Motivated Reasoning and Social Accounts in Promoting

Organizational Change," *Journal of Applied Psychology* 84 (1999), pp. 514–28.

94. K. Hope, "Are Executive Sleepovers the Best Way for Staff of Bond?" BBC News (online), April 7, 2014, www.bbc.com.

95. Deutschman, *Change or Die,* p. 202.

96. Ibid, pp. 187–93.

97. C. F. Leana and B. Barry, "Stability and Change as Simultaneous Experiences in Organizational Life," *Academy of Management Review* 25 (2000), pp. 753–59.

98. O. Gadiesh and J. Gilbert, "Transforming Corner-Office Strategy into Frontline Action," *Harvard Business Review,* May 2001, pp. 72–79.

99. B. Schneider, A. Brief, and R. Guzzo, "Creating a Climate and Culture for Sustainable Organizational Change," *Organizational Dynamics,* Spring 1996, pp. 7–19.

100. Price Waterhouse Change Integration Team, *Better Change: Best Practices for Transforming Your Organization* (Burr Ridge, IL: Irwin, 1995).

101. M. Beer and N. Nohria, "Cracking the Code of Change," *Harvard Business Review,* May–June 2000, pp. 133–41.

102. N. Nohria and J. Berkley, "Whatever Happened to the Take-Charge Manager?" *Harvard Business Review,* January–February 1994, pp. 128–37.

103. D. Miller, J. Hartwick, and I. Le Breton-Miller, "How to Detect a Management Fad—and Distinguish It from a Classic," *Business Horizons,* July–August 2004, pp. 7–16.

104. Price Waterhouse Change Integration Team, *Better Change.*

105. Ibid.

106. E. M. Heffes, "You Need Urgency Now!" *Financial Executive,* January–February 2009 (interview with John P. Kotter).

107. J. P. Kotter, *Leading Change* (Boston: Harvard Business School Press, 1996).

108. Lawler, *From the Ground Up.*

109. Kotter, *Leading Change.*

110. Schneider, Brief, and, "Creating a Climate and Culture."

111. R. Beckhard and R. Harris, *Organizational Transitions* (Reading, MA: Addison-Wesley, 1977).

112. Kotter, *Leading Change.*

113. E. Boens, "Positive Communication," *Industrial Safety and Hygiene News,* June 2006.

114. G. Hamel, "Waking Up IBM," *Harvard Business Review,* July–August 2000, pp. 137–46; and Deutschman, *Change or Die.*

115. Kotter, *Leading Change.*

116. D. Smith, *Taking Charge of Change* (Reading, MA: Addison-Wesley, 1996).

117. M. J. Mandel, "This Way to the Future," *BusinessWeek,* October 11, 2004, pp. 92–98, quoting p. 93.

118. S. Zuboff and J. Maxim, *The Support Economy* (New York: Penguin, 2004).

119. Company website, www.uber.com; C. Clifford, "Car-Service Company Uber Reportedly Valued at $3.5 Billion," *Entrepreneur* (online), August 23, 2013, www.entrepreneur.com; and

A. Vaccaro, "Uber Isn't a Car Service. It's the Future of Logistics," *Inc.* (online), December 13, 2013, www.inc.com.

120. H. Courtney, J. Kirkland, and P. Viguerie, "Strategy under Uncertainty," *Harvard Business Review,* November–December 1997, pp. 66–79.

121. J. O'Shea and C. Madigan, *Dangerous Company: The Consulting Powerhouses and the Business They Save and Ruin* (New York: Times Books, 1997).

122. G. Hamel and C. K. Prahalad, *Competing for the Future* (Boston: Harvard Business School Press, 1994).

123. Ibid.

124. Ibid.

125. R. D. Hof, "How to Hit a Moving Target," *BusinessWeek,* August 21, 2006.

126. S. E. Rickert, "Taking the NanoPulse: Sizing Up Nanotechnology," *Industry Week,* May 9, 2007, www.industryweek.com; M. David, "Into the Nano Frontier—Closer Than You Might Think," *Electronic Design,* May 10, 2007, and S. Baker and A. Aston, "The Business of Nanotech," *BusinessWeek,* February 14, 2005, pp. 569–70.

127. David, "Into the Nano Frontier"; and M. Haiken, "Eight Nanotech Takes on Water Pollution," *Business 2.0,* July 2007.

128. M. C. Bellas, "Very Small and Unfathomably Huge," *Beverage World,* June 15, 2007.

129. Hamel and Prahalad, *Competing for the Future.*

130. J. Kotter, *The New Rules: How to Succeed in Today's Post-Corporate World* (New York: Free Press, 1995).

131. Ibid.

132. T. Bateman and C. Porath, "Transcendent Behavior," in *Positive Organizational Scholarship,* ed. K. Cameron, J. Dutton, and R. Quinn (San Francisco: Barrett-Koehler, 2003).

133. L. A. Hill, "New Manager Development for the 21st Century," *Academy of Management Executive,* August 2004, pp. 121–26.

134. Lawler, *From the Ground Up;* and Kotter, *The New Rules.*

135. Lawler, *Treat People Right!*

136. "Life After a Layoff," *Kiplinger's Personal Finance* (online), February 2012, www.kiplinger.com; and M. Peiperl and Y. Baruck, "Back to Square Zero: The Post-Corporate Career," *Organizational Dynamics,* Spring 1997, pp. 7–22.

137. Ibid.

138. Conner, *Managing at the Speed of Change,* pp. 235–45.

139. J. W. Slocum Jr., M. McGill, and D. Lei, "The New Learning Strategy Anytime, Anything, Anywhere," *Organizational Dynamics,* Autumn 1994, pp. 33–37.

140. G. Binney and C. Williams, *Leaning into the Future: Changing the Way People Change Organizations* (London: Nicholas Brealey, 1997).

141. Kotter, *The New Rules.*

142. Hill, "New Manager Development for the 21st Century," p. 125.

143. J. A. Raelin, "Don't Bother Putting Leadership into People," *Academy of Management Executive,* August 2004, pp. 131–35.

144. Binney and Williams, *Leaning into the Future.*

Photo Credits

Index

SUMMARY

LO 1 Describe the four functions of management.

Planning refers to making decisions about which goals and activities the organization should pursue. *Organizing* means assembling and coordinating resources to achieve those goals. *Leading* is about stimulating high performance by employees. Once a goal or activity is being pursued, *controlling* is used to monitor performance and make needed changes. Managers perform these four functions in an *efficient* (achieving goals with minimal waste) and *effective* (achieve important organizational goals) manner.

LO 2 Understand what managers at different organizational levels do.

Top-level managers are responsible for the overall management and effectiveness of the organization. They establish performance standards, institutionalize norms to support cooperation, and create overarching corporate purpose. *Middle-level managers* support, develop, and control frontline managers and report to top-level managers. They share knowledge and skills across business units, and manage tension between short- and long-term issues. *Frontline managers* are lower-level managers who supervise the operational activities of the organization. As aggressive entrepreneurs, they attract and develop resources, create and pursue growth opportunities, and manage continuous improvement efforts within the unit. *Team leaders* facilitate team effectiveness. They structure teams and define their purpose, remove obstacles so teams can accomplish their goals, and develop team members' skills and abilities. In addition, managers of all types perform three different roles: *interpersonal* (leader, liaison, and figurehead), *informational* (monitor, disseminator, and spokesperson), and *decisional* (entrepreneur, disturbance handler, resource allocator, and negotiator).

LO 3 Define the skills needed to be an effective manager.

Managers need three broad skill sets to be successful. *Technical skills* are the ability to perform a specialized task involving a particular method or process. *Conceptual and decision skills* refer to a manager's ability to identify and resolve problems for the benefit of the organization and its members. *Interpersonal and communication skills* are the important people skills that give a manager the ability to lead, motivate, and communicate effectively with others. The importance of these skills varies by managerial level. Technical skills are more important earlier in your career as a team leader or frontline manager. Conceptual and decision skills become more important as you reach the middle and top management levels of an organization. Interpersonal, communication, and emotional intelligence skills are very important during every stage of your career, from team leader to executive manager or chief executive officer.

LO 4 Summarize the major challenges facing managers today.

Five challenges facing managers today include (1) managing globalization, (2) staying on top of changing technology and using it to develop social capital, (3) leveraging the power of knowledge and knowledge workers, (4) encouraging collaboration across the organization and within business units (the T-shaped manager), and (5) leveraging diversity.

KEY TERMS

conceptual and decision skills Skills pertaining to the ability to identify and resolve problems for the benefit of the organization and its members.

controlling The management function of monitoring performance and making needed changes.

cost competitiveness Keeping costs low to achieve profits and to be able to offer prices that are attractive to consumers.

emotional intelligence The skills of understanding yourself, managing yourself, and dealing effectively with others.

frontline managers Lower-level managers who supervise the operational activities of the organization.

innovation The introduction of new goods and services.

interpersonal and communication skills People skills; the ability to lead, motivate, and communicate effectively with others.

knowledge management Practices aimed at discovering and harnessing an organization's intellectual resources.

leading The management function that involves the manager's efforts to stimulate high performance by employees.

management The process of working with people and resources to accomplish organizational goals.

middle-level managers Managers located in the middle layers of the organizational hierarchy, reporting to top-level executives.

organizing The management function of assembling and coordinating human, financial, physical, informational, and other resources needed to achieve goals.

planning The management function of systematically making decisions about the goals and activities that an individual, a group, a work unit, or the overall organization will pursue.

quality The excellence of your products (goods or services).

service The speed and dependability with which an organization delivers what customers want.

social capital Goodwill stemming from your social relationships.

speed Fast and timely execution, response, and delivery of results.

team leaders Employees who are responsible for facilitating successful team performance.

technical skills The ability to perform a specialized task involving a particular method or process.

top-level managers Senior executives responsible for the overall management and effectiveness of the organization.

LO 5 Recognize how successful managers achieve competitive advantage.

One of the major reasons why some companies thrive while other fail can be attributed to managers' ability to create competitive advantage. Managers can achieve this by helping their firms excel at all of the following: (1) innovating to stay ahead of competitors, (2) producing quality products and services, (3) meeting and exceeding customers' needs, (4) moving with speed and agility, and (5) keeping costs low to increase sales.

chapter two

The Evolution of Management

REVIEW CARD

SUMMARY

LO 1 Describe the origins of management practice and its early concepts and influences.

Early contributors developed many of today's widely accepted management practices and concepts such as efficiency, division of labor, pay for performance, and equitable treatment of employees. Civilizations as diverse as the Sumerians, Egyptians, Chinese, Greeks, and Venetians practiced one or more of the functions of management: planning, organizing, leading, and controlling. For centuries, many managers operated on a trial-and-error basis until the advent of the industrial revolution in the 18th and 19th centuries. Fueled by major advances in manufacturing and transportation technologies, and large numbers of unskilled laborers, companies and factories grew in size and complexity. Managers discovered that improvements in management tactics and economies of scale produced large increases in production quantity and quality.

LO 2 Summarize the five classical approaches to management.

The classical period extended from the mid-19th century through the early 1950s. To address problems of poor coordination and frequent breakdowns in the manufacturing process, the *systematic management* approach attempted to build internal procedures and processes into operations to improve coordination efforts. To increase production efficiency, Frederick Taylor introduced *scientific management,* an approach that applied scientific methods to analyze work and to determine how best to complete production tasks in an efficient manner. Other important contributors to the scientific management approach were Henry Gantt and Frank and Lillian Gilbreth. The *bureaucracy* approach, developed by Max Weber, was based on the assumption that organizations could be more efficient and consistent if several management principles were followed, including a clearly specified division of labor, a well-established chain of command, selection and promotions based on qualifications, ownership separated from management, and consistent application of rules and controls. The *administrative management* approach emphasized the perspective of senior managers within the organization, and assumed that management was a profession that could be taught. Key contributors to this approach were Henri Fayol, Chester Barnard, and Mary Parker Follett. The final approach of the classical period, *human relations,* focused on understanding how psychological and social processes interacted with the work situation to influence performance. Researchers Elton Mayo and Fritz Roethlisberger conducted extensive research and identified the Hawthorne Effect, basically, that workers perform and react differently when they are being observed.

LO 3 Discuss the four contemporary approaches to management.

Developed at different times since World War II, contemporary approaches continue to have a major influence on modern management thought. The first approach, *sociotechnical systems,* suggests that organizations are successful when their employees (the social system) have the right tools, training, and knowledge (the technical system) to make products and services valued by customers. The second approach, *quantitative management,* emphasizes the application of quantitative analysis (using mathematical models and computer analysis) to management decisions and problems. The third approach, *organizational behavior,* assumes that employee effectiveness is based on understanding the complex interplay of individual, group, and organizational processes. The last approach, *systems theory,* assumes that organizations are open systems that depend on inputs from the external environment that need to be transformed into outputs that meet the market's needs for goods and services.

KEY TERMS

administrative management A classical management approach that attempted to identify major principles and functions that managers could use to achieve superior organizational performance.

bureaucracy A classical management approach emphasizing a structured, formal network of relationships among specialized positions in the organization.

contingencies Factors that determine the appropriateness of managerial actions.

contingency perspective An approach to the study of management proposing that the managerial strategies, structures, and processes that result in high performance depend on the characteristics, or important contingencies, or the situation in which they are applied.

economies of scale Reductions in the average cost of a unit of production as the total volume produces increases.

Hawthorne Effect People's reactions to being observed or studied resulting in superficial rather than meaningful changes in behavior.

human relations A classical management approach that attempted to understand how human psychological and social processes interact with the formal aspects of the work situation to influence performance.

inputs Goods and services organizations take in and use to create products or services.

organizational behavior A contemporary management approach that studies and identifies management activities that promote employee effectiveness by examining the complex and dynamic nature of individual, group, and organizational processes.

outputs The products and services organizations create.

quantitative management A contemporary management approach that emphasizes the application of quantitative analysis to managerial decisions and problems.

scientific management A classical management approach that applied scientific methods to analyze and determine the "one best way" to complete production tasks.

sociotechnical systems theory An approach to job design that attempts to redesign tasks to optimize operation of a new technology while preserving employees' interpersonal relationships and other human aspects of the work.

systematic management A classical management approach that attempted to build into operations the specific procedures and processes that would ensure coordination of effort to achieve established goals and plans.

systems theory A theory stating that an organization is a managed system that changes inputs into outputs.

LO 4 Identify modern contributors who have shaped management thought and practices.

Through their leadership, interviews, presentations, or writings, a number of individuals have contributed to modern management thought and practices. A sample of these contributors include Jim Collins, author of *Good to Great;* Jack Welch, ex-CEO of General Electric, who often is acknowledged as one of the most influential CEOs in recent times; Peter Drucker, a visionary who added several concepts to the language of modern management, including management by objective, decentralization, and knowledge workers; Gary Hamel, author of *The Future of Management* and "The Core Competence of the Corporation" (with C.K. Prahalad); and Michael Porter, who has written extensively about competitive strategy.

chapter three

The Organizational Environment and Culture

REVIEW CARD

SUMMARY

LO 1 Describe the five elements of an organization's macroenvironment.

The macroenvironment is a general environment that exerts indirect pressure on managers of generally all organizations. It consists of (1) laws and regulations, (2) the economy, (3) technological changes, (4) demographics, and (5) social issues. Although it is not under the direct control of managers, there are ways that managers attempt to influence it in their organization's favor.

LO 2 Explain the five components of an organization's competitive environment.

An organization's competitive environment exerts influence in a closer, more direct and immediate manner. It consists of five components, including rivalry with existing competitors and the threat of new entrants, the influence of substitute products or services, and the bargaining power of suppliers and customers. Changes in one or more of these components can present significant opportunities and threats to an organization.

LO 3 Understand how managers stay on top of changes in the external environment.

Environmental uncertainty arises from complexity and dynamism. Complexity refers to the number of issues to which a manager must deal with in his or her industry; the automobile industry is complex relative to the dairy farming industry. Dynamism refers to the degree of change that occurs within an industry. The smartphone industry is more dynamic than the utilities industry. Managers stay on top of changes in their industries by (1) engaging in environmental scanning, (2) developing worst-case and best-case scenarios, and (3) forecasting and using data to predict the future.

LO 4 Summarize how managers respond to changes in the external environment.

Managers can respond to environmental uncertainty in three different ways. First, they can adapt to it. The approach they take depends on whether the uncertainty arises from complexity, dynamism, or both. Managers adjust their organizations to become more (or less) decentralized and more (or less) bureaucratic to deal with environmental uncertainty. Also, managers have the option of adapting their organization at its boundaries (e.g., employing temporary workers) or at its core (e.g., use flexible processes). The second way to decrease uncertainty occurs when managers proactively attempt to influence their environment through independent action that includes competitive aggression and pacification, public relations, and voluntary, legal, and political action. Also, two or more organizations working together to manage uncertainty use contracts, cooptation, and coalitions. The third approach that managers use is to change the boundaries of the environment. This can be done through domain selection, diversification, mergers and acquisitions, and divestiture.

LO 5 Discuss how organization cultures can be leveraged to overcome challenges in the internal environment.

The internal environment, or organization culture, consists of three levels, including visible artifacts, values, and unconscious assumptions. Visible artifacts can be anything you can see or hear, including office layout, organization charts, dress code, and so on. Values are less apparent and consist of the underlying qualities and desirable behaviors that the organization rewards. You can infer what the organization's values are by

KEY TERMS

acquisition One firm buying another.

barriers to entry Conditions that prevent new companies from entering an industry.

benchmarking The process of comparing an organization's practices and technologies with those of other companies.

buffering Creating supplies of excess resources in case of unpredictable needs.

competitive environment The immediate environment surrounding a firm; includes suppliers, customers, rivals, and the like.

competitive intelligence Information that helps managers determine how to compete better.

cooperative strategies Strategies used by two or more organizations working together to manage the external environment.

defenders Companies that stay within a stable product domain as a strategic maneuver.

demographics Statistical characteristics of a group or population such as age, gender, and education level.

diversification A firm's investment in a different product, business, or geographic area.

divestiture A firm selling one or more businesses.

domain selection Entering a new market or industry with existing expertise.

empowerment The process of sharing power with employees to enhance their confidence in their ability to perform their jobs and contribute to the organization.

environmental scanning Searching for and sorting through information about the environment.

environmental uncertainty Lack of information needed to understand or predict the future.

external environment All relevant forces outside a firm's boundaries, such as competitors, customers, the government, and the economy.

final consumer A customer who purchases products in their finished form.

flexible processes Methods for adapting the technical core to changes in the environment.

forecasting Method for predicting how variables will change the future.

independent strategies Strategies that an organization acting on its own uses to change some aspect of its current environment.

intermediate consumer A customer who purchases raw materials or wholesale products before selling them to final customers.

internal environment All relevant forces inside a firm's boundaries, such as its managers, employees, resources, and organization culture.

macroenvironment The general environment; includes governments, economic conditions, and other fundamental factors that generally affect all organizations.

merger One or more companies combining with another.

open systems Organizations that are affected by, and that affect, their environment.

organization culture The set of assumptions that members of an organization share to create internal cohesion and adapt to the external environment.

prospectors Companies that continuously change the boundaries for their task environments by seeking new products and markets, diversifying and merging, or acquiring new enterprises.

scenario A narrative that describes a particular set of future conditions.

smoothing Leveling normal fluctuations at the boundaries of the environment.

strategic maneuvering An organization's conscious efforts to change the boundaries of its task environment.

supply chain management The managing of the network of facilities and people that obtain materials from outside the organization, transform them into products, and distribute them to customers.

switching costs Fixed costs buyers face when they change suppliers.

unconscious assumptions The strongly held and taken-for-granted beliefs that guide behavior in the firm.

values The underlying qualities and desirable behaviors that are important to the organization.

visible artifacts The components of an organization that can be seen and heard, such as office layout, dress, orientation, stories, and written material.

observing managerial and employee behavior. Unconscious assumptions are deeply held beliefs that govern the behavior within the organization. Organization cultures can be strong or weak. Companies provide many clues about their cultures, including corporate mission statements; business practices; symbols, rites, and ceremonies; and stories about organizational heroes. There are four major types of organization cultures: group, hierarchical, rational, and adhocracy. Effective managers can leverage the strengths of their organization cultures to address uncertainty in the external environment by crafting an inspirational vision of "what can be" as a way to align the internal and external environments; "walking the talk" by showing employees that the manager is committed to long-term culture change; and celebrating and rewarding members who exemplify the desired behaviors of the culture.

chapter four

Ethics and Corporate Responsibility

SUMMARY

LO 1 Describe how different ethical perspectives guide managerial decision making.

Ethics refers to the moral principles and standards that guide the behavior of an individual or group. Ethical decisions are guided by an individual's values or principles of conduct, such as honesty, fairness, integrity, respect for others, and responsible citizenship. Different ethical systems include universalism, egoism, utilitarianism, relativism, and virtue ethics. These philosophical systems, as practiced by different individuals according to their level of cognitive moral development and other factors, underlie the ethical stances of individuals and organizations.

LO 2 Identify the ethics-related issues and laws facing managers.

Business ethics refers to the moral principles and standards that guide behavior in the world of business. Managers and employees are often confronted with ethical dilemmas such as how to react to manipulative or deceptive marketing practices, manage perceptions of excessive CEO compensation when many workers feel underpaid, or react to public disdain over the use of sweatshops. In 2002 the Sarbanes-Oxley Act was passed requiring companies to have more independent board directors, adhere strictly to accounting rules, and have senior managers personally sign off on financial results. An organization's ethical climate, or the processes by which decisions are evaluated and made on the basis of right or wrong, can influence employee behavior. Danger signs that organizations are allowing or even encouraging unethical behavior include excessive emphasis on short-term revenues, failure to establish a written code of ethics, pursuit of "quick fix" solutions to ethical problems, unwillingness to take an ethical stand that may impose financial costs, consideration of ethics solely as a legal issue or a public relations tool, and responsiveness to the demands of shareholders at the expense of other stakeholders.

LO 3 Explain how managers influence their ethics environment.

Different managers apply different ethical perspectives and standards. Ethics codes sometimes are helpful, although they must be implemented properly. Ethics programs can range from compliance-based to integrity-based. An increasing number of organizations are adopting ethics codes. Such codes address employee conduct, community and environment, shareholders, customers, suppliers and contractors, political activity, and technology.

LO 4 Outline the process for making ethical decisions.

Making ethical decisions requires moral awareness, moral judgment, and moral character. When faced with ethical dilemmas, the veil of ignorance is a useful metaphor. More precisely, you can use the model of ethical decision making in this chapter to inform your choices and actions, including knowing various moral standards (universalism, relativism, and so on); recognizing the moral impact of your decision (whom it will harm, whom it will benefit, and so forth); defining the complete moral problem; considering the economic, legal, and ethical components of the decision; and proposing a convincing moral solution. The business costs associated with ethical failures can be large: government fines and penalties, audits, customer defections, loss of reputation, and employee turnover. The Sarbanes-Oxley Act and the Dodd-Frank Wall Street Reform and Consumer Protection Act provide protection for employees who report fraudulent activities.

KEY TERMS

business ethics The moral principles and standards that guide behavior in the world of business.

Caux Principles for Business Ethical principles established by international executives based in Caux, Switzerland, in collaboration with business leaders from Japan, Europe, and the United States.

compliance-based ethics programs Company mechanisms typically designed by corporate counsel to prevent, detect, and punish legal violations.

corporate social responsibility Obligation toward society assumed by business.

ecocentric management Its goal is the creation of sustainable economic development and improvement of quality of life worldwide for all organizational stakeholders.

economic responsibilities To produce goods and services that society wants at a price that perpetuates the business and satisfies its obligations to investors.

egoism An ethical principal holding that individual self-interest is the actual motive of all conscious action.

ethical climate In an organization, the processes by which decisions are evaluated and made on the basis of right and wrong.

ethical issue A situation, problem, or opportunity in which an individual must choose among several actions that must be evaluated as morally right or wrong.

ethical leader One who is both a moral person and a moral manager influencing others to behave ethically.

ethical responsibilities Meeting other social expectations, not written as law.

ethics The moral principles and standards that guide the behavior of an individual or group.

integrity-based ethics programs Company mechanisms designed to instill in people a personal responsibility for ethical behavior.

Kohlberg's model of cognitive moral development Classification of people based on their level of moral judgment.

legal responsibilities To obey local, state, federal, and relevant international laws.

life cycle analysis (LCA) A process of analyzing all inputs and outputs, through the entire "cradle-to-grave" life of a product, to determine total environmental impact.

moral philosophy Principles, rules, and values people use in deciding what is right or wrong.

philanthropic responsibilities Additional behaviors and activities that society finds desirable and that the values of the business support.

relativism A philosophy that bases ethical behavior on the opinions and behaviors of relevant other people.

Sarbanes-Oxley Act An act that established strict accounting and reporting rules to make senior managers more accountable and to improve and maintain investor confidence.

shareholder model Theory of corporate social responsibility that holds that managers are agents of shareholders whose primary objective is to maximize profits.

stakeholder model Theory of corporate social responsibility that suggests that managers are obliged to look beyond profitability to help their organizations succeed by interacting with groups that have a stake in the organization.

sustainable growth Economic growth and development that meet present needs without harming the needs of future generations.

transcendent education An education with five higher goals that balance self-interest with responsibility to others.

universalism The ethical system stating that all people should uphold certain values that society needs to function.

utilitarianism An ethical system stating that the greatest good for the greatest number should be the overriding concern of decision makers.

virtue ethics A perspective that what is moral comes from what a mature person with "good" moral character would deem right.

LO 5 Summarize the important issues surrounding corporate social responsibility.

Corporate social responsibility is the extension of the corporate role beyond economic pursuits. It includes not only economic but also legal, ethical, and philanthropic responsibilities. Advocates of this stakeholder model believe managers should consider societal and human needs in their business decisions because corporations are members of society and carry a wide range of responsibilities. Critics of corporate responsibility believe in the shareholder model, in which managers' first responsibility is to increase profits for the shareholders who own the corporation. The two perspectives are potentially reconcilable, especially if managers choose to address areas of social responsibility that contribute to the organization's strategy.

LO 6 Discuss the growing importance of managing the natural environment.

In the past, most companies viewed the natural environment as a resource to be used for raw materials and profit. But consumer, regulatory, and other pressures arose. Executives often viewed these pressures as burdens, constraints, and costs to be borne. Now more companies view the interface between business and the natural environment as a potential win–win opportunity. Some are adopting a "greener" agenda for philosophical reasons and personal commitment to sustainable development. Many also are recognizing the potential financial benefits of managing with the environment in mind, and are integrating environmental issues into corporate and business strategy. Organizations also have the capability to help solve environmental problems. Ecocentric management attempts to minimize negative environment impact, create sustainable economic development, and improve the quality of life worldwide. Relevant actions are described in the chapter, including strategic initiatives, life cycle analysis, and interorganizational alliances.

chapter five

Planning and Decision Making

SUMMARY

LO 1 Summarize the basic steps in any planning process.

The planning process begins with a situation analysis of the external and internal forces affecting the organization. This examination helps identify and diagnose issues and problems and may bring to the surface alternative goals and plans for the firm. Next the advantages and disadvantages of these goals and plans should be evaluated against one another. Goals that follow the SMART framework motivate and direct employees. Common plans used by organizations fall into three categories, including single-use, standing, or contingency. Once a set of goals and a plan have been selected, implementation involves communicating the plan to employees, allocating resources, and making certain that other systems such as rewards and budgets support the plan. Finally, planning requires instituting control systems to monitor progress toward the goals.

LO 2 Discuss how strategic planning should be integrated with tactical and operational planning.

Strategic planning is different from operational planning in that it involves making long-term decisions about the entire organization and is performed by top-level managers. Tactical planning translates broad goals and strategies into specific actions to be taken within parts of the organization and is done by middle-level managers. Operational planning identifies the specific short-term procedures and processes required at lower levels of the organization and is developed by frontline managers.

LO 3 Describe the strategic management process and the importance of SWOT analysis in strategy formulation.

The strategic management process begins with the establishment of a mission, vision, and goals for the organization. A strategic vision is also important because it provides a perspective on where the organization is headed and what it can become. Next the competitive environment and macroenvironment are assessed for opportunities and threats, including industry growth, competitor analysis, legislative and regulatory activities, macroeconomic conditions, and technological factors. Managers also analyze the internal strengths and weaknesses of the organization by conducting financial analyses, human resource assessments, and marketing audits. During this stage, managers seek to identify core capabilities and use benchmarking to enhance performance. Drawing on the most relevant and useful facts from the external and internal analyses, a SWOT analysis allows managers to prioritize the key issues and formulate a strategy that leverages the firm's strengths while neutralizing its weaknesses and countering potential threats. The four basic corporate strategies range from very specialized to highly diverse: concentration, vertical integration, related diversification, and unrelated diversification.

KEY TERMS

brainstorming A process in which group members generate as many ideas about a problem as they can; criticism is withheld until all ideas have been proposed.

business strategy The major actions by which a business competes in a particular industry or market.

certainty The state that exists when decision makers have accurate and comprehensive information.

concentration A strategy employed for an organization that operates a single business and competes in a single industry.

core capability A unique skill and/or knowledge an organization possesses that gives it an edge over competitors.

corporate strategy The set of businesses, markets, or industries in which an organization competes and the distribution of resources among those entities.

custom-made solutions New, creative solutions designed specifically for the problem.

devil's advocate A person who has the job of criticizing ideas to ensure that their downsides are fully explored.

dialectic A structured debate comparing two conflicting courses of action.

differentiation strategy A strategy an organization uses to build competitive advantage by being unique in its industry or market segment along one or more dimensions.

discounting the future A bias weighting short-term costs and benefits more heavily than longer-term costs and benefits.

framing effects A decision bias influenced by the way in which a problem or decision alternative is phrased or presented.

functional strategies Strategies implemented by each functional area of the organization to support the organization's business strategy.

goal A target or end that management desires to reach.

goal displacement A condition that occurs when a decision-making group loses sight of its original goal and a new, less important goal emerges.

groupthink A phenomenon that occurs in decision making when group members avoid disagreement as they strive for consensus.

illusion of control People's belief that they can influence events, even when they have no control over what will happen.

low-cost strategy A strategy an organization uses to build competitive advantage by being efficient and offering a standard, no-frills product.

maximizing A decision realizing the best possible outcome.

mission An organization's basic purpose and scope of operations.

operational planning The process of identifying the specific procedures and processes required at lower levels of the organization.

optimizing Achieving the best possible balance among several goals.

plans The actions or means managers intend to use to achieve organizational goals.

ready-made solutions Ideas that have been seen or tried before.

related diversification A strategy used to add new businesses that produce related products or are involved in related markets and activities.

resources Inputs to a system that can enhance performance.

risk The state that exists when the probability of success is less than 100 percent and losses may occur.

satisficing Choosing an option that is acceptable, although not necessarily the best or perfect.

scenario A narrative that describes a particular set of future conditions.

situational analysis A process planners use, within time and resource constraints, to gather, interpret, and summarize all information relevant to the planning issue under consideration.

stakeholders Groups and individuals who affect and are affected by the achievement of the organization's mission, goals, and strategies.

strategic control system A system designed to support managers in evaluating the organization's progress regarding its strategy and, when discrepancies exist, taking corrective action.

strategic goals Major targets or end results relating to the organization's long-term survival, value, and growth.

strategic management A process that involves managers from all parts of the organization in the formulation and implementation of strategic goals and strategies.

strategic planning A set of procedures for making decisions about the organization's long-term goals and strategies.

strategic vision The long-term direction and strategic intent of a company.

strategy A pattern of actions and resource allocations designed to achieve the organization's goals.

SWOT analysis A comparison of strengths, weaknesses, opportunities, and threats that helps executives formulate strategy.

tactical planning A set of procedures for translating broad strategic goals and plans into specific goals and plans that are relevant to a particular portion of the organization, such as a functional area like marketing.

uncertainty The state that exists when decision makers have insufficient information.

unrelated diversification A strategy used to add new businesses that produce unrelated products or are involved in unrelated markets and activities.

vertical integration The acquisition or development of new businesses that produce parts or components of the organization's product.

LO 4 Analyze how companies can achieve competitive advantage through business strategy.

A business strategy defines the major actions by which an organization builds and strengthens its competitive position in the marketplace. Companies gain competitive advantage in two primary ways: they can attempt to be unique in some way by pursuing a differentiation strategy, or they can focus on efficiency and price by pursuing a low-cost strategy.

LO 5 Identify the keys to effective strategy implementation.

Many good plans are doomed to failure because they are not implemented correctly. Strategy implementation typically involves four steps: (1) define strategic tasks, (2) assess organization capabilities, (3) develop an implementation agenda, and (4) create an implementation plan. To increase the likelihood of successful implementation, top managers need to be actively involved in communicating and sharing information about the plan with all levels of the organization. Also, coaching and training should be made available to lower-level managers so they have the tools required to implement the strategy in an effective manner. A strategic control system needs to be designed to support managers in evaluating progress with the strategy and, when discrepancies exist, taking corrective action.

LO 6 Explain how to make effective decisions as a manager.

Managerial decisions are often made without perfect information and under conditions of uncertainty. Good decision makers try to anticipate, minimize, and control risk. The ideal decision-making process has six stages: (1) indentify and diagnose the problem, (2) generate alternative solutions, (3) evaluate alternatives, (4) make the choice, (5) implement the decision, and (6) evaluate the decision.

LO 7 Give examples of some individual barriers that affect rational decision making.

Psychological biases, time pressures, and social realities can all negatively affect the quality of decisions. Psychological biases include the illusion of control, framing effects, and discounting the future. Most managers are under a lot of pressure to make quality decisions in a timely manner. If managers can make decisions more quickly without sacrificing quality, that may help their firms achieve competitive advantage over their slower-moving competitors. Few if any managers make decisions in a vacuum. Important managerial decisions often can affect the interests of third parties like other departments or employees. Therefore, many decisions are the result of intensive social interactions, bargaining, and politicking.

LO 8 Summarize principles for group decision making.

Advantages of group decision making include (1) more information and facts are generated about a decision; (2) a greater number of perspectives and approaches contribute to more optimal solutions; (3) intellectual stimulation unleashes creativity to a greater extent than is possible with individual decision making; (4) people involved in a group discussion are more likely to understand why the decision was made; and (5) group discussion leads to greater commitment to the decision. Disadvantages of group decision making include (1) one group member dominates the discussion, undermining the contribution of others and the quality of the decision; (2) most people do not like meetings and may settle for a satisficing, not an optimizing or maximizing, decision; (3) groupthink, or the pressure to avoid disagreement, can lower the quality of group decisions; and (4) goal displacement can occur, whereby new goals emerge and replace the original goal of the group.

chapter six

Entrepreneurship

REVIEW CARD

SUMMARY

LO 1 Describe why people become entrepreneurs and what it takes, personally.

People become entrepreneurs because of the profit potential, the challenge, and the satisfaction they anticipate (and often receive) from participating in the process, and sometimes because they are blocked from more traditional avenues of career advancement. Successful entrepreneurs are innovators, and they have good knowledge and skills in management, business, and networking. While there is no single "entrepreneurial personality," certain characteristics are helpful: commitment and determination; leadership skills; opportunity obsession; tolerance of risk, ambiguity, and uncertainty; creativity, self-reliance, the ability to adapt; and motivation to excel.

LO 2 Summarize how to assess opportunities to start new businesses.

You should always be on the lookout for new ideas, monitoring the current business environment and other indicators of opportunity. Franchising offers an interesting opportunity, and the potential of the Internet is being tapped (after entrepreneurs learned some tough lessons from the dot-bomb era). Trial and error and preparation play important roles. Assessing the business concept on the basis of how innovative and risky it is, combined with your personal interests and tendencies, will also help you make good choices. Ideas should be carefully assessed via opportunity analysis and a thorough business plan.

LO 3 Identify common causes of success and failure.

New ventures are inherently risky. The economic environment plays an important role in the success or failure of the business, and the entrepreneur should anticipate and be prepared to adapt in the face of changing economic conditions. Entrepreneurs can think about their ventures in terms of the degree of innovation and the risk of a major loss. Products and services with low innovation and low risk are likely to have low returns but higher security. The opposite is likely to be true of high-innovation and high-risk ventures. Entrepreneurs should pursue new venture ideas that fit their objectives and preferences. How you handle a variety of common management challenges also can mean the difference between success and failure, as can the effectiveness of your planning and your ability to mobilize nonfinancial resources, including other people who can help.

LO 4 Discuss common management challenges.

When new businesses fail, the causes often can be traced to some common challenges that entrepreneurs face and must manage well. You might not enjoy the entrepreneurial process. Survival—including getting started and fending off competitors—is difficult. Growth creates new challenges, including reluctance to delegate work to others. Funds may be put to improper use, and financial controls may be inadequate. Many entrepreneurs fail to plan well for succession. When needing or wanting new funds, initial public offerings provide an option, but they represent an important and difficult decision that must be considered carefully.

LO 5 Explain how to increase your chances of success, including good business planning.

The business plan helps you think through your idea thoroughly and determine its viability. It also convinces (or fails to convince) others to participate. The plan describes the venture and its future, provides financial projections, and includes plans for marketing,

KEY TERMS

advertising support model Charging fees to advertise on a site.

affiliate model Charging fees to direct site visitors to other companies' sites.

bootlegging Informal work on projects, other than those officially assigned, of employees' own choosing and initiative.

business incubators Protected environments for new small businesses.

business plan A formal planning step that focuses on the entire venture and describes all the elements involved in starting it.

entrepreneur An individual who establishes a new organization without the benefit of corporate sponsorship.

entrepreneurial orientation The tendency of an organization to identify and capitalize successfully on opportunities to launch new ventures by entering new or established markets with new or existing goods or services.

entrepreneurial venture A new business having growth and high profitability as primary objectives.

entrepreneurship The process by which enterprising individuals initiate, manage, and assume the risks and rewards associated with a business venture.

franchising An entrepreneurial alliance between a franchisor (an innovator who has created at least one successful store and wants to grow) and a franchisee (a partner who manages a new store of the same type in a new location).

initial public offering (IPO) Sale to the public, for the first time, of federally registered and underwritten shares of stock in the company.

intermediary model Charging fees to bring buyers and sellers together.

intrapreneurs New venture creators working inside big companies.

legitimacy People's judgment of a company's acceptance, appropriateness, and desirability, generally stemming from company goals and methods that are consistent with societal values.

opportunity analysis A description of the good or service, an assessment of the opportunity, an assessment of the entrepreneur, and specification of activities and resources needed to translate your idea into a viable business and your source(s) of capital.

side street effect As you head down a road, unexpected opportunities begin to appear.

skunkworks A project team designated to produce a new, innovative product.

small business A business having fewer than 100 employees, independently owned and operated, not dominant in its field, and not characterized by many innovative practices.

social capital A competitive advantage in the form of relationships with other people and the image other people have of you.

subscription model Charging fees for site visits.

transaction fee model Charging fees for goods and services.

manufacturing, and other business functions. The plan should describe the people involved in the venture and should include a full assessment of the opportunity (including customers and competitors), the environmental context (including regulatory and economic issues), and the risk (including future risks and how you intend to deal with them). Successful entrepreneurs also understand how to develop social capital, which enhances legitimacy and helps develop a network of others including customers, talented people, partners, and boards.

LO 6 Describe how managers of large companies can foster entrepreneurship.

Intrapreneurs work within established companies to develop new goods or services that allow the corporation to reap the benefits of innovation. To facilitate intrapreneurship, organizations use skunkworks—special project teams designated to develop a new product—and allow bootlegging—informal efforts beyond formal job assignments in which employees pursue their own pet projects. Organizations should select projects carefully, have an ongoing portfolio of projects, and fund them appropriately. Ultimately a true entrepreneurial orientation in a company comes from encouraging independent action, innovativeness, risk taking, proactive behavior, and competitive aggressiveness.

chapter seven

Organizing for Success

SUMMARY

LO 1 Define the fundamental characteristics of organization structure.

Mechanistic organizations seek to maximize internal efficiency, whereas organic organizations emphasize flexibility. Differentiation is created through specialization and division of labor. Specialization means that various individuals and units throughout the organization perform different tasks. The assignment of tasks to different people or groups often is referred to as the division of labor. But the specialized tasks in an organization cannot all be performed independently of one another. Coordination links the various tasks to achieve the organization's overall mission. An organization with many different specialized tasks and work units is highly differentiated; the more differentiated the organization is, the more integration or coordination is required.

LO 2 Distinguish among the four dimensions of an organization's vertical structure.

An organization's vertical structure consists of authority, span of control, delegation, and centralization. Authority is the legitimate right to make decisions and to tell others what to do. It traditionally resides in positions (rather than in people) such as chief executive officer or executive vice president. Span of control refers to the number of subordinates who report directly to an executive or supervisor. Narrow spans create tall organizations, and wide spans create flat ones. Span of control must be narrow enough to permit managers to maintain control over subordinates. Delegation occurs when managers or supervisors assign new or additional responsibilities to a subordinate. Managers who delegate tasks should also grant the subordinate enough authority to get the job done. The subordinate is often held accountable for performing the job and taking corrective action as needed. Decentralized organizations allow lower-level managers to make important decisions. This approach works well when the business environment is fast-changing and decisions need to be made quickly. Centralization is valuable when departments have different priorities or conflicting goals, which need to be mediated by top management.

LO 3 Give examples of four basic forms of horizontal structures of organizations.

As the tasks of organizations become increasingly complex, the organization must be subdivided or departmentalized. In a functional organization, jobs are specialized and grouped according to business functions such as production, marketing, and human resources. A divisional organization groups all functions into a single division and duplicates functions across all of the divisions. Divisions can be created around products, customers, or geographic regions. A matrix organization consists of dual reporting relationships in which some managers report to two superiors: a functional manager and divisional manager. A network organization, which relies on collaboration, consists of a collection of independent, mostly single-function firms that collaborate on a good or service.

KEY TERMS

accountability The expectation that employees will perform a job, take corrective action when necessary, and report upward on the status and quality of their performance.

authority The legitimate right to make decisions and to tell other people what to do.

broker A person who assembles and coordinates participants in a network.

centralized organization An organization in which high-level executives make most decisions and pass them down to lower levels for implementation.

continuous process A process that is highly automated and has a continuous production flow.

coordination The procedures that link the various parts of an organization for the purpose of achieving the organization's overall mission.

coordination by mutual adjustment Units interact with one another to make accommodations in order to achieve flexible coordination.

coordination by plan Interdependent units are required to meet deadlines and objectives that contribute to a common goal.

decentralized organization An organization in which lower-level managers make important decisions.

delegation The assignment of new or additional responsibilities to a subordinate.

departmentalization Subdividing an organization into smaller subunits.

differentiation An aspect of the organization's internal environment created by job specialization and the division of labor.

division of labor The assignment of different tasks to different people or groups.

divisional organization Departmentalization that groups units around products, customers, or geographic regions.

formalization The presence of rules and regulations governing how people in the organization interact.

functional organization Departmentalization around specialized activities such as production, marketing, and human resources.

high-involvement organization An organization in which top management ensures that there is consensus about the direction in which the business is heading.

integration The degree to which differentiated work units work together and coordinate their efforts.

ISO 9001 A series of quality standards developed by a committee working under the International Organization for Standardization to improve total quality in all businesses for the benefit of producers and consumers.

just-in-time (JIT) A system that calls for subassemblies and components to be manufactured in very small lots and delivered to the next stage of the production process just as they are needed.

large batch Technologies that produce goods and services in high volume.

lean manufacturing An operation that strives to achieve the highest possible productivity and total quality, cost-effectively, by eliminating unnecessary steps in the production process and continually striving for improvement.

learning organization An organization skilled at creating, acquiring, and transferring knowledge, and at modifying its behavior to reflect new knowledge and insights.

line departments Units that deal directly with the organization's primary goods and services.

mass customization The production of varied, individually customized products at the low cost of standardized, mass-produced products.

matrix organization An organization composed of dual reporting relationships in which some managers report to two superiors—a functional manager and a divisional manager.

mechanistic organization A form of organization that seeks to maximize internal efficiency.

modular network Temporary arrangements among partners that can be assembled and reassembled to adapt to the environment; also called virtual network.

network organization A collection of independent, mostly single-function firms that collaborate on a good or service.

organic structure An organizational form that emphasizes flexibility.

organization chart The reporting structure and division of labor in an organization.

responsibility The assignment of a task that an employee is supposed to carry out.

small batch Technologies that produce goods and services in low volume.

span of control The number of subordinates who report directly to an executive or supervisor.

specialization A process in which different individuals and units perform different tasks.

staff departments Units that support line departments.

standardization Establishing common routines and procedures that apply uniformly to everyone.

strategic alliance A formal relationship created among independent organizations with the purpose of joint pursuit of mutual goals.

technology The systematic application of scientific knowledge to a new product, process, or service.

total quality management (TQM) An integrative approach to management that supports the attainment of customer satisfaction through a wide variety of tools and techniques that result in high-quality goods and services.

unity-of-command principle A structure in which each worker reports to one boss, who in turn reports to one boss.

LO 4 Describe important mechanisms used to coordinate work.

Managers can coordinate interdependent units through standardization, plans, and mutual adjustment. Standardization occurs when routines and standard operating procedures are put in place. They typically are accompanied by formalized rules. Coordination by plan is more flexible and allows more freedom in how tasks are carried out but keeps interdependent units focused on schedules and joint goals. Mutual adjustment involves feedback and discussions among related parties to accommodate each other's needs. It is the most flexible and simple to administer, but it is time-consuming.

LO 5 Discuss how organizations can improve their agility through their strategy, commitment to customers, and use of technology.

Firms can improve their agility through their strategy by organizing around core capabilities, forming strategic alliances, becoming learning organizations, creating high-involvement organizations, and using downsizing to help regain responsiveness. Another way that organizations can improve their agility is through focusing on customers. To meet customer needs, organizations focus on quality improvement. Total quality management (TQM) is a comprehensive approach to improving product and service quality, and thereby customer satisfaction. Many firms use Six Sigma quality and ISO 9001 to enhance quality. Technology can also support organizational agility. In manufacturing companies, technology can be configured as small batch, large batch, or continuous process technologies. Today's flexible manufacturing factories attempt to produce both high-volume and high-variety products at the same time. Speed in manufacturing can be an important source of competitive advantage and is supported by just-in-time (JIT) operations.

SUMMARY

LO 1 Discuss how companies use human resources management to gain competitive advantage.

To succeed, companies must align their human resources to their strategies. Effective planning is necessary to make certain that the right number and type of employees are available to implement a company's strategic plan. It is clear that hiring the most competent people is a very involved process. Companies that compete on cost, quality, service, and so on also should use their staffing, training, appraisal, and reward systems to elicit and reinforce the kinds of behaviors that underlie their strategies.

LO 2 Give reasons why companies recruit both internally and externally for new hires.

Some companies prefer to recruit internally to make certain that employees are familiar with organizational policies and values. In other instances, companies prefer to recruit externally, such as through employee referrals, job boards, online and newspaper advertising, and campus visits, to find individuals with new ideas and fresh perspectives. External recruiting is also necessary to fill positions when the organization is growing or needs skills that do not exist among its current employees.

LO 3 Understand various methods for selecting new employees and HR-related laws.

There are myriad selection techniques from which to choose. Interviews and reference checks are the most common. Personality tests and cognitive ability tests measure an individual's aptitude and potential to do well on the job. Other selection techniques include assessment centers and integrity tests. Background and reference checks verify that the information supplied by employees is accurate. Regardless of the approach used, any test should be able to demonstrate reliability (consistency across time and different interview situations) and validity (accuracy in predicting job performance). In addition, selection methods must comply with equal opportunity laws, which are intended to ensure that companies do not discriminate in any employment practices.

LO 4 Evaluate the importance of spending on training and development.

People cannot depend on a static set of skills for all of their working lives. In today's changing, competitive world, old skills quickly become obsolete, and new ones become essential for success. Refreshing or updating an individual's skills requires continuous training, designed with measurable goals and methods that will achieve those goals. Companies must understand that gaining a competitive edge in quality of service depends on having the most talented, flexible workers in the industry.

LO 5 Explain alternatives for who appraises an employee's performance.

While many organizations rely on managers and supervisors to gather performance appraisal information, an increasing number of companies use multiple sources of appraisal because different people see different sides of an employee's performance. Typically a superior is expected to evaluate an employee, but peers and team members are often well positioned to see aspects of performance that a superior misses. Even an employee's subordinates are being asked more often today to give their input to get yet another perspective on the evaluation. Particularly in companies concerned about quality,

KEY TERMS

adverse impact When a seemingly neutral employment practice has a disproportionately negative effect on a protected group.

arbitration The use of a neutral third party to resolve a labor dispute.

assessment center A managerial performance test in which candidates participate in a variety of exercises and situations.

cafeteria benefit program An employee benefit program in which employees choose from a menu of options to create benefit packages tailored to their needs.

comparable worth Principle of equal pay for different jobs of equal worth.

development Teaching managers and professional employees broad skills needed for their present and future jobs.

diversity training Programs that focus on identifying and reducing hidden biases against people with differences and developing the skills needed to manage a diversified workforce.

employment-at-will The legal concept that an employee may be terminated for any reason.

flexible benefit programs Benefit programs in which employees are given credits to spend on benefits that fit their unique needs.

human resources management (HRM) System of organizational activities to attract, develop, and motivate an effective and qualified workforce. Also known as talent, human capital, or personnel management.

job analysis A tool for determining what is done on a given job and what should be done on that job.

labor relations The system of relations between workers and management.

management by objectives (MBO) A process in which objectives set by a subordinate and a supervisor must be reached within a given time period.

needs assessment An analysis identifying the jobs, people, and departments for which training is necessary.

orientation training Training designed to introduce new employees to the company and familiarize them with policies, procedures, culture, and the like.

outplacement The process of helping people who have been dismissed from the company to regain employment elsewhere.

performance appraisal (PA) Assessment of an employee's job performance.

recruitment The development of a pool of applicants for jobs in an organization.

reliability The consistency of test scores over time and across alternative measurements.

right-to-work Legislation that allows employees to work without having to join a union.

selection Choosing from among qualified applicants to hire into an organization.

structured interview Selection technique that involves asking all applicants the same questions and comparing their responses to a standardized set of answers.

team training Training that provides employees with the skills and perspectives they need to collaborate with others.

termination interview A discussion between a manager and an employee about the employee's dismissal.

360-degree appraisal Process of using multiple sources of appraisal to gain a comprehensive perspective on one's performance.

training Teaching lower-level employees how to perform their present jobs.

union shop An organization with a union and a union security clause specifying that workers must join the union after a set period of time.

validity The degree to which a selection test predicts or correlates with job performance.

internal and external customers also are surveyed. Finally, employees should evaluate their own performance to get them thinking about their own contribution, as well as to engage them in the appraisal process.

LO 6 Describe the fundamental aspects of a reward system.

Reward systems include pay and benefits. Pay systems have three basic components: pay level, pay structure, and individual pay determination. To achieve an advantage over competitors, executives may want to pay a generally higher wage to their company's employees, but this decision must be weighed against the need to control costs (pay level decisions often are tied to strategic concerns such as these). To achieve internal equity (paying people what they are worth relative to their peers within the company), managers must look at the pay structure, making certain that pay differentials are based on knowledge, effort, responsibility, working conditions, seniority, and so on. Individual pay determination is often based on merit or the different contributions of individuals. In these cases, it is important to make certain that men and women receive equal pay for equal work, and managers may wish to base pay decisions on the idea of comparable worth (equal pay for an equal contribution).

LO 7 Summarize how unions and labor laws influence human resources management.

Labor relations involve the interactions between workers and management. One mechanism by which this relationship is conducted is unions. Unions seek to present a collective voice for workers, to make their needs and wishes known to management. Unions negotiate agreements with management regarding issues such as wages, hours, working conditions, job security, and health care. One important tool that unions can use is the grievance procedure established through collective bargaining, which gives employees a way to seek redress for wrongful action on the part of management. In this way, unions make certain that the rights of all employees are protected. Labor laws seek to protect the rights of both employees and managers so that their relationship can be productive and agreeable.

chapter nine

Managing Diversity and Inclusion

REVIEW CARD

SUMMARY

LO 1 Describe how changes in the U.S. workforce make diversity a critical organizational and managerial issue.

The labor force is getting older and more racially and ethnically diverse, with a higher proportion of women. And while the absolute number of workers is increasing, the growth in jobs is outpacing the numerical growth of workers. In addition, the jobs that are being created frequently require higher skills than the typical worker can provide; thus we are seeing a growing skills gap. To be competitive, organizations can no longer take the traditional approach of depending on white males to form the core of the workforce. Today managers must look broadly to use talent wherever it can be found. As the labor market changes, organizations that can recruit, develop, motivate, and retain a diverse workforce will have a competitive advantage.

LO 2 Explain how diversity, if well managed, can give organizations a competitive edge.

Managing diversity is a bottom-line issue. If managers are effective at managing diversity, they will have an easier time attracting, retaining, and motivating the best employees. They will be more effective at marketing to diverse consumer groups in the United States and globally. They will have a workforce that is more creative, more innovative, and better able to solve problems. In addition, they are likely to increase the flexibility and responsiveness of the organization to environmental change.

LO 3 Identify challenges associated with managing a diverse workforce.

The challenges for managers created by a diverse workforce include decreased group cohesiveness, communication problems, mistrust and tension, and stereotyping. These challenges can be overcome by training and effective management.

LO 4 Define monolithic, pluralistic, and multicultural organizations.

These categories are based on the organization's prevailing assumptions about people and cultures. Monolithic organizations have a low degree of structural integration, so their population is homogeneous. Pluralistic organizations have a relatively diverse employee population and try to involve various types of employees (e.g., engaging in affirmative action and avoiding discrimination). Multicultural organizations not only have diversity but value it, and they fully integrate men and women of various racial and ethnic groups, as well as people with different types of expertise. Conflict is greatest in a pluralistic organization.

LO 5 List steps managers and their organizations can take to cultivate diversity.

To be successful, organizational efforts to manage diversity must have top management support and commitment. Organizations should first thoroughly assess their cultures, policies, and practices, as well as the demographics of their labor pools and customer bases. Only after this diagnosis has been completed can a company initiate programs designed to attract, develop, motivate, and retain a diverse workforce.

KEY TERMS

affirmative action Special efforts to recruit and hire qualified members of groups that have been discriminated against in the past.

culture shock The disorientation and stress associated with being in a foreign environment.

diversity and inclusion initiatives Managing a culturally diverse workforce by recognizing the characteristics common to specific groups of employees while dealing with such employees as individuals and supporting, nurturing, and utilizing their differences to the organization's advantage.

ethnocentrism The tendency to judge others by the standards of one's group or culture, which are seen as superior.

expatriates Parent-company nationals who are sent to work at a foreign subsidiary.

glass ceiling Metaphor for an invisible barrier that makes it difficult for women and minorities to rise above a certain level in the organization.

host-country nationals Individuals from the country where an overseas subsidiary is located.

inpatriates Foreign nationals transferred to work at the parent company.

mentors Higher-level managers who help ensure that high-potential people are introduced to top management and socialized into the norms and values of the organization.

monolithic organization An organization that has a low degree of structural integration—employing few women, minorities, or other groups that differ from the majority—and thus has a highly homogeneous employee population.

multicultural organization An organization that values cultural diversity and seeks to utilize and encourage it.

pluralistic organization An organization that has a relatively diverse employee population and makes an effort to involve employees from different gender, racial, or cultural backgrounds.

sexual harassment Conduct of a sexual nature that has negative consequences for employment.

third-country nationals Individuals from a country other than the home country or the host country of an overseas subsidiary.

LO 6 Summarize the skills and knowledge about cultural differences needed to manage globally.

Managers need a variety of skills and knowledge to help their firms succeed in the global marketplace. They need to cope with the initial shock that often accompanies working and living in a different culture. Also, global managers can become more effective through learning the language of the host country and interpreting accurately the work values of their foreign counterparts. The following traits may be associated with candidates who are likely to succeed in international contexts: flexibility, sensitivity to cultural differences, business knowledge, cultural adventurousness, and desire for feedback. Before doing business with people from different cultures, managers can familiarize themselves with research that describes important cultural differences in work values. Geert Hofstede, a cross-cultural researcher, identified four dimensions on which different cultures can be compared: power distance, individualism/collectivism, uncertainty avoidance, and masculinity/femininity.

SUMMARY

LO 1 Explain how a good vision helps you be a better leader.

Outstanding leaders have vision. A vision is a mental image that goes beyond the ordinary and perhaps beyond what others thought possible. The vision provides the direction in which the leader wants the organization to move and inspiration for people to pursue it.

LO 2 Discuss the similarities and differences between leading and managing.

Managers can be effective leaders. While management deals with the ongoing, day-to-day complexities of organizations, leadership includes effectively orchestrating important change. Managers structure the organization, staff it with capable people, and monitor activities; leaders inspire people to attain a vision and motivate them to overcome obstacles. Perhaps a less judgmental way to distinguish between managers and leaders is to classify these individuals as supervisory leaders and strategic leaders.

LO 3 Identify sources of power in organizations.

Having power and using it appropriately are essential to effective leadership. Managers at all levels of the organization have five potential sources of power. Legitimate power is company-granted authority to direct others. Reward power is control over rewards valued by others in the organization. Coercive power is control over punishments that others in the organization want to avoid. Referent power consists of personal characteristics that appeal to others, so they model their behavior on the leader's and seek the leader's approval. Expert power is expertise or knowledge that can benefit others in the organization.

LO 4 Know the three traditional approaches to understanding leadership.

The trait approach is the oldest leadership perspective and assumes the existence of a leadership personality—that leaders are born, not made. Some personality characteristics (which people can strive to acquire) distinguish effective leaders from other people: drive, leadership motivation, integrity, self-confidence, and knowledge of the business. The behavioral approach to leadership tries to identify what good leaders do. For example, should leaders be task focused by ensuring that the work unit reaches its performance goals? Or should leaders exhibit group maintenance behaviors by making sure group members are satisfied and working well with one another? The situational approach assumes that universal traits and behaviors don't exist, but rather effective leader behaviors vary from situation to situation. Leaders should first analyze the situation and then decide what to do.

LO 5 Understand the important contemporary perspectives on leadership.

Charismatic leaders are dominant, self-confident, and have a strong conviction in the moral righteousness of their beliefs. They are able to arouse a sense of excitement and adventure in followers through such means as highly effective communication, a compelling vision, and motivational goals. Transformational leaders also generate excitement among followers. They translate a vision into reality by getting people to transcend their individual interests for the good of the larger community. They do this through charisma, individualized attention to followers, intellectual stimulation, formation and communication of their vision, building of trust, and positive self-regard. Level 5 leaders transform their organizations through a combination of strong professional will (determination) and personal humility. Authentic leaders strive for honesty, genuineness,

KEY TERMS

authentic leadership A style in which the leader is true to himself or herself while leading.

autocratic leadership A form of leadership in which the leader makes decisions on his or her own and then announces those decisions to the group.

behavioral approach A leadership perspective that attempts to identify what good leaders do—that is, what behaviors they exhibit.

bridge leaders Leaders who bridge conflicting value systems or different cultures.

charismatic leader A person who is dominant, self-confident, convinced of the moral righteousness of his or her beliefs, and able to arouse a sense of excitement and adventure in followers.

democratic leadership A form of leadership in which the leader solicits input from subordinates.

Fiedler's contingency model of leadership effectiveness A situational approach to leadership postulating that effectiveness depends on the personal style of the leader and the degree to which the situation gives the leader power, control, and influence over the situation.

group maintenance behaviors Actions taken to ensure the satisfaction of group members, develop and maintain harmonious work relationships, and preserve the social stability of the group.

Hersey and Blanchard's situational theory A life cycle theory of leadership postulating that a manager should consider an employee's psychological and job maturity before deciding whether task performance or maintenance behaviors are more important.

job maturity The level of the employee's skills and technical knowledge relative to the task being performed.

laissez-faire A leadership philosophy characterized by an absence of managerial decision making.

lateral leadership Style in which colleagues at the same hierarchical level are invited to collaborate and facilitate joint problem solving.

leader–member exchange (LMX) theory Highlights the importance of leader behaviors not just toward the group as a whole but toward individuals on a personal basis.

Level 5 leadership A combination of strong professional will (determination) and humility that builds enduring greatness.

path–goal theory A theory that concerns how leaders influence subordinates' perceptions of their work goals and the paths they follow toward attainment of those goals.

power The ability to influence others.

pseudotransformational leaders Leaders who talk about positive change but allow their self-interest to take precedence over followers' needs.

psychological maturity An employee's self-confidence and self-respect.

relationship-motivated leadership Leadership that places primary emphasis on maintaining good interpersonal relationships.

servant–leader A leader who serves others' needs while strengthening the organization.

shared leadership Rotating leadership, in which people rotate through the leadership role based on which person has the most relevant skills at a particular time.

situational approach Leadership perspective proposing that universally important traits and behaviors do not exist, and that effective leadership behavior varies from situation to situation.

strategic leadership Behavior that gives purpose and meaning to organizations, envisioning and creating a positive future.

substitutes for leadership Factors in the workplace that can exert the same influence on employees as leaders would provide.

supervisory leadership Behavior that provides guidance, support, and corrective feedback for day-to-day activities.

task-motivated leadership Leadership that places primary emphasis on completing a task.

task performance behaviors Actions taken to ensure that the work group or organization reaches its goals.

trait approach A leadership perspective that attempts to determine the personal characteristics that great leaders share.

transactional leaders Leaders who manage through transactions, using their legitimate, reward, and coercive powers to give commands and exchange rewards for services rendered.

transformational leaders Leaders who motivate people to transcend their personal interests for the good of the group.

vision A mental image of a possible and desirable future state of the organization.

Vroom model A situational model that focuses on the participative dimension of leadership.

reliability, integrity, and trustworthiness. They care about the greater good and will sacrifice their own interests for others.

LO 6 Identify types of opportunities to be a leader in an organization.

There's plenty of opportunity to be a leader; being a manager of others who report to you is just the traditional one. You can also take or create opportunities to be a servant–leader or bridge leader and engage in shared leadership and lateral leadership. A servant–leader serves others' needs while strengthening the organization. A bridge leader uses experiences of other cultures to create a bridge between systems. Shared leadership involves taking on a leadership role when your skills are most relevant to a particular situation. Lateral leadership is inspiring people to work collaboratively and solve problems together.

SUMMARY

LO 1 Understand principles for setting goals that motivate employees.

Goal setting is a powerful motivator. Specific, quantifiable, and challenging but attainable goals motivate high effort and performance. Goal setting can be used for teams as well as for individuals. Care should be taken to avoid setting single goals to the exclusion of other important dimensions of performance. Managers also should keep sight of the other potential downsides of goals.

LO 2 Give examples of how to reward good performance effectively.

Organizational behavior modification programs influence behavior at work by arranging consequences for people's actions. Most programs use positive reinforcement as a consequence, but other important consequences are negative reinforcement, punishment, and extinction. Care must be taken to reinforce appropriate, not inappropriate, behavior. Innovative managers use a wide variety of rewards for good performance. They also understand how to "manage mistakes" and provide useful feedback.

LO 3 Describe the key beliefs that affect people's motivation.

Expectancy theory describes three important work-related beliefs. Motivation is a function of people's (1) expectancies, or effort-to-performance links; (2) instrumentalities, or performance-to-outcome links; and (3) the valences people attach to the outcomes of performance. For employees to feel motivated, all three beliefs must be high.

LO 4 Explain ways in which people's individual needs affect their behavior.

According to Maslow, important needs arise at five levels of a hierarchy: physiological, safety, social, ego, and self-actualization needs. Focusing more on the context of work, Alderfer's ERG theory describes three sets of needs: existence, relatedness, and growth. McClelland says people vary in the extent to which they have needs for achievement, affiliation, and power. Because people are inclined to satisfy their various needs, these theories suggest to managers the kinds of rewards that motivate people.

LO 5 Define ways to create jobs that motivate.

Job rotation and job enlargement are two job design methods that alleviate boredom in jobs, while job enrichment makes jobs more rewarding and satisfying. An approach to satisfying needs and motivating people is to create intrinsic motivation through the improved design of jobs. Incorporating more skill variety, task identity, task significance, autonomy, and feedback can enrich jobs. Empowerment, the most recent development in the creation of motivating jobs, includes the perceptions of meaning, competence, self-determination, and impact. These qualities come from an environment in which people have necessary information, knowledge, power, and rewards.

LO 6 Summarize how people assess and achieve fairness.

Equity theory states that people compare their inputs and outcomes to the inputs and outcomes of others. Perceptions of equity (fairness) are satisfying; feelings of inequity (unfairness) are dissatisfying and motivate people to change their behavior or their perceptions to restore equity. In addition to fairness of outcomes, as described in equity theory, fairness is also appraised and managed through procedural justice.

KEY TERMS

Alderfer's ERG theory A human needs theory postulating that people have three basic sets of needs that can operate simultaneously.

empowerment The process of sharing power with employees, thereby enhancing their confidence in their ability to perform their jobs and their belief that they are influential contributors to the organization.

equity theory A theory stating that people assess how fairly they have been treated according to two key factors: outcomes and inputs.

expectancy Employees' perception of the likelihood that their efforts will enable them to attain their performance goals.

expectancy theory A theory proposing that people will behave based on their perceived likelihood that their effort will lead to a certain outcome and on how highly they value that outcome.

extinction Withdrawing or failing to provide a reinforcing consequence.

extrinsic rewards Rewards given to a person by the boss, the company, or some other person.

goal-setting theory A motivation theory stating that people have conscious goals that energize them and direct their thoughts and behaviors toward a particular end.

growth need strength The degree to which individuals want personal and psychological development.

hygiene factors Characteristics of the workplace, such as company policies, working conditions, pay, and supervision, that can make people dissatisfied.

instrumentality The perceived likelihood that performance will be followed by a particular outcome.

intrinsic reward Reward a worker derives directly from performing the job itself.

job enlargement Giving people additional tasks at the same time to alleviate boredom.

job enrichment Changing a task to make it inherently more rewarding, motivating, and satisfying.

job rotation Changing from one routine task to another to alleviate boredom.

law of effect A law formulated by Edward Thorndike in 1911 stating that behavior that is followed by positive consequences will likely be repeated.

Maslow's need hierarchy A human needs theory postulating that people are motivated to satisfy unmet needs in a specific order.

motivation Forces that energize, direct, and sustain a person's efforts.

motivators Factors that make a job more motivating, such as additional job responsibilities, opportunities for personal growth and recognition, and feelings of achievement.

negative reinforcement Removing or withholding an undesirable consequence.

organizational behavior modification (OB MOD) The application of reinforcement theory in organizational settings.

outcome A consequence a person receives for his or her performance.

positive reinforcement Applying a consequence that increases the likelihood of a person repeating the behavior that led to it.

procedural justice Using a fair process in decision making and making sure others know that the process was as fair as possible.

psychological contract A set of perceptions of what employees owe their employers, and what their employers owe them.

punishment Administering an aversive consequence.

quality of work life (QWL) programs Programs designed to create a workplace that enhances employee well-being.

reinforcers Positive consequences that motivate behavior.

stretch goals Targets that are particularly demanding, sometimes even thought to be impossible.

two-factor theory Herzberg's theory describing two factors affecting people's work motivation and satisfaction.

valence The value an outcome holds for the person contemplating it.

LO 7 Identify causes and consequences of a satisfied workforce.

A satisfied workforce has many advantages for the firm, including lower absenteeism and turnover; fewer grievances, lawsuits, and strikes; lower health costs; and higher-quality work. One general approach to generating higher satisfaction for people is to implement a quality of work life program. QWL seeks to provide a safe and healthy environment, opportunity for personal growth, a positive social environment, fair treatment, and other improvements in people's work lives. These and other benefits from the organization, exchanged for contributions from employees, create a psychological contract. Over time, how the psychological contract is upheld or violated, and changed unfairly or fairly, will influence people's satisfaction and motivation.

SUMMARY

LO 1 Discuss how teams can contribute to an organization's effectiveness.

Teams are building blocks for organization structure and forces for productivity, quality, cost savings, speed, change, and innovation. They have the potential to provide many benefits for both the organization and individual members.

LO 2 Distinguish the new team environment from that of traditional work groups.

Compared with traditional work groups that were closely supervised, today's teams have more authority and often are self-managed. Teams now are used in many more ways, for many more purposes, than in the past. Generally, types of teams include work teams, project and development teams, parallel teams, management teams, transnational teams, and virtual teams. Types of work teams range from traditional groups with low autonomy to self-designing teams with high autonomy.

LO 3 Summarize how groups become teams.

Groups carry on a variety of important developmental processes, including forming, storming, norming, and performing. For a group to become a team, it should move beyond traditional supervisory leadership, become more participative, and ultimately enjoy team leadership. A true team has members who complement one another; who are committed to a common purpose, performance goals, and approach; and who hold themselves accountable to one another.

LO 4 Explain why groups sometimes fail.

Teams do not always work well. Some companies underestimate the difficulties of moving to a team-based approach. Teams require training, empowerment, and a well-managed transition to make them work. Groups may fail to become effective teams unless managers and team members commit to the idea, understand what makes teams work, and implement appropriate practices.

LO 5 Describe how to build an effective team.

Create a team with a high-performance focus by establishing a common purpose, translating the purpose into measurable team goals, designing the team's task so it is intrinsically motivating, designing a team-based performance measurement system, and providing team rewards. Work to develop a common understanding of how the team will perform its task. Make it clear that everyone has to work hard and contribute in concrete ways. Establish mutual accountability and build trust among members. Examine the team's strategies periodically and be willing to adapt. Make sure members contribute fully by selecting them appropriately, training them, and checking that all important roles are carried out. Take a variety of steps to establish team cohesiveness and high-performance norms. And don't just manage inwardly—manage the team's relations with outsiders, too.

LO 6 List methods for managing a team's relationships with other teams.

Perform important roles such as gatekeeping, informing, parading, and probing. Identify the types of lateral role relationships you have with outsiders. This can help coordinate efforts throughout the work system. As teams carry out their roles, several patterns of working relationships emerge, including work flow, service, advisory, audit, stabilization, and liaison relationships.

KEY TERMS

accommodation A style of dealing with conflict involving cooperation on behalf of the other party but not being assertive about one's own interests.

autonomous work groups Groups that control decisions about and execution of a complete range of tasks.

avoidance A reaction to conflict that involves ignoring the problem by doing nothing at all, or deemphasizing the disagreement.

cohesiveness The degree to which a group is attractive to its members, members are motivated to remain in the group, and members influence one another.

collaboration A style of dealing with conflict emphasizing both cooperation and assertiveness to maximize both parties' satisfaction.

competing A style of dealing with conflict involving strong focus on one's own goals and little or no concern for the other person's goals.

compromise A style of dealing with conflict involving moderate attention to both parties' concerns.

conflict A process in which one party perceives that its interests are being opposed or negatively affected by another party.

gatekeeper A team member who keeps abreast of current developments and provides the team with relevant information.

group A collection of people who interact to undertake a task but do not necessarily perform as a unit or achieve significant performance improvements.

informing A team strategy that entails making decisions with the team and then informing outsiders of its intentions.

management teams Teams that coordinate and provide direction to the subunits under their jurisdiction and integrate work among subunits.

mediator A third party who intervenes to help others manage their conflict.

norms Shared beliefs about how people should think and behave.

parading A team strategy that entails simultaneously emphasizing internal team building and achieving external visibility.

parallel teams Teams that operate separately from the regular work structure, and exist temporarily.

probing A team strategy that requires team members to interact frequently with outsiders, diagnose their needs, and experiment with solutions.

project and development teams Teams that work on long-term projects but disband once the work is completed.

quality circles Voluntary groups of people drawn from various production teams who make suggestions about quality.

roles Different sets of expectations for how different individuals should behave.

self-designing teams Teams with the responsibilities of autonomous work groups, plus control over hiring, firing, and deciding what tasks members perform.

self-managed teams Autonomous work groups in which workers are trained to do all or most of the jobs in a unit, have no immediate supervisor, and make decisions previously made by first-line supervisors.

semiautonomous work groups Groups that make decisions about managing and carrying out major production activities but get outside support for quality control and maintenance.

social facilitation effect Working harder when in a group than when working alone.

social loafing Working less hard and being less productive when in a group.

superordinate goals Higher-level goals taking priority over specific individual or group goals.

task specialist An individual who has more advanced job-related skills and abilities than other group members possess.

team A small number of people with complementary skills who are committed to a common purpose, set of performance goals, and approach for which they hold themselves mutually accountable.

team maintenance specialist Individual who develops and maintains team harmony.

traditional work groups Groups that have no managerial responsibilities.

transnational teams Work groups composed of multinational members whose activities span multiple countries.

virtual teams Teams that are physically dispersed and communicate electronically more than face-to-face.

work teams Teams that make or do things like manufacture, assemble, sell, or provide service.

LO 7 Give examples of ways to manage conflict.

Managing lateral relationships well can prevent some conflict. But conflict arises because of the sheer number of contacts, ambiguities, goal differences, competition for scarce resources, and different perspectives and time horizons. Depending on the situation, five basic interpersonal approaches to managing conflict can be used: avoidance, accommodation, compromise, competition, and collaboration. Superordinate goals offer a focus on higher-level organizational goals that can help generate a collaborative relationship. Techniques for managing conflict between other parties include acting as a mediator and managing virtual conflict.

SUMMARY

LO 1 Discuss important advantages of two-way communication.

One-way communication flows from the sender to the receiver with no feedback loop. In two-way communication, each person is both a sender and a receiver as both parties provide and react to information. One-way communication is faster and easier but less accurate than two-way; two-way communication is slower and more difficult but is more accurate and results in better performance.

LO 2 Identify communication problems to avoid.

The communication process involves a sender who conveys information to a receiver. Problems in communication can occur in all stages: encoding, transmission, decoding, and interpreting. Noise in the system further complicates communication, creating more distortion. Moreover, feedback may be unavailable or misleading. Subjective perceptions and filtering, as well as inaccurate interpretation of verbal and nonverbal behavior, add to the possibility of error.

LO 3 Describe when and how to use the various communication channels.

Communications are sent through oral, written, and electronic channels. All have important advantages and disadvantages that you should consider before choosing a channel. Electronic media have a huge impact on interpersonal and organizational communications and make possible the virtual office. Key advantages of electronic media are speed, cost, and efficiency, but the downsides are also significant, including information overload. Media richness, or how much and what sort of information a channel conveys, is one factor to consider as you decide which channels to use and how to use them both efficiently and effectively.

LO 4 Give examples of ways to become a better "sender" and "receiver" of information.

Practice writing, be critical of your work, and revise. Train yourself to become a more persuasive speaker. Use language carefully and well, and work to overcome cross-cultural language differences. Be alert to the nonverbal signals that you send, including your use of time as perceived by other people. Know the common bad listening habits, and work to overcome them. Read widely, and engage in careful, firsthand observation and interpretation.

LO 5 Explain how to improve downward, upward, and horizontal communication.

Actively manage communications in all directions. Engage in two-way communication more than one-way. Make information available to others. Useful approaches to downward communication include coaching, special communications during difficult periods, and open-book management. You should also both facilitate and motivate people to communicate upward. Many mechanisms exist for enhancing horizontal communications.

LO 6 Summarize how to work with the company grapevine.

The informal flow of information can contribute as much as formal communication can to organizational effectiveness and morale. Managers must understand that the grapevine cannot be eliminated and should be managed actively. Many of the suggestions for

KEY TERMS

boundaryless organization Organization in which there are no barriers to information flow.

coaching Dialogue with a goal of helping another be more effective and achieve his or her full potential on the job.

communication The transmission of information and meaning from one party to another through the use of shared symbols.

downward communication Information that flows from higher to lower levels in the organization's hierarchy.

filtering The process of withholding, ignoring, or distorting information.

grapevine Informal communication network.

horizontal communication Information shared among people on the same hierarchical level.

media richness The degree to which a communication channel conveys information.

one-way communication A process in which information flows in only one direction—from the sender to the receiver, with no feedback loop.

open-book management Practice of sharing with employees at all levels of the organization vital information previously meant for management's eyes only.

perception The process of receiving and interpreting information.

reflection Process by which a person states what he or she believes the other person is saying.

two-way communication A process in which information flows in two directions—the receiver provides feedback, and the sender is receptive to the feedback.

upward communication Information that flows from lower to higher levels in the organization's hierarchy.

virtual office A mobile office in which people can work anywhere as long as they have the tools to communicate with customers and colleagues.

Web 2.0 A set of Internet-based applications that encourage user-provided content and collaboration.

managing formal communications apply also to managing the grapevine. Moreover, managers can take steps to prevent rumors or neutralize the ones that arise.

LO 7 Describe the boundaryless organization and its advantages.

Boundaries—psychological if not physical—exist between different organizational levels, units, and organizations and external stakeholders. The ideal boundaryless organization is one in which no barriers to information flow exist. Ideas, information, decisions, and actions move to where they are most needed. Information is available as needed and freely accessible so that the organization as a whole functions far better than as separate parts.

chapter fourteen

Managerial Control

SUMMARY

LO 1 Explain why companies develop control systems for employees.

Left to their own devices, employees may act in ways that do not benefit the organization. Control systems are designed to eliminate idiosyncratic behavior and keep employees directed toward achieving the goals of the firm. Control systems are a steering mechanism for guiding resources and for helping each individual act on behalf of the organization.

LO 2 Summarize how to design a basic bureaucratic control system.

The design of a basic control system involves four steps: (1) setting performance standards, (2) measuring performance, (3) comparing performance with the standards, and (4) eliminating unfavorable deviations by taking corrective action. Performance standards should be valid and should cover issues such as quantity, quality, time, and cost. Once performance is compared with the standards, the principle of exception suggests that the manager needs to direct attention to the exceptional cases that have significant deviations. Then the manager takes the action most likely to solve the problem.

LO 3 Describe the purposes for using budgets as a control device.

Budgets combine the benefits of feedforward, concurrent, and feedback controls. They are used as an initial guide for allocating resources, a reference point for using funds, and a feedback mechanism for comparing actual levels of sales and expenses with their expected levels. Recently companies have modified their budgeting processes to allocate costs over basic processes (such as customer service) rather than to functions or departments. By changing the way they prepare budgets, many companies have discovered ways to eliminate waste and improve business processes.

LO 4 Recognize basic types of financial statements and financial ratios used as controls.

The basic financial statements are the balance sheet and the profit and loss statement. The balance sheet compares the value of company assets to the obligations the company owes to owners and creditors. The profit and loss statement shows company income relative to costs incurred. In addition to these statements, companies look at liquidity ratios (whether the company can pay its short-term debts), leverage ratios (the extent to which the company is funding operations by going into debt), and profitability ratios (profit relative to investment). These ratios provide a goal for managers as well as a standard against which to evaluate performance.

LO 5 List procedures for implementing effective control systems.

To maximize the effectiveness of controls, managers should (1) establish valid performance standards, (2) provide adequate information to employees, (3) ensure acceptability, (4) maintain open communication, and (5) see that multiple approaches are used (such as bureaucratic, market, and clan control).

LO 6 Discuss ways in which market and clan control influence performance.

Market controls can be used at the level of the corporation, the business unit or department, or the individual. At the corporate level, business units are evaluated against

KEY TERMS

accounting audits Procedures used to verify accounting reports and statements.

activity-based costing (ABC) A method of cost accounting designed to identify streams of activity and then to allocate costs across particular business processes according to the amount of time employees devote to particular activities.

assets The values of the various items the corporation owns.

balanced scorecard Control system combining four sets of performance measures: financial, customer, business process, and learning and growth.

balance sheet A report that shows the financial picture of a company at a given time and itemizes assets, liabilities, and stockholders' equity.

budgeting The process of investigating what is being done and comparing the results with the corresponding budget data to verify accomplishments or remedy differences; also called *budgetary controlling*.

bureaucratic control The use of rules, regulations, and authority to guide performance.

clan control Control based on the norms, values, shared goals, and trust among group members.

concurrent control The control process used while plans are being carried out, including directing, monitoring, and fine-tuning activities as they are performed.

control Any process that directs the activities of individuals toward the achievement of organizational goals.

current ratio A liquidity ratio that indicates the extent to which short-term assets can decline and still be adequate to pay short-term liabilities.

debt–equity ratio A leverage ratio that indicates the company's ability to meet its long-term financial obligations.

external audit An evaluation conducted by one organization, such as a CPA firm, on another.

feedback control Control that focuses on the use of information about previous results to correct deviations from the acceptable standard.

feedforward control The control process used before operations begin, including policies, procedures, and rules designed to ensure that planned activities are carried out properly.

internal audit A periodic assessment of a company's own planning, organizing, leading, and controlling processes.

liabilities The amounts a corporation owes to various creditors.

management audit An evaluation of the effectiveness and efficiency of various systems within an organization.

management myopia Focusing on short-term earnings and profits at the expense of longer-term strategic obligations.

market control Control based on the use of pricing mechanisms and economic information to regulate activities within organizations.

principle of exception A managerial principle stating that control is enhanced by concentrating on the exceptions to or significant deviations from the expected result or standard.

profit and loss statement An itemized financial statement of the income and expenses of a company's operations.

return on investment (ROI) A ratio of profit to capital used, or a rate of return from capital.

standard Expected performance for a given goal: a target that establishes a desired performance level, motivates performance, and serves as a benchmark against which actual performance is assessed.

stockholders' equity The amount accruing to the corporation's owners.

transfer price Price charged by one unit for a good or service provided to another unit within the organization.

one another based on profitability. Within business units, transfer pricing may be used to approximate market mechanisms to control transactions among departments. At the individual level, market mechanisms control the wage rate of employees and can be used to evaluate the performance of individual managers. Some organizations find it difficult to program "one best way" to approach work and monitor employee performance. To be responsive to customers, these companies use clan controls to harness the expertise of employees and give them the freedom to act on their own initiative. To maintain control while empowering employees, companies should (1) use self-guided teams, (2) allow decision making at the source of the problems, (3) build trust and mutual respect, (4) base control on a guiding framework of norms, and (5) use incentive systems that encourage teamwork.

SUMMARY

LO 1 Summarize how to assess technology needs.

Assessing the technology needs of a company begins by benchmarking, or comparing, the technologies it employs with those of both competitors and noncompetitors. Benchmarking should be done on a global basis to understand practices used worldwide. Technology scanning helps identify emerging technologies and those still under development in an effort to project their eventual competitive impact. Managers should be aware of and engage in disruptive innovation that could potentially displace established competitors in their industry.

LO 2 Identify the criteria on which to base technology decisions.

After analyzing the firm's current technological position, managers consider several criteria when planning how to develop or exploit emerging technologies. First, they consider the market demand for the technological innovation. Second, managers assess whether the development and use of the innovation is feasible in light of significant technical barriers. Third, they calculate the amount of financial return for implementing the technological innovation. Fourth, managers link technology and innovation strategies to their organizations' core capabilities. Last, technology adoption decisions should take into account the culture of the organization, the interests of the managers, and the expectations of stakeholders.

LO 3 Compare key ways of acquiring new technologies..

In many industries, the primary sources of new technology are the organizations that use it. However, new technologies can come from many sources, including suppliers, manufacturers, users, other industries, universities, and overseas companies. The question of how to acquire new technology is a make-or-buy decision. There are advantages and disadvantages associated with both approaches. A few basic questions can help managers decide whether to make their own new technology or to purchase or license it from others: (1) Is it important (and possible) that the technology remain proprietary? (2) Are the time, skills, and resources for internal development available?, (3) Is the technology readily available outside the company?

LO 4 Evaluate the elements of an innovative organization.

Organizing for innovation involves unleashing the creative energies of employees while directing their efforts toward meeting market needs in a timely manner. Companies can unleash creativity by establishing a culture that values intrapreneurship; accepts and even celebrates failure as a sign of innovation; and reinforces innovation through goal setting, rewards, and stories of creative employees. The organization's structure should balance bureaucracy for controlling existing processes with a flexibility that allows innovation to take place. Development projects provide an opportunity for cross-functional teamwork aimed at innovation. Job design should take into account both social relationships and the technical efficiency of work so that jobs are within employees' ability but also empower them to work cooperatively and creatively.

LO 5 Discuss what it takes to be world-class.

You should strive for world-class excellence, which means using the very best and latest knowledge and ideas to operate at the highest standards of any place anywhere. Sustainable greatness comes from, among other things, having strong core values, living

KEY TERMS

adapters Companies that take the current industry structure and its evolution as givens, and choose where to compete.

development project A focused organizational effort to create a new product or process via technological advances.

disruptive innovation A process by which a product, service, or business model takes root initially in simple applications at the bottom of a market and then moves "up market," eventually displacing established competitors.

force-field analysis An approach to implementing Lewin's unfreezing/moving/refreezing model by identifying the forces that prevent people from changing and those that will drive people toward change.

make-or-buy decision The question an organization asks itself about whether to acquire new technology from an outside source or develop it itself.

moving Instituting the change.

organization development (OD) The systemwide application of behavioral science knowledge to develop, improve, and reinforce the strategies, structures, and processes that lead to organizational effectiveness.

performance gap The difference between actual performance and desired performance.

refreezing Strengthening the new behaviors that support the change.

shapers Companies that try to change the structure of their industries, creating a future competitive landscape of their own design.

technology audit Process of clarifying the key technologies on which an organization depends.

unfreezing Realizing that current practices are inappropriate and that new behavior is necessary.

those values constantly, striving for continuous improvement, experimenting, and always trying to do better tomorrow than today. It is essential to not fall prey to the tyranny of the *or*—that is, the belief that one important goal can be attained only at the expense of another. The genius of the *and* is that multiple important goals can be achieved simultaneously and synergistically.

LO 6 Describe how to manage change effectively.

Effective change management occurs when the organization moves from its current state to a desired future state without excessive cost to the organization or its people. People resist change for a variety of reasons, including inertia, poor timing, surprise, peer pressure, self-interest, misunderstanding, different information about (and assessments of) the change, and management's tactics. Motivating people to change requires a general process of unfreezing, moving, and refreezing, with the caveat that appropriate and not inappropriate behaviors be "refrozen." More specific techniques to motivate people to change include education and communication, participation and involvement, facilitation and support, negotiation and rewards, manipulation and cooptation, and coercion. Each approach has strengths, weaknesses, and appropriate uses, and multiple approaches can be used. It is important to harmonize the multiple changes that are occurring throughout the organization. Effective change requires active leadership, including creating a sense of urgency, forming a guiding coalition, developing a vision and strategy, communicating the change vision, empowering broad-based action, generating short-term wins, consolidating gains and producing more change, and anchoring the new approaches in the culture.

LO 7 List tactics for creating a successful future.

Preparing for an uncertain future requires a proactive approach. You can proactively forge the future by being a shaper more than an adapter, creating new competitive advantages, actively managing your career and your personal development, and becoming an active leader and a lifelong learner.